D1285513

THE EIGHTH AMENDMENT AND ITS FUTURE
IN A NEW AGE OF PUNISHMENT

This book provides a theoretical and practical exploration of the constitutional bar against cruel and unusual punishments, excessive bail, and excessive fines. It explores the history of this prohibition, the current legal doctrine, and future applications of the Eighth Amendment. With contributions from the leading academics and experts on the Eighth Amendment and the wide range of punishments and criminal justice actors it touches, this volume addresses constitutional theory, legal history, federalism, constitutional values, the applicable legal doctrine, punishment theory, prison conditions, bail, fines, the death penalty, juvenile life without parole, execution methods, prosecutorial misconduct, race discrimination, and law and science.

MEGHAN J. RYAN is the Associate Dean for Research and Altshuler Distinguished Teaching Professor at Southern Methodist University (SMU) Dedman School of Law in Dallas, TX. An award-winning scholar and teacher, her work spans the areas of criminal law and procedure, law and science, and torts. Her writing focuses primarily on the U.S. Supreme Court's Eighth Amendment jurisprudence, wrongful convictions and sentencing, and the roles of science and technology in the law. She is also engaged in interdisciplinary projects such as collaborating with engineers and statisticians to find a scientific basis for various forms of forensic evidence.

WILLIAM W. BERRY III is Professor of Law and Montague Professor at the University of Mississippi School of Law, where he teaches and writes about criminal law, focusing on issues related to criminal sentencing and the death penalty. He has published extensively on the Eighth Amendment, including articles in the *Texas Law Review*, *Southern California Law Review*, *UCLA Law Review*, and *Washington University Law Review*, among others. He is also co-author of several books, including *Criminal Law* (9th ed., 2020).

The Eighth Amendment and Its Future in a New Age of Punishment

Edited by

MEGHAN J. RYAN

Southern Methodist University, Dedman School of Law

WILLIAM W. BERRY III

University of Mississippi School of Law

CAMBRIDGE
UNIVERSITY PRESS

CAMBRIDGE
UNIVERSITY PRESS

University Printing House, Cambridge CB2 8BS, United Kingdom

One Liberty Plaza, 20th Floor, New York, NY 10006, USA

477 Williamstown Road, Port Melbourne, VIC 3207, Australia

314–321, 3rd Floor, Plot 3, Splendor Forum, Jasola District Centre, New Delhi – 110025, India

79 Anson Road, #06–04/06, Singapore 079906

Cambridge University Press is part of the University of Cambridge.

It furthers the University's mission by disseminating knowledge in the pursuit of education, learning, and research at the highest international levels of excellence.

www.cambridge.org
Information on this title: www.cambridge.org/9781108498579
DOI: 10.1017/9781108653732

© Cambridge University Press 2020

First published 2020

A catalogue record for this publication is available from the British Library.

Library of Congress Cataloging-in-Publication Data
NAMES: Ryan, Meghan J, editor. | Berry, William W., III, 1974– editor.
TITLE: The Eighth Amendment and its future in a new age of punishment / edited by Meghan J. Ryan, Southern Methodist University, Texas [and] William W. Berry III, University of Mississippi
DESCRIPTION: Cambridge, United Kingdom ; New York, NY, USA : Cambridge University Press, 2020. | Includes bibliographical references and index.
IDENTIFIERS: LCCN 2020009503 (print) | LCCN 2020009504 (ebook) | ISBN 9781108498579 (hardback) | ISBN 9781108724210 (paperback) | ISBN 9781108653732 (epub)
SUBJECTS: LCSH: United States. Constitution. 8th Amendment. | Punishment–United States. | Criminal justice, Administration of–United States. | Law reform–United States.
CLASSIFICATION: LCC KF4558 8th .E374 2020 (print) | LCC KF4558 8th (ebook) | DDC 345.73/0773–dc23
LC record available at https://lccn.loc.gov/2020009503
LC ebook record available at https://lccn.loc.gov/2020009504

ISBN 978-1-108-49857-9 Hardback

To Tré and Jack – MJR

To Stephanie, Eleanor, William, and Caroline – WWB

Contents

Contributors

William W. Berry III is Professor of Law and Montague Professor at the University of Mississippi School of Law, where he teaches and writes about criminal law, focusing on issues related to criminal sentencing and the death penalty. He has published extensively on the Eighth Amendment, including articles in the *Texas Law Review, Southern California Law Review, UCLA Law Review,* and *Washington University Law Review,* among others. He is also coauthor of several books, including *Criminal Law* (9th ed.) by Carolina Academic Press.

Eric Berger is the Earl Dunlap Distinguished Professor of Law and Associate Dean for Faculty at the University of Nebraska College of Law, where he teaches and researches in the area of Constitutional Law. His article *Individual Rights, Judicial Deference, and Administrative Law Norms in Constitutional Decision Making,* 91 B.U. L. Rev. 2029 (2011) was named the 2011 winner of the American Constitution Society's Richard D. Cudahy Writing Competition on Regulatory and Administrative Law. Professor Berger has also written extensively about lethal injection litigation.

John D. Bessler is Associate Professor at the University of Baltimore School of Law and Adjunct Professor at the Georgetown University Law Center. He has also taught at the University of Minnesota Law School, The George Washington University Law School, the Rutgers School of Law, and the University of Aberdeen in Scotland. He has written multiple books on capital punishment, including *Cruel and Unusual: The American Death Penalty and the Founders' Eighth Amendment* (2012) and *The Death Penalty as Torture: From the Dark Ages to Abolition* (2017).

Richard A. Bierschbach is Dean and Professor of Law at Wayne State University Law School. He previously taught at Cardozo Law School in New York City, where he also served as Vice Dean, and, before entering academia, was a law clerk to United States Supreme Court Justice Sandra Day O'Connor. His teaching and research interests are in criminal law and procedure, administrative law, and corporations (especially corporate, white collar, and regulatory crimes). His scholarship explores how the criminal justice system's institutional and procedural structure intersects with its substantive and regulatory aims. Dean Bierschbach's work has appeared in numerous leading law journals, including the *Yale Law Journal*, *Michigan Law Review*, *Virginia Law Review*, *University of Pennsylvania Law Review*, *Northwestern University Law Review*, and *Georgetown Law Journal*.

Beth A. Colgan is Professor of Law at the UCLA School of Law. She is one of the country's leading experts on constitutional and policy issues related to the use of economic sanctions as punishment and particularly on the Eighth Amendment's Excessive Fines Clause. In addition to her interest in the intersection between criminal legal systems and poverty, Professor Colgan's research and teaching also investigate the treatment of juveniles in juvenile and adult criminal legal systems and indigent defense representation.

Deborah W. Denno is Arthur A. McGivney Professor of Law and Founding Director of the Neuroscience and Law Center at Fordham Law School. Seven of Professor Denno's articles have been cited by the United States Supreme Court, some multiple times and/or in different cases, and primarily in conjunction with her scholarship on execution methods. In 2016, the Fordham Student Bar Association named Professor Denno Teacher of the Year. Her forthcoming book, *Changing Law's Mind: How Neuroscience Can Help Us Punish Criminals More Fairly and Effectively* (Oxford University Press), focuses on her study of how criminal cases use neuroscientific evidence.

Sharon Dolovich is Professor of Law at the UCLA School of Law, and Faculty Director of the UCLA Prison Law and Policy Program. Her scholarship focuses on the law, policy, and theory of prisons and punishment, with particular attention to prison conditions and the legal and moral implications of the way the state treats people in custody. Dolovich has been a visiting professor at New York University, Harvard University, and Georgetown University, and a fellow at the Radcliffe Institute for Advanced Study. She has written extensively on the Eighth Amendment and on prison law more generally and has conducted award-winning ethnographic research in the Los Angeles County Jail. Her book, *The New Criminal Justice Thinking* (NYU Press: coedited with Alexandra Natapoff) appeared in paperback in December 2018.

Cara H. Drinan is Professor of Law at The Catholic University of America, Columbus School of Law, in Washington, DC. She teaches criminal law, criminal procedure, and seminars related to criminal justice reform and constitutional law. Professor Drinan's research focuses on the ways in which the American criminal justice system is broken and possible avenues to reform at the state and federal levels. She is especially interested in the vulnerable group of minors in the criminal justice system.

Richard S. Frase is Benjamin N. Berger Professor of Criminal Law at the University of Minnesota Law School and Co-Director of the Robina Institute of Criminal Law and Criminal Justice. His principal teaching and research interests are Minnesota and other state sentencing guidelines, punishment and proportionality theories, comparative criminal procedure, and comparative sentencing between the United States and other nations and within the United States (between states). His most recent books are *Paying for the Past: The Case against Prior Record Sentence Enhancements* (Oxford University Press, 2019), and *Just Sentencing: Principles and Procedures for a Workable System* (Oxford University Press, 2013).

Jeffrey L. Kirchmeier is Professor of Law at City University of New York (CUNY) School of Law and the author of *Imprisoned by the Past: Warren McCleskey, Race, and the American Death Penalty*, which chronicles the death penalty's history and its connection with race. His other writings include articles about criminal procedure, constitutional law, and the death penalty. Before joining CUNY, he taught at Tulane School of Law, worked as an associate at Arnold & Porter, and was a staff attorney at the Arizona Capital Representation Project. He received his B.A. and J.D. degrees from Case Western Reserve University.

Corinna Barrett Lain is S. D. Roberts & Sandra Moore Professor of Law at the University of Richmond. A constitutional law scholar, Professor Lain writes about the influence of extralegal norms on Supreme Court decision making, with a particular focus on the field of capital punishment. Her scholarship, which often uses the lens of legal history, has appeared in the *Stanford Law Review*, *University of Pennsylvania Law Review*, *Duke Law Journal*, *UCLA Law Review*, and *Georgetown Law Journal*, among other venues. Professor Lain is an elected member of the American Law Institute and has received the University of Richmond's Distinguished Educator Award in 2006. She is a former prosecutor and an Army veteran.

Michael Mannheimer is a Professor of Law at Northern Kentucky University, Salmon P. Chase College of Law, where he teaches Criminal Law, Criminal Procedure, and related courses. His scholarship has appeared or is forthcoming in such journals as the *Columbia Law Review*, *Texas Law Review*, *Notre Dame Law Review*, *Emory Law Journal*, *Indiana Law Journal*, and *Iowa Law Review*. He was recipient of the 2010 AALS Criminal Justice Section Junior Scholar Paper Award. His current research focuses on the under-appreciated federalism component of the Bill of Rights. He received his J. D. from Columbia Law School.

Meghan J. Ryan is the Associate Dean for Research and Altshuler Distinguished Teaching Professor at Southern Methodist University Dedman School of Law in Dallas, Texas. An award-winning scholar and teacher, her work spans the areas of criminal law and procedure, law and science, and torts. Many of her publications focus on the U.S. Supreme Court's Eighth Amendment jurisprudence, wrongful convictions and sentencing, and the roles of science and technology in the law.

Carol Steiker is Henry J. Friendly Professor of Law and Director of the Criminal Justice Policy Program at Harvard Law School. She specializes in the broad field of criminal justice, where her work ranges from substantive criminal law to criminal procedure to institutional design, with a special focus on capital punishment. Her most recent books are *Comparative Capital Punishment Law*, coedited with her brother Jordan Steiker (Edward Elgar, 2019) and *Courting Death: The Supreme Court and Capital Punishment*, coauthored with Jordan Steiker (The Belknap Press of Harvard University Press, 2016). In addition to her scholarly work, Professor Steiker has done pro bono work for indigent criminal defendants, including death penalty cases in the United States Supreme Court. She also has served as a consultant and expert witness on issues of criminal justice for nonprofit organizations and has testified before the United States Congress and state legislatures.

Jordan Steiker is Judge Robert M. Parker Chair in Law and Director of the Capital Punishment Center at the University of Texas School of Law. His work focuses primarily on the administration of capital punishment in the United States (including *Courting Death: The Supreme Court and Capital Punishment*, coauthored with his sister Carol Steiker). With her, he produced the report that led the American Law Institute to withdraw the death penalty provision from the Model Penal Code.

John F. Stinneford is Professor of Law at the University of Florida Levin College of Law. Professor Stinneford teaches and writes about criminal law, criminal procedure, constitutional law, and legal ethics. The primary focus of his scholarship has been the original meaning of the Cruel and Unusual Punishments Clause. His work has been cited by the United States Supreme Court, several state supreme courts and federal courts of appeal, and numerous scholars.

Sherod Thaxton is Professor of Law at the UCLA School of Law. He also holds courtesy appointments in the Department of African American Studies and the Department of Sociology. Prior to joining the law faculty, he served as a staff attorney in the Capital Habeas Unit of the Office of the Federal Defender for the Eastern District of California. Before law school, he was the principal investigator of the Death Penalty Tracking Project for the Office of the Multi-County Public Defender in Atlanta, Georgia. His primary research and teaching interests are in the areas of criminal law and procedure, capital punishment, habeas corpus, the sociology of law, and empirical legal studies.

Samuel R. Wiseman is McConnaughhay and Rissman Professor at Florida State University College of Law. Since graduating from Yale Law School in 2007, he has written a number of articles on the Eighth Amendment's Excessive Bail Clause and bail reform more generally. These include "Pretrial Detention and the Right to Be Monitored," which appeared in the *Yale Law Journal*, "Fixing Bail," which appeared in the *George Washington Law Review*, and "Bail and Mass Incarceration," which appeared in the *Georgia Law Review*.

Preface

In 2002, the United States Supreme Court decided *Atkins v. Virginia*, opening the door to the Court's application of the Eighth Amendment on an almost annual basis – *Roper v. Simmons* (2005), *Kennedy v. Louisiana* (2007), *Baze v. Rees* (2008), *Graham v. Florida* (2010), *Brown v. Plata* (2011), *Miller v. Alabama* (2012), *Hall v. Florida* (2014), *Glossip v. Gross* (2015), *Moore v. Texas* (2017), *Bucklew v. Precythe* (2019), *Timbs v. Indiana* (2019), *Kahler v. Kansas* (2019-2020 term), and *Mathena v. Malvo* (2019-2020 term). These decisions generated a number of interesting conversations and papers by many of the contributors to this book.

Some particularly memorable conversations included a Southeastern Association of Law Schools panel in the summer of 2011 in Hilton Head, South Carolina, with John Stinneford and Corinna Lain; a Law & Society panel in Boston, Massachusetts, in 2013 with Rick Bierschbach and Beth Colgan; a Law & Society panel in Minneapolis, Minnesota, in 2014 with Richard Frase; an Association of American Law Schools panel in 2016 in New York City with Corinna Lain, Debby Denno, and Eric Berger; and a Law & Society panel in Washington, DC, in 2019 with Corinna Lain and John Bessler. And of course, we should mention the SEALS panel we had in August 2018 in Fort Lauderdale, Florida, with many of the contributors in preparation for this volume: Rick Bierschbach, Mike Mannheimer, Debby Denno, John Bessler, Corinna Lain, John Stinneford, and Cara Drinan.

Unaware of any collection of Eighth Amendment work by a variety of authors, we found it important to collect the many ideas that these stimulating conversations generated in one place. We wanted to share how constitutional doctrine connects to the hot-button issues of the day – mass incarceration, the death penalty, juvenile life-without-parole, and innocence – and offer our thoughts about how the Court will shape the Eighth Amendment in the future. We hope this volume of chapters on the Eighth Amendment will generate many future conversations exploring this often overlooked constitutional amendment, and its capacity to regulate the excessive punishment (and related) practices of federal and state governments. We are indebted to this book's many contributors for the sophistication and acumen of their contributions; we hope their insights will be of use to practitioners and academics alike.

We also appreciate the willingness of Cambridge University Press to publish this manuscript and allow for the collection of the interwoven and interconnected ideas and theories contained within a single volume. To be sure, there is much to say about the Court's Eighth Amendment jurisprudence, and we believe this volume is a good start to the conversation and a precursor to many fruitful conversations in the future.

Meghan Ryan **Will Berry**
Dallas, Texas *Oxford, Mississippi*

Introduction

The Eighth Amendment to the United States Constitution proscribes governments from imposing "cruel and unusual punishments," as well as excessive bail and fines.[1] The Amendment has roots in a similar provision in the English Bill of Rights, which historically sought to prevent extreme punishments like the whipping, pillorying, defrocking, and life imprisonment of Titus Oates for perjury. Despite the historical importance of the Amendment, U.S. courts and scholars have given the Amendment and its prohibitions relatively little attention. In particular, the Supreme Court has construed its text quite narrowly, especially outside of the capital context.

Although the Eighth Amendment has, for decades, remained largely a dead letter, during the past decade or two there have been signs that the U.S. Supreme Court and its litigants are awakening to the possibility of using the Eighth Amendment as a tool to counteract the punishment practices of federal and state governments. In 2002, the Supreme Court held that the Eighth Amendment bars death sentences for intellectually disabled offenders — a decision further clarified by the Court twice in the last four years.[2] In 2005, the Court found that death sentences for juvenile offenders violate the Eighth Amendment.[3] And three years later, the Court created an exception to the death penalty for virtually all non-homicide crimes against individuals.[4] These developments limiting the imposition of capital punishment are important, but these cases affect only a small subset of offenders.[5]

---

[1] U.S. Const. amend. VIII.
[2] Moore v. Texas, 137 S. Ct. 1039 (2017); Hall v. Florida, 572 U.S. 701 (2014); Atkins v. Virginia, 536 U.S. 304 (2002).
[3] Roper v. Simmons, 543 U.S. 551 (2005).
[4] Kennedy v. Louisiana, 554 U.S. 407 (2008).
[5] Although we use the term "offender," it is of course important to remember that the Eighth Amendment regulates the punishment of *people*. Further, even if someone is a convicted offender, there may be a chance that the individual is actually innocent of the crimes for which he was convicted.

Continuing to revitalize the Eighth Amendment, the Court in recent years has expanded its analysis in this area beyond the boundaries of capital punishment. In 2010, for example, the Court held that juveniles could not receive life-without-parole (LWOP) sentences for non-homicide crimes,[6] and the next year it found California prison conditions unconstitutional because of overcrowding.[7] In 2012, the Court barred the imposition of mandatory juvenile life-without-parole (JLWOP) sentences.[8] By placing real limitations on punishments outside of the capital arena, the Court has opened the door to broader inquiry into the reach of the Eighth Amendment — particularly now that litigants and the Court have recognized the Amendment's vitality in this new line of cases.

The Court's expanded view of the Eighth Amendment is consistent with the doctrine it has espoused since 1958 — that the meaning of the Amendment evolves over time as society advances. More specifically, in its landmark case of *Trop v. Dulles*, a plurality of the Court explained that "the Amendment must draw its meaning from the evolving standards of decency that mark the progress of a maturing society."[9] While the Court has waffled in other legal areas about whether the Constitution stands still in time or whether it evolves to meet society's changing needs, in the area of Eighth Amendment analysis, the Court seems to have explicitly endorsed the idea of a living Constitution.

In addition to the Court's living constitutional basis for the Eighth Amendment, which has made the Amendment more broadly applicable in recent years, the Eighth Amendment and its protections are perhaps more necessary currently than they have been for a long time. The U.S. criminal justice system — and in particular its punishment system — is broken. Despite the Eighth Amendment prohibitions, the United States engages in punishment practices that are, by the standards of much of the rest of the world, draconian and excessive. The United States remains one of the few Western nations to still use capital punishment regularly.[10] It has more than fifty thousand inmates serving life-without-parole sentences, while no other country in the world has more than five hundred people serving such a sentence.[11] The United States currently is the only country in the world that permits LWOP sentences for juvenile offenders. And its prisons house more than 2.3 million people — a mass incarceration epidemic locking up twenty-five percent of the world's prison population, even though the United States claims less than five percent of the world's population. This proliferation of harsh

---

[6] Graham v. Florida, 560 U.S. 48 (2010).
[7] Brown v. Plata, 563 U.S. 493 (2011).
[8] Miller v. Alabama, 567 U.S. 460 (2012).
[9] Trop v. Dulles, 356 U.S. 86, 100 (1958) (plurality opinion).
[10] *See, e.g.,* ROGER HOOD & CAROLYN HOYLE, THE DEATH PENALTY: A WORLDWIDE PERSPECTIVE (5th ed. 2015).
[11] *See, e.g.,* MARC MAUER & ASHLEY NELLIS, THE MEANING OF LIFE: THE CASE FOR ABOLISHING LIFE SENTENCES (2019).

punishments has cemented America's status as the country with the most incarcerated people on Earth.

At the same time, the criminal justice system and the harsh punishments it often imposes have become very expensive. This has propelled some jurisdictions to experiment in their approaches to punishment. While some of these approaches — such as eliminating LWOP sentences for juveniles — might be laudable, others — such as experimenting with drug cocktails to carry out executions — remain concerning and questionable. Concerns about the expense of punishment are especially true in the capital context. The constitutional protections that accompany the imposition of the death penalty and the fact that a life is at stake translate into numerous expensive legal fees, procedures, and appeals. In response to these spiraling expenses — and constrained resources among the states — a number of states have abandoned the death penalty altogether. Today, although the United States is one of only a handful of nations that regularly imposes capital punishment, and although twenty-nine U.S. states have technically retained it, most death sentences are imposed within just two percent of U.S. counties. They, alone, are almost entirely responsible for the death penalty retaining its vitality in the United States. This geographic rarity of the imposition of death sentences raises questions about the constitutionality of this ultimate punishment. Further, the diminished numbers of total death sentences imposed and of actual offender executions indicate that this punishment may have become too unusual to be constitutionally imposed.

Also, new evidence suggests that capital punishment has perhaps become too cruel to impose. New evidence from cognitive neuroscience, various fields of social science, and other disciplines suggest that this may be the case. Questions linger about the true culpability and deterrability of many defendants. Further, there are real questions about whether particular techniques for imposing lethal injection — the main way states carry out death sentences — are humane or actually impose torture, which the Eighth Amendment clearly prohibits.

In examining the applicability of the Eighth Amendment, questions likewise arise about how judges and litigants should interpret the individual terms of the Amendment — like "cruel" and "unusual" — and whether they should evolve with time under the "evolving standards of decency" test or whether they apply only to punishments prohibited at the time the Bill of Rights was ratified. These questions also speak to broader questions of federalism, including to what extent states are free to experiment with their punishments and to what extent states can prohibit punishments within their borders when imposed by the separate sovereign of the federal government.

In analyzing the Eighth Amendment, the Court has imbued its interpretation of the Amendment with several concepts that still guide its application. First, the Court has announced that the basic concept underlying the Eighth Amendment is "nothing less than the dignity of man." The question of human dignity undergirds the Court's evolving standards of decency framework, with the clear import being that disproportionate punishments incongruent with societal standards threaten the human dignity of the punished. The Court has also embraced the concept of differentness with respect to its application of the Eighth Amendment. As "death is different" both in its severity and irrevocability, the Court has generally accorded capital cases a greater level of scrutiny than all other criminal cases. In its recent JLWOP cases, though, the Court has announced that juveniles are also different. This step may signal a willingness to broaden the application of the Eighth Amendment to additional categories of "different" offenders or offenses, or, alternatively, to migrate away from the differentness concept altogether. The Court has also concluded that capital punishment cannot be imposed arbitrarily — requiring some modicum of consistency in sentencing outcomes — a concept in tension with the idea that this unique punishment should be reserved for the worst offenders.

Despite looking to these Eighth Amendment values, the Court often heavily relies on its evolving standards of decency doctrine, which depends in part on counting state legislative enactments. This majoritarian practice thus may provide the substantive content for the Eighth Amendment. If the constitutional provision in theory exists to protect an individual right against excessive punishments imposed by a majority will as reflected in the legislature, it seems odd to define the scope of that right by the practices of the legislatures themselves. Under this scheme, the Eighth Amendment protects against outlier jurisdictions but provides little protection against excessive punishments adopted by a majority of jurisdictions. Although this practice may be contrary to most constitutional norms, the Court has applied a similar analysis in other areas of constitutional law, as under the doctrine of substantive due process. One might look for similarities in these other areas and question why they deserve this treatment. Also important is the Eighth Amendment's interplay with other constitutional clauses, like the Fourteenth Amendment. Viewing the Eighth Amendment as part of a larger constitutional scheme, and viewing it through various lenses, may be enlightening.

Although most Eighth Amendment analysis focuses on this prohibition of cruel and unusual punishments, that amounts to only one-third of the Amendment. It also prohibits excessive bail and excessive fines. The meager case law that exists in these areas provides little limitation on bail and fines, but expansion of the prohibition of punishments might signal expansion of limitations in these other Eighth Amendment spheres as well. Considering the bail crisis in this nation, and the great number of criminal cases in which states impose fines, further exploring these lesser-examined areas of the Eighth Amendment is also important.

Beyond the many questions highlighted so far, shifts in the types and amounts of punishments regularly imposed in criminal cases raise a series of interesting considerations. Imposition of death sentences and JLWOP sentences are waning, but adult

LWOP sentences continue to balloon. The Eighth Amendment has something to say about these shifts and potentially could mandate additional punishment prohibitions. These could occur on the micro level — prohibiting punishments for particular offenses or offenders — or on the macro level — prohibiting entire categories of punishments. For example, the Court could expand its limitation on JLWOP to include even juvenile offenders who committed homicides. Or, the Court could prohibit imposing LWOP sentences on offenders with intellectual disabilities. Pushing further, one might fathom the Court prohibiting altogether the use of JLWOP or even capital punishment. Indeed, with states abandoning these practices, the evolving standards of decency could lead the Court in these directions.

To be sure, the Eighth Amendment has historically been an under-litigated, under-studied, and under-theorized area of constitutional law. The Court's limits on punishment are often unclear, the doctrine has recently shifted to accompany new lethal injection techniques, and there are parts of the Amendment on which there is very little case law — like bail and fines. Yet, the Eighth Amendment, in addition to continuously evolving, is becoming increasingly relevant to our complex and broken punishment system.

This book attempts to depict the landscape of the Eighth Amendment — from its history to its current state — and, along the way, explain how the Amendment can help sort out the boundaries of permissible punishment and address new issues that are yet to emerge. It aims to take a step toward remedying the dearth of understanding and study related to the Amendment by engaging with a number of underlying Eighth Amendment principles and offering several avenues by which to explore future litigation strategies.

At its core, the central thesis of this book is that the Eighth Amendment has increasing value and application in the modern criminal justice system, and the Court's decisions continue to confirm this constitutional expansion. The chapters that follow explore the Amendment — past, present, and particularly future — to assess the many applications of the Amendment to the governments and punishments it regulates.

Part I of the book explores the broader historical context of the Eighth Amendment. In Chapter 1, "From the Founding to the Present: An Overview of Legal Thought and the Eighth Amendment's Evolution," John Bessler describes the origins of the Eighth Amendment and their connection to its modern interpretation. Chapter 2, "Back to the Future: Originalism and the Eighth Amendment," written by John Stinneford, provides an originalist account of the Eighth Amendment and argues for its incorporation into the Court's current doctrine. Further, in Chapter 3, "Eighth Amendment Federalism," Michael Mannheimer explains the historical connection between federalism and the Eighth Amendment, and suggests some modern applications in light of this history.

Part II of the book assesses the current landscape of the Eighth Amendment, particularly its doctrinal underpinnings and applications. In Chapter 4, "Eighth

Amendment Values," Will Berry and Meghan Ryan provide an overview of the values inherent in the Court's Eighth Amendment cases, both implicit and explicit, and map possible implications of these values. Chapter 5, "The Power, Problems, and Potential of 'Evolving Standards of Decency,'" written by Corinna Lain, connects the history of the evolving standards of decency doctrine, what the doctrine has accomplished, and the potential of the doctrine to shape the application of the Eighth Amendment. In Chapter 6, "Judicial Hesitancy and Majoritarianism," Will Berry describes the judicial hesitancy toward applying the Eighth Amendment and argues that the majoritarian component of the Court's doctrine offers an invitation for increased Court intervention. Chapter 7, "Punishment Purposes and Eighth Amendment Disproportionality" by Richard Frase, analyzes the connection between proportionality and the Eighth Amendment and the role that the purposes of punishment should play in the Court's application of the Amendment. In Chapter 8, "The Administrative Law of the Eighth (and Sixth) Amendment," Rick Bierschbach explores the hidden connection between administrative law and sentencing in the context of Eighth Amendment limitations. Chapter 9, "Evading the Eighth Amendment: Prison Conditions and the Courts," written by Sharon Dolovich, assesses the scope of Eighth Amendment limitations on the conditions of confinement. In Chapter 10, "Excessive Deference — The Eighth Amendment Bail Clause," Sam Wiseman explores the consequences of the Court's excessive deference to states in the context of bail in applying the Eighth Amendment. Finally, in Chapter 11, "Nor Excessive Fines Imposed," Beth Colgan makes the case for expanding the Excessive Fines Clause under the Eighth Amendment.

In Part III, the book transitions to consider the future of the Eighth Amendment. Chapter 12, "Judicial Abolition of the American Death Penalty under the Eighth Amendment: The Most Likely Path" by Carol Steiker and Jordan Steiker, considers the future of the death penalty amid its decline over the past two decades. In Chapter 13, "Back to the Future with Execution Methods," Debby Denno explores the recent shifts in execution methods and assesses where capital punishment methods might go in the future. Chapter 14, "Evolving Standards of Lethal Injection" by Eric Berger, examines the changing landscape of lethal injection drug protocols. In Chapter 15, "The Future of Juvenile Life Without Parole Sentences," Cara Drinan investigates the recent move toward abolition of JLWOP sentences in light of the recent Eighth Amendment cases in this area. Chapter 16, "Metrics of Mayhem: Quantifying Capriciousness in Capital Cases" by Sherod Thaxton, assesses the role of capriciousness in the exercise of prosecutorial discretion in capital cases and its connection to the Eighth Amendment. In Chapter 17, "Race Discrimination in Punishment," Jeffrey Kirchmeier explores the role that race has played under the Eighth Amendment in discussing the *McCleskey* case and the consequences of that decision. Finally, in Chapter 18, "Science and the Eighth Amendment," Meghan Ryan examines the role that science has played in the Court's Eighth Amendment decision-making and suggests how new science can further shape the Court's Eighth Amendment jurisprudence.

Together, these chapters endeavor to explore the past, present, and future of the Eighth Amendment. Over time, the Eighth Amendment has grown in importance and will likely continue to shape punishment practices in the United States.

A History of the Eighth Amendment

From the Founding to the Present

An Overview of Legal Thought and the Eighth Amendment's Evolution

*John D. Bessler**

On June 8, 1789, James Madison — then a member of the U.S. House of Representatives — rose in the First Congress to propose a set of amendments to the
recently ratified U.S. Constitution. "This day, Mr. Speaker," he said, "is the day
assigned for taking into consideration the subject of amendments to the constitution."[1] Some of his congressional colleagues thought the discussion premature,
but Madison persisted, contending that "[t]he applications for amendments come
from a very respectable number of our constituents, and it is certainly proper for
Congress to consider the subject, in order to quiet that anxiety which prevails in the
public mind."[2] Madison had sorted through nearly two hundred recommendations
for constitutional amendments, and he wanted Congress to act promptly.[3] "I hold it
to be my duty to unfold my ideas, and explain myself to the House in some form or
other without delay," Madison stressed.[4]

Representative William Loughton Smith of South Carolina was one of the
skeptics. Smith, alluding to Madison, asserted that "the gentleman who brought
forward the subject had done his duty," but Smith then argued "[t]hat, however
desirous this House may be to go into the consideration of amendments to the
constitution, in order to establish the liberties of the people of America on the
securest foundation, yet the important and pressing business of the Government
prevents their entering upon that subject at present."[5] The First Congress had a
tremendous amount of work to do, but Madison would not be deterred. "I am sorry
to be accessary to the loss of a single moment of time by the House," Madison

---

* Associate Professor of Law, University of Baltimore School of Law.
[1] 1 ANNALS OF CONG. 440–41 (Gales & Seaton eds., 1834).
[2] *Id.* at 441–44.
[3] JOHN D. BESSLER, CRUEL AND UNUSUAL: THE AMERICAN DEATH PENALTY AND THE FOUND-
ERS' EIGHTH AMENDMENT 162–71 (2012).
[4] 1 ANNALS OF CONG. 444 (Gales & Seaton eds., 1834).
[5] *Id.* at 446.

replied to Smith's line of argument, requesting that Congress appoint a committee to propose what amendments the country's state legislatures should quickly consider for ratification.[6] Asking that Congress "devote but one day to this subject, so far as to satisfy the public that we do not disregard their wishes," Madison said, "this House is bound by every motive of prudence, not to let the first session pass over without proposing to the State Legislatures some things to be incorporated into the constitution, that will render it as acceptable to the whole people of the United States, as it has been found acceptable to a majority of them."[7]

Madison — encouraged by his fellow Virginian, Thomas Jefferson — had specific reasons for pushing for the adoption of the constitutional amendments that would become known as the U.S. Bill of Rights.[8] "I wish, among other reasons why something should be done," Madison said on June 8th, "that those who have been friendly to the adoption of this constitution may have the opportunity of proving to those who were opposed to it that they were as sincerely devoted to liberty and a Republican Government, as those who charged them with wishing the adoption of this constitution in order to lay the foundation of an aristocracy or despotism."[9] In the wake of the U.S. Constitution's ratification, Madison hoped to bring the country — and its people — together. He stressed, "It will be a desirable thing to extinguish from the bosom of every member of the community, any apprehensions that there are those among his countrymen who wish to deprive them of the liberty for which they valiantly fought and honorably bled."[10]

Some of the amendments that Madison had in mind that day were grounded in the Glorious Revolution of 1688–1689. The Glorious Revolution, which installed William and Mary as England's new king and queen, had produced the English Bill of Rights, which, among other things, forbade "excessive" bail and fines and "cruel and unusual punishments."[11] Exorbitant fines, abusive

---

[6]   *Id.* at 448.

[7]   *Id.* at 448–49.

[8]   1 John R. Vile, The Constitutional Convention of 1787: A Comprehensive Encyclopedia of America's Founding 376 (2005) ("Jefferson wrote to Madison suggesting that 'a bill of rights is what the people are entitled to against every government on earth, general or particular, and what no just government should refuse, or rest on inferences'. He sent a series of letters to Madison between October 1787 and March 1789 advocating such a bill and especially commending it for the power that it would give to members of the judiciary to strike down unconstitutional legislation."); *cf.* Weems v. United States, 217 U.S. 349, 372 (1910) ("Patrick Henry said that there was danger in the adoption of the Constitution without a Bill of Rights. Mr. Wilson considered that it was unnecessary, and had been purposely omitted from the Constitution.").

[9]   1 Annals of Cong. 449 (Gales & Seaton eds., 1834).

[10]   *Id.*

[11]   *See, e.g.,* John D. Bessler, *A Century in the Making: The Glorious Revolution, the American Revolution, and the Origins of the U.S. Constitution's Eighth Amendment,* 27 Wm. & Mary Bill of Rts. J. 989, 996, 1001 (2019); Anthony F. Granucci, *"Nor Cruel and Unusual Punishments Inflicted:" The Original Meaning,* 57 Calif. L. Rev. 839 (1969); *see also* John D. Bessler, *The Concept of "Unusual Punishments" in Anglo-American Law: The Death Penalty*

detentions, and horrendous punishments — many at the hands of England's tyrannical Lord Chief Justice George Jeffreys — were a hallmark of the reign of King James II, and the English Bill of Rights set out the English people's civil liberties.[12] America's founders were well versed in English history, and they insisted upon historically rooted legal protections that they felt were owed to them. The English Bill of Rights, adopted by Parliament in the late seventeenth century, contained important safeguards against tyranny that Americans, too, felt should be part of their own constitutional order. "[I]n the late eighteenth century," Yale Law School professor Akhil Amar has observed, "every schoolboy in America knew that the English Bill of Rights' 1689 ban on excessive bail, excessive fines, and cruel and unusual punishments — a ban repeated virtually verbatim in the Eighth Amendment — arose as a response to the gross misbehavior of the infamous Judge Jeffreys."[13]

On the House floor, Madison pointed out that, notwithstanding the ratification of the U.S. Constitution by eleven of the thirteen states,[14] it was no secret that "there is a great number of our constituents who are dissatisfied with it."[15] As Madison argued, urging the adoption of a U.S. Bill of Rights: "We ought not to disregard their inclination, but, on principles of amity and moderation, conform to their wishes, and expressly declare the great rights of mankind secured under this constitution."[16] In seeking to protect American liberty and rights, Madison expressed the view that "the great mass of the people who opposed" the ratification of the Constitution had done so because "it did not contain effectual provisions against encroachments on particular rights, and those safeguards which they had been long accustomed to have interposed between them and the magistrate who exercises the sovereign power ... ."[17] Like the English Bill of Rights, America's revolutionary state constitutions and declarations of rights had set forth specific protections for individual rights. "[I]t will be practicable," Madison asserted, asking his colleagues to join him, "to obviate the objection, so far as to satisfy the public mind that their liberties will be perpetual ... ."[18] One of the people's consistent demands: outlaw excessive fines and bail and prohibit cruel and unusual punishments.[19]

---

as *Arbitrary, Discriminatory, and Cruel and Unusual*, 13 Nw. J.L. & Soc. Pol'y 307 (2018) (discussing the difference between "usual" and "unusual" punishments).

[12] Akhil Reed Amar, The Bill of Rights: Creation and Reconstruction 279 (1998).

[13] *Id.* at 87.

[14] The U.S. Constitution became effective after the ninth state, New Hampshire, ratified it on June 21, 1788. At the time of Madison's speech, North Carolina and Rhode Island had not yet ratified the Constitution. Jacqueline R. Kanovitz, Constitutional Law 7 (13th ed. 2012).

[15] 1 Annals of Cong. 449 (Gales & Seaton eds., 1834).

[16] *Id.*

[17] *Id.* at 449–50.

[18] *Id.* at 450.

[19] Bessler, *supra* note 3, at 173–85.

Drawing upon the text of the 1688 English Declaration of Rights (and its statutory counterpart, the English Bill of Rights of 1689),[20] as well as Virginia's Declaration of Rights (1776),[21] which contained similar language,[22] Madison proposed that these sixteen words be added to the U.S. Constitution: "Excessive bail shall not be required, nor excessive fines imposed, nor cruel and unusual punishments inflicted."[23] The idea of a bill of rights, Madison contended, was "to limit and qualify the powers of Government," with Madison taking note of the country's existing revolutionary state constitutions.[24] "The people of many States," he underscored, "have thought it necessary to raise barriers against power in all forms and departments of Government, and I am inclined to believe, if once bills of rights are established in all the States as well as the federal constitution, we shall find that although some of them are rather unimportant, yet, upon the whole, they will have a salutary tendency."[25] Madison spoke of declarations of rights as "paper barriers," but he felt that they were worthwhile because they would "have a tendency to impress some degree of respect" for the rights set forth in them.[26]

The Revolutionary War (1775–1783) severed America's political ties to its mother country, but legal language — on both sides of the Atlantic — was deeply rooted in custom and tradition. The early American state constitutions and declarations of rights, in fact, borrowed heavily from English law, although they were inspired, too, by the Enlightenment,[27] not by the same set of circumstances that fueled the

---

[20] Gerard N. Magliocca, *The Bill of Rights as a Term of Art*, 92 NOTRE DAME L. REV. 231, 241 n.44 (2016) ("The English Declaration of Rights was issued by an irregular Parliament sitting without a king, and after William III was crowned the Declaration was reenacted as the Bill of Rights.").

[21] VA. DECLARATION OF RIGHTS OF 1776.

[22] RAY RAPHAEL, FOUNDERS: THE PEOPLE WHO BROUGHT YOU A NATION 299 (2009).

[23] 1 ANNALS OF CONG. 450–52 (Gales & Seaton eds., 1834).

[24] *Id.* at 454.

[25] *Id.*

[26] *Id.* at 455.

[27] *See* JOHN D. BESSLER, THE BARON AND THE MARQUIS: LIBERTY, TYRANNY, AND THE ENLIGHTENMENT MAXIM THAT CAN REMAKE AMERICAN CRIMINAL JUSTICE (2019) (documenting Montesquieu's creation of a popular eighteenth-century maxim — one later publicized by Cesare Beccaria — that any punishment that goes beyond necessity is "tyrannical"); JOHN D. BESSLER, THE BIRTH OF AMERICAN LAW: AN ITALIAN PHILOSOPHER AND THE AMERICAN REVOLUTION (2014) (documenting Beccaria's influence in America); JOHN D. BESSLER, THE CELEBRATED MARQUIS: AN ITALIAN NOBLE AND THE MAKING OF THE MODERN WORLD (2018) (describing Beccaria's influence on punishment practices); JOHN D. BESSLER, *The Marquis Beccaria: An Italian Penal Reformer's Meteoric Rise in the British Isles in the Transatlantic Republic of Letters*, 4 DICIOTTESIMO SECOLO 107 (2019) (detailing the reception of Beccaria's *Dei delitti e delle pene* (1764), translated into English as *An Essay on Crimes and Punishments* (1767)). The Enlightenment not only shaped Americans' understanding of the Eighth Amendment proscriptions against "excessive" bail and fines and "cruel and unusual punishments," but it spawned Article 8 of the French Declaration of the Rights of Man and of the Citizen (1789), which only permits punishments that are "strictly and evidently necessary." LOUIS HENKIN, THE AGE OF RIGHTS 162 (1990); ROBERT NARES, PRINCIPLES OF GOVERNMENT DEDUCED FROM REASON, SUPPORTED BY ENGLISH EXPERIENCE, AND OPPOSED TO FRENCH ERRORS 154 (1792).

Glorious Revolution.[28] After the Virginia Declaration of Rights, drafted by George Mason[29] and adopted on June 12, 1776, had barred excessive bail and fines and cruel and unusual punishments, other states had quickly followed suit. Section 9 of the Virginia Declaration, like Section 10 of the English Bill of Rights, used the hortatory "ought not," specifically providing: "That excessive bail ought not to be required, nor excessive fines imposed, nor cruel and unusual punishments inflicted."[30]

Other American lawmakers also used the "ought" verbiage in framing their own declarations and bills of rights. On August 14, 1776, for example, the State of Maryland adopted two separate clauses — one directed at the legislative branch and another targeted at the judicial branch. Clause 14 read: "That sanguinary laws ought to be avoided, so far as is consistent with the safety of the State; and no law, to inflict cruel and unusual pains and penalties, ought to be made in any case, or at any time hereafter."[31] And Clause 22 provided "[t]hat excessive bail ought not to be required, nor excessive fines imposed, nor cruel or unusual punishments inflicted, by the courts of law."[32]

From the 1770s to the 1790s, American lawmakers throughout the United States adopted legal prohibitions on cruel punishments and excessive governmental actions. Although those proscriptions were rarely litigated in the early days of the republic,[33] they were seen as important constitutional guarantees. On September 11, 1776, for instance, Delaware adopted this provision: "[t]hat excessive bail ought not to be required, nor excessive fines imposed, nor cruel or unusual punishments inflicted."[34] The use of the disjunctive "or" between "cruel" and "unusual" would later show up in the Massachusetts Constitution of 1780[35] and in the Northwest Ordinance of 1787.[36] Other states adopted similar variations, with Pennsylvania's 1776 constitution forbidding "[e]xcessive bail," providing that "all fines shall be moderate," and stating that the penal laws "shall be reformed by the legislature of

---

[28] *Foundations of American Government*, USHISTORY.ORG, http://www.ushistory.org/gov/2.asp (last visited Nov. 4, 2018).

[29] JEFF BROADWATER, GEORGE MASON: FORGOTTEN FOUNDERS 80–81, 87–88 (2006) (noting Mason's role in drafting the Virginia Declaration of Rights and how he drew on a variety of sources, including the English Bill of Rights, in drafting that document).

[30] Jeremy Rabkin, *Constitutional Firepower: New Light on the Meaning of the Second Amendment*, 86 J. CRIM. L. & CRIMINOLOGY 231, 232–35 (1995).

[31] MD. CONST. cl. 14 (1776).

[32] *Id.* at cl. 22.

[33] *See, e.g.*, STUART BANNER, THE DEATH PENALTY: AN AMERICAN HISTORY 232 (2009) ("Neither the Eighth Amendment's cruel and unusual punishments clause nor its state constitutional analogues were used much in the century that followed. The lack of much early litigation on the subject, combined with the virtual absence of recorded debate over the Eighth Amendment and its antecedents, has left little evidence of exactly what Americans of the late eighteenth century understood by the concept of cruel and unusual punishment.").

[34] DEL. DECL. OF RTS. § 16 (Sept. 11, 1776).

[35] BESSLER, *supra* note 3, at 179–80.

[36] *Id.* at 118–19.

this state, as soon as may be, and punishments made in some cases less sanguinary, and in general more proportionate to the crimes."[37]

Safeguards at the federal level were seen by American revolutionaries as indispensable to liberty. As "Brutus" wrote in the *New York Journal* on November 1, 1787: "For the security of liberty it has been declared, 'that excessive bail should not be required, nor excessive fines imposed, nor cruel or unusual punishments inflicted ... .'" "These provisions," Brutus argued, "are as necessary under the general government as under that of the individual states; for the power of the former is as complete to the purpose of requiring bail, imposing fines, inflicting punishments ... in certain cases, as the other."[38] On November 7, 1787, in Philadelphia's *Independent Gazetteer*, "Philadelphiensis" wrote of the original Constitution's lack of adequate protections as drafted at the Constitutional Convention:

> To such lengths have these bold conspirators carried their scheme of despotism, that your most sacred rights and privileges are surrendered at discretion. When government thinks proper, under the pretense of writing a libel, &c. it may imprison, inflict the most cruel and unusual punishment, seize property, carry on prosecutions, &c. and the unfortunate citizen has no *magna charta*, no *bill of rights*, to protect him; nay, the prosecution may be carried on in such a manner that even a *jury* will not be allowed him.[39]

By 1790, the year before the ratification of the U.S. Bill of Rights, nine states had constitutional provisions barring "cruel and unusual," "cruel or unusual," or "cruel" punishments.[40] Those prohibitions[41] were explained, in part, by James Iredell, a future U.S. Supreme Court Justice.[42] North Carolina's attorney general from 1779 to 1782, Iredell, in replying to George Mason's objections to the original Constitution's lack of a federal bill of rights, clarified in 1788 why — in his judgment — such prohibitions ended up in early American constitutions. Mason had begun his objections to the federal constitution: "There is no declaration of rights: and the laws of the general government being paramount to the laws and constitutions of the

[37] *Id.* at 178–80.
[38] 1 THE COMPLETE ANTI-FEDERALIST 375 (Herbert J. Storing ed., 1981).
[39] BESSLER, *supra* note 3, at 163.
[40] *Id.* at 177–81.
[41] ROLAND ADICKES, THE UNITED STATES CONSTITUTION AND CITIZENS' RIGHTS: THE INTERPRETATION AND MIS-INTERPRETATION OF THE AMERICAN CONTRACT FOR GOVERNANCE 132–33 (2001); THE COMPLETE BILL OF RIGHTS: THE DRAFTS, DEBATES, SOURCES, AND ORIGINS 922–25 (Neil H. Cogen ed., 2d ed. 2015). Such prohibitions became a standard feature of American constitutions. BANNER, *supra* note 33, at 231–32 ("By the time the Constitution was up for ratification, the prohibition of cruel and unusual punishments was such a standard element in documents of the sort that its absence was a common source of complaint among the Constitution's opponents. There was accordingly almost no debate over the constitutional amendment that became number eight.").
[42] Iredell served on the nation's highest court from 1790 until his death in 1799. THE SUPREME COURT JUSTICES: ILLUSTRATED BIOGRAPHIES, 1789–2012, 23 (Clare Cushman ed., 3d ed. 2013).

several states, the declarations of rights, in the separate states, are no security."[43] While some of America's founders believed that the U.S. Congress, like Parliament, should have absolute power to decide what punishments to inflict, a majority of them felt that the U.S. Constitution needed a written bill of rights, just like so many of the states had already put in place.

The majority of early American state constitutions had the familiar prohibitions against excessive bail and fines and cruel punishments. But not every lawmaker believed that similar prohibitions were needed in the federal constitution, leading to friction as America's founders vocally debated the necessity of a U.S. Bill of Rights. In fact, in 1788, Iredell specifically opposed the inclusion of a prohibition against cruel and unusual punishments in the U.S. Constitution, which was debated one hundred years after the Glorious Revolution. He did so — albeit unsuccessfully, as others insisted on what became the Eighth Amendment's written safeguards — because of his belief that Congress should have the prerogative to decide for itself upon the punishments for crimes in the areas over which it had jurisdiction to legislate (e.g., counterfeiting, piracy, felonies committed on the high seas, offenses against the law of nations, and treason).[44]

In discussing the prohibitions in early American state constitutions, Iredell looked to English history even as he recognized that Americans were making their own history.[45] "It may be observed, in the first place," he wrote, "that a declaration against 'cruel and unusual punishments' formed part of an article in the Bill of Rights at the revolution in England in 1688."[46] "The prerogative of the Crown having been grossly abused in some preceding reigns," Iredell stressed of Stuart abuses, "it was thought proper to notice every grievance they had endured, and those declarations went to an abuse of power in the Crown only, but were never intended to limit the authority of Parliament."[47] "Many of these articles of the Bill of Rights in England, without a due attention to the difference of the cases," Iredell continued, "were eagerly adopted when our constitutions were formed, the minds of men then being so warmed with their exertions in the cause of liberty as to lean too much perhaps towards a jealousy of power to repose a proper confidence in their own government."[48]

Iredell put more faith in federal lawmakers, asserting that Congress had "a just right" to delineate crimes and punishments, pondering "whether it is practicable and proper to prescribe limits to its exercise, for fear that they should inflict

---

[43] George Mason, *Objections to the Constitution* (Oct. 1787), *in* 1 JON L. WAKELYN, BIRTH OF THE BILL OF RIGHTS: ENCYCLOPEDIA OF THE ANTIFEDERALISTS 233 (2004).

[44] James Iredell, *Marcus, Answers to Mr. Mason's Objections to the New Constitution*, THE FOUNDERS' CONSTITUTION, http://press-pubs.uchicago.edu/founders/documents/amendVIIIs11 .html (last visited Nov. 4, 2018).

[45] *Id.*

[46] *Id.*

[47] *Id.*

[48] *Id.*

punishments unusual and severe."[49] Article I, Section 8 of the U.S. Constitution, for example, gives Congress the power "[t]o provide for the Punishment of counterfeiting the Securities and current Coin of the United States" and "[t]o define and punish Piracies and Felonies committed on the high Seas, and Offences against the Law of Nations."[50] The question that America's founders so vigorously debated was whether such legislative power should be checked in any way.

For Iredell, the prohibition against cruel and unusual punishments was too ambiguous to warrant inclusion in the U.S. Constitution.[51] "From these articles in the State constitutions," Iredell explained, "many things were attempted to be transplanted into our new Constitution, which would either have been nugatory or improper."[52] "This is one of them," Iredell offered of the proscription.[53] "The expressions 'unusual and severe' or 'cruel and unusual,'" Iredell emphasized, "surely would have been too vague to have been of any consequence, since they admit of no clear and precise signification."[54] "If to guard against punishments being too severe," Iredell observed, the Constitutional Convention in Philadelphia had enumerated a vast variety of cruel punishments, and prohibited the use of any of them, let the number have been ever so great, an inexhaustible fund must have been unmentioned, and if our government had been disposed to be cruel their invention would only have been put to a little more trouble."[55]

"If to avoid this difficulty," he added, "they had determined, not negatively what punishments should not be exercised, but positively what punishments should, this must have led them into a labyrinth of detail which in the original constitution of a government would have appeared perfectly ridiculous, and not left a room for such changes, according to circumstances, as must be in the power of every Legislature that is rationally formed."[56] "[W]hen we enter into particulars," Iredell concluded, "we must be convinced that the proposition of such a restriction would have led to nothing useful, or to something dangerous, and therefore that its omission is not chargeable as a fault in the new Constitution."[57] In short, Iredell believed a constitutional restraint was neither necessary nor advisable, with Iredell instead trusting Congress to set the rules of the road.

[49] *Id.*
[50] U.S. Const. art. I, § 8.
[51] *See* Iredell, *supra* note 44.
[52] *Id.*
[53] *Id.*
[54] *Id.*
[55] *Id.*
[56] *Id.*
[57] The Federalists and Other Contemporary Papers on the Constitution of the United States 907–08 (E. H. Scott ed., 1894); 2 Griffith J. McRee, Life and Correspondence of James Iredell, One of the Associate Justices of the Supreme Court of the United States 206–07 (1858); Pamphlets on the Constitution of the United States, Published during Its Discussion by the People 1787–1788, at 32, 359–60 (Paul Leicester Ford ed., 1888); Iredell, *supra* note 44.

But James Iredell's views did not prevail, and the broad prohibitions against "excessive" bail and fines and "cruel and unusual punishments" — ones now set forth in the U.S. Constitution's Eighth Amendment — were included in the U.S. Bill of Rights without much debate. At the First Congress, only two mentions were made about the prohibitions, both of which tracked Iredell's concerns about the vagueness or indefiniteness of the text. William Loughton Smith, a South Carolina attorney who had studied law in Europe during the Revolutionary War and who, in Congress, defended the institution of slavery, "objected to the words 'nor cruel and unusual punishments,' the import of them being too indefinite."[58]

Samuel Livermore of New Hampshire, another lawyer, also offered this perspective: "The clause seems to express a great deal of humanity, on which account I have no objection to it; but as it seems to have no meaning in it, I do not think it necessary."[59] Livermore raised these questions: "What is meant by the terms excessive bail? Who are to be the judges? What is understood by excessive fines?"[60] Livermore's answer: "It lies with the court to determine." "No cruel and unusual punishment is to be inflicted," Livermore added of the other proposed prohibition, offering this commentary: "it is sometimes necessary to hang a man, villains often deserve whipping, and perhaps having their ears cut off; but are we in future to be prevented from inflicting these punishments because they are cruel?"[61] "If a more lenient mode of correcting vice and deterring others from the commission of it could be invented," Livermore concluded, "it would be very prudent in the Legislature to adopt it; but until we have some security that this will be done, we ought not to be restrained from making necessary laws by any declaration of this kind."[62] In spite of these concerns, the Eighth Amendment's text "was agreed to by a considerable majority" of legislators in the First Congress.[63] Just as early American state constitutions checked the power of state legislatures, the U.S. Bill of Rights checked the power of the national government, including its legislative branch.

Since its ratification in 1791, the Eighth Amendment has been endlessly debated.[64] In the generations that came after America's founders, everyone — but

---

[58] BESSLER, *supra* note 3, at 186; THE COMPLETE BILL OF RIGHTS: THE DRAFTS, DEBATES, SOURCES, AND ORIGINS 926–27 (Neil H. Cogen ed., 2d ed. 2015); DUNCAN J. MACLEOD, SLAVERY, RACE AND THE AMERICAN REVOLUTION 101 (1974); 51 PROCEEDINGS OF THE MASSACHUSETTS HISTORICAL SOCIETY 21–22 (1917).

[59] 1 ANNALS OF CONG. 754 (James Gales ed. 1789).

[60] *Id.*

[61] *Id.*

[62] *Id.*

[63] *Id.*

[64] Joseph L. Hoffmann, *"The 'Cruel and Unusual Punishment' Clause,"* in DAVID J. BODENHAMER & JAMES W. ELY, JR., THE BILL OF RIGHTS IN MODERN AMERICA 173 (rev. & expanded 2000) ("The cruel and unusual punishment clause of the Eighth Amendment today remains a constitutional enigma.").

especially lawyers and judges — had their own take on the meaning of its words.[65]
For example, Joseph Story, an Associate Justice of the U.S. Supreme Court who
served in that position from 1811 to 1845, explained why, in his view, the Eighth
Amendment was adopted. In his *Commentaries on the Constitution of the United
States* (1833), written before the Fourteenth Amendment's ratification, Story gave
this history and context, taking note of how the Eighth Amendment, at that time,
only served to restrain the *federal* government:

> Sec. 1896. The next amendment is: "Excessive bail shall not be required; nor
> excessive fines imposed; nor cruel and unusual punishments inflicted." This is an
> exact transcript of a clause in the bill of rights, framed at the revolution of 1688. The
> provision would seem to be wholly unnecessary in a free government, since it is
> scarcely possible, that any department of such a government should authorize, or
> justify such atrocious conduct. It was, however, adopted, as an admonition to all
> departments of the national government,[66] to warn them against such violent
> proceedings, as had taken place in England in the arbitrary reigns of some of the
> Stuarts. In those times, a demand of excessive bail was often made against persons,
> who were odious to the court, and its favourites; and on failing to procure it, they
> were committed to prison. Enormous fines and amercements were also sometimes
> imposed, and cruel and vindictive punishments inflicted. Upon this subject
> Mr. Justice Blackstone has wisely remarked, that sanguinary laws are a bad symptom
> of the distemper of any state, or at least of its weak constitution . . . .
>
> Sec. 1897. It has been held in the state courts, (and the point does not seem ever to
> have arisen in the courts of the United States,) that this clause does not apply to
> punishments inflicted in a state court for a crime against such state; but that the
> prohibition is addressed solely to the national government, and operates, as a
> restriction upon its powers.[67]

---

[65] The debate has divided jurists and legal scholars into two competing camps: originalists and
living constitutionalists. ROBERT W. BENNETT & LAWRENCE B. SOLUM, CONSTITUTIONAL
ORIGINALISM: A DEBATE (2016). *Compare* RONALD DWORKIN, LIFE'S DOMINION: AN ARGU-
MENT ABOUT ABORTION, EUTHANASIA, AND INDIVIDUAL FREEDOM 127 (1994) ("The Eighth
Amendment forbids 'cruel and unusual punishment,' but it does not indicate whether any
particular methods of executing criminals — hanging or electrocution, for example — are cruel
or, indeed, whether the death penalty is itself cruel no matter what method of execution is used."),
with ANTONIN SCALIA, REFLECTIONS ON LAW, FAITH, AND LIFE WELL LIVED 192 (Christopher
J. Scalia & Edward Whelan eds., 2017) ("[P]erhaps the area of our jurisprudence that most clearly
reflects the 'living Constitution's philosophy is that which pertains to the Eighth Amendment, the
provision of our Bill of Rights that proscribes cruel and unusual punishments.'").

[66] Other public officials around that time also saw the Eighth Amendment as an admonition.
Gov. Gabriel Moore, Governor's Message (Tuscaloosa, Alabama) (Nov. 16, 1830), THE DEMO-
CRAT (Huntsville, AL), Nov. 25, 1830, at 2 ("[T]he federal compact points emphatically to the
protection of the personal rights of the citizen, as one of its prominent objects: — thus we find
it forbidding . . . the exaction of unreasonable fines, and the infliction of cruel and unusual
punishments. These, gentlemen, we should receive as powerful admonitions to us, and great
incentives in this work of humanity.").

[67] 3 JOSEPH L. STORY, COMMENTARIES ON THE CONSTITUTION OF THE UNITED STATES ch. 44,
§§ 1896–1897 (1833).

The Eighth Amendment's prohibitions against "excessive" bail and fines and "cruel and unusual punishments" are broad and sweeping, and they apply not just to judicial discretion but restrain the conduct of all three branches of government: legislative, executive, and judicial.[68] The rub has always been to determine precisely *what* they prohibit.[69] In *A Treatise on the Constitutional Limitations which Rest upon the Legislative Power of the States of the American Union* (1868), Thomas Cooley — a Michigan supreme court justice — wrote in a section on "Excessive Fines and Cruel and Unusual Punishments" that "the question what fine shall be imposed is one addressed to the discretion of the court."[70] "But," Cooley added, "it is a discretion to be judicially exercised, and it would be error in law to inflict a punishment clearly excessive."[71] As Cooley emphasized: "A fine should have some reference to the party's ability to pay it. By Magna Charta a freeman was not to be amerced for a small fault, but according to the degree of the fault, and for a great crime in proportion to the heinousness of it, *saving to him his contenement;*[72] and after the same manner a merchant, *saving to him his merchandise.*"[73] "The merciful spirit of these provisions addresses itself to the criminal courts of the American States through the provisions of their constitutions," Cooley declared.[74]

In another section of his treatise, Cooley continued: "It is somewhat difficult to determine precisely what is meant by cruel and unusual punishments."[75] "Probably a punishment declared by statute for an offence which was punishable in the same way at the common law," he wrote, "could not be regarded as cruel or

[68] BESSLER, *supra* note 3, at 294; JOHN C. KLOTTER & JACQUELINE R. KANOVITZ, CONSTITUTIONAL LAW 531 (6th ed. 1991); Granucci, *supra* note 11, at 840. Article 10 of the English Bill of Rights, by contrast, was aimed at curtailing runaway judicial discretion. BESSLER, *supra* note 3, at 173 (noting that Blackstone's *Commentaries on the Laws of England* describes how the arbitrariness of judges is limited by the proscriptions in the English Bill of Rights against excessive fines and cruel and unusual punishments).

[69] *See, e.g.,* O'Neil v. Vermont, 144 U.S. 323, 325–37 (1892) (finding the Eighth Amendment inapplicable to a state law punishment in which a defendant had been found guilty of 307 offenses of selling intoxicating liquors in violation of Vermont law and sentenced to be fined and to be imprisoned at hard labor for 19,914 days in the event the fine was not paid); *id.* at 337, 339–40 (Field, J., dissenting) (labeling the punishment at issue "unusual and cruel" while noting that such a designation "is usually applied" to punishments "which inflict torture, such as the rack, the thumbscrew, the iron boot, the stretching of limbs and the like, which are attended with acute pain and suffering").

[70] THOMAS M. COOLEY, A TREATISE ON THE CONSTITUTIONAL LIMITATIONS WHICH REST UPON THE LEGISLATIVE POWER OF THE STATES OF THE AMERICAN UNION 328–29 (1868).

[71] *Id.*

[72] In old English law, a *contenement* was understood to be "that which is held together with another thing; that which is connected *with a tenement* or thing holden; countenance, appearance, credit or reputation." ALEXANDER M. BURRILL, A NEW LAW DICTIONARY AND GLOSSARY 272 (1850); *see also* Nicholas M. McLean, *Livelihood, Ability to Pay, and the Original Meaning of the Excessive Fines Clause,* 40 HASTINGS CONST. L.Q. 833, 853–57 (2013) (reviewing the history of the legal concept of *salvo contenemento* in English law).

[73] *See* COOLEY *supra* note 70, at 328–29.

[74] *Id.*

[75] *Id.* at 329–30.

unusual in the constitutional sense."[76] "And probably any new statutory offence," he added, "may be made punishable to the extent permitted by the common law for similar offences."[77] "But those degrading punishments which in any State had become obsolete before its existing constitution was adopted," Cooley opined, "we think may well be held to be forbidden by it as cruel and unusual."[78] As Cooley editorialized: "We may well doubt the right to establish the whipping-post and the pillory in States where they were never recognized as instruments of punishment, or in States whose constitutions, revised since public opinion had banished them, had forbidden cruel and unusual punishments."[79] "In such a case," Cooley explained, "the public sentiment had condemned them as cruel, and they had not merely become unusual, but altogether ceased to be inflicted."[80]

How legal commentators viewed the Eighth Amendment's prohibitions were, necessarily, shaped by their own times — and by their own understanding of history and the meaning of the words. For example, in 1824,[81] Peter Du Ponceau — the provost of the Law Academy of Philadelphia — distinguished America's prohibition on cruel and unusual punishments from the earlier one contained in the English Bill of Rights. Du Ponceau wrote of "certain harsh punishments which our modern manners reprove, but which still stain the page of the common law; as for instance the punishment of petty treason in men by drawing and quartering, and in women by burning."[82] On the difference between American and English law, he offered:

> But the 10th amendment of our Constitution has sufficiently provided that "no cruel and unusual punishment shall be inflicted," which word "unusual" evidently refers to the United States, and the time when the Constitution was made, and therefore is not to be confounded with the same clause in the English bill of rights, which referring to another period and to another country, may have been differently construed.[83]

Du Ponceau emphasized that *peine forte et dure* (pressing to death) and burning in the hand for manslaughter had been abolished, with "milder substitutes

---

[76] *Id.*

[77] *Id.*

[78] *Id.*

[79] COOLEY, *supra* note 70, at 329–30.

[80] *Id.*

[81] PETER S. DU PONCEAU, A DISSERTATION ON THE NATURE AND EXTENT OF THE JURISDICTION OF THE COURTS OF THE UNITED STATES, BEING A VALEDICTORY ADDRESS DELIVERED TO THE STUDENTS OF THE LAW ACADEMY OF PHILADELPHIA, AT THE CLOSE OF THE ACADEMIC YEAR, ON THE 22ND OF APRIL, 1824 (1824).

[82] *Id.* at 95.

[83] James Madison originally proposed twelve amendments to the U.S. Constitution. What became the Eighth Amendment was originally proposed as *"Article the Tenth." Congress of the United States*, LIBRARY OF CONGRESS, Printed Ephemera Collection, Portfolio O, Folder 6 (1789), https://www.loc.gov/item/90898145/.

provided by our national statutes."[84] As Du Ponceau wrote, reflecting his view of what he perceived as the progressive nature of his own time: "the common law as modified by our Constitution, by our laws, manners and usages, is as wholesome and as harmless a system, in criminal as well as in civil cases, as any that can be devised."[85] Du Ponceau continued, giving his assessment of the state of the law and expressing his views on American life: "As to offences not capital, cruel and unusual punishments being forbidden by our Constitution, there remains none but fine, imprisonment and, perhaps, whipping and the pillory. I hope I shall hear nothing of the ducking stool and other obsolete remains of the customs of barbarous ages."[86] "The pillory and whipping," Du Ponceau added, "are out of use in most of the States, imprisonment at hard labour having been substituted in lieu of them."[87] "I see nothing inhuman in the moderate infliction of either of these penalties, nor any reason why we should reject the common law on their account," he emphasized.[88]

The debate over the Eighth Amendment has important — sometimes life or death — consequences for persons accused or convicted of crimes,[89] as the U.S. Supreme Court's jurisprudence has made clear.[90] That debate has played out in countless law review articles,[91] in state and federal courts,[92] and before the highest

---

[84] Du Ponceau, *supra* note 81, at 95–96.

[85] *Id.*

[86] *Id.*

[87] *Id.*

[88] *Id.* at 96–97. The pillory and the whipping post were once usual punishments in colonial and early America. Peter C. Holloran, Historical Dictionary of New England 496 (2d ed. 2017); Howard O. Sprogle, The Philadelphia Police, Past and Present 56 (1887).

[89] *See* Michael Meltsner, Cruel and Unusual: The Supreme Court and Capital Punishment (2011).

[90] John D. Bessler, *Introduction, in* Stephen Breyer, Against the Death Penalty (John D. Bessler ed., 2016) (discussing the U.S. Supreme Court's death penalty jurisprudence).

[91] *E.g.*, William W. Berry III, *Evolved Standards, Evolving Justices? The Case for a Broader Application of the Eighth Amendment*, 98 Wash. U. L. Rev. 105 (2018); Laurence Claus, *The Antidiscrimination Eighth Amendment*, 28 Harv. J. L. & Pub. Pol'y 119 (2004); Phyllis Goldfarb, *Arriving Where We've Been: Death's Indignity and the Eighth Amendment*, 103 Iowa L. Rev. Online 386 (2018); Scott W. Howe, *The Implications of Incorporating the Eighth Amendment Prohibition on Excessive Bail*, 43 Hofstra L. Rev. 1039 (2015); Meghan J. Ryan, *Taking Dignity Seriously: Excavating the Backdrop of the Eighth Amendment*, 2016 U. Ill. L. Rev. 2129 (2016).

[92] In the 1970s, political scientist Larry Berkson put it this way:

[T]he concept of cruel and unusual punishment has, until very recently, remained an obscure, if important, part of the Bill of Rights. For example, after an exhaustive search of opinions reported prior to 1870, only 20 cases were found that dealt with the prohibition. Beginning with that date, however, larger numbers of cases raising the issue did begin appearing before state and federal courts. The total by 1916 was slightly over 200 cases. The number of cases reported during each subsequent ten-year period rose in rather even increments until the 1955–66 era. At that time, litigation of the inhibition nearly doubled (253 cases).

Larry C. Berkson, *The Eighth Amendment: A New Frontier of Creative Constitutional Law, in* Civil Liberties: Policy and Policy Making 107 (Stephen L. Wasby ed., 1976).

court in the land, the U.S. Supreme Court.[93] Although the Eighth Amendment's prohibitions originally applied only against the federal government,[94] the Supreme Court — using its selective incorporation doctrine[95] — made the ban on "cruel and unusual punishments" applicable against the states in 1962[96] in *Robinson v. California*.[97] In 1971, consistent with the history surrounding the Fourteenth Amendment's post-Civil War ratification,[98] the Supreme Court also assumed that the bar on "excessive bail" is a fundamental legal protection applicable against the states.[99] And more recently, in 2019 in *Timbs v. Indiana*, the Court held that the Eighth Amendment's Excessive Fines Clause applies against the states.[100]

The Eighth Amendment's protections have been part of America's national conversation for multiple centuries. It was only in the 1950s and 1960s, however, that modern Eighth Amendment jurisprudence emerged. In 1958, the U.S. Supreme Court crafted its now famous "evolving standards of decency" test.[101] Ten years later, in 1968, Harry Blackmun — then a judge on the U.S. Court of

---

[93] *See generally* CAROL S. STEIKER & JORDAN M. STEIKER, COURTING DEATH: THE SUPREME COURT AND CAPITAL PUNISHMENT (2016).

[94] Barron v. Baltimore, 32 U.S. (7 Pet.) 243 (1833); Pervear v. Massachusetts, 72 U.S. (5 Wall.) 475 (1866); *see also* GEORGE F. COLE ET AL., THE AMERICAN SYSTEM OF CRIMINAL JUSTICE 169 (15th ed. 2017) ("For most of U.S. history, the Bill of Rights did not apply to most criminal cases, because it was designed to protect people from abusive actions by the federal government.").

[95] KÄREN MATISON HESS & CHRISTINE HESS ORTHMANN, INTRODUCTION TO LAW ENFORCE-MENT AND CRIMINAL JUSTICE 55 (10th ed. 2012) ("The selective incorporation doctrine holds that only those provisions of the Bill of Rights fundamental to the American legal process are made applicable to the states through the due process clause.").

[96] William J. Brennan, Jr., *State Constitutions and the Protections of Individual Rights*, 90 HARV. L. REV. 489, 493 (1977) (noting that the Eighth Amendment's prohibition against cruel and unusual punishments "was applied to state action in 1962"); *cf.* Louisiana ex rel. Francis v. Resweber, 329 U.S. 459, 462 (1947) (assuming, *arguendo*, that the prohibition against "cruel and unusual punishment" applied to the states).

[97] 370 U.S. 660 (1962); *see also* NANCY D. CAMPBELL, DISCOVERING ADDICTION: THE SCIENCE AND POLITICS OF SUBSTANCE ABUSE RESEARCH 135 (2007) ("The U.S. Supreme Court inter-preted addiction as a condition akin to illness in *Robinson v. California* (1962), opining that 'even one day in prison would be a cruel and unusual punishment for the 'crime' of having a common cold.'").

[98] John D. Bessler, *The Inequality of America's Death Penalty: A Crossroads for Capital Punish-ment at the Intersection of the Eighth and Fourteenth Amendments*, 73 WASH. & LEE L. REV. ONLINE 487, 541 (2016), https://scholarlycommons.law.wlu.edu/wlulr-online/vol73/iss1/22; *see also* Steven G. Calabresi & Sarah E. Agudo, *Individual Rights under State Constitutions When the Fourteenth Amendment Was Ratified in 1868: What Rights Are Deeply Rooted in American History and Tradition?*, 87 TEX. L. REV. 7, 83 (2008) ("Thirty-four states — or an Article V, three-quarters consensus — in 1868 had clauses in their state constitutions that banned cruel and unusual punishments."); *id.* at 83 ("Ninety-one percent of all Americans in 1868 — again a huge supermajority — lived in states with bans on cruel and unusual punishments.").

[99] Schilb v. Kuebel, 404 U.S. 357, 365 (1971) (noting that bail is "basic to our system of law" and that the "Eighth Amendment's proscription of excessive bail has been assumed to have application to the States through the Fourteenth Amendment").

[100] State v. Timbs, 139 S. Ct. 682 (2019).

[101] Trop v. Dulles, 356 U.S. 86, 101 (1958) (plurality opinion).

Appeals for the Eighth Circuit — applied that test, ruling in *Jackson v. Bishop*[102] that the prohibition against "cruel and unusual punishments" outlawed the use of the strap in Arkansas prisons.[103] After citing language from *Trop v. Dulles*[104] about "the dignity of man" anchoring that prohibition, Blackmun wrote: "we have no difficulty in reaching the conclusion that the use of the strap in the penitentiaries of Arkansas is punishment which, in this last third of the 20th century, runs afoul of the Eighth Amendment; that the strap's use, irrespective of any precautionary conditions which may be imposed, offends contemporary concepts of decency and human dignity and precepts of civilization which we profess to possess."[105]

Each generation — from Glorious Revolution participants, to America's framers, to nineteenth-century legal commentators, to modern-day jurists — has put its own indelible stamp upon the "excessive bail," "excessive fines," and "cruel and unusual punishments" prohibitions.[106] And that process will continue, with the law inevitably evolving as American society evolves. How one generation views what is "excessive" or "cruel and unusual" will not — and should not — inhibit a later generation's views.[107] If the Eighth Amendment

---

[102] 404 F.2d 571 (8th Cir. 1968).

[103] TINSLEY E. YARBROUGH, HARRY A. BLACKMUN: THE OUTSIDER JUSTICE 101 (2008).

[104] *Trop*, 356 U.S. at 100.

[105] *Jackson*, 404 F.2d at 579–80. The fact that *non-lethal* corporal punishments have been declared unconstitutional makes the continued use of *lethal* punishments a particular enigma. *See, e.g.,* John D. Bessler, *The Anomaly of Executions: The Cruel and Unusual Punishments Clause in the 21st Century*, 2 BRIT. J. AM. LEG. STUDIES 297 (2013); John D. Bessler, *Tinkering around the Edges: The Supreme Court's Death Penalty Jurisprudence*, 49 AM. CRIM. L. REV. 1913 (2012).

[106] *E.g.,* J. L. DE LOLME, THE CONSTITUTION OF ENGLAND; OR, AN ACCOUNT OF THE ENGLISH GOVERNMENT, IN WHICH IT IS COMPARED, BOTH WITH THE REPUBLICAN FORM OF GOVERN-MENT, AND THE OTHER MONARCHIES IN EUROPE 371–72 (corr. ed. 1796) (after noting that "the use of Torture has, from the earliest times, been utterly unknown in England," emphasizing that "[f]rom the same cause also arose that remarkable forbearance of the English laws, to use any cruel severity in the punishments which experience shewed it was necessary for the preservation of Society to establish" and that "so anxious has the English Legislature been to establish mercy, even to convicted Offenders, as a fundamental principle of the Government of England, that they made it an express article of that great public Compact which was framed at the important era of the Revolution, that 'no cruel and unusual punishments should be used.'") (citing English Bill of Rights, Art. x — "Excessive bail ought not to be required, nor excessive fines imposed; nor cruel and unusual punishments inflicted.").

[107] Early English legal commentators, such as William Blackstone, did not view death sentences as violating the "cruel and unusual punishments" prohibition, though they frequently recounted how the English common law had renounced the use of torture. *E.g.,* 4 WILLIAM BLACKSTONE, COMMENTARIES ON THE LAWS OF ENGLAND 320–21 (1769) ("[T]he trial by rack is utterly unknown to the law of England; though once when the dukes of Exeter and Suffolk, and other ministers of Henry VI, had laid a design to introduce the civil law into this kingdom as the rule of government, for a beginning thereof they erected a rack of torture; which was called in derision the duke of Exeter's daughter, and still remains in the tower of London: where it was occasionally used as an engine of state, not of law, more than once in the reign of queen Elizabeth."); *id.* at 370 (noting the law's authorization of capital punishment and hanging, embowelling alive, beheading, quartering, and burning alive as methods of execution, but adding that "the humanity of the English nation has authorized, by a tacit consent, an almost

were read in a static manner,[108] an approach the U.S. Supreme Court explicitly rejected decades ago, its prohibitions — originally targeted at only the most extreme and grotesque of Stuart excesses[109] — would be rendered moot or meaningless in the modern age.[110] Nonetheless, in 2019, a bare majority of the Supreme Court, in its 5-4 decision in *Bucklew v. Precythe*, purported to "examine the original and historical understanding of the Eighth Amendment" without even alluding to the Court's long-prevailing "evolving standards of decency" test.[111] It remains to be seen how the Court will rule in future cases.

general mitigation of such part of these judgments as favour of torture or cruelty: a sledge or hurdle being usually allowed to such traitors as are condemned to be drawn, and there being very few instances (and those accidental or by negligence) of any person's being embowelled or burned, till previously deprived of sensation by strangling").

[108] Greg Roza, Preventing Cruel and Unusual Punishment 42 (2011) (noting that, in *Trop v. Dulles* (1958), Chief Justice Earl Warren wrote that "[t]he words of the [Eighth] Amendment are not precise, and their scope is not static.").

[109] Andrew Novak, The Global Decline of the Mandatory Death Penalty: Constitutional Jurisprudence and Legislative Reform in Africa, Asia, and the Caribbean 14 (2016) ("[T]he only contemporaneous use of the phrase 'cruel and unusual punishment' before the drafting of the English Bill of Rights was in a minority report in the House of Lords condemning the overly harsh punishment on Titus Oates, including an excessive fine, life imprisonment, whipping, pillorying four times per year, and defrocking, none of which would have been considered barbarous or cruel per se at the time."); John W. Palmer, Constitutional Rights of Prisoners 237 (9th ed. 2015) ("The proscription of cruel and unusual punishments has been attributed to reaction to barbaric, torturous punishments imposed by the Stuarts, and to illegal punishments (such as defrocking) imposed by the King's Bench."); *cf.* Meghan J. Ryan, *Does the Eighth Amendment Punishments Clause Prohibit Only Punishments That Are Both Cruel and Unusual?*, 87 Wash. U.L. Rev. 567, 578–79 (2010) ("[M]ost scholars conclude that, in the context of the English Bill of Rights, 'cruel and unusual' seems to have meant simply 'cruel and illegal.'").

[110] While the U.S. Constitution's Eighth Amendment was understood in America's founding era to prohibit torture, *see* Bessler, *supra* note 3, at 188, I have argued elsewhere that capital punishment — which was not seen as a form of torture in the eighteenth century — should now be classified under the rubric of torture. John D. Bessler, The Death Penalty as Torture: From the Dark Ages to Abolition (2017); John D. Bessler, *Torture and Trauma: Why the Death Penalty Is Wrong and Should Be Strictly Prohibited by American and International Law*, 58 Washburn L.J. 1 (2019); *see also* John D. Bessler, Death in the Dark: Midnight Executions in America (1997) (discussing the history of capital punishment in early America); John D. Bessler, *The American Death Penalty: A Short (But Long) History*, in Routledge Handbook on Capital Punishment (Robert M. Bohm & Gavin Lee eds., 2017); John D. Bessler, *Capital Punishment Law and Practices: History, Trends, and Developments*, in James R. Acker et al., America's Experiment with Capital Punishment: Reflections on the Past, Present, and Future of the Ultimate Penal Sanction (3d ed. 2014); John D. Bessler, *The Law's Evolution: From Medieval Executions to a Peremptory, International Law Norm Against Capital Punishment*, 3 Beccaria: Revue d'Histoire du droit de punir 255 (2017); John D. Bessler, *Taking Psychological Torture Seriously: The Torturous Nature of Credible Death Threats and the Collateral Consequences for Capital Punishment*, 11 Ne. U. L. Rev. 1 (2019).

[111] Bucklew v. Precythe, 139 S. Ct. 1112 (2019). The majority opinion in *Bucklew*, which upheld Missouri's lethal injection protocol, was written by Justice Neil Gorsuch, a self-described "originalist." Ed Pilkington, *Originalism: Neil Gorsuch's Constitutional Philosophy Explained*, The Guardian, Feb. 2, 2017, https://www.google.com/amp/s/amp/theguardian.com/law/2017/feb/02/originalism-constitution-supreme-court-neil-gorsuch.

The law is constantly in motion, with archaic punishments such as drawing and quartering, ducking, the pillory, and the whipping post no longer with us.[112] In fact, the Fourteenth Amendment, which made the Eighth Amendment applicable to the states, added the Equal Protection Clause to the Constitution in 1868, thus fundamentally transforming the Eighth Amendment calculus because of the equality principle it embodies.[113] The Eighth and Fourteenth Amendments use common, everyday language, and each generation is bound to interpret — and to re-interpret — their prohibitions and their language in their own time on a case-by-case basis.[114] The Supreme Court's own, often closely divided opinions interpreting the Eighth Amendment have come in cases challenging everything from conditions of confinement[115] to terms of imprisonment[116] to the death penalty.[117] The Eighth Amendment thus remains as relevant as ever, because how the Eighth Amendment is read and interpreted is a reflection of how far American society has — or has not yet — advanced.

---

[112] The "evolving standards of decency" test adopted by the U.S. Supreme Court ensures the evolution of Eighth Amendment jurisprudence. The most recent Supreme Court case that refers to the "evolving standards of decency" test in a majority opinion is *Moore v. Texas*, 137 S. Ct. 1039, 1048 (2017). That opinion was written by Justice Ruth Bader Ginsburg, joined by Justices Kennedy, Breyer, Sotomayor, and Kagan. Justice Kennedy retired from the Court in 2018 and was replaced by Brett Kavanaugh.

[113] Bessler, *supra* note 98, at 515 (discussing how the Fourteenth Amendment constitutionalized the Civil Rights Act of 1866, which required "like punishment" for citizens of "every race and color").

[114] DWORKIN, *supra* note 65, at 127.

[115] Brown v. Plata, 563 U.S. 493 (2011).

[116] E. THOMAS SULLIVAN & RICHARD S. FRASE, PROPORTIONALITY PRINCIPLES IN AMERICAN LAW: CONTROLLING EXCESSIVE GOVERNMENT ACTIONS 134 (2009) ("Since 1980 the Supreme Court has decided six cases in which the duration of a prison sentence was attacked on Eighth Amendment grounds. All six cases were 5-4 decisions in form or substance . . . .").

[117] The Supreme Court's decision in *Glossip v. Gross*, 135 S. Ct. 2726 (2015), which upheld the State of Oklahoma's lethal injection protocol, was decided on a 5-4 vote.

2

Back to the Future

Originalism and the Eighth Amendment

John F. Stinneford[*]

Over the past half-century, the Supreme Court has generally refused to rely on the original meaning of the Cruel and Unusual Punishments Clause in deciding Eighth Amendment cases. Instead, it has held that Eighth Amendment claims must be evaluated in light of contemporary standards: "the evolving standards of decency that mark the progress of a maturing society."[1] The result has been an almost unmitigated disaster for criminal offenders. Although the Court has occasionally intervened to limit the (already rarely used) death penalty, it has taken a hands-off approach to the 99.999% of adult offenders subject to a punishment other than death.

This result was entirely predictable because the evolving standards test makes the definition of "cruel and unusual punishments" dependent upon current public opinion. If there is a current societal consensus in favor of leniency, the test asks the Court to interpret the Eighth Amendment to require lenient punishments. But if there is a current societal consensus in favor of greater harshness, the test dictates that harsher punishments should be permissible. In short, when public opinion turns against criminal offenders — as it often does — the Eighth Amendment disappears. Under the evolving standards regime, the Supreme Court has turned a blind eye to drastic increases in prison sentences, the imposition of long-term solitary confinement on tens of thousands of prisoners, the invention of new methods of punishment such as chemical castration and lethal injection, and legislative innovation designed to impose serious punishment even in the absence of individual culpability.

This may all be changing. In *Bucklew v. Precythe*,[2] a majority of the Supreme Court explicitly relied — for the first time in more than a generation — on what it

[*] Professor of Law, University of Florida School of Law.
[1] Trop v. Dulles, 356 U.S. 86, 100-01 (1958) (plurality opinion).
[2] 139 S. Ct. 1112 (2019).

took to be the "original and historical understanding of the Eighth Amendment."[3] The future of the Eighth Amendment may turn out to be originalist. Given this fact, it is important to understand what the original meaning of the Cruel and Unusual Punishments Clause is and how it would work in practice.

THE ORIGINAL MEANING OF THE CRUEL AND UNUSUAL PUNISHMENTS CLAUSE

The Cruel and Unusual Punishments Clause was originally understood to prohibit cruel innovation in punishment. More specifically, the word "cruel" was originally understood to mean "unjustly harsh" and the word "unusual" was understood to mean "contrary to long usage." Taken as a whole, the Clause prohibited punishments that are unjustly harsh in light of longstanding prior practice, either because they involve a barbaric method of punishment or because they are significantly disproportionate to the offender's culpability as measured against longstanding prior practice.

The Cruel and Unusual Punishments Clause had, and was publicly understood to have, a preexisting legal meaning when it became part of the Eighth Amendment in 1791. The word unusual was a term of art derived from the common law. Although most lawyers today think of the common law as judge-made law, it was traditionally described as the law of "custom" and "long usage."[4] The key idea underlying the common law was that a practice or custom could attain the status of law if it were used throughout the jurisdiction for a very long time. These two characteristics — universality and long usage — justified legal enforcement of the practice. The theoretical basis for common law judging was not that judges had the power to make law, but that they had the power to identify and enforce universal, longstanding customs.

In English and American legal thought, the terms custom and long usage were tied closely together as a matter of both logic and grammar. Whereas today we normally say that we "follow" a custom, it was more common in the seventeenth and eighteenth centuries to say that we "use" a custom. For example, Edward Coke

---

[3] *Id.* at 1122. Unfortunately, the core holding of *Bucklew* — that condemned offenders cannot challenge a given method of execution unless they are able to identify a feasible, readily implementable alternative method that significantly reduces the chance of pain — is completely unsupported by the text and history of the Eighth Amendment, and the earliest precedent supporting the decision is a mere ten years old. *See* Baze v. Rees, 553 U.S. 35, 52 (2008) (plurality opinion) (inventing this requirement without citation to authority).

[4] *See* John F. Stinneford, *The Original Meaning of "Cruel,"* 105 GEO. L.J. 441, 468–71 (2017) [hereinafter Stinneford, *Cruel*]; John F. Stinneford, *The Original Meaning of "Unusual": The Eighth Amendment as a Bar to Cruel Innovation*, 102 Nw. U. L. REV. 1739 (2008) [hereinafter Stinneford, *Unusual*].

wrote: "And note that no custome is to bee allowed, but such custome as hath bin used by title of prescription, that is to say, from time out of minde."[5]

Coke argued that customary practices that enjoyed "long" or "immemorial usage" were inherently just and reasonable. "The Law of England," Coke wrote, "by many successions of ages . . . has been fined and refined by an infinite number of grave and learned men, and by long experience grown to such a perfection, for the government of this realm, that the old rule may be justly verified of it, *Neminem oportet esse sapientiorem legibus*: no man, out of his own private reason, ought to be wiser than the law, which is the perfection of reason."[6] Similarly, in America, James Wilson — one of the primary drafters of the U.S. Constitution — wrote: "[L]ong customs, approved by the consent of those who use them, acquire the qualities of a law."[7]

In seventeenth century England, departures from settled and longstanding practice were described as unusual.[8] Similarly, Americans in the late eighteenth and early nineteenth centuries also used the term unusual to describe actions that were contrary to long usage. In 1769, for example, the Virginia House of Burgesses described Parliament's attempt to revive a long-defunct statute that would permit the trial of American protesters in England — in derogation of the cherished right to a local criminal venue — as "new, unusual, . . . unconstitutional and illegal."[9] In the Declaration of Independence, the Continental Congress complained of the recent English practice of calling colonial legislatures at "places unusual."[10]

The notion of long usage as a basis for law is important because it gave rise to the idea of rights enforceable against the sovereign. Influential jurists asserted that the common law is normatively superior to laws ordered by king or Parliament because it does not become law until long usage shows that it is just, reasonable, and enjoys the stable, multi-generational consent of the people. In other words, tradition and prior practice were considered guides to the application of moral principles in practice: they helped show which moral principles were relevant to a given case, how they were to be balanced against competing principles, and how they were to be applied to a given set of facts. Laws enacted by the sovereign, by contrast, become law before they have been used and often turn out to be unjust or unworkable in practice.

---

[5] 1 Edward Coke, Institutes of the Lawes of England (1608), *as reprinted in* 2 The Selected Writings and Speeches of Sir Edward Coke §170, at 701 (Steve Sheppard ed., 2003).

[6] 1 Edward Coke, Systematic Arrangement of Lord Coke's First Institute of the Laws of England 1 (J. H. Thomas ed., 2d American ed. 1836).

[7] 1 The Works of James Wilson 435-36 (James DeWitt Andrews ed., 1896).

[8] *See* discussion of Titus Oates case, *infra* notes 15–24 and accompanying text.

[9] Journals of the House of Burgesses, 1766–1769, at 215 (John Pendleton Kennedy ed., 1906).

[10] The Declaration of Independence, para. 6 (U.S. 1776).

A growing chorus in England, and especially in America, argued that the sovereign lacked legitimate authority to enact or enforce laws that violate rights established through long usage — particularly rights relating to life, liberty, or property. To say that something was "unusual" was to say that it was new and that it violated rights established through long usage and settled practice. Thus, in the ratification debates, Antifederalists argued that without a Bill of Rights the Constitution would not bind Congress to respect common law rights, particularly those relating to criminal trial and punishment. The lack of common law constraints on the proposed new federal government led Patrick Henry to describe the government itself as a series of "new and unusual experiments."[11] Similarly, George Mason, who had been a principal drafter of the Virginia Declaration of Rights a decade earlier, warned that the lack of common law constraints in the new Constitution would empower Congress to "constitute new crimes, inflict *unusual and severe punishments*, and extend their powers as far as they shall think proper[.]"[12]

The phrase "cruel and unusual punishments" first appeared, as best we can tell, in the late seventeenth century English Bill of Rights. Seventeenth century England experienced a period of intense constitutional struggle. Efforts to constrain the sovereign to follow the rule of law were directed first against the absolutist Stuart kings, then against the absolutist Parliament that succeeded them after the English Civil War, and finally against the Stuart kings who returned to power after the Restoration. In 1688–89, these conflicts culminated in the Glorious Revolution. Members of the English aristocracy invited William and Mary to invade England and depose King James II on the ground that the king had violated the rights of English subjects in a variety of ways — including through the imposition of "excessive Bayle," "excessive fynes," and "illegal and cruell punishments."[13]

Parliament offered to recognize William and Mary as king and queen on the condition that they accept a declaration of rights designed to limit the arbitrary exercise of the monarch's power. This declaration was followed by the Bill of Rights of 1689, which codified and entrenched the constitutional settlement that followed the overthrow of James II, specified certain actions that the sovereign should not take — including that "excessive Baile ought not to be required, nor excessive Fines imposed; nor cruell and unusuall Punishments inflicted."[14] This appears to have been the first use of the phrase "cruell and unusuall Punishments."

We have compelling evidence of the contemporary meaning of the phrase "cruell and unusuall Punishments" in England because the same Parliament that drafted

---

[11] 3 Jonathan Elliot, The Debates in the Several State Conventions on the Adoption of the Federal Constitution 170–72 (photo. reprint 2d ed. 1974) (1968).

[12] George Mason, Objections to this Constitution of Government (1787) (emphasis added).

[13] Decl. of Rgts. (Feb. 12, 1689), *reprinted in* Lois G. Schwoerer, The Declaration of Rights, 1689 295, 296 (1981) [hereinafter Schwoerer, Declaration].

[14] 1 Wm. & Mary, 2d Sess., ch. 2, 9 Stat. at Large 67, 69 (1764 ed.).

the Bill of Rights was called upon to debate the meaning of this prohibition the year after it was adopted. The reason for this debate was a disgraced former Anglican clergyman named Titus Oates. A few years earlier, Oates had been convicted of perjury for falsely claiming that there was a plot — the so-called "Popish plot" — to kill the King.[15] Oates had named some fifteen members of this alleged conspiracy, including the queen's physician, and had testified against them at their trials. His story was eventually exposed as false.

At Oates' sentencing, Chief Justice Jeffreys expressed his regret that the death penalty was not available for this crime and declared that "it is left to the discretion of the court to inflict such punishment as they think fit" so long as it "extend not to life or member."[16] Oates was sentenced to be whipped continuously as he crossed the city of London "from Aldgate to Newgate," and then two days later "from Newgate to Tyburn."[17] He was also sentenced to life imprisonment, pillorying four times a year for life, a fine of 2,000 marks, and defrockment.[18] Shortly after the English Bill of Rights was enacted, Oates petitioned Parliament to review his sentence, arguing that it violated, among other things, the prohibition of "cruell and unusuall Punishments."

Representatives from the House of Commons asserted that the House had Oates' case specifically in mind when it drafted the Bill of Rights.[19] A majority of the House of Lords agreed the punishment was illegal but refused to lift the judgment against "so ill a man." A minority protested against this decision, arguing that Oates' punishments were "contrary to law and ancient practice," "barbarous, inhuman and unchristian," and given with "no precedent" to support them.[20] The Titus Oates case demonstrates that in prohibiting "cruell and unusuall Punishments," Parliament drew upon the idea that long usage tends to reveal what is just and that lack of long usage tends to reveal what is unjust. The fact that Oates' punishment was "contrary to law and ancient practice" and was supported by "no precedent" demonstrated that it was "extravagant,"[21] "exorbitant,"[22] and "barbarous, inhuman and unchristian."[23] The punishment was cruel and unusual because it was significantly harsher than the punishments that had previously been given for the crime of perjury.

---

[15] See JOHN H. LANGBEIN, THE ORIGINS OF ADVERSARY CRIMINAL TRIAL 69–73 (2003) (discussing Oates' perjury and the "Popish Plot").

[16] Trial of Titus Oates, 10 Howell's State Trials 1079, 1314–15 (K.B. 1685).

[17] Id. at 1316–17.

[18] Id.

[19] See 10 H.C. JOUR. 247 (1689) ("[T]he Commons had a particular Regard to these Judgments, amongst others, when that Declaration [i.e., the English Cruell and unusuall Punishments Clause] was first made; and must insist upon it, That they are erroneous, cruel, illegal, and of ill Example to future Ages.").

[20] 14 H.L. JOUR. 228 (1689).

[21] Id.

[22] 10 H.C. JOUR. 249 (1689).

[23] 14 H.L. JOUR. 228 (1689).

In America, the Cruel and Unusual Punishments Clause was publicly under-stood to have a preexisting legal meaning when it became part of the Eighth Amendment in 1791.[24] The prohibition of cruel and unusual punishments was part of the lexicon of rights that was familiar to well-informed members of the public. Americans justified their break from England during the American Revolution by arguing that they were acting to vindicate fundamental common law rights against a government that sought arbitrarily to deny them.[25] Bills of rights in both state and federal constitutions were modeled after the English Bill of Rights, Magna Carta, and other key documents from English constitutional history. They were designed, by and large, to protect the rights the colonists understood themselves to possess as English subjects.[26]

The provisions in the various state constitutions and bills of rights for prohibiting cruel punishments varied somewhat — prohibiting "cruel and unusual," "cruel or unusual," or "cruel" punishments, respectively.[27] But these provisions reflected a general consensus on two points: First, the government should not impose cruel punishments. Second, because the common law was presumptively reasonable, governmental efforts to "ratchet up" punishment beyond what was permitted by longstanding prior practice were presumptively contrary to reason. Given this dual consensus, the words "cruel" and "unusual" acted as synonyms when employed in the context of punishment. The word "cruel" stated the abstract moral principle,

---

[24] This account is consistent with the view that "the founding generation generally did not consider many of the rights identified in these amendments as new entitlements, but as inalienable rights of all men, given legal effect by their codification in the Constitution's text." McDonald v. City of Chicago, 561 U.S. 742, 818 (2010) (Thomas, J., concurring). Accordingly — and in light of the fact that "one of the consistent themes of the era was that Americans had all the rights of English subjects" — the Supreme Court has concluded that "[w]hen the Framers of the Eighth Amendment adopted the language of the English Bill of Rights, they also adopted the English principle of proportionality." Solem v. Helm, 463 U.S. 277, 285-86 (1983).

[25] In Americans' view, "English law — as authority, as legitimizing precedent, as embodied principle, and as the framework of historical understanding — stood side by side with Enlightenment rationalism in the minds of the Revolutionary generation." BERNARD BAILYN, THE IDEOLOGICAL ORIGINS OF THE AMERICAN REVOLUTION 31 (1967). The leading English expositors of the law were held in high esteem: Coke's "Institutes 'were read in the American Colonies by virtually every student of the law," Kerry v. Din, 135 S. Ct. 2128, 2133 (2015) (plurality opinion) (internal quotations omitted), and Blackstone was "the preeminent author-ity on English law for the founding generation," District of Columbia v. Heller, 554 U.S. 570, 593-94 (2008) (internal quotations omitted).

[26] See, e.g., Edmund Randolph, *Essay on the Revolutionary History of Virginia* (c. 1809–1813), *reprinted in* 1 BERNARD SCHWARTZ, THE BILL OF RIGHTS: A DOCUMENTARY HISTORY 246, 248 (noting that the Cruel and Unusual Punishments Clause in the Virginia Declaration of Rights was one of several provisions "borrowed from England"); *see also, e.g.*, ALLAN NEVINS, THE AMERICAN STATES DURING AND AFTER THE REVOLUTION, 1775-1789, 146 (1924) (noting that the Virginia Declaration of Rights was in large measure "a restatement of English principles — the principles of Magna Charta, the Petition of Rights, the Commonwealth Parliament, and the Revolution of 1688").

[27] Stinneford, *Cruel, supra* note 4, at 465–66; Stinneford, *Unusual, supra* note 4, at 1799.

and the word "unusual" provided a concrete reference point for determining whether that principle had been violated. Thus, it makes sense that some states outlawed "cruel punishments," some outlawed "cruel and unusual punishments," and some outlawed "cruel or unusual punishments." Each formulation is simply a different way of saying the same thing.

In sum, historical evidence suggests that the founding generation understood the Cruel and Unusual Punishments Clause to prohibit cruel innovations in punishment. Punishment practices that enjoyed long usage were considered to be presumptively just and reasonable, and to enjoy the stable, multigenerational consent of the people. New punishment practices that were significantly harsher than the baseline established by longstanding prior practice were considered cruel and unusual.

THE PROPORTIONALITY REQUIREMENT

The principle that punishment should be commensurate with fault or culpability is deeply rooted in Western history.[28] It is also deeply rooted in English law.[29] Magna Carta stated, "[a] Free-man shall not be amerced for a small fault, but after the manner of the fault; and for a great fault after the greatness thereof."[30] By the early seventeenth century, the English common law courts had distilled from Magna Carta the general principle that punishments should be reasonable and proportional, with one prominent case from 1615 reasoning that "[e]xcess in any thing is reprehended by common law."[31] Courts extended the principle of proportionality to cases involving imprisonment — although this form of punishment was rare prior to the eighteenth century. In *Hodges v. Humkin*,[32] Hodges was incarcerated for insulting a local mayor with vulgar words and gestures. He petitioned for a writ of habeas corpus. The Court of King's Bench ordered his release, holding that under Magna Carta and the Statute of Marlbridge, "imprisonment ought always to be according to the quality of the offence."[33] Thus, Magna Carta's prohibition of excessive amercements came to embody a broader fundamental principle in English law — that the governmental power to punish should be limited by customary retributive notions of proportionality.

---

[28] *See, e.g., Exodus* 21:25; *Leviticus* 24:19–20 ("An eye for an eye; a tooth for a tooth."); 4 THOMAS AQUINAS, SUMMA CONTRA GENTILES 304 (1929 ed.)(1264) ("[T]he punishment should correspond with the fault, so that the will may receive a punishment in contrast with that for love of which it sinned."); V ARISTOTLE, NICOMACHEAN ETHICS ch. 3 (Roger Crisp trans., Cambridge Univ. Press 2004) (350 B.C.E.) ("What is just in this sense, then, is what is proportionate. And what is unjust is what violates the proportion.").

[29] *See, e.g.,* SCHWOERER, DECLARATION, *supra* note 13, at 92 (1981) (stating that "the prohibition of excessive punishments and the concern for equating crime and punishment were ancient concerns in English law and custom").

[30] Magna Carta, 9 Hen. III, Ch. 14, in 1 Eng. Stat. at Large 5 (1225).

[31] Godfrey's Case, 77 Eng. Rep. 1199, 1202 (K.B. 1615), *as translated in* 2 JOHN BOUVIER, A LAW DICTIONARY 179 (15th ed. 1890).

[32] 80 Eng. Rep. 1015 (K.B. 1615).

[33] *Id.* at 1016.

It was against this common law backdrop that the ban on "cruell and unusuall Punishments" in the English Bill of Rights of 1689 was enacted.

The Titus Oates case discussed above demonstrates that the English Cruell and Unusuall Punishments Clause was designed to prohibit excessive or disproportionate punishments. As noted, Oates was sentenced to repeated floggings, a large monetary fine, imprisonment for life, pillorying four times a year for life, and defrocking. Every element of Oates' punishment (except defrocking) was accepted under the common law at the time; none appears to have been considered an inherently barbarous *method* of punishment.[34] Thus, if the punishments inflicted on Oates were unacceptably cruel, this must have been because they were disproportionate to the crime of perjury. This conclusion is supported by the fact that the punishments were described in the parliamentary debates as "extravagant" and "exorbitant,"[35] both of which are synonyms for excessive or disproportionate. The purpose of the Cruell and Unusuall Punishments Clause — as members of the House of Commons put it during the debate over Oates' case — was to ensure that "*such excessive punishment* should not be inflicted for the future."[36]

In the years following the Glorious Revolution, prominent English jurists attested to the common law's proportionality limitations on punishments. Consider, for instance, the discussion of common law principles that appeared in Sollom Emlyn's preface to the 1730 edition of *State Trials*. As Emlyn observed:

> As to smaller Crimes and Misdemeanors, they are differenc'd with such a variety of extenuating or aggravating Circumstances, that the Law has not, nor indeed could affix to each a certain and determinate Penalty; this is left to the Discretion and Prudence of the Judge, who may punish it either with Fine or Imprisonment, Pillory or Whipping, as he shall think the nature of the Crime deserves: but tho' he be intrusted with so great Power, yet he is not at liberty to do as he lists, and inflict what arbitrary Punishments he pleases; due regard is to be had to the Quality and Degree, to the Estate and Circumstances of the Offender, and to the greatness or smallness of the Offence . . . .[37]

---

[34] Today, most of the *modes* of punishment associated with *Titus Oates's Case* — having "fall[en] completely out of usage for a long period of time," *Bucklew v. Precythe*, 139 S. Ct. 1112, 1123 (2019) (internal quotations omitted) — might well be considered categorically "cruel and unusual" within the original meaning of the text of the Cruel and Unusual Punishment Clause. *See generally* John F. Stinneford, *Death, Desuetude, and Original Meaning*, 56 Wm. & Mary L. Rev. 531 (2014) [Stinneford, *Death, Desuetude*]. The Cruel and Unusual Punishments Clause's text, as originally understood, is appropriately regarded as enacting a *principle of legal development* — not merely a fixed set of particular applications that a given reader might have anticipated in 1791. *Cf.* Steven G. Calabresi & Andrea Matthews, *Originalism and* Loving v. Virginia, 2012 B.Y.U. L. Rev. 1393, 1462 (2012) (suggesting that "it is not the original expected applications of a legal text that bind us, but it is instead the words that are enacted into law").

[35] 14 H.L. Jour. 228 (1689); 10 H.C. Jour. 249 (1689).

[36] 10 H.C. Jour. 264 (emphasis added).

[37] Sollom Emlyn, *Preface*, in A Complete Collection of State-Trials (3d ed. 1742) (*reprinted in* Preface to 2d ed., 1730) (footnote omitted).

Emlyn further stated:

> It is indeed no easy matter to settle the precise Limits, how far a Court of Justice may go; every Case must depend upon its own particular Circumstances. But *some* Fines and *some* Punishments are so monstrously extravagant, that no body can doubt their being so; such were the Fines of Sir *Samuel Barnardiston* and Mr. *Hapden,* such were the repeated Pilloryings and barbarous Whippings of *Oates, Dangerfield,* and *Johnson.*
>
> These Punishments may no doubt be properly inflicted, *where they are in a moderate degree and proportioned to the Offence* . . . .[38]

The historical evidence thus demonstrates that the English Cruell and Unusuall Punishments Clause was originally understood to entrench traditional common law norms regarding proportionality and to prohibit new punishments that were excessive in light of prior practice. But because the English version of the Clause was directed only at judges, not Parliament, its significance in England was limited. As the doctrine of parliamentary supremacy developed over the course of the eighteenth century, Parliament repeatedly innovated in a manner contrary to fundamental common law principles. These innovations included imposition of the "bloody code," which punished more than two hundred crimes, major and minor, with death.[39] Though Parliament's actions in this area were both "cruel" and "unusual" — contrary to long usage — the doctrine of parliamentary supremacy precluded any challenge against them on this ground.

In America, things were different. The American Revolution represented a fundamental *rejection* of the doctrine of parliamentary supremacy.[40] Accordingly, the provisions of the Bill of Rights — including the Eighth Amendment's prohibition of cruel and unusual punishments — bound Congress as well as the courts. Because the Eighth Amendment was "adopted as an admonition to *all* departments" of government[41] — to Congress as well as the courts[42] — there is no reason to suppose that the founding generation wished Congress to have the same power to impose arbitrary and disproportionate punishments as was then enjoyed by Parliament. Indeed, a critical purpose of the Bill of Rights was to ensure that Congress did *not* assume such arbitrary power unto itself.

Americans understood the phrase "cruel and unusual" to embody the concept of excessiveness or disproportionality. In America, as in England, the phrase "cruel and unusual" was regularly used within the legal system as a synonym for "excessive" or

---

[38] *Id.* at xii (final emphasis added).

[39] *See* RANDALL McGOWAN, LAW, CRIME, AND ENGLISH SOCIETY, 1660–1830, 117–21 (2002).

[40] *See, e.g.,* AKHIL REED AMAR, AMERICA'S CONSTITUTION: A BIOGRAPHY 105–06 (2005).

[41] 3 JOSEPH STORY, COMMENTARIES ON THE CONSTITUTION OF THE UNITED STATES § 1896, at 750–51 (1833).

[42] And, following the adoption of the Fourteenth Amendment, it served as an admonition to all branches of the state governments as well. *See, e.g.,* Robinson v. California, 370 U.S. 660, 675 (1962).

"disproportionate." This occurred in two major areas of law outside of criminal punishment.

First, in the late eighteenth and nineteenth centuries, several states referenced "cruel and unusual" killings in their homicide laws. In virtually every case involving such a killing, the phrase "cruel and unusual" was used as a synonym for "excessive."[43] Some states treated "cruel and unusual" homicide as a form of murder. In these states, a beating was considered "cruel and unusual" if it was so excessive that it demonstrated intent to kill or its equivalent. Other states treated "cruel and unusual" homicide as a form of manslaughter. In these states, a beating was considered "cruel and unusual" if it was disproportionate to any threat or provocation that came from the victim. In both sets of cases, the phrase "cruel and unusual" was used as a synonym for "excessive"; none limited the phrase to situations involving a barbaric mode or method.[44]

Second, several federal and state laws prohibited those in positions of authority over others — including ship's officers, parents, and teachers — from inflicting "cruel and unusual punishments." Parents were permitted to use moderate force to discipline their children; teachers were permitted to use moderate force to discipline students. When excessive force was used, this discipline was described as a "cruel and unusual punishment." Notably, in none of these cases was it suggested that the phrase only applied to inherently barbaric modes of punishment.[45]

The relationship of punishment to an offender's *culpability* was central to the question of whether the punishment was cruel and unusual by virtue of its disproportionality.[46] Indeed, on the few occasions in the late eighteenth and early nineteenth centuries when legislatures passed laws that authorized punishment *without* culpability, courts did not hesitate to declare such laws unconstitutional. In determining

---

[43] See John F. Stinneford, *Rethinking Proportionality under the Cruel and Unusual Punishments Clause*, 97 VA. L. REV. 899, 938–42 (2011) [Stinneford, *Rethinking*].

[44] *Id.* at 940.

[45] *See* Stinneford, *Rethinking*, at 939–42 (surveying cases); *see also* Alexander A. Reinert, *Reconceptualizing the Eighth Amendment: Slaves, Prisoners, and "Cruel and Unusual" Punishment*, 94 N.C. L. REV. 817 (2016) (discussing additional cases in the slavery context). Notably, in only one case decided prior to 1866 did a court explicitly state that a state analogue to the Cruel and Unusual Punishments Clause forbids only barbaric methods of punishment. *See* Aldridge v. Commonwealth, 4 Va. (2 Va. Cas.) 447, 447–50 (Va. Gen. Ct. 1824). That dictum in *Aldridge*, however, ought to be of limited persuasive force as it contradicts actual holdings of Virginia courts made both before and after that case was decided. *See* Stinneford, *Rethinking*, *supra* note 43, at 951.

[46] In practice, this approach is similar to what modern criminal-law theorists have referred to as "limiting retributivism" or the use of retributivism as a "side constraint" on punishment. *See* Richard S. Frase, *Excessive Prison Sentences, Punishment Goals, and the Eighth Amendment: "Proportionality" Relative to What?*, 89 MINN. L. REV. 571, 590–92 (2005); Youngjae Lee, *The Constitutional Right against Excessive Punishment*, 91 VA. L. REV. 677, 737–45 (2005). According to this idea, criminal sentences may be imposed to serve multiple purposes (incapacitation, deterrence, etc.), but the retributive concept of disproportionality relative to culpability nevertheless represents an upper bound on legitimate punishment.

whether a challenged punishment was unconstitutionally excessive, early courts compared the punishment to what had previously been permitted at common law.

For example, in an 1820 case — *Ely v. Thompson*[47] — the Kentucky Court of Appeals held that it would be unconstitutional under a state analogue to the Cruel and Unusual Punishments Clause to punish a person for exercising the common law right of self-defense, even though the criminal statute purported to permit such punishment. The Court held that it would be "cruel indeed" to impose a whipping on a defendant whose actions were justified under the common law doctrine of self-defense, for such a defendant did not deserve punishment at all.[48]

Similarly, in *Commonwealth v. Wyatt*,[49] the General Court of Virginia stated that a judge could violate the cruel and unusual punishments clause by ordering the defendant to undergo excessive floggings, although a statute giving the judge discretion to impose flogging on operators of an illegal gambling business was not facially unconstitutional.

And in *Jones v. Commonwealth*,[50] the Supreme Court of Appeals of Virginia held that abrogation of the common law rule prohibiting imposition of a joint fine in a criminal case would be cruel and unusual because it could require some defendants to bear the punishment for others. In *Jones*, the defendants were convicted of assaulting a magistrate. As punishment, they were given a joint fine and ordered to be imprisoned until the fine was paid. The court invalidated this punishment on the ground that it violated the common law prohibition of joint fines in criminal cases. The problem with a joint fine, as one of the two judges in the majority explained, was that it could require the defendant to "endure a longer confinement or to pay a greater sum than his own proportion of the fine" if one of his codefendants died, escaped, or became insolvent.[51] Because the sentence subjected the defendant to a punishment "beyond the real measure of his own offence," the Court held that it violated both the constitutional command that "excessive bail ought not to be required, nor excessive fines imposed, nor cruel and unusual punishments inflicted," as well as a statutory command that any "fine or amercement ought to be according to the degree of the fault and the estate of the defendant."[52] A second judge on the three-judge panel concurred in the judgment, explaining that "principles of natural justice ... forbid that one man should be punished for the fault of another[.]"[53]

---

[47] 10 Ky. (3 A.K. Marsh.) 70 (Ky. 1820).

[48] *Id.*

[49] 27 Va. (6 Rand.) 694 (1828).

[50] 5 Va. (1 Call) 555 (1799).

[51] *Id.* at 558 (Carrington, J.).

[52] *Id.*

[53] *Id.* at 556 (Roane, J.). Judge Roane continued: "This is so unjust and contrary to the spirit of the constitution, that even if it were established by adjudged cases to be the law, nay even if an act of Assembly should pass authorizing it, in express terms, I should most probably be of opinion that the one should be exploded and the other declared unconstitutional and not law." *Id.* at 557.

The approaches outlined above were consistent with settled understandings and longstanding traditions regarding the centrality of individual culpability to criminal punishment. Indeed, as late as 1877, the Supreme Court implied that it would be beyond the authority of government to punish even knowing violations of a criminal statute, where the violations were committed in good faith and with no "evil intent": "All punitive legislation contemplates some relation between guilt and punishment. To inflict the latter where the former does not exist would shock the sense of justice of every one."[54]

In reaching these conclusions, jurists were guided by traditional views regarding criminal culpability that had been universally held for more than five hundred years. For example, the medieval jurist Henry de Bracton, whose influential work *On the Laws and Customs of England* was the most comprehensive treatment of English law before Blackstone, wrote that "a crime is not committed unless the intention to injure exists . . . . It is will and purpose which mark maleficia . . . ."[55] William Blackstone likewise maintained that it was unjust to impose punishment without culpability. He wrote that "punishments are . . . only inflicted for [the] abuse of . . . free will,"[56] and that "an unwarrantable act without a vitious will is no crime at all."[57]

IMPLICATIONS FOR THE FUTURE

If the Supreme Court adopts an originalist reading of the Cruel and Unusual Punishments Clause in future cases, the result will be greater consistency and less subjectivity in the Court's decisions, combined with greater protection for most criminal offenders. The evolving standards of decency test asks the Court to determine whether a traditional punishment still meets contemporary standards. But this sort of question is better directed to the legislature than to a court. If a traditional punishment no longer enjoys public support, it should fall out of usage without judicial intervention. The original meaning of the Cruel and Unusual Punishments Clause directs the Court to ask precisely the opposite question: Does this new punishment meet our traditional standards? This is precisely the sort of question that should be asked by judges. Legislatures sometimes get caught up in the panic of the moment and ratchet up the harshness of punishment well beyond traditional levels. The Eighth Amendment asks judges to prevent drastic increases of this sort.

We have experienced more than fifty years of harsh governmental innovation. We incarcerate seven times as many people as we did in 1970. We subject tens of

[54] Felton v. United States, 96 U.S. 699, 703 (1877).
[55] 2 Henry de Bracton, On the Laws and Customs of England 384 (Samuel E. Thorne trans. & ed., Harvard Univ. Press 1968) (c. 1300).
[56] 4 William Blackstone, Commentaries *27.
[57] Id. at *21.

thousands of offenders to long-term solitary confinement in supermax prisons. We use experimental corporal punishments such as chemical castration and lethal injection. We even permit convictions for some felonies without any showing of individual culpability. At least some of these innovations are likely unconstitutional under the original meaning of the Cruel and Unusual Punishments Clause.

On the other hand, the original meaning of the Cruel and Unusual Punishments Clause would not permit the Court to continue outlawing traditional applications of the death penalty. If the death penalty is to be abolished, this result must be achieved through the political process. But if a given application of the death penalty does fall out of usage and remains out of usage for a period of multiple generations, the Court could appropriately block it on the ground that it is no longer part of our tradition — for the common law tradition is not static.[58] The great seventeenth century jurist Edward Coke Edward Coke wrote that "Custome ... lose[s its] being, if usage faile."[59] Similarly, Sir John Davies maintained that if a traditional legal practice has "been found inconvenient" it is "used no longer" and thus "los[es] the virtue and force of a lawe."[60] James Wilson, an important participant in the drafting and ratification of the Constitution, argued that gradual changes wrought by practices coming into and falling out of usage over time gave the common law its dual character as stable and durable but also sensitive to cultural change:

> It is the characteristic of a system of common law, that it may be accommodated to the circumstances, the exigencies, and the conveniences of the people, by whom it is appointed. Now, as these circumstances, and exigencies, and conveniences insensibly change; a proportioned change, in time and in degree must take place in the accommodated system ... [Time] silently and gradually introduces; it silently and gradually withdraws its customary laws.[61]

In short, the common law tradition that serves as the foundation for the Cruel and Unusual Punishments Clause is not the tradition as it existed at some point in the distant past, but the tradition as it has survived up to today. Once-traditional punishments that fall out of usage for a significant period of time are no longer part of our tradition because they have not withstood the test of time. Should a legislature attempt to revive them, they should not be automatically approved simply because they were once part of the tradition. Rather, courts should compare them to the tradition as it still exists today. The death penalty was once permissible in America

---

[58] See Stinneford supra note 34.

[59] Edward Coke, The Compleat Copyholder (1630), reprinted in 2 THE SELECTED WRITINGS AND SPEECHES OF SIR EDWARD COKE 563, 564 (Steve Sheppard ed., 2003).

[60] John Davies, A Preface Dedicatory, in LE PRIMER REPORT DES CASES & MATTERS EN LEY RESOLUES & ADIUDGES EN LES COURTS DEL ROY EN IRELAND *2 (Dublin, 1615); see also J. G. A. POCOCK, THE ANCIENT CONSTITUTION AND THE FEUDAL LAW 30-55 (1987).

[61] Id.

for crimes that we now consider relatively minor, such as counterfeiting.[62] But this punishment was eliminated so long ago that any attempt to revive it should be met with a healthy dose of judicial skepticism. Similarly, if the death penalty as a whole were to fall out of usage for multiple generations, a court could appropriately find that it was no longer "usual," and perhaps that it was cruel and unusual in light of the tradition as it developed up to that time.

---

[62] *See* Act for the Punishment of Certain Crimes Against the United States, Ch. 9, §14, 1 Stat. 112 (1790).

3

Eighth Amendment Federalism

Michael J. Zydney Mannheimer[*]

Disagreements over the original understanding of the Cruel and Unusual Punishments Clause of the Eighth Amendment generally center around whether the Clause covers only methods of punishment or is also concerned with proportionality of punishment. Few discussions about the Clause's original public meaning ever recognize federalism as a goal furthered by the Clause. My claim is that, on an original understanding of the Cruel and Unusual Punishments Clause, federalism is a central value of the Clause that has long been overlooked.

Like much of the Bill of Rights, the Cruel and Unusual Punishments Clause can be understood only by recognizing that a good many of the framers and ratifiers of the Bill understood individual rights and federalism to be intertwined. They sought to secure the former by preserving the latter. Because the states, through their own laws and constitutions, were the guardians of the common-law rights of Englishmen, the framers and ratifiers of the Bill of Rights sought to secure individual rights against the federal government by tying many of the constraints on that government to state norms. In that way, at least some of the rights against the federal government would "float" on a body of underlying state law, rising when state law provided greater protections, diminishing when state law provided fewer protections. Thus, federal rights would not be static but dynamic, changing in content across borders and over time.

The Bill did this, for example, by requiring that the federal government abide by "due process of law," that it not conduct searches and seizures that are "unreasonable," and that it not inflict "unusual" punishments. These vague and open-ended words have vexed courts and scholars for generations. But the best way to understand them is by using state law as a baseline for the process that is "due," for what searches and seizures are "unreasonable," and for what punishments are "unusual." These

[*] Professor of Law, Salmon P. Chase College of Law, Northern Kentucky University.

constraints on government stemmed from English common law, and the common law that was adopted in North America varied by colony and then by state.

Thinking about the Cruel and Unusual Punishments Clause in this way provides an accommodation between originalism and living constitutionalism. Assuming that we should consider ourselves bound by the framers' and ratifiers' understanding of the Eighth Amendment, that understanding itself was likely that the Clause would not be interpreted in a static manner. Instead, the framers and ratifiers likely understood that the content of the Clause would change over time. But their understanding was not akin to the free form "evolving standards of decency" approach that the Court has adopted. Instead, their understanding was that constraints on the federal government's power to punish would evolve only when, and only to the extent that, the People, through their representatives in the state legislatures and judiciaries, changed their views on the outer bounds of the state's power to punish. Thus, "evolving standards" should be closely tethered to local, accountable, democratic institutions, not left to the normative judgments formed by transient Court majorities.

STATE-SPECIFIC USE OF THE TERM "CRUEL OR UNUSUAL" IN THE 1780S

One powerful clue that the phrase "cruel and unusual" was understood in a state-specific way was the explicitly state-specific use of the nearly identical term "cruel or unusual" in state legislation ratifying the proposed 1783 confederal impost. Congress under the Articles of Confederation found itself sorely in need of revenue to pay off debts accruing as a result of the recent war, but was without power to raise revenue directly. On April 18, 1783, the Confederal Congress asked the states to confer upon it the power to enact an impost on certain imports, including molasses, rum, sugar, tea, and wine.[1] Because it was asking for a power not granted by the Articles, the proposal could not take effect unless it were ratified by all thirteen states. All of those states except New York eventually enacted ratification legislation deemed acceptable by Congress.

However, the state ratifications came with caveats. Six states sought to ensure that confederal criminal penalties for smuggling not be too severe. Rhode Island provided that Congress must not "inflict punishments which are cruel or unusual" for violations of any impost, and Pennsylvania similarly prohibited Congress from "imposing any unusual punishments or penalty."[2] But Georgia, Massachusetts,

---

[1] 24 Journals of The Continental Congress, 1774–1789, at 256–57 (Gaillard Hunt ed., 1922).
[2] The Resolution of Congress of the 18th of April, 1783: Recommending the States to Invest Congress with the Power to Levy an Impost, for the Use of the States; and the Laws of the Respective States Passed in Pursuance of the Said Recommendation, Together with Remarks on the Resolutions of Congress, and Laws of the Different States 11–13 (Rhode Island), 27, 30–31 (Pennsylvania) (1787).

New Hampshire, and South Carolina each framed its proviso in a state-specific way: each forbade Congress from "inflict[ing] punishments which are either cruel or unusual *in this State*" (or in Massachusetts, "in this commonwealth").[3]

This language in the ratifying legislation of four of the thirteen states demonstrates that the term "cruel or unusual" was used, at least sometimes, to describe punishments harsher than those authorized by the law of a given jurisdiction, and not necessarily punishments too harsh according to some more general standard. True, the language of the Eighth Amendment does not match up precisely, for the Cruel and Unusual Punishments Clause does not explicitly forbid punishments that are "cruel and unusual in the State in which they are inflicted." But this structure would have been extremely unwieldy given that the Excessive Bail Clause, the Excessive Fines Clause, and the Cruel and Unusual Punishments Clause were all joined together in the single sentence that constitutes the Eighth Amendment. When James Madison penned that Amendment, he decided to copy verbatim the analogous provision in the constitution of his home state of Virginia, which in turn was a nearly verbatim copy of the 1689 English version forbidding "cruel and unusual punishments." But whether Madison failed to recognize that the same four words can have different meanings depending on the context, or whether he simply chose eloquence over precision, need not detain us long. For Madison's was simply the pen through which the phrase was proposed as an addition to the Constitution. Far more important, for purposes of an originalist account, was the public meaning of the words at the time they were adopted.

THE ORIGINAL UNDERSTANDING OF THE CRUEL AND UNUSUAL PUNISHMENTS CLAUSE

The most persuasive view of the original public meaning of the Cruel and Unusual Punishments Clause is that it forbade, as Professor John Stinneford has put it, "cruel innovations" in the law of punishments.[4] Specifically, the Clause was understood as prohibiting deviations in punishments from longstanding practice in the direction of greater severity. The word "unusual" was understood as implicating the common law of punishment, the law of long custom and usage. At the time of the framing, and for centuries before, the common law was seen as customary law, the end result of a long, iterative process that transformed practice into social norms, norms into customs, and customs into enforceable rights and interests. When the framers and ratifers barred punishments that were "cruel and unusual," their benchmark for unusualness was the common law of punishment, as it had evolved out of long

---

[3]   *Id.* at 6 (New Hampshire), 9–10 (Massachusetts), 43–45 (South Carolina), 46, 48 (Georgia) (emphasis added).

[4]   *See generally* John Stinneford, *The Original Meaning of "Unusual": The Eighth Amendment as a Bar to Cruel Innovation*, 102 Nw. U. L. Rev. 1739 (2008).

custom and usage. In essence, then, "unusual" meant "contrary to common law," broadly defined to cover (1) judge-made law, (2) statutory emendations thereto, and (3) law established by long custom and usage.

But in what way did the framers understand "common law?" Did they understand it in what we think of as the pre-*Erie* sense as being declaratory, uniform, and regardless of sovereignty? Or did they understand it in a more modern sense, as instrumental, differentiated, and tied to sovereignty? The answer to that question is complex and requires a brief detour into a discussion of the origin of the Bill of Rights as a demand made by the foes of the Constitution, the Anti-Federalists.

THE ANTI-FEDERALIST ORIGINS OF THE BILL OF RIGHTS

The average person, perhaps even the average lawyer, would say that we have a Bill of Rights to keep the government from infringing our rights, that is, to keep the majority from infringing the rights of the minority. But that is only partly right. The Bill of Rights protects us only from the federal government. It is the Fourteenth Amendment that protects us from state governments. We sometimes forget that for seventy-seven years, from 1791 to 1868, the Bill of Rights applied only to the federal government. And it took about another century after that for the Supreme Court to hold that the Bill of Rights applies to the states via incorporation through the Fourteenth Amendment. It is only within the lifetimes of many reading these words that we can speak of the states as violating the Bill of Rights and, even when we do so, it is still only a shorthand for "the Bill of Rights as incorporated by the Fourteenth Amendment."

Understanding the Bill of Rights as a set of limitations on the federal government alone helps us understand why the Bill was demanded by the Anti-Federalists. They were opposed to ratification for two main reasons.[5] First, they argued, the Constitution gave the federal government too much power at the expense of the states. Second, the Constitution did not guarantee individual rights. We moderns tend to view these as two separate reasons: the distribution of power between the federal and state governments — federalism — is a wholly separate issue from the preservation of individual rights as against the government. In law schools across the nation, law students learn constitutional law in two semesters, the first focused on structure and the second on rights.

Strange as it might seem to us, the Anti-Federalists saw structure and rights to be inextricably intertwined, "marbled together" in Akhil Amar's evocative phrase.[6] Prior to ratification, each state had a constitution, bill of rights, or (in the case of

---

[5] *See* Michael J.Z. Mannheimer, WHEN THE FEDERAL DEATH PENALTY IS "CRUEL AND UNUSUAL," 74 U. CIN. L. REV. 819, 850–55 (2006).
[6] Akhil Reed Amar, *The Bill of Rights and the Fourteenth Amendment*, 101 YALE L.J. 1193, 1265 (1992).

Connecticut) at least a very strong common law tradition protecting individual rights. The Anti-Federalists saw these state constitutions, bills of rights, and common-law constraints as the primary repository of the people's rights. Thus, the best prospect for preserving individual rights was to keep the states vibrant. Robust state power meant preservation of these repositories of rights.

The proposed Constitution posed a grave danger along these lines. The primary hazard the Anti-Federalists saw in the Constitution was that wide-ranging federal power could be read into the Commerce and Necessary and Proper Clauses, permitting Congress to legislate across a broad range of subjects. Unlike the Articles of Confederation, the Constitution would allow the federal government to act directly upon the people, without needing to go through the states as intermediaries. By virtue of the Supremacy Clause, a potentially vast code of federal law applicable directly to the people could largely supplant state law. The states could, in essence, be destroyed as separate and independent sovereign entities because state law could be rendered largely nugatory. This meant that state-law constraints against the government in favor of individual rights would be ineffectual in preserving human freedom because these formed a barrier only between the states and the people.[7] The new federal government, for the first time acting directly upon the people themselves, would be able to sidestep these constraints. Recall that this was the same concern implicated by the proposed impost of 1783, which triggered a protective response by the states.

When the issue of a federal Bill of Rights was first raised by Anti-Federalists Elbridge Gerry and George Mason at the tail end of the Constitutional Convention, Federalist Roger Sherman denied that such a bill was needed, arguing that "[t]he State Declarations of Rights" would be "sufficient" to guarantee individual rights. Mason responded that this was not so because, based on the Supremacy Clause of Article VI, "the laws of the U.S. are to be paramount to State Bills of Rights."[8] Mason followed up this thought within a few weeks with his *Objections to the Constitution of Government Formed by the Convention*, "the first salvo in the paper war over ratification,"[9] and an extraordinarily influential missive in Anti-Federalist circles. Mason began his *Objections* by repeating his lament that any state-law protection of individual rights would be ineffectual against the proposed federal government because of the Supremacy Clause: "There is no declaration of rights; and, the laws of the general government being paramount to the laws and constitutions of the several states, the declarations of rights in the separate states are no security."[10]

[7] Michael J.Z. Mannheimer, *Cruel and Unusual Federal Punishments*, 98 Iowa L. Rev. 69, 100–05 (2012).

[8] 2 The Records of the Federal Convention of 1787, at 587–88 (Max Farrand ed., 1911).

[9] Robert A. Rutland, *Framing and Ratifying the First Ten Amendments, in* The Framing and Ratification of the Constitution 305, 305 (L. Levy & D. Mahoney eds., 1987).

[10] George Mason, *Objections to the Constitution of Government Formed by the Convention* (1787), *reprinted in* 2 The Complete Anti-Federalist 11 (Herbert J. Storing ed., 1981).

Anti-Federalists were soon echoing these words in pamphlets and state ratifying conventions up and down the continent, explicitly tying together state power with individual rights.[11] For example, Pennsylvania Anti-Federalist Centinel (George and/or Samuel Bryan) wrote in a widely distributed piece that under the proposed Constitution, "the general government would necessarily annihilate the particular [i.e., state] governments, and . . . the security of the personal rights of the people by the state governments is superseded and destroyed."[12] Thomas Tredwell in the New York ratifying convention said of the proposed Constitution: "Here we find no security for the rights of individuals, no security for the existence of our state governments; here is no bill of rights, no proper restriction of power; our lives, our property, and our consciences, are left wholly at the mercy of the [national] legislature."[13] Another Anti-Federalist essayist asserted that the proposed Constitution would "expunge[] your [state] bill of rights by rendering ineffectual, all the state governments."[14] And Robert Whitehill in the Pennsylvania ratifying convention stated that he viewed the proposed Constitution "as the means of annihilating the constitutions of the several States, and consequently the liberties of the people."[15]

If the problem was that the new federal government could easily sidestep the constraints established by state law that were designed to protect individual freedom, then the solution seemed obvious to the Anti-Federalists: replicate those same constraints in a federal bill of rights. That is, the Anti-Federalists sought to take the same constraints that the states imposed upon themselves and impose them on the new federal government. "[H]ence results the necessity," wrote Centinel, "of such security being provided for by a bill of rights to be inserted in the new plan of federal government."[16]

And what was the nature of those constraints? The second sentence of Mason's *Objections* tells us, when he complains that the proposed Constitution would not secure the people "even in the enjoyment of the benefit of the common law."[17] The constraints the states imposed on themselves comprised the common-law rights of Englishmen. That is, after all, the reason we fought a revolution — because the colonists felt that they were not being afforded the common-law rights of

[11] *See* Michael J.Z. Mannheimer, *The Contingent Fourth Amendment*, 64 Emory L.J. 1229, 1265–66 (2015); Mannheimer, *supra* note 7, at 103–05.

[12] Letter from Centinel to the People of Pennsylvania (Nov. 30, 1787), *reprinted in* 2 The Complete Anti-Federalist, *supra* note 10, at 143, 152.

[13] 2 The Debates in the Several State Conventions on the Adoption of the Federal Constitution 401 (Jonathan Elliot ed., Philadelphia, J.B. Lippincott & Co. 1876) [hereinafter Elliot's Debates].

[14] Essay by the Impartial Examiner (Mar. 5, 1788), *reprinted in* 5 The Complete Anti-Federalist, *supra* note 10, at 185.

[15] Pennsylvania And The Federal Constitution, 1787–1788, at 287 (John Bach McMaster & Frederick Dawson Stone eds., 1888).

[16] Letter from Centinel to the People of Pennsylvania (Nov. 30, 1787), *reprinted in* 2 The Complete Anti-Federalist, *supra* note 10, at 143.

[17] *See* Mason, *supra* note 10.

Englishmen. And that is why virtually all of the former colonies, as among their very first acts as "free and independent States," adopted constitutions and bills of rights that ensured that these common-law rights would be respected by the new state governments.

That raises the question we put off earlier regarding the nature of these common-law rights and, indeed, the common law itself: was the common law viewed during the framing period as being uniform or differentiated? It turns out that this was one of the many things the Federalists and Anti-Federalists disagreed on.

DIFFERING VIEWS OF THE COMMON LAW AT THE FOUNDING

Did the framers and ratifiers of the Bill of Rights view the common law in the pre-Realist sense, as being unitary, declarative, and regardless of sovereignty? Or did they view it, as we do, as being particularized, instrumental, and tied to sovereignty?

The conventional wisdom is that the framers and ratifiers took the pre-Realist view. Take, just as one example, this description by Justice Scalia:

> [T]he prevailing image of the common law [at the founding] was that of a preexisting body of rules, uniform throughout the nation (rather than different from state to state), that judges merely "discovered" rather than created. It is only in th[e] [twentieth] century, with the rise of legal realism, that we came to acknowledge that judges in fact "make" the common law, and that each state has its own.[18]

This is, more or less, an accurate description of the prevalent view before 1776. Prior to the break with Britain, it was easier to see the common law as unitary, general, undifferentiated, and declaratory. Britain and her colonies were, at least in theory, one land with one law. And the stirring words of the Declaration of Independence evoke a strong sense of natural rights, based in natural law, transcending colonial boundaries.

But even vis-à-vis 1776, this is an oversimplified view. The oldest colony, Virginia, had been around for nearly 170 years. During this time, the colonies had developed their own legal personalities and their own versions of "the" common law. We can see this in the reception statutes passed in the wake of independence, which enacted the common law of England as it existed on July 4, 1776 (or some other date) but which generally adopted only those parts of English common law that had previously been accepted by the colony as consistent with local conditions.[19] We can also see the recognition of the different varieties of common law in the various colonial

---

[18] Antonin Scalia, *Common-Law Courts in a Civil-Law System: The Role of United States Federal Courts in Interpreting the Constitution and Laws, in* A MATTER OF INTERPRETATION: FEDERAL COURTS AND THE LAW 3, 10 (Amy Gutmann ed., 1997).

[19] *See* Mannheimer, *supra* note 7, at 112-13.

adaptations of the "law of the land" provision from chapter 29 of Magna Carta[20] to refer, not to some generalized law, but to the law of the colony itself. For example, in 1639, Maryland reenacted chapter 29 with "the law of the land" replaced by "the Laws of this province."[21] New York's Charter of Liberties and Privileges of 1683 likewise contained a jurisdiction-specific version of chapter 29, using "by the Law of this province."[22] In all, at least seven colonies were home to iterations of chapter 29 that referred specifically to the laws of those jurisdictions, suggesting that as early as the late seventeenth century, common-law rights were viewed, at least for some purposes, as jurisdiction specific.[23]

This view really took off following independence. With the stroke of a pen, thirteen separate sovereigns were created, with potentially thirteen different versions of the common law. While the older view of the common law as unitary still had vitality, it had to compete with the more modern view that had just been given the opportunity to develop with the sudden creation of thirteen sovereign states ruled by English common law. Suddenly, the common law could be viewed as one common religion with thirteen different sects, one common language with thirteen different dialects. As Professor Henry Monaghan put it, "the instrumental (rather than the declaratory) nature of the common law increasingly began to take hold in legal thinking" during this period.[24] Thus, the conventional wisdom voiced by Justice Scalia does not fully capture the complexity of legal thought regarding the common law near the turn of the eighteenth century.

Most importantly, it does not fully capture the views of the Anti-Federalists, for this issue broke down along party lines. Federalists generally took the pre-Realist position that there was a general common law untethered to sovereignty, while Anti-Federalists tended to take a proto-Realist position that the common law was tied to political boundaries.[25] Recall the words of Federalist Roger Sherman after Anti-Federalists Elbridge Gerry and George Mason proposed at the Constitutional Convention that a federal bill of rights be adopted: "The State Declarations of Rights are not repealed by this Constitution; and being in force are sufficient."[26] In Sherman's pre-Realist view of the law, the common law protections enshrined in state law simply existed "in the air," as it were, and thus could be interposed between

[20] The provision states: "No freeman shall be taken, or imprisoned, or be disseised of his freehold, or liberties, or free customs, or be outlawed, or exiled, or any otherwise destroyed; nor will we not pass upon him, nor condemn him, but by lawful judgment of his peers, or by the law of the land." 2 EDWARD COKE, INSTITUTES OF THE LAWS OF ENGLAND 45 (1642).

[21] *See* Ryan C. Williams, *The One and Only Substantive Due Process Clause*, 120 YALE L.J. 408, 436 (2010) (quoting 1639 MARYLAND ACT FOR THE LIBERTIES OF THE PEOPLE).

[22] The Charter of Liberties and privileges granted by his Royall Highnesse to the Inhabitants of New Yorke and its Dependencyes (Oct. 30, 1683), *reprinted in* 1 THE COLONIAL LAWS OF NEW YORK: YEAR 1664 TO THE REVOLUTION 111, 113 (1894).

[23] *See* Mannheimer, *supra* note 11, at 1277–78.

[24] Henry P. Monaghan, *Supremacy Clause Textualism*, 110 COLUM. L. REV. 731, 774 (2010).

[25] *See* Mannheimer, *supra* note 7, at 109–20; Mannheimer, *supra* note 11, at 1268–74.

[26] *See* 3 ELLIOT'S DEBATES, *supra* note 13, at 588.

the individual and the new federal government. (It is perhaps significant, in this regard, that Sherman hailed from Connecticut, the only state not to have adopted a Constitution or Declaration of Rights in the wake of independence, relying instead on common-law protections of liberty).

Mason responded in an entirely positivistic fashion: "[T]he laws of the U.S. are to be paramount to State Bills of Rights."[27] That is to say, the rights created by state law are worthless when it comes to providing a barrier between the individual and the proposed federal government, because, in that context, the Supremacy Clause sweeps them away. He expanded upon this view in the first paragraph of his *Objections.* "[T]he common law," Mason tells us, "stands here upon no other Foundation than it's [sic] having been adopted by the respective Acts forming the Constitutions of the several States."[28] This line could have been written by any twentieth-century Realist. The common law does not simply exist in the ether; it exists only to the extent that it has been adopted as positive law of each individual state. Indeed, that was precisely the premise behind the reception statutes. Even the great common law rights of Englishmen — the "benefit of the common law" to which Mason had just adverted — have no authority unless adopted as the positive law of the polity: they have "no other [f]oundation."[29]

If the common law existed, according to the Anti-Federalists, only as positive law, it stands to reason that it could and would differ by jurisdiction. Indeed, the thrust of Mason's ideas was sometimes expressed by the Anti-Federalists alongside the cognate idea that the common law was different in every state. For example, Maryland Farmer (probably John Francis Mercer) in his essay of Feb. 15, 1788, expressed this view:

> If a citizen of Maryland can have no benefit of his own bill of rights in the confederal courts, and there is no bill of rights of the United States — how could he take advantage of a natural right founded in reason, could he plead it and produce Locke, Sydney, or Montesquieu as authority? How could he take advantage of any of the common law rights, which have heretofore been considered as the birthright of Englishmen and their descendants, could he plead them and produce the authority of the English judges in his support? Unquestionably not, for *the authority of the common law arises from the express adoption by the several States in their respective constitutions, and that in various degrees and under different modifications.*[30]

That is very different from the conventional wisdom regarding the common law during the framing period. Maryland Farmer was not talking about, as Justice Scalia

---

[27] *Id.*
[28] Mason, *supra* note 10, at 11.
[29] *Id.*
[30] Essay by A [Maryland] Farmer No. I (Feb. 15, 1788), *reprinted in* 5 THE COMPLETE ANTI-FEDERALIST, *supra* note 10, at 13 (emphasis added).

put it, "a preexisting body of rules, uniform throughout the nation ... that judges merely 'discovered' rather than created." While he does mention "natural right[s] founded in reason," these rights are worthless without some positive-law manifest-ation, something to plead in court when the full authority of the federal government brings itself to bear against the lone citizen. While natural rights, such as freedom from cruel and unusual punishment, existed across borders in some nebulous form, they existed in a practical sense only if operationalized by positive law. Moreover, they could be operationalized in different ways in different states. Americans, in short, were evolving toward a more positivistic way of thinking about common-law rights and the Anti-Federalists were leading the charge.

Of course, the Federalists tended to retain the more traditional view. So if the Federalists generally accepted a declaratory, uniform, undifferentiated view of common law, and the Anti-Federalists tended to take a more instrumental, variable, heterogeneous view of common law, where does that leave us in terms of original understanding?

HEEDING THE ANTI-FEDERALIST VIEW

The Anti-Federalist take on the common law should guide our interpretation of the Bill of Rights because the Bill was the concession made by the Federalists to the Anti-Federalists for their reluctant acquiescence to ratification. While the Consti-tution was a Federalist project, the Bill of Rights – and, in turn, the nation itself — owes its existence to the Anti-Federalists.[31]

Why should we care about the Anti-Federalists? History, they say, is written by the victors and the Anti-Federalist foes of the Constitution clearly lost. But ratification was not an unmitigated victory for the Federalists. It was a compromise between Federalists and more moderate Anti-Federalists who obtained an important conces-sion in the Bill of Rights. Reading the Bill of Rights from the Federalist perspective ignores the other side of that compromise.

It is easy to look back and imagine that the Constitution was inevitable. But Anti-Federalists were initially in the majority in the key states of Massachusetts, New York, and Virginia, as well as in New Hampshire and North Carolina. In all those states, the initial votes in the ratifying conventions were either against ratification or, in the case of Virginia, split down the middle. Ratification in Massachusetts, New York, and Virginia was obtained only on the condition that a bill of rights would be added to placate the more moderate faction of the Anti-Federalists. Without that promise, ratification almost certainly would have failed.

True, Virginia and New York were the tenth and eleventh states to ratify, respectively, and were therefore technically unnecessary, given that Article VII of the Constitution required only nine states to ratify it in order for it to become

---

[31] *See* Mannheimer, *supra* note 7, at 108–09; Mannheimer, *supra* note 11, at 1278–84.

effective in those states. But imagine a United States without New York and Virginia. In 1788, before being split up into the three states that now occupy its territory, Virginia stretched from the Atlantic to the Mississippi, and reached to the southern border of Pennsylvania. New York, while not as grand, separated New England from the rest of the country and, of course, contained one of the nation's busiest ports. Survival of the fledgling republic required buy-in from these two states, Article VII notwithstanding.

Let us look at the Anti-Federalist opposition in New York in particular, where ratification was contingent on the promise of a bill of rights. The Anti-Federalist faction was led by Melancton Smith, a moderate who ultimately softened his position from outright opposition to the Constitution to reluctant acquiescence, so long as the quick passage of a bill of rights was assured. Satisfied with this concession, Smith ultimately voted in favor of ratification, taking eleven other Anti-Federalists with him. The final tally in New York in favor of ratification was 30-27.

As for James Madison's home state of Virginia, Madison himself acknowledged that the state would not have ratified the Constitution but for the promise of a bill of rights. He knew that ratification in that early period was tenuous and contingent, and that failure to adopt a bill of rights would likely precipitate a second constitutional convention threatening to undo his handiwork. Madison also saw his own political future hinge on his pledge to push a bill of rights through Congress that was acceptable to the states. Virginia was controlled by Anti-Federalists, who had not only blocked Madison from being chosen for the U.S. Senate but also gerrymandered his House district in an unsuccessful attempt to keep him out of Congress altogether. Failure to fulfill his pledge to adopt a bill of rights, and quickly, would have been political suicide for the rising star from Virginia.

Thus, the Bill of Rights, though penned by Madison, was the culmination of Anti-Federalist opposition to the Constitution and a clear victory for them. "[W]hile the Federalists gave us the Constitution," Murray Dry has said, "the Anti-Federalists gave us the Bill of Rights."[32] The underlying premises of the Anti-Federalists, then, are critical to a proper understanding of the Bill of Rights, for without their assent, the Constitution might never have been ratified and the country we know today might not exist. As Saul Cornell said: "Anti-Federalist political thought is essential to understanding the meaning of the Bill of Rights."[33] This translates, as Robert Palmer has put it, into "a state-oriented approach to the Bill of Rights."[34]

---

[32] Murray Dry, *The Anti-Federalists and the Constitution, in* PRINCIPLES OF THE CONSTITU-TIONAL ORDER: THE RATIFICATION DEBATES 63, 80 (Robert L. Utley, Jr. ed., 1989).

[33] Saul A. Cornell, *The Changing Historical Fortunes of the Anti-Federalists*, 84 Nw. U. L. REV. 39, 67 (1989).

[34] Robert C. Palmer, *Liberties as Constitutional Provisions, 1776–1791, in* CONSTITUTION AND RIGHTS IN THE EARLY AMERICAN REPUBLIC 55, 105 (Robert C. Palmer & William E. Nelson eds. 1987).

CRUEL AND UNUSUAL PUNISHMENT IN GEORGE MASON'S
OBJECTIONS

The view that the Cruel and Unusual Punishments Clause tied individual rights to state power is reinforced by what George Mason wrote about the subject in his *Objections*.[35]

The Anti-Federalists did not say much about the common-law proscription against cruel and unusual punishments and much of what they did say is fairly unenlightening. Abraham Holmes and Patrick Henry, in the Massachusetts and Virginia ratifying conventions, respectively, each lamented the lack of a constraint on Congress from, in Holmes's words, "inventing the most cruel and unheard-of punishments."[36] But neither one elaborated upon what that meant beyond a proscription against torture and adherence to common law. Again, we must turn to George Mason for further insight. In paragraph twelve of his *Objections*, he wrote:

> Under their own Construction of the general Clause at the End of the enumerated powers [i.e., the Necessary and Proper Clause] the Congress may grant Monopolies in Trade and Commerce, constitute new Crimes, inflict unusual and severe Punishments, and extend their Power as far as they shall think proper; so that the State Legislatures have no Security for the Powers now presumed to remain to them; or the People for their Rights.[37]

This passage reinforces a number of observations already made about the Anti-Federalists. First, notice that Mason mentions Congress's unbridled power to "grant Monopolies in Trade and Commerce" in virtually the same breath as he mentions its power to "inflict unusual and severe Punishments."[38] Though we think of the former as implicating structural concerns — that power would be overly centralized — and the latter as sounding in individual rights, this passage demonstrates the intertwined nature of structure and rights in Anti-Federalist ideology.

Even more telling along these lines is Mason's fear that "State Legislatures [will] have no Security for the Powers now presumed to remain to them,"[39] which follows closely on the heels of his concern regarding three potential incursions on those powers by Congress: the "grant[ing of] Monopolies in Trade and Commerce," the creation of "new Crimes," and the "inflict[ion of] unusual and severe Punishments."[40] The first two make sense on a conventional understanding of the Anti-Federalists' structural critique of the proposed Constitution. Congress's power

[35] *See* Mannheimer, *supra* note 5, at 865; Mannheimer, *supra* note 7, at 101–02.
[36] 2 ELLIOT'S DEBATES, *supra* note 13, at 111; *see also* 3 ELLIOT'S DEBATES, *supra* note 13, at 447–48 (statement of Patrick Henry) ("In this business of legislation, your members of Congress will loose the restriction of not . . . inflicting cruel and unusual punishments.").
[37] Mason, *supra* note 10, at 13.
[38] *Id.*
[39] *Id.*
[40] *Id.*

to regulate trade and create federal crimes would necessarily detract from the states' heretofore exclusive domain over those subjects. But his third example of federal incursion into state territory — the power to "inflict unusual and severe Punishments"— cannot be taken at face value. Mason surely did not mean that the new Constitution would interfere with the state legislatures' power to "inflict unusual and severe Punishments."[41] After all, Virginia's own 1776 Declaration of Rights, drafted by Mason himself, forbade the infliction of "cruel and unusual punishments." The only way that this passage makes sense is if the "unusual and severe Punishments" to which he referred were those that were more severe than those authorized by the state legislatures.[42] That is to say, "the Powers [then] presumed to remain" with the state legislatures included the power to set the outer bounds of criminal punishment; any punishment devised by the central government that were to go beyond those bounds would be, by definition, "unusual and severe."[43] And this objection, of course, led to the adoption of the Cruel and Unusual Punishments Clause.

MODERN IMPLICATIONS OF EIGHTH AMENDMENT FEDERALISM

This view, were it to be adopted by the courts, would have far-reaching implications in two separate directions. First, it would mean that federal punishments for crimes could not exceed the punishment authorized for the same offense in the state in which the crime occurred. Most starkly, the federal government would no longer be able to inflict the death penalty for a crime committed in a state that does not authorize capital punishment.[44] Until relatively recently, the federal government seemed to recognize an informal constraint upon the use of the federal death penalty for crimes committed in non-death-penalty states. It appears that only once in the 231-year history of the Republic has the federal government executed someone under those circumstances: Anthony Chebatoris, who killed a bystander in the course of an attempted bank robbery in Midland, Michigan in 1937. Chebatoris was hanged the following year, having declined to appeal his conviction or sentence, in the face of protests by then-Michigan Governor (later U.S. Supreme Court Justice) Frank Murphy. Since 1993, however, the federal government has sought the death penalty eighty times for crimes committed in non-death-penalty states, obtaining eleven death sentences.[45] A handful of district courts and the U.S. Court of Appeals for the Second Circuit have addressed but

---

[41] *Id.*

[42] *Id.*

[43] Mason, *supra* note 10, at 13.

[44] *See* Mannheimer, *supra* note 5, at 866–76.

[45] See Michael J.Z. Mannheimer, *The Coming Federalism Battle in the War over the Death Penalty*, 70 Ark. L. Rev. 309, 312–19 (2017).

rejected federalism-based challenges to these sentences.[46] One federal capital defendant, Dustin Honken, who committed five murders in Iowa, a non-death state, might soon join Chebatoris. His execution had been scheduled for January 15, 2020, but, as of this writing, has been stayed pending a challenge to the proposed method of execution.[47]

But the greater impact would be on carceral punishments for ordinary street crime, which the federal government has pursued vigorously in the past fifty years. Federal carceral sentences for these types of crimes, typically involving guns and/or drugs, often greatly exceed the sentences authorized by state law for the same conduct, sometimes by a factor of ten or twenty.[48] This disparity has been exacerbated by the fact that sentencing reform recently has been robust in the states but sluggish at the federal level.[49] As states make strides in reducing carceral sentences in an effort to downsize their prison populations while federal sentencing reform remains spotty, the disconnect grows between what some states, on the one hand, and the federal government, on the other, believe is appropriate punishment for what are, in essence, the same crimes. But if the central point of the Cruel and Unusual Punishments Clause is to tie federal punishments to the policy preferences of the respective states, this disconnect raises constitutional difficulties. A federalism-centered view of the Eighth Amendment would, in effect, force reform at the federal level through constitutional dictate, at least vis-à-vis federal prosecutions for ordinary street crime in reform-minded states.

A second implication of Eighth Amendment federalism is that we would have to rethink the reflexive incorporation of the Cruel and Unusual Punishments Clause against the states through the Fourteenth Amendment. If the central constraint of the Clause is one sounding in federalism, it is logically impossible to apply that constraint against the states. It is likely that the Fourteenth Amendment should be read as imposing some constraints on the states' power to punish. Adoption of that Amendment was motivated in large part by the Black Codes of the immediate post-Civil War South, which meted out different punishments for blacks and whites, explicitly in some provisions but also through the creation of wide prosecutorial and judicial discretion by facially race-neutral but loosely worded vagrancy statutes. Thus, a Fourteenth Amendment constraint on punishment should be guided by the twin pillars of equal protection and due process. The Court's landmark decisions

---

[46] *See* United States v. Aquart, 912 F.3d 1, 65–69 (2d Cir. 2018); United States v. Andrews, No.1:12CR100–1, 2015 WL 1191146, at *7 (N.D. W. Va. Mar. 16, 2015); United States v. Johnson, 900 F. Supp. 2d 949, 961–63 (N.D. Iowa 2012); United States v. McCluskey, CR. No. 10-2734 JCH, 2012 WL 13076173, at *10–11 (D. N.M. Sept. 24, 2012); United States v. Jacques, No. 2:08-cr-117, 2011 WL 3881033, at *3–5* (D. Vt. Sept. 2, 2011).
[47] *See* Barr v. Roane, No. 19A615, 2019 WL 6649067 (U.S. Dec. 6, 2019).
[48] *See* Mannheimer, *supra* note 7, at 78–79.
[49] *See* Rebecca Silber et al., *Justice in Review: New Trends in State Sentencing and Corrections 2014–2015*, VERA INST. OF JUST., at 20–28 (May 2016), https://www.vera.org/publications/justice-in-review-new-trends-in-state-sentencing-and-corrections-2014-2015.

in *Furman* v. *Georgia*[50] and *Gregg* v. *Georgia*,[51] which require that the states cabin the sentencing authority's discretion to sentence someone to death, are consistent with, though not necessarily compelled by, a due process constraint on excessive sentencing discretion. And statistical evidence that powerfully suggests that killers of whites are far more likely to be sentenced to death than killers of blacks raises the troubling specter that blacks are not being afforded "the equal protection of the laws" in some states.[52] On the other hand, it is difficult to defend on either due process or equal protection grounds the Court's exemption of certain categories of offenders and offenses from the death penalty.[53] But these are only preliminary thoughts and whether and to what extent Fourteenth Amendment due process and equal protection constraints match up with the Court's current Eighth Amendment jurisprudence remains an area for further study.

CONCLUSION

The Anti-Federalists' Bill of Rights was first and foremost an instrument to protect individual rights through the preservation of a robust form of state sovereignty. They demanded a bill of rights to fill the gap left by the Constitution, that is, to apply against the federal government the common-law rights of Englishmen already secured by state law. And they conceived of the common law as having no force other than as positive law of each individual state, and therefore varying by state in its particulars. Indeed, some of the Anti-Federalist proposals for amendments would have explicitly required the federal government to obey the laws of each individual state when acting therein. One amendment proposed by the New York ratifying convention, for example, would have required all federal officers "to be bound, by oath or affirmation, not to infringe the constitutions or rights of the respective states."[54] Who was the author of that proposal? It was none other than Melancton Smith, perhaps the man most responsible for the creation of our Union.

True, Smith's proposal was not expressly adopted. But its spirit, the idea of carving out some state-created rights for preservation against federal power, infuses the provisions of the Bill of Rights. Just as Georgia, Massachusetts, New Hampshire, and South Carolina insisted on setting the outer bounds of punishment for smuggling in their states under the Articles of Confederation, the Anti-Federalists sought through the Bill of Rights a preservation of state power in furtherance of individual rights. While the shift from the Articles to the Constitution occasioned a

---

[50] 408 U.S. 238 (1972) (per curiam).
[51] 428 U.S. 153 (1976) (plurality opinion).
[52] *But see* McCleskey v. Kemp, 481 U.S. 279 (1987) (rejecting this claim).
[53] *See* Kennedy v. Louisiana, 554 U.S. 407 (2008); Roper v. Simmons, 543 U.S. 551 (2005); Atkins v. Virginia, 536 U.S. 304 (2002); Enmund v. Florida, 458 U.S. 782 (1982); Coker v. Georgia, 433 U.S. 584 (1977) (plurality opinion).
[54] 2 ELLIOT'S DEBATES, *supra* note 13, at 409–10.

tremendous transfer of power to the central government at the expense of the states, the Bill represented a restoration of some of that power back to the states. The centripetal force of the Constitution, drawing power to the center, was tempered by the centrifugal force of the Bill, returning power to the states.

Thus, it makes some sense, at least if we give primacy to the views of the Anti-Federalists — and we should — to read the word "unusual" in the Eighth Amendment as a way of calibrating federal punishments to those permitted by the laws in each state. That is to say, "cruel and unusual" is best interpreted as "more severe than is permitted by the law of the state."

PART II

The Landscape of Eighth Amendment Doctrine

4

Eighth Amendment Values

William W. Berry III * & *Meghan J. Ryan* **

As with many constitutional provisions, the language of the Eighth Amendment is open-ended and vague in its proscription of excessive bail, excessive fines, and cruel and unusual punishments. Because the language of the Constitution does not provide any additional descriptive information concerning what might make bail or fines excessive, or punishments cruel and unusual, courts must look beyond the text itself to ascertain the meaning of the Eighth Amendment. With respect to the prohibition on cruel and unusual punishments, the U.S. Supreme Court has, over the course of several decades, articulated a number of relevant underlying values that offer some guidance in interpreting this Eighth Amendment provision. These values are also helpful in assessing the excessiveness of bail and fines.[1]

This Chapter explores several of these core Eighth Amendment values, providing an overview of their origin and indicating how such values might apply in interpreting the Eighth Amendment in the future. Specifically, this Chapter discusses the principles of dignity, individualized sentencing, proportionality — both absolute and comparative, humanness, non-arbitrariness, and differentness. The Court has explicitly or implicitly invoked each of these values in its Eighth Amendment cases and detailed the scope and importance of these values to varying degrees. For the most part, though, the Court has remained opaque about how much each of these values influences, and should influence, its Eighth Amendment decisions.

While the scope and reach of the various Eighth Amendment values remain uncertain, the Court has made it clear that the meaning of the Amendment — e.g., which punishments are unconstitutionally cruel and unusual — changes over time.[2]

---

* Professor of Law and Montague Professor, University of Mississippi School of Law.
** Associate Dean for Research, Altshuler Distinguished Teaching Professor, and Professor of Law, SMU Dedman School of Law.
[1] *See* Chs. 10 & 11.
[2] *Cf.* Meghan J. Ryan, *The Missing Jury: The Neglected Role of Juries in Eighth Amendment Punishments Clause Determinations*, 64 FLA. L. REV. 549, 566 (2012) (explaining that the

In *Weems v. United States*, the Court explained that, for "a principle[] to be vital, [it] must be capable of wider application than the mischief which gave it birth" and that "[t]his is peculiarly true of constitutions."[3] As such, the Court emphasized that the Eighth Amendment is progressive and may acquire broader meaning over time.[4] The Court cemented this principle in its 1958 landmark opinion of *Trop v. Dulles*,[5] indicating that "the words of the [Eighth] Amendment are not precise, and that their scope is not static." Accordingly, when determining whether a punishment is unconstitutionally cruel and unusual, courts must interpret the prohibition in light of "the evolving standards of decency that mark the progress of a maturing society."[6]

To capture these changing values, the Court has adopted a two-part test to assess whether a particular punishment violates the evolving standards of decency, at least in capital cases. The first step, an objective inquiry, generally consists of state-counting — surveying primarily legislatures' determinations, as well as decisions by sentencing juries, about whether the particular jurisdiction has rejected the punishment at issue, at least in the relevant circumstances.[7] In the second step, the Court "brings its own independent judgment to bear"[8] in assessing whether a punishment has become unconstitutionally cruel and unusual in light of the purposes of punishment.[9]

Viewing the Eighth Amendment's meaning as evolving over time reflects the changing nature of punishments over the course of generations and also the changing views and values of Americans and even other citizens of the world. The various Eighth Amendment values should be understood in light of this gradual movement toward greater enlightenment.

DIGNITY

An important Eighth Amendment value woven into the Eighth Amendment case law is that of dignity. In fact, the Court has been more explicit about this Eighth Amendment value than others. In 1958, the Court first articulated the requirement

---

Court's Punishments Clause analysis is "atypical in that [it is] more securely tethered to a particular method of constitutional interpretation": "[b]y focusing on ... 'evolving standards' ... , the Court's primary standard[] for constitutionality in th[is] context[] seem[s] to be tied to a notion of living constitutionalism rather than rooted in history as many originalists would prefer").

[3] Weems v. United States, 217 U.S. 349, 373 (1910).

[4] *Id.*

[5] Trop v. Dulles, 356 U.S. 86 (1958) (plurality opinion).

[6] *Id.*

[7] *See* Meghan J. Ryan, *Does Stare Decisis Apply in the Eighth Amendment Death Penalty Context?*, 85 N.C. L. Rev. 847, 855 (2007). For a discussion concerning filling the content of a counter-majoritarian constitutional provision with a majoritarian assessment, see Ch. 6.

[8] Coker v. Georgia, 433 U.S. 584 (1977) (plurality opinion).

[9] *See* Meghan J. Ryan, *Judging Cruelty*, 44 U.C. Davis L. Rev. 81, 90–95 (2010).

that punishments respect human dignity in its case of *Trop v. Dulles*.[10] There, a plurality of the Court explained:

> The basic concept underlying the Eighth Amendment is nothing less than the dignity of man. While the State has the power to punish, the Amendment stands to assure that this power be exercised within the limits of civilized standards. Fines, imprisonment and even execution may be imposed depending upon the enormity of the crime, but any technique outside the bounds of these traditional penalties is constitutionally suspect.[11]

This focus on dignity has been a touchstone for the Court in its Eighth Amendment cases. In case after case, the Court has stated that "[t]he basic concept underlying the Eighth Amendment is nothing less than the dignity of man."[12]

Despite the Court's emphasis that dignity is the backdrop of the Eighth Amendment, the Court has never clearly explained what dignity means in this context. As a philosophical concept, and even as a legal one, dignity has a complicated history. Although the concept "has been around since antiquity," dignity really blossomed in the aftermath of World War II.[13] Reacting to Nazi atrocities, various nations established the United Nations (UN), the UN adopted the Universal Declaration of Human Rights, and countries around the world have created constitutions protective of human dignity. Yet, at both the international and national levels, there has been disagreement — among various nations, among various Supreme Court Justices, and even among commentators — about what dignity actually means and how it should apply to particular situations.

Although the Court has neglected to explicitly define Eighth Amendment dignity, and although there are various conceptions of dignity among legislators, courts, scholars, and commentators, there seems to be at least a common kernel of dignity that persists in the Eighth Amendment case law. Some thinkers have more robust notions of dignity, but, at the heart of the concept is a respect for individuals as individuals. As Emmanuel Kant put it, "a human being cannot be used merely as a means by any human being ... but must also be used at the same time as an end."[14] Examining the many Eighth Amendment cases in which the Court explicitly invoked the concept of dignity, one sees a focus on individualism — viewing individuals as ends rather than merely as means.

---

[10] 356 U.S. 86 (1958) (plurality opinion).

[11] *Id.* at 100.

[12] *See, e.g.*, Hope v. Pelzer, 536 U.S. 730, 738 (2002) (quoting *Trop*, 356 U.S. at 100–01); Atkins v. Virginia, 536 U.S. 304, 311–12 (2002) (same).

[13] Meghan J. Ryan, *Taking Dignity Seriously: Excavating the Backdrop of the Eighth Amendment*, 2016 ILL. L. REV. 2129, 2135–36 (2016); *see also* Christopher McCrudden, *Human Dignity and Judicial Interpretation of Human Rights*, 19 EUR. J. INT'L L. 655, 662–64 (2008).

[14] IMMANUEL KANT, THE METAPHYSICS OF MORALS 209 (Mary J. Gregor trans. & ed., Cambridge University Press 1996) (1797).

Preserving this minimum non-instrumentalization core of dignity has at least two facets — imposing only proportionate punishments on criminal offenders and treating offenders as human beings.[15] For example, in the famous case of *Gregg v. Georgia*,[16] a plurality of the Court suggested that respecting dignity prohibits excessive punishments. And in *Brown v. Plata*,[17] the Court explained that, "[a]s a consequence of their own actions, prisoners may be deprived of rights that are fundamental to liberty" but that "the law and the Constitution demand [that] . . . [p]risoners retain the essence of human dignity inherent in all persons." In fact, in examining all of the Court's Eighth Amendment cases — the procedural, type-of-offense, class-of-offender, method-of-punishment, and prison-condition cases — it seems that the Court has been consistent in adopting an individualism-directed notion of dignity, which incorporates both proportionality and humanness principles.[18]

To be sure, this basic conception of Eighth Amendment dignity is still vague and, in many ways, cannot unambiguously police the constitutionality of punishments under the Amendment. At the same time, many commentators would argue that this conception of dignity is too narrow and does not go far enough in proscribing suspect methods, durations, and conditions of many punishments. While the Court seems to be cutting back on the breadth of Eighth Amendment protection against cruel and unusual punishments,[19] this non-instrumentalization core of dignity does not necessarily define the outer bounds of what this backdrop of the Eighth Amendment proscribes. Rather, it is the kernel of protection that the Court has consistently determined is essential to guarding against unconstitutionally cruel and unusual punishments.[20]

Taken seriously, this minimum non-instrumentalization core of dignity would limit punishment in significant ways — ways not necessarily yet captured in court opinions. Staying true to this conception of dignity would mean that purely utilitarian punishment is unconstitutional.[21] Punishments may certainly be partially instrumentalist, such as under the popular theory of limiting retributivism, where retribution sets the outer boundaries of punishment and instrumentalist approaches like deterrence determine the exact punishment within those endpoints. But punishments that treat individuals as means rather than ends in themselves would be

---

[15] *See* Ryan, *supra* note 13.
[16] 428 U.S. 153 (1976) (plurality opinion).
[17] 563 U.S. 493 (2011).
[18] *See* Ryan, *supra* note 13, at 2156–65.
[19] *See, e.g.*, Bucklew v. Precythe, 139 S. Ct. 1112 (2019) (rejecting the petitioner's Eighth Amendment challenge because he failed to sufficiently establish that he had identified a feasible alternative execution method that would "significantly reduce a substantial risk of severe pain"). *But see* Timbs v. Indiana, 139 S. Ct. 682 (2019) (incorporating — finally — the Excessive Fines Clause such that it applies to the states). Note that recent changes to the Supreme Court — the appointment of Justices Gorsuch and Kavanaugh, and the retirement of Justice Kennedy — will likely have a limiting impact on the breadth of Eighth Amendment protections in future years.
[20] *See* Ryan, *supra* note 13, at 2156–65.
[21] *See id.*

impermissible. This suggests that punishing innocent persons is unconstitutional.[22] While this may not seem shocking, there are numerous court opinions suggesting that, if a convicted offender is later found innocent, he has no constitutional right to avoid punishment if he received a fair trial, because federal habeas courts review for constitutional violations rather than factual errors.[23]

The minimum non-instrumentalization core of dignity, and thus of the Eighth Amendment, also suggests that mandatorily imposed punishments are constitutionally impermissible.[24] The Supreme Court has already struck down the mandatory imposition of capital punishment and the mandatory imposition of life without the possibility of parole (LWOP) for juvenile offenders,[25] but mandatory sentences are very common in other areas, and taking the Eighth Amendment dignity requirement seriously would mean finding these practices unconstitutional.

INDIVIDUALIZED SENTENCING

The Court's focus on individualism logically translates to the more specific value of individualized sentencing. Under the Court's decisions, individualized sentencing means that the sentencing court, at least in capital cases, must examine the individual characteristics of the offender and the offense prior to making a sentencing determination.

This idea germinates from the Court's decision in *McGautha v. California*,[26] in which the Court rejected Fourteenth Amendment due process challenges to the capital jury sentencing procedures of California and Ohio. In that case, the Court discussed the troubling consequences of jury nullification in response to mandatory death statutes. Without the ability to decide whether death was an appropriate sentence for the individual offender in question, juries often chose to find the offender not guilty instead of entering a guilty verdict that mandated death. In reaffirming the importance of juror sentencing discretion in capital cases, even when unguided, the Court explained that juries are critical to "maintain a link between contemporary community values and the penal system."[27]

The Court constitutionalized this idea in *Woodson v. North Carolina*,[28] holding that the Eighth Amendment bars mandatory death sentences. Specifically, the

---

[22] *See id.* at 2168–73.

[23] *See id.*

[24] *See id.* at 2177–78.

[25] *See* Miller v. Alabama, 567 U.S. 460 (2012) (striking down the mandatory imposition of LWOP sentences for juvenile offenders); Woodson v. North Carolina, 428 U.S. 280 (1976) (plurality opinion).

[26] 402 U.S. 183 (1971).

[27] *Id.*

[28] 428 U.S. 280 (1976) (plurality opinion). The Court applied the same rule in another case decided the same day, *Roberts v. Louisiana*, 428 U.S. 325 (1976) (plurality opinion), in which it struck down Louisiana's mandatory death statute.

Court held that the Eighth Amendment requires "the particularized consideration of relevant aspects of the character and record of each convicted defendant before the imposition upon him of a sentence of death."[29]

The Court reaffirmed this value of individualized sentencing determinations in *Lockett v. Ohio*,[30] where it struck down an Ohio statute that limited the mitigating evidence available to capital defendants at sentencing to enumerated statutory factors. A plurality of the Court made clear that the sentencing judge or jury must consider "*as a mitigating factor,* any aspect of a defendant's character or record and any of the circumstances of the offense that the defendant proffers as a basis for a sentence less than death."[31]

While the Court has primarily focused on this concept of individualized sentencing in capital cases, the Court expanded the concept to juvenile life-without-parole (JLWOP) sentences in *Miller v. Alabama*,[32] finding that mandatory JLWOP sentences violate the Eighth Amendment. In that case, the Court relied on the same individualized sentencing concept, emphasizing the unique nature of cases and the need to consider the particularized circumstances and conduct of the offender in determining whether a death-in-prison sentence is appropriate.

While LWOP sentences are still permissible for adult offenders, a logical expansion of the individualized sentencing concept would be to prohibit mandatory LWOP sentences even for adults.[33] This extension would result from the Court acknowledging that these death-in-prison sentences share many similarities with death sentences, something the Court has already done in *Miller*. A further expansion, though perhaps less likely, would be to ban all mandatory sentences.[34]

ABSOLUTE PROPORTIONALITY

In debating the bounds of the Eighth Amendment proscription on cruel and unusual punishments, various U.S. Supreme Court Justices have considered whether the Clause prohibits only certain torturous methods of punishment, or, alternatively, whether the Clause offers broader protection to criminal offenders. Several Justices would require, and indeed several cases indicate, that such broader protection demands that imposed sentences are proportionate to the crimes committed, accounting for both the characteristics of the particular offender and the details of

---

[29] *Woodson*, 428 U.S. at 303.

[30] 438 U.S. 586 (1976).

[31] *Id.* at 604 (opinion of Burger, J.).

[32] 567 U.S. 460 (2012).

[33] *See* William W. Berry III, *More Different than Life, Less Different than Death*, 71 Oнio St. L. J. 1109 (2010) (arguing for expansion of *Miller* to adult LWOP).

[34] *See* William W. Berry III, *Individualized Executions*, 52 U.C. Davis L. Rev. 1779 (2019) (arguing for an application of individualized sentencing to methods of execution); William W. Berry III, *Individualized Sentencing*, 76 Wash. & Lee L. Rev. 13 (2019) (arguing for an expansion of individualized sentencing to all felony offenses).

the offense. Although Justices Scalia, Thomas, and Rehnquist have famously argued that proportionality has no place in the application of the Eighth Amendment,[35] a majority of the Court has embraced the value of proportionality.[36]

Beginning with the Court's decision in *Coker v. Georgia*,[37] the Supreme Court has used the concept of proportionality to hold that, in certain types of cases, death sentences constitute cruel and unusual punishments. To date, the Supreme Court has proscribed the death penalty for rape,[38] child rape,[39] certain felony murders,[40] juvenile offenders,[41] "insane" persons,[42] and intellectually disabled offenders.[43] The concept of proportionality embedded in these decisions — "absolute" proportionality — relates to the excessiveness of the death penalty in light of the underlying crime or the characteristics of the offender.

The Court's analysis in these capital cases begins with the objective assessment of jurisdictions' legislation and jury sentences to determine whether society has generally condemned the punishment.[44] The second prong of the analysis considers the question of whether one or both of the relevant purposes of punishment — retribution and deterrence — justify the imposition of death.[45] The idea championed by the Court is that, when capital punishment does not achieve the purpose of retribution or deterrence, that punishment is disproportionate and thus violates the Eighth Amendment. For example, in *Atkins v. Virginia*, the Court expressed concern that certain types of defendants, such as those with intellectual disabilities, are at a special risk of wrongful execution.[46]

In non-capital cases, the Court has fashioned the concept of proportionality in a different manner, electing not to apply its more robust test used in capital cases and instead using a narrow gross disproportionality standard. Ordinarily, the Court has

---

[35] *See, e.g.*, Graham v. Florida, 560 U.S. 48 (2010) (Thomas, J., dissenting); Harmelin v. Michigan, 501 U.S. 957 (1991) (opinion of Scalia, J.).

[36] Ewing v. California, 538 U.S. 11 (2003) (plurality opinion).

[37] 433 U.S. 584 (1977) (plurality opinion).

[38] *Id.*

[39] Kennedy v. Louisiana, 554 U.S. 407 (2008).

[40] *See* Tison v. Arizona, 481 U.S. 137 (1987); Enmund v. Florida, 458 U.S. 782 (1982).

[41] Roper v. Simmons, 543 U.S. 551 (2005).

[42] Panetti v. Quarterman, 551 U.S. 930 (2007); Ford v. Wainwright, 477 U.S. 399 (1986).

[43] Moore v. Texas, 137 S. Ct. 1039 (2017); Hall v. Florida, 572 U.S. 701 (2014); Atkins v. Virginia, 536 U.S. 304 (2002).

[44] One of us has argued that proportionality extends beyond *just deserts* retribution conceptions of proportionality. *See* William W. Berry III, *Separating Retribution from Proportionality*, 97 Va. L. Rev. In Brief 61 (2011); *see also* Ch. 7.

[45] The other two purposes of punishment — incapacitation and rehabilitation — have generally not been part of the Court's analysis. Incapacitation seems inappropriate, *see* William W. Berry III, *Ending Death by Dangerousness*, 52 Ariz. L. Rev. 889 (2010), but rehabilitation may surprisingly be more relevant than the Court has perceived, *see* Meghan J. Ryan, *Death and Rehabilitation*, 46 U.C. Davis L. Rev. 1231 (2013).

[46] *See Atkins*, 536 U.S. at 321 (expressing concern that "[m]entally retarded defendants in the aggregate face a special risk of wrongful execution").

held that non-capital sentences are generally proportionate punishments regardless of the offenses at issue. This deferential standard has, in essence, created two tracks of Eighth Amendment application.[47]

In more recent years, though, the Court has carved out a significant exception to applying the narrow gross disproportionality standard in non-capital cases: JLWOP sentences. In these cases, the Court has used the same two-part test it uses in capital cases instead of the gross proportionality test. In *Graham v. Florida*,[48] for example, the Court held that the Eighth Amendment bars LWOP sentences for juveniles who committed non-homicide offenses. In *Miller*, the Court barred mandatory JLWOP sentences.[49]

One of the most logical extensions of the value of absolute proportionality would be to prohibit capital punishment for additional categories of defendants like those suffering from various types of brain injuries. Another extension of the proportionality principle would be to prohibit JLWOP sentences for particular classes of defendants or even prohibit these sentences altogether.[50] Further, the Court could take the additional step of entirely dismantling the bright line between capital and non-capital cases, applying the Eighth Amendment's capital case approach to additional kinds of non-capital sentences.

COMPARATIVE PROPORTIONALITY

A corollary to the concept of absolute proportionality that has inhabited the Court's Eighth Amendment cases is the concept of "comparative" or "relative" proportionality. While absolute proportionality assesses whether a particular kind of sentence is excessive under certain circumstances, comparative proportionality assesses whether a sentence is disproportionate in light of sentencing decisions in other cases.

In *Gregg v. Georgia*,[51] part of the state's solution to the problem of sentencing disparities arising from jury sentencing decisions was its adoption of comparative proportionality review. Under this approach, the state supreme court reviewed jury verdicts in capital cases to assess whether a death sentence was consistent with prior jury decisions in capital cases. After the Court affirmed this approach in *Gregg*, a number of states have employed similar approaches in their capital sentencing procedures.

The idea behind comparative proportionality is to eliminate outlier sentencing decisions by juries. While such an approach cannot guarantee complete consistency, it can, at the very least, minimize sentencing outcomes that fall outside of

---

[47] See Rachel E. Barkow, *The Court of Life and Death: The Two Tracks of Constitutional Sentencing Law and the Case for Uniformity*, 107 MICH. L. REV. 1145, 1145 (2009).

[48] 560 U.S. 48 (2010).

[49] 567 U.S. 460 (2012).

[50] *See* William W. Berry III, *Evolved Standards, Evolving Justices*, 96 WASH. U. L. REV. 105 (2018).

[51] 428 U.S. 153 (1976) (plurality opinion).

mainstream sentencing decisions. This is particularly important because states employ a wide variety of aggravating factors in capital sentencing, meaning that cases with widely differing levels of offender culpability within a jurisdiction can nonetheless be subject to capital sentencing determinations. Comparative proportionality review allows state supreme courts to strike down capital sentences that are excessive by comparison to previous cases in which the state imposed the death penalty.

Although many jurisdictions have adopted this comparative proportionality approach, they have mostly conducted the analysis in a cursory, toothless manner. State supreme courts have reversed a negligible number of sentences based on comparative proportionality review. Most states limit this review to prior capital cases, meaning the court never considers the cases in which juries imposed a life sentence. In addition, the proportionality review in most states consists simply of identifying other cases relying on the same aggravating factor and, based upon that factor alone, declaring the sentence proportionate.[52]

Nonetheless, in *Pulley v. Harris*,[53] the Supreme Court made clear that the Eighth Amendment does not require a comparative proportionality analysis at all. The Eighth Amendment simply requires meaningful appellate review of jury-imposed death sentences. While comparative proportionality review can be one way to satisfy the Eighth Amendment concern of arbitrary and capricious imposition of punishment, the Constitution does not mandate such an approach.

While remaining a constitutionally approved but not required approach in the death penalty context, comparative proportionality review has also played a role in the assessment of non-capital sentences, but it is similarly ordinarily not constitutionally required. In *Solem v. Helm*, the Court used comparative proportionality concepts in assessing gross disproportionality, including the sentences imposed on other criminals in the same jurisdiction, and in other jurisdictions.[54] While the contours of the Court's gross disproportionality jurisprudence remain hazy, the Court made clear in *Harmelin v. Michigan* that such comparisons, while useful, were not constitutionally required in most cases.[55]

HUMANNESS

In addition to focusing on proportionality in sentencing, the Court's Eighth Amendment analysis has highlighted the importance of ensuring that punishments

---

[52] *See, e.g.*, William W. Berry III, *Practicing Proportionality*, 64 FLA. L. REV. 687 (2012).

[53] 465 U.S. 37 (1984).

[54] Solem v. Helm, 463 U.S. 277 (1983).

[55] *See* Harmelin v. Michigan, 501 U.S. 957, 1004–05 (2003) (Kennedy, J., concurring) ("*Solem* is best understood as holding that comparative analysis within and between jurisdictions is not always relevant to proportionality review.... [I]ntrajurisdictional and interjurisdictional analyses are appropriate only in the rare case in which a threshold comparison of the crime committed and the sentence imposed leads to an inference of gross disproportionality.").

acknowledge the humanness of even the worst convicted criminal offenders.[56] There are some punishments, such as torture, that are simply too horrendous to impose regardless of the offense committed. In *Trop*, for example, the Court found that the punishment of denationalization "subject[ed] the individual to a fate forbidden by the principle of civilized treatment guaranteed by the Eighth Amendment."[57] In fact, the Court found the punishment even "more primitive than torture."[58] In addressing the unconstitutionality of insufficient prison medical care under the Eighth Amendment, the Court was similarly concerned about how such medical neglect could "actually produce physical 'torture or a lingering death,'" which would amount to cruel and unusual punishment.[59] And in striking down the practice of executing "insane" offenders, the Court emphasized the sheer inhumanity of the practice.[60]

The Supreme Court's command that punishments must reflect the humanness of individuals is important in this modern era of mass incarceration where thousands of individuals are convicted each year.[61] To many prosecutors, judges, and citizens, these offenders must seem to be faceless numbers — the causes of victims' pain and suffering and in part the source of staggering criminal justice expenses. But the Eighth Amendment requires that we remember the humanity of even the worst offenders. Although some prosecutors have been known to label these offenders as "animals,"[62] we cannot treat them like that under the Constitution. Depending on how far one takes this principle, it could raise significant questions about a number of current punishment practices, such as LWOP, solitary confinement, certain techniques used to carry out execution, and even the death penalty itself.

NON-ARBITRARINESS

The Court has also adopted an Eighth Amendment value of non-arbitrariness. In 1972, the Court struck down the death penalty as applied throughout the United States in the landmark opinion of *Furman v. Georgia*.[63] The Justices were unable to reach a consensus about whether the death penalty was unconstitutional in its entirety or just as it was applied in this (and other) case(s), but there was significant

---

[56] See Ryan, *supra* note 13.
[57] Trop v. Dulles, 356 U.S. 86, 100 (1958) (plurality opinion).
[58] *Id.*
[59] *See* Estelle v. Gamble, 429 U.S. 97, 103 (1976).
[60] *See* Ford v. Wainwright, 477 U.S. 399, 406–10 (1986).
[61] *See, e.g.*, THE SENTENCING PROJECT, *Criminal Justice Facts*, https://www.sentencingproject .org/criminal-justice-facts/ (last visited, Oct. 1, 2019).
[62] *See, e.g.*, Darden v. Wainwright, 477 U.S. 168, 179 (1986) (noting that the prosecutor referred to the defendant as an animal and stating that this "deserves the condemnation it has received from every court to review it, although no court has held that the argument rendered the trial unfair").
[63] Furman v. Georgia, 408 U.S. 238 (1972) (per curiam).

agreement that, to the extent the punishment was unconstitutional, it was unconstitutional because of its unusualness. Some of the Justices noted the racially discriminatory way in which judges and juries had imposed the death penalty. But even more Justices focused on the arbitrary way in which capital punishment was imposed and carried out. For example, Justice White explained that, as applied, "the penalty [was] so infrequently imposed that the threat of execution [was] too attenuated to be of substantial service to criminal justice."[64] Justice Brennan pointed to the "steady decline in the infliction of the punishment in every decade since the 1930's," the increase in the number of capital crimes committed, and the resulting "rarity of the infliction of th[e] punishment."[65] He explained that "[w]hen the punishment of death is inflicted in a trivial number of cases in which it is legally available, the conclusion is virtually inescapable that it is being inflicted arbitrarily. Indeed, it smacks of little more than a lottery system."[66] Justice Stewart characterized it as akin to "being struck by lightning."[67]

When the Supreme Court later upheld capital punishment in *Gregg v. Georgia*[68] in 1976, it emphasized the importance of ensuring that states did not impose capital punishment arbitrarily or capriciously. The Court explained that capital punishment cannot "be imposed under sentencing procedures that create[] a substantial risk that [the penalty] w[ill] be inflicted in an arbitrary and capricious manner."[69] Instead, a jurisdiction's statutes must guide jury sentencing discretion, providing the jury with the tools to distinguish the offenders deserving of death from those who are not. The new Georgia scheme cured the Eighth Amendment arbitrariness concerns articulated in *Furman* in two important ways. First, the scheme mandated the use of aggravating and mitigating circumstances in sentencing, requiring a factual finding for death eligibility and then requiring the jury to weigh such findings against mitigating evidence. Second, the state supreme court reviewed the determination of the jury in light of other cases, conducting a comparative proportionality review to promote consistency among jury decisions. Although not identical, jurisdictions across the country now provide capital sentencing juries with such guidance on their discretion, attempting to comply with the requirements of *Furman* under the Eighth Amendment.[70]

It is worth noting that this value of non-arbitrariness is sometimes in tension with the value of individualized sentencing. Every case is unique, so when attempting to achieve some uniformity or consistency in sentencing across cases, it often comes at the expense of considering individual differences in each case. Justice Scalia made

---

[64] *Id.* at 313 (White, J., concurring).
[65] *Id.* at 291 (Brennan, J., concurring).
[66] *Id.* at 293.
[67] *Id.* at 309 (Stewart, J., concurring).
[68] Gregg v. Georgia, 428 U.S. 153 (1976) (plurality opinion).
[69] *Id.* at 188.
[70] Some have argued, though, that the guidance is, as a practical matter, insufficient to affect disparity concerns. *See* Berry, *supra* note 52.

this argument in *Walton v. Arizona*, finding that individualized sentencing and non-arbitrariness are inconsistent because individualized discretion is the source of arbitrary outcomes.[71] Justice Stevens disagreed, though, explaining that narrowing the class of death-eligible offenders through requiring a finding of aggravating circumstances minimizes the concern of arbitrary outcomes, whereas individualized sentencing discretion is exercised within that narrowed group.[72] Regardless of whether they are in tension, the Court's cases have made clear that both individualized sentencing and non-arbitrariness are Eighth Amendment requirements.

Applying a strong version of the non-arbitrariness value could result in, once again, striking down capital punishment.[73] The current use of the death penalty, with its consistent decline over the past decade, mirrors the conditions that the Court addressed in *Furman*. Today, only a few counties are responsible for most executions,[74] resulting in a lack of uniformity in the punishment's imposition. Further, only half of the states authorize the death penalty, and fewer than a quarter of them actively use it.[75] The same is true for JLWOP sentences, with many states abandoning the punishment after *Miller* and fewer than half of them currently imposing JLWOP sentences.[76]

DIFFERENTNESS

Unlike the previous values that seem to bear some connection to dignity, the pervasive value of differentness appears to move further afield. The Supreme Court has, for the most part, treated capital cases differently than non-capital cases under the Eighth Amendment. While not the Court's original approach, this distinction arose from the Court's determination that "death is different."[77] This oft-repeated concept stems from the idea that death is a unique punishment, both in its severity

---

[71] Walton v. Arizona, 497 U.S. 639, 656 (1990) (Scalia, J., concurring in part), *rev'd in part*, Ring v. Arizona, 536 U.S. 584 (2002).

[72] *Id.* at 708 (Stevens, J., dissenting). Comparative proportionality review could, in theory, help to reconcile the apparent incompatibility of non-arbitrariness and individualized sentencing discretion. *See* Berry, *supra* note 52.

[73] *See* Berry, *supra* note 52.

[74] *See* Frank R. Baumgartner, *A Few Counties Are Responsible for the Vast Majority of Executions. This Explains Why*, WASH. POST, Feb. 1, 2008, https://www.washingtonpost.com/news/monkey-cage/wp/2018/02/01/a-handful-of-counties-are-responsible-for-the-vast-majority-of-executions-this-explains-why/?noredirect=on.

[75] *See State by State*, DEATH PENALTY INFO. CTR. (2019), https://deathpenaltyinfo.org/state-and-federal-info/state-by-state.

[76] *See* Berry, *supra* note 52.

[77] Justice Brennan's concurrence in *Furman v. Georgia* is the source of the Court's "death is different" capital jurisprudence. Carol S. Steiker & Jordan M. Steiker, *Sober Second Thoughts: Reflections on Two Decades of Constitutional Regulation of Capital Punishment*, 109 HARV. L. REV. 355, 370 (1995) (crediting Justice Brennan as the originator of this line of argument); *see also* Furman v. Georgia, 408 U.S. 238, 286 (1972) (Brennan, J., concurring) ("Death is a unique punishment in the United States.").

and its irrevocability. There is no more serious punishment than the death penalty. And once a state carries out an execution, there is no way to reverse it.

Using this principle, the Court has accorded capital cases heightened scrutiny under the Eighth Amendment. This value has served as the basis for categorical exclusions to the death penalty. It also has served as the basis for heightened procedural requirements in capital cases.

More recently, the court has decided that juveniles are also different.[78] This has meant, at the very least, that some of the categorical exclusions that apply to the death penalty also apply to juvenile offenders, at least in LWOP cases. It is possible that the procedural safeguards available in capital cases might also extend to JLWOP cases, but to date that has not happened.

It is also unclear what the broadening of differentness might mean for future expansions of the Eighth Amendment. As death is a punishment but juveniles are a class of offenders, it suggests that expansion is possible, albeit not likely in the near future. If death is different, the Court could in theory also find that other punishments are different such that they might deserve heightened substantive or procedural safeguards. These might include LWOP sentences, life sentences, or sentences that extend beyond an offender's life expectancy. If juveniles are different, other categories of offenders could, in theory, be different as well. One might imagine groups such as veterans, the elderly, or those with certain mental illnesses receiving the label of "different."

The consequence of the Court using the value of differentness has largely been positive for the "different" offenders and "different" offenses but has unfortunately had the consequence of preventing heightened scrutiny for "non-different" offenders and offenses. In other words, the Court has elected to limit Eighth Amendment scrutiny in non-capital cases in a comparatively restrictive manner.

With respect to future applications of this principle, another approach would be simply to de-emphasize the value rather than create new categories of differentness. Continuing to create new categories of differentness could exacerbate the inconsistency and fragmented nature of existing Eighth Amendment jurisprudence. Rather than creating a constitutional doctrine that mandates separation for death sentences in the form of higher scrutiny, it would also be possible to require a higher level of Eighth Amendment scrutiny for all cases. Although death may indeed be different, and children and LWOP sentences may also be different, courts may be able to accommodate these different characteristics within proportionality analyses and the more robust analyses typically applied in capital cases.

THE FUTURE OF EIGHTH AMENDMENT VALUES

The Eighth Amendment values discussed in this Chapter shed light on the constitutionality of a variety of criminal justice practices — from regularly litigated

---

[78] Miller v. Alabama, 567 U.S. 460 (2012); Graham v. Florida, 560 U.S. 48 (2010).

punishments like the death penalty to areas less considered like bail. These values help explain past Supreme Court decisions, but they also provide tools for Eighth Amendment litigants. Indeed, the question remains of how such values relate to the scope of the Eighth Amendment with respect to punishments that do not fit neatly into the Court's currently defined categories. While not dispositive, these values can help explain why the Court's doctrine should shift in particular circumstances over time.

With respect to the death penalty, for instance, Eighth Amendment values have much to say. As use of the death penalty in the United States continues to decline, the strength of the argument that the punishment contravenes the evolving standards of decency grows.[79] In addition, states increasingly impose the death penalty in an arbitrary way, as demonstrated by statistics on the impact of geography, race, and socio-economic status on capital decisions.[80] Further, commentators have argued that the death penalty is a disproportionate punishment for all criminal offenses[81] and that it violates human dignity. An overwhelming number of nations have also adopted this position. In light of all of this evidence and the values illuminating Eighth Amendment meaning, there are real questions about the continuing constitutional viability of capital punishment, even though the Bill of Rights itself contemplates the punishment's use.

Juvenile LWOP sentences also create tension with a number of Eighth Amendment values. As the only country that imposes such sentences, the United States does not comply with evolving standards internationally. In addition, since the *Miller* decision in 2012, there has been a significant movement away from JLWOP even within the United States, with a number of states abolishing the punishment and many courts reducing sentences in light of *Miller's* retroactive application.[82] Currently, more than half of the states do not have anyone serving a JLWOP sentence, raising real questions about arbitrariness and proportionality when a court imposes such a sentence.

The use of LWOP sentences in the United States similarly makes our nation an outlier internationally. There are more than 50,000 people serving LWOP sentences in the United States; the next three countries combined have fewer than 1,000 individuals serving such sentences. As with the punishments of death and JLWOP, adult LWOP sentences spark questions about offender dignity and proportionality — issues that have formed the basis for most other countries rejecting the practice. Further, many of the LWOP sentences imposed in the United States are the result

---

[79] *See* Berry, *supra* note 52. Such an outcome becomes magnified if one examines the use of the death penalty on a county level. *See* William W. Berry III, *Unusual State Capital Punishments*, 72 FLA. L. REV. __ (forthcoming 2020).

[80] *See* Glossip v. Gross, 135 S. Ct. 2726, 2760–63 (Breyer, J., dissenting).

[81] Dan Markel, *State, Be Not Proud: A Retributivist Defense of the Commutation of Death Row and the Abolition of the Death Penalty*, 40 HARV. C.R.-C.L. L. REV. 407 (2005).

[82] *See* Montgomery v. Louisiana, 136 S. Ct. 718 (2016).

of the abolition of parole, not a carefully considered decision that the offender deserves to die in prison. This creates significant concerns about respecting the values of individualized sentencing, non-arbitrariness, and humanness.

Similarly, mandatory sentences undermine some of the core values of the Eighth Amendment. They deny individualized consideration, can threaten human dignity, and often result in disproportionate sentences. Almost every single value animating the Eighth Amendment counsels against allowing mandatory punishments. Considering that the Court has generally refused to strike down mandatory punishments across the board, its intervention in at least select mandatory sentencing cases would be a step in the right direction.

Finally, these Eighth Amendment values can shed light on practices such as solitary confinement and even other Eighth Amendment areas like excessive bail and fines. Practices such as solitary confinement that leave lasting psychological damage on individuals clearly implicate questions about how to treat other human beings, even if they have committed terrible offenses. But if lasting psychological damage is a human dignity concern, then even relatively short stints in prison should receive serious Eighth Amendment scrutiny. Although Eighth Amendment application comes loaded with relevant values like dignity, it does not necessarily provide us with clear answers about the permissiveness of any particular practice. Still, these values remain important and help shape our understanding of the Eighth Amendment. Although most references to these values are in Eighth Amendment Punishments Clause cases, they are also relevant to the important, but generally less litigated, Excessive Bail and Excessive Fines Clauses as well.

To be sure, the current conservative tilt of the Supreme Court makes the expansion of Eighth Amendment protection less likely in the near future. Nonetheless, it is likely that these values will continue to inform the Court's Eighth Amendment decisions irrespective of whether the doctrine expands or contracts.

5

The Power, Problems, and Potential of "Evolving Standards of Decency"

Corinna Barrett Lain[*]

The "evolving standards of decency" doctrine, which affords Eighth Amendment protection to punishment practices that violate contemporary standards, has historically played a key role in interpreting the nebulous Cruel and Unusual Punishments Clause, although the journey has been marked by controversy and contradictions. Today, as the continued vitality of the evolving standards doctrine has been increasingly called into question,[1] it is worth pausing to remember where the doctrine came from, how and why it came about, and the work it has done and is poised to do going forward. This chapter touches upon each of those topics, first discussing the origins of the evolving standards doctrine and how it revitalized the Eighth Amendment, then turning to the power of the doctrine and the problems that developed as it came into full flower, and then finally turning to the doctrine's potential going forward. The power, problems, and potential of the evolving standards doctrine are what make the doctrine a lightning rod of criticism as well as a beacon of hope for progressive decisions to come, rendering it one of the most interesting and important areas of Eighth Amendment law.

[*] S.D. Roberts & Sandra Moore Professor of Law, University of Richmond School of Law. I thank Will Berry and Meghan Ryan for taking on this important project, and for inviting me to be a part of it.

[1] *See* Garrett Epps, *Unusual Cruelty at the Supreme Court*, THE ATLANTIC, April 4, 2019, https://www.theatlantic.com/ideas/archive/2019/04/bucklew-v-precythe-supreme-court-turns-cruelty/586471/ (noting that the majority in *Bucklew v. Precythe*, a recent death penalty case, pretended like the evolving standards doctrine did not even exist, and questioning its continued vitality on an increasingly conservative Supreme Court); *Justice Kennedy: His Departure from the Court and Possible Consequences for Capital Cases*, AMERICAN BAR ASS'N (Nov. 6, 2018), https://www.americanbar.org/groups/committees/death_penalty_representation/project_press/2018/fall/kennedy-in-retrospective/ (questioning the future of the evolving standards doctrine in light of Justice Kennedy's retirement from the Supreme Court and the appointment of Justice Kavanaugh in his stead).

THE EVOLUTION OF EVOLVING STANDARDS

The standard story of the evolving standards doctrine starts with the Supreme Court's 1958 decision in *Trop v. Dulles*, which contains the famous line: "The [Eighth] Amendment must draw its meaning from the evolving standards of decency that mark the progress of a maturing society."[2] But starting there misses the larger context in which *Trop* was decided. It treats *Trop* as the major doctrinal move, whereas in truth, those moves occurred before and after *Trop*. *Trop* just gave us the words that would give the doctrine its name.

The real story starts with the Supreme Court's 1910 decision in *Weems v. United States*.[3] Before *Weems*, the Supreme Court had decided only two Eighth Amendment cases on the merits — one in 1878, and one in 1890.[4] Both were execution method challenges, and there was a reason that was true: the Framers had understood the phrase "cruel and unusual punishments" to mean punishments that were *unusually cruel*, as in torturous, and so the only question under the Constitution was whether a particular execution method qualified as torture.[5] In 1878, the Court's answer was "no" as to the firing squad, and in 1890, it was "no" as to death by electrocution.[6]

That brings us to *Weems* in 1910. *Weems* considered a fifteen-year sentence of *cadena temporal* — hard labor while chained at the ankles and wrists — for the crime of forging a public document. The punishment was not torture, but it was unusually cruel in light of the crime. The Supreme Court held that such grossly disproportionate punishments violated the Cruel and Unusual Punishments Clause, stating:

> Time works changes, brings into existence new conditions and purposes. Therefore a principle to be vital must be capable of wider application than the mischief which gave it birth. This is peculiarly true of constitutions ... The [Cruel and Unusual Punishments Clause] may be therefore progressive, and is not fastened to the obsolete but may acquire meaning as public opinion becomes enlightened by a humane justice.[7]

Cadena temporal may not be torture per se, the Court concluded, but it was torturous for the crime, and that was close enough.

---

[2] 356 U.S. 86, 100–01 (1958).

[3] 217 U.S. 349 (1910).

[4] Wilkerson v. Utah, 99 U.S. 130 (1878) (upholding death by firing squad); *In re* Kemmler, 136 U.S. 436 (1890) (upholding death by electrocution). *Wilkerson* applied the Eighth Amendment to the territory of Utah; *Kemmler* was technically a Fourteenth Amendment case that applied the Eighth Amendment's prohibition against cruel and unusual punishments at the state level.

[5] *See* Harmelin v. Michigan, 501 U.S. 957, 979–85 (1991) (discussing commentary in depth from the First Congress, state ratification debates, contemporary observers, and early common law, all supporting the conclusion that the Framers understood the Cruel and Unusual Punishments Clause to prohibit torture).

[6] *See supra* note 4.

[7] *Weems*, 217 U.S. at 373, 378.

Weems is known for its recognition of the proportionality principle, but its reason for doing so is the doctrinal move worth noting here. In *Weems*, the Supreme Court explicitly rejected a reading of the Eighth Amendment that was limited to its original understanding, a stance that the Court viewed as necessary to ensure that the Eighth Amendment remained "vital." Here again, there was a reason that was true. Torturous punishments — what the Supreme Court in 1890 referred to as "burning at the stake, crucifixion, breaking at the wheel, or the like"[8] — were long gone by 1910. So if that is what the Eighth Amendment's Cruel and Unusual Punishments Clause prohibited, and *all* that it prohibited, the Clause would be a dead letter in constitutional law. Indeed, the fact that the Court had decided only three cases under the Cruel and Unusual Punishments Clause in the first hundred years of its existence suggested that it already was.

It was *Weems* that unmoored the Cruel and Unusual Punishments Clause from its original understanding and set the stage for *Trop v. Dulles*,[9] the next proportionality case after *Weems*. *Trop* considered a soldier's expatriation — complete loss of citizenship — as punishment for his wartime desertion for a day. Once again, the Supreme Court found the punishment to be grossly disproportionate to the crime and invalidated it under the Eighth Amendment. With only *Weems* to rely on as precedent, the Court in *Trop* wrote:

> [In *Weems*, the Supreme Court] did not hesitate to declare that the penalty was cruel in its excessiveness and unusual in its character. The Court recognized in that case that the words of the Amendment are not precise, and that their scope is not static. The Amendment must draw its meaning from the evolving standards of decency that mark the progress of a maturing society.[10]

The last line would turn out to be gold, but the Court in *Trop* could not have known that; it was just paraphrasing *Weems*, echoing the recognition of an Eighth Amendment whose meaning would evolve over time.

Importantly, neither *Weems* nor *Trop* advocated using societal standards as a constitutional constraint in and of themselves; that doctrinal move was made in *Furman v. Georgia*, decided in 1972.[11] *Furman* invalidated the death penalty as it then existed, and while it was deeply problematic as a doctrinal matter, the decision was eminently understandable in light of the larger sociopolitical context in which it was decided.[12] For present purposes, what mattered in *Furman* was that two Justices — Brennan and Marshall — argued that a punishment could be "cruel and unusual" for no reason other than it had become unpopular, citing *Trop*'s

---

8   *In re* Kemmler, 136 U.S. at 446.
9   356 U.S. 86 (1958) (plurality opinion).
10 *Id.* at 100–01.
11 408 U.S. 238 (1972) (per curiam).
12 For a discussion of the point, see Corinna Barrett Lain, Furman *Fundamentals*, 82 WASH. L. REV. 1 (2007).

reference to evolving standards of decency.[13] But Brennan and Marshall stood alone on this point, and the *Furman* decision came to be known for something else — a prohibition against arbitrary and capricious death sentencing.[14]

In 1976, when the Supreme Court in *Gregg v. Georgia* decided that the death penalty was constitutional after all, the Justices once again found themselves in a doctrinal tight spot, and turned to evolving standards of decency to get themselves out of it. By then, thirty-five states had passed new death penalty statutes, death sentences had hit the highest year-end figure ever recorded, and public opinion polls showed support for the death penalty at a ratio of two-to-one — a twenty-five-year high.[15] The one thing that the Justices could say with confidence was that their ruling comported with society's evolving standards of decency, and that's exactly what the Justices did say, adopting Brennan and Marshall's notion of evolving standards as a substantive constitutional command and then announcing that the death penalty met it.[16] In that moment, the evolving standards doctrine was born.

Why does all this matter? For starters, the origin story of the evolving standards doctrine is a reminder that the Supreme Court has rejected a reading of the Eighth Amendment that is limited to its original understanding for well over a hundred years. And for good reason — no one is actually trying to torture anyone anymore, so for the Eighth Amendment to have any relevance at all, it must be relevant to something beyond torture. The evolving standards language was a recognition of this truth, reviving the Eighth Amendment from its otherwise dead letter status and giving birth to the Amendment's key modernizing function.

The origin story of the evolving standards doctrine also reveals the power that the doctrine had from the start. Evolving standards was part of the reason that the Justices invalidated the death penalty in 1972 and was a key component of the Supreme Court's reason for bringing the death penalty back in 1976. *Gregg v. Georgia* inaugurated the modern death penalty era, and the evolving standards doctrine was the tool that the Court used to do it. Yet all this was just the start; the doctrine's power would only grow as the Court used it to trim some of the worst excesses of death penalty practice.

EVOLVING STANDARDS IN FULL FLOWER

In the wake of *Gregg*, the Supreme Court used the evolving standards doctrine to eradicate a number of the most categorically offensive uses of the death penalty, and

---

[13] *See Furman*, 408 U.S. at 270 n.10, 277–306 (Brennan, J., concurring); *id.* at 329–32 (Marshall, J., concurring).
[14] *See* Lain, *supra* note 12, at 14–15 (discussing the five concurring opinions in *Furman* and the rationale for the decision that emerged as a result).
[15] *See id.* at 46–50.
[16] *See* Gregg v. Georgia, 428 U.S. 153, 179–82 (1976) (plurality opinion) (discussing legislation and jury verdicts in the wake of *Furman*, and concluding that "it is now evident that a large proportion of American society continues to regard [the death penalty] as an appropriate and necessary criminal sanction").

there the doctrine came into full flower. First, the Court used the evolving standards doctrine to invalidate the death penalty for rape of an adult that did not result in death,[17] then it used evolving standards to categorically exclude from the death penalty those offenders who were deemed insane at the time of execution.[18] Eventually, the Court used the doctrine to invalidate the death penalty for juvenile offenders and the intellectually disabled as well,[19] although not before first taking the position that evolving standards of decency did not prohibit such executions.[20] The Court went back and forth on whether evolving standards prohibited the death penalty for those who were accessories to murder but did not actually kill, leaving the law on that issue muddled,[21] but it spoke clearly when it reiterated in 2008 that the death penalty for rape not resulting in death violated evolving standards, even when the victim was a child.[22]

In all these cases, the Supreme Court ostensibly took aim at outlier practices, using the evolving standards doctrine to invalidate the death penalty where its application was unduly harsh and out of line with mainstream punishment practices. At the time, it seemed that nibbling around the edges was all that the evolving standards doctrine could do. Indeed, some lamented the doctrine for this very reason, observing that it got rid of the ugliest parts of the death penalty — the so-called "'poster children' of the abolition movement" — while stabilizing the center that remained.[23]

But the practical implications of the evolving standards doctrine for abolitionists paled in comparison to the problems with the doctrine itself. Those problems were two-fold. One was a theoretical problem with the sort of "sheep dog" judicial review that the evolving standards doctrine offered. The other was a problem with how the doctrine played out over time.

The theoretical problem with the evolving standards doctrine stems from the fact that it affords Eighth Amendment protection only after society has largely rejected a punishment practice on its own. In no small measure, the very point of constitutional protection is to protect minorities from democratic majorities. But this is a

---

[17] *See* Coker v. Georgia, 433 U.S. 584 (1977) (plurality opinion).

[18] *See* Ford v. Wainwright, 477 U.S. 399 (1986).

[19] *See* Roper v. Simmons, 543 U.S. 551 (2005) (invalidating the death penalty for juvenile offenders); Atkins v. Virginia, 536 U.S. 304 (2002) (invalidating the death penalty for offenders with intellectual disabilities).

[20] *See* Stanford v. Kentucky, 492 U.S. 361 (1989) (upholding the death penalty for juvenile offenders older than the age of fifteen); Penry v. Lynaugh, 492 U.S. 302 (1989) (upholding the death penalty for offenders with intellectual disabilities).

[21] *See* Tison v. Arizona, 481 U.S. 137 (1987) (upholding the death penalty for accomplices who did not take life but exhibited reckless indifference to doing so); Enmund v. Florida, 458 U.S. 782 (1982) (invalidating the death penalty for accomplices who neither took life, attempted to take life, nor intended to take life).

[22] *See* Kennedy v. Louisiana, 554 U.S. 407 (2008).

[23] Carol S. Steiker, *Things Fall Apart, but the Center Holds: The Supreme Court and the Death Penalty*, 77 N.Y.U. L. REV. 1475, 1488 (2002).

nonstarter under the evolving standards doctrine, which uses prevailing societal standards to determine whether a punishment practice violates the Cruel and Unusual Punishments Clause, resulting in constitutional protection that depends on, because it is defined by, majority will. Forget about protecting unpopular minorities from tyrannical majorities, and the fact that capital defendants are about as unpopular a minority as minorities get. The Eighth Amendment context may be the one place we would expect to see countermajoritarian protection, but it is also the place where the doctrine renders that moot. As John Hart Ely wrote, "It makes no sense to employ the value judgments of the majority as a vehicle for protecting minorities from the value judgments of the majority."[24] That is not going to work out well for the minorities in need of protection.

Defenders of the evolving standards doctrine have typically countered this criticism by pointing to the text of the Eighth Amendment. By its very terms, the Amendment prohibits punishments that are cruel *and unusual*, the argument goes, and so whether or not it makes constitutional sense, the notion of Eighth Amendment protection when a punishment practice becomes unusual — that is, when society has largely rejected it — is textually based and justified here. To quote the late Justice Scalia (who, for the record, came to despise the evolving standards doctrine),[25] "If a punishment is not unusual, that is, if an objective examination of laws and jury determinations fails to demonstrate society's disapproval of it, the punishment is not unconstitutional even if out of accord with the theories of penology favored by the Justices of this Court."[26]

As I have discussed elsewhere, this textual defense of the evolving standards doctrine makes sense until one realizes that for better or worse, the Supreme Court uses the same doctrinal framework to decide questions of constitutional law even when the text does not support it.[27] The substantive due process context is perhaps the most obvious example; there the Court engages in exactly the same sort of state counting that we see under the evolving standards doctrine[28] and has even imported

---

[24] John Hart Ely, Democracy and Distrust 69 (1980).

[25] *See, e.g.,* Glossip v. Gross, 135 S. Ct. 2726, 2749 (2015) (Scalia, J., concurring) ("I would ask that counsel also brief whether our cases that have abandoned the historical understanding of the Eighth Amendment, beginning with *Trop,* should be overruled. That case has caused more mischief to our jurisprudence, to our federal system, and to our society than any other that comes to mind.").

[26] Penry v. Lynaugh, 492 U.S. 302, 351 (1989) (Scalia, J., concurring in part and dissenting in part). In full disclosure, the fact that this Chapter is quoting Justice Scalia for a textual defense of the evolving standards doctrine would probably make him roll over in his grave.

[27] *See* Corinna Barrett Lain, *The Unexceptionalism of Evolving Standards,* UCLA L. Rev. 365 (2009).

[28] *Compare* Lawrence v. Texas, 539 U.S. 558 (2003) (invalidating state statutes that criminalized same sex sodomy under the Due Process Clause), *with* Roper v. Simmons, 543 U.S. 551 (2005) (invalidating the death penalty for juvenile offenders under the evolving standards of decency doctrine). For a side-by-side comparison, see Lain, *supra* note 27, at 372–73.

language from evolving standards cases to do it.[29] But that is not the only place where one can see the Supreme Court invalidating outlier practices using explicitly majoritarian constitutional doctrine. The Court's decisions in the procedural due process context, equal protection context, and First, Fourth, and Sixth Amendment contexts all feature the sort of state-counting and consensus-following for which the evolving standards doctrine is famous.[30] By and large, the phenomenon has simply escaped notice.

Unexceptional as it may be, the inherently majoritarian nature of the evolving standards doctrine is one problem, and the way it has played out is yet another. In *Gregg*, the Supreme Court held that society's evolving standards of decency could be ascertained by looking at state legislative positions and jury verdicts, as each provided an indication of what society thought of a particular punishment practice.[31] And so that is what the evolving standards doctrine entailed, *at first*. But where the doctrine's most basic formulation did not produce the outcome that the Justices wanted, it evolved, growing more capacious over time. Sometimes the evolving standards doctrine considered only death penalty states in determining what practices society had rejected;[32] sometimes it counted abolitionist states too.[33] Sometimes the Court bolstered a weak state count by considering the direction of legislative change and "near misses" in other states.[34] And sometimes it considered broader sociopolitical indicators under the evolving standards doctrine, such as international opinion, the stance of respected professional organizations, and public

---

[29] *See* Washington v. Glucksberg, 521 U.S. 702, 711 (1997) (noting that "the primary and most reliable indication of [a national] consensus is ... the pattern of enacted laws") (quoting and citing *Stanford v. Kentucky*, 492 U.S. 361, 373 (1989) (upholding death penalty for juvenile offenders under the evolving standards doctrine)).

[30] *See* Lain, *supra* note 27, at 380–400 (discussing state counting in the procedural due process, equal protection, and First, Fourth, and Sixth Amendment contexts).

[31] *See* Gregg v. Georgia, 428 U.S. 153, 179–182 (1976) (plurality opinion).

[32] *See, e.g.*, Enmund v. Florida, 458 U.S. 782, 789 (1982) ("Thirty-six state and federal jurisdictions presently authorize the death penalty. Of these, only eight jurisdictions authorize imposition of the death penalty solely for participation in a robbery in which another robber takes life."); Coker v. Georgia, 433 U.S. 584, 594–95 (1977) (plurality opinion) (noting that only three of the thirty-five states that reinstated the death penalty authorized the punishment for rape of an adult woman).

[33] *See, e.g.*, Roper v. Simmons, 543 U.S. 551, 564 (2005) ("When *Atkins* was decided, 30 States prohibited the death penalty for the mentally retarded. This number comprised 12 that had abandoned the death penalty altogether, and 18 that maintained it but excluded the mentally retarded from its reach. By a similar calculation in this case, 30 States prohibit the juvenile death penalty, comprising 12 that have rejected the death penalty altogether and 18 that maintain it but, by express provision or judicial interpretation, exclude juveniles from its reach."); Penry v. Lynaugh, 492 U.S. 302, 334 (1989) ("In our view, the two state statutes prohibiting execution of the mentally retarded, even when added to the 14 States that have rejected capital punishment completely, do not provide sufficient evidence at present of a national consensus.").

[34] *See, e.g.*, Atkins v. Virginia, 536 U.S. 304, 315–16 (2002).

opinion polls.[35] Whether the evolving standards doctrine was read narrowly or in a broad, more expansive fashion depended mostly on where a majority of the Justices wanted to go. As I have noted elsewhere, the Justices have not followed the evolving standards doctrine so much as the doctrine has followed them.[36]

None of that is to say that the Supreme Court got its more capacious evolving standards decisions wrong. When the Court in *Atkins v. Virginia* invalidated the death penalty for intellectually disabled offenders in 2002, for example, it may have stretched the evolving standards doctrine to the limit,[37] but it did in fact manage to eradicate a practice that was clearly on its way out. Famous death row exonerees Anthony Porter and Earl Washington had brought national attention to the danger of wrongful conviction for the intellectually disabled, causing a number of prominent death penalty supporters to oppose the death penalty for this class of offenders, the public to turn against it, and a slew of state legislatures to quickly fall into line.[38] Even Virginia was in the midst of abolishing the death penalty for intellectually disabled offenders when the Supreme Court granted certiorari in *Atkins*.[39]

The same was true of the Supreme Court's 2005 decision invalidating the death penalty for juvenile offenders in *Roper v. Simmons*. *Roper* was an even tougher sell than *Atkins* under the evolving standards doctrine,[40] but for all its doctrinal difficulties, the decision did in fact invalidate a practice that had pretty much died out on its own. Death sentences for juveniles were never high, but they had dwindled over the

---

[35] *See, e.g., Roper*, 543 U.S. at 575–78 (considering international opinion against the death penalty for juvenile offenders and noting that only the United States and Somalia expressly allow the practice); *Atkins*, 536 U.S. at 316–17 n.21 (considering views of professional organizations, religious denominations, the world community, and pollsters).

[36] *See* Corinna Barrett Lain, *Deciding Death*, 57 DUKE L.J. 1, 6 (2007) ("[T]he 'evolving standards' doctrine might be problematic in theory, but in practice, majoritarian doctrine imposes too little constraint to be the crux of the majoritarian problem. The Justices do not follow doctrine in any meaningful way. Doctrine follows them.").

[37] *See Atkins*, 536 U.S. at 347 (Scalia, J., dissenting) (awarding the majority "the Prize for the Court's Most Feeble Effort to fabricate 'national consensus'").

[38] Those supporters included President George W. Bush and his brother, Florida Governor Jeb Bush. *See* Raymond Bonner, *President Says the Retarded Should Never Be Executed*, N.Y. TIMES, June 12, 2001, at 28; *Jeb Bush Signs Bill Barring Executing the Retarded*, N.Y. TIMES, June 13, 2001, at A30. For an in-depth discussion of the larger sociopolitical context in which *Atkins* was decided, see Lain, *supra* note 36, at 43–52.

[39] Linda Greenhouse, *The Death Penalty: Citing "National Consensus," Justices Bar Death Penalty for Retarded Defendants*, N.Y. TIMES, June 21, 2002, at A1 (noting that the Virginia Senate had voted unanimously to abolish the death penalty for intellectually disabled offenders, but the Virginia House decided to delay any action until after the Supreme Court had decided *Atkins*); *see also id.* (noting that the Supreme Court initially agreed to hear a North Carolina case on this issue, but North Carolina abolished the death penalty for intellectually disabled offenders in the meantime so the Justices dismissed the appeal).

[40] Only four legislatures had abandoned the death penalty for juveniles between 1989, when the Supreme Court upheld the practice, and 2005, when it invalidated the death penalty for juveniles in *Roper*, so even the considerations that the Court had used to bolster the holding in *Atkins* cut the other way. *See Roper*, 543 U.S. at 611–12 (Scalia, J., dissenting).

years and by 2003 and 2004, the annual tally of juvenile death sentences was just two.[41] Moreover, only two states in the country, Texas and Virginia, actively embraced the death penalty for juveniles – together, they accounted for more than seventy-five percent of all juvenile offender executions in the modern death penalty era[42] — and Virginia's use of the punishment was fading fast.[43]

In both *Atkins* and *Roper*, the Court might have gotten the doctrine wrong, but it managed to get the ruling itself right. How this could be so is a more complicated story than can be fully told here, but the short of it is that the evolving standards doctrine had become so capacious that it was hard to say it was doing any real work, yet by the time the Supreme Court could muster a majority to invalidate a practice, the practice had — for reasons often having nothing to do with doctrine — truly come to be viewed as unduly punitive and obsolete.[44] The doctrine was majoritarian, and the decisions were majoritarian, but it was hard to say the decisions were the result of the doctrine.

The sort of doctrinal manipulation that made all this work drew the ire of some and offered a beacon of hope to others. For conservatives on the Supreme Court, the evolving standards doctrine was bearable as initially conceived; it was not originalism but it was textually defensible, and as long as constitutional protection was following state legislative positions, it stood no chance of getting ahead of them. At least as initially conceived, the evolving standards doctrine was a doctrine of conservative constitutional protection. But the broader reading of the doctrine allowed for progressive decisions too. Progressive decisions under the auspices of a conservative doctrine — *that* was infuriating.[45] And so it came to be that the evolving standards doctrine inspired fear and loathing on the right and optimism on the left, rendering it one of the most controversial doctrines in Eighth Amendment law.

Looking back, it is fair to say that as the power of the evolving standards doctrine grew over time, so did its doctrinal problems. But with power and problems also came tremendous potential. And the potential of the evolving standards doctrine going forward brings us to where we are now.

EVOLVING STANDARDS AND THE FUTURE OF THE DEATH PENALTY

Thus far, the evolving standards doctrine has been used to effectuate categorical exclusions to the death penalty. Sometimes the category is the type of offender;

---

[41] See Lain, *supra* note 36, at 52 (discussing death sentencing for juvenile offenders from the 1990s to 2005).

[42] See *id.* at 53.

[43] Not even Lee Boyd Malvo, one of the two Washington beltway snipers who terrorized the mid-Atlantic region and killed ten people, received a death sentence in 2003, and he was tried in Virginia just to maximize the possibility that he would. See Henri E. Cauvin, *Malvo's Age Was the Deciding Factor*, WASH. POST, Dec. 24, 2003, at A1.

[44] This is the point I make in *Deciding Death*. See Lain, *supra* note 36.

[45] For prominent examples of Justice Scalia blowing his judicial gasket, see *Roper*, 543 U.S. at 607–30 (Scalia, J., dissenting); *Atkins*, 536 U.S. 304, 337–54 (2002) (Scalia, J., dissenting).

sometimes it is the crime. But all of the Supreme Court's evolving standards cases since *Gregg* have considered discrete applications of the death penalty for categorical exclusion.

And that may well continue. Ever since *Atkins* categorically excluded the intellectually disabled from the death penalty, court watchers have predicted that offenders who suffer from severe mental illness are next.[46] That would be a feat fit for Houdini under the evolving standards doctrine, because to date, not a single state has categorically exempted this group of offenders, although a number of states have considered doing so over the last few years and momentum for change appears to be growing.[47] Time is likely to make other categorical exclusions a possibility in the future as well.

That said, the practice that the evolving standards doctrine is perhaps best poised to invalidate is not a discrete application of the death penalty at all, but rather the death penalty itself. The only thing holding the Supreme Court back is the Justices' own inclinations. The numbers under the evolving standards doctrine are there — or *could be,* for a Court inclined to find them — showing for all to see the awesome potential of the doctrine not just going forward, but also at this moment in time.

Consider first the number of death penalty states. To date, twenty-one states have abolished the death penalty, nine since 2007 alone.[48] For a Supreme Court that looks at state trends, this is a strong one. Obviously, that figure is less than one-half the states, but the Justices could easily get to half or more if they wanted; that figure does not include the four states that have declared an official moratorium on executions, bringing the tally to twenty-five,[49] or the states that are known as "de facto" abolitionist states because they have not had an execution in ten years, which would put the tally at thirty-one.[50] And if one included states that have not executed in at least five years, as opposed to ten, that number would jump to thirty-seven.[51]

---

[46] For one of my personal favorites, see Scott E. Sundby, *The True Legacy of Atkins and Roper: The Unreliability Principle, Mentally Ill Defendants, and the Death Penalty's Unraveling,* 23 WM. & MARY BILL RTS. J. 487, 512–13 (2014).

[47] In 2017 alone, seven states considered such legislation, and momentum appears to be rising. *See* Laura Vozzella, *Bill to Ban Death Penalty for Severely Mentally Ill Clears GOP-Controlled Va. Senate,* WASH. POST, Jan. 17, 2019, https://www.washingtonpost.com/local/virginia-polit ics/bill-to-ban-death-penalty-for-severely-mentally-ill-clears-gop-controlled-va-senate/2019/01/ 17/afe1981c-1a87-11e9-8813-cb9dec761e73_story.html; Rebecca Beitsch, *States Consider Barring Death Penalty for Severely Mentally Ill,* PEW RESEARCH CENTER (April 17, 2017), https:// www.pewtrusts.org/en/research-and-analysis/blogs/stateline/2017/04/17/states-consider-barring- death-penalty-for-severely-mentally-ill.

[48] *See* DEATH PENALTY INFO. CTR., *State by State,* https://deathpenaltyinfo.org/state-and-federal- info/state-by-state (last accessed Sept. 6, 2019).

[49] *See id.*

[50] *See* DEATH PENALTY INFO. CTR., *States with No Recent Executions,* https://deathpenaltyinfo .org/executions/executions-overview/states-with-no-recent-executions (last accessed Sept. 6, 2019).

[51] *See id.*

Viewing the death penalty from the vantage point of executions, as opposed to states, provides yet another data point. In 2018, the country saw just twenty-five executions nationwide.[52] For a sense of perspective, that is one-fourth of the ninety-eight executions that the country saw more than twenty years ago in 1998, representing a seventy-five percent decline over time.[53] Granted, part of the decline in executions over the last several years reflects the difficulty states have had in procuring lethal injection drugs.[54] But the strong downward trend in executions predates that development and is in large part a reflection of a state's institutional commitment to carrying out death sentences.[55] The year 2018's executions are no exception. Just over one-half of the country's twenty-five executions — thirteen — took place in Texas alone.[56]

Even more significant than the national decline in executions is the decline in death sentencing. In 2018, the entire country produced only forty-three new death sentences.[57] For a sense of perspective, that is around one-third of the one hundred twenty new death sentences that the country saw ten years ago in 2008, and just under fifteen percent of the 295 new death sentences that the nation saw twenty years ago in 1998.[58] That is right — in the last twenty years, death sentencing has seen a whopping eighty-five percent decline.

Even more telling are the negligible death sentences coming out of states traditionally known as death penalty strongholds. Virginia is the third most executing state in the country but has not had a single new death sentence in the past seven years.[59] Oklahoma is the second most executing state in the country and produced just one death sentence in 2018 (and two the year before that).[60] Texas is by far the most executing state in the country, and it produced just seven new death sentences in 2018 (and four the year before that).[61]

For a Supreme Court that looks at death sentencing as a core consideration under the evolving standards doctrine (and has from the start), these numbers

---

[52] *See* Death Penalty Info. Ctr., *Executions by State and Region since 1976*, https://death penaltyinfo.org/executions/executions-overview/number-of-executions-by-state-and-region-since-1976 (last accessed Sept. 6, 2019).

[53] *See id.*

[54] For a detailed discussion of the death penalty drug saga and its impact on the American Death Penalty, see James Gibson & Corinna Barrett Lain, *Death Penalty Drugs and the International Moral Marketplace*, 103 Geo. L.J. 1215 (2015).

[55] For a discussion of the topic, see Corinna Barrett Lain, *Following Finality: Why Capital Punishment Is Collapsing under Its Own Weight*, *in* Final Judgments: The Death Penalty in American Law and Culture 30, 44 (Austin Sarat, ed., 2017).

[56] *See* Death Penalty Info. Ctr., *supra* note 50.

[57] *See* Death Penalty Info. Ctr., *Death Sentences in the United States since 1977*, https:// deathpenaltyinfo.org/facts-and-research/sentencing-data/death-sentences-in-the-united-states-from-1977-by-state-and-by-year (last accessed Sept. 6, 2019).

[58] *See id.*

[59] *See id.*

[60] *See id.*

[61] *See id.*

are potent indicators.[62] But death sentences are also important wholly aside from their relevance under the evolving standards doctrine, for they provide the clearest indication of the death penalty's continued vitality going forward. Today's death sentences are tomorrow's executions. Without death sentences to feed the capital justice system, the pipeline will wither and the costly capital justice system will become even more so, making it all the more likely to eventually collapse under its own weight.[63]

None of this is to say that the Supreme Court will use the evolving standards doctrine to abolish the death penalty. (In fact, here is a shocking prediction given the Court's current composition — it will not.) Nor is this is to say that the Supreme Court *should* do so; the lessons of *Furman* continue to haunt the prospect of judicial abolition.[64] The point of the discussion here is simply to say that the evolving standards doctrine *could* bring about the end of the death penalty itself; it is poised to do so for a Court inclined to reach that result. As a practical matter, that potential is more likely to put the evolving standards doctrine on the doctrinal endangered species list than come to fruition anytime soon (at least if the Court's more blood-thirsty Justices have their way),[65] but the very possibility that the same doctrine that revived the death penalty could, forty years later, be the cause of its death is a testament to the evolving standards doctrine's tremendous power and potential.

In the end, the evolving standards doctrine's power, problems, and potential are what make it the mass of contradictions and controversy that it is today. But the driving force behind the doctrine — the notion that the Eighth Amendment should

---

[62] The discussion of death sentences in this essay has considered those sentences at the state-level only, and only in the context of the evolving standards doctrine. But within death sentencing states, the vast majority of death sentences occur in just a few counties — a mere two percent nationwide. This disparity has typically been noted in discussions of how arbitrary the death penalty's application is, but it is also a testament to the rarity of its use. *See* DEATH PENALTY INFO. CTR., THE 2% DEATH PENALTY: HOW A MINORITY OF COUNTIES PRODUCE MOST DEATH CASES AT ENORMOUS COST TO ALL (Oct. 2013), https://files.deathpenaltyinfo.org/legacy/documents/TwoPercentReport.pdf (in 2012, less than two percent of counties in the country accounted for all death sentences nationwide); *see also* Glossip v. Gross, 135 S. Ct. 2726, 2761–62 (2015) (Breyer, J., dissenting) (discussing county-by-county disparity in death sentencing as a feature of arbitrariness).

[63] This is the theme of my essay *Following Finality: Why Capital Punishment Is Collapsing under Its Own Weight.* For an extended discussion of the point, see Lain, *supra* note 55.

[64] For an extended discussion of the lessons of *Furman*, see Furman *Fundamentals, supra* note 12. For a thoughtful discussion of why judicial abolition of the death penalty now would not likely trigger a repeat of the backlash of *Furman*, see Jordan Steiker, *The American Death Penalty from a Consequentialist Perspective,* 47 TEX. TECH. L. REV. 211 (2014).

[65] *See Glossip,* 135 S. Ct. at 2752 (Thomas, J., concurring) ("In my decades on the Court, I have not seen a capital crime that could not be considered sufficiently 'blameworthy' to merit a death sentence (even when genuine constitutional errors justified a vacatur of that sentence)."); *id.* at 2753–55 (Thomas, J., concurring) (reexamining the Supreme Court's categorical exclusions under the evolving standards doctrine for juveniles, offenders who are intellectually disabled, and offenders who commit rape that does not result in death, and disagreeing with the Court's exemption from the death penalty in those cases).

do more than protect against something that no one was doing anymore anyway — was what saved the Eighth Amendment from being a dead letter in constitutional law and made it relevant to a variety of punishment practices over time. The evolving standards doctrine was what brought the death penalty back to life in 1976, ushering in the modern death penalty era. And it is responsible for eradicating the ugliest, most categorically offensive applications of the death penalty over the last forty years. Today, it stands as a vanguard of protection against egregiously punitive practices in and outside the death penalty context. At a time when the United States is known for having the most punitive punishment practices in the world, that is not a bad doctrine to have.

6

Judicial Hesitancy and Majoritarianism

William W. Berry III

The story of the Supreme Court's Eighth Amendment jurisprudence has been one of judicial hesitancy and restraint.[1] This chapter explores the reluctance of the Supreme Court Justices to apply their normative views to develop a clear constitutional line that limits excessive punishment practices. It then explains why the majoritarian principles of the evolving standards of decency doctrine make this judicial reluctance less warranted. The chapter concludes by exploring the possible consequences of the Court abandoning its hesitant posture and infusing the Eighth Amendment with normative values and limits on state and federal punishment practices.

THE COUNTERMAJORITARIAN BILL OF RIGHTS

At the core of the individual rights provisions in the Constitution's Bill of Rights is the idea that the constitutional amendment protects individuals against government infringement of the right in question. With respect to the Eighth Amendment, this includes protection against government infliction of punishments that are cruel and unusual. In essence, as with other similar provisions, this language protects the minority — the individual — against the overreach of the majority — the legislature. It is the role of the Supreme Court to interpret this language, the proscription against cruel and unusual punishments, in such a way as to protect the individual against the imposition of such punishments by the state. Put another way, when the majority infringes upon the individual rights of citizens, the Court has a countermajoritarian role— to place limits on the scope of majority power consistent with the language of the Constitution.

In a number of other contexts, the Court has embraced this role. To be sure, the Court's First Amendment free speech cases, the Court's Fourth Amendment search

---

[1] *See* William W. Berry III, *Evolved Standards, Evolving Justices*, 96 Wash. U. L. Rev. 105 (2018).

and seizure cases, and the Court's Fourteenth Amendment substantive due process and equal protection cases all offer examples of the Court delineating the scope of the individual constitutional right in question, in some cases serving as a counter-majoritarian check upon the unconstitutional infringement upon individual rights by the majority.[2]

As explored below, this has generally not been the case with the Court's Eighth Amendment cases. The Court has largely deferred to the actions of state legislatures with respect to their punishment practices. Before assessing the possible reasons for the Court's hesitancy in this context, it is instructive to highlight one core tenet of the Eighth Amendment — it evolves over time. From its earliest Eighth Amendment cases, the Court has made this clear. In *Weems v. United States*, the Court explained that, "a principle, to be vital, must be capable of wider application than the mischief which gave it birth. This is peculiarly true of constitutions."[3] And in *Trop v. Dulles*, the Court emphasized, "the words of the [Eighth] Amendment are not precise, and that their scope is not static."[4] Indeed, as *Trop* explained, the meaning of the Eighth Amendment derives from "the evolving standards of decency that mark the progress of a maturing society."[5] Even originalist scholars have concluded that the best reading of the Eighth Amendment is as a provision that changes over time.[6]

JUDICIAL RELUCTANCE AND HESITANCY

In applying the Eighth Amendment, the Court has only rarely held that it limits the state's power to use a particular punishment. In *Weems*, the Court held that a punishment of *cadena temporal* (fifteen years of hard labor) for the falsification of a government document violated the Eighth Amendment. In *Trop*, the Court found that a punishment of loss of citizenship for the crime of treason also violated the Eighth Amendment.

The most significant use of the Court's power in applying the Eighth Amendment came in *Furman v. Georgia*, in which the Court held in a 5-4 *per curiam* opinion that the death penalty violated the Eighth Amendment.[7] The splintered decision had three of the five Justices in the majority finding the death penalty not unconstitutional *per se*, but only unconstitutional *as applied* by Georgia. Four years later in *Gregg v. Georgia* and other cases, the Court backtracked and held that the death

---

[2] *See* Corinna Barrett Lain, *The Unexceptionalism of Evolving Standards*, 57 UCLA L. REV. 365 (2009).

[3] Weems v. United States, 217 U.S. 349, 373 (1910).

[4] Trop v. Dulles, 356 U.S. 86, 100–01 (1958) (plurality opinion).

[5] *Id.* at 101.

[6] See, e.g., John Stinneford, *The Original Meaning of 'Unusual': The Eighth Amendment as a Bar to Cruel Innovation*, 102 NW. U. L. REV. 1739 (2008).

[7] Furman v. Georgia, 408 U.S. 238 (1972) (per curiam).

penalty was constitutional, provided acceptable safeguards existed to prevent arbitrary and random sentencing outcomes.[8] The Court also barred the imposition of mandatory death sentences in two cases, *Woodson v. North Carolina* and *Roberts v. Louisiana*, decided on the same day as *Gregg*.[9]

An important consequence of *Gregg* was that the Court established the principle that "death is different."[10] Because the death penalty is unique in its severity as a punishment and in its irrevocability, the Court reasoned that it deserved heightened scrutiny under the Eighth Amendment. The unfortunate corollary to the differentness principle has been that the Court has presumed that all non-capital adult punishments do not violate the Eighth Amendment.[11]

A second consequence of *Furman* and *Gregg* has been the hesitancy of the Court to apply the Eighth Amendment in a rigorous way to state-imposed sentences, capital and non-capital. At the time of *Furman*, the death penalty appeared to be extinct in America, with no executions occurring in more than a decade prior to the decision. The effect of the Court's decision, however, was a strong public backlash, with over forty legislatures passing new capital statutes in its aftermath.[12] It is possible that the Court's hesitancy to apply the Eighth Amendment to punishments in the decades that followed might stem from the public response to *Furman*.

In the more than forty years since *Furman*, the Court has struck down punishments under the Eighth Amendment only a few times, and only with respect to particular applications of punishments otherwise deemed constitutional. For instance, in *Coker v. Georgia*, the Court held that the death penalty was an excessive punishment for the crime of rape.[13] In *Enmund v. Florida*, the Court held that a felony murder in which the offender "did not kill, attempt to kill, or intend to kill" could not serve as the basis for a death sentence under the Eighth Amendment.[14] In *Tison v. Arizona*, however, the Court narrowed this holding by finding that the death penalty could be a constitutional punishment for felony murder where the offender was a major participant in the crime and acted with a reckless indifference to human life.[15]

In the non-capital context concerning adult offenders, the Court, with one exception, has rejected every substantive claim of excessive punishment involving adult offenders under the Eighth Amendment. For instance, in *Rummel v. Estelle*,

---

[8] Jurek v. Texas, 428 U.S. 262 (1976); Proffitt v. Florida, 428 U.S. 242 (1976); Gregg v. Georgia, 428 U.S. 153 (1976) (plurality opinion).

[9] Roberts v. Louisiana, 428 U.S. 325 (1976); Woodson v. North Carolina, 428 U.S. 280 (1976) (plurality opinion).

[10] *See* Carol S. Steiker & Jordan M. Steiker, *Sober Second Thoughts: Reflections on Two Decades of Constitutional Regulation of Capital Punishment*, 109 HARV. L. REV. 355 (1995).

[11] *See* William W. Berry III, *Individualized Sentencing*, 76 WASH. & LEE L. REV. 13 (2019).

[12] *See* Corinna Barrett Lain, *Furman Fundamentals*, 82 WASH L. REV. 1 (2007).

[13] Coker v. Georgia, 433 U.S. 584 (1977) (plurality opinon).

[14] Enmund v. Florida, 458 U.S. 782 (1982).

[15] Tison v. Arizona, 481 U.S. 137 (1987).

the Court affirmed a life with parole sentence for felony theft of $120.75 by false pretenses where the defendant had two prior convictions.[16] Similarly, the Court in *Hutto v. Davis* upheld two consecutive sentences of twenty years for possession with intent to distribute and distribution of nine ounces of marijuana.[17]

The one non-capital case where the Court granted relief to an adult offender under the Eighth Amendment was *Solem v. Helm*, where the Court reversed a sentence of life without parole (LWOP) for presenting a no account check for $100, where defendant had six prior felony convictions.[18] But the Court narrowed the *Solem* outcome in *Harmelin v. Michigan*, where it affirmed a LWOP sentence for first offense of possessing 672 grams of cocaine.[19]

The pattern continued in *Ewing v. California*, where the Court upheld the California three-strikes law, affirming a sentence of twenty-five years to life for the theft of approximately $1,200 of golf clubs, where the defendant had four prior felony convictions.[20] In the same term in *Lockyer v. Andrade*, the Court affirmed on habeas review two consecutive sentences of twenty-five years to life for stealing approximately $150 of videotapes, where the defendant had three prior felony convictions.[21]

For twenty years, the Court's rejection of non-capital Eighth Amendment claims coincided with the absence of any capital claims of excessive punishment accepted by the Court under the Eighth Amendment. In 2002, however, the Court held in *Atkins v. Virginia* that the execution of an intellectually disabled offender constituted a cruel and unusual punishment under the Eighth Amendment.[22] Three years later, the Court held in *Roper v. Simmons* that the execution of a juvenile offender violated the Eighth Amendment.[23] In *Kennedy v. Louisiana*, the Court expanded its decisions to hold that the imposition of the death penalty for the rape of a minor violated the Eighth Amendment.[24]

The difference in the capital and non-capital cases related centrally to the test used by the Court in applying the Eighth Amendment. In capital cases, the Court used the evolving standards of decency test. In non-capital cases, however, the Court has used a gross disproportionality standard. Under this standard, punishments do not violate the Eighth Amendment unless they are so excessive that they shock the conscience. Practically, this means almost no non-capital adult punishments violate the Eighth Amendment.[25]

[16]   Rummel v. Estelle, 445 U.S. 263 (1980).
[17]   Hutto v. Davis, 454 U.S. 370 (1982)(per curiam).
[18]   Solem v. Helm, 463 U.S. 277 (1983).
[19]   Harmelin v. Michigan, 501 U.S. 957 (1991).
[20]   Ewing v. California, 538 U.S. 11 (2003) (plurality opinion).
[21]   Lockyer v. Andrade, 538 U.S. 63 (2003).
[22]   Atkins v. Virginia, 536 U.S. 304 (2002).
[23]   Roper v. Simmons, 543 U.S. 551 (2005).
[24]   Kennedy v. Louisiana, 554 U.S. 407 (2008).
[25]   William W. Berry III, *Unusual Deference*, 70 Fla. L. Rev. 315 (2018).

In capital cases, because "death is different," the doctrine applied by the Court is the "evolving standards of decency," in which the Court assesses the proportionality of the punishment in light of the offense. In its capital cases, the Court has used a two-part test, relying on both objective and subjective indicia to assess the constitutionality of punishments under the Eighth Amendment. The objective test relies upon an assessment of the majoritarian practice among the states, mostly examining the state laws, but also sometimes considering the direction of legislative movement, jury decisions, and international norms. In a sense, this part of the test examines the unusualness or rarity of the practice in question.[26]

The subjective part of the inquiry, where the Justices bring their own judgment to bear, employs a type of proportionality test, assessing whether the punishment is proportional to the offense in light of the purposes of punishment — retribution, deterrence, incapacitation, and rehabilitation. Where none of the purposes justify the punishment in question, it is disproportionate in contravention of the Eighth Amendment. This part of the test serves as a proxy for assessing the cruelty or excessiveness of the punishment in question.

Subsequently, the Court partially abandoned its bright line between capital and non-capital cases, expanding its notion of "differentness" from death to include juvenile life-without-parole sentences (JLWOP). If death is different, the Court explained, juveniles are also different. In *Graham v. Florida*, the Court held that the JLWOP was an excessive punishment for non-homicide crimes, building on its decisions in *Roper* and *Kennedy*.[27] Two years later, the Court held in *Miller v. Alabama* that the Eighth Amendment proscribed mandatory JLWOP sentences, combining its holdings in *Woodson* and *Roberts* with its decision in *Roper*.[28] The Court reemphasized the importance of minimizing JLWOP sentences in *Montgomery v. Louisiana*, where the Court concluded that *Miller* applied retroactively.[29] The Court may narrow the scope of *Miller* and *Montgomery* in a pending case in the 2019–2020 term, *Mathena v. Malvo*.[30]

Even with this recent Eighth Amendment expansion in the past decade, the Court's few categorical exceptions amount more to baby steps than paradigm shift. The cases themselves actually impact a small number of offenders, particularly when considered in light of the more than two million currently incarcerated. The Court has ignored many of the drivers of mass incarceration, including increased sentences for low-level offenses, the movement toward mandatory sentences, and the proliferation of LWOP sentences. Part of the hesitancy, at least for some Justices, may stem from the perception that the legislature, not the courts, should make such decisions, despite the role of the Court as protector of individual rights.

[26] *See* William W. Berry III, *Promulgating Proportionality*, 46 GA. L. REV. 69 (2011).
[27] Graham v. Florida, 560 U.S. 48 (2010).
[28] Miller v. Alabama, 567 U.S. 460 (2012).
[29] Montgomery v. Louisiana,136 S. Ct. 718 (2016).
[30] 139 S.Ct. 1317 (2019) (granting certiorari).

THE MAJORITARIAN EVOLVING STANDARDS

The countermajoritarian difficulty focuses this tension.[31] The worry of counter-majoritarian judicial decision-making relates to the Court, through a mere five Justices, substituting its views for the legislature and the presumptive will of the people by interpreting the Constitution to prohibit the actions of the legislature. Of course, if the Court always defers to the legislative view, the Constitution will be unable to protect individuals against majoritarian legislative overreach. This dilemma can become particularly pronounced when applying constitutional language written deliberately in a vague and open-ended manner. The proscription against cruel and unusual punishments certainly falls into this category.

The evolving standards of decency approach, however, largely mitigates this set of concerns. The Court's test relies upon objective indicia of majoritarian legislative practices to assess society's standard of decency. In other words, the content of the standard that the countermajoritarian Justices use to determine the meaning of the Eighth Amendment reflects the practice of a supermajority of legislatures in the country. Where the Court strikes down a state statute, it might reflect the will of the majority of citizens as represented by the legislature within the state in question, but the practice is an outlier nationally, and sometimes internationally. Under the evolving standards of decency, the five Justices in the majority thus are not substituting their own judgment in the place of the people writ large. Instead, the Justices are striking down a practice that has fallen out of line with the evolution of a supermajority of jurisdictions nationally. As such, the judicial activism of striking down a statute under the Eighth Amendment operates more like Congress preempting a state's laws to achieve national consistency or uniformity than the countermajoritarian problem of substituting its own normative views to contradict the will of the people.

To be sure, there is a second part of the evolving standards of decency test in which the Court brings its own normative judgment to the equation. But the Court has never struck down a punishment that passed one part of the test but failed the other. Indeed, the Court has never reached opposing conclusions under its subject-ive and objective tests. As a practical matter, then, the evolving standards of decency test reflects the Court's application of a majority approach to which it subscribes. The judgment of the Court in this context suggests a view that the degree to which the state practice is an outlier has risen to a level that it is unusually or particularly cruel.[32] The Court is only acting as a countermajoritarian check against state punishment practices where they fall significantly out of line with the modern standard embraced by a supermajority of other jurisdictions.

---

[31] *See* ALEXANDER BICKEL, THE LEAST DANGEROUS BRANCH (1962).

[32] See Samuel L. Bray, *"Necessary AND Proper" and "Cruel AND Unusual": Hendiadys in the Constitution*, 102 VA. L. REV. 687, 690 (2016).

AN INVITATION TO JUDICIAL INTERVENTION

Given the majoritarian nature of the evolving standards doctrine, then, the Court should view the Eighth Amendment as providing an open invitation to intervene where states continue to engage in practices largely abandoned. The Court should not remain hesitant to curb excessive punishment practices where they persist. As discussed, broadening the Eighth Amendment in this way does not mean that the Court is merely substituting its judgment for that of a state legislature; rather, it is bringing the state legislature in line with a supermajority of other jurisdictions where it has exceeded its constitutional authority.

The application of the Eighth Amendment to punishment can occur in both per se and applied contexts. The Court can declare a particular punishment per se unconstitutional as a cruel and unusual punishment, meaning that the imposition of the punishment will always violate the constitution. For instance, Justices Brennan and Marshall voted in *Furman* to hold that the death penalty constituted a per se violation of the Eighth Amendment.

Alternatively, the Court can determine that a particular punishment violates the death penalty as applied. This means that the particular use of the punishment is what is unconstitutional, not necessarily the use of the punishment generally. Justices Stewart, White, and Douglas, for example, all found in *Furman* that the death penalty violated the Eighth Amendment as applied, because its use was random and arbitrary.

Beyond the common constitutional dichotomy of per se and as applied challenges to state and federal law, it is also possible to conceptualize the applications of the Eighth Amendment to punishments in terms of micro and macro incursions. A micro incursion does not bar the punishment entirely, but instead forbids certain applications altogether. The Court's evolving standards of decency cases have all fallen into this category. The Court, for example, has proscribed the imposition of the death penalty for certain types of offenders — insane, juvenile, and intellectually disabled ones. Similarly, the Court has barred the imposition of the death penalty for certain crimes — rape, child rape, and certain types of felony murder — under the Eighth Amendment. The Court has also barred the use of a mandatory death penalty. All of these are micro incursions to the use of the death penalty. They merely restrict the use of the punishment in certain contexts. The Court's JLWOP cases follow the same pattern. The Court has proscribed the imposition of JLWOP sentences for non-homicide crimes. As with the death penalty, mandatory JLWOP sentences also constitute Eighth Amendment violations.

The Court has not, although could, impose a macro ban against a particular punishment, barring it altogether. The Court's decision in *Furman* did this, but since it reversed that outcome in *Gregg*, the Court has not barred any other punishment altogether. Presumably, some punishments involving overt torture would cross this line, but states have not employed such punishments outside of the context of the death penalty, so the Court has not had occasion to apply the Eighth Amendment in such a way. As discussed below, the declining use of the death penalty and JLWOP make both likely candidates for Eighth Amendment expansion in the future in the form of macro proscriptions.

One other way in which the Court could engage with the Eighth Amendment relates to methods of execution. The Court's current test, as developed in *Baze v. Rees* and *Glossip v. Gross*, examines the degree to which the execution is likely to create an unnecessary risk of pain.[33] This is an as applied standard, and does not consider the question of evolving standards. Even worse, the standard requires the offender to demonstrate that another less painful execution method exists.

Although ignored by the Court, there are three different possible categories of Eighth Amendment inquiry with respect to an execution.[34] First, the type of punishment — the death penalty — is a category for Eighth Amendment scrutiny as indicated previously. Second, the method of execution — lethal injection, electrocution, hanging, firing squad, or nitrogen gas — provides a second category of inquiry for the Court in terms of evolving standards. Finally, the technique itself — the kind of lethal injection, for example — provides a third level of Eighth Amendment inquiry in this taxonomy. For each level, the questions are the same — the objective question of whether states use the type of punishment, the method of punishment, and the technique of punishment at issue — and whether the use of that type, method, and technique of punishment will satisfy one or more of the purposes of punishment.

REASSESSING THE EVOLVING STANDARDS: THE DEATH PENALTY

The declining use of the death penalty in the United States increasingly suggests that as a punishment, it violates the evolving standards of decency, or will very soon do so. Justices Breyer and Ginsburg have suggested as much, and the current trends reflect the same possibility.[35] The total number of annual executions has not exceeded thirty in the past five years, with the number of new death sentences annually decreasing to less than forty per year over the same period. The number of states that still allow the death penalty is twenty-nine, but four of those states currently have a moratorium on the death penalty. Thirty-seven states have not carried out an execution in the past five years, and thirty-one of those have not executed anyone in the past ten years. With Texas being responsible for a high percentage of executions in conjunction with the diminished use of the death penalty in most jurisdictions, one could easily conclude that the evolving standards

---

[33] Glossip v. Gross, 135 S.Ct. 2726 (2014); Baze v. Rees, 553 U.S. 35 (2008) (plurality opinion).

[34] *See* William W. Berry III & Meghan J. Ryan, *Cruel Techniques, Unusual Secrets*, 77 OHIO ST. L. J. 403 (2017).

[35] *See generally* DEATH PENALTY INFO. CTR., https://deathpenaltyinfo.org/.

of decency bars or will soon bar the use of the death penalty under the Eighth Amendment. Given the current conservative lean of the Supreme Court, such a determination is unlikely anytime soon, but the factual case for evolving standards abolition grows stronger by the day under the Court's doctrine.

In addition to the possibility for a macro exclusion of the death penalty under the Eighth Amendment, there are several possible categories of micro exclusions that exist as well. The Court could build upon its prior cases to exclude the death penalty for other kinds of mental illness, not just intellectual disability. The question becomes the ability to execute individuals suffering from certain mental illnesses in light of the frequency of such executions.

Similarly, the Court could limit the use of the death penalty under the evolving standards of decency with respect to methods of execution. As lethal injection faces a series of challenges related to the availability of drugs and the degree to which certain procedures torture offenders as they kill them, states have used electrocution and have also made plans to use nitrogen gas. It is possible that neither return to a prior but largely rejected method of execution would survive the evolving standards of decency test. The jurisdiction counting approach might indicate that a super-majority of jurisdictions forbid a certain method, and then the question would be whether a purpose of punishment supports the use of that technique. As there is a consensus that the death penalty does not deter crime, the question would be whether the technique can achieve the purpose of retribution.

REASSESSING THE EVOLVING STANDARDS: JUVENILE LIFE WITHOUT PAROLE

As with the death penalty, JLWOP sentences increasingly appear to violate the evolving standards of decency under the Eighth Amendment. Currently, twenty-eight states have abolished JLWOP or do not have offenders serving JLWOP sentences. Since the Court's decision in *Miller* in 2012, seventeen states have abolished JLWOP, indicating a clear trend toward abolition.[36] And the United States remains the only country in the world to permit JLWOP sentences. There has also been a decrease in JLWOP sentences after *Montgomery*, which made the *Miller* holding retroactive, and has resulted in a resentencing of a number of JLWOP sentences.

In addition to the increasing trend of objective indicia toward abolition, the subjective criteria that the Court uses to apply the Eighth Amendment also point toward proscribing JLWOP. Certainly, a JLWOP sentence forecloses the possibility of rehabilitation in terms of the offender rejoining society. With respect to incapacitation, it seems difficult and inaccurate to predict that an offender will always be dangerous, particularly when making the prediction for a juvenile offender. It is not clear that JLWOP sentences have any deterrent effect, as many

---

[36] *See* JUVENILE LIFE WITHOUT PAROLE, https://juvenilelwop.org/map/.

juvenile offenses stem from lack of maturity and the ability to exert self-control. Finally, it is not likely that allowing reconsideration of an offense will undermine the goal of just deserts retribution. The opportunity for parole at some point does not compromise the purpose of retribution — if the offender deserves life in prison, reconsideration of the sentence does not mean that the state will release the offender.

While a macro abolition of JLWOP sentences under the Eighth Amendment constitutes the most logical next result, there are other micro limitations the Court could place on JLWOP if it elects to pursue a more incremental approach. Mirroring the Court's death penalty jurisprudence, the Court could limit JLWOP in relation to the offense or the kind of offender. With respect to the former, felony murder cases seem to provide a logical place to start. Felony murder allows the state to increase the available punishment in spite of the lack of intent to kill on the part of the offender, and in some cases, in the absence of the offender killing anyone. As in *Enmund*, but not *Tison*, the Court could limit the imposition of JLWOP sentences in cases where the juvenile offender did not kill, intend to kill, or otherwise facilitate the killing that occurred during the felony. A central rationale for the felony murder doctrine is the purpose of deterrence, and as described above, that rationale carries significantly less force with juvenile offenders.

With respect to the offender, the Court could, as with capital cases, place limits on the imposition of JLWOP sentences for intellectually disabled offenders. As with death sentences, intellectually disabled juvenile offenders bear less responsibility than other offenders, making such factors counsel in favor of proscribing such sentences. As LWOP constitutes its own kind of death sentence, the same considerations relate to the imposition of such a sentence on an intellectually disabled juvenile offender. This is particularly true with respect to the purposes of punishment, as there exists a lower level of culpability, a decreased ability to deter, a likelihood of lower dangerousness (at some point prior to death), and an increased opportunity for rehabilitation.

BEYOND JLWOP AND THE DEATH PENALTY

Beyond JLWOP sentences and the death penalty, the Eighth Amendment can also apply to non-capital cases to restrict excessive and outlier practices. Part of the way forward in light of the Court's current doctrine could include broadening the "differentness" principle. To date, the Court has held that the death penalty and juvenile offenders are both different, entitling these categories of offense and offender to heightened scrutiny under the evolving standards of decency. The corollary of this principle, though, has meant that non-different sentences receive almost no scrutiny under the Eighth Amendment and receive a strong presumption of constitutionality.

In terms of offenders, differentness could embrace elderly offenders, veterans, mentally ill individuals, and others that demonstrate some mitigating characteristics.[37] With respect to offenses, LWOP and its similarity to a death sentence might warrant higher scrutiny, as well as mandatory sentences, particularly because the Court has already restricted these kinds of sentences in certain contexts under the Eighth Amendment.

A broader approach might contemplate the many collateral consequences of felony offenses more generally.[38] Such an inquiry would treat all felony offenses as "different," and explore the trends with respect to the many collateral consequences to felony convictions — loss of right to vote, inability to own a firearm, supervised release — to determine whether such approaches constituted outliers in certain situations and whether the purposes of punishment justified such conditions as proportional punishments.

Another line of inquiry altogether could frame the Eighth Amendment as creating a set of presumptions that legislatures could overcome upon certain showings.[39] Addressing the countermajoritarian critique from a different lens, such an approach would allow the Court to guide legislatures without placing hard limits on their punitive practices. Certain punishments might be disfavored — the death penalty, LWOP, mandatory sentences — but states could overcome the presumption against constitutionality with a strict scrutiny-type showing of the necessity of the punishment in a certain instance or set of circumstances.

THE NEED FOR INTERVENTION

Without some constitutional limiting principles, states will continue to engage in excessive, abusive punishment practices. As penal populism has demonstrated, the popularity of overpunishment will dictate unreasonable, draconian punishment outcomes in many cases, particularly in light of the common misunderstandings the average citizen has about the American criminal justice system.[40]

Given the majoritarian underpinnings of the Eighth Amendment evolving standards of decency doctrine, Supreme Court Justices should not be hesitant about protecting individuals against excessive punishment practices rejected by a supermajority of states. Even so, the prospects for reform in this area appear bleak in the short term. With the retirement of Justice Kennedy, the 5-4 majority that decided the series of evolving standards Eighth Amendment cases beginning with *Atkins* in 2002 has disappeared. The conservative lean of the current Court is more likely to narrow the Eighth Amendment than expand it. Perhaps a movement in popular

---

[37] William W. Berry III, *Eighth Amendment Differentness*, 78 Mo. L. Rev. 1053 (2013).
[38] Berry, *supra* note 11, at 13.
[39] William W. Berry III, *Eighth Amendment Presumptions*, 89 S. Cal. L. Rev. 67 (2015).
[40] *See* Rachel Barkow, Prisoners of Politics: Breaking the Cycle of Mass Incarceration (2019).

opinion away from excessive punishment, as is happening with the death penalty and JLWOP, might nonetheless spur change in the use of these punishments, but it is unlikely to come in the form of an Eighth Amendment restriction. This is unfortunate, particularly given the Court's hesitancy to apply this constitutional provision for the past half century, alongside the proliferation of excessive punishments in the United States in building the largest prison population in the history of the world. To be sure, the door will remain open, but it remains to be seen whether the current Court will have the inclination to walk through it.

7

Punishment Purposes and Eighth Amendment Disproportionality

Richard S. Frase[*]

INTRODUCTION

This chapter examines how Eighth Amendment standards banning disproportionately severe penalties could and should take account of traditional purposes of punishment, in particular, retributive and non-retributive (crime-control) goals and limitations.

Supreme Court opinions frequently state that the Eighth Amendment forbids criminal penalties that are "disproportionate" in their severity (or "grossly" disproportionate).[1] But the Court has never specified a normative frame of reference — disproportionate (or constitutionally excessive) relative to what punishment goals or other criteria.[2] In several of his opinions, Justice Antonin Scalia rejected any Eighth Amendment proportionality limits, at least for prison sentences.[3] He argued that sentencing proportionality is a concept inherently tied to retributive punishment goals, and he pointed out that the Court has never expressly endorsed purely retributive upper limits on prison sentences. Indeed, some of the Court's opinions have asserted that Congress and state legislatures are permitted to select and give priority to any of the traditional punishment purposes, including widely endorsed crime control goals such as deterrence and incapacitation.[4] Thus, Scalia concluded, a prison sentence cannot be deemed disproportionately severe because that concept has no meaning relative to the crime control purposes that legislatures are permitted

---

[*] Benjamin N. Berger Professor of Criminal Law, and Co-Director of the Robina Institute of Criminal Law and Criminal Justice.

[1] In recent decisions, the Court has omitted the "gross" modifier but has not said why. *See* Richard S. Frase, *What's "Different" (Enough) in Eighth Amendment Law?*, 11 OHIO ST. J. CRIM. L. 9, 19 (2013).

[2] *See generally* Richard S. Frase, *Excessive Prison Sentences, Punishment Goals, and the Eighth Amendment: "Proportionality" Relative to What?*, 89 MINN. L. REV. 571 (2005).

[3] *See, e.g.*, Harmelin v. Michigan, 501 U.S. 957, 965–96 (1991) (opinion of Scalia, J.).

[4] *See, e.g., id.* at 998–99 (opinion of Kennedy, J.).

to endorse and prioritize. Notwithstanding Scalia's objection, however, a majority of the Justices in recent decades have agreed that some prison sentences are disproportionately severe and in violation of the Eighth Amendment.

The simplest answer to Scalia's objection is that the Court could, and should, expressly endorse retributive upper limits on the severity of all punishments, including prison sentences. This chapter will defend that position, and point out supporting language in some of the Court's opinions. Another way to respond to Scalia's objection, and to rationalize the Court's occasional findings of unconstitutional disproportionality without necessarily adopting the retributive upper limit described above, is to posit one or more non-retributive proportionality principles. The question then becomes, what does it mean to say that a penalty is excessive, and thus in that sense disproportionate, relative to non-retributive punishment goals? None of the Justices have ever addressed this question directly, but I will argue that the answers to this question can be found in a number of the Court's cases. As I have done in previous writings, this chapter identifies two non-retributive proportionality principles that are implicit in Eighth Amendment decisions and well established in utilitarian philosophy. They are also frequently found in cases from other fields of U.S. constitutional law, as well as in constitutional cases from other Western countries and in regional and international law.[5]

The first part of this chapter defines and briefly explains retributive and utilitarian proportionality principles. Each of these proportionality principles is logically independent of the others although, as will be explained, they have certain features in common. The next part summarizes the Supreme Court's Eighth Amendment decisions, showing their lack of any explicit and consistent normative frame of reference grounded in punishment theory. But this part also argues that there is support in many of these opinions for each of the three proportionality principles described initially. The last part of the chapter examines four ways to define Eighth Amendment proportionality limitations relative to traditional punishment purposes, employing one or more of the three proportionality principles summarized earlier. All four approaches find support in the Court's cases. The first approach is based on limiting retributive proportionality — a penalty is unconstitutional if it clearly exceeds the offender's just deserts. A second approach provides broader Eighth Amendment protection — a penalty is unconstitutional if it is very excessive under any of the three proportionality principles. The third approach also provides fairly broad protection — a penalty is unconstitutional if it is either clearly excessive on retributive grounds, or there is significant disproportionality under both retributive and non-retributive principles. Finally, the fourth and least-protective approach holds that a penalty is unconstitutional only if it is very excessive under *all three* of the proportionality principles.

---

[5]   *See generally* E. Thomas Sullivan & Richard S. Frase, Proportionality Principles in American Law: Controlling Excessive Government Actions (2009).

RETRIBUTIVE AND UTILITARIAN (CRIME-CONTROL) PROPORTIONALITY PRINCIPLES DEFINED AND COMPARED

The concept of disproportionality is meaningless without a normative or definitional frame of reference — "disproportionate" relative to what? For example, if a CEO's high salary is said to be disproportionate, we mean relative to his or her merits as a manager and leader. When speaking about disproportionality under the Eighth Amendment's Cruel and Unusual Punishments and Excessive Fines clauses, the purposes of punishment should define the relevant frame of reference; a sentence is disproportionately severe if it is more punitive than can be justified by applicable punishment purposes — the reasons why punishments are inflicted.

Although sentencing proportionality is sometimes assumed to be relevant only under a retributive (or "just deserts") theory of punishment, several proportionality principles are also recognized by advocates of non-retributive punishment purposes. Before describing and contrasting each of these proportionality principles, however, it is necessary to recognize some overarching punishment principles and concepts.

Punishment purposes can serve as positive, justifying principles, or as negative, restraining principles. Such justifications and limitations are generally viewed as falling into two categories: utilitarian and non-utilitarian. The former seek to achieve beneficial effects (or a net benefit) and, in particular, lower frequency and/or seriousness of future criminal acts by this or other offenders. Non-utilitarian punishment purposes and limitations embody principles of justice and/or fairness that are deemed to be ends in themselves, without regard to whether they produce any net social or individual benefits. Retribution is the most widely recognized non-utilitarian sentencing principle. Of course, any given sentence can reflect both retributive and utilitarian principles, and it seems likely that, in practice, most sentences do — very few judges, attorneys, or other sentencing actors or policy makers subscribe to a one-dimensional punishment model; all modern systems reflect some sort of hybrid blend of retributive and utilitarian purposes and limitations.[6]

Retributive (Just Deserts) Proportionality Principles

Under a retributive theory of punishment, offenders should be punished in proportion to their blameworthiness (or desert) in committing the crime being sentenced. An offender's degree of blameworthiness depends on two factors: the nature and seriousness of the harm caused or threatened by the crime and the offender's degree of culpability in committing the crime.[7] Culpability depends on such things as

---

[6] *See* RICHARD S. FRASE, JUST SENTENCING: PRINCIPLES AND PROCEDURES FOR A WORKABLE SYSTEM 81–120 (2013).

[7] ANDREW VON HIRSCH, PAST OR FUTURE CRIMES 64–74 (1985).

intent (intentional wrongdoing is more culpable than negligence); diminished capacity to obey the law due to mental disease or defect, or situational factors such as threats of harm if the crime is not committed; motives for the crime (some mitigate and others aggravate culpability); and, in group crimes, the defendant's role as instigator, leader, follower, primary actor, or minor player. It should be noted that, unlike the utilitarian (crime-control) sentencing purposes identified below, retributive punishment is backward looking; it focuses on the defendant's crime, not the future.

Some writers (but as noted above, very few sentencing actors and policy makers) view retribution as a positive and sufficient justification for punishment — offenders should be punished simply because they deserve to be, and their punishment should be no more and no less severe than they deserve. A more widely accepted view is that an offender's blameworthiness places an upper limit on the permissible severity of punishment, and sometimes also places a lower limit on punishment severity, at least for serious crimes. In writings on the philosophy of punishment, this is known as the theory of limiting retributivism.[8] Upper retributive limits embody the belief that it is fundamentally unfair and an abuse of governmental power to punish an offender more severely than he or she deserves; this view also corresponds to the core function of constitutionally protected rights. However, in defining the most severe constitutionally permissible punishment, especially for extremely serious crimes, courts must also address retribution-based claims that a given punishment is the minimum penalty such an offender deserves.

Utilitarian (Crime-Control) Proportionality Principles

Utilitarian sentencing principles usually focus on using criminal penalties to prevent or lessen the frequency or seriousness of future criminal acts by this offender or other would-be offenders. Criminal penalties can achieve crime-control effects through at least five mechanisms:[9] rehabilitation (addressing offender characteristics that cause him or her to offend); incapacitation (preventing crime by imprisoning or otherwise physically restraining offenders); specific deterrence (discouraging future crimes by this offender through fear of receiving further penalties); general deterrence (discouraging future crimes by other offenders through fear of punishment); and denunciation (using punishment to define and reinforce important social norms of law-abiding behavior and relative crime seriousness).

In addition to the positive purposes summarized above, utilitarian theory also provides two negative or limiting principles that place proportionality limits on punishment severity:

---

[8]   *See, e.g.*, NORVAL MORRIS, THE FUTURE OF IMPRISONMENT (1974); Richard S. Frase, *Limiting Retributivism, in* THE FUTURE OF IMPRISONMENT (Michael Tonry ed., 2004).

[9]   *See generally*, Richard S. Frase, *Punishment Purposes*, 58 STAN. L. REV. 67, 67–84 (2005).

1. *"Ends-benefits" proportionality* is a limiting principle reflecting core utilitarian cost-benefit concerns: a severe penalty is excessive if its burdens exceed the likely crime-control or other practical benefits of the penalty (or if the added benefits of the severe penalty, compared to a lesser penalty, are outweighed by the added burdens).

2. The *"alternative means" proportionality* principle reflects basic utilitarian efficiency concerns: a severe penalty is excessive if the same benefits can be achieved with a less severe penalty. In Anglo-American jurisprudence, this principle is usually referred to as parsimony, necessity, or narrow tailoring, but in some foreign legal systems it is viewed as an aspect of proportionality.[10]

Utilitarian philosophers have recognized each of these punishment-limiting principles since the eighteenth century.[11] The same two limiting principles are also frequently found in many fields of U.S. constitutional law, in constitutional cases from other Western countries, and in regional and international law.[12]

Major Differences and Similarities among the Three Proportionality Principles

Ends-Benefits Compared to Retributive Proportionality. Retributive and utilitarian ends-benefits principles both require proportionality relative to the harms caused or threatened by the offender's crime, but each set of principles also considers other factors. As noted, offender culpability (intent, motives, etc.) is a critical, second aspect of retributive proportionality; utilitarianism considers culpability only if it is related to the likely future benefits of punishment. (For example, intentional killers might be deemed to be more dangerous and/or more amenable to deterrent threats.) Conversely, utilitarianism considers not only the harms associated with the defendant's crimes but also the aggregate harms caused by all similar crimes, and the possibility that more severe punishment is needed to compensate for the greater difficulty of detecting and deterring certain crimes. Utilitarian theory also takes into account the costs and possible undesirable consequences of severe punishments. (For example, if all crimes are severely punished, this may reduce incentives to prefer less harmful crimes, send confused messages about relative crime seriousness, and cause a loss of public respect for and cooperation with the law.)

Alternative-Means Compared to Retributive Proportionality. The alternative-means proportionality principle might seem so grounded in utilitarian efficiency

---

[10] *See, e.g.,* SULLIVAN & FRASE, *supra* note 5, at 28, 167–68.

[11] *See* Richard S. Frase, *Limiting Excessive Prison Sentences under Federal and State Constitutions,* 11 U. PA. J. CONST. L. 39, 44–46 (2008) (discussing the writings of Cesare Beccaria and Jeremy Bentham).

[12] *See generally,* SULLIVAN & FRASE, *supra* note 5.

concerns that it lacks any retributive counterpart. But just as utilitarians emphasize the special importance of avoiding punishments that are more severe than necessary, it can be argued that retributivists should emphasize the special importance of avoiding punishments more severe than the offender deserves. Alternative-means proportionality is an asymmetric principle — it forbids penalties more severe than necessary to achieve their practical purposes, but not penalties less severe than necessary. This asymmetry reflects the inescapable reality that assessments of such necessity can err in either direction — a penalty can be too severe or too lenient. Moreover, we know that criminal penalties are costly and usually hurtful to offenders and their families, whereas the crime-control benefits are often uncertain. Therefore, it is better to err on the side of too little punishment rather than too much. Similarly, retributive assessments can err in either direction — a penalty can be more severe than the offender deserves, or less severe. The former is arguably a "worse" kind of error, from a retributive standpoint, so special attention should be paid to avoiding above-desert penalties.[13] A similar asymmetric assessment of error risks underlies the many pro-defendant rules found in American criminal law and procedure (proof beyond a reasonable doubt, jury unanimity, strict construction of criminal statutes, etc.) — it is normatively better to have too few convictions than too many.

HOW THE COURT'S EIGHTH AMENDMENT DECISIONS HAVE (AND HAVE NOT) DEFINED PROPORTIONALITY

As noted earlier, the concept of disproportionality requires a normative or definitional frame of reference, and, under the Eighth Amendment punishment clauses, purposes of punishment provide the relevant frame. It is thus rather surprising that the Supreme Court has never clearly stated how "disproportionality" under the Amendment relates to each of the traditional punishment purposes. Indeed, as further discussed below, the Court has sometimes gone out of its way to avoid answering this question, and the answers it has given have been contradictory. Nevertheless, as shown below, there is support in many of these opinions for one or more of the three proportionality principles described above, each of which is grounded in punishment theory.

The Court's Refusal to Recognize Clear Purpose-Based Proportionality Principles

For many years the Court's cases recognizing (or rejecting) Eighth Amendment limits on punishment severity fell into two separate, non-overlapping groups – death

---

[13] Some versions of limiting retributivism expressly endorse an asymmetric, parsimony-type principle, under which upper retributive limits on penalty severity are quite firm while lower limits are more flexible. *See, e.g.,* FRASE, *supra* note 6, at 25–31.

penalty cases and prison-sentence cases — with very different analytic methods and punishment-purpose rationales applied to each group. That distinction began to break down in two recent cases involving juveniles who received sentences of life without parole (LWOP). But as shown below, the distinction between death and non-death cases has not been totally abandoned. To further complicate matters, the Court has addressed the proportionality of economic penalties (applying the Excessive Fines Clause) only once, and the standards applied in that case were likewise unclear and possibly different from standards applied in death penalty and prison cases.

Death Penalty Cases — Categorical Bans, Applying the *Gregg-Coker* Standards

In a series of cases beginning in the mid-1970s, the Court held that the death penalty cannot be imposed in certain types of cases, usually defined by either the nature of the crime or the offender's role in it, or the nature of the offender.[14] The first of these "categorical" bans on capital punishment was announced in the 1977 case of *Coker v. Georgia* and applied to cases involving rape of an adult victim.[15] Subsequent cases banned capital punishment for low-culpability felony murder accomplices,[16] mentally retarded offenders,[17] offenders under the age of eighteen at the time of the offense,[18] and rape of a juvenile victim.[19] *Coker* provides the most complete — and also probably the most pro-defendant — statement of the Court's substantive tests for determining whether a categorical ban should be adopted.

In *Coker*, citing and building on language in *Gregg v. Georgia*,[20] the Court announced two main tests, the second composed of two sub-tests. First, the Court looks at legislation, prosecution charging policies, jury verdicts, and judges' sentences to see whether there is a "national consensus" against applying capital punishment to this category of crimes or offenders; the Court then applies its own "independent judgment" about whether such a ban should apply.[21] In making that judgment, the Court in *Coker* announced two grounds for finding an Eighth Amendment violation:

---

[14] A third group of cases banned the death penalty under statutes that eliminated or constrained the sentencing court's or jury's power to consider mitigating circumstances. *See, e.g.*, Lockett v. Ohio, 438 U.S. 586, 602–69 (1978). These cases, however, do not apply the *Gregg-Coker* standards discussed below, and they say almost nothing related to purposes of punishment.

[15] Coker v. Georgia, 433 U.S. 584 (1977) (plurality opinion).

[16] Enmund v. Florida, 458 U.S. 782 (1982).

[17] Atkins v. Virginia, 536 U.S. 304 (2002).

[18] Roper v. Simmons, 543 U.S. 551 (2005).

[19] Kennedy v. Louisiana, 554 U.S. 945 (2008).

[20] Gregg v. Georgia, 428 U.S. 153 (1976) (plurality opinion).

[21] Graham v. Florida, 560 U.S. 48, 61 (2010) (describing the Court's death penalty standards).

[the] punishment . . . (1) makes no measureable contribution to acceptable goals of punishment and hence is nothing more than the purposeless and needless imposition of pain and suffering; or (2) is grossly out of proportion to the severity of the crime. A punishment might fail the test on either ground.[22]

The last sentence above implies that sub-tests (1) and (2) are independent and that only one need be met. Indeed, the Court went on to invalidate Mr. Coker's death sentence solely under the second standard. However, only one later Eighth Amendment case has repeated the quoted passage above; moreover, in that case, *Kennedy v. Louisiana*, the Court examined both sub-tests, which seems to suggest that they must both be met (or at least that both must be considered if neither gives a definitive result).

In all of the other cases that categorically banned the death penalty for certain offenders, the Court expressly addressed only the first (purposes of punishment) sub-test. However, the second *Coker* test (proportionality to the crime) was perhaps implicit in each of those cases (*Enmund*, *Atkins*, and *Roper*); before addressing how the death penalty might serve traditional purposes of punishment, the Court first discussed the reasons why that category of offenders has substantially diminished culpability.

Some of the *Coker* standards seem closely linked to particular purposes of punishment, but others lack any clear link. "National consensus" is opaque and could reflect any or all purposes. As for the court's "independent judgment," the first sub-test (purposes of punishment) is expressly linked to the two purposes that the Court deems to be valid justifications for the death penalty: retribution and deterrence.[23] The *Coker* opinion also briefly discussed incapacitation in a footnote, but no subsequent death penalty case has even mentioned it.

The second sub-test, gross disproportionality to the severity of the defendant's crime, could reflect either retributive or ends-benefits proportionality since, as discussed above, both of the latter principles consider the seriousness of the harm caused or threatened by the defendant's crime. But as noted above, in several post-*Coker* categorical-ban cases the Court has stressed the diminished culpability of offenders in that group of cases. Culpability is clearly a retributive concept; so if that factor has replaced or is a proxy for the *Coker* offense disproportionality sub-test, the latter is strongly grounded in retributive principles.

A further difficulty with the *Coker* standards is the seeming overlap between the two sub-tests — retribution appears to be included in both! One answer to this puzzle is that the culpability test (second sub-test) asks whether a severe penalty exceeds the offender's deserts, while, on the issue of whether retribution can justify the challenged death penalty (first sub-test), the question is whether the state can plausibly claim that death is the minimum required penalty on retributive grounds.

---

[22] Coker v. Georgia, 433 U.S. 584, 592 (1977) (plurality opinion).
[23] *Gregg*, 428 U.S. at 183.

If it cannot, and if there is minimal deterrent value, then the challenged death penalty violates the Eighth Amendment (under the first sub-test) even if it does not exceed the offender's desert (under the second).

Prison-Sentence Cases — As-Applied Bans, under *Solem*, *Harmelin*, and *Ewing*

Prior to the juvenile LWOP cases discussed below, Eighth Amendment challenges to severe prison sentences were always assessed on the specific facts of the case, not categorically. In *Solem v. Helm* the Court announced a three-factor test, involving comparisons of (1) "the gravity of the offense and the harshness of the penalty;" (2) penalties imposed for other crimes in that jurisdiction; and (3) penalties imposed for the same crime in other jurisdictions.[24] But two later decisions added criteria that greatly limit the number of cases that can meet these standards. In *Harmelin v. Michigan*, a three-judge plurality opinion held that the second and third *Solem* factors need only be considered "in the rare case in which a threshold comparison of the crime committed and the sentence imposed [— the first *Solem* factor —] leads to an inference of gross disproportionality."[25] And in *Ewing v. California*, another three-judge plurality held that, under the first *Solem* factor, the "gravity of the offense" must include consideration of the offender's prior conviction record, not just the new offense(s) for which he is being sentenced.[26]

The first *Solem* factor (offense gravity versus penalty severity) is consistent with most traditional punishment purposes, but does not name them or suggest how to weigh them against each other; the second and third factors are completely opaque with respect to punishment purposes. In fact, the only clear reference to such purposes in *Solem* is in a footnote, stating that giving Mr. Helm an LWOP sentence "is unlikely to advance the goals of our criminal justice system in any substantial way."[27] This statement was made in connection with discussion of Helm's prior convictions, which the Court noted were all "relatively minor [and] nonviolent."[28]

The *Harmelin* plurality opinion did expressly mention punishment purposes, but only as part of its rationale for relaxing Eighth Amendment standards. The opinion states that the choice of prison terms for specific crimes involves "a substantive penological judgment ... about the nature and purposes of punishment" that is primarily for the legislature, not the courts; the opinion further states, "the Eighth Amendment does not mandate adoption of any one penological theory [such as] retribution, deterrence, incapacitation, [or] rehabilitation."[29] Similarly, the *Ewing* plurality opinion cited punishment purposes as a reason to limit Eighth Amendment

---

[24] Solem v. Helm, 463 U.S. 277, 290–92 (1983).
[25] Harmelin v. Michigan, 501 U.S. 957, 1005 (1991) (opinion of Kennedy, J.).
[26] Ewing v. California, 538 U.S. 11, 29–30 (2003) (opinion of O'Connor, J.).
[27] *Solem*, 463 U.S. at 297 n.22.
[28] *Id.* at 296–97.
[29] *Harmelin*, 501 U.S. at 998–99.

protections even further. It is doubtful that the Court in *Solem* intended its first factor, "gravity of the offense," to include the offender's prior convictions,[30] but the *Ewing* plurality felt that this addition was needed "[t]o give full effect to the State's choice" among legitimate punishment purposes, including "the State's public safety interest in incapacitating and deterring recidivist felons."[31] The Court's acceptance of all traditional punishment purposes thus seems to imply that an unconstitutional penalty must be grossly disproportionate relative to all such purposes.

The Court's (Sole) Excessive Fines Case — Neither Death Penalty nor *Solem* Standards?

In *United States v. Bajakajian*,[32] the Court invalidated the criminal forfeiture of $357,144 in cash under the Excessive Fines Clause. The Court cited *Solem*'s "gross disproportionality" test,[33] but not the three *Solem* factors or the *Harmelin* decision modifying those factors. The Court also did not cite any death penalty cases and made no express reference to punishment purposes that might justify or invalidate the forfeiture. But the rationale seemed to be retributive, since all of the factors examined by the Court are related to retributive principles: the harshness of the penalty, the lack of any concrete harm to the government or any person, the technical nature of the charged non-reporting violation (the defendant's possession and transportation of the funds was perfectly legal), the lack of relationship between the money and any illegal behavior (i.e., no criminal motive), and the defendant's very limited culpability relative to other potential violators of the currency-reporting statute.[34]

Juvenile LWOP Cases — Applying (Modified) Death Penalty Standards

In *Graham v. Florida*,[35] the Court held that the Eighth Amendment prohibits imposing an LWOP sentence for a non-homicide crime committed by a person under eighteen years of age. Noting the almost-like-death severity of LWOP, the Court chose not to apply the modified *Solem* standards to the particular facts of the defendant's crime; instead, the Court applied the categorical approach (all cases of this type) it had previously used only in death penalty cases, and also applied a version of the *Gregg-Coker* tests.

---

[30] Although the *Solem* Court noted that prior convictions are relevant in sentencing, it stated that, for Eighth Amendment purposes, "[w]e must focus on the [conviction offense] since Helm already has paid the penalty for each of his prior offenses." *Solem*, 463 U.S. at 296 n.21. Accordingly, the Court's application of its first factor focused on the defendant's current offense, only briefly noting his prior convictions.

[31] *Ewing*, 538 U.S. at 29.

[32] 524 U.S. 321 (1998).

[33] *Id.* at 336–37.

[34] *Id.* at 337–40; *see also id.* at 339 n.14.

[35] 560 U.S. 48 (2010).

Justice Kennedy's majority opinion first looked at legislation and sentencing practices and concluded that a national consensus had formed against authorizing and imposing LWOP in cases such as Mr. Graham's. His opinion then applied the Court's own independent judgment to this issue and concluded that the challenged LWOP sentence violated the Eighth Amendment. The Court's independent judgment analysis followed the same steps it had used in all death penalty cases except *Coker*: Justice Kennedy first noted the substantially diminished culpability of juvenile offenders (which, as discussed above, seems to be a proxy for the second *Gregg-Coker* factor — gross disproportionality to the severity of the crime); he also noted the reduced culpability associated with all non-homicide crimes (citing *Coker* and *Kennedy*) — death is "different" on the offense side.

Justice Kennedy then addressed each of the four traditional purposes of punishment (the first *Gregg-Coker* factor, but including incapacitation and rehabilitation, not just retribution and deterrence). He concluded that none of those purposes "provides an adequate justification" for an LWOP sentence imposed on a juvenile non-homicide offender.[36] Finally, Justice Kennedy argued that it was necessary to impose a categorical ban on LWOP sentencing for juvenile non-homicide crimes. Given the punitive urges triggered by the seriousness of LWOP-eligible offenses and the difficulties juveniles have in defending themselves, case-specific analysis would pose an unacceptable risk of allowing some juvenile offenders to receive unconstitutionally severe punishment.[37] A similar unacceptable-risk/necessary-overbreadth concept had been cited in earlier cases imposing categorical bans on death penalty eligibility.[38]

Two years later, in *Miller v. Alabama* and a companion case,[39] the Court applied a similar categorical approach and similar *Gregg-Coker* standards, and held that the Eighth Amendment prohibits mandatory LWOP sentences for any juvenile offense, including homicide. Unlike *Graham* and the death penalty cases, however, the *Miller* opinion began with what amounted to the Court's independent assessment, and then examined evidence suggesting a national consensus against the penalty in question. In place of the diminished culpability associated with non-homicide crimes (*Graham*), the *Miller* majority opinion by Justice Kagan pointed to the inherent overbreadth of a mandatory LWOP penalty — neither the sentencing court nor a subsequent parole board can factor in the mitigating circumstances of the offender's current and prior offenses, and changes in the offender's character and dangerousness while in prison. This is particularly problematic for juvenile offenders since, as the Court had noted in several prior cases, one of the distinguishing

---

[36] *Id.* at 71, 74.

[37] *Id.* at 74–79.

[38] *See* Kennedy v. Louisiana, 554 U.S. 407, 441–44 (2008); Roper v. Simmons, 543 U.S. 551, 572–73 (2005); Atkins v. Virginia, 536 U.S. 304, 320–21 (2002).

[39] Miller v. Alabama, 567 U.S. 460 (2012).

features of juveniles is their greater capacity to change as they grow older.[40] Given these features, a mandatory LWOP sentence "poses too great a risk of disproportionate punishment."[41]

A later case, *Montgomery v. Louisiana*,[42] held that *Miller*'s protections extend to offenders whose convictions had already become final when *Miller* was decided. The Court again stressed the unacceptable-risk/necessary-overbreadth principle — because LWOP for juvenile crime is impermissible for "the vast majority of juvenile offenders," many offenders would receive excessive punishment if *Miller* were not made fully retroactive.[43]

In *Montgomery*, the Court used four terms to describe the "rare" juveniles who may properly be given LWOP: these are offenders whose crime did not reflect "transient immaturity" but rather "irretrievable depravity," "permanent incorrigibility," or "irreparable corruption."[44] All four terms seem related to the offender's future dangerousness, and thus to crime-control purposes (especially the need for long-term incapacitation). On the other hand, "transient immaturity" implies that the crime stemmed from contextual and other external factors that reduce culpability. Moreover, *non-transient* immaturity, depravity, incorrigibility, or corruption suggests that the defendant, albeit youthful when the crime was committed, was and remains a wicked person; such fundamental character flaws — which might not be fully apparent until years later when the defendant continues to show no sign of rehabilitation — arguably have retributive (culpability-enhancing) as well as crime control significance.

Implicit Recognition of the Three Proportionality Principles in the Court's Opinions

Retributive Disproportionality. As shown above, all of the Court's cases finding an Eighth Amendment violation have applied retributive proportionality principles — each case examined one or both of the two major elements of retributive blame-worthiness: offense harm and offender culpability. At least three and possibly four cases have come close to recognizing reduced offender blameworthiness as a sufficient basis for finding an Eighth Amendment violation:

- In *Coker*, the Court stated that disproportionality of the death penalty to the offender's crime could, by itself, violate the Amendment, and then proceeded to examine only the lesser harms of non-homicide crimes; the Court ignored the offender's substantial record of violent crimes, which could have been cited to justify the death penalty on deterrent grounds (i.e., the need to deter other violent recidivists).

---

[40] *Graham*, 560 U.S. at 68; *Roper*, 543 U.S. at 570.
[41] *Miller*, 567 U.S. at 479.
[42] 136 S. Ct. 718 (2016).
[43] *Id.* at 733–36.
[44] *Id.* at 734–35.

- In *Solem*, the Court focused almost entirely on offense harm and offender culpability — using those terms — and made only one indirect reference, in a footnote, to non-retributive punishment goals.[45]
- In *Bajakajian*, the factors examined by the Court were all related to retribution, and non-retributive punishment purposes that might have justified the forfeiture were not mentioned.
- In *Kennedy*, the Court, citing *Coker*, emphasized the "fundamental moral distinction" between homicide and non-homicide crimes. The use of the term "moral" suggests a primarily retributive assessment. And although the Court conceded that the death penalty for child rape might have some general deterrent benefit, it stated that "[t]his argument does not overcome other objections," in particular, "the risk of overpunishment," if the death penalty were permitted for non-homicide crimes.[46]

Non-Retributive Disproportionality. Implicit support for limits based on ends-benefits and alternative-means proportionality principles can be found in several of the Court's death penalty cases and in the juvenile LWOP cases. The Court has noted the limited general deterrent benefits of the death penalty for would-be offenders who are minor felony murder accomplices, mentally retarded, or juveniles.[47] This is essentially an ends-benefits argument — the severity of the death penalty outweighs its deterrent value. Alternatively, the added severity of the death penalty outweighs any added deterrent benefits, relative to the most likely lesser alternative of LWOP.[48] Likewise, an implicit alternative-means argument may explain why the Court does not consider incapacitation to be a justification for the death penalty — given the LWOP alternative, execution is unnecessary, and thus excessive, as a way to protect the public from very dangerous offenders.

In the juvenile LWOP cases, both of the non-retributive proportionality principles were implicitly endorsed. In each case the Court rejected deterrence as a justification for LWOP on essentially ends-benefits grounds: because juveniles are relatively undeterrable, "any limited deterrent effect [of LWOP] is not enough to justify the sentence."[49] In both cases the Court also rejected incapacitation as a justification, on essentially alternative-means grounds: for many juvenile offenders, an LWOP sentence will prove to have been unnecessarily severe in terms of incapacitation, given the capacity for change that is typical of most juveniles.[50]

[45] Solem v. Helm, 463 U.S. 277, 292–94, 296 n. 22 (1983).
[46] Kennedy v. Louisiana, 554 U.S. 407, 441–42 (2008).
[47] Roper v. Simmons, 543 U.S. 551, 571–72 (2005); Atkins v. Virginia, 536 U.S. 304, 318–19 (2002); Enmund v. Florida, 458 U.S. 782, 798–99 (1982).
[48] Only in *Roper* did the Court expressly note the LWOP alternative. *See Roper*, 543 U.S. at 572.
[49] Graham v. Florida, 560 U.S. 48, 72 (2010); *see also* Miller v. Alabama, 567 U.S. 460, 472 (2012).
[50] *Miller*, 567 U.S. at 472–73; *Graham*, 560 U.S. at 72–74. As for rehabilitation, the Court noted that LWOP "foreswears altogether the rehabilitative ideal," so this penalty does not even purport to be justified on those grounds. *Miller*, 567 U.S. at 473.

The categorical approach used in some cases may, itself, embody the alternative-means proportionality principle, and perhaps also retributive proportionality. In most of the death penalty cases, and the first juvenile LWOP case (*Graham*), the Court felt that a case-specific (non-categorical) approach would pose too great a risk of disproportionate punishment.[51] As noted earlier, a categorical approach is consistent with the alternative-means proportionality principle that sentences should not be more severe than necessary to achieve applicable sentencing purposes; use of an overly broad, categorical approach essentially requires courts to err on the side of leniency, and this helps to ensure that the alternative-means proportionality principle is respected. But as was also noted, such an asymmetric proportionality principle can and should be applied even under a purely retributive justification for punishment — it is normatively worse to give an offender an above-desert penalty, than to impose below-desert punishment.

Summary. The preceding review of the four groups of Supreme Court cases interpreting the Eighth Amendment's punishment clauses reveals many differences on the surface, some greater degree of consistency in substance, and much that is still unclear. The differences relate to the choice between case-specific and categorical rulings, and the specific tests used to decide which severe punishments are unconstitutionally excessive. Death penalty cases remain "different" from the other three groups in several ways that render death penalties more likely to be struck down: the applicable punishment purposes are more limited; penalties are more likely to be invalidated on what seem like solely retributive grounds; and categorical rulings are often applied, even to adult sentencing. The underlying consistency is this: the Court usually (but not always) considers whether the challenged penalty exceeds the offender's culpability for the crime(s) being sentenced and whether it helps to achieve any of the applicable purposes of (justifications for) punishment. The Court has never articulated how unconstitutional "disproportionality" relates to non-retributive purposes of punishment, but several decisions seem to implicitly adopt one or both of the non-retributive proportionality principles examined in this chapter. Finally, the Court has not articulated how retributive and non-retributive proportionality principles relate to each other. That is the topic of the next section.

FOUR WAYS TO LINK EIGHTH AMENDMENT PROPORTIONALITY TO TRADITIONAL PUNISHMENT PURPOSES

The Court's opinions state or imply several standards, grounded in various traditional punishment purposes, for finding a punishment to be unconstitutionally disproportionate. Does any such standard, by itself, provide sufficient grounds for such a finding? Or must a penalty be disproportionate under every one of the

[51] *See, e.g., Graham,* 560 U.S. at 77–79.

standards? This part examines four ways in which these standards have been or could be applied.

Limiting Retributivism: Punishment Is Barred If It Clearly Exceeds the Offender's Just Deserts

The limiting retributivism approach has been endorsed by several writers,[52] and there is much to be said for it. The argument is simply that, as a matter of principle, it is fundamentally unfair and an abuse of government power to punish offenders much more than they deserve — even if an undeservedly severe penalty might be justifiable on crime-control grounds. This is essentially a human rights argument, based on the core concept that courts, when interpreting constitutionally protected civil rights, have an essential role to play in protecting individuals, especially the politically powerless, from government and/or majoritarian oppression and unfairness.[53] As noted above, the Court has come close to adopting this rule in at least three cases; it should do so expressly, and for all cases.

Disjunctive Limits: Punishment Is Barred if It Clearly Violates Any of the Proportionality Principles

The disjunctive limits approach yields broader Eighth Amendment protection — a penalty is unconstitutional if it is very excessive under any of the three proportionality principles. That is because each principle protects against a separate and distinct form of excessive punishment. Because of its breadth, and given the limits of federalism and democratic accountability, this second approach would be easier to implement under state than under federal constitutional provisions.[54]

Cumulative Disproportionality: The Three Proportionality Tests Lend Support to Each Other

Another way to interpret the Court's Eighth Amendment punishments clause decisions is through the lens of cumulative disproportionality – retributive and non-retributive proportionality limits are all potentially relevant and may all be considered in any case, but retributive disproportionality is sometimes so great that

---

[52] *See, e.g.,* Frase, *supra* note 2; Youngjae Lee, *The Constitutional Right against Excessive Punishment*, 91 VA. L. REV. 677 (2005); John F. Stinneford, *Rethinking Proportionality under the Cruel and Unusual Punishments Clause*, 97 VA. L. REV. 899 (2011).

[53] *Cf.* United States v. Carolene Products, Co., 304 U.S. 144, 152 n.4 (1938) (noting that heightened judicial scrutiny of legislation is needed to protect "discrete and insular minorities" that are not adequately protected by ordinary political processes).

[54] For further discussion of state constitutional protections, *see* Frase, *supra* note 11.

it is sufficient.[55] Thus, if a case shows strong evidence of retributive disproportionality (or a category of cases presents a high risk of such disproportionality), that alone
makes the sentence unconstitutional. This was arguably the case in *Coker* (most-
severe penalty/not the most severe offense harm), in *Solem* (next-most-severe pen-
alty/minor non-violent offenses), and in *Bajakajian* (very severe monetary penalty/
minor regulatory offense). If the degree of retributive disproportionality is significant
but not deemed sufficient to violate the Eighth Amendment, a severe penalty can
still be found unconstitutional if it has very little justification on crime-control
grounds (i.e., there is also a significant violation of one or both of the non-retributive
proportionality principles). This was arguably the situation in all of the other cases
where the Court has found a violation of the Amendment on substantive grounds:
the death penalty cases of *Enmund, Atkins, Roper,* and *Kennedy*; and the juvenile
LWOP cases of *Graham* and *Miller*. It might also have been part of the rationale in
Solem, the adult LWOP case.[56] In other words, weak crime-control justifications can
add support to a finding of retributive disproportionality — disproportionality is
cumulative, across these principles[57] — but in extreme cases retributive disproportionality suffices.

Conjunctive Limit: Punishment Is Barred if It Clearly Violates All Three Proportionality Principles

The conjunctive limit approach is the narrowest of the four — a penalty is
unconstitutional only if it is very excessive under *all three* of the proportionality
principles: the penalty is undeservedly severe, its burdens (or added burdens)
exceed its crime-control benefits (or added benefits), and the same benefits could
be achieved with a less burdensome penalty. An alternative, more protective version
of this approach would require a penalty to be undeservedly severe and also in
violation of *one* of the utilitarian proportionality principles (either ends-benefits or
alternative-means). The latter is arguably the rule the Supreme Court has already
implicitly adopted, at least for adult prison sentences. But this approach would
provide — and has provided — inadequate protection from grossly excessive
punishment. Nevertheless, if that is what the Court really means, then its standard
should be made explicit so as to provide clear and consistent guidance to lower
courts (and to the Court itself).

---

[55] It is less clear (and none of the Court's cases hold) that a penalty could violate the Eighth
Amendment solely because of extreme non-retributive disproportionality.

[56] *See supra* text accompanying notes 27–28.

[57] A finding of cumulative disproportionality is especially justified in the presence of one or more
recognized "different" factors (e.g., the death penalty, LWOP, nonhomicide offense), suggesting a heightened risk of disproportionality relative to some or all punishment purposes. *See*
Frase, *supra* note 1.

CONCLUSION

The Supreme Court has abdicated its responsibility to protect politically powerless criminal defendants from unreasonably severe punishments. Although the Cruel and Unusual Punishments Clause does not expressly protect against excessive penalties, the unifying theme of the entire Amendment is the prevention of excessive penal measures, whether in the form of excessive bail, excessive fines, or other severe punishments.[58] As American jurisdictions gradually replaced corporal punishment with lengthy prison sentences, and public opinion turned against widespread use of the death penalty, Supreme Court Justices began to recognize that death penalties and very severe prison terms could likewise be unconstitutionally excessive — or, in the Court's preferred terminology, "disproportionate." The Court, however, has failed to provide a coherent and consistent set of principles to explain what it means by Eighth Amendment "disproportionality," and in particular, how this concept relates to traditional purposes of punishment. This chapter discusses three proportionality principles, one related to retributive punishment purposes and two related to crime-control purposes, each of which has been implicitly applied in the Court's decisions. The chapter proposes four ways in which the Court could use these principles to more clearly articulate constitutional limits on excessive punishments

---

[58] Atkins v. Virginia, 536 U.S. 304, 311 n.7 (2005).

8

The Administrative Law of the Eighth (and Sixth) Amendment

Richard A. Bierschbach[*]

On the surface, few similarities exist between modern administrative law and the modern constitutional law of sentencing. Administrative law is preoccupied with structural constitutional law, statutory interpretation, and regulatory policy. Constitutional sentencing law — much of which springs from the Eighth Amendment, as well as the Sixth — is overwhelmingly concerned with individual constitutional rights, blame, and punishment. Scholars thus almost never draw connections between the two.

This Chapter does just that. Administrative law and the constitutional law of sentencing can be seen as sharing an underlying concern about the structure of decision-making — how to ensure that difficult, value-laden judgments best reflect and filter the viewpoints and concerns of those they affect. Administrative law usually casts this concern in terms of accountability or democratic legitimacy. Constitutional sentencing law usually casts this concern in terms of the community's norms or conscience. One might also label this concern one of "voice" or "perspective." Just as the institutional and procedural structure of administrative law evolved in large part to address problems of voice and perspective in the regulatory context, we might understand the arc of constitutional sentencing law over the last half-decade as slowly moving in a parallel direction in the criminal justice field.

I briefly trace the contours of this development below. My approach is self-consciously descriptive and attributional. Though I offer a certain way of looking at the evolution of modern constitutional sentencing law, I make no strong historical, causal, or motivational claims explaining its evolution. Rather, my aim is the far more limited one of noting an underappreciated conceptual overlap between it and

[*] Dean and Professor of Law, Wayne State University Law School. I thank Will Berry and Meghan Ryan for inviting me to contribute to this book, my fellow contributors for valuable comments on an earlier sketch of this Chapter, and Emma Trivax for outstanding research assistance.

the field of administrative law, without positing any deeper cross-pollination. Likewise, while I make several observations about what that overlap might augur for the future, those observations necessarily are conjectural. I make no prescriptive claims about what should or should not happen in light of that overlap, and leave to the reader what, if any, lessons to carry away.

THE ADMINISTRATIVE LAW STORY

I begin with the administrative law side of the story. The history and structure of American administrative law exhibits two features that situate it roughly alongside the modern constitutional law of sentencing. First, a significant part of that history involves grappling with how to give content to indeterminate, contested, and often competing conceptions of the public good. Second, a significant part of the solution to that struggle involves opening channels for meaningful input into agency decision-making from citizens and other actors holding a broad range of views and perspectives, thereby legitimating the regulatory process by helping to ensure that agency decisions are both accountable and just. This participatory approach to addressing difficult issues of governance and morality — the idea that citizens should have some input into thorny regulatory decisions — has become a cornerstone of modern administrative law. It is why, as Ronald Wright and Marc Miller put it, "the history of administrative government in the United States can be framed as a story about combining expertise and public input."[1]

It was not always that way. The Progressives who established the framework of the modern regulatory state aimed to insulate agencies from citizen involvement, not to encourage it. At best, they saw laypersons as incompetent in affairs of government; at worst, they saw them as corrupt instruments of majoritarian politics.[2] Professional agency personnel, by contrast, were viewed as skilled technocrats — dispassionate and unbiased experts who merely called upon their training to execute congressional judgments or to ascertain and implement some objective version of the public interest.[3]

But that view quickly changed as the federal government exploded in size and the power delegated to agencies ballooned. It soon became clear that even the most expert and well-intentioned agency personnel engaging in the most seemingly

---

[1] Ronald F. Wright & Marc L. Miller, *The Worldwide Accountability Deficit for Prosecutors*, 67 WASH. & LEE L. REV. 1587, 1591 (2010).

[2] Ronald F. Wright, *Why Not Administrative Grand Juries?*, 44 ADMIN. L. REV. 465, 495–96 (1992) (discussing the Progressive concern that lay citizens could not serve competently or independently).

[3] *See* BENJAMIN P. DE WITT, THE PROGRESSIVE MOVEMENT 299–318 (1915); JAMES M. LANDIS, THE ADMINISTRATIVE PROCESS 154–55 (1938); MARTIN J. SCHIESL, THE POLITICS OF EFFICIENCY: MUNICIPAL ADMINISTRATION AND REFORM IN AMERICA: 1880–1920, at 6–25 (1977); RUSSELL STORY, THE AMERICAN MUNICIPAL EXECUTIVE 218–20 (1918); Morris L. Cooke, *Scientific Management of the Public Business*, 9 AM. POL. SCI. REV. 488 (1915).

technical of inquires could not avoid making deeply discretionary, highly value-laden decisions in the name of the public interest.[4] One cannot, for instance, set the limit on airborne benzene that is "reasonably necessary . . . to provide safe or healthful employment" without confronting hard trade-offs of dollars versus lives or lives versus jobs; even "safety" is a fundamentally normative question that implicates unavoidable value judgments.[5] At the same time, scholars began to recognize that agencies were not the enlightened Platonic guardians that the Progressives had envisioned, but were imperfectly attuned to the public interest, with their own agendas, preferences, and incentives. In short, "the public interest is a texture of multiple strands"[6] and "not a monolith."[7] Even if it were monolithic, we could not blindly trust agencies to pursue it. Those realizations undermined the notion of the impartial administrator and opened up a legitimacy gap in the field. The project of administrative law then shifted from protecting agencies from citizen interference to cabining agency discretion and "explaining how unelected bureaucrats, making their choices without resort to a scientific method that produces a single correct answer, can claim to exercise legitimate power in a democracy."[8]

Participation became a cornerstone of that project for several reasons. It enhances the soundness and thoroughness of agency deliberations by improving the quality and variety of information the agency considers, whether factual or relating to the public's viewpoints. It creates feedback loops between agencies, citizens, and courts, improving communication and helping policy to evolve over time. It improves accountability by placing the onus on agencies to justify their actions publicly. And, by requiring agencies to "balanc[e] all elements essential to a just determination of the public interest," it forces agencies to confront the many challenging questions before them in the light of competing public and regulatory priorities.[9]

---

[4]   *See* Richard B. Stewart, *Reformation of American Administrative Law*, 88 Harv. L. Rev. 1669, 1676 (1975).

[5]   *See* Indus. Union Dep't, AFL-CIO v. Am. Petroleum Inst., 448 U.S. 607, 615 (1980).

[6]   FPC v. Hope Nat. Gas Co., 320 U.S. 591, 627 (1944) (Frankfurter, J., dissenting).

[7]   Ernest Gellhorn, *Public Participation in Administrative Proceedings*, 81 Yale L.J. 359, 360 (1972).

[8]   Wright, *supra* note 2, at 495–96 (citing Christopher F. Edley, Administrative Law: Rethinking Judicial Control of Administrative Agencies 217 (1990)); *see also* William Funk, *Public Participation and Transparency in Administrative Law — Three Examples as an Object Lesson*, 61 Admin. L. Rev. 171, 172–80 (2009) (discussing the history and legal and political context of the development of public participation as a cornerstone of modern American administrative law).

[9]   Air Line Pilots Ass'n v. Civil Aeronautics Bd., 475 F.2d 900, 905 (D.C. Cir. 1973); *see also* Sierra Club v. Costle, 657 F.2d 298, 400–01 (D.C. Cir. 1981) ("[T]he very legitimacy of general policymaking performed by unelected administrators depends in no small part on the openness, accessibility, and amenability of these officials to the needs and ideas of the public."); Palisades Citizens Ass'n v. Civil Aeronautics Bd., 420 F.2d 188, 191–92 (D.C. Cir. 1969).

A broad range of mechanisms exists to help administrative law realize these benefits of participation. I am less concerned with their details than with the gestalt of what they accomplish, but here are some highlights. In informal rulemakings, the notice-and-comment process of the Administrative Procedure Act (APA) requires agencies to accept public comment on proposed rules and (as interpreted by courts) lays down further procedures intended to make that input meaningful, including the requirement that agencies' final rules address comments of significance in some way.[10] Broad standing rules enhance public input by allowing any "person ... adversely affected or aggrieved" by agency action to challenge it in court.[11] The Negotiated Rulemaking Act encourages agencies to work closely with affected stakeholders to reach consensus on proposed rules before agencies issue them;[12] other statutes and agency practices provide for similar consultation in more specific cases.[13] At the level of individual adjudications, some agencies, such as the Federal Communications Commission (FCC), allow interested parties wide latitude to intervene in formal proceedings.[14] Some statutes and regulations provide for public comments in agency enforcement actions where civil penalties or consent decrees are at issue.[15] Finally, courts reviewing agency action use all of this as a foil for bringing their own judicial expertise to bear on agency decision-making. They make sure that agencies base their decisions on the information before them, do not act arbitrarily or capriciously, and adequately explain their reasoning by taking a "hard look" at agency action to ensure they have done so.[16]

The result is a system that leans heavily on multiple perspectives and interests — a sort of rough-and-tumble version of Madisonian checks and balances for the administrative state — to constrain and channel the exercise of agency discretion. Normally we think of the great virtues of this arrangement as protecting individual liberty and preventing tyranny.[17] But (to use Jon Michaels' words) its "democratic,

---

[10] 5 U.S.C. § 553(c) (2006); Auto. Parts & Accessories Ass'n v. Boyd, 407 F.2d 330, 338 (D.C. Cir. 1968).

[11] 5 U.S.C. § 702 (2006); *see* Ass'n of Data Processing Serv. Org., Inc. v. Camp, 397 U.S. 150, 154 (1970).

[12] *See* Negotiated Rulemaking Act, 5 U.S.C. §§ 561–570 (2006); RICHARD PIERCE, JR. ET AL., ADMINISTRATIVE LAW AND PROCESS § 6.4.6f at 342–42 (5th ed. 2008) (describing negotiated rulemaking).

[13] *See, e.g.,* Forest and Rangeland Renewable Resources Planning Act, 16 U.S.C. § 1612 (2006) (providing that the Secretary of Agriculture shall establish procedures to give the public adequate notice and an opportunity to comment on the formulation of standards, criteria, and guidelines applicable to Forest Service programs).

[14] *See* 47 C.F.R. § 1.223 (2012).

[15] *See* 33 U.S.C. § 1319(g)(4) (2006); FTC Regulations, 16 C.F.R. §§ 2.34(c)–(e) (2012); Consumer Product Safety Conservation and Recovery Act, 42 U.S.C. § 6973(d) (2006); Clean Air Act, 42 U.S.C. § 7413(g) (2006); Comprehensive Environmental Response, Compensation, and Liability Act, 42 U.S.C. § 9622(d)(2) (2006); 28 C.F.R. § 50.7 (2012) (adopting procedures for public comment on proposed consent judgments under CERCLA).

[16] *See* PIERCE ET AL., *supra* note 12, § 7.5, at 391–403 (describing the hard-look doctrine).

[17] *See* THE FEDERALIST No. 51, p. 349 (J. Cooke ed. 1961).

pluralistic, inclusive, and deliberative" nature also serves another function: it helps give content to the messy questions of values that agencies routinely face.[18] The process by which it does so is not especially efficient or orderly, and it does not provide a single right answer. What it does do, however, at least ideally, is legitimate, in the most basic sense, whatever answer emerges.[19] The substantive question of what is the public interest or public good thus in many ways collapses into the procedural one. At the end of the day, within the limits of an agency decision-maker's organic statute and other applicable law, the "public interest" or "public good" just is what comes out of this process.[20]

THE CONSTITUTIONAL LAW OF SENTENCING

The constitutional law of sentencing broadly shares these features. Substantively, while administrative law wrestles with the problem of how to give content to the notion of the public interest, much of constitutional sentencing law wrestles with the equally slippery and intractable problem of how to give content to the notion of just punishment. Procedurally, while administrative law addresses that problem by leavening agency decision-making with participation from various actors, sentencing law has moved in that same direction in fits and starts. And it has done so with the same ultimate goal: to legitimate — not only democratically, but also morally — the state's meting out of punishment by helping to ensure that sentencing decisions reflect the views of a range of stakeholders with different perspectives.

One sees this most readily in the Supreme Court's capital sentencing decisions under the Eighth Amendment.[21] The goal in all capital cases is to ensure morally appropriate judgments by ensuring that punishment is "tailored to [the offender's] personal responsibility and moral guilt."[22] The Eighth Amendment cases that grapple with this end speak the general language of retributive desert.[23] The Court's

---

[18] Jon D. Michaels, Constitutional Coup: Privatization's Threat to the American Republic 6 (2017).

[19] Nina A. Mendelson, *Regulatory Beneficiaries and Informal Agency Policymaking*, 92 Cornell L. Rev. 397, 419–20 (2007) (explaining how virtually all of the major theories that seek to legitimate administrative decision-making see participation as important).

[20] *Cf.* K. Sabeel Rahman, *Reconstructing the Administrative State in an Era of Economic and Democratic Crisis*, 131 Harv. L. Rev. 1671, 1682 (2017) (noting the connection between the structure of administrative government and the need to ensure that the powers of the regulatory state are deployed in ways consistent with liberal democratic values).

[21] Again, I am less concerned with details than with the gestalt of the framework the decisions set up.

[22] Enmund v. Florida, 458 U.S. 782, 801 (1982).

[23] *See, e.g.*, Tison v. Arizona, 481 U.S. 137, 149 (1987); *Enmund*, 458 U.S. at 801; Woodson v. North Carolina, 428 U.S. 280, 304–05 (1976) (plurality opinion). *See generally* Carol S. Steiker & Jordan M. Steiker, *Sober Second Thoughts: Reflections on Two Decades of Constitutional Regulation of Capital Punishment*, 109 Harv. L. Rev. 355, 364–66, 372–78 (1995) (discussing the Court's goal of ensuring deserved punishment in capital sentencing and its doctrinal efforts to implement it).

retributivism, however, is neither pure nor static. It is pluralistic and popular, not monistic and philosophical. The Court looks to evidence of community consensus to help give substantive content to punishment norms, placing great weight on state legislative judgments, on-the-ground practices, and other indicia of popular views of moral appropriateness.[24] The Court also weighs punishments against a spectrum of other non-retributive ends that most people believe should matter to sentencing, such as deterrence, incapacitation, rehabilitation, and reformation.[25] When it comes to tailoring punishment, the *Woodson/Lockett/Eddings* trilogy emphasizes that sentencers can ensure "a just and appropriate sentence" only by "consider[ing] ... the character and record of the individual offender and the circumstances of the particular offense."[26] In implementing that principle, the Court requires sentencers to consider a nearly unlimited range of factors from a nearly unlimited range of sources as potential mitigating circumstances.[27]

The institutional and procedural structure that has grown up around this scheme has resulted in a system in which capital sentencing determinations are filtered through multiple actors and viewpoints. Legislatures make initial, broad, ex ante sentencing judgments by laying out criteria for death-eligible crimes.[28] The Court weighs in as well, barring death sentences for certain categories of crimes (such as rape) and defendants (such as juveniles and insane and intellectually disabled defendants).[29] Prosecutors then make first-cut, individualized, ex post sentencing judgments when they decide whether to file capital charges. Juries individualize

[24] *See, e.g.,* Graham v. Florida, 130 S. Ct. 2011, 2023–26 (2010); Roper v. Simmons, 543 U.S. 551, 564–67 (2005); Atkins v. Virginia, 536 U.S. 304, 314–17 (2002); *Woodson,* 428 U.S. at 295–96 (plurality opinion).

[25] *See, e.g.,* Ewing v. California, 538 U.S. 11, 30 (2003) (plurality opinion); *Atkins,* 536 U.S. at 319–20; Gregg v. Georgia, 428 U.S. 153, 184–86 (1976) (plurality opinion); *see also* Youngjae Lee, *The Purposes of Punishment Test,* 23 FED. SENT'G REP. 58, 58–59 (2010) (discussing the "purposes of punishment test" and stating that the Court has resisted commitment to a specific theory of punishment); Carol S. Steiker, *Commentary,* Panetti v. Quarterman: *Is There a "Rational Understanding" of the Supreme Court's Eighth Amendment Jurisprudence?,* 5 OHIO ST. J. CRIM. L. 285, 290 (2007) ("In the [Eighth Amendment] morass ... one theme has remained consistent: the Court insists that the Constitution is agnostic when it comes to penological purposes.").

[26] *Woodson,* 428 U.S. at 304; *see* Eddings v. Oklahoma, 455 U.S. 104 (1982); Lockett v. Ohio, 438 U.S. 586 (1978) (plurality opinion in part).

[27] *See, e.g.,* McKoy v. North Carolina, 494 U.S. 433, 436–37 (1990); Penry v. Lynaugh, 492 U.S. 302, 340 (1989) (plurality opinion), *abrogated by Atkins,* 536 U.S. at 321; Mills v. Maryland, 486 U.S. 367, 370 (1988); Sumner v. Shuman, 483 U.S. 66, 82 (1987); Hitchcock v. Dugger, 481 U.S. 393, 397 (1987); Skipper v. South Carolina, 476 U.S. 1, 6–7, 14 (1986); *Eddings,* 455 U.S. at 115–16; *Lockett,* 438 U.S. at 605.

[28] *See Gregg,* 428 U.S. at 206–07 (requiring statutorily defined aggravating circumstances before capital punishment may be constitutionally imposed).

[29] *See, e.g., Roper,* 542 U.S. at 568 (forbidding the death penalty for crimes committed while under the age of eighteen); *Atkins,* 536 U.S. at 321 (forbidding execution of intellectually disabled defendants); Ford v. Wainwright, 477 U.S. 399, 409–10 (1986) (forbidding execution of insane defendants); Coker v. Georgia, 433 U.S. 584, 597–600 (1977) (plurality opinion) (forbidding the death penalty for the crime of raping an adult woman).

further, assessing every capital case both at the guilt phase and at the sentencing phase.[30] Judges also independently review the pursuit of capital sentences at various points, including charging, immediately after trial, and again on direct and collateral appeal (the former of which is automatic in capital cases).[31] Even governors get involved, paying closer attention to clemency in capital cases than they do for non-capital crimes. Although the Court has not formally required the vast bulk of these procedures as an Eighth Amendment matter, it has viewed most of them as critical to the constitutionality of capital sentencing.[32]

That pattern has continued more recently as the Court has extended the constitutional regulation of punishment beyond capital cases. *Graham v. Florida* and *Miller v. Alabama* invoked the Eighth Amendment to prohibit discretionary imposition of life imprisonment without the possibility of parole (LWOP) for juveniles who have not committed homicide (*Graham*) and mandatory LWOP for those who have (*Miller*).[33] Taking moral appropriateness and individual tailoring as their baseline and relying again on an eclectic and elastic conception of desert, the decisions appear in many ways as substantive proportionality cases. But their real thrust is procedural and structural. They inserted more actors, information, and viewpoints into juvenile LWOP determinations. Like *Woodson/Lockett/Eddings*, *Miller* required front-line sentencers to weigh the complete "wealth of characteristics and circumstances attendant to" a juvenile and his crime before imposing LWOP, bringing in the spectrum of factors, sources, and perspectives that come with that.[34] *Graham* required an additional actor, the parole board — which, at least ideally, itself also channels a spectrum of input and views from affected community members and stakeholders — periodically to re-evaluate a juvenile's continued imprisonment in light of a wide-ranging set of considerations.[35] In doing so, both

---

[30] Douglas Berman, *Encouraging (and Even Requiring) Prosecutors to Be Second-Look Sentencers*, 19 TEMP. POL. & CIV. RTS. L. REV. 429, 432 (2010); *see also* Alyssa Connell Lareau & Grant Henrichsen Willis, *Thirty-First Annual Review of Criminal Procedure: Capital Punishment*, 90 GEO. L.J. 1838, 1845–47 (2002).

[31] *See Gregg*, 428 U.S. at 204–07 (1976) (discussing Georgia's statutory requirement for a trial court to review a jury's verdict for the death penalty against the facts of the case before affirming the penalty's imposition, as well as the Georgia Supreme Court's "sentence-review function"); *see also* VA. CODE ANN. § 19.2-264.5 (2008) ("When the punishment of any person has been fixed at death, the court shall, before imposing sentence, direct a probation officer of the court to thoroughly investigate the history of the defendant and any and all other relevant facts, to the end that the court may be fully advised as to whether the sentence of death is appropriate and just."); Berman, *supra* note 29, at 431.

[32] *See, e.g., Gregg*, 428 U.S. at 198 (emphasizing the importance of a state's automatic appellate review of death sentences in determining whether the state's death penalty statute is constitutional); Steiker & Steiker, *supra* note 23, at 371–96 (reviewing the constitutional framework for regulation of capital punishment).

[33] Graham v. Florida, 560 U.S. 48 (2010); Miller v. Alabama, 567 U.S. 460 (2012).

[34] *Miller*, 567 U.S. at 476.

[35] *Graham*, 560 U.S. at 75 ("[T]he State must ... give [juvenile, nonhomicide] defendants ... some meaningful opportunity to obtain release based on demonstrated maturity and rehabilitation.");

decisions noted ways in which the structure of juvenile justice — from the incentives it creates for district judges, to the broad waiver discretion it confers on prosecutors, to the barriers it imposes to presenting mental health and similar experts, and more — has squeezed other checks out of the system.[36]

The Court's watershed line of Sixth Amendment cases that began with *Apprendi v. New Jersey* echoes that theme. In injecting the jury back into punishment determinations, cases like *Apprendi* and *Ring v. Arizona* emphasized jurors' role as a critical institutional check on other governmental actors in the criminal process.[37] As Jenia Iontcheva explains, "[b]ecause of their deliberative capacity and democratic makeup, juries are better situated ... to perform the sensitive tasks of deciding between contested sentencing goals and applying the law with due regard for the individual circumstances of each offender."[38] These structural aspects of the jury's role in ensuring just punishment underscore a deep connection between the Sixth and Eighth Amendments. They even have prompted some Justices to argue that the Eighth Amendment requires jury sentencing in capital cases because juries "more accurately reflect the conscience of the community than can a single judge" and therefore are best suited for making the textured, granular, and normative judgments that give punishment decisions their "moral and constitutional legitimacy."[39] Later decisions in the *Apprendi* line — holding binding guidelines unconstitutional, establishing a reasonableness standard for review of sentences, and allowing district court judges to (reasonably) depart from guidelines based both on case-specific facts and policy disagreements — draw the theme out more, stressing the importance of inter-branch dialogue, effective communication, and different perspectives in the

---

see also Richard A. Bierschbach, *Proportionality and Parole*, 160 U. PA. L. REV. 1745, 1776 (2012) (observing that *Graham* "diversif[ied] sentencing across time and institutions").

[36] Richard A. Bierschbach & Stephanos Bibas, *Constitutionally Tailoring Punishment*, 112 MICH. L. REV. 397, 411–13 (2013).

[37] Apprendi v. New Jersey, 530 U.S. 466, 477 (2000) (quoting JOSEPH STORY, COMMENTARIES ON THE CONSTITUTION OF THE UNITED STATES 540–41 (4th ed. 1873)); *see also* Hurst v. Florida, 136 S. Ct. 616 (2016); Ring v. Arizona, 536 U.S. 584, 606–08 (2002) (majority opinion); Jones v. United States, 526 U.S. 227, 245 (1999) (noting the jury's historical "power to thwart Parliament and Crown").

[38] Jenia Iontcheva, *Jury Sentencing as Democratic Practice*, 89 VA. L. REV. 311, 350 (2003); *see also* Cunningham v. California, 549 U.S. 270, 295–97 (2007) (Kennedy, J., dissenting); Blakely v. Washington, 542 U.S. 296, 327 (2004) (Kennedy, J., dissenting); Akhil Reed Amar, *The Bill of Rights as a Constitution*, 100 YALE L.J. 1131, 1189 (1991); Rachel E. Barkow, *Recharging the Jury: The Criminal Jury's Constitutional Role in an Era of Mandatory Sentencing*, 152 U. PA. L. REV. 33, 72–93 (2003); Stephanos Bibas, *Blakely's Federal Aftermath*, 1 FED. SENT'G REP. 333, 341 (2004); Stephanos Bibas, *How Apprendi Affects Institutional Allocations of Power*, 87 IOWA L. REV. 465, 468 (2002); Stephanos Bibas, *Judicial Fact-Finding and Sentence Enhancements in a World of Guilty Pleas*, 110 YALE L.J. 1097, 1158–73, 1150–70 (2001).

[39] Spaziano v. Florida, 468 U.S. 447, 483, 487 (1984) (Stevens, J., concurring in part and dissenting in part); *see also* Ring, 536 U.S. at 615 (Breyer, J., concurring in the judgment) ("[Juries] are more attuned to the community's moral sensibility ... ." (internal citations and quotation omitted)); Harris v. Alabama, 513 U.S. 504, 515–26 (1995) (Stevens, J., dissenting).

development of sentencing policy and splitting up sentencing power in ways consistent with *Apprendi*'s overarching mission, if not its formalistic approach.[40]

Viewing all of this together, the consequence is a system that increasingly looks to multiple viewpoints and interests to channel and guide discretion, this time in the context of punishment. This development has not been nearly as self-conscious, explicit, or complete as it has in administrative law. Nor has it been theoretically or doctrinally pure. But the basic idea of a Madisonian fragmentation of the power to punish inhabits the interstices of the Court's constitutional sentencing decisions. Together those decisions evince a shared (if imperfectly realized) motif: in sentencing, as elsewhere, no single actor should hold all the cards.

Much as it does in administrative law, this theme has special purchase when it comes to punishment. The exercise of unchanneled and unconstrained sentencing authority by a single actor raises the specter not only of the arbitrary or oppressive use of power that Madison feared. It also raises the specter of morally — and also democratically — illegitimate sentencing that fails adequately to grapple with the many competing priorities, trade-offs, and value judgments that should inform just punishment in a constitutional democracy. Especially in a pluralistic democracy like ours, the indeterminate and irreducibly normative nature of punishment decisions demands "multivalued rather than . . . single-valued thinking."[41] That is in part why the Court has steadfastly resisted commitment to any single purpose of punishment as a matter of constitutional law, instead insisting that the Constitution leaves room to effectuate a "constantly shifting adjustment of the tension between the evolving aims of the criminal law and changing religious, moral, philosophical, and medical views of the nature of man."[42]

Procedurally, that adjustment process involves a host of actors, each with its own strengths and perspectives on the demands of justice. In our system, just punishment is not a matter of a priori philosophical principles. It is a matter of democratic processes, of dialogue and deliberation that engages all of the considerations that plausibly inform punishment — not only its multiplicity of values, but also the different viewpoints, practical needs, and interests of stakeholders.[43] The Constitution embodies that notion in a set of arrangements designed to give content to punishment by filtering those variegated inputs through different institutional actors and mechanisms. Just and morally appropriate punishment, ideally, is what comes out of that process; it is defined by the process that produces it.

---

[40] Pepper v. United States, 131 S. Ct. 1229, 1247–50 (2011); Kimbrough v. United States, 552 U.S. 85, 111 (2007); Rita v. United States, 551 U.S. 338, 353–54 (2007); United States v. Booker, 543 U.S. 220, 258–65 (2005); *Blakely*, 542 U.S. at 303–04.

[41] Henry M. Hart, Jr., *The Aims of the Criminal Law*, 23 Law & Contemp. Probs. 401, 401 (1958).

[42] Powell v. Texas, 392 U.S. 514, 536 (1968) (plurality opinion).

[43] Variants of this theme appear repeatedly in the Court's sentencing cases. *See, e.g.*, Graham v. Florida, 560 U.S. 48, 67–68 (2010); *Rita*, 551 U.S. at 350; *Blakely*, 542 U.S. at 326 (Kennedy, J., dissenting); Skipper v. South Carolina, 476 U.S. 1, 4–5 (1986).

THE ADMINISTRATIVE LAW OF THE EIGHTH (AND SIXTH)
AMENDMENT

So we can understand the institutional and procedural framework of constitutional sentencing law to have evolved in ways that roughly parallel those of administrative law, and for roughly parallel reasons. It bears repeating here that I do not posit any necessary, historical, causal, or conscious connection between the two, or even that this pattern of evolution on the sentencing side was conscious at all. And without any such connection, attempting to draw lessons from the earlier and now more mature evolution of administrative law for the still-evolving field of sentencing law can be a hazardous and unwise business.

At the same time, one has to wonder whether the broad conceptual overlap between the two, as rough and imperfect as it may be, is more than just coincidental. After all, with some limited exceptions, neither the text of the APA nor that of the Eighth and Sixth Amendments require the frameworks I described above. Those frameworks instead are largely a construct of judicial interpretations, ones that courts have built out over time. It might just be that, in our socio-legal, cultural, and especially democratic tradition, this is how courts approach intractable questions of values — whether the meaning of public safety of just punishment — that have been delegated to governmental actors, whether agency heads or sentencers.[44]

Against that backdrop, then, let me speculate — and do no more than that — about some possible takeaways from the more-evolved realm of administrative law for the less-evolved realm of the law of sentencing. In particular, let me make three brief observations about what the history of administrative law might portend for the future of sentencing law.

First. As the law of sentencing proceeds farther and farther down the road I have outlined above, the Constitution — specifically, the particular provisions of the Eighth and Sixth Amendments — will become less and less relevant. This trend has been unmistakable in administrative law, where courts — most notably, the D.C. Circuit — have engaged in common-law elaboration of the APA in ways that have largely rendered certain parts of its text (especially those related to informal procedures) an afterthought.[45] For various reasons — inertia, path dependency, the tendency of judicial involvement to reassure outsiders that something is being

---

[44] As Stephanos Bibas and I have explained elsewhere, as a matter of political theory, a process that attempts to aggregate and reconcile the competing considerations at issue is more democratically legitimate and responsive than one left entirely to a single perspective. *See* Richard A. Bierschbach & Stephanos Bibas, *Notice-and-Comment Sentencing*, 97 MINN. L. REV. 1, 20–24 (2019).

[45] *See, e.g.*, GARY LAWSON, FEDERAL ADMINISTRATIVE LAW 262 (6th ed. 2013) (noting that "[m]-odern developments have rendered the APA's provisions for informal procedures unrecognizable to their 1946 drafters").

done — the resulting judicialization of process is difficult to roll back, as both the administrative law experience and the experience of the Court's procedural regulation of capital punishment show.[46] We can expect the judicial management of non-capital sentencing to follow a similar path, the beginnings of which I already have sketched, with courts trading their traditional roles as arbiters of truth for a more regulatory function in which their focus is to erect and oversee the best procedural and institutional structures for addressing polycentric problems.[47] This phenomenon, too, is nothing new. It occurs in many areas in which the Court starts out adjudicating a basic right, the Fourth Amendment being an obvious one.[48] Even so, acknowledging that the Court is moving from adjudicating text-based rights into designing decision-making structures for sentencing is important because it ought to prompt us to ask the comparative institutional question whether another actor or regime could do that better.[49]

Second. As reviewing courts attempt to design fair and inclusive processes for reconciling competing values and perspectives in sentencing without taking a strong substantive position on those values themselves, time-honored judicial concepts like reasonableness and reason-giving will become increasingly important. Insistence that agencies act reasonably and explain themselves on the record has long been a hallmark of judicial review of administrative agency decision-making, allowing courts — at least in theory — to ensure that an agency has grappled with the views and information before it without substituting their own judgment for that of the agency.[50] We might expect sentencing to proceed along a similar track. And indeed, outside of jury sentencing (almost exclusively the province of capital cases), where reason-giving and similar requirements would upend decades of law,[51] it already is.

---

[46] *See* Jack M. Beerman & Gary Lawson, *Reprocessing Vermont Yankee*, 75 GEO. WASH. L. REV. 856, 882–900 (2007) (noting various judicially created administrative law doctrines that substantially depart from the text of the APA despite *Vermont Yankee*'s general admonition against doing so); Carol S. Steiker & Jordan M. Steiker, *Lessons for Law Reform from the American Experiment with Capital Punishment*, 87 S. CAL. L. REV. 733, 753–54 (2014) (discussing entrenchment of capital sentencing procedures).

[47] *See* Malcolm M. Feeley, *How to Think about Criminal Court Reform*, 98 B.U. L. REV. 673, 719–20 (2018) (discussing the panoply of criminal justice problems that appellate courts theoretically must address and their limited ability to do so).

[48] *See* Orin S. Kerr, *The Fourth Amendment and New Technologies: Constitutional Myths and the Case for Caution*, 102 MICH. L. REV. 801 (2004) (discussing the evolution of the judicial role in protecting the reasonable expectation of privacy under the Fourth Amendment).

[49] *Cf. id.* at 858–59 (arguing that courts are less competent than legislatures to regulate new technologies in the Fourth Amendment context).

[50] *See* Motor Vehicle Mfrs. Ass'n v. State Farm Mut. Auto. Ins. Co., 463 U.S. 29, 43 (1983) (holding that a court reviewing agency action under the arbitrary and capricious standard should ensure that the agency has considered relevant data, statutory factors, and important aspects of the problem, but should not "substitute its judgment for that of the agency"); PIERCE ET AL., *supra* note 12, § 7.5, at 407–13 (discussing review of agency reasoning).

[51] *See* Rachel E. Barkow, *The Ascent of the Administrative State and the Demise of Mercy*, 121 HARV. L. REV. 1332, 1340 (2008) (observing that explanations are not required from jury decisionmakers).

Some courts implementing *Graham v. Florida*'s command that juvenile non-homicide offenders receive a "meaningful" opportunity for parole have tied that language to more robust requirements for back-end sentencing explanations instead of the pro forma denials that routinely come out of parole hearings.[52] Likewise, lower federal courts implementing the post-*Booker* advisory federal guidelines scheme have taken seriously the dictates that sentencing courts must "state . . . the reasons"[53] for their sentences and that appellate courts will review those sentences for "reasonableness"[54]; they are now confronting a broad and growing set of issues about how far those requirements go.[55]

As the common law of these and similar cases develops, we should be cognizant of the history of administrative law and any cautionary notes it might sound. As courts have fleshed out reasonableness and reason-giving standards under the APA, and especially in informal rulemaking, the process demands on administrative decision-makers have increased dramatically.[56] While one can argue about whether that is a good development, one undeniable consequence of it is that deciding and making policy is more cumbersome and slow moving for agencies than ever. Perhaps in response to these increased procedural and analytic demands, agencies increasingly are searching for ways around or simply not following the APA's judicially established rules.[57] We might worry that the continued fleshing out of reasonableness and reason-giving requirements for sentencing will create parallel incentives for front-line sentencers, pushing them toward paths of least resistance in the form of rote or mechanical sentences and explanations that might seem more efficient and more likely to satisfy appellate review.[58] Along similar lines, we might worry that reviewing courts will use the reasonableness standard as a hook for an especially searching inquiry, effectively substituting their own judgment for that of the actor closer to the totality of the circumstances that should inform sentencing and thereby frustrating the ability of front-line sentencers to settle on the morally

---

[52] Graham v. Florida, 560 U.S. 48, 75 (2010); Hayden v. Keller, 134 F. Supp. 3d 1000, 1008 (E.D.N.C. 2015) (holding North Carolina's typical parole review process unconstitutional under *Graham* for juvenile offenders serving life sentences).

[53] 18 U.S.C. § 3553(c) (2006).

[54] United States v. Booker, 543 U.S. 220, 261 (2005); *see also* Kimbrough v. United States, 552 U.S. 85, 90–91 (2007); Gall v. United States, 552 U.S. 38, 51 (2007); Rita v. United States, 551 U.S. 338, 350–51 (2007).

[55] For a sampling of lower court cases discussing some of the issues in play, see United States v. Marin-Castano, 688 F.3d 899, 904 (7th Cir. 2012); United States v. Rosales, 413 F. App'x. 748, 749 (5th Cir. 2011); United States v. Cereceres-Zavala, 499 F.3d 1211, 1216–18 (10th Cir. 2007); United States v. Scott, 312 F. App'x. 527, 528 (4th Cir. 2009).

[56] *See* LAWSON, *supra* note 45, at 343–44.

[57] *See* Connor Raso, *Agency Avoidance of Rulemaking Procedures*, 67 ADMIN. L. REV. 65, 67–68 & n.7 (2015).

[58] *See, e.g., Booker*, 543 U.S. at 288 (Stevens, J., dissenting in part) (arguing that a reasonableness standard of review might discourage sentencing judges from considering "relevant conduct" under 18 U.S.C. § 3553(a)).

appropriate punishment at which all sentencing aims.[59] Alternatively, we might worry that the sheer volume of sentencing cases will make reasonableness review anemic, causing appellate courts to rubber stamp all but the most egregious sentences that come before them. Clear evidence of both tendencies exists in the record of administrative law also.[60]

Attention to that record might shine some light on the future of sentencing law, despite the vastly different context. As one example, federal appellate courts continue to wrestle with the scope and limits of procedural versus substantive reasonableness review of sentences in the post-*Booker* world.[61] While a similar debate accompanied the evolution of reasonableness review of agency decision-making in the 1970s, courts now have coalesced around a "hard look" approach that includes some elements of both, even if they typically cast their reasoning in proceduralist terms.[62] Against that backdrop, the current debates in sentencing ultimately might prove overblown.

Third. As avenues of input into sentencing from different perspectives and interests increase, so too will corresponding opportunities for well-resourced actors to turn those avenues to their advantage. We see this in administrative law not only in the well-known example of agency capture, but also in the more prosaic and day-to-day ways that heavily-financed targets of regulation adeptly find and exploit procedural mechanisms that others often cannot. No reason exists to believe that sentencing will be immune from this paradox of process. Just as the coal industry lobbies and litigates against tougher clean air standards or a giant investment bank pulls every procedural lever it can to press for a favorable settlement with the Securities and Exchange Commission, so too prosecutors and prison guard unions lobby for tougher sentencing laws, corporate executives marshal teams of lawyers to negotiate deferred prosecution agreements that spare them and their companies serious sanctions, and wealthy defendants submit reams of letters to sentencing

---

[59] *Cf. id.* at 301 (questioning how courts of appeals will review district courts' decisions for reasonableness).

[60] For one illuminating discussion famous in administrative law circles, see the dueling concurring opinions of Chief Judge Bazelon and Judge Leventhal in the D.C. Circuit's en banc opinion in *Ethyl Corp. v. EPA*, 541 F.2d 1, 66–69 (D.C. Cir. 1976) (en banc).

[61] *See, e.g.*, D. Michael Fischer, *Still in Balance? Federal District Court Discretion and Appellate Review Six Years After Booker*, 49 DUQUESNE L. REV. 641, 650–54 (2011) (discussing different approaches and open questions in the courts of appeals); Craig D. Rust, *When "Reasonableness" Is Not So Reasonable: The Need to Restore Clarity to Appellate Review of Federal Sentencing Decisions after Rita, Gall, and Kimbrough*, 26 TOURO L. REV. 75, 90–102 (2010) (same). Analogous debate is appearing over procedural and substantive dimensions of *Graham*'s "meaningfulness" requirement for second-look sentencing. Sarah F. Russell & Tracy L. Denholtz, *Procedures for Proportionate Sentences: The Next Wave of Eighth Amendment Noncapital Litigation*, 48 Conn. L. Rev. 1121, 1139–50 (2016) (reviewing growing litigation over "second look" procedures after *Graham* and its progeny).

[62] LAWSON, *supra* note 44, at 752–53.

judges extolling their positive influence on their communities.[63] Less resourced and less visible interests — your average street criminal, for instance — do not have the wherewithal to do so. Unsurprisingly, the groups, communities, and individuals who bear the greatest costs of punishment are among the least well-organized and well-represented in the political process.[64] Under such circumstances, opening more nodes of influence and participation could further amplify some interests over others, with troubling substantive and distributive implications.[65]

Administrative law has not solved this problem, and it is unlikely that sentencing will either. But at least some institutional players — think of watchdog groups and public interest organizations like the National Wildlife Federation and the Sierra Club in the area of environmental law — exist in administrative law to try to add a little counterbalance to the scales, both at the level of policy and in critical individual cases. In the world of sentencing, organizations adding new and important perspectives at the policy level and in policy-making cases are growing in strength and number. Groups that can intervene and air different perspectives in the mill run of individual sentencings are comparatively rare, though recent years have seen the development of more state and local organizations that seek to influence outcomes at other stages of the criminal process.[66] Beyond external groups, policymakers designing sentencing institutions might focus on making them as inclusive as possible. That could mean, for instance, making sure that state sentencing commissions and parole boards, among other bodies, contain or work with a wide cross-section of stakeholders, including victims, ex-offenders, members of their families, community members, and representatives of various professional and public interest groups.[67]

---

[63] *See, e.g.*, Rachel E. Barkow, *Federalism and the Politics of Sentencing*, 105 Colum. L. Rev. 1276, 1281–83 (2005) (explaining how interest group pressures push politicians and policymakers toward ever-harsher sentencing laws).

[64] *Id.* at 1282 (observing that the direct targets of sentencing policy and their allies "have little political weight" and "do not have a strong voice in the political process"); Darryl K. Brown, *Street Crime, Corporate Crime, and the Contingency of Criminal Liability*, 149 U. Pa. L. Rev. 1295, 1343 (2001) (noting that those wealthy enough to have a political voice in lawmaking and enforcement and to increase the costs that criminal procedures impose on the government "have had more success responding to the … criminal law that they face"); Darryl K. Brown, *Third-Party Interests in Criminal Law*, 80 Tex. L. Rev. 1383, 1401 (2002) (discussing weight given to third-party interests at charging and sentencing in white-collar criminal cases).

[65] For two excellent treatments of this effect, one dealing with policing and one dealing with criminal justice policymaking, see Lisa L. Miller, The Perils of Federalism: Race, Poverty, and the Politics of Crime Control (2008), and Rachel A. Harmon, *Federal Programs and the Real Costs of Policing*, 90 N.Y.U. L. Rev. 870 (2015).

[66] *See, e.g.*, Jocelyn Simonson, *Bail Nullification*, 115 Mich. L. Rev. 585 (2017) (analyzing the growing phenomenon of community bail funds).

[67] *See* Rachel E. Barkow, *Administering Crime*, 52 UCLA L. Rev. 715, 782–84 (2005) (reviewing design and membership of the North Carolina Sentencing and Policy Advisory Commission, one of the country's "most diverse"); *cf.* W. David Ball, *Normative Elements of Parole Risk*, 22 Stan. L. & Pol'y Rev. 395, 407–10 (2011) (proposing the idea of a "parole jury").

* * *

Administrative law and the constitutional law of sentencing are vastly different beasts. We cannot and should not glibly compare the two, and readers should not take this chapter as suggesting otherwise. But the paths they tread — and some of the forces that impel them — might not be as radically dissimilar as their appearances lead us to believe. As constitutional and sub-constitutional sentencing law evolves, we might do well to ruminate on possible parallels between the two fields, and what insights, if any, the history of the one holds for the future of the other. [68]

---

[68] Some scholars — most notably, Rachel Barkow — have made valuable contributions to this general project already. *See, e.g.,* Barkow, *supra* note 51; Barkow, *supra* note 63; Barkow, *supra* note 67.

9

Evading the Eighth Amendment

Prison Conditions and the Courts

Sharon Dolovich[*]

The Eighth Amendment prohibition on "cruel and unusual punishment" places moral limits on what the state may do to people convicted of crimes.[1] But because constitutional norms "are too vague to serve as rules of law," courts need doctrinal standards to guide their analysis in concrete cases.[2] In the American constitutional scheme, it falls to the Supreme Court to craft these standards. Translating constitutional values into workable rules will inevitably entail some cost to the full enforcement of those values, which makes the Court a site of ongoing struggle over the scope of constitutional protections.[3] On paper, this struggle plays out in legal abstractions. Yet when the claimants are prisoners seeking to challenge the conditions of their confinement, the human stakes could not be higher. The greater

---

[*] Professor of Law, UCLA School of Law. Thanks to Will Berry and Meghan Ryan for inviting me to contribute to this volume, Sasha Natapoff for characteristically insightful comments, and Tiffany Sarchet and the UCLA Hugh & Hazel Darling Law Library reference librarians for their research assistance.

[1] *See* Furman v. Georgia, 408 U.S. 238, 382 (1972) (Burger, C. J., dissenting) ("The standard of extreme cruelty is not merely descriptive, but necessarily embodies a moral judgment.").

[2] Richard H. Fallon, Jr., *Foreword: Implementing the Constitution*, 111 HARV. L. REV. 54, 57 (1997).

[3] *See* Richard H. Fallon, Jr., *Judicially Manageable Standards and Constitutional Meaning*, 119 HARV. L. REV. 1275 (2006). Some commentators have endorsed what has come to be called the "pragmatic" view, on which the Constitution encompasses only those protections provided by the governing judicial doctrine, and no more. *See, e.g.*, Roderick M. Hills, Jr., *The Pragmatist's View of Constitutional Implementation and Constitutional Meaning*, 119 HARV. L. REV. F. 173 (2006); Daryl J. Levinson, *Rights Essentialism and Remedial Equilibration*, 99 COLUM. L. REV. 857 (1999). Others take a more aspirational view, on which the limited constitutional protections typically afforded by courts do not represent the whole of constitutional meaning, but instead indicate a gap between constitutional doctrine and normative constitutional entitlements. *See, e.g.*, Fallon, *supra*, at 1317; Lawrence Gene Sager, *Fair Measure: The Legal Status of Underenforced Constitutional Norms*, 91 HARV. L. REV. 1212, 1213 (1978). As should be clear, I subscribe to the latter, aspirational view, which forms the backdrop to this chapter.

the "slippage" between Eighth Amendment norms and their enforcement,[4] the broader the judicial permission conferred on correctional officers to treat the incarcerated with cruelty — an effect that will cash out, every day, in increased physical suffering and psychological trauma for the real live flesh-and-blood people living in American prisons.[5]

This chapter traces the evolution of the governing standards for Eighth Amendment prison conditions claims. It argues that the Supreme Court's early efforts to shape those standards looked set to enable judicial determinations consistent with fundamental Eighth Amendment moral imperatives, but that, in later cases, the Court betrayed that early promise by, among other things, conditioning findings of unconstitutional conditions on defendants' subjective awareness of the risk of harm. Though seemingly simple, this move in fact entailed a radical shift away from meaningful enforcement, allowing courts to dismiss prisoners' claims without ever squarely confronting either the character of the challenged conditions or their consistency with core Eighth Amendment values. The effect was to leave the people we incarcerate — fellow human beings — wholly dependent for their survival on state officials with no constitutional obligation even to notice obvious dangers to prisoners' health and safety. This arrangement all but guarantees needless pain and suffering for people in prison, a result directly at odds with the Court's repeated assertion that the Eighth Amendment prohibits the "unnecessary and wanton infliction of pain."[6] And recent signs from the new Roberts Court suggest that people in prison may soon face an Eighth Amendment regime even less protective than the already diminished standards that currently govern.

THE FEDERAL COURTS OPEN THE DOORS

Today, it is taken for granted that prison conditions are open to Eighth Amendment challenge. But it was not always so. For much of the twentieth century, the federal courts largely took a "hands-off" posture toward prisoners' constitutional claims. However brutal prison conditions were during this period — and they were brutal indeed[7] — the federal courts almost uniformly subscribed to the view that

---

[4] *See* Sager, *supra* note 3, at 1213.

[5] *See* Robert Cover, *The Bonds of Constitutional Interpretation: Of the Word, the Deed, and the Role*, 20 GA. L. REV. 815, 818 (1986) ("The Constitution's connection to violence is not confined to our Revolutionary origins . . . . [J]udges also deal in pain and death . . . . Even the violence of weak judges is utterly real . . . . Take a short trip to your local prison and see.").

[6] *See, e.g.,* Whitley v. Albers, 475 U.S. 312, 319 (1986); Rhodes v. Chapman, 452 U.S. 337, 347 (1981); Estelle v. Gamble, 429 U.S. 97, 102–03 (1976).

[7] *See, e.g.,* Atterbury v. Ragen, 237 F.2d 953, 954 (7th Cir. 1956); Pugh v. Locke, 406 F. Supp. 318 (M.D. Ala. 1976); MONA LYNCH, SUNBELT JUSTICE: ARIZONA AND THE TRANSFORMATION OF AMERICAN PUNISHMENT (2009); ROBERT PERKINSON, TEXAS TOUGH: THE RISE OF AMERICA'S PRISON EMPIRE (2010); Matthew L. Myers, *The Alabama Case: 12 Years after James v. Wallace*, 13 NAT'L PRISON PROJECT J. 8 (1987), *reprinted in* LYNN S. BRANHAM, THE LAW AND POLICY OF SENTENCING AND CORRECTIONS 472 (9th ed. 2013); WRIT WRITER (New Day Films 2009).

"it is not the function of the courts to superintend the treatment and discipline of prisoners in penitentiaries."[8] As a consequence, even people whose conditions of confinement plainly transgressed constitutional values had no forum in which to bring their claims.

Despite the evident unwillingness of the judiciary to entertain prisoner suits, federal judges had long received complaints from people incarcerated in state prisons.[9] By the 1960s, motivated at least in part by the "soul-chilling" conditions described in those missives,[10] a number of federal courts had started to soften their hands-off posture.[11] And once they began to look behind the walls, what they saw led at least some judges to abandon that posture completely. This dramatic shift occurred first in Arkansas, where litigation begun in 1965 revealed "the savage and quasi-feral character of the Arkansas prisons."[12] By 1970, Judge J. Smith Henley of the Eastern District of Arkansas had held the state's prison system "in its entirety [to be] in violation of the Eighth Amendment," and had "placed the system under a comprehensive court order that was tantamount to federal receivership."[13] In the ensuing decades, prison officials in Alabama, Georgia, Louisiana, Mississippi and countless other states found themselves in the same situation as their Arkansas counterparts.[14]

---

[8]   *Atterbury*, 257 F.2d at 955 (internal quotation marks omitted).

[9]   *See* MALCOM M. FEELEY & EDWARD L. RUBIN, JUDICIAL POLICY MAKING AND THE MODERN STATE: HOW THE COURTS REFORMED AMERICA'S PRISONS 34–35 (1998) ("It is somewhat curious, given the evident hostility of most federal courts to prisoner complaints, that these prisoner complaints kept coming [to the courts]."); *see also Atterbury*, 237 F.2d at 955 (expressing concern "at the ever-increasing number of [complaints] which are filed in this Circuit" that allege "brutal treatment by prison officials or other complaints with reference to the regulations pertaining to prison discipline," and emphasizing that "for the most part, such . . . suits are futile").

[10]   *Rhodes*, 452 U.S. at 354 (Brennan, J., concurring) (quoting Inmates of Suffolk County Jail v. Eisenstadt, 360 F. Supp. 676, 684 (Mass. 1973)).

[11]   FEELEY & RUBIN, supra note 9, at 37.

[12]   *Id.* at 39.

[13]   *See id.* at 39; *see also id.* at 51–79 (discussing the Arkansas prison litigation in detail).

[14]   *See* Williams v. Edwards, 547 F.2d 1206 (5th Cir. 1977) (Louisiana); Pugh v. Locke, 406 F. Supp. 318 (M.D. Ala. 1976); Guthrie v. Evans, No. 73-3068 (S.D. Ga. 1973); Gates v. Collier, 349 F. Supp. 881 (N.D. Miss. 1972); *see also* FEELEY & RUBIN, *supra* note 9, at 39–92 (discussing the spread of judicial prison reform). That these prisons were almost exclusively Southern reflects the deep connection in the American South between incarceration and the practice and culture of slavery. As the mechanism for controlling black bodies shifted from slavery to criminal punishment, brutality against the enslaved readily turned into brutality against the imprisoned, the vast majority of whom were black. *See* DOUGLAS A. BLACKMON, SLAVERY BY ANOTHER NAME: THE RE-ENSLAVEMENT OF BLACK AMERICANS FROM THE CIVIL WAR TO WORLD WAR II (2008); DAVID M. OSHINSKY, WORSE THAN SLAVERY: PARCHMAN FARM AND THE ORDEAL OF JIM CROW JUSTICE (1997); Taja-Nia Henderson, *Property, Penality and (Racial) Profiling*, 12 STAN. J. C.R. & C.L. 177 (2016) (describing the role local jails played in supporting enslavers and the institution of chattel slavery itself in the antebellum South); John Bardes, *The Problem of Incarceration in the Age of Slavery* 5, 43–47 (draft copy on file with the author) (describing a network of carceral institutions forming a "statewide penal system for

It was not until 1962, in *Robinson v. California*, that the Supreme Court incorporated the Eighth Amendment against the states via the Fourteenth Amendment.[15] With *Robinson* being so new, governing Eighth Amendment precedent in the 1960s was thin, leaving those courts newly open to hearing conditions claims to mine past decisions for whatever principles seemed most appropriate to this new context. When it came time to apply those principles, the reasoning was mostly conclusory. The focus was instead on the facts, with judges largely taking a totality of the circumstances/totality of the conditions approach. Given the barbarism of the conditions courts were confronting — "dangerously overcrowded,"[16] "a dark and evil world,"[17] "unfit for human habitation"[18] — the tendency to cut analytical corners should not have been surprising. But at some point, "[o]nce the very worst practices were successfully attacked" and the follow-on cases began to emerge, more formal legal analysis would be required.[19] At that point, judges would need workable standards against which to assess challenged conditions, to allow them to determine whether, given their nature and impact, those conditions violated Eighth Amendment limits on state punishment.

This last point bears emphasizing: to enable courts hearing Eighth Amendment prison conditions claims to reach valid judgments of constitutionality, the applicable doctrine would need to (1) direct courts to examine the impact of the conditions at issue, and (2) provide evaluative standards that, in their application, would operationalize the Eighth Amendment's governing moral imperatives. Otherwise, even if dispositive on constitutional liability, a judicial finding for defendants would have no bearing on what is, after all, the essential question when evaluating the constitutionality of carceral punishment: whether the challenged conditions are consistent with prison officials' Eighth Amendment obligations to prisoners.[20]

Given the broad and novel authority being claimed by the federal courts to regulate state prisons during this period, it was only a matter of time before the Supreme Court weighed in. The Court's earliest efforts came in 1976 and 1981

enslaved convicts" in Louisiana, Mississippi, Tennessee, and elsewhere in the antebellum South, and describing the brutal methods of torture employed to humiliate and "discipline" the enslaved people held in those facilities).

[15] *See* Robinson v. California, 370 U.S. 660 (1962).

[16] Costello v. Wainwright, 397 F. Supp. 20, 34 (1975).

[17] Hutto v. Finney, 437 U.S. 678, 681 (1970) (quoting Holt v. Sarver, 309 F. Supp. 362, 382 (E.D. Ark. 1970)) (opinion of Judge Henley).

[18] *Pugh*, 406 F. Supp. at 323–24; *Gates*, 349 F. Supp. at 894; *see also* Ramos v. Lamm, 639 F.2d 559, 567 (10th Cir. 1980).

[19] Malcom M. Feeley & Roger A. Hanson, *The Impact of Judicial Intervention on Prisons and Jails: A Framework for Analysis and a Review of the Literature, in* COURTS, CORRECTIONS, AND THE CONSTITUTION 12, 28 (John J. Dilulio, Jr. ed., 1990).

[20] *See* Sharon Dolovich, *Canons of Evasion in Constitutional Criminal Law, in* THE NEW CRIMINAL JUSTICE THINKING (Sharon Dolovich & Alexandra Natapoff, eds., 2017); *see also* *supra* note 3 (acknowledging the overtly aspirational approach to constitutional interpretation this chapter embraces).

with *Estelle v. Gamble*[21] and *Rhodes v. Chapman*.[22] Together, this pair of cases addressed the two types of conditions claims prisoners might bring: micro-level assertions of personal mistreatment by individual officers, and macro-level challenges to system-wide failures of care. Although the defendants prevailed in both cases, *Gamble* and *Rhodes* nonetheless laid a foundation for doctrinal standards that would have allowed courts to effectively operationalize the Eighth Amendment's animating moral commitments and thus to meaningfully enforce prisoners' constitutional rights.

Then, with a second pair of cases in the early 1990s — *Wilson v. Seiter*[23] and *Farmer v. Brennan*[24] — the Court shifted the inquiry, directing courts away from the conditions themselves and toward what defendants did or did not know about the risk of harm to prisoners. This is where the law currently stands. To the extent that, in the wake of *Wilson* and *Farmer*, courts are still to consider the conditions themselves, it is only within the narrowest possible frame, from a perspective that inevitably leaves unaddressed or even unacknowledged conditions that deeply compromise the overall safety and well-being of those inside. This shift substantially narrowed prison officials' constitutional obligations and has left prisoners' constitutional rights correspondingly underenforced — with the price to be paid by the incarcerated in increased physical pain and psychological trauma.

The sections that follow trace this doctrinal evolution from early promise to eventual contraction and also consider what the Court's 2019 decision in *Bucklew v. Precythe* portends for the future of Eighth Amendment prison conditions claims.[25] But first, it is necessary to briefly consider the normative limits the Eighth Amendment places on the treatment of prisoners. If we had a system of Eighth Amendment enforcement that sought to reflect this provision's animating values, what obligations would the state be held to owe the people we have collectively chosen to incarcerate? Only once we have answered this question will we be equipped to recognize which standards would best enable judicial enforcement of Eighth Amendment imperatives in the conditions context and why the current regime falls so far short of the mark.

THE EIGHTH AMENDMENT ROOTS OF THE STATE'S CARCERAL BURDEN

What limits does the Eighth Amendment place on the conditions of prisoners' confinement? In our constitutional system, it is widely agreed that the state may not, in the name of criminal punishment, inflict torture or "other barbarous

---

[21] Estelle v. Gamble, 429 U.S. 97 (1976).
[22] Rhodes v. Chapman, 452 U.S. 337 (1981).
[23] Wilson v. Seiter, 501 U.S. 294 (1991).
[24] Farmer v. Brennan, 511 U.S. 825 (1994).
[25] Bucklew v. Precythe, 139 S. Ct. 1112 (2019).

methods of punishment."[26] Nor may accepted forms of punishment be applied in ways that cause gratuitous pain and suffering. As the Supreme Court has recognized, such treatment would at worst amount to torture, and at best constitute the "unnecessary and wanton infliction of pain," serving no legitimate penal purpose.[27] Either way, it would represent an abuse of the state's penal power.

The prohibition on gratuitously harmful prison conditions is thus a fundamental Eighth Amendment principle. The Supreme Court has explicitly acknowledged as much, holding that, under the Eighth Amendment, the state is obliged to provide people in custody with "the minimal civilized measure of life's necessities"[28] and to protect them from "substantial risk[s] of serious harm"[29] — by, among other things, treating their serious medical needs[30] and keeping them safe from violence at the hands of other prisoners.[31] As Chief Justice Rehnquist explained in *DeShaney v. Winnebago County*, "when the State takes a person into its custody and holds him there against his will, the Constitution imposes upon it a corresponding duty to assume some responsibility for his safety and general well-being."[32] This "affirmative duty to protect" arises "from the limitation which [the State] has imposed on [the detained individual's] freedom to act on his own behalf."[33] The state's obligation, in other words, arises from prisoners' total dependence on prison officials, a function of the government's own decision to incarcerate people under conditions depriving them of the capacity to meet their own needs.[34]

Even in the Court's later cases, one finds overt acknowledgment of this obligation. In *Farmer*, for example, the Court emphasized just how dangerous prisons can be and how vulnerable the people inside would be without state aid. As Justice Souter put it, "having stripped [incarcerated persons] of virtually every means of self-protection and foreclosed their access to outside aid, the government and its officials are not free to let the state of nature take its course."[35] It must instead "provide

---

[26] Estelle v. Gamble, 429 U.S. 97, 102 (1976) (internal quotations omitted); *see also* Wilkerson v. Utah, 99 U.S. 130, 135 (1879) (citing cases "where the prisoner was drawn or dragged to the place of execution . . . [or] embowelled alive, beheaded, and quartered" as examples of tortures forbidden by the Eighth Amendment).

[27] *See Estelle*, 429 U.S. at 103.

[28] Rhodes v. Chapman, 452 U.S. 337, 347 (1981).

[29] Farmer v. Brennan, 511 U.S. 825, 828 (1994).

[30] *See Estelle*, 429 U.S. at 103–04.

[31] *See Farmer*, 511 U.S. at 833.

[32] DeShaney v. Winnebago County Department of Social Services, 489 U.S. 189, 199–200 (1989).

[33] *Id.* at 200.

[34] *See id.* (explaining that the state's duty of care towards the incarcerated arises because "the State by the affirmative exercise of its power so restrains an individual's liberty that it renders him unable to care for himself"); *see also* Sharon Dolovich, *Cruelty, Prison Conditions, and the Eighth Amendment*, 84 N.Y.U. L. REV. 881, 911–23 (2009).

[35] *Farmer*, 511 U.S. at 833 (citing *DeShaney*, 489 U.S. at 199–200, along with other opinions) (internal citations and quotation marks omitted); *see also* Estelle, 429 U.S. at 103 ("An [incarcerated person] must rely on prison authorities to treat his medical needs; if the authorities fail to do so, those needs will not be met.").

humane conditions of confinement[,] . . . ensure that [people] receive adequate food, clothing, shelter, and medical care, and . . . 'take reasonable measures to guarantee [their] safety.'"[36]

In short, when the state opts to incarcerate people convicted of crimes, it commits itself to providing for their basic needs as long as they are in custody. This, as I have argued elsewhere, is *the state's carceral burden*.[37] More than simply a moral imperative, meeting this burden is a fundamental constitutional requirement, arising directly from the Eighth Amendment prohibition on "cruel and unusual punishment," which forbids "the unnecessary and wanton infliction of pain."[38]

The state, however, is not a natural person, but rather a complex organization. As such, it cannot act independently of the officials authorized to act on its behalf. This means that, if the state's carceral burden is to be fulfilled, prison officials must make it happen. It is therefore to prison officials themselves that the constitutional duty attaches.[39] What is the nature of this duty? Here, the answer emerges from the Court's own reasoning: The incarcerated are held against their will in close quarters with people who are possibly dangerous and are wholly dependent on state officials for their basic needs. This being so, Chief Justice Rehnquist was right to label this duty an *affirmative* one[40] — not a passive obligation on the part of prison officials to respond to the problems they happen to notice, but an ongoing responsibility to monitor, to investigate, to stay on top of potential threats and to be proactive in their alleviation. Although constitutional in origin, this affirmative obligation is no different from any duty of care pursuant to which duty holders are expected to take all appropriate steps to keep their charges safe. It is not episodic but continuous. At the same time, as with any duty of care, prison officials' liability is not unlimited. Here, failures of care amounting to the "wanton and unnecessary infliction of pain" warrant condemnation as unconstitutional. If the burden the Eighth Amendment imposes on prison officials is considerable, it is not strict liability. When people suffer harm in custody as a result of forces about which no correctional officer knew or could have reasonably been expected to know even had he been paying proper attention,[41] the resulting treatment could in no way be said to be "cruel." In such cases, Eighth Amendment liability would be inappropriate.[42]

The key takeaway is this: the Eighth Amendment imposes on prison officials an affirmative duty to ensure in an ongoing way the health and safety of incarcerated

---

[36] *Farmer*, 511 U.S. at 832 (quoting Hudson v. Palmer, 468 U.S. 517, 526–27 (1984)).

[37] Dolovich, *supra* note 34, at 911–23.

[38] *Estelle*, 429 U.S. at 103.

[39] *See* Dolovich, *supra* note 34, at 923–30.

[40] *See DeShaney*, 489 U.S. at 200 (explaining that the State's "affirmative duty to protect arises not from the State's knowledge of the individual's predicament or from its expressions of intent to help him, but from the limitation which it has imposed on his freedom to act on his own behalf").

[41] *See* Dolovich, *supra* note 34, at 940–43.

[42] For discussion, see *id.* at 924–26, 940–42.

persons. This is not simply the thin obligation of providing people only with the minimum inputs they need to remain alive and perhaps protected from the worst forms of physical violence. For one thing, psychological trauma can cause severe pain and suffering even when there is no accompanying physical harm.[43] Thus, even on a thin reading of the state's carceral burden, prison officials would still be obliged not to leave people, for example, living daily with a justifiable fear of violence or of inadequate treatment should they receive a serious medical or mental health diagnosis.

Even beyond the need to protect prisoners from ongoing trauma, to read prison officials' constitutional obligations as solely about keeping people alive is to strip the Eighth Amendment of much of its moral force. As the Court has made clear, the Eighth Amendment embodies "broad and idealistic concepts of dignity, civilized standards, humanity and decency."[44] These are the values that give shape to the state's carceral burden. If the Constitution "does not mandate comfortable prisons,"[45] it nonetheless prohibits treatment at odds with basic decency and with the humanity and dignity of the people we punish.[46] It therefore obliges state officials to engage with people inside, not as some lower form of life that merely needs to keep drawing breath for the state's burden to be discharged, but as fellow human beings whose suffering and despair demand a moral response regardless of whether some measure of criminal punishment may be warranted.

As we will see, the Court's initial efforts to shape the doctrine seemed to reflect this understanding. But when the Court revisited the issue in the 1990s, it radically minimized the state's carceral burden. The effect was to leave the people we punish, and society itself, lacking an effective channel for ensuring that the treatment of prisoners comports with fundamental Eighth Amendment values.

A PROMISING START

Estelle v. Gamble was the first Supreme Court case to directly apply the Eighth Amendment to prison conditions. Gamble, a Texas prisoner, alleged that prison officials violated the Eighth Amendment by failing to adequately treat a back injury

---

[43] *See, e.g.*, Wisniewski v. Kennard, 901 F.2d 1276, 1277 (5th Cir. 1990) (explaining that the correctional officer "placed his revolver in [the plaintiff's] mouth [and] threatened to blow his head off"), *cited in* Hudson v. McMillian, 503 U.S. 1, 16 (1992) (Blackmun, J., concurring).

[44] Estelle v. Gamble, 429 U.S. 97, 102 (1976) (quoting Jackson v. Bishop, 404 F.2d 571, 579 (8th Cir. 1968) (opinion of then-Judge Harry Blackmun)); *see also infra* note 47.

[45] Rhodes v. Chapman, 452 U.S. 337, 349 (1981).

[46] *See* Furman v. Georgia, 408 U.S. 238, 271 (1972) (Brennan, J., concurring) ("The primary principle [of the Eighth Amendment] is that a punishment must not be so severe as to be degrading to the dignity of human beings."); Trop v. Dulles, 356 U.S. 86, 100 (1958) (plurality opinion) ("The basic concept underlying the Eighth Amendment is nothing less than the dignity of man.").

he sustained when "a 600-pound bale of cotton fell upon him during a prison work assignment."[47] Using language acknowledging the state's carceral burden, Justice Marshall, writing for the majority, noted that prisoners are completely dependent on prison officials to treat their medical needs and that, if "the authorities fail to [provide treatment], those needs will not be met."[48] In the worst cases, Justice Marshall found, such a failure would amount to "physical torture or a lingering death," and even in "less serious cases, ... may result in [gratuitous] pain and suffering."[49] Finding "[t]he infliction of such unnecessary suffering ... inconsistent with contemporary standards of decency," the Court held that "deliberate indifference to serious medical needs of prisoners constitutes the 'unnecessary and wanton infliction of pain' proscribed by the Eighth Amendment."[50]

Gamble's deliberate indifference standard established the constitutional relevance of the defendant's state of mind vis-à-vis the challenged condition. That any attention at all should be paid to this matter may at first seem wrongheaded: if the issue is the way people are treated in prison, surely the only relevant consideration is the harm prison conditions inflict. This view, suggestive of strict liability, seemed to underpin Justice Stevens's *Gamble* dissent, in which he charged the majority with "improperly attach[ing] significance to the subjective motivation of the defendant."[51] As Justice Stevens saw it, "whether the constitutional standard has been violated should turn on the character of the punishment rather than the motivation of the individual who inflicted it."[52]

As already noted, if the Eighth Amendment imposes a considerable burden on prison officials, it cannot fairly be read to establish strict liability. There was, however, another way to understand *Gamble*'s deliberate indifference standard, one that would still accommodate Justice Stevens's view that the primary focus should be on the character of the conditions themselves: as a constructive knowledge standard, on which prison officials would be constitutionally liable for failing to address those risks of which they should have known. As we will see, this approach would substantially capture the state's carceral burden and thus enable courts to operationalize prison officials' Eighth Amendment obligation to meet this burden. At the same time, appropriately, it would shield prison officials from liability for harms that could not reasonably be anticipated even by those officers fully committed to protecting people from gratuitous physical and psychological harm.

In *Gamble*, the Court did not specify the precise mental state that constituted deliberate indifference. But it said enough to narrow it down to two possibilities:

---

[47] Gamble v. Estelle, 516 F.2d 937, 938 (5th Cir. 1975), *rev'd*, 429 U.S. 97 (1976).
[48] *Estelle*, 429 U.S. at 103.
[49] *Id.*
[50] *Id.* at 104 (quoting Gregg v. Georgia, 428 U.S. 153, 182–83 (1976)).
[51] *Id.* at 116 (Stevens, J., dissenting).
[52] *Id.*

heightened (a.k.a. "gross") negligence and criminal recklessness. Unlike intentional conduct, which is undertaken purposely, these two intermediate mental states represent the available states of mind with which actors engage in risky conduct and unintentionally cause harm to others. The difference between the two is the defendant's level of knowledge with respect to the risk they have created: on criminal recklessness, the defendant must have actually realized the risk, whereas on gross negligence it is enough to show constructive knowledge, i.e. that the defendant should have realized the risk.

Were deliberate indifference read as an actual knowledge standard, the focus would be on whether the defendant in fact recognized the risk of harm posed by the conditions at issue. On this approach, correctional officers who failed to notice the risk could not be found constitutionally liable, no matter how great the danger or how obvious it would have been to the defendants had they been paying proper attention. A credible showing that defendants lacked such subjective awareness would be the end of it, leaving no need to consider either the character of the conditions or any harm they may have caused the plaintiffs.

By contrast, on a constructive knowledge standard, the relevant perspective would be that of a reasonable correctional officer committed to fulfilling the state's carceral burden. To establish this state of mind, courts would have to squarely address the conditions at issue. Any reasonableness standard, of course, has subjective elements. As the Model Penal Code explains, the factfinder is to consider what a reasonable person would have known in the situation in which the defendant found himself, given "the nature and purpose of the [defendant's conduct] and the circumstances known to him."[53] Reasonable people, appropriately committed to fulfilling their obligations, can still miss things. But even taking the defendant's perspective into account in these ways, no constructive knowledge finding could be made without careful consideration of the reality on the ground. And the worse the conditions, the more one could expect a reasonable correctional officer to have recognized the dangers they represented.

If the goal is to minimize the gap between constitutional meaning and constitutional doctrine,[54] the question then becomes: which standard — actual knowledge or constructive knowledge — best comports with the moral imperatives animating the Eighth Amendment? Given the nature of prison officials' constitutional obligations canvassed above, the answer should be obvious. Under the Eighth Amendment, state officials have an affirmative obligation to the incarcerated — an ongoing responsibility to pay attention to the conditions they face, to notice potential dangers as those dangers arise, and to be proactive in taking the necessary steps to mitigate any risks of harm. It is a constructive knowledge standard

---

[53] MODEL PENAL CODE § 2.02 (d) (AM. LAW INST. 1985).
[54] See text accompanying notes 90–93 for a discussion (and refutation) of the most likely institutional justifications for underenforcement in this context.

that best reflects this obligation and thus represents the better reading of *Gamble*'s deliberate indifference requirement. Although on this approach the defendant's state of mind would constitute a component of the analysis (thus foreclosing strict liability), such a standard would still channel judicial attention in the direction Justice Stevens advocated: toward "the character of the punishment and not the motivation of the individual who inflicted it."[55]

After *Gamble*, prisoners alleging Eighth Amendment medical neglect were required to show that defendants were deliberately indifferent to their serious medical needs. Yet when, in the 1981 case of *Rhodes v. Chapman*, the Court next entertained an Eighth Amendment prison conditions challenge, it mentioned no state of mind requirement at all, deliberate indifference or otherwise. This silence, and *Rhodes*'s exclusive focus on the nature and impact of the conditions themselves, may seem at odds with *Gamble*'s central holding. However, once we recognize the essential difference between the types of conditions the two cases address, it becomes clear that what may appear to be a doctrinal conflict is only a matter of emphasis. It also becomes apparent just how close the Court came in this pair of cases to mapping an approach that, had it been solidified as governing doctrine, could have bridged the gap between Eighth Amendment values and constitutional doctrine for the prison context.

Rhodes involved a challenge out of Southern Ohio Correctional Facility (SOCF) to the use of double celling — i.e., housing two people in cells designed for one.[56] The District Court enjoined the practice, and the Sixth Circuit affirmed.[57] Although not a model of clarity, Justice Powell's majority opinion emphasized that, under the Eighth Amendment, "conditions must not involve the wanton and unnecessary infliction of pain." It also invoked as guiding authority the Court's 1978 holding in *Hutto v. Finney*, which had found conditions in two Arkansas prisons unconstitutional "because they resulted in unquestioned and serious deprivations of basic human needs."[58] On the strength of these principles, Justice Powell concluded that conditions, "alone or in combination, may deprive [people in custody] of the minimal civilized measure of life's necessities" and thus "could be cruel and unusual under the contemporary standard of decency."[59]

It was left to Justice Brennan in his *Rhodes* concurrence to provide courts with legible guidelines for applying this holding. First, Justice Brennan explained, courts are to scrutinize the conditions themselves, mindful that "individual conditions

---

[55] Estelle v. Gamble, 429 U.S. 97, 116 (1976) (Stevens, J., dissenting).

[56] Double celling emerged as a standard practice in the late 1970s and early 1980s, when the increase in the incarceration rate began to outpace the speed with which prison officials could authorize and build new prisons. It is now the norm in most American carceral facilities.

[57] *See* Rhodes v. Chapman, 452 U.S. 337, 344 (1981).

[58] *Id.* at 347 (citing Hutto v. Finney, 437 U.S. 678 (1978)).

[59] *Id.*

'exist in combination ... and taken together they may have a cumulative impact.'"[60] Second, they must apply "realistic yet humane standards to the conditions as observed." Although acknowledging the "elusive" nature of this "aspect of the judicial inquiry," Justice Brennan emphasized that the "touchstone is the effect on the imprisoned."[61] And when the "'cumulative impact of the conditions of incarceration threatens [the] physical, mental, and emotional health and well-being' [of those in custody] ... the court must conclude that the conditions violate the Constitution."[62]

Justice Brennan's "totality of the circumstances" framework makes sense.[63] If it is possible to individually itemize the basic requirements for sustaining life and even for ensuring a humane and decent existence, any determination as to whether a carceral experience is bearable, much less humane, can only be made holistically. Conditions that may be scarcely endurable in isolation — say, persistently unpalatable food or crowded living quarters or an absence of meaningful pursuits — may well become wholly *un*endurable when lived all at once. It was this view — that to assess the constitutionality of prison conditions, those conditions must be considered *in toto* — that the district courts largely adopted in the omnibus conditions cases that predated *Gamble*. In his *Rhodes* opinion, Justice Brennan gave shape to this understanding, explaining that courts should determine constitutionality by asking whether "exposure to the cumulative effects of prison conditions" amounts "to cruel and unusual punishment."[64]

In *Rhodes*, the Court clearly endorsed a focus on the conditions themselves, "alone or in combination." But Justice Powell's opinion was also notable for what it did not say, i.e., anything to suggest the doctrinal relevance of defendants' culpability for the harm caused.[65] It would, however, be a mistake to read this silence as an endorsement of strict liability. For one thing, as already noted, this reading would stretch the scope of the state's carceral burden well beyond its constitutional moorings. Moreover, the Court made clear in *Gamble* that ordinary civil negligence would be insufficient to ground an Eighth Amendment medical neglect claim,[66] a constraint plainly incompatible with a strict liability standard.

---

[60] *Id.* at 362 (quoting Holt v. Sarver, 309 F. Supp. 362, 373 (E.D. Ark. 1970)).

[61] *Id.* at 363–64 (quoting Laaman v. Helgemoe, 437 F. Supp. 269, 323 (N.H. 1977)).

[62] *Id.* at 364 (quoting *Laaman*, 437 F. Supp. at 323).

[63] Rhodes v. Chapman, 452 U.S. 337, 362–63 (1981) (Brennan, J., concurring).

[64] *Id.* at 363 (quoting *Laaman*, 437 F. Supp. at 322–23).

[65] Indeed, the term "deliberate indifference" surfaced only once in the *Rhodes* majority, in Justice Powell's recounting of *Gamble*'s holding. *See id.* at 347 (majority opinion).

[66] *See* Estelle v. Gamble, 429 U.S. 97, 105 (1976) ("An accident, although it may produce added anguish, is not on that basis alone [unconstitutional]."); *see also id.* ("[I]n the [prison] medical context, an inadvertent failure to provide adequate medical care cannot be said to constitute an unnecessary and wanton infliction of harm [violating the Eighth Amendment]." (internal quotation marks omitted)).

If just five years after *Gamble*, the Court meant to reverse itself on this salient point, it is unlikely to have done so *sub silentio*.

In any case, *Rhodes* lends itself to a very different reading, one that is still entirely consistent with the understanding of *Gamble* offered above: that under some circumstances, prison officials' culpability for failures of care may be inferred from the character of the conditions themselves. It is plain that double celling at SOCF could only have been implemented via an affirmative decision on the part of prison administrators to respond to overcrowding by putting bunk beds in single-person cells. And, as any prison official will know, all decisions affecting the living environment in prison can potentially impact physical safety and psychological well-being. For this reason, responsible officials, concerned with maintaining prisoners' health and safety, would only ever institute double celling after carefully considering the consequences of doing so — and having done so, would continuously monitor the effects and remain alert to any danger signs. If double celling at SOCF proved to put people at risk of "serious mental, emotional, and physical deterioration," this is something about which the defendants *should* have known, if not immediately, then certainly once enough time had passed for any potential risks to become apparent.[67] This being so, the only remaining issue concerns the nature of the deprivation itself, which explains why, in *Rhodes*, the issue of defendants' culpability never came up.

Seen in this light, *Rhodes*'s failure to address defendants' mental state need not be taken to mean that state of mind is irrelevant. It may only indicate — rightly — that when conditions are ongoing and plainly dangerous to prisoners, courts may infer that prison officials knew of the risk. In such cases, no separate focus on the defendant's state of mind would be necessary, so none should be required.

Gamble offers a way to characterize more precisely when such an inference would be appropriate. As noted, in his *Gamble* dissent, Justice Stevens took issue with the emphasis on the defendant's state of mind in Justice Marshall's majority opinion. For Justice Stevens, "whether the constitutional standard has been violated should turn on the character of the punishment rather than the motivation of the individual who inflicted it."[68] But Justices Marshall and Stevens seem to have viewed *Gamble*'s facts in two very different lights. Justice Marshall read Gamble's experience as a series of one-on-one micro-level interactions — seventeen of them — with individual members of the prison's medical team. In contrast, Justice Stevens's dissent adopts a more macro-level perspective. As Justice Stevens saw it, Gamble's suffering may well have been traceable to system-wide deficiencies in the structure and culture of the prison health care system. That Gamble may have been seen seventeen times and that no individual member of the medical staff may have been "guilty of [anything] more than negligence or malpractice" was to Justice Stevens beside the point if — as Gamble's complaint suggested — it should turn out that "an

---

[67] *Rhodes*, 452 U.S. at 371 (Marshall, J., dissenting).
[68] *Estelle*, 429 U.S. at 116 (Stevens, J., dissenting).

overworked, undermanned medical staff in a crowded prison [was] following the expedient course of routinely prescribing nothing more than pain killers when a thorough diagnosis would disclose an obvious need for remedial treatment."[69] In that case, the problem was not a micro-level failure of care on the part of any individual prison official,[70] but instead a macro-level failure to provide a health care system with adequate resources to meet the needs of those in custody.

This distinction suggests that the burden on plaintiffs to demonstrate the defendants' culpability for the challenged conditions should vary depending on the nature of the claim. In cases of micro-level failure, fairness may demand that defendants have an opportunity to demonstrate an absence of culpability. When the need is localized, it is possible for incarcerated persons to suffer serious harm without even those correctional officers who are fully committed to fulfilling their constitutional obligations having any reason to suspect that a danger exists. In such cases, no liability should lie. But with macro-level failures, it is a different matter. When there is a system-wide failure sufficient to cause serious harm, it will always be the case that *some* prison official, specifically the officer or officers responsible for that aspect of the prison's operations, should have known of the risk. In such cases, the demonstrated inadequacies of the system would be proof enough of official culpability.[71] For example, if, as Justice Stevens suggested, the real problem in Gamble's case was a grossly inadequate system for providing medical care, proof of that gross inadequacy should suffice to make out a claim, since that showing alone would establish that the official(s) in charge of the prison's medical services should have known of the dangers the system's deficiencies posed.[72] This reading reflects the appropriate allocation of responsibility in the bureaucratic operation of the prison, where the heads of medical services, security, food services, etc., are responsible for — and thus should be expected to know about — what goes on in their departments. It is also consistent with *Rhodes*'s explicit emphasis on the harm

---

[69] *Id.* at 110 (citations omitted).

[70] Although Justice Stevens acknowledged that human error can create risks of harm to people in prison, he emphasized that this risk may be exacerbated when the medical staff do "not meet minimum standards of competence or diligence or . . . cannot give adequate care because of an excessive caseload or inadequate facilities . . . ." *Id.* at 116–17 n.13.

[71] Arguably, even at a macro level, there may be rare cases in which a presumption of constructive knowledge could be overcome. As Wilson argued, in cases involving "'short-term' or 'one-time conditions,'" it seems appropriate to allow defendants the opportunity to rebut this presumption. By contrast, in macro-level cases involving "'continuing' or 'systemic'" conditions, prison officials' affirmative obligations would be at their height, and the presumption should thus be irrebuttable. *See, e.g.*, Wilson v. Seiter, Br. of United States as amicus curiae at 14 n.16 ("An unheated prison during a cold winter may be viewed as inflicting unnecessary pain, but if the problem is a temporary one caused by a broken boiler [and] officials have endeavored to fix the situation," this case would "not involve the kind of pervasive conditions that can be viewed as an integral part of the penal confinement").

[72] *See, e.g.*, Brown v. Plata, 563 U.S. 493, 505 n.3 (2011) ("Plaintiffs rely on systemwide deficiencies in the provision of medical and mental health care that, taken as a whole, subject sick and mentally ill prisoners in California to 'substantial risk of serious harm.'").

inflicted, an emphasis that translates into the need for courts to "scrutin[ize] the actual conditions under challenge,"[73] to determine whether their "cumulative impact ... threatens [the] physical, mental and emotional health and well-being" of the people inside.[74]

When *Rhodes* was decided, the Court had not yet defined "deliberate indifference" with any precision. But as we have seen, the state has an obligation to provide prisoners with "the minimal civilized measure of life's necessities" and to keep them safe from "pain [that lacks] any penological purpose."[75] This imperative makes an actual knowledge standard ill-suited to the task. After *Gamble* and *Rhodes*, deliberate indifference ought to have been taken as the equivalent of gross negligence, on which prison officials would be liable for any conditions creating a substantial risk of serious harm[76] of which they should have known.

Read in this light, these two cases thus laid the groundwork for an interpretively appropriate two-pronged approach. Plaintiffs alleging micro-level failures of care would need to show both that they faced a substantial risk of serious harm in some form *and* that defendants had constructive knowledge of that risk, whereas in cases alleging macro-level failures, it would be enough for plaintiffs to demonstrate the risk of harm itself. In the latter set of cases, the state of mind showing would not be irrelevant but simply inferred from the conditions themselves.[77] Though the line between micro- and macro-level failures of care may not always be clear, some indeterminacy in this regard would be an insufficient reason to demand an affirmative state-of-mind showing in all cases. Courts, after all, are constantly called upon to draw distinctions of this sort. The imperative here is to avoid the imputation of official culpability in cases where even reasonably attentive prison officials committed to satisfying the state's carceral burden could well have remained unaware of a given risk. There is no reason to think that, guided by this concern, courts would be unable to draw appropriate lines.

In sum, with *Gamble* and *Rhodes*, the Court charted a course toward doctrinal standards that closely tracked prison officials' non-negotiable constitutional

---

[73] Rhodes v. Chapman, 452 U.S. 344, 362 (1981) (Brennan, J., concurring).

[74] *Id.* (quoting Laaman v. Helgemoe, 437 F. Supp. 269, 323 (N.H. 1977)).

[75] *Id.* at 347 (majority opinion).

[76] *See* Dolovich, *supra* note 34, at 917–18 ("If prisoners should suffer minor harms while incarcerated, it seems inapt to call the imposition of such harms 'cruel' even if they have arisen from official neglect and even if they may be thought to induce some deprivation of prisoners' basic needs. But when a threshold is crossed such that the victim's suffering is 'serious, not trivial,' the harm suffered would be sufficient to qualify as cruel." (quoting John Kekes, *Cruelty and Liberalism*, 106 ETHICS 834, 837 (1996))).

[77] Justice Scalia appears to have misunderstood this point. In the 1991 case of *Wilson v. Seiter*, 501 U.S. 294 (1991) (discussed below), Justice Scalia chided the petitioner for arguing that, in cases involving "'continuous' or 'systemic' conditions ... official state of mind would be irrelevant." *Id.* at 300. In fact, what Wilson had argued was that, in such cases, any state of mind showing would be *redundant*, a claim consistent with the framework I lay out here. *See* Reply Br. for the Petitioner at 16, Wilson v. Seiter, 501 U.S. 294 (No. 89-7376).

obligation to fulfill the state's carceral burden, on terms — i.e., via the totality of conditions approach — that would have acknowledged the humanity of people in prison. But in the years following *Rhodes*, the practical import of the case quickly eclipsed this doctrinal promise. Despite the considerable evidence introduced at trial that the floor space afforded at SOCF to people subjected to double celling fell well short of what human beings require "to avoid serious mental, emotional and physical deterioration,"[78] the *Rhodes* Court declined to declare double celling per se unconstitutional.[79] In fairness, the case left open the possibility that, in future cases, the overall pathological effects of overcrowding might yet tip a given institution into unconstitutionality. But *Rhodes* nonetheless wound up providing constitutional cover for prison officials nationwide to respond to ever-increasing prison populations by jamming two people into cells built to the minimum adequate specifications for a single person. It thus set the stage for broad judicial acquiescence to the endemic overcrowding that came to define American carceral institutions from the 1980s to the present day.

This effect, however, was in no way required by the doctrinal framework established in the case. To the contrary, had the Court's understanding of prisoners' Eighth Amendment protections continued to develop along the lines staked out in *Gamble* and *Rhodes* — and had the federal courts rigorously enforced that understanding — judicial enforcement of Eighth Amendment prison conditions claims could have come close to operationalizing core constitutional values and thus ensuring meaningful Eighth Amendment protections for people in prison.

EVADING THE EIGHTH AMENDMENT

The doctrine, however, did not develop this way. The first sign of divergence came in the 1991 case of *Wilson v. Seiter*. Wilson had brought an omnibus challenge to a raft of macro-level conditions in Hocking Correctional Facility (HCF), the Ohio prison where he was housed. Arguing that *Rhodes* required only "an objective examination of prison conditions,"[80] Wilson maintained that when conditions are "continuous" or "ongoing," some prison official may be presumed to know of

---

[78] *Rhodes*, 452 U.S. at 371 (Marshall, J., dissenting); *see also id.* at 375 (noting "the concurrent conclusions of two courts that the overcrowding and double celling here in issue are sufficiently severe that they will, if left unchecked, cause deterioration in [residents'] mental and physical health").

[79] Justice Brennan's vote for the government in *Rhodes* appears to have stemmed, at least in part, from a reluctance to endorse a constitutional conclusion that would wholly upend the structural foundations of a regulatory institution as massive, complex, and costly to reform as the carceral system. *See id.* at 367 n.15 (Brennan, J., concurring) ("If it were true that ... providing less than 63 square feet of cell space per [person] were [per se unconstitutional], then approximately two-thirds of all federal, state, and local [prisoners] today would be unconstitutionally confined.").

[80] Br. for Petitioner at 10–11, Wilson v. Seiter, 501 U.S. 294 (1990) (No. 89-7376).

them. Thus, Wilson suggested that, in cases like his, such a showing would be "redundant."[81]

Writing for the *Wilson* majority, Justice Scalia rejected this view. "*Rhodes* had not," Justice Scalia insisted, "eliminated the subjective component."[82] As Justice Scalia explained, the "holding in *Rhodes* turned on the objective component . . . (Was the deprivation sufficiently serious?)." It therefore had no occasion to consider the equally necessary "subjective component (Did the officials act with a sufficiently culpable state of mind?)."[83] And, the *Wilson* Court now held, even in cases alleging macro-level failures of care, a showing of deliberate indifference is always required.[84]

Although foreclosing any judicial inference of deliberate indifference, *Wilson* still left open the question of precisely what state of mind deliberate indifference represented. Were constructive knowledge ultimately held to suffice, *Wilson's* holding need not have greatly blunted the scope of Eighth Amendment protections, nor diverted judicial attention unduly from a focus on the conditions themselves. To minimize the gap between constitutional meaning and constitutional doctrine, the operative question could simply have been whether reasonable correctional officers, committed to fulfilling the state's carceral burden, would have recognized the risk and acted to alleviate it. If, even in macro-level cases like *Wilson*, the plaintiff would now bear the burden of making the showing, judicial focus could still remain on the character of the conditions themselves and their "effect on the imprisoned."

Then, just three years after *Wilson*, the Court decided otherwise. In the 1994 case of *Farmer v. Brennan*, the Court defined deliberate indifference as the equivalent of criminal recklessness, on which defendants are liable only if they actually realized the risk of harm.[85] To make this showing, the conditions themselves need not be wholly irrelevant. As the *Farmer* Court observed, "a factfinder may conclude that a prison official knew of a substantial risk from the very fact that the risk was obvious,"[86] and to assess this possibility, courts would presumably need to consider the conditions giving rise to the risk. But after *Farmer*, such relevance would be only contingent. As the Court hastened to note, any inference of defendants' subjective awareness "cannot be conclusive, for we know that people are not always conscious of what reasonable people would be conscious of."[87] In other words, however obvious the circumstances, people may at times remain oblivious. And when this

---

[81] *See* Reply Br. for the Petitioner, *supra* note 77, at 16, (arguing that a state of mind showing "is unnecessary or redundant in the context of continuing practices and customs"); *see also supra* note 77.

[82] Reply Br. for the Petitioner at 16, *supra* note 77, at 16.

[83] *Wilson*, 501 U.S. at 298.

[84] *See id.* at 299–303.

[85] Farmer v. Brennan, 511 U.S. 825, 837 (1994).

[86] *Id.* at 842.

[87] *See id.* (noting the possibility of inferring actual knowledge from obvious circumstances) (quoting WAYNE LaFAVE & AUSTIN SCOTT, SUBSTANTIVE CRIMINAL LAW § 3.7 (1st ed.)).

is true of prison officials, no constitutional liability may lie, however "soul-chilling" the conditions and however painful their impact. *Farmer's* holding thus recasts the affirmative obligation of the state's carceral burden into something more episodic and random. The effect is to incentivize the failure to pay attention, setting the stage for innumerable institutional pathologies carrying great potential for harm.[88]

Lawrence Sager famously argued that the Court will sometimes fail to enforce a constitutional provision "to its full conceptual boundaries" out of "institutional concerns."[89] But the gap *Farmer* creates between Eighth Amendment values and the governing doctrine cannot be explained away on institutional grounds. For one thing, culpability standards being the judiciary's bread and butter, application of a constructive knowledge standard in this context is hardly beyond the ken of the courts — a reality that negates any plausible institutional competence concerns.[90] Nor does the need for judicial deference to prison officials — perhaps the strongest theme in the Court's prison law jurisprudence more generally[91] — provide sufficient justification for standards so directly at odds with the state's Eighth Amendment obligations. Deference might be appropriate in contexts where state officials may be relied upon to fulfill their duties without abusing their authority. But the long and troubling history of unspeakable maltreatment against incarcerated people by the very actors charged with their protection[92] has shown that, absent meaningful external scrutiny, the power that prison officials have over incarcerated persons is sure to be abused. Executive branch corrections agencies, in other words, have demonstrated unequivocally their inability to police themselves. Add to this picture the broad political disenfranchisement of people in prison and their families and communities, and it becomes clear that courts represent the only available mechanism for overseeing the state's treatment of incarcerated persons. Without judicial review, people in custody would be left not only without recourse for constitutional violations but also constantly vulnerable to the "wanton and unnecessary infliction of pain" by state officials who would know their own prerogatives to be absolute. For these reasons, judicial deference to prison officials is entirely inappropriate for this context.

In any case, it was not Sager's "institutional concerns" but instead the language of the Eighth Amendment itself that the Court invoked to justify defining deliberate indifference as requiring subjective awareness of the risk. As the Court put it in *Wilson*, "[t]he source of the intent requirement is . . . the Eighth Amendment itself,

---

[88] *See Wilson*, 501 U.S. at 310 (White, J., concurring) ("Inhumane prison conditions often are the result of cumulative actions and inactions by numerous officials inside and outside a prison, sometimes over a long period of time.").

[89] *See* Sager, *supra* note 3, at 1213.

[90] Note, *Beyond the Ken of the Courts: A Critique of Judicial Refusal to Review the Complaints of Convicts*, 72 Yale L.J. 506 (1963).

[91] *See* Dolovich, *supra* note 20; Dolovich, *supra* note 34, at 961–63 n.306; Sharon Dolovich, *Forms of Deference in Prison Law*, 24 Fed. Sent'g Rep. 245 (2012).

[92] *See supra* note 7 and accompanying text.

which bans only cruel and unusual *punishment.*"[93] And punishment, Justice Scalia maintained, is "'a deliberate act intended to chastise or deter.'"[94] Thus, "[i]f the pain inflicted is not formally meted out *as punishment* by the statute or the sentencing judge, some mental element must be attributed to the inflicting officer before it can qualify."[95] But this interpretive move, relied upon by the Court in *Farmer*, in no way justifies *Farmer*'s holding. The problem lies in the theory of punishment Justice Scalia implicitly (and inappropriately) invokes — an individualistic conception of punishment wholly unsuited to governmental action in general and to the Eighth Amendment context in particular.

In the private sphere, individuals *qua* individuals may and do inflict punishment on others. It is, however, the distinct practice of *state* punishment with which the Eighth Amendment is exclusively concerned. And state punishment cannot be inflicted by one person acting alone, even a person wearing a correctional officer's uniform. It is instead, and can only be, inflicted through the combined actions of the linked institutions that comprise the state's criminal justice apparatus. This means that prison conditions constitute punishment for Eighth Amendment purposes regardless of what responsible officers happened to know or believe or intend regarding the effects of their own conduct on individual prisoners. To echo Justice Scalia's phrasing in *Wilson*, it is the penalty itself — that of being deliberately consigned to prison for the specified term under whatever conditions prison officials impose — that is "intended to chastise or deter."[96] Prison conditions necessarily constituting punishment,[97] the only question is whether the punishment they represent in any given case is one the state is constitutionally entitled to inflict — a question to which the state's carceral burden forms the answer.[98]

Flawed reading notwithstanding, after *Farmer*, Eighth Amendment challenges may be defeated by a showing that defendants did not personally realize the risk — a determination that will often be made with no reference to the conditions themselves or to prisoners' experience of those conditions. True, even on a recklessness standard, courts finding actual knowledge of the risk will then move to examining the challenged conditions to determine whether "the deprivation [was] sufficiently

---

[93] *Wilson*, 501 U.S. at 300 (emphasis in the original); *see also* Farmer v. Brennan, 511 U.S. 825, 837 (1994) ("The Eighth Amendment does not outlaw cruel and unusual 'conditions'; it outlaws cruel and unusual 'punishments.'").

[94] *Wilson*, 501 U.S. at 300 (quoting Duckworth v. Franzen, 780 F.2d 645, 652 (7th Cir. 1985)).

[95] *Id.* (emphasis in the original).

[96] Wilson, 501 U.S. at 300 (quoting Duckworth v. Franzen, 780 F.2d 645, 652 (7th Cir. 1985)).

[97] *See* Dolovich, *supra* note 34, at 897–910 (fleshing out this argument in more detail and describing a narrow exception to this general rule).

[98] To put it another way, the real question for Eighth Amendment purposes is not, as the Court put it in *Wilson* and *Farmer*, when prison conditions constitute *punishment*, but when they may be said to be *cruel*. For discussion grounding the imperative of the state's carceral burden in the meaning of "cruelty," see Dolovich, *supra* note 34, at 910–31. For an authoritative historical account, see John F. Stinneford, *The Original Meaning of "Cruel,"* 105 GEO. L. J. 441 (2017).

serious." But here too the Court has narrowed the scope of the inquiry in a way that undercuts basic Eighth Amendment values.

Rhodes, recall, held that prison conditions, "*alone or in combination, may deprive* [incarcerated persons] of the minimal civilized measure of life's necessities" in violation of the Eighth Amendment.[99] As Justice Brennan emphasized in his concurrence, this meant that "various deficiencies in prison conditions 'must be considered together'" since "[e]ven if no single condition of confinement would be unconstitutional in itself, exposure to the cumulative effect of prison conditions may subject [people] to cruel and unusual punishment."[100] This view gives life to the constitutional imperative affirmed by the Court in *Gamble*, that punishment must comport with the requirements of "dignity, civilized standards, humanity, and decency."[101] Human experience being cumulative, and physical and psychological health informed by the totality of a person's circumstances, any other approach would risk willful blindness to the nature and extent of human suffering in custody.[102]

But in *Wilson*, Justice Scalia recast the requisite showing in ways fundamentally at odds with this basic feature of human life. On appeal, the Sixth Circuit had dismissed several of Wilson's claims — including those concerning "inadequate cooling, housing with mentally ill inmates, and overcrowding" — on the grounds that, "even if proved, they did not involve the serious deprivation required by *Rhodes*."[103] Wilson had argued that this was in error because "each condition must be considered as part of the overall conditions challenged."[104] Justice Scalia, however, rejected this notion as a misunderstanding of *Rhodes*. Yes, he acknowledged, "[s]ome conditions of confinement may establish an Eighth Amendment violation 'in combination' when each would not do so alone."[105] But this is the case "only when they have a mutually enforcing effect that produces the deprivation of a *single, identifiable human need* such as food, warmth, or exercise — for example, a low cell temperature at night combined with a failure to issue blankets."[106] Dismissing the "totality of the conditions" approach that had prevailed since federal courts first began to entertain Eighth Amendment conditions claims in the 1960s, Justice Scalia held that "[n]othing so amorphous as 'overall conditions' can rise to the level of cruel and unusual punishment when no specific deprivation of a single human need exists."[107]

---

[99] Rhodes v. Chapman, 452 U.S. 337, 347 (1981) (emphasis added).

[100] *Id.* at 362–63 (Brennan, J., concurring) (internal citations and quotations omitted).

[101] *See* Estelle v. Gamble, 429 U.S. 97, 102 (1976) (quoting Jackson v. Bishop, 404 F.2d 571, 579 (8th Cir. 1968) (opinion of then-Judge Harry Blackmun)).

[102] *See supra* text accompanying notes 63–64.

[103] Wilson v. Seiter, 501 U.S. 294, 304 (1991).

[104] *Id.* (internal citations and quotations omitted).

[105] *Id.* (emphasis in the original).

[106] *Id.* (emphasis added).

[107] *Id.* at 305.

After *Wilson*, courts may consider only those conditions bearing directly on clear and specific requisites of human health and safety. All other aspects of the carceral experience, however much they may compromise plaintiffs' quality of life, become constitutionally irrelevant. But just as free people do not generally evaluate their everyday life experience by considering their various needs in isolation, the character of the prison experience — and thus of carceral punishment — cannot properly be assessed other than holistically. Take, for example, one aspect of life in HCF included in Wilson's complaint: housing with mentally ill inmates. The Sixth Circuit dismissed this claim because, although plaintiffs contended that this practice "place[d] them in fear for their safety," they failed to "cite any particular episodes of violence supporting this fear."[108] And, the Sixth Circuit found, in the absence of "allegations of prior physical violence" involving people with mental illness, "th[is] fear is not reasonable."[109] But the potential danger of being housed in close quarters with people who are mentally ill cannot be reduced simply to whether the experience instills a fear of imminent assault. Nor is the fear of assault by residents with mental illness the only potentially harmful or oppressive aspect of such an arrangement.

In his complaint, among other issues, Wilson alleged "overcrowding, excessive noise . . . inadequate heating and cooling, improper ventilation [and] unclean and inadequate restrooms."[110] Assuming the truth of these allegations, imagine what these conditions meant for the daily life of Wilson and his fellow HCF residents. The dorms were hot, crowded, noisy, and malodorous. Privacy would be virtually nonexistent, and everyone would feel compelled to be on constant alert for potential threats. Now add to this volatile mix the additional fact that some subset of the dorm's population suffers from (likely insufficiently treated) mental illness. Even if none of these individuals is violent or aggressive, they may still behave in ways that increase the unpleasantness of the environment and thus the general levels of stress and irritability that can make prison both physically harmful and psychologically traumatic.[111] Perhaps some of those with mental illness do not bathe, or, lacking a sense of proper interpersonal boundaries, continually invade the space of others. Or they may say inappropriate things, things that could set off hostile and even violent reactions on the part of other residents. Or it may simply fall to others in the dorm to provide the care that should be given by mental health professionals, thereby creating new sources of pressure in an environment already close to the breaking point.

---

[108] Wilson v. Seiter, 893 F.2d 861, 865 (6th Cir. 1990).
[109] *Id.*
[110] Wilson v. Seiter, 501 U.S. 294, 296 (1991).
[111] *See* Terry A. Kupers, *Prisons and the Decimation of Pro-social Life Skills*, *in* THE TRAUMA OF PSYCHOLOGICAL TORTURE 127, 130 (Almerindo Ojeda ed. 2008) ("In crowded, noisy, unhygienic environments, human beings tend to treat each other terribly.").

As this brief account suggests, without knowing more, it is impossible to fix precisely in what ways, and how much, the practice of placing people with mental illness in general population units increases the tension, frustration, and threat of violence faced by all residents.[112] We might, for example, want to know: How much time are residents able to spend out of the unit? What is the extant level of violence and tension in the dorms? What kind of support, if any, is provided those residents who take it upon themselves to help those who are mentally ill? It is, however, already clear that this practice would contribute in innumerable ways to the instability of an environment that is already inherently fragile — a fragility, it bears emphasizing, that would only be further exacerbated by overcrowding and inadequate cooling, to name the other two conditions the Sixth Circuit struck from Wilson's complaint as not representing "the type of seriously inadequate and indecent surroundings necessary to establish an Eighth Amendment violation."[113]

After *Wilson*, a plaintiff's inability to state with precision the reinforcing effect of a particular condition on the deprivation of a "single, identifiable human need" renders those conditions constitutionally irrelevant.[114] They drop out entirely, to be treated by the court as if they did not exist. But if specific conditions can be erased for constitutional purposes, they cannot be erased as a matter of lived experience. For Wilson and other residents of HCF, the conditions the Sixth Circuit dismissed would have continued to negatively shape their daily reality and thus also — and this is key — the character of the punishment the state was inflicting on them. It is worth recalling that courts will not impose constitutional liability unless they have found that defendants actually realized the risk of harm. This aspect of *Wilson* may thus shield from Eighth Amendment scrutiny even conditions known by state officials to compromise overall health and safety and thus to cause gratuitous pain and suffering to people inside.

THE NEXT FRONTIER IN EIGHTH AMENDMENT EVASION?

Taken together, *Wilson* and *Farmer* enable courts to reject claims of unconstitutional conditions without ever squarely addressing either the character of those conditions or the suffering they cause the people subjected to them. Thanks to this

---

[112] Note that people with untreated mental illness will personally have an Eighth Amendment claim for medical neglect. But the fact of such a claim hardly guarantees that treatment will be provided, *see* Dolovich, *supra* note 20 (describing the many obstacles to the successful prosecution of constitutional claims by prisoners), and the situation described in the text remains a standard experience in many prisons and jails around the country. *See, e.g.*, Sharon Dolovich, *Two Models of the Prison: Accidental Humanity and Hypermasculinity in the L.A. County Jail*, 102 J. CRIM. L. & CRIMINOLOGY 965, 982, 991 & n.110 (2012) (describing the practice in the L.A. County Jail of housing people with untreated mental illness in the dorms and the problems this practice creates for other dorm residents).

[113] *Wilson*, 893 F.2d at 865 (internal citations and quotations omitted).

[114] *Wilson*, 501 U.S. at 304.

regime, a victory for defendants in any given case can tell us little or nothing about the constitutional adequacy of the punishment the state is inflicting, via its designated agents, on the people we have collectively consigned to prison. Given the judicial monopoly on constitutional enforcement in the American system, the effect is to leave prisoners in most cases to endure without recourse whatever conditions prison officials choose to inflict.

Twenty-five years on, this is still where things stand. It is unknown whether the new Roberts Court, with its Trump-appointed additions of Justices Gorsuch and Kavanaugh, will revisit the standards governing Eighth Amendment prison conditions claims, or what changes they will make if they do. But for those committed to ensuring that state punishment comports with the basic values of "dignity, civilized standards, humanity, and decency" embraced by the Court in *Gamble*, the early signs are not promising.

In 2019, the Court decided *Bucklew v. Precythe*, a death penalty case that raised an as-applied challenge to Missouri's lethal injection protocol. Justice Gorsuch,[115] writing for the majority, framed his holding as a clarification of *Baze*[116] and *Glossip*,[117] the Court's prior decisions concerning the constitutionality of lethal injection. But the opinion reflects a greatly diminished view of the Eighth Amendment in general, one that, were it extended to conditions cases, could portend still broader permission for prison officials to inflict gratuitous suffering with constitutional impunity.

Bucklew suffered from a rare medical condition that caused "tumors filled with blood vessels to grow throughout his body," including his throat.[118] He argued that, because of this condition, execution by lethal injection would likely cause him "prolonged feelings of suffocation and excruciating pain."[119] In turning back Bucklew's challenge, Justice Gorsuch made clear that the "Eighth Amendment does not guarantee a prisoner a painless death." Instead, "when it comes to determining whether a punishment is unconstitutionally cruel because of the pain involved," the question is "whether the punishment '*superadds*' pain well beyond what's needed to effectuate a death sentence."[120] What might this standard mean for people wishing to challenge their conditions of confinement? Optimistically, it might seem to promise careful judicial attention to the nature and impact of the conditions at issue. Incarceration is a punishment of exile, its essence being the loss of liberty for a fixed term. And banishment, even when effectuated through confinement in locked institutions, need not entail the infliction of either physical

---

[115] Bucklew v. Precythe, 139 S. Ct. 1112 (2019). Justice Gorsuch was joined in the majority by Chief Justice Roberts and Justices Alito, Kavanaugh, and Thomas.
[116] Baze v. Rees, 553 U.S. 35 (2008).
[117] Glossip v. Gross, 135 S. Ct. 2726 (2015).
[118] *Bucklew*, 139 S. Ct. at 1137 (Breyer, J., dissenting).
[119] *Id.* at 1138 (internal citations and quotations omitted).
[120] *Id.* at 1124, 1126–27 (emphasis added) (majority opinion).

harm or undue psychological trauma. Perhaps, therefore, courts applying *Buck-lew's* standard of "superadding pain beyond that required to effectuate the penalty" could wind up condemning many conditions that produce gratuitous physical or psychological suffering.

Bucklew, however, offers several indications that this optimistic reading is neither intended nor warranted. For one thing, as already indicated, Justice Gorsuch emphasized that what is constitutionally prohibited is the infliction of pain "well beyond" what is needed to effectuate the penalty. As he put it, "what unites the punishments the Eighth Amendment was understood to forbid" is that they intensify the sentence "with a (cruel) 'superadd[ition]' of 'terror, pain, or disgrace.'"[121] This language alone indicates a minimalist version of Eighth Amendment protections, on which baseline levels of "terror, pain, and disgrace" are an acceptable part of criminal punishment. On this standard, the mere fact that state officials inflict gratuitous pain and suffering would be insufficient to trigger Eighth Amendment protections. And what, for Justice Gorsuch, constitutes this baseline? Is it set with any reference to the demands of humane treatment? *Bucklew* suggests otherwise. Instead, it tells us, assessing whether an execution method "cruel[ly] superadd[s]" pain "involve[s] a comparison with available alternatives" — i.e., "to other known methods" of carrying out the sentence. Courts seeking an appropriate reference point should look to current practice or "some other feasible and readily available" means of "carry[ing] out [a] lawful sentence ... that would have significantly reduced [the] substantial risk of pain."[122] If, in death penalty cases, this imperative requires defendants to identify a substantially less painful method of execution, applying this standard to prison conditions could leave prisoners with the burden of having to demonstrate the state's capacity to establish less brutal conditions. This approach could allow defendants to defeat Eighth Amendment conditions claims by demonstrating the combined intractability of current incarceration rates and resource constraints, thereby — perversely — allowing conditions of the state's own making to justify reducing its constitutional obligations to keep people safe from harm while they are in prison.

Other features of *Bucklew* also carry the potential to narrow still further prisoners' Eighth Amendment protections. Most notably, Justice Gorsuch takes pains to emphasize the majority's originalist commitments,[123] thus plainly signaling a repudiation — long advocated by the Court's conservative wing — of a "living

---

[121] *Id.* at 1124 (quoting *Baze*, 553 U.S. at 48 (brackets in the original)).

[122] *Id.* at 1127.

[123] Among other things, Justice Gorsuch identified certain methods of execution as "'cruel and unusual,' as a reader at the time of the Eighth Amendment's adoption would have understood those words"; bolstered an interpretation of "cruel and unusual" based on "confirm[ing] that people who ratified the Eighth Amendment would have understood it in just this way"; invoked "the Constitution's original understanding" when explicating early death penalty precedent; and contrasted "the modes of execution the Eighth Amendment was understood to forbid with those it was understood to permit [a]t the time of its adoption." *Id.* at 1112, 1123–24.

Constitution" approach to Eighth Amendment interpretation, with its emphasis on the "evolving standards of decency that mark the progress of a maturing society."[124] The full practical implications of this shift remain to be seen. But for our purposes, a return to originalism could mean that courts assessing prison conditions for any "superadding" of pain will soon be taking as the baseline the carceral experience of people in nineteenth-century American prisons.

In his opinion in the 2003 case of *Overton v. Bazzetta*, Justice Thomas provided a chilling preview of this approach. *Overton* involved a First Amendment freedom of association challenge brought by Michigan prisoners against new limits on prison visitation.[125] The Court upheld the regulations, and, in his concurrence, Justice Thomas canvassed the limits on prisoners' interactions with the outside world that defined life in the nation's earliest penitentiaries. At the time, as Justice Thomas described it, people in prison were "permitted virtually no visitors" and "even their letters were censored."[126] In some facilities, they were permitted "to send one letter every six months, provided it was penned by the chaplain and censored by the warden"; were entitled to only "one visit from ... relatives during [their entire] sentence"; and had access to "[n]o reading materials of any kind, except a Bible." Justice Thomas was not offering these details to condemn the regime they represented. It was simply that, for him, this historical experience set the relevant point of comparison against which the constitutionality of Michigan's new restrictions on visitors should be measured.

In his *Overton* concurrence, Justice Thomas focused only on practices in the early nineteenth-century penitentiaries of New York and Pennsylvania. But after the Civil War, the Southern states adopted a different carceral model: the plantation prison.[127] And when, in the 1960s, the first federal judges began to investigate claims of "brutal and dehumanizing" treatment in those Southern prisons, they unearthed an almost unimaginable level of physical barbarity. In his *Rhodes* concurrence, Justice Brennan offered a snapshot of those findings, as recounted "in gruesome detail" by Judge Frank Johnson of the Alabama District Court in the 1976 omnibus prison conditions case of *Pugh v. Locke*. As Justice Brennan explained, Judge Johnson found the Alabama prisons to be

> "horrendously overcrowded," to the point where some inmates were forced to sleep on mattresses spread on floors in hallways and next to urinals. The physical facilities were "dilapidat[ed]" and "filthy," the cells infested with roaches, flies, mosquitoes,

---

[124] Trop v. Dulles, 356 U.S. 86, 100 (1958) (plurality opinion).

[125] Overton v. Bazzetta, 539 U.S. 126 (2003). Justice Thomas agreed with the *Overton* majority that the regulation should be upheld, but he based this view on an idiosyncratic theory of incarcerated persons' First Amendment rights, on which the challenged regulation should be upheld if the state legislature intended prison sentences to encompass the termination of those rights. *See id.* at 140–43 (Thomas, J., concurring in the judgment).

[126] *Id.* at 144 (Thomas, J., concurring in the judgment).

[127] *See, e.g.*, OSHINSKY, *supra* note 14.

and other vermin. Sanitation facilities were limited and in ill repair, emitting an "overpowering odor"; in one instance, over 200 men were forced to share one toilet. Inmates were not provided with toothpaste, toothbrush, shampoo, shaving cream, razors, combs, or other such necessities. Food was "unappetizing and unwholesome," poorly prepared, and often infested with insects, and served without reasonable utensils. There were no meaningful vocational, educational, recreational, or work programs . . . . [There was also] "rampant violence" within the prison. Weaker inmates were "repeatedly victimized" by the stronger; robbery, rape, extortion, theft, and assault were "everyday occurrences among the general inmate population."[128]

Nor was Alabama an outlier. As Justice Brennan noted, "[s]imilar tales of horror are recounted in dozens of other cases."[129]

This is not the place to engage either *Bucklew*'s originalist turn or Justice Thomas's particular brand of originalism, on which conditions in the earliest American carceral facilities would set the bar on unconstitutional cruelty. Here, what matters is that, were the Court to follow Justice Thomas's lead, evidence that a given carceral environment is currently no worse than the "gruesome" conditions that prevailed in the nation's first prisons would be sufficient to warrant dismissal of plaintiffs' claims. This suggestion, however, is perverse. It was just such unalloyed freedom from external discipline afforded prison officials during the hands-off era that left prisoners so profoundly vulnerable to abuse. The "foul [and] inhuman" conditions that eventually came to light through litigation proved the folly — and cruelty — of such constitutional impunity.[130] The promise of judicial enforcement lies in the ability of courts to measure state action against the moral imperatives that animate the Eighth Amendment. An originalist approach in the Justice Thomas mold would instead turn this system on its head, allowing the long and sordid history of brutality against people in prison to justify continuing abuse.[131]

Two other seeds planted by the *Bucklew* majority also carry the potential to dramatically contract prisoners' Eighth Amendment protections. The first would

---

[128] Rhodes v. Chapman, 452 U.S. 337, 355 (1981) (Brennan, J., concurring) (internal citations omitted) (quoting Pugh v. Locke, 406 F. Supp. 318 (M.D. Ala. 1976)); *see also infra* note 129.

[129] *Rhodes*, 452 U.S. at 356.

[130] Gates v. Collier, 349 F. Supp. 881, 894 (N.D. Miss. 1972).

[131] There is good reason to fear the real-life consequences of a constitutional standard that would validate current abuses in light of historical practices. Forty-three years after *Pugh v. Locke* first brought Eighth Amendment scrutiny to bear on Alabama's prisons, an April 2019 Department of Justice investigation into conditions in that state's prisons found "severe, systemic" violations "exacerbated by serious deficiencies in staffing and supervision; overcrowding; ineffective housing and classification protocols; inadequate incident reporting; inability to control the flow of contraband into and within the prisons, including illegal drugs and weapons; ineffective prison management and training; insufficient maintenance and cleaning of facilities; the use of segregation in solitary confinement to both punish and protect victims of violence and/or sexual abuse; and a high level of violence that is too common, cruel, of an unusual nature, and pervasive." U.S. Dept. of Just. Civ. Rts. Div. & U.S. Att'y Off. for the N., Middle, & S. Dist. of Ala., Investigation of Ala. St. Prisons for Men (Apr. 2, 2019).

considerably raise the bar on the requisite state of mind showing, thereby expanding even further the capacity of courts to reject conditions challenges with minimal attention to the nature and impact of the conditions themselves. In *Baze*, Justice Thomas, joined by Justice Scalia, took the position that "the evil the Eighth Amendment targets is intentional infliction of gratuitous pain" and therefore that "a method of execution violates the Eighth Amendment only if it is deliberately designed to inflict pain."[132] Although Justice Gorsuch did not explicitly endorse this view in *Bucklew*, he nonetheless implied the readiness of the Court's conservative wing to consider doing so in the future.[133] Should Justice Thomas's preferred approach be applied to conditions claims, *Farmer*'s already high standard would be raised further still, to deny plaintiffs any constitutional recourse unless conditions were imposed deliberately, "for the very purpose of causing harm."[134] This standard would place beyond constitutional concern an enormous range of gratuitous pain and suffering daily inflicted by officers who, although not themselves sadistic (i.e., not inclined to impose pain for no reason other than making prisoners suffer), still know that people for whom they are responsible are in danger of harm and yet fail to take the necessary steps to keep them safe. This is a long way from Chief Justice Rehnquist's recognition in *DeShaney* of the constitutional status of the state's carceral burden.

A second seed planted by Justice Gorsuch in *Bucklew* could, if it takes root, have an even more extreme effect: the foreclosure of virtually any conditions claims at all. In *Bucklew*, Justice Gorsuch cites with approbation Justice Story's view, expressed at the time of ratification, that "the prohibition of cruel and unusual punishments [is] likely unnecessary because no free government would ever authorize atrocious methods of execution like [those that concerned the framers]."[135] Justice Story's

---

[132] Baze v. Rees, 553 U.S. 35, 94, 102 (2008) (Thomas, J., concurring in the judgment). This view echoes the standard that currently applies to Eighth Amendment excessive force claims. Under *Whitley v. Albers*, incarcerated plaintiffs alleging excessive force must show that defendants used force "maliciously and sadistically for the very purpose of causing harm." 475 U.S. 312, 321 (1991). The Eighth Amendment theory that Justice Thomas staked out in *Baze* and again in *Bucklew* would effectively extend the *Whitley* standard to all Eighth Amendment claims.

[133] *See* Bucklew v. Precythe, 139 S. Ct. 1112, 1125–26 (2019) (explaining that, for Justices Thomas and Scalia, a person facing the death penalty "must show that the state intended its method to inflict [unnecessary] pain," but that "revisiting that debate isn't necessary here, because ... the State was entitled to summary judgment even under the more forgiving *Baze/Glossip* test").

[134] *Whitley*, 475 U.S. at 321.

[135] *Id.* at 1123 (internal quotation marks omitted). In fairness, states arrived at the standard lethal injection protocol by searching for less obviously painful and traumatic methods of execution. *See* Deborah W. Denno, *Execution Methods in a Nutshell*, in ROUTLEDGE HANDBOOK ON CAPITAL PUNISHMENT 427, 427 (Robert M. Bohm & Gavin Lee eds., 2017) ("This country's centuries-long search for a medically humane method of execution landed at the doorstep of lethal injection."). But Bucklew's situation indicates that best intentions do not always suffice to avert agonizing pain. And as innumerable federal judges discovered in the 1960s as soon as they started to look, left to their own devices, state prison systems are in no way guaranteed to prioritize reducing gratuitous suffering and ensuring the humane treatment of people in custody.

assertion was echoed by Justice Thomas, who in his *Bucklew* concurrence expressed his "thankful[ness] ... that the Eighth Amendment is 'wholly unnecessary in a free government'" and that "States do not attempt to devise such diabolical punishments."[136] Read alongside the assertion that the Eighth Amendment prohibits only "the intentional infliction of gratuitous pain," it is not difficult to see how Justice Story's notion could lead the Court to reject any conditions challenges at all — on the ground that, in a free society like the United States, no government officials would ever deliberately subject prisoners to conditions causing them needless pain and suffering. And if this (stipulated) possibility could never arise, then the courts need never even entertain allegations of unconstitutional prison conditions.

To arrive at such a total evisceration of prisoners' Eighth Amendment protections, the Court would have to cross many a Rubicon. One hopes we never reach that point. Still, *Bucklew* clearly endorses a much a diminished normative vision of the Eighth Amendment, one that, were it implemented, would enable yet further loosening of the already limited constitutional constraints on how state officials treat people in prison. Depending on how things play out, a new hands-off era could well soon be upon us.

---

[136] *Bucklew*, 139 S. Ct. at 1123 (quoting J. STORY, COMMENTARIES ON THE CONSTITUTION OF THE UNITED STATES § 1986 750 (1883)); *id.* at 1135 (Thomas, J., concurring in the judgment) (quoting same).

Excessive Deference — The Eighth Amendment Bail Clause

Samuel R. Wiseman[*]

Despite the fact that many times more defendants are subject to cash bail and pretrial detention than face the death penalty or life without parole, the Eighth Amendment's prohibition against cruel and unusual punishments has been the subject of far more litigation and scholarly attention than the Excessive Bail Clause. The Clause simply reads: "Excessive bail shall not be required . . . . " and it has been rarely used in litigation.[1] One might have expected otherwise, given the injustice and inefficiency of current U.S. bail practices. But the Bail Clause has so far played almost no role in the recent bail reform movement, with advocates instead focusing on due process and equal protection under the Fourteenth Amendment.[2] This chapter provides an account of the history of the Bail Clause and the court interpretations that have rendered it peripheral to current reform efforts before briefly exploring proposals for revitalizing what should be an important constitutional safeguard of pretrial liberty.

THE PROBLEMS OF U.S. BAIL PRACTICES AND THE REFORM MOVEMENT

The pretrial justice system in the United States is deeply flawed. Approximately sixty-five percent of individuals in U.S. jails — more than 480,000 people — have not been convicted of a crime but have only been charged and are awaiting

---

[*] Professor of Law, Florida State University College of Law.
[1] *See* Galen v. County of Los Angeles, 477 F.3d 652, 659 (9th Cir. 2007) (noting that the Excessive Bail Clause is "one of the least litigated provisions in the Bill of Rights").
[2] *See* Christine S. Scott-Hayward & Sarah Ottone, *Punishing Poverty, California's Unconstitutional Bail System*, 70 STAN. L. REV. ONLINE 167, 175 (2018) (noting that "claims challenging state bail systems have ... focused on the Fourteenth Amendment" and that, pursuant to "recent state and federal precedent, arguments based on the Fourteenth Amendment appear to be more likely to succeed").

"court action."[3] Many of these defendants face low-level charges and are not dangerous; they are detained because they cannot afford the bail set in their case or the fees charged by a bail bond company, and they are disproportionately minority defendants.[4] The primary driver of this massive problem is courts' widespread reliance on money bail and bail schedules. More than half of county courts look to bail schedules when determining whether criminal defendants should be released pretrial, released with a bond, or jailed with no bond.[5] The bond amounts listed on the schedule are based solely on the nature of the crime charged.[6] Thus, bail is initially set with no attention to a defendant's individual ability to pay, and even relatively low bond amounts are effectively detention orders for the many poor defendants to which they apply.[7] Wealthy defendants, on the other hand — even those facing relatively serious charges and who have dangerous tendencies — can often afford to pay, and the bond imposed might provide little pressure for good behavior pending trial or for appearance on trial day.

This system causes a range of problems for defendants and society.[8] Low-income defendants become even poorer each day they sit in jail. They — and the families they support — often face the loss of their jobs and housing.[9] Offered a plea deal that imposes fines, court fees, and/or probation but lets them walk out of jail, they are very likely to plead guilty to the charge even if they are innocent, thus adding convictions to their criminal record and making future employment even more difficult. Further, the defendants jailed pretrial — the majority of whom are poor — also tend to develop violent tendencies. Thus, the widespread jailing of poor defendants pulls away productive members of the workforce, and it costs society

---

[3] Zhen Zeng, *Jail Inmates in 2016*, U.S. Dep't. of Just., Bureau of Justice Stats., at 4 (Feb. 2018), www.bjs.gov/content/pub/pdf/ji16.pdf.

[4] *See* David Arnold et al., Racial Bias in Bail Decisions (2018), https://academic.oup.com/ qje/article/133/4/1885/5025665 ("Racial disparities are particularly prominent in the setting of bail: in our data, black defendants are 3.6 percentage points more likely to be assigned monetary bail than white defendants and, conditional on being assigned monetary bail, receive bail amounts that are $9,923 greater."); Thomas H. Cohen, U.S. Dep't of Just., Pretrial Detention and Misconduct in Federal District Courts, 1995–2010, at 1 (2013), www.bjs .gov/content/pub/pdf/pdmfdc9510.pdf (observing that eighty-four percent of defendants charged with drug-related offenses are jailed pretrial).

[5] Pretrial Just. Inst., Pretrial Justice in America: A Survey of County Pretrial Release Policies, Practices, and Outcomes 8 (2009), https://university.pretrial.org/HigherLogic/ System/DownloadDocumentFile.ashx?DocumentFileKey=d4c7feb2–55be-ccd0-f06a-0280218e eee&forceDialog=0.

[6] Scott-Hayward & Ottone, *supra* note 2, at 169.

[7] Thomas H. Cohen & Brian A. Reaves, U.S. Dep't of Just., Pretrial Release of Felony Defendants in State Courts 1 (2007), http://bjs.gov/content/pub/pdf/prfdsc.pdf (observing that five out of six state court defendants are jailed pretrial because they could not afford the bail assigned to them).

[8] *See* Cohen, *supra* note 4, at 1 (observing that eighty-four percent of defendants charged with drug-related offenses are jailed pretrial); *supra* note 5.

[9] *See, e.g.,* Samuel R. Wiseman, *Pretrial Detention and the Right to Be Monitored*, 123 Yale L.J. 1344, 1356–57 (2014) (describing the effects on jobs and housing).

billions of dollars, often for little reason. Inexpensive alternatives for ensuring defendants' presence at trial include phone call reminders and rides to the courthouse, and perhaps electronic monitoring for the relatively rare defendants facing more serious charges who might seek to flee the jurisdiction.

More broadly, current bail practices likely contribute to the U.S. mass incarceration problem.[10] Most convictions are now obtained through plea bargains,[11] and bail appears to play a large role in driving guilty pleas.[12] The majority of defendants in the criminal justice system are charged with misdemeanors or low-level crimes, and as noted above, these defendants have a strong incentive to plead guilty when they are detained pretrial.[13] Particularly when time served before conviction counts toward their sentence, they will have completed or nearly completed their sentence by the time the plea deal is offered.[14] And even defendants facing longer sentences may prefer to plead guilty rather than waiting months in jail for a trial with an indeterminate outcome. Indeed, statistics show that, as compared to defendants released pretrial, those detained, who have less access to witnesses, counsel, and supportive family, are more likely to be convicted.[15] Thus, pretrial detention strongly incentivizes pleas. The systemic result of these incentives is that prosecutors, knowing that many defendants will be unable to afford the bond amount and will be detained pretrial, can "cheaply" obtain large numbers of convictions.

An alternative system, with lower pretrial detention rates and fewer pleas, would mean that there would either be fewer convictions, or, if conviction rates were to remain the same, convictions would be more expensive to obtain.[16] More prosecutors would be necessary to invest more time in trials, more judges would have to be hired to preside over the trials, and more public defenders would have to be appointed to represent indigent defendants. At the same time, the wealthier people who would be most likely to successfully lobby for bail reform, with results that

---

[10] *See generally* Samuel R. Wiseman, *Bail and Mass Incarceration*, 53 GA. L. REV. 235 (2018) (describing the link between bail and mass incarceration and the associated disincentives for reform).

[11] Missouri v. Frye, 566 U.S. 134, 143 (2012) (observing that ninety-seven percent of federal convictions and ninety-four percent of state convictions are the result of pleas).

[12] *See* Wiseman, *supra* note 10, at 250–52 (describing empirical studies that show that pretrial detention drives higher plea rates).

[13] Alexandra Natapoff, *Misdemeanors*, 85 S. CAL. L. REV. 1313, 1314–15, 1320–21 (2012).

[14] *See* Josh Bowers, *Punishing the Innocent*, 156 U. PA. L. REV. 1117, 1136 (2008) (describing the link between time served and pleas).

[15] *See, e.g.*, LAURA & JOHN ARNOLD FOUND., PRETRIAL CRIMINAL JUSTICE RESEARCH SUMMARY 2 (2013) (showing higher conviction rates for those detained pretrial than those who were not detained and faced similar charges).

[16] *See, e.g.*, Chief Justice Warren Burger, *The State of the Judiciary – 1970*, 56 A.B.A. J. 929, 931 (1970) (estimating that a ten percent reduction in guilty pleas would double the resources needed for the criminal justice system); Wiseman, *supra* note 10, at 252–53 (describing the connection between reduced guilty pleas and increased needs for prosecutors, judges, and public defenders).

might extend to poorer, less influential defendants, have little incentive to do so.[17] The bail-mass-incarceration link creates two classes of defendants — those with meaningful assets, who can avoid pretrial detention by paying their bond or hiring sophisticated attorneys to argue for pretrial release, and all other defendants. This stark separation leaves reform efforts to nonprofits and other entities that are not directly affected by the bail system but care about its impact.

REFORM EFFORTS AND THE WEAK EXCESSIVE BAIL CLAUSE

Scholars and activists began to focus on the massive problem of U.S. money bail as early as the 1920s,[18] and there was a resurgence of interest in reform in the 1960s,[19] with some change but no widespread deviation from the norm.[20] The most recent reform movement began around the time of the last economic recession. It combines a focus on the massive inefficiencies and costs to taxpayers associated with locking up millions of defendants despite cheaper, effective alternatives,[21] with the deep injustice of systematically discriminating against indigent defendants, many of whom are also minorities.[22] More and more large cities and counties are moving

[17] *See* Wiseman, *supra* note 10, at 262–65 (describing the two classes of defendants created by the U.S. bail system).

[18] ARTHUR LAWTON BEELEY, THE BAIL SYSTEM IN CHICAGO 164 (1927) (noting the unfairness of bail for indigent defendants).

[19] *See, e.g.*, Anne Rankin, *The Effect of Pretrial Detention*, 39 N.Y.U. L. REV. 641, 641 (1964) (documenting the problems associated with money bail and pretrial detention, and particularly the higher conviction rates for pretrial detainees); John N. Mitchell, Att'y Gen., U.S. Dep't of Just., *Address at the 92nd Annual Meeting of the American Bar Association* 10 (Aug. 13, 1969), www.justice.gov/ag/aghistory/mitchell/1969/08-13-1969a.pdf (highlighting the connection between pretrial release and ability to afford bail bonds); *see also* Charles E. Ares et al., *The Manhattan Bail Project: An Interim Report on the Use of Pre-trial Parole*, 38 N.Y.U. L. REV. 67 (1963) (describing the Manhattan Bail Project, an early reform project to show that defendants could be successfully released pretrial without negative effects on appearance rates).

[20] *See, e.g.*, Pretrial Services Agency for the District of Columbia, *PSA's History*, www.psa.gov/?q=about/history (noting that Washington, DC's pretrial services agency, which allows for more pretrial release, "was among the handful of pioneer pretrial agencies established in the 1960s").

[21] *See* CHRISTIAN HENRICHSON & RUTH DELANEY, VERA INST. OF JUST., THE PRICE OF PRISONS: WHAT INCARCERATION COSTS TAXPAYERS 6 (2012), https://storage.googleapis.com/vera-web-assets/downloads/Publications/price-of-prisons-what-incarceration-costs-taxpayers/legacy_downloads/price-of-prisons-updated-version-021914.pdf (describing the tax burden); Wiseman, *supra* note 5, at 1357–58 (same). The cost of bail has inspired some bipartisan efforts for reform — for example, a proposed federal bill that would have supported state bail reform efforts. *See* Kamala D. Harris & Rand Paul, Opinion: *Kamala Harris and Rand Paul: To Shrink Jails, Let's Reform Bail*, N.Y. TIMES, July 20, 2017, https://nyti.ms/2tu17jc [https://perma.cc/2HXM-RWZH] (describing proposed legislation).

[22] *See, e.g.*, Laura I. Appleman, *Justice in the Shadowlands: Pretrial Detention, Punishment, & the Sixth Amendment*, 69 WASH. & LEE L. REV. 1297, 1361–68 (2012)(focusing on the injustices and proposing reforms);Shima Baradaran & Frank L. McIntyre, *Predicting Violence*, 90 TEX. L. REV. 497, 558 (2012)(describing the problems with the current system and arguing for a more data-based system for predicting dangerousness, which would lower pretrial detention rates without negatively impacting community safety);Shima Baradaran, *Restoring the*

away from money bail and bail schedules to more nuanced ways of preventing non-appearance and dangerousness.[23] And a growing number of successful cases have challenged money bail systems because of their discriminatory effects. But there has been almost no mention of the Excessive Bail Clause in this increasingly successful reform effort. Reformers have instead focused almost exclusively on the Due Process and Equal Protection clauses, paying little attention to the Constitutional language that directly addresses bail.

The inattention paid to the Excessive Bail Clause by modern bail reformers arises from the cramped interpretation given to the Clause by the courts. From the beginning, the precise meaning of the Clause has been unclear. As a member of the House of Representatives observed during the congressional debate over the Bill of Rights, "The clause seems to express a great deal of humanity, on which account I have no objection to it; but as it seems to have no meaning in it, I do not think it necessary. What is meant by the terms excessive bail? Who are to be the judges?"[24]

The language of the Clause is nearly identical to that within the English Bill of Rights, which aimed to prevent judges from discriminating against defendants for illegitimate reasons — denying bail to individuals with religious, political, or other views that differed from those of the King. But the meaning of "excessive" still remained unclear, leaving unsettled the questions of whether the Clause created a right to bail — preventing Congress from denying the availability of bail altogether for certain types of charges, for example — and whether it limited the purpose of bail to ensuring the defendant's presence at trial and the integrity of the trial process.

A pair of cases from the mid-twentieth century did little to clarify matters. The first significant case addressing the substantive meaning of the Excessive Bail Clause was *Stack v. Boyle*, decided by the Supreme Court in 1951. Individuals charged under the Smith Act for advocating the overthrow of government filed a habeas petition challenging the imposition of a $50,000 bail amount in their cases as excessive.[25] Here, the Federal Rules of Criminal Procedure gave the defendants a right to bail, so the question of whether the Excessive Bail Clause secures this

---

Presumption of Innocence, 72 OHIO ST. L. J. 723, 766–75 (2011) (making a due process argument for pretrial release); Note, *Bail Reform and Risk Assessment: The Cautionary Tale of Federal Sentencing*, 131 HARV. L. REV. 1125 (2018) (describing the injustice of the current system and supporting a more empirical, risk-based approach to predicting dangerousness and pretrial detention but warning of the dangers associated with reliance on risk-based data, including legislative meddling with the metrics).

[23] See, e.g., LAURA & JOHN ARNOLD FOUND., MORE THAN 20 CITIES AND STATES ADOPT RISK ASSESSMENT TOOL TO HELP JUDGES DECIDE WHICH DEFENDANTS TO DETAIN PRIOR TO TRIAL (June 26, 2015), www.courts.wa.gov/subsite/mjc/docs/ArnoldFoundation.pdf.

[24] 1 ANNALS OF CONG. 754 (Joseph Gales & William Seaton eds., 1834), *reprinted in* 5 THE FOUNDERS' CONSTITUTION 377 (Philip B. Kurland & Ralph Lerner eds., 1987).

[25] Stack v. Boyle, 342 U.S. 1, 3 (1951).

right was not at issue.[26] But in dictum, the Court suggested that the Clause does indeed prohibit the outright erasure of the bail option by Congress for particular crimes or types of defendants, finding that, "[u]nless this right to bail before trial is preserved, the presumption of innocence, secured only after centuries of struggle, would lose its meaning."[27]

Regarding the meaning of an "excessive" bail amount under the Clause, the Court in *Stack* tied the definition of excessive to the purpose of bail in preventing pretrial flight, finding that "[b]ail set at a figure higher than an amount reasonably calculated to fulfill this purpose [of assuring "the presence of an accused"] is 'excessive' under the Eighth Amendment."[28] Under this standard, "the fixing of bail for any individual defendant must be based upon standards relevant to the purpose of assuring the presence of that defendant."[29] In *Stack*, the court had set bail at an amount much higher than the fine imposed upon conviction, and the amounts were "much higher than that usually imposed for offenses with like penalties."[30] Yet there was no indication that the judge had considered any factual evidence that justified this higher amount in order to prevent the defendants' flight. Instead, the government argued that it was clear from the indictment that the defendants were part of a conspiracy and were likely to flee.[31] The Court found that the lower court had not followed proper procedures in setting the bond amount but that a habeas petition was not the proper way to address the problem.[32]

Although the Court in *Stack* ultimately concluded that the defendants had used the wrong procedure for challenging bail amounts, its dictum was promising in terms of its suggestion that bail amounts would be too high if they accounted for any factors unrelated to securing defendants' presence at trial. The question remained, however, whether the Clause even provides a right to bail — in other words, whether it applies to Congress, and would prevent Congress from denying bail to certain classes of defendants or charges. Just one year after *Stack*, the Court in *Carlson v. Landon* — addressing a lower court's denial of bail to alien communists facing deportation under the civil Internal Security Act — suggested that the Excessive Bail Clause contains no right to bail in a given case and applies only to judges, not Congress. The Court concluded that "the very language of the Amendment fails to say all arrests must be bailable" and that bail was not required in this case.[33] The Court also noted that the language was lifted nearly verbatim

---

[26] *Id.* at 4 (observing that, under the Federal Rules of Criminal Procedure, "federal law has unequivocally provided that a person arrested for a non-capital offense shall be admitted to bail").

[27] *Id.*

[28] *Id.* at 5.

[29] *Id.*

[30] *Id.*

[31] *Stack*, 342 U.S. at 5–6.

[32] *Id.* at 6.

[33] Carlson v. Landon, 342 U.S. 524, 546 (1952).

from the English Bill of Rights and that "[i]n England that clause has never been thought to accord a right to bail in all cases."[34] Rather, it required that in cases where a judge determined that bail was appropriate, bail should not be set in an excessive amount.[35] But this case — which addressed a civil statute — did not definitively determine whether the Clause applies only to the judiciary or also to Congress and thus whether it protects a right to bail. And *Carlson* still left open the possibility that the Clause would set some meaningful limit on bail amounts. Thus, as of 1952, there were just two major cases addressing the Clause, which pointed in different directions in terms of suggesting any meaningful substantive limits that the Clause might place on bail. That issue remained undecided until 1987, when the Court in *United States v. Salerno* strongly implied the lack of any right to bail under the Clause and offered a very narrow reading of *Stack's* suggestion that the Clause limits bail amounts.[36]

Salerno addressed the Bail Reform Act of 1984, which requires courts to deny bail and detain pretrial defendants charged with serious felonies if the government shows after an adversary hearing that no release conditions "will reasonably assure ... the safety of any other person and the community."[37] The government had charged the defendants in the case under various provisions of the Racketeer Influenced and Corrupt Organizations Act, and it had persuaded the courts under the newly enacted Bail Reform Act that no amount of bail would protect community safety while the defendants awaited trial.[38] The defendants, who were detained pretrial due to the denial of bail, challenged the Bail Reform Act as unconstitutional because it allowed for the pretrial detention of individuals based on future predictions of dangerousness. This, they argued, violated the Excessive Bail Clause and Substantive Due Process.[39] Chief Justice Rehnquist, writing for the majority, disagreed. Citing *Landon* extensively, he strongly implied that the Excessive Bail Clause places no limits on Congress and does not guarantee a right to bail in any given case.[40] Justice Rehnquist concluded that *Landon* "squarely rejected" the proposition that the Clause required that bail be available to defendants.[41]

Further, the issue previously addressed in *Stack* dictum – the extent to which the Excessive Bail Clause provides substantive protections against unreasonably high

---

[34] *Id.* at 545.
[35] *Id.*
[36] United States v. Salerno, 481 U.S. 739, 752–53 (1987).
[37] *Id.* at 741.
[38] *Id.* at 743.
[39] *Id.* at 746.
[40] *Id.* at 754 (quoting *Landon's* assertion that "[t]he Eighth Amendment has not prevented Congress from defining the classes of cases in which bail shall be allowed in this country"). *But see* Appleman, *supra* note 22, at 1361–68 (arguing that "the *Salerno* Court was careful to note that its decision did not implicate the question of whether the Excessive Bail Clause affects the legislative power to delineate who might be eligible for bail").
[41] *Salerno*, 481 U.S. at 753–54.

bail amounts – also arose in *Salerno*. This was because the defendants argued that, by requiring the detention of certain defendants on the ground of dangerousness, Congress was essentially requiring courts to set "infinite" bail amounts for reasons unrelated to flight, which was prohibited by *Stack*.[42] Justice Rehnquist rejected the argument that bail could be set only on the basis of protecting the judicial process by preventing defendant flight, finding that the "[t]he only arguable substantive limitation of the Bail Clause is that the Government's proposed conditions of release or detention not be 'excessive' in light of the perceived evil."[43]

The *Salerno* decision strongly implies that the Excessive Bail Clause provides no, or at most a very limited, right to bail. Congress can simply prohibit courts from releasing certain types of defendants pretrial, on bail or other conditions, and that the amount of bail (even an "infinite" amount) may be set for purposes well beyond assuring defendants' presence pretrial. Since this decision, there has been very little litigation addressing bail under the Excessive Bail Clause because it is clear that the Clause will do very little work. Thus interpreted, the Clause has in fact done so little work that its incorporation against the states was settled only in 2010, in a footnote.[44]

In an example of just how narrow the Clause now is, in *Galen v. County of Los Angeles*, the U.S. Court of Appeals for the Ninth Circuit determined that bail set at $1 million for a domestic violence defendant was not excessive, citing *Salerno*.[45] The few cases in which courts have found a violation of the Clause involve bail being set for clearly impermissible purposes. For example, in *Wagenmann v. Adams*, a county clerk set bail at $500 for a case in which the police had no cause to arrest the defendant. The police charged the defendant as driving without a license and registration and disturbing the peace, but they had never asked him to produce these documents, and there was no indication of the defendant having caused any disturbance.[46] The police also directly recommended to the county clerk that she set the bail at $500 after observing that the defendant had $480 in cash, suggesting that their purpose in setting bail was to ensure that he would be detained, not to prevent flight or accomplish other legitimate purposes.[47] The court affirmed a jury verdict that this bail amount was excessive.[48]

---

[42] *Id.* at 753.

[43] *Id.* at 754.

[44] McDonald v. City of Chicago, 561 U.S. 742, 764 n.12 (2010) (misleadingly citing to *Schilb v. Kuebel* as holding that the Excessive Bail Clause was incorporated against the states, as that case merely noted that courts had long assumed that the Clause was incorporated); Samuel R. Wiseman, *McDonald's Other Right*, 97 VA. L. REV. IN BRIEF 23, 24–26 (2011) (describing and analyzing the footnote, and noting that neither party in *Schilb* raised an Eighth Amendment issue).

[45] Galen v. Cty. of Los Angeles, 477 F.3d 652, 660 (9th Cir. 2007).

[46] Wagenmann v. Adams, 829 F.2d 196, 203 (1987).

[47] *Id.* at 204.

[48] *Id.* at 213.

MODERN BAIL REFORM AND THE MARGINALIZATION
OF THE EXCESSIVE BAIL CLAUSE

Despite the exceedingly narrow reading of the Excessive Bail Clause in *Salerno* – which was essentially the final nail in the coffin for a right once thought to be potentially meaningful — some modern scholars have suggested ways in which the Excessive Bail Clause could play a role in reforming our flawed bail system. As I have noted in other work, the Court in *Salerno* did not clarify the meaning of "excessive," leaving unresolved the required closeness of the fit between the purpose of detention or of the bail amount, such as preventing flight or protecting the community against dangerousness, and the actual amount of bail set or denied altogether.[49] For instance, if there are reasonable, low-cost alternatives to detention that will fulfill the government's purposes of preventing non-appearance or dangerous acts, would the imposition of money bail or detention count as "excessive"?[50] This leaves open the possibility that recent developments, such as the availability of low-cost, effective means of assuring presence at trial — including phone call reminders, rides, and perhaps pretrial monitoring — could render cash bail and pretrial detention excessive under the Clause, at least in some circumstances. Some courts have ventured into this territory. For example, the Southern District of New York concluded that the Clause "must preclude bail conditions that are more onerous than necessary" and that "result in deprivation of the defendant's liberty."[51]

Other scholars more forcefully argue that the Excessive Bail Clause remains alive. Scott Howe, for example, argues that the fact that the Supreme Court incorporated the Clause gives it important meaning, including a "right to bail in broad circumstances;" he has also argued that the courts must better define excessiveness by determining the "proper function of bail" under the Clause.[52] He has suggested that bail is excessive if it is set at an amount higher than necessary to achieve three functions — appearance, "non-interference with the judicial process," and "compliance with the criminal law."[53] Building from this argument, Christine S. Scott-Hayward and Sarah Ottone have argued that bail schedules such as those used in California, which set bail amounts based on the offense charged, fail to include "any individualized consideration of either dangerousness or likelihood of appearance" and thus violate the Excessive Bail Clause.[54] They concede, though, that Fourteenth Amendment arguments are likely to be more successful.[55]

---

[49] Wiseman, *supra* note 9, at 1349.
[50] *Id.*
[51] United States v. Arzberger, 592 F. Supp. 2d 590, 605 (S.D.N.Y. 2008).
[52] Scott W. Howe, *The Implications of Incorporating the Eighth Amendment Prohibition on Excessive Bail*, 43 HOFSTRA L. REV. 1039, 1084–85 (2015).
[53] *Id.* at 1058.
[54] Scott-Hayward & Ottone, *supra* note 1, at 175.
[55] *Id.*

Despite some modern attention to the Clause, most reformers who have focused their efforts on the courts have ignored the Clause entirely, relying instead on due process and equal protection. Addressing the money bail system in Harris County, Texas, the U.S. Court of Appeals for the Fifth Circuit observed that the system causes judges to "almost always set a bail amount that detains the indigent" and found that it violated due process by taking away a state-created liberty interest in bail without adequate minimum procedures.[56] The court found that the system also violated the Equal Protection Clause because "poor arrestees in Harris County are incarcerated where similarly situated wealthy arrestees are not, solely because the indigent cannot afford to pay a secured bond," and this failed to withstand heightened scrutiny.[57] Other challenges to money bail systems have been similarly successful — again using only due process and equal protection claims.[58]

The burgeoning reform arguments that rely on various parts of the Constitution, but not the very portion of the Constitution that addresses bail, demonstrate the Supreme Court's marginalization of the Excessive Bail Clause — leaving a system in which only the most extreme legislative or judicial decision involving bail would disrupt a court's nearly blind deference to these decisions.

---

[56] ODonnell v. Harris County, 892 F.3d 147, 159 (5th Cir. 2018).

[57] *Id.* at 162.

[58] *See, e.g.*, Buffin v. San Francisco, 2019 WL 1017537 (N.D. Cal., Mar. 4, 2019) (showing a successful equal protection and due process challenge to San Francisco City and County's money bail system); *In re* Humphrey, 228 Cal. Rptr. 3d 513, 545 (Ct. App. 2018) (finding that California's bail system violated the Fourteenth Amendment); Varden v. City of Clanton, 2015 WL 5387219 (N.D. Ala., Sept. 14, 2015) (showing that the *Varden* case settled); Varden v. City of Clanton, Class Action Complaint, Case no. 2:14-cv-00034-MHT-WC, U.S. District Court for the Middle District of Alabama (Jan. 15, 2015) (raising equal protection and due process claims against the City of Clanton, Alabama's money bail system, in which bail schedules required a $500 bond for defendants facing minor misdemeanors and most defendants could not afford bail); Note, *Bail Reform and Risk Assessment: The Cautionary Tale of Federal Sentencing, supra* note 22 (describing these and other cases).

Nor Excessive Fines Imposed

Beth A. Colgan[*]

Across America, federal, state, and local governments use economic sanctions to punish juveniles and adults in cases ranging from low-level traffic tickets, to truancy, to theft, to murder.[1] Millions of people now struggle with debt resulting from these practices. Increasingly, people report having to forgo basic necessities, such as food, housing, winter coats for their children,[2] toilet paper,[3] necessary medical care,[4] and more, in an attempt to extract themselves from these debts. For those who cannot pay immediately, lawmakers have directed the imposition of further punishments, in the form of additional debt, loss of driver's licenses and voting rights, and even incarceration.[5] Still others lose their homes, their cars, business equipment, and

---

[*] Professor of Law, UCLA School of Law.
[1] For overviews of the use of economic sanctions in jurisdictions around the country, see, for example, ALA. APPLESEED CTR. FOR LAW & JUST., UNDER PRESSURE: HOW FINES AND FEES HURT PEOPLE, UNDERMINE PUBLIC SAFETY, AND DRIVE ALABAMA'S RACIAL WEALTH DIVIDE (2018); DICK M. CARPENTER II ET AL., INST. FOR JUST., POLICING FOR PROFIT: THE ABUSE OF CIVIL ASSET FORFEITURE (2d ed. 2015); CIV. RIGHTS DIV., U.S. DEP'T OF JUST., INVESTIGATION OF THE FERGUSON POLICE DEPARTMENT (2015); JESSICA FEIERMAN ET AL., JUVENILE LAW CTR., DEBTORS' PRISON FOR KIDS?: THE HIGH COST OF FINES AND FEES IN THE JUVENILE SYSTEM (2016); HUMAN RIGHTS WATCH, PROFITING FROM PROBATION: AMERICA'S "OFFENDER-FUNDED" PROBATION INDUSTRY (2014); ACLU, IN FOR A PENNY: THE RISE OF AMERICA'S NEW DEBTORS' PRISONS (2010); LAWYERS COMM. FOR CIV. RIGHTS ET AL., NOT JUST A FERGUSON PROBLEM (2015); Alexes Harris et al., *Drawing Blood from Stones: Legal Debt and Social Inequality in the Contemporary United States*, 115 AM. J. OF SOCIOLOGY 1753 (2010); Nathan Link, *Criminal Justice Debt during the Prisoner Reintegration Process: Who Has It and How Much?*, 46 CRIM. JUSTICE & BEHAVIOR 154 (2019).
[2] ACLU OF WASH. & COLUMBIA LEGAL SERVS., MODERN-DAY DEBTORS' PRISONS: HOW COURT-IMPOSED DEBTS PUNISH POOR PEOPLE IN WASHINGTON 13–14 (2010).
[3] HUMAN RIGHTS WATCH, *supra* note 1, at 34–35.
[4] *See, e.g.,* ALA. APPLESEED, *supra* note 1, at 4, 31.
[5] *See, e.g.,* ACLU, *supra* note 1; Beth A. Colgan, *Wealth-Based Penal Disenfranchisement*, 72 VAND. L. REV. 55 (2019); BRANDON L. GARRETT & WILLIAM CROZIER, DRIVER'S LICENSE SUSPENSION IN NORTH CAROLINA (Duke Law Sch. Pub. Law & Legal Theory Series No. 2019-27, 2019).

other possessions to forfeiture[6] — cutting them off from stable housing, disrupting access to employment and educational services, and restricting the availability of food and medical care[7] — at times without ever having been convicted of a crime.

These practices have been subject to heavy criticism in recent years. They are now commonly described as both "modern debtors' prisons" given the consequences for those who cannot pay,[8] and as "policing for profit" in light of government incentives to abuse the use of such punishments to generate revenue.[9]

As the detrimental effects of economic sanctions on the well-being of people and their families and the potentially perverse incentives caused by their revenue-generating power has come to light, it has begged the question: Can the government's imposition of such punishments be constitutional? The answer to that question may be found in part in the Eighth Amendment.

Though overshadowed by its cruel and unusual punishments counterpart in the courts, in scholarship, and even in this book, the Eighth Amendment does prohibit the imposition of "excessive fines."[10] In 2019, in *Timbs v. Indiana*, the U.S. Supreme Court held for the first time that the Excessive Fines Clause was incorporated against the states, and in doing so, described the Clause as a "constant shield" against the risk that the government will use economic sanctions "in a measure out of accord with the penal goals of retribution and deterrence," in order to generate revenue, particularly against politically vulnerable people and communities.[11] Yet, despite the deep historical foundations of the Clause and the longstanding use of questionable practices related to economic sanctions — reaching back through the Jim Crow Era, to the Stuart kings of England, to the abuses leading to Magna Carta in 1215 — prior to *Timbs*, the Court had only interpreted the Clause's meaning on four other occasions. As a result, the story of the Excessive Fines Clause is as much about what has not been decided as about what has.

Before surveying the excessive fines doctrine, it is worth considering why it may be that the Clause has received so little attention, particularly given that economic sanctions are by far the most common form of punishment. One answer may be that the vast majority of economic sanctions are not, in fact, constitutionally excessive. For many people in the United States, the cost of a traffic ticket would cause a slight pinch on their pocketbooks, a minor inconvenience far from what one thinks of

---

[6] *See GSA Auctions*, https://gsaauctions.gov/gsaauctions/gsaauctions (listing types of forfeited property for sale including real property, vehicles, household/personal items, electronic equipment, and various forms of business equipment).

[7] Beth A. Colgan & Nicholas M. McLean, *Financial Hardship and the Excessive Fines Clause: Assessing the Severity of Property Forfeitures after Timbs*, 129 Yale L.J. Forum 430 (2020).

[8] *See, e.g.*, Kate Gibson, *Poor Defendants Say They Face Modern-Day Debtors' Prison*, CBS Moneywatch (Aug. 23, 2016).

[9] *See, e.g.*, Carpenter et al., *supra* note 1.

[10] U.S. Const. amend. VIII.

[11] Timbs v. Indiana, 139 S. Ct. 682, 689 (2019) (quoting Harmelin v. Michigan, 501 U.S. 957, 979 n.9 (1991) (opinion of Scalia, J.) (internal quotations omitted)).

when contemplating government behavior that offends the constitution — punishments such as execution, long-term incarceration, or grueling prison conditions detailed elsewhere in this book. But that answer rests on not one faulty premise, but two. First, it assumes that fines are imposed at minimal amounts. In some cases, economic sanctions can be in the tens of thousands, or even millions, of dollars. Even for traffic tickets and other low-level offenses, lawmakers have in many places tacked on multiple surcharges and fees that can far outpace base fines, in some cases tripling, quadrupling, or more the total amount imposed. And while forfeitures may involve the deprivation of small amounts of cash,[12] they also may result in the loss of major assets such as vehicles and homes even when the property is only tangentially related to the underlying offense.[13] Second, it assumes that most people subject to economic sanctions have the ability to absorb such losses. Yet, recent studies show that four of ten Americans adults could not cover an unexpected $400 expense without having to sell personal property or borrow money.[14] Further, in many jurisdictions, policing is heavily targeted at poor communities and communities of color.[15] More than nine million households — concentrated in such communities — are unbanked, meaning they have little to no savings upon which to draw and no access to reasonable lending options that may otherwise help them extract themselves from these debts.[16]

Assuming that some meaningful percentage of cases raise colorable issues, the lack of attention to the Excessive Fines Clause may be attributable to the fact that in many cases in which economic sanctions are imposed, there is no Sixth Amendment right to counsel. In the landmark decision, *Gideon v. Wainwright*,[17] the Court held that the Sixth Amendment requires state governments to provide counsel in felony cases to indigent defendants. The Court later expanded the right to misdemeanor cases in which terms of incarceration are imposed[18] but stopped there. In a 1977 case, *Scott v. Illinois*,[19] the Court held that the Sixth Amendment right to counsel did not extend to cases in which the only punishment imposed was a fine, no matter the complexity of the factual, evidentiary, or constitutional

---

[12] *See, e.g.*, Robert O'Harrow, Jr. & Steven Rich, *D.C. Police Plan for Future Seizure Proceeds Years in Advance in City Budget Documents*, WASH. POST, Nov. 15, 2014.

[13] *See, e.g.*, Pamela Brown, *Parent's House Seized after Son's Drug Bust*, CNN.COM (10:45 a.m., Sept. 8, 2014), www.cnn.com/2014/09/03/us/philadelphia-drug-bust-house-seizure/index.html.

[14] BOARD OF GOVERNORS OF THE FEDERAL RESERVE SYSTEM, REP. ON THE ECONOMIC WELL-BEING OF AMERICAN HOUSEHOLDS IN 2017 (2018).

[15] *See, e.g.*, Leonard v. Texas, 137 S. Ct. 847, 848 (2017) (Thomas, J., statement respecting the denial of certiorari) ("These forfeiture operations frequently target the poor and other groups least able to defend their interests in forfeiture proceedings."); CIV. RIGHTS DIV., *supra* note 1.

[16] ALA. APPLESEED, *supra* note 1, at 29–30; FEDERAL DEPOSIT INSURANCE CORP., NATIONAL SURVEY OF UNBANKED AND UNDERBANKED HOUSEHOLDS (2015); Mehrsa Baradaran, *It's Time for Postal Banking*, 127 HARV. L. REV. F. 165 (2014).

[17] Gideon v. Wainwright, 372 U.S. 335 (1963).

[18] Argersinger v. Hamlin, 407 U.S. 25 (1972).

[19] Scott v. Illinois, 440 U.S. 367 (1979).

issues involved in such a case. While the Court subsequently opened the door to the possibility of a right to counsel in cases in which economic sanctions are made a condition of probation,[20] and while a person could attempt to claim a due process right to counsel on a case-by-case basis,[21] the result has been that there is effectively no right to counsel in proceedings in which the most problematic practices may occur.[22] With no attorney, it is unlikely that people will have the capacity to raise and preserve excessive fines claims to set the wheels of Supreme Court review in motion.

Even in cases where defense counsel is available, it is also possible that the potential protections offered by the Excessive Fines Clause will be shunted aside due to the pressures inherent in plea bargaining. People often accept the imposition of significant economic sanctions in plea bargains in exchange for release without further incarceration or, increasingly, to access pretrial diversion programs. While these may be rational bargains in some cases, further study is needed to investigate whether people — or their attorneys — fully understand the long-term consequences of these debts and forfeitures when making these decisions.

No matter the reason, the Excessive Fines Clause remains a constitutional provision with great promise, but with more questions open than resolved. As detailed below, these questions involve both the threshold consideration of what constitutes a fine subject to the Clause's protections, as well as the question of how to assess whether such a fine is constitutionally excessive.

What Constitutes a Fine

Economic sanctions take on myriad forms. Statutory fines have now been extended to include "surcharges" or "assessments," which are imposed in the same manner as fines but are often targeted at funding particular governmental projects that may or may not have anything to do with the underlying offense.[23] Restitution is also common in cases involving harm to a victim. In addition, lawmakers also often require or allow for the imposition of fees, designed at least nominally to cover system costs, such as the cost of pretrial incarceration, prosecution, or one's indigent defense counsel, as well as downstream costs associated with incarceration, probation and parole supervision, or collections.

In addition to economic sanctions that create an ongoing obligation to pay, another type involves the forfeiture of cash or property. Criminal forfeitures are imposed as a component of sentencing following a finding of guilt beyond a

---

[20] Alabama v. Shelton, 535 U.S. 654 (2002).

[21] Turner v. Rogers, 564 U.S. 431 (2011); Powell v. Alabama, 287 U.S. 45 (1932).

[22] *See, e.g.,* Beth A. Colgan, *Lessons from Ferguson on Individual Defense Representation as a Tool for Systemic Reform,* 58 Wm. & Mary L. Rev. 1179 (2017).

[23] *See, e.g.,* Beth A. Colgan, *The Excessive Fines Clause: Challenging the Modern Debtors' Prison,* 65 UCLA L. Rev. 2, 32–33 (2018).

reasonable doubt, whereas the government may secure civil, "civil asset," or "administrative" forfeitures without obtaining a conviction.[24] Though the requirements of such proceedings vary from jurisdiction to jurisdiction, typically after the government makes a showing of evidence linking the cash or property subject to civil forfeiture to alleged criminal conduct, the burden shifts to the owner to prove his or her innocence. Whether criminal or civil, there are several stated rationales for forfeitures. The government might seek to forfeit property on the theory that it served as an "instrumentality" because it contributed in some way to the person's ability to commit the offense; for example, a vehicle used to drive to the location of a drug deal.[25] Alternatively, the government might seek to forfeit property because, while not inherently illegal to possess, it is rendered illegal by a person's actions; for example, legally obtained cash that a person fails to report at customs.[26] The government may also seek the forfeiture of the proceeds of a criminal offense, including items of real or personal property purchased in whole or in part with proceeds, as well as substitute assets in cases where proceeds cannot be located or otherwise obtained.

Despite the wide variety of economic sanctions, the Court to date has decided only that punitive damages awarded in private civil suits do not constitute fines,[27] but that both criminal[28] and civil forfeitures do.[29] In other words, whether statutory fines, surcharges, restitution, and fees — as well as any monies paid to private entities rather than the government — constitute fines remains an open question. Further, as detailed below, the application of the Clause to civil forfeitures is currently under attack.

Even though the doctrine is limited, the Court's conception of the Clause as a bulwark against the prosecutorial power, particularly where such abuses are motivated by a desire to generate revenue or to punish the politically vulnerable, provides important guidance. The Court has heavily relied on the Clause's historical pedigree for this understanding. For example, when first interpreting the Clause in 1989's *Browning-Ferris Industries of Vermont, Inc. v. Kelco Disposal, Inc.*, the Court focused on abuses committed by King James II, in which he imposed heavy fines on his political enemies. This led to the adoption of a prohibition on excessive fines in the English Bill of Rights, which ultimately served as the basis for its American constitutional counterpart.[30] Thus, from its initial foray into setting the scope of the Clause's protections, the Court has recognized that the Clause was designed to serve as a meaningful restriction on government overreach.

[24] *See generally* CARPENTER ET AL., *supra* note 1.
[25] *See, e.g.,* Timbs v. Indiana, 139 S. Ct. 682, 686 (2019).
[26] *See, e.g.,* United States v. Bajakajian, 524 U.S. 321 (1998).
[27] Browning-Ferris Indus. of Vt., Inc. v. Kelco Disposal, Inc., 492 U.S. 257 (1989).
[28] Alexander v. United States, 509 U.S. 544 (1993).
[29] Austin v. United States, 509 U.S. 602 (1993).
[30] *Browning-Ferris Indus. of Vt.*, 492 U.S. at 266–68.

That conception of the Clause as highly protective ultimately led the Court to adopt an expansive vision of what constitutes a fine — subject to a restriction addressed below — under which an economic sanction falls within the Clause's scope so long as it is at least partially punitive, even if it is nominally civil. The Court expounded this test in *Austin v. United States,* which involved the civil forfeiture of a person's home and business.[31] After noting that the text did not limit the Clause to criminal matters as other constitutional provisions had done, the *Austin* Court turned to the historical use of forfeitures. The Court described early forfeitures as a governmental response to wrongdoing or engagement in prohibited behavior. In addition, the *Austin* Court considered modern forfeiture practices, explaining that they were associated with other forms of punishment both by proximity in statutory text and by legislative history, showing that civil forfeitures are seen by lawmakers as substitute or additional punishments. In light of the text, history, and modern usage, the Court held that civil forfeitures did constitute fines — even if they served some remedial purposes and despite being labeled "civil"— because they also served retributive and consequentialist aims.

Arguably substantiating the Court's understanding of a need for constitutional restraint on governments that may unjustifiably impose economic sanctions to reap revenue, states are now attempting to dislodge from the doctrine the partially punitive test in general, and the protections afforded to civil forfeitures in particular. Though the test as articulated in *Austin* is relatively straightforward, the Court gave fodder to these arguments by muddying the waters a few years after *Austin* in *United States v. Bajakajian.*[32] Though the case involved a criminal forfeiture, the *Bajakajian* majority engaged in an extended discussion calling into question whether civil forfeitures would have been understood to be punitive at the time of the Clause's ratification in 1791. While the Court ultimately stated that modern civil forfeitures had departed enough from their historical roots that they would meet the partially punitive test and thus constitute fines regardless,[33] the dictum has caused confusion in some lower courts.[34] In litigating *Timbs,* the State of Indiana — which generates significant revenue from civil forfeitures, taking in $3.4 million in 2017 alone[35] — seized upon the *Bajakajian* dictum. In both its briefing and at oral argument, Indiana argued that *Bajakjaian's* recitation of historical records suggesting that civil forfeitures were originally non-punitive should lead the Court to overturn the partially punitive test and remove civil forfeitures from the Clause's protection.

---

[31] *Austin,* 509 U.S. at 605.

[32] United States v. Bajakajian, 524 U.S. 321 (1998).

[33] *Id.* at 330–34, 331 n.6, 334 n.9, 343 n.18.

[34] *See, e.g.,* United States v. Ahmad, 213 F.3d 805, 812–13 (4th Cir. 2000) (describing the conflict between *Austin's* holding and *Bajakajian's* dictum); United States v. 1866.75 Bd. Feet and 11 Doors and Casings, 587 F. Supp. 2d 740, 755 (E.D. Va. 2008) (describing the *Bajakajian* dictum as "unworkable and pointless").

[35] *Indiana High Court to Hear Civil Forfeiture, Schools Case,* Assoc. Press, July 4, 2018.

The Court, however, declined to reframe the question in front of it — whether to incorporate the Clause against the states — to include reconsideration of *Austin*, given that it had not been properly presented in the lower courts. In doing so, the majority pointedly noted that *Austin* was unanimously decided,[36] suggesting that the partially punitive test is on firm ground.

Not only do challenges to the partially punitive test and the treatment of civil forfeitures as fines appear unlikely to gain traction, application of the test to other common forms of economic sanction suggest that the Clause's scope could be far-reaching. Governments would be hard pressed to argue that statutory fines, surcharges, and restitution serve no punitive purpose for three reasons: the Court has previously described these types of sanctions as serving retributive and consequentialist goals;[37] they typically cannot be imposed absent a finding that prohibited conduct occurred; and they are often directly linked to other forms of punishment, including by requiring payment as a condition of probation or parole.

Though fines, surcharges, and restitution likely meet the partially punitive test, the outcome is less clear with respect to administrative fees. On the surface, administrative fees are designed as a mechanism for cost recoupment, not punishment. Yet, in most cases — just like other forms of economic sanction — they cannot be imposed absent a determination of wrongdoing, and may be intertwined with other forms of punishment. More complicated still are those jurisdictions that impose fees absent a conviction — for example, requiring payment of a fee to apply for indigent defense representation regardless of whether the person is ultimately convicted. While such practices may fall outside of the Clause's protections (though perhaps unconstitutional on other grounds[38]), there may be some room to argue that such fees are within the Clause's scope. If, for example, statutory fines that could only be imposed upon conviction and fees imposed without conviction are treated identically during collections, a person would have a stronger argument that the fee was merely a fine by another name.

Yet, despite the capaciousness of the partially punitive test and the likelihood that most if not all forms of economic sanction in use today would pass it, the *Browning-Ferris* Court also significantly cabined the Clause's scope by limiting fines to those economic sanctions paid directly to the government.[39] At first glance this cramped interpretation of the Clause seems like an insignificant restriction, as government entities have traditionally received monies collected for economic sanctions. In many

---

[36] Timbs v. Indiana, 139 S. Ct. 682, 690 (2019).

[37] *See, e.g.*, Paroline v. United States, 572 U.S. 434, 456 (2014) (explaining that restitution "serves punitive purposes"); Southern Union Co. v. United States, 132 S. Ct. 2344, 2351 (2012) (noting that the term "punishment" "undeniably embrace[s statutory] fines").

[38] *Cf.* Nelson v. Colorado, 137 S. Ct. 1249 (2017) (striking down a statute that required people to prove their innocence to obtain refunds of economic sanctions paid in relation to cases later reversed or vacated).

[39] Browning-Ferris Indus. of Vt., Inc. v. Kelco Disposal, Inc., 492 U.S. 257, 265 (1989).

cases, however, the largest component of economic sanctions ordered is restitution, made payable to crime victims rather than the government. Further, with the increased privatization of the criminal legal system, including the provision of proba- tion and parole supervision, chemical dependency and mental health treatment, electronic monitoring, and more, it is increasingly likely that economic sanctions will be awarded to private entities rather than the state. For example, in a case in which the trial court ordered a man to attend psychiatric counseling sessions, the District of Connecticut held that the fees for those sessions did not constitute fines within the scope of the Clause solely because "the money appear[ed] to have been paid [to the psychiatrist] and not the government."[40] Under current doctrine, therefore, privatiza- tion would allow the government to sidestep the Clause's protections.

Unlike the partially punitive test, however, the requirement that economic sanctions be paid to the government is on shaky ground, as the restriction was called into question on the day it was announced and the Court has expressed reticence about it in a subsequent opinion. The *Browning-Ferris* Court based this restriction on the definition of a "fine" in three dictionaries — one published before the Clause's ratification in 1791 and two published forty-five and sixty-one years after — as well as the historical relationship between the Clause and the English Bill of Rights, the latter of which was intended to curb abuses by the Stuart kings. Those few sources served as the sole basis for the idea that fines were limited to monies paid to the government. The Court's reliance on that paltry historical record drew immediate fire from Justice O'Connor, who wrote that the determin- ation was "neither compelled by history nor supported by precedent."[41] Her conviction is supported by subsequent research showing that, in the colonies and early American states, both fines and forfeitures were made payable to non- governmental entities including crime victims and other private actors.[42] Apart from Justice O'Connor's immediate critique, a majority of the Court also later questioned the ongoing validity of restricting the Clause to monies paid to the government, noting that such a restriction was inconsistent with the partially punitive test, given that restitution serves both retributive and consequentialist aims, and because of the importance of the Clause serving as a limitation on the prosecutorial power of the state.[43]

In short, the Court has taken a broad view of what constitutes a fine and has indicated a willingness to further expand that definition to ensure the Clause can fulfill its role as a protection against government overreach. Whether an economic sanction constitutes a fine, however, is merely the threshold inquiry. As detailed

---

[40] Parsons v. Pond, 126 F. Supp. 2d 205, 209, 222 (D. Conn. 2000), *aff'd*, 25 F. App'x 77 (2d Cir. 2002).

[41] *Browning-Ferris Indus. of Vt.*, 492 U.S. at 283 (O'Connor, J., concurring in part and dissenting in part).

[42] Beth A. Colgan, *Reviving the Excessive Fines Clause*, 102 CAL. L. REV. 277, 300–10 (2014).

[43] Paroline v. United States, 572 U.S. 434, 455–56 (2014).

below, how courts should determine whether such fines are constitutionally excessive remains largely undecided.

Assessing Excessiveness

Though the Supreme Court has only considered what it means for a fine to be "excessive" on one occasion, it has expressly adopted the gross disproportionality test from the neighboring Cruel and Unusual Punishments Clause.[44] In its plainest terms, the test requires a court to compare the severity of the punishment against the seriousness of the offense; if the punishment is grossly disproportionate to the offense, the punishment is constitutionally excessive.

Members of the Court have telegraphed a complex conceptual problem triggered by the use of a common test to determine the constitutionality of punishment under the two clauses. During the *Timbs* oral argument, Justices Alito, Breyer, and Kagan all expressed discomfort with the idea that the forfeiture of a vehicle may be constitutionally excessive for the drug offense at issue in the case, even though a six-year term of incarceration — to which the individual may also have been subjected under Indiana law — would be unlikely deemed cruel and unusual, even though both forms of punishment are, in theory, measured by using the same gross disproportionality test.[45]

This conundrum exists in part because the Court has been loath to find term-of-incarceration sentences to be cruel and unusual. While the Court has struck down a life-without-parole sentence imposed under a habitual offender law when the final offense was issuing a no account check for $100,[46] it has also, for example, upheld a forty-year sentence for the possession and distribution of nine ounces of marijuana valued at $200,[47] and a life-with-the-possibility-of-parole sentence for a third felony conviction (following two prior convictions for frauds netting $80 and $28.36) for obtaining $120.75 under false pretenses.[48] In other words, as Justice Kagan has remarked, the Court has "made it awfully, awfully hard to assert a disproportionality claim with respect even to imprisonment," let alone fines.[49]

One response to this concern that allows the Excessive Fines Clause to retain its focus on proportionality but still have teeth is that, while the two clauses may approach the question of constitutionality by weighing offense seriousness against punishment severity, the application of that test must be less deferential in the excessive fines context because of the greater risk of government overreach given the

---

[44] United States v. Bajakajian, 524 U.S. 321, 337 (1998).
[45] *See* Transcript of Oral Argument at 10:9–12, 13:24–14:6, 19:12–21:16, 22:9–21; 23:21–24:5, Timbs v. Indiana, 139 S. Ct. 682 (2019) (No. 17-1091).
[46] Solem v. Helm, 463 U.S. 277 (1983).
[47] Hutto v. Davis, 454 U.S. 370 (1982).
[48] Rummel v. Estelle, 445 U.S. 263 (1980).
[49] Transcript of Oral Argument, *supra* note 45, at 23:23–24:5.

revenue-generating capacity of the punishment involved. The *Timbs* Court gave a nod to this concept, quoting from a passage in which Justice Scalia had staked out this position in arguing for a narrow interpretation of the Cruel and Unusual Punishments Clause years earlier.[50] He wrote:

> There is good reason to be concerned that fines, uniquely of all punishments, will be imposed in a measure out of accord with the penal goals of retribution and deterrence. Imprisonment, corporal punishment, and even capital punishment cost a State money; fines are a source of revenue. As we have recognized in the context of other constitutional provisions, it makes sense to scrutinize governmental action more closely when the State stands to benefit.[51]

This distinction may have particular resonance because states — as well as the federal and local governments — do stand to significantly benefit from the revenue generation afforded by the use of fines. Though practices vary across the country, lawmakers at times even include targeted increases in the imposition of economic sanctions into proposed budgets.[52] Fines and forfeitures have also been linked to distortions in law enforcement priorities, potentially pushing police and prosecutors to focus on traffic, public order, and drug offenses that carry a high likelihood of the imposition of economic sanctions, to the detriment of solving violent and property crimes.[53] Further, there is significant evidence that such practices are targeted at politically vulnerable communities. One study, for example, showed an increased use of traffic tickets during economic downturns, while "marginal increases in political activity" were associated with a reduced reliance on ticketing.[54] Complicating this concern is that people of color, and particularly African Americans, are disproportionately subject to penal disenfranchisement practices, which deny them the vote.[55] Perhaps unsurprisingly, then, another study of more than 9,000 cities found that "municipal governments with higher black populations rely more heavily on fines and fees for revenue."[56]

Despite signals that the Court may differentiate the two clauses on these grounds, there are other avenues available. The Court could, of course, restrict the Excessive

---

[50] *Timbs*, 139 S. Ct. at 689 (quoting Harmelin v. Michigan, 501 U.S. 957, 979 n.9 (1991) (opinion of Scalia, J.).

[51] *Harmelin*, 501 U.S. at 979 n.9 (opinion of Scalia, J.).

[52] *See, e.g.*, Thomas A. Garrett & Gary A. Wagner, *Red Ink in the Rearview Mirror: Local Fiscal Conditions and the Issuance of Traffic Tickets*, 52 J.L. & ECON. 71, 72 (2009); O'Harrow & Rich, *supra* note 12.

[53] Rebecca Goldstein et al., *Exploitative Revenues, Law Enforcement, and the Quality of Government Service*, 56 URBAN AFFAIRS REV. 5, 8, 17, 21–22 (2018).

[54] Garrett & Wagner, *supra* note 52, at 86.

[55] *See, e.g.*, SENT'G PROJECT, STATE-BY-STATE DATA: FELONY DISENFRANCHISEMENT RATE (2016); Marc Meredith & Michael Morse, *Discretionary Disenfranchisement: The Case of Legal Financial Obligations*, 46 J. LEGAL STUD. 309, 311, 327–28 (2017).

[56] Michael W. Sances & Hye Young You, *Who Pays for Government? Descriptive Representation and Exploitative Revenue Sources*, 79, J. OF POLITICS 1090, 1091–92 (2017).

Fines Clause to the narrow form of proportionality review through which it has given lawmakers wide deference in setting terms of incarceration.[57] It could also use the tension between the two clauses as an opportunity to rethink the validity of that deference in both settings.

In addition to the question of deference, the Court's conundrum also exists because it forces the question of whether incarceration is necessarily more severe than economic sanctions. Though at the extremes, the answer seems obvious — life without the possibility of parole is undoubtedly more severe than a $60 parking ticket — whether the same would be true when comparing a short term of incarceration to the perpetual instability caused by ongoing debt from fines and fees or from the loss of a home or automobile through forfeiture is unclear. Not only has that question been fodder for debate by the Court in the past,[58] but in at least some cases people with no means to pay and facing the risk of arrest and other consequences of nonpayment actually seek to serve jail time as a mechanism for paying off debt in order to avoid the burdens caused by economic sanctions.

Beyond these broader conceptual difficulties raised by the adoption of the gross disproportionality test, there remain a plethora of open questions about how to assess the seriousness of the offense and the severity of economic sanctions, many of which are already percolating up through the lower courts.

The Supreme Court has provided some guidance on the question of assessing offense seriousness. In the sole case in which it examined the excessiveness of a fine, the Court focused on the offense seriousness side of the scale. The punishment at issue in *Bajakajian* was the forfeiture of $357,144 in cash Mr. Bajakajian lawfully owned but had failed to report when attempting to transport it outside of the country in violation of U.S. customs laws. The Court described Mr. Bajakajian's actions as "solely a reporting offense" unrelated to any other illegal activity, leading it to describe Mr. Bajakajian himself as falling outside of the "class of persons for whom the statute was principally designed: money launderers, drug traffickers, and tax evaders."[59] The Court also noted that in failing to report Mr. Bajakajian caused minimal harm, and only to the government, and that the forfeiture far exceeded the maximum six-month sentence and $5,000 fine available for the offense under the U.S. Sentencing Guidelines. Given the minimal degree of offense seriousness, the Court deemed the forfeiture to be grossly disproportionate and thus an excessive fine.

The lower courts have largely followed the *Bajakajian* Court's lead on assessing offense seriousness, with a critical distinction. In *Bajakajian*, the Court used the available penalties under the Sentencing Guidelines as an indication of the "minimal level of culpability" Congress had assigned to the offense, signaling a

---

[57] *See* Harmelin v. Michigan, 501 U.S. 957, 996–97 (Kennedy, J., concurring in part).
[58] Colgan, *supra* note 5, at 111 n.283.
[59] United States v. Bajakajian, 524 U.S. 321, 337–38 (1998).

lack of offense seriousness, and it also took into account an individualized assessment of the actual crime and Mr. Bajakajian's culpability for it.[60] Several lower
courts, in contrast, have treated available statutory fines and other penalties as
dispositive, whereby any forfeiture within the range of those sanctions are deemed
constitutional regardless of any facts related to the person's culpability for the
offense, the lack of harm caused, or other mitigating information that might
reduce offense seriousness.[61]

In addition to misreading *Bajakajian*'s treatment of culpability, in cases involving instrumentality forfeitures in which property is forfeited on the theory that it
contributed in some way to the commission of the offense, some courts have taken
a hybrid approach, combining a *Bajakajian*-style proportionality review with a
consideration of the nexus of the forfeited property to the offense.[62] This consideration may, in fact, provide greater protection in cases in which the relationship
between the property and offense is tenuous, such as the forfeiture of a home
because a family member sold a small quantity of drugs from the home on a one-
time basis.[63] As Justice Breyer has suggested, however, the usefulness of a nexus
inquiry is less clear in cases where the validity of a forfeiture might be most
questionable, as would be the case, for example, if a state were to forfeit an
automobile for a minor traffic offense.[64] As with the apparent misinterpretation
of *Bajakajian* noted above, this division in the lower courts regarding the relevance of the nexus between property and offense to the excessiveness inquiry may
require intervention by the Supreme Court.

A separate question left open in *Bajakajian* is how to assess offense seriousness in
cases in which the government is not required to prove the facts of an offense
beyond a reasonable doubt. In addition to the civil forfeiture setting, this is an issue
that may arise out of the use of economic sanctions in juvenile court. In many
jurisdictions, parents may be made liable for the economic sanctions imposed on
juveniles adjudicated delinquent. In some places, that liability is dependent upon a
determination at a standard far less than beyond a reasonable doubt that the child's
delinquent behavior is related to a lapse in parental oversight, and in others, parents
are subject to economic sanctions without any such determination.[65] In either case,
as well as in the civil forfeiture context, it is arguable that offense seriousness should
be given less weight in the proportionality inquiry when the government's burden of
proof is reduced or even eliminated.

---

[60] *Id.* at 338–39.
[61] *See, e.g.,* State v. One 1987 Toyota Truck, 964 So.2d 60, 64–65 (Ala. Civ. App. 2007).
[62] *See, e.g.,* Howell v. State, 656 S.E.2d 511, 512 (Ga. 2008).
[63] *See* Brown, *supra* note 13.
[64] *See* Transcript of Oral Argument, *supra* note 45, at 43:11–45:10.
[65] *Compare, e.g.,* WYO. STAT. ANN. § 14-6-247(a)(xiii) (allowing imposition of fines against parents
if the court finds "that the child's act was proximately caused by the failure or neglect of
the parent or child to subject the child to reasonable parental control and authority"), *with id.*
§ 14-6-247(a)(v) (allowing imposition of restitution against parents without such a finding).

The other half of the proportionality analysis — also the subject of a wide array of open questions — is the assessment of punishment severity. Perhaps the most pressing issue that the Court has so far declined to decide,[66] and that has divided the lower courts,[67] is whether the effect fines have on the financial condition of people and their families, including the ability to meet basic needs, is relevant to the question of excessiveness.

The Court's previous reliance on the Clause's historical foundations suggests that it may ultimately deem the consequences of the deprivation, and not just its dollar value, relevant to understanding the severity of a fine. From its first analysis of the Clause in *Browning-Ferris* to its most recent assessment in *Timbs*, the Court has repeatedly tied the concept of excessiveness to individualized consideration of such effects.[68] In particular, the Court has understood the Clause to be rooted in Magna Carta, which expressly mandated that economic sanctions be limited to ensure they did not deprive a person of his livelihood.[69] It has also relied upon Blackstone's writings — which stated that "[t]he value of money itself changes from a thousand causes; and at all events, what is ruin to one man's fortune may be a matter of indifference to another's,"[70] and thus fines should be prohibited if they are beyond what "his circumstances or personal estate will bear."[71]

In addition to its reliance on the historical record, the Court's adoption of the gross disproportionality test also supports the inclusion of a fine's effects on one's financial condition.[72] A key concept underlying the doctrine is the use of proportionality as a means of ensuring equality in sentencing, whereby two people equally culpable for the same offense should receive the same punishment. In circumstances in which people are charged additional fees, placed or retained on

---

[66] Mr. Bajakajian did not raise an argument as to the effect of the forfeiture on his financial condition, and the Court did not address the issue. *See* United States v. Bajakajian, 524 U.S. 321, 339, 340 n.15 (1998); *see also* Timbs v. Indiana, 139 S. Ct. 682, 687–88 (2019). Shortly after the Court decided *Timbs*, the State of Colorado and a corporation it had fined both asked the Court to accept review of the Colorado Supreme Court's determination that financial effect is relevant to excessiveness — as well as the application of the Clause's protections — but the Court denied certiorari. Colo. Dep't of Labor & Employ. v. Dami Hospitality, LLC, 442 P.3d 94 (Colo. 2019), *cert. denied* 2020 WL 129639 (Jan. 13, 2020).

[67] *Compare, e.g.,* United States v. Seher, 562 F.3d 1344, 1371 (11th Cir. 2009), *with* United States v. Levesque, 546 F.3d 78, 84–85 (1st Cir. 2008).

[68] For a more detailed discussion of the historical record regarding consideration of financial effect, see generally Eighth Amendment Scholars Brief Amici Curiae in Support of Neither Party, Timbs v. Indiana, 2018 WL 4522295 (Sept. 10, 2018); Colgan, *supra* note 42, at 330–35; Nicholas M. McLean, *Livelihood, Ability to Pay, and the Original Meaning of the Excessive Fines Clause,* 40 HASTINGS CONST. L.Q. 833 (2013).

[69] *Timbs,* 139 S. Ct. at 687–88; Browning-Ferris Indus. of Vt., Inc. v. Kelco Disposal, Inc., 492 U.S. 257, 270 n.14 (1989).

[70] *Browning-Ferris,* 492 U.S. at 300 (O'Connor, J., concurring in part and dissenting in part) (quoting 4 W. BLACKSTONE, COMMENTARIES ON THE LAWS OF ENGLAND 371 (1769)).

[71] *Timbs,* 139 S. Ct. at 688 (quoting BLACKSTONE, *supra* note 70, at 372).

[72] For a more detailed discussion of the principles underlying the gross disproportionality test described here, see Colgan, *supra* note 23, at 48–76.

probation or parole, or subject to other forms of punishment due to an inability to pay immediately or in full, the punishment is inherently unequal as compared to a person who, though committing the same offense, could pay upon imposition. If those additional penalties are set aside — leaving only the fine (whether a cash fine or forfeiture of cash or property) — it raises the question of whether equality should be understood formally (by dollar value) or substantively (by effect). The Court has yet to opine on this issue, but even theorists who oppose the use of subjective considerations in assessing the severity of the length and conditions of incarceration agree that the formal approach, and the use of "one-size fits all" economic sanctions, is unjustifiable given their inherently regressive nature.[73] This agreement is due in part to the difficulty in separating the consequences of a deprivation to one's financial condition and ability to access basic needs from the imposition of the fine; in other words, the government must intend economic sanctions to have a fiscal effect and thus it is an appropriate consideration in assessing punishment severity. Further, failing to account for such effects would be likely to exacerbate inequalities rather than promote equality. For example, because a luxury vehicle has a higher dollar value than a jalopy, if dollar value alone is relevant, a person of means would have greater access to the Clause's protections because the larger dollar amount would be more likely to be disproportionately severe as compared to the offense. In contrast, the jalopy's more limited dollar value would be less likely to be disproportionate even if jalopy owners would be hit hardest by the deprivation. Therefore, consideration of the effect of the fine along with its dollar value does a better job at ensuring equality in sentencing.

Beyond equality, the Court has relied on several additional principles when conceptualizing proportionality that also comport with a more expansive approach to assessing punishment severity. It has, for example, expressed an interest in ensuring comparative proportionality, by which the punishment for a more serious offense must be more severe than the punishment for a less serious offense. Failing to include financial effect when assessing punishment severity dilutes that goal, particularly in cases where people cannot reach the principle debt or where the level of debt is high enough that completing payment in the foreseeable future is unlikely. In such cases, the perpetual requirement to pay means that it no longer matters whether the debt stems from a minor offense such as a traffic violation or a major offense such as robbery, rendering the seriousness of the offense effectively irrelevant. A lack of attention to the consequences of economic sanctions also distorts the expressive goals of punishment, both by suggesting to those against whom unmanageable fines are imposed that the justice system prizes revenue

---

[73] Kenneth W. Simons, *Retributivists Need Not and Should Not Endorse the Subjectivist Account of Punishment*, 109 Colum. L. Rev. Sidebar 1, 6 n.11 (2009); *see also, e.g.*, Dan Markel & Chad Flanders, *Bentham on Stilts: The Bare Relevance of Subjectivity to Retributive Justice*, 98 Calif. L. Rev. 907, 915 (2010); Adam J. Kolber, *The Subjective Experience of Punishment*, 109 Colum. L. Rev. 182, 226 (2009).

generation over fairness, and by imposing punishment that often outweighs the public's desire to condemn. Failing to attend to the consequences for one's financial condition may also cut against the Court's interest in avoiding criminogenic effects and other social harms caused by excessive punishments. Recent studies, for example, suggest that the inability to pay economic sanctions leads some people to commit new offenses, such as theft, drugs sales, and prostitution, in order to obtain money to pay off the debt, and tie such debts to increases in homelessness, decreases in child support, family disunification, and other social harms.[74] Finally, the Court's declaration that the "basic concept underlying the Eighth Amendment is nothing less than the dignity of man"[75] is at stake. If that dignity demand is to mean anything, the fact that an economic sanction may place people in a position where they must engage in the drug or sex trades or otherwise risky behavior, or must forgo necessities such as food, shelter, or medicine, in order to pay off economic sanctions or recover from forfeiture, certainly must be relevant to excessiveness.

Though splits in the lower courts and increased public attention to the negative consequences of fines for those deprived of money and property makes the question of individualized assessments of punishment severity the likely subject of litigation in the near future, open questions regarding the scope of the Clause's protections extend well beyond that issue. For example, the Court has afforded categorical protections for juveniles in the cruel and unusual punishments context,[76] but has yet to consider whether similar categorical rules should apply with respect to fines. That inquiry may be particularly important in light of recent studies showing that the imposition of economic sanctions on juveniles contributes to increased recidivism rates and other short- and long-term negative outcomes.[77] Another example involves the burden of proof for establishing excessiveness. While most lower courts

---

[74] Ala. Appleseed, *supra* note 1, at 31–33; Foster Cook, Jefferson Cty.'s Cmty. Corr. Program, The Burden of Criminal Justice Debt in Alabama: 2014 Participant Self-Report Survey 12 (2014); Harris et al., *supra* note 1, at 1785; *see also* Beth A. Colgan, Brookings Institute, Addressing Modern Debtors' Prisons with Graduated Economic Sanctions that Depend on Ability to Pay 10–11 (2019) (summarizing empirical studies of the deterrent effects of economic sanctions, which generally support the conclusion that higher rates of economic sanctions and the imposition of sanctions beyond a person's ability to pay can increase recidivism).

[75] Trop v. Dulles, 356 U.S. 86, 99 (1958) (plurality opinion).

[76] Miller v. Alabama, 567 U.S. 460 (2012) (holding that mandatory imposition of life without parole sentences on juveniles violates the Cruel and Unusual Punishments Clause); Graham v. Florida, 560 U.S. 48 (2010) (prohibiting life without parole sentences for juveniles convicted of non-homicide offenses); Roper v. Simmons, 543 U.S. 551 (2005) (striking down as cruel and unusual the use of capital punishment against juveniles).

[77] Alex R. Piquero & Wesley G. Jennings, *Research Note: Justice System-Imposed Financial Penalties Increase the Likelihood of Recidivism in a Sample of Adolescent Offenders*, 15 Youth Violence & Juv. Just. 325, 334 (2017) (finding that, in the juvenile context, the imposition of restitution, higher amounts of economic sanctions, and the continuation of debt upon case closing "all significantly increased the odds of a youth recidivating . . . even after controlling for relevant youth demographics and case characteristic variables").

have simply assumed that the person raising the constitutional challenge bears the burden,[78] the foundation for that assumption is on shakier ground in cases where the government is not held to establish guilt beyond a reasonable doubt.

* * *

Though only four words long — "nor excessive fines imposed"[79] — a plethora of open questions as to what constitutes a fine and what renders a fine excessive remain. Those questions are of no small matter given both the serious, long-term consequences that economic sanctions may have on people and their families, and the potentially perverse incentives that their revenue-generating capacity can have on lawmakers. There are good reasons to doubt whether the Excessive Fines Clause will ultimately spur reform of these modern debtors' prisons and policing for profit problems, whether due to misunderstandings regarding the nature and scope of the harms economic sanctions cause, the unavailability of counsel to litigate excessive fines claims, or the pressure to waive such claims in plea bargaining. But there is also reason for cautious optimism. The members of the *Timbs* Court disagreed as to whether the proper vehicle for incorporation of the Clause's protections against the states was a determination that it was "fundamental to our scheme of ordered liberty" and "deeply rooted in this nation's history and traditions,"[80] or instead because freedom from excessive fines has long been understood to be a "fundamental right of American citizenship" and thus a privilege or immunity that states may not abridge.[81] But the Court was unanimous in its understanding that government abuses of economic sanctions are "scarcely hypothetical,"[82] leading lawmakers to abuse the prosecutorial power in order to generate revenue, and leaving the financial security and well-being of people and their families devastated in their wake. And though the Supreme Court's Excessive Fines cases are few in number, in each one, the Court has cemented the role of the Excessive Fines Clause as a safeguard against those very abuses.

---

[78] *See, e.g.*, United States v. Jose, 499 F.3d 105, 108 (1st Cir. 2007).

[79] U.S. Const. amend. VIII.

[80] Timbs v. Indiana, 139 S. Ct. 682, 689 (2019) (internal citations omitted) (quoting McDonald v. Chicago, 561 U.S. 742, 767 (2010)).

[81] *Id.* at 698 (Thomas, J. concurring); *see also id.* at 691 (Gorsuch, J., concurring).

[82] *Id.* at 689.

PART III

The Future of the Eighth Amendment

Rubberball / Mike Kemp / Getty Images

Judicial Abolition of the American Death Penalty under the Eighth Amendment: The Most Likely Path

*Carol Steiker & Jordan Steiker**

INTRODUCTION: THE DECLINE OF THE AMERICAN DEATH PENALTY

Over the past fifty years, the death penalty has rapidly declined around the world. In 1965, only twenty-five countries were in the abolitionist camp.[1] By 2018, 106 countries had legally abolished the death penalty for all crimes, and another thirty-six countries were deemed "de facto" abolitionist by Amnesty International (reflected in part by not carrying out any executions over the past ten years).[2] The magnitude of the shift from majority retentionist to majority abolitionist jurisdictions does not capture the depth of the world's turn away from the death penalty, what is fairly characterized as a true "global movement toward the universal abolition of capital punishment."[3] During this turn, countries have increasingly viewed the death penalty not as a local issue of criminal justice policy but rather as an issue of fundamental human rights, with an imperative to end the practice through international advocacy and treaties. During this period, the United States came quite close to being on the early side of this global movement, having experienced an informal moratorium on executions for almost ten years (June 1967–January 1977), followed by what many thought at the time was the end of the American death penalty — the Supreme Court's invalidation of prevailing capital statutes in *Furman v. Georgia* 1972.[4] But state legislatures reasserted their commitment to the death

---

[*] Carol Steiker is the Henry J. Friendly Professor of Law and Faculty Co-Director of the Criminal Justice Policy Program, Harvard Law School; Jordon Steiker is the Judge Robert M. Parker Endowed Chair in Law and Director of the Capital Punishment Center, University of Texas School of Law.

[1] Richard Dieter, *Introduction: International Perspectives on the Death Penalty, in* COMPARATIVE CAPITAL PUNISHMENT (Carol Steiker & Jordan Steiker eds., 2019).

[2] *Death Penalty in 2018: Facts and Figures,* AMNESTY INT'L, www.amnesty.org/en/latest/news/2019/04/death-penalty-facts-and-figures-2018/ (last visited Sept. 26, 2019).

[3] DEATH PENALTY WORLDWIDE INT'L HUMAN RTS. CLINIC, PATHWAYS TO ABOLITION OF THE DEATH PENALTY 2 (June 2016), www.deathpenaltyworldwide.org/pdf/pathways-english.pdf.

[4] 408 U.S. 238 (1972).

penalty in response to *Furman*, the Court affirmed the basic constitutionality of the death penalty in 1976,[5] executions resumed in 1977, and the United States emerged as one of the world's leading executioners by the mid-1990s. The revitalization of the American death penalty, coinciding as it did with the marked decline of capital punishment in the rest of the world, led many to wonder what accounted for American exceptionalism — its emergence as the sole developed Western democracy with both the death penalty on the books and active execution chambers.

Over the past two decades, though, the American death penalty has experienced an enormous decline — mirroring the weakening of capital punishment around the world. Beginning with New York and New Jersey in 2007, nine states have abandoned the death penalty over the past twelve years — a seismic shift given that the most recent abolition (not triggered by a judicial decision) before 2007 was a half-century ago (1965).[6] Executions, too, have declined substantially, to about twenty-three executions per year nationwide from 2016 to 2018, down over seventy-five percent from the high of ninety-eight executions nationwide in 1999.[7] The most dramatic and important development, though, is the extraordinary decline in capital sentencing. Death sentences have dropped from their highs in the mid-1990s of more than 300 sentences per year to about forty death sentences per year nationwide from 2015 to 2018;[8] with only fourteen death sentences nationwide recorded by mid-year 2019,[9] the United States may see the fewest number of death sentences in the modern era of the American death penalty, stretching back to the early 1970s. Given the lag between death sentences and executions, death sentences are the "leading indicator" of American capital practice, and the prevailing historic lows in death sentencing suggest a significantly diminished presence of the death penalty going forward.

The declines in death sentencing and executions understate the extent to which the death penalty in the United States has become marginalized and confined to a very small number of states and counties: four states (Texas, Alabama, Georgia, and Florida) account for over seventy-five percent of all executions since 2016, and a slightly different combination of states (California, Florida, Ohio, and Texas) accounts for over half the death verdicts issued in that time.[10] Opinion polls reflect a significant decline in public support for capital punishment as well. In 1995, only

---

[5] *Gregg v. Georgia*, 428 U.S. 153 (1976).

[6] *State by State*, DEATH PENALTY INFO. CTR., https://deathpenaltyinfo.org/state-and-federal-info/state-by-state (last visited Sept. 26, 2019).

[7] *Executions by State and Region Since 1976*, DEATH PENALTY INFO. CTR., https://deathpenalty info.org/executions/executions-overview/number-of-executions-by-state-and-region-since-1976 (last visited Sept. 26, 2019).

[8] *Death Sentences in the United States Since 1977*, DEATH PENALTY INFO. CTR., https://death penaltyinfo.org/facts-and-research/sentencing-data/death-sentences-in-the-united-states-from-1977-by-state-and-by-year (last visited Sept. 26, 2019).

[9] *DPIC Mid-Year Review: At Midpoint of 2019, Death Penalty Remains Near Historic Lows*, DEATH PENALTY INFO. CTR. (July 1, 2019), https://deathpenaltyinfo.org/news/dpic-mid-year-review-at-midpoint-of-2019-death-penalty-use-remains-near-historic-lows.

[10] *Death Sentences in the United States Since 1977*, *supra* note 8.

thirteen percent of Americans polled by Gallup answered "no" to the question: "Are you in favor of the death penalty for a person convicted of murder," compared to forty-one percent who answered "no" in the two recent (2018, 2017) Gallup polls asking the identical question, an increase of over two hundred percent.[11] That level of opposition to the death penalty was last achieved in 1972, just before the Court's invalidation of prevailing statutes.[12]

Is the present weakening of the American death penalty a harbinger of abolition? American abolition of the death penalty will occur, if it does, through a judicial decision invalidating the practice as inconsistent with the Eighth Amendment. The current weakening of the death penalty has marginalized the death penalty to a handful of jurisdictions, but those jurisdictions — including Texas, Alabama, Florida — are unlikely to abolish in the near future. Even if Congress were to have an appetite to ban the death penalty (and there is no indication of the type of coordinated opposition among congressional and executive decision-makers necessary for such legislation), substantial doubts remain about the ability of Congress to use its powers under Article I or section 5 of the Fourteenth Amendment to preclude the use of the death penalty.

Judicial abolition became much less likely in the short term with the recent replacement of Justices Scalia and Kennedy with Justices Gorsuch and Kavanaugh. The significance of those replacements became clear in the Court's recent decision in *Bucklew v. Precythe*,[13] rejecting an as-applied challenge to Missouri's lethal injection protocol. In evaluating the inmate's claim, the Court began with its observation that the "Constitution allows capital punishment."[14] That observation was not new: in both of the Court's prior lethal injection cases, *Baze v. Rees*[15] and *Glossip v. Gross*,[16] the Court assumed that "because it is settled that capital punishment is constitutional . . . there must be a constitutional means of carrying it out."[17] It is fair to read *Baze* and *Glossip* as simply reflecting the holding in *Gregg v. Georgia*[18] that the death penalty remains consistent with "evolving standards of decency," the approach to Eighth Amendment analysis that the Court first embraced more than six decades ago in *Trop v. Dulles*.[19]

But Justice Gorsuch's majority opinion in *Bucklew* made clear, in a manner that *Baze* and *Glossip* did not, that the majority views the issue of the death penalty's constitutionality as essentially foreclosed by the text and history of the Constitution. Justice Gorsuch cites the language in the Fifth Amendment "expressly contemplat

[11] *Death Penalty*, GALLUP, https://news.gallup.com/poll/1606/death-penalty.aspx (last visited Sept. 26, 2019).

[12] *Id.*

[13] 139 S. Ct. 1112 (2019).

[14] *Id.* at 1122.

[15] 553 U.S. 35 (2008).

[16] 135 S. Ct. 2726, 2732–33 (2015).

[17] *Id.* (quoting *Baze*, 553 U.S. at 47).

[18] 428 U.S. 153 (1976).

[19] 356 U.S. 86 (1958).

[ing] that a defendant may be tried for a 'capital' crime and 'deprived of life' as a penalty," as well as the fact that the First Congress "made a number of crimes punishable by death."[20] On these grounds, Justice Gorsuch insists that although states may choose to abandon the death penalty, "the judiciary bears no license to end a debate reserved for the people and their representatives."[21] *Bucklew's* approach to the constitutionality of the death penalty is an implicit assault on the Court's longstanding proportionality analysis, which the Court has deployed in striking down the death penalty as applied to persons with intellectual disability,[22] juveniles,[23] and offenders convicted of non-homicidal crimes against persons (including the rape of a child).[24] *Bucklew* suggests strongly that the current majority would not be inclined to evaluate the constitutionality of the death penalty in the same manner as it evaluated those particular practices by assessing current indicia of societal support. Nonetheless, *Bucklew* is not an enormous obstacle to a future Court revisiting the constitutionality of the death penalty: the constitutionality of the death penalty was not contested in *Bucklew* and the case is not fairly read to overrule *sub silentio* the *Trop* framework, which was decisive to numerous Court holdings (whereas *Bucklew's* discussion of the constitutionality of the death penalty is plainly dictum).

If the Court were to revisit the constitutionality of the American death penalty, what would judicial abolition look like? On this score, there is a surprising disconnect between the concerns that have animated growing discontent about the American death penalty and prevailing capital doctrines. In particular, it is unlikely that the Court would invalidate the death penalty based on its racially discriminatory imposition, the risk (or demonstrated presence) of wrongful convictions or executions, or its denial of human dignity. Each of these concerns has played a significant role in catalyzing opposition to the death penalty. Concerns about the death penalty's racially discriminatory administration led to the initial efforts by the NAACP Legal Defense Fund (LDF) in the 1960s to challenge the practice. Concerns about wrongful convictions brought a new circumspection about capital punishment in the late 1990s, contributing significantly to the drop in public support (and in capital sentencing). The argument that capital punishment is inconsistent with human dignity is by far the most frequently voiced ground for abolition around the world. Yet each of these arguments would encounter formidable jurisprudential obstacles as stand-alone grounds for constitutional abolition of the death penalty. The first section of this chapter will examine those obstacles, and the next section will discuss the more likely path to judicial abolition — the Court's

---

[20] *Bucklew v. Precythe*, 139 S. Ct. 1112, 1122 (2019).
[21] *Id.* at 1123.
[22] *Atkins v. Virginia*, 536 U.S. 23 (2002).
[23] *Roper v. Simmons*, 543 U.S. 551 (2005).
[24] *Kennedy v. Louisiana*, 554 U.S. 407 (2008).

proportionality doctrine — as well as the subsidiary role concerns about race, wrongful convictions, and human dignity might play within that doctrine.

JURISPRUDENTIAL OBSTACLES TO INVALIDATION OF THE DEATH PENALTY BASED ON RACE, WRONGFUL CONVICTIONS, OR INCOMPATIBILITY WITH HUMAN DIGNITY

Many problems haunt the American death penalty. Capital trial lawyers are often underfunded, poorly trained, and insufficiently committed to their clients. Prosecutors routinely fail to comply with basic ethical duties in capital litigation, particularly their responsibility to disclose exculpatory information to the defense. Death-row incarceration has become increasingly cruel, as most states have gravitated toward solitary confinement as the sole means of incarcerating death-row inmates, a problem exacerbated by mental health challenges among the death-row population and the length of time between sentencing and execution. Clemency has all but disappeared as a check on the fundamental justice of capital sentences. But three concerns stand out as especially vexing, having plagued the American death penalty since its inception: the role of race discrimination in the application of the death penalty, the proneness of the capital system to error, and the incompatibility of capital punishment with fundamental conceptions of human dignity. Despite the compelling nature and urgency of these concerns, the Court has marginalized them within constitutional discourse, making them unlikely stand-alone grounds for constitutional abolition of the death penalty.

Race

Race discrimination has played an outsized role in the American death penalty from the colonial period to the present day. During the antebellum period, Southern capital codes explicitly made the death penalty's availability turn on the race of the accused and the victim.[25] Modes of execution were more draconian for African-American offenders.[26] After the conclusion of the Civil War and the passage of the Fourteenth Amendment, racial discrimination continued despite the command of equal protection of the laws. In many parts of the country but particularly the South, African Americans were effectively precluded from serving as jurors in capital trials (despite the Court's rejection of formal discrimination in state juror qualifications[27]), and disparate treatment was the norm in all aspects of capital litigation — in charging decisions, trials, appeals, and executive clemency. In the period spanning

---

[25] Carol S. Steiker & Jordan M. Steiker, *The American Death Penalty and the (In)Visibility of Race*, 82 U. CHI. L. REV. 243, 245–46 (2015).
[26] *Id.* at 246.
[27] Strauder v. West Virginia, 100 U.S. 303 (1880).

the Civil War to the Depression, discriminatory capital trials were sometimes better than the alternative, as the specter of lynching often cast a shadow over the proceedings. Cases involving accusations of black-on-white crime were often litigated swiftly and without a pretense of process, earning the sobriquet "legal lynchings." During the twentieth century, the role of race discrimination was particularly evident in rape prosecutions, as the vast majority of those executed for rape were African-American defendants convicted of raping white victims.

Concerns about race discrimination in capital cases prompted the Legal Defense Fund to lead the effort against the death penalty in the 1960s. As part of its effort, the LDF enlisted Marvin Wolfgang, an eminent sociologist, to document the discriminatory application of the death penalty in the South. Wolfgang's empirical study ultimately served as the basis of a constitutional challenge to the use of the death penalty in rape cases in Arkansas.[28]

In *Maxwell v. Bishop*,[29] then-Judge Harry Blackmun, writing for a panel of the U.S. Court of Appeals for the Eighth Circuit, rejected the claim of race discrimination and expressed deep skepticism about the possibility of the defendant ever prevailing on the basis of statistical showings of statewide racial discrimination.[30] The U.S. Supreme Court, though it agreed to hear Maxwell's appeal of the panel's denial of federal habeas relief, declined to grant review of his race discrimination claim — one of many occasions in which the Supreme Court declined to address directly claims of race discrimination in the administration of the death penalty.[31] Indeed, when the Court ruled almost a decade later that the death penalty was excessive as applied to the crime of rape, it selected the case of a white defendant as a vehicle for its decision and made no mention of race — though it was plainly aware of the evidence of longstanding race discrimination in capital rape cases.[32]

When the Court invalidated prevailing statutes in *Furman* based largely on the death penalty's unpredictable and unprincipled administration, the opinions supporting the judgment generally avoided discussing race discrimination directly, instead referring euphemistically to broader concerns about "arbitrariness" in the American capital system.[33] After the Court upheld several of the new capital statutes enacted post-*Furman*, the LDF again sought to document the role of race in a Southern capital jurisdiction, this time in Georgia's post-*Furman* regime. Eventually, the Supreme Court addressed an extensive empirical study by the Baldus group finding a significant role of race — particularly the race of victims — in the

---

[28] Steiker & Steiker, *supra* note 25, at 255–57.
[29] 398 F.2d 138 (8th Cir. 1968).
[30] *Id.* at 148 ("We are not certain that, for Maxwell, statistics will ever be his redemption.").
[31] Steiker & Steiker, *supra* note 25, at 265. Justice Douglas alone offered a sustained critique of the operation of racial discrimination within the American death penalty. *See* Furman v. Georgia, 408 U.S. 238, 249–50 (1972) (Douglas, J., concurring).
[32] *Id.* at 273–77 (discussing the Court's choice of a white defendant and avoidance of race in *Coker v. Georgia*, 433 U.S. 584 (1977) (plurality opinion)).
[33] *Coker*, 433 U.S. at 584.

distribution of capital verdicts in Georgia. The Court rejected the constitutional claim in *McCleskey v. Kemp*.[34]

The most striking aspect of *McCleskey* is the fact that the Court assumed for the purposes of its decision that the Baldus study was methodologically sound.[35] An early draft of Justice Powell's majority decision had criticized the study and left open the possibility that stronger evidence of the role of race in capital sentencing might justify relief; but Justice Scalia objected to this approach in a memorandum, insisting that he did not want to pretend that more "proof" of the role of irrational prejudice, including racial prejudice, would change the outcome.[36] Instead, at Justice Scalia's urging, the majority opinion concluded that statistical evidence of racial discrimination is insufficient to establish a constitutional violation under either the Eighth Amendment or the Fourteenth Amendment's guarantee of equal protection.

The Court's decision seemed to rest on its view of the disruptiveness of a contrary holding. The Court recognized that discretion inevitably invites arbitrariness, including race discrimination,[37] and that the Court's individualization doctrine *requires* states to afford significant discretion in the capital context. Accordingly, the Court seemed to suggest (as Justice Scalia stated explicitly in his memorandum) that a demand that capital sentencing be free of racial influences was unrealistic and incompatible with its continued retention.[38] Moreover, the Court feared that the successful use of statistical evidence in the capital context might threaten the administration of non-capital punishments, given that the Eighth Amendment applies "to all penalties."[39]

Apart from these concerns, the Court was likely influenced by several other considerations. If it were to entertain challenges based on statistical studies, the Court would have to decide the difficult question of how much racial influence on capital sentencing is constitutionally unacceptable, a determination that itself would be arbitrary. The Court would also have to decide upon an appropriate remedy. Given that the most powerful finding of the Baldus study was the unwillingness of prosecutors and jurors to produce death sentences in minority victim cases, it is not at all clear that exempting offenders with white victims from the death penalty

[34] 481 U.S. 279 (1987).

[35] *Id.* at 291 n.7.

[36] Justice Antonin Scalia, *Memorandum to the Conference Re: No. 84-6811-*McCleskey v. Kemp (Jan. 6, 1987), *available at* Library of Congress, Thurgood Marshall Papers, *McCleskey v. Kemp* file ("Since it is my view that the unconscious operation of irrational sympathies and antipathies, including racial, upon jury decisions and (hence) prosecutorial decisions is real, acknowledged in the decisions of this court, and ineradicable, I cannot honestly say that all I need is more proof.").

[37] *McCleskey*, 481 U.S. at 312.

[38] *Id.* at 319 ("As we have stated specifically in the context of capital punishment, the Constitution does not place totally unrealistic conditions on its use." (internal quotation marks and citation omitted)).

[39] *Id.* at 315.

(as the Court was asked to do in *McCleskey*) is responsive to the underlying discrimination; it does little to address the indifference to minority victims that produced the disparate results. And the Court lacks the power to command prosecutors to seek, and jurors to return, death verdicts in minority victim cases. More generally, these sort of line-drawing and remedial problems underscore why the Court is much more comfortable making *procedural* rather than *substantive* interventions as it regulates capital punishment. Most of the Court's decisions focus on structuring the capital decision-making process and the duties of the various institutional actors (prosecutors, defense attorneys, judges). The Court's jurisprudence is designed to reduce arbitrariness and discrimination, but it has never sought — outside a set of proportionality decisions restricting the death penalty's application to certain offenders and offenses — to regulate capital outcomes directly.

McCleskey is a formidable obstacle to challenging the continued use of the death penalty based on its racially-discriminatory administration. The Court's justifications for refusing relief to an individual defendant based on systemic racial discrimination would likely be invoked in a case globally challenging the continued use of the death penalty. Moreover, *McCleskey*'s seeming indifference to the quantity and quality of evidence demonstrating the influence of race in capital sentencing was self-consciously designed to foreclose race-based challenges in the future. Simply put, from the Court's perspective, a decision rejecting the death penalty as racially discriminatory would have too much disruptive potential by opening the door to challenges to a host of racially skewed American criminal justice practices — including disparate policing policies, fees and fines, and the severity of non-capital sentences.

Innocence

Concerns about the possibility of wrongful convictions and executions are likely as old as the death penalty. Some countries in the abolitionist camp were motivated in part to abolish because of high-profile wrongful convictions (as in the case of the United Kingdom following the execution and subsequent exoneration of Timothy Evans). In the United States, such concerns surfaced in some of the most famous capital prosecutions of the twentieth century, including in the cases of Leo Frank, Sacco and Vanzetti, and the Rosenbergs. But concerns about wrongful convictions reached a new level of urgency in the late 1990s, as advances in technology facilitated more accurate testing of DNA evidence.[40] As the technology was applied to preserved genetic material in criminal cases, numerous inmates — including some death-sentenced inmates — were found to have been wrongly convicted.[41]

---

[40] Carol S. Steiker & Jordan M. Steiker, *The Seduction of Innocence: The Attraction and Limitations of the Focus on Innocence in Capital Punishment Law and Advocacy*, 95 J. CRIM. L. & CRIMINOLOGY 587, 594–95 (2005).

[41] *Id.*

Even though most criminal cases lack available genetic material for testing, the sudden technological shift prompted a growth industry in uncovering error in the criminal justice system, reflected in the establishment of "Innocence Projects" dedicated exclusively to such efforts. The most dramatic spate of exonerations occurred in Illinois, where the discovery of more than a dozen wrongly death-sentenced inmates produced a firestorm of popular and political outcry. In 2000, Illinois Governor George Ryan declared a moratorium on executions, which was followed three years later by his decision to commute the death sentences of all inmates on the state's death row. The Illinois legislature subsequently abolished the death penalty.

The revelation that capital verdicts could be returned with some frequency against innocent defendants shook American confidence in the death penalty. The "exoneration" phenomenon, brought home to the wider public through both journalistic and artistic efforts (including stage and film productions of "The Exonerated"), seemed to significantly shift public discourse around the death penalty. Beginning in the early 2000s, death-sentencing rates began to plummet, dropping below two hundred sentences a year in 2001, and below one hundred sentences a year by 2011.[42] Support for the death penalty in the Gallup poll fell below seventy percent in 2000 (having never been below that number in the 1990s), and support fell to sixty-one percent by 2011.[43] By 2006, executions fell below forty-five a year for the first time since 1994, and they have remained below forty-five every year since 2010.[44] Within two decades of the high-profile exonerations in Illinois, numerous states repealed their capital statutes, with concerns about innocence in the forefront of the public debates of repeal.

Despite its power to move public opinion, the fear of wrongful convictions has had little traction in shaping the constitutional jurisprudence around the death penalty. Since the Court "constitutionalized" capital punishment law in the 1970s, it has crafted numerous doctrines regulating capital practices, including jury selection, the use of aggravating and mitigating factors to guide sentencer discretion, the essential duties of counsel in preparing for the punishment phase, and so on. But the Court has resisted any special protections to guard against the possibility of executing innocents. In the early 1990s — before the spate of exonerations in Illinois — the Court was confronted in *Herrera v. Collins*[45] with a claim of innocence by Leonel Herrera, a death-sentenced inmate in Texas. After Herrera had been convicted and sentenced to death, his attorneys discovered new evidence of his innocence, including the statement of his brother's attorney that the brother had confessed to the murder underlying Herrera's death sentence. Prevailing Texas procedural rules, though, like those of other states at the time, precluded revisiting any criminal verdict (including a death verdict) based on new evidence of innocence unless such evidence was discovered and presented within thirty days of trial. In federal habeas proceedings, Herrera argued that the refusal of the state courts to consider new evidence of innocence in a capital case violated the Constitution, and that the federal court should address his evidence to determine whether he had been wrongly convicted. The Court of Appeals for the Fifth Circuit denied the claim, stating that "the existence merely of newly discovered evidence relevant to the guilt of a state prisoner is not a ground for relief on federal habeas corpus."[46]

Herrera filed a petition for certiorari raising the question of whether the Constitution prohibits the execution of an innocent person. Chief Justice William Rehnquist, writing for the Court, suggested strongly that the Constitution does not mandate relief based on post-trial evidence of actual innocence, even in a capital case; he insisted that as a matter of longstanding practice, the appropriate forum for such claims is executive clemency. Ultimately, the Court left open whether a "truly persuasive demonstration of 'actual innocence' made after trial" in a capital case might require judicial relief.[47] In the quarter decade since Herrera's claim was rejected, though, the Court has never embraced the proposition that courts are obligated to provide a forum to vindicate claims of actual innocence, even to prevent a wrongful execution.

Herrera suggests strongly that the Court would not invalidate the death penalty based on concerns of wrongful conviction or execution. If the Constitution does not afford a remedy to an individual inmate based on demonstrated innocence in his own case, it seems unlikely that capital punishment as a practice would be deemed unconstitutional based on fears of a pervasive *risk* of error within the capital system. Indeed, when a federal district judge invalidated the federal death penalty based on such fears (in the wake of the exonerations of the late 1990s),[48] that decision was promptly reversed by the Court of Appeals for the Second Circuit.[49] Though several Justices have lamented the failure of the Court to develop a jurisprudence responsive to the discovery of wrongful capital convictions,[50] the Court shows no signs of reversing course. Individual wrongful executions do not currently violate the Constitution, and systemic error — even in capital cases — appears to be an unlikely stand-alone basis for judicial abolition of the death penalty.

---

[46] *Id.* at 398.
[47] *Id.* at 417.
[48] United States v. Quinones, 196 F. Supp. 2d 416, (S.D.N.Y. 2002).
[49] United States v. Quinones, 313 F.3d 49 (2d Cir. 2002).
[50] Kansas v. Marsh, 548 U.S. 163, 207–08 (2006) (Souter, J., joined by Justices Stevens, Ginsburg, & Breyer) ("Today, a new body of fact must be accounted for in deciding what, in practical terms, the Eighth Amendment guarantees should tolerate, for the period starting in 1989 has seen repeated exonerations of convicts under death sentences, in numbers never imagined before the development of DNA tests.").

The Court's reluctance to shape its doctrine in response to wrongful convictions is likely rooted in many of the same concerns as its reluctance to police systemic race discrimination. Here, too, the Court confronts the difficult problem of quantifying the level of intolerable error. What percentage of inaccurate verdicts (or executions) renders the death penalty unconstitutional? Would a high rate of error in one jurisdiction call for the abolition of the death penalty in other jurisdictions? Moreover, there is the additional question of what counts as a "wrongful" conviction or execution. Is a conviction "wrongful" when an inmate can establish a reasonable doubt in later proceedings? Or is it wrongful only when an inmate can *prove* his innocence? And, if an affirmative showing is required, what quantum of proof is required (must an inmate establish his innocence by a preponderance of the evidence or beyond a reasonable doubt)? As the questions make clear, the difficulty in structuring a doctrine around the problem of wrongful conviction mirrors the problems of remedy in the race context: without a clear baseline of acceptable results in capital cases, it is hard to conclude that a particular jurisdiction (or the nation as a whole) has crossed the constitutional line.

Human Dignity

The belief that the death penalty violates human dignity has fueled the remarkable and unprecedented global movement of death penalty abolition over the past four decades. This belief is reflected in the European Union's insistence on death penalty abolition as a condition of membership, confirming that Europe no longer views the death penalty as a mere policy choice but as a basic issue of human rights. It is also reflected in the Vatican's opposition to capital punishment, with its 2007 declaration that the death penalty is an "affront to human dignity."[51] In the United States, too, opponents of the death penalty are likely motivated by their view that the death penalty creates an unacceptable relation between the state and its people and that executing offenders is intrinsically (not simply instrumentally) wrong. But American discourse around the death penalty has gravitated away from human dignity concerns. Part of the reason for this turn away from human dignity is the desire to build a winning coalition against the death penalty. Opponents of the death penalty are more likely to convert supporters by noting problems with its administration (such the risk of error or the extravagant costs associated with capital trials and subsequent appeals) than by insisting on the fundamental wrongness of the practice. The shift in emphasis is reflected in contemporary efforts of opponents to "repeal" the death penalty rather than "abolish" it, as they seek to avoid the

---

[51] *Vatican Says Death Penalty Is "Affront to Human Dignity,"* DEATH PENALTY INFO. CTR. (Feb. 19, 2017), https://deathpenaltyinfo.org/news/vatican-says-death-penalty-is-affront-to-human-dignity.

moralistic overtones of "abolition" (with the connotation that the end of capital punishment is rooted in a moral imperative akin to the end of slavery).

But the diminished presence of human dignity concerns in popular capital punishment discourse rests as well on a pragmatic assessment of the Court's unwillingness to reject the death penalty based on such concerns. Throughout its history, the Court has been underwhelmed by the proposition that the death penalty is by its nature unconstitutionally cruel. When New York embraced electrocution as its means of execution, and the method was challenged under the Eighth Amendment, the Court insisted that capital punishment is not cruel in the constitutional sense so long as it does not involve "something more than the mere extinguishment of life."[52] When a subsequent effort to electrocute a prisoner in Louisiana failed, and the inmate sought to prevent the state from attempting to electrocute him a second time (what was derided as "death by installments"), the Court rejected the claim, announcing that "[a]ccidents happen for which no man is to blame," and "[t]he traditional humanity of Anglo-American law" forbids only "unnecessary pain in the execution of the death sentence."[53] Even when the Court took up the question of the sustainability of the death penalty in its landmark decision in *Furman*, the five Justices who voted to invalidate prevailing statutes seemed to strain to avoid addressing whether the death penalty is incompatible with human dignity. Instead, the opinions in that case focused primarily on a variety of pragmatic considerations, including the death penalty's arbitrary administration, its lack of a proven deterrent effect, its cost, and the potential brutalization effect of executions.[54] Only Justice William Brennan spoke at length about the basic morality of the death penalty, claiming that capital punishment necessarily amounts to a "denial of the executed person's humanity."[55] Since *Furman*, the Court has been preoccupied with policing specific state practices rather than confronting whether the death penalty itself is fundamentally wrong. Accordingly, there are essentially no doctrinal building blocks for a judicial decision invalidating the death penalty as violative of human dignity.

RACE, INNOCENCE, AND CRUELTY AS CONTRIBUTORS TO CONSTITUTIONAL ABOLITION UNDER THE EIGHTH AMENDMENT

Despite the difficulties faced by arguments based on race, innocence, and cruelty as stand-alone constitutional challenges, these widespread concerns have played a powerful role in generating skepticism about the death penalty, both in and outside of the courts. Several Supreme Court Justices have announced their support for constitutional abolition based on some combination of these concerns, as have other

---

[52] *In re* Kemmler, 136 U.S. 426, 447 (1890).
[53] Louisiana v. Resweber, 329 U.S. 459, 462–63 (1947) (plurality opinion).
[54] *See, e.g.,* Furman v. Georgia, 408 U.S. 238, 362–63 (1972) (Marshall, J., concurring).
[55] *Id.* at 290 (Brennan, J., concurring).

federal judges. State court judges, as well as other state actors such as governors and legislators, have also based decisions to reform, restrict, or repeal the death penalty on such concerns. More broadly, the general public's appetite for executions and new death sentences has diminished in response to media reports about these endemic problems, especially exonerations of people wrongfully convicted and sentenced to death. It is unlikely that race, innocence, or cruelty will be the central focus of a constitutional ruling that ends the American death penalty, as we believe that such a decision, if it ever comes, is more likely to be rooted in the Supreme Court's Eighth Amendment proportionality doctrine. However, these three issues will help create the conditions for an ultimate proportionality challenge and also play a supporting role within that doctrinal structure.

Changing Hearts and Minds in the Federal Courts

Some of the most dramatic moments in the past two decades of "the Great American death penalty decline"[56] have been statements from members of the nation's highest court to the effect that the death penalty no longer comports with the U.S. Constitution. In their Eighth Amendment analyses, these Justices elaborated on what they viewed as the most important dysfunctions of prevailing capital practices, with special attention to concerns about race, innocence, and/or cruelty.

Justice John Paul Stevens joined the Court in late 1975, just in time for the 1976 revival of the death penalty in *Gregg v. Georgia*,[57] merely four years after the Court had constitutionally invalidated all prevailing capital statutes.[58] Justice Stevens was one of the three Justices who authored the influential plurality opinion in *Gregg* that upheld a new generation of reformed capital statutes, and for decades thereafter, he was a reliable member of a centrist coalition on the Court that sought to reform the death penalty rather than to abolish or deregulate it. But thirty-two years after he joined the Court, Justice Stevens had seen enough. Invoking his extensive exposure to death penalty cases over the years, Justice Stevens concluded in 2008 in *Baze v. Rees* that the death penalty categorically violates the Eighth Amendment, though he continued to vote to uphold executions as a matter of *stare decisis*.[59]

Justice Stevens' concurring opinion in *Baze* provided a lengthy list of problems with the American death penalty and failures of the Court's decisions to adequately address those problems. Justice Stevens began by describing the death penalty's diminishing contributions to its penological rationales of deterrence and retribution.

---

[56] *See* Brandon L. Garrett, End of Its Rope: How Killing the Death Penalty Can Revive Criminal Justice 79 (2017) (describing the "remarkable decline" in the use of the death penalty in the United States since the late 1990s).

[57] 428 U.S. 153 (1976).

[58] *See* Furman v. Georgia, 408 U.S. 238 (1972).

[59] *See* Baze v. Rees, 553 U.S. 35, 86–87 (2008) (Stevens, J., concurring in judgment).

He then moved on to procedural issues, listing four primary concerns, three of which addressed either racial discrimination or innocence. As for discrimination, Justice Stevens acknowledged that the risk of discriminatory application of the death penalty had been "dramatically reduced," but lamented that "the Court has allowed it to continue to play an unacceptable role in capital cases."[60] As for innocence, Justice Stevens critiqued precedents that he believed increased the risk of error in capital cases by "placing a thumb on the prosecutor's side of the scales."[61] But what he declared to be of "decisive importance" was the irrevocable nature of the death penalty, given the "risk of executing innocent defendants."[62]

Less than a decade later in 2015, Justice Stephen Breyer wrote a lengthy, empirically supported dissent in *Glossip v. Gross*,[63] joined by Justice Ruth Bader Ginsburg, urging the Court to take up the constitutionality of the death penalty under the Eighth Amendment. Although Justice Breyer stopped just shy of unequivocally declaring the death penalty unconstitutional, his opinion left no doubt where he stood. Like Justice Stevens before him, Justice Breyer emphasized both innocence and race as among the most important problems in the administration of the death penalty. With regard to race, Justice Breyer canvassed studies documenting the influence of race on the imposition of the death penalty under the broader rubric of "arbitrariness," which the Court's precedents have long identified as violating the Eighth Amendment.[64] Unlike Justice Stevens, Justice Breyer did not treat racial discrimination as distinctive or focus his attention primarily on the Court's decision in *McCleskey*, which rejected an Eighth Amendment challenge based on proven racial disparities in capital sentencing. Rather, Justice Breyer considered studies about the influence of race in capital cases alongside of studies about the influence of gender, geography, and the availability of resources for defense counsel. Ultimately, Justice Breyer echoed Justice Stevens in referencing his long experience with capital cases, though he widened his lens to include multiple sources of arbitrariness: "The studies bear out my own view, reached after considering thousands of death penalty cases ... over the course of more than 20 years. I see discrepancies for which I can find no rational explanations."[65]

Also similar to Justice Stevens, Justice Breyer placed strong emphasis on concerns about innocence. He marshaled extensive social science research suggesting that the

---

[60] *Id.* at 85 (critiquing the Court's decision in *McCleskey v. Kemp*, 481 U.S. 279 (1987).

[61] *Id.*

[62] *Id.* at 85–86. Despite the fact that he expressed concerns about the cruelty of the lethal injection protocol at issue in *Baze*, Justice Stevens did not list the cruelty of the death penalty among his reasons for its categorical unconstitutionality. Rather, he invoked the very *lack* of cruelty of most current execution methods as a reason to find the death penalty unconstitutional — because it no longer could be thought to serve retributive ends by mirroring the defendant's own wrongdoing. *See id.* at 80–81.

[63] *Glossip v. Gross*, 135 S. Ct. 2726 (2015).

[64] *Id.* at 2759 (Breyer, J., dissenting).

[65] *Id.* at 2763.

risk of error in capital cases is substantial and in fact greater than the risk of wrongful conviction in non-capital cases. In considering what constitutes a wrongful conviction, Justice Breyer once again widened his lens and included "individuals who may well be actually innocent *or* whose convictions (in the law's view) do not warrant the death penalty's application."[66] Although he acknowledged that the research and figures he presented were "likely controversial," Justice Breyer argued that they "suggest a serious problem of reliability" and that their very contestability was an argument in favor of full briefing of the question before the Court.

Finally, Justice Breyer also focused on the cruelty of the death penalty in terms of the suffering of the condemned, an issue that Justice Stevens had omitted from his categorical constitutional analysis. Although Justices Breyer and Ginsburg both joined Justice Sonia Sotomayor's dissent from the Court's constitutional validation of Oklahoma's lethal injection protocol, Justice Breyer focused his concerns about cruelty not on prevailing modes of execution but rather on excessive delays between sentence and execution. Explaining that extraordinarily lengthy stays on death row are common, Justice Breyer emphasized the "dehumanizing effect" of solitary confinement (which nearly all death penalty states use for death row prisoners) and the "horrible feelings" of uncertainty that death row inmates endure over the years as they await execution.[67] Justice Breyer also argued that excessive delays undermine the death penalty's primary penological rationales of deterrence and retribution, rendering the suffering of the condemned "patently excessive" and "gratuitous."[68]

In an unusual move, Justice Breyer published his dissent in *Glossip* as a book entitled *Against the Death Penalty*, edited and introduced by law professor John Bessler and published by Brookings Institution Press.[69] This decision reflects the view that a wider audience than readers of U.S. Reports would be interested in the arguments and empirical information presented in Justice Breyer's dissent. This view finds support in the broad swath of people, among both institutional actors and the general public, who appear to have been moved by many of the same concerns that animated Justice Breyer.

Justice Antonin Scalia derided Justice Breyer's *Glossip* dissent by declaring "Welcome to Groundhog Day,"[70] a reference to the film in which a newscaster lives through the same day over and over again. Justice Scalia sarcastically described the Court's "long-running drama" in which new Justices "take[] on the role of the abolitionists."[71] But Justice Scalia's mockery is telling about the traction that the kinds of arguments marshaled by Justice Breyer have had. Justices Breyer, Ginsburg,

[66] *Id.* at 2759(emphasis added).
[67] *Id.* at 2765 (internal quotation marks and citation omitted).
[68] *Id.* at 2771 (quoting the Court's opinions in *Gregg* and *Furman*).
[69] Stephen Breyer, Against the Death Penalty (John D. Bessler ed., 2016).
[70] Glossip v. Gross, 135 S. Ct. 2726, 2746 (2015) (Scalia, J., concurring).
[71] *Id.* at 2747.

and Stevens represent only the latest in a longer line of Supreme Court Justices who have declared the death penalty categorically unconstitutional,[72] and they almost certainly will not be the last. Lower federal court judges, too, have begun to respond to the dysfunctions of the American capital justice system with opinions questioning or invalidating the federal death penalty. Judge Jed Rakoff was the first of such judges, who struck down the federal death penalty in 2002 on the ground that it created "an undue risk of executing innocent people."[73] Although his decision was reversed on the merits by the Second Circuit Court of Appeals, concerns about innocence and other problems in the administration of the death penalty have continued to reverberate. In 2016, Judge Geoffrey Crawford took the unusual step of holding a two-week hearing on the constitutionality of the federal death penalty, explicitly citing Justice Breyer's dissent in *Glossip* as raising serious constitutional concerns about the practice of capital punishment. Although Judge Crawford concluded that a federal trial judge "is without authority to rewrite the law so as to overrule the majority position at the Supreme Court,"[74] he nonetheless noted that "a trial court has its own contribution to make to the debate."[75] By holding hearings and permitting witnesses to testify, Judge Crawford added to Justice Breyer's empirical record, tracking the same four categories (unreliability, arbitrariness, excessive delay, and decline in use of the death penalty) that Justice Breyer used to organize his *Glossip* dissent. Although Judge Crawford believed that he lacked institutional authority to invalidate the federal death penalty, he nonetheless concluded that "the [] findings and the fuller record of the hearing conducted before the court substantiate the questions and the criticism expressed in the *Glossip* dissent."[76]

Influencing Death Penalty Decisions in the States

Concerns about race, innocence, and cruelty also have had tremendous influence on state governmental actors — influence that has driven the steep decline in death sentences and executions over the past decades. This influence is seen not only in state courts, but also across all branches of state government.

At the judicial level, the two most recent state supreme court decisions declaring the death penalty unconstitutional under state constitutional law relied either substantially or exclusively on concerns about racial discrimination and innocence. In contrast to the U.S. Supreme Court's rejection of an Eighth Amendment challenge to the death penalty based on patterns of racial disparities, the Washington

---

[72] *See* Carol S. Steiker, *The Marshall Hypothesis Revisited*, 52 How. L.J. 525 (2009) (describing the repeated phenomenon of Supreme Court Justices concluding that the death penalty is unconstitutional after years of observing it from the bench).

[73] United States v. Quinones, 205 F. Supp.2d 256 (S.D.N.Y. 2002).

[74] United States v. Fell, 224 F. Supp.3d 327, 328 (D. Vt. 2016).

[75] *Id.* at 329.

[76] *Id.* at 358.

State Supreme Court in 2018 declared its state's death penalty unconstitutional solely on the ground that it was administered "in an arbitrary and racially biased manner."[77] The court relied on a statistical study that demonstrated that black defendants were four and a half times more likely to be sentenced to death than similarly situated white defendants. In 2015, the Connecticut Supreme Court declared its state's death penalty unconstitutional in a sweeping opinion that relied on concerns about both racial discrimination and innocence, among other issues.[78] That decision, too, relied upon a statistical study demonstrating racial discrimination in the imposition of the death penalty within the state, as well as upon more general studies of the problems of racial discrimination and wrongful conviction in the administration of the death penalty, citing Justice Breyer's opinion in *Glossip*, among other sources.

State governors have been motivated the most by concerns about innocence — most likely because they often have the power to prevent the consummation of a death sentence with an execution and thus often bear direct responsibility for the execution of those who may have been wrongfully convicted. Republican Governor George Ryan of Illinois most dramatically responded to these concerns by granting mass clemency to all of the state's 167 death row inmates in 2003, after a spate of condemned prisoners were exonerated, some at the last minute.[79] Most recently, Governor Gavin Newsom of California early in 2019 declared a moratorium on executions in that state — which is home to the country's largest death row of more than seven hundred condemned prisoners — for as long as he holds office. Newsom cited a variety of problems in the administration of the California death penalty, but he emphasized that "most of all, the death penalty is absolute, irreversible and irreparable in the event of a human error."[80]

The problems of error and racial discrimination are also routinely aired in legislative hearings that culminate in the repeal of state capital statutes. For example, when Illinois repealed its death penalty in 2011, that decision was deeply marked by the exonerations and mass commutations that preceded it, reflecting the fact that, in former Governor Ryan's words, the state's death penalty system was "haunted by the demon of error."[81] When Maryland abolished the death penalty in 2013, its capital statute was the narrowest in the country, and it had only five people on death row — but four of the five were black men whose victims had been white. Governor Martin O'Malley, a former prosecutor and mayor of Baltimore, explained that his reasons

---

[77] State v. Gregory, 427 P.3d 621 (Wash. 2018).

[78] State v. Santiago, 122 A.3d 1 (Conn. 2015).

[79] *See* Jodi Wilgoren, *Citing Issue of Fairness, Governor Clears Out Death Row in Illinois*, N.Y. TIMES, Jan. 12, 2003, www.nytimes.com/2003/01/12/us/citing-issue-of-fairness-governor-clears-out-death-row-in-illinois.html.

[80] Scott Shafer & Marisa Lagos, *Gov. Gavin Newsom Suspends Death Penalty in California*, NPR MORNING EDITION, Mar. 11, 2019.

[81] *See How the Death Penalty Was Abolished in Illinois*, CHICAGO TRIB., May 15, 2018, www .chicagotribune.com/news/ct-met-illinois-death-penalty-timeline-gfx-20180514-htmlstory.html.

for signing the repeal bill into law included that the death penalty "cannot be administered without racial bias" and that "there is no way to reverse a mistake if an innocent person is put to death."[82]

Even some locally elected district attorneys who have donned the mantle of progressive prosecution have questioned the death penalty. When Aramis Ayala, the first black person elected prosecutor in Florida, announced that she would refuse to seek the death penalty in her county, she based her decision on standard law enforcement grounds of cost and ineffectiveness. However, the president of the Florida NAACP greeted Ayala's decision as a step toward racial justice, stating, "A powerful symbol of racial injustice has now been discarded in Orange County."[83] Philadelphia District Attorney Larry Krasner, a former public defender, has mounted a categorical challenge to the Pennsylvania death penalty under the state constitution on the grounds that it has been imposed in an "unreliable" and "arbitrary" fashion.[84] Krasner's brief relies heavily on a study by his office that analyzed the 155 cases in which death sentences were imposed in Philadelphia between 1978 and 2017. The District Attorney's Office study revealed "troubling data" regarding the race of the Philadelphia defendants currently on death row, eighty-two percent of whom are black, and ninety-one percent of whom are members of a minority group.[85] Krasner's brief also invokes the findings of the Pennsylvania Supreme Court's Committee on Racial and Gender Bias, which concluded that there were "strong indicators that Pennsylvania's capital justice system does not operate in an evenhanded manner."[86]

Cruelty, whether of execution methods or lengthy stays on death row, is less commonly offered as a rationale from public officials for abolishing or limiting the death penalty. However, concerns about botched executions have led some chief executives to study or halt executions. For example, in the wake of the apparently torturous execution of Clayton Lockett in Oklahoma in 2016, Oklahoma Governor Mary Fallin ordered an independent review of the execution, and then-President

---

[82] Joe Sutton, *Maryland Governor Signs Death Penalty Repeal*, CNN, May 2, 2013, www.cnn .com/2013/05/02/us/maryland-death-penalty/index.html.

[83] Frances Robles & Alan Blinder, *Florida Prosecutor Takes a Bold Stand against Death Penalty*, N.Y. TIMES, Mar. 16, 2017, www.nytimes.com/2017/03/16/us/orlando-prosecutor-will-no-longer-seek-death-penalty.html. Ayala's refusal to seek the death penalty evoked pushback from the governor of Florida, who took the controversial step of removing her from capital cases in her county. The controversy ultimately led Ayala to decline to seek reelection in 2019. *See* Monivette Cordeiro & Jeff Weiner, *Aramis Ayala Won't Seek Re-election as Orange-Osceola State Attorney; Belvin Perry May Enter Race*, ORLANDO SENTINEL, May 28, 2019, www .orlandosentinel.com/news/breaking-news/os-ne-aramis-ayala-no-re-election-run-orange-osceola-state-attorney-20190528-z65rv7rmqjdqfoyxsd6rp6junu-story.html.

[84] *See* Commonwealth's Br. for Respondent, Cox v. Commonwealth of Pennsylvania, No. 102 EM 2018, July 15, 2019, at i.

[85] *Id.* at 3, 5.

[86] *Id.* at 48–49 (citing FINAL REPORT OF THE PENNSYLVANIA SUPREME COURT COMMITTEE ON RACIAL AND GENDER BIAS IN THE JUDICIAL SYSTEM 201 (Mar. 2003)).

Barack Obama ordered a study of the federal death penalty, specifically referencing the events in Oklahoma.[87] In Ohio, Republican Governor Mike DeWine ordered a series of reprieves for death row prisoners while a new execution protocol is developed after an Ohio magistrate judge likened the use of midazolam in the state's lethal injection process to "waterboarding."[88] More generally, as other contributions to this volume describe in more detail, the intensive litigation over execution protocols and the increasing unavailability of lethal injection drugs have slowed or stopped executions in many states across the country.[89] Arguments about cruelty may not top the list of rationales that public officials offer for decisions to restrict or repeal the death penalty, but the controversy over lethal injection protocols has nonetheless played a substantial role in limiting the pace of executions over the past two decades.

Declining Public Appetite

General public support for the death penalty has declined significantly over the past two and a half decades in response to some of the same concerns that have moved judges and public officials, reaching lows not seen since the early 1970s.[90] In particular, public opinion polls show that people are especially concerned that the death penalty is unfair because "sometimes an innocent person is executed."[91] In the period following the so-called DNA revolution of the late 1990s, which produced a spate of exonerations through new technology, the percent of the public that reported concerns about wrongful conviction in the capital context more than doubled, moving from eleven percent to twenty-five percent.[92] But concerns about racial discrimination and cruelty seem to play less of a role in public skepticism about the death penalty. Indeed, one study showed that white respondents favored the death penalty *more* rather than less if they believed it was imposed in a racially discriminatory manner.[93] And families of murder victims sometimes evince

---

[87] *See* Corinna Barrett Lain, *The Politics of Botched Executions*, 49 RICH. L. REV. 825, 838–39 (2015); Eyder Peralta, *Oklahoma Governor Calls for Review of Botched Execution*, NPR NEWS, Apr. 30, 2014.

[88] *See* Jessie Balmert, *Ohio Gov. Mike DeWine Delays 3 More Executions after Judge Compares Method to "Waterboarding,"* CINCINNATI ENQ., Mar. 7, 2019, www.cincinnati.com/story/news/politics/2019/03/07/ohio-governor-delays-3-more-executions/3091289002/.

[89] *See generally* Lincoln Caplan, *The End of the Open Market for Lethal-Injection Drugs*, NEW YORKER, May 21, 2016, www.newyorker.com/news/news-desk/the-end-of-the-open-market-for-lethal-injection-drugs (describing the increasing unavailability of lethal injection drugs and the litigation surrounding lethal injection protocols).

[90] *See Death Penalty, supra* note 11.

[91] GARRETT, *supra* note 56, at 91.

[92] *Id.*

[93] Mark Peffley & Jon Hurwitz, *Persuasion and Resistance: Race and the Death Penalty in America*, 51 AM. J. POL. SCI. 996, 1001 (2007).

disappointment that current methods of execution are relatively painless,[94] a view that may extend past those immediately impacted by heinous crimes.

It is difficult to determine how much and in what ways waning public support has contributed to the dramatic decline in the use of the death penalty over the past two decades. It is unlikely that changes in public attitudes about the death penalty translate directly into jury verdicts in capital cases, because capital juries are "death qualified" to remove prospective jurors who have serious reservations about capital punishment. Rather, public opinion likely affects the discretionary decision-making of institutional actors through ordinary politics — through the election of state and local officials, including governors, legislators, prosecutors, and often judges as well. Thus, whatever public opinion may show about changes in public attitudes over time, it seems fair to view the statements and actions of public officials as reasonably reliable proxies for attitudes of the general public among their constituents, especially on an issue with as much emotional salience as the death penalty.

Constitutional Abolition under the Eighth Amendment

Despite the retentionist views of the current Republican presidential administration and the conservative majority on the U.S. Supreme Court, we continue to believe that a categorical constitutional abolition of the death penalty under the Eighth Amendment will eventually occur if recent trends in death penalty practices continue (or even merely stabilize) on the ground. For the reasons elaborated above, we think it is unlikely that such an Eighth Amendment ruling will be premised on race, innocence, or cruelty as a stand-alone rationale for constitutional abolition. Rather, we think the most likely route to constitutional abolition is through application of the Court's Eighth Amendment proportionality doctrine.[95] In sketching the likely contours of a proportionality ruling abolishing the death penalty, we nonetheless see a role for concerns about race, innocence, and cruelty — in both creating the conditions on the ground that will permit a proportionality challenge to succeed and in bolstering the doctrinal analysis.

Just one year after the Court reauthorized capital punishment in 1976, it issued its first proportionality limitation on the scope of the death penalty, ruling that a sentence of death was constitutionally excessive for the crime of the rape of an adult woman.[96] In the more than forty years since, the Court has continued to

---

[94] *See* Joan Bundy, *Should the Condemned Suffer through Painful Executions? Victims' Families Torn,* Associated Press, July 28, 2014, www.masslive.com/news/2014/07/should_the_con demned_suffer_th.html.

[95] For an elaboration of the constitutional path that we predict, see Carol S. Steiker & Jordan M. Steiker, Courting Death: The Supreme Court and Capital Punishment 255–89 (2016).

[96] *See* Coker v. Georgia, 433 U.S. 584 (1977) (plurality opinion).

restrict the scope of the death penalty under the Eighth Amendment, declaring it unconstitutional for some offenders convicted of felony murder as accomplices who did not themselves kill,[97] for offenders with intellectual disability,[98] for juvenile offenders,[99] and for offenders convicted of any interpersonal crimes other than murder.[100] In doing so, the Court has developed an elaborate proportionality analysis under the Eighth Amendment, a doctrine that it has even exported from the capital context to apply to the imposition of sentences of life without possibility of parole (LWOP) on juvenile offenders — reasoning that LWOP is like capital punishment in that it is the most severe punishment that may constitutionally be imposed on juveniles.[101]

The basic structure of the Court's Eighth Amendment proportionality doctrine is simple, despite numerous refinements wrought by repeated application over the years. The analysis has two parts. First, the Court considers "objective evidence" that a challenged punishment practice violates the Eighth Amendment by running afoul of "evolving standards of decency."[102] Such evidence tends to focus on the extent to which the challenged practice is permitted by state legislatures, invoked by prosecutors, and actually imposed by juries and judges. Second, the Court brings its "own judgment" to bear on the question of proportionality.[103] In doing so, the Court primarily addresses whether the challenged practice adequately advances the twin penological goals of capital punishment (deterrence and retribution). In every case in which the Court has either invalidated or upheld a practice under its proportionality doctrine, it has found that both parts of the analysis have pointed in the same direction, so it is not clear what would happen should "objective evidence" and the Court's "own judgment" diverge.

The issues of race, innocence, and cruelty have a dual role to play in supporting an eventual categorical constitutional challenge to the death penalty under the Eighth Amendment. First, as elaborated above, these concerns have played a substantial role in driving the tremendous decline in the use of the death penalty over the past two decades. Given the centrality of "objective evidence" that societal views about a practice have changed to the Court's proportionality analysis, the rising number of legislative repeals and the declining number of executions and new death sentences will be of crucial importance in a categorical challenge to capital punishment under the Eighth Amendment. Unfortunately, the problems of

---

[97] *See* Tison v. Arizona, 481 U.S. 137 (1987); Enmund v. Florida, 458 U.S. 782 (1982).
[98] *See* Atkins v. Virginia, 536 U.S. 304 (2002).
[99] *See* Roper v. Simmons, 543 U.S. 551 (2005).
[100] *See* Kennedy v. Louisiana, 554 U.S. 407 (2008).
[101] *See* Miller v. Alabama, 567 U.S. 460 (2012) (holding that mandatory LWOP is constitutionally excessive for juvenile homicide offenders); Graham v. Florida, 560 U.S. 48 (2010) (holding that LWOP is constitutionally excessive for juvenile offenders convicted of non-homicide crimes).
[102] *See, e.g., Atkins*, 536 U.S. at 312.
[103] *Id.*

discrimination, wrongful conviction, and cruel suffering in the use of the death penalty have not been and are not likely to be substantially ameliorated by policy reform, so it seems probable that the declines in the use of capital punishment that have resulted from such concerns are not a mere temporary blip but rather a more enduring feature of death penalty practice. Thus, concerns about race, innocence, and cruelty will likely continue to play an important role in creating the conditions that make the death penalty vulnerable to a categorical Eighth Amendment proportionality challenge.

Second, there is some room for direct consideration of the issues of race, innocence, and cruelty within the Court's proportionality doctrine — not as freestanding claims, but as part of the considerations that the Court addresses under the rubric of bringing its "own judgment" to bear. The issue of innocence, in particular, has been invoked by the Court on more than one occasion with regard to its "own judgment." For example, the Court raised the concern that offenders with intellectual disability might be wrongfully convicted or sentenced to death because of the difficulties that their disability would likely raise in the investigation and trial contexts, concluding that such defendants "face a special risk of wrongful execution."[104] Similarly, the Court raised the concern that offenders charged with child rape might be wrongfully convicted because of manipulation of child witnesses, noting "the special risks of unreliable testimony with respect to this crime."[105] In this way, evidence of a heightened risk of wrongful conviction in capital cases more generally may play a role in the Court's doctrinal evaluation of the constitutionality of the death penalty under the Eighth Amendment. As for concerns about racial discrimination, they may enter the Court's proportionality analysis through the Court's consideration, under its "own judgment," of whether the death penalty promotes the goal of retribution. If death sentences are imposed on the basis of arbitrary or invidious characteristics of the offender such as race and ethnicity, then by definition, the death penalty is not being imposed according to offenders' just deserts and thus runs afoul of the core principle of retributive justice. Evidence of racially discriminatory patterns in capital sentencing is directly relevant to whether the death penalty meets retributive goals *as practiced*, rather than in abstract theory. Finally, concerns about the cruelty of modes of execution or lengthy stays on death row have a less obvious place in the Court's doctrine. However, as Justice Breyer explained in his *Glossip* dissent, excessive delays make the death penalty unable to deliver on its deterrent and retributive promises and thus render the suffering of prisoners on death row gratuitous and excessive.[106]

[104] *See id.* at 321.
[105] *See Kennedy*, 554 U.S. at 444.
[106] *See supra* text accompanying notes 63–68.

The Court's proportionality doctrine represents both the most established and the most capacious avenue for a categorical constitutional challenge to the death penalty under the Eighth Amendment. Such a challenge would build on and incorporate the concerns about racial discrimination, wrongful conviction of the innocent, and excessive cruelty that are prevalent in public discourse and that have deeply influenced the trajectory of death penalty practices in recent decades.

13

Back to the Future with Execution Methods

Deborah W. Denno[*]

INTRODUCTION

Lethal injection, the most common method of execution in the United States, is at an impasse. Despite three U.S. Supreme Court decisions upholding particular lethal injection protocols,[1] inmates continue to challenge this method on the grounds that it is inhumane and unconstitutional, and states continue to cling to scientifically uninformed procedures in an effort to ensure the death penalty's survival generally.[2] Yet lethal injection is simply the last in a long line of disastrous execution methods.

The history of the United States' five execution methods and the transitions from one method to another is replete with detailed accounts at the legislative, judicial, and correctional levels that explain why each new method failed so appreciably in its goal to be more humane than the method it superseded. Hanging, lethal gas, and electrocution were adopted and initially used with celebration, only to be criticized and replaced after decades of technical problems and botched executions.[3]

[*] Arthur A. McGivney Professor of Law, Founding Director, Neuroscience and Law Center, Fordham University School of Law. I am most grateful to the following individuals for their contributions to this chapter: William Berry, Marianna Gebhardt, Jennifer Moreno, Ngozi Ndulue, Meghan Ryan, and Erica Valencia-Graham. I give special thanks to Erica Valencia-Graham for her incredible skill and care in creating the chapter's charts.

[1] Bucklew v. Precythe, 139 S. Ct. 112 (2019); Glossip v. Gross, 135 S. Ct. 2726 (2015); Baze v. Rees, 553 U.S. 35 (2008).

[2] For a discussion of the nature, range, and content of these challenges in modern and historical contexts, see generally William W. Berry III, *Individualized Executions*, 52 U.C. DAVIS L. REV. 1779 (2019); William W. Berry III & Meghan J. Ryan, *Cruel Techniques, Unusual Secrets*, 78 OHIO ST. L.J. 403 (2017); Deborah W. Denno, *Execution Methods in a Nutshell*, in ROUTLEDGE HANDBOOK ON CAPITAL PUNISHMENT 427, 427–45 (Robert M. Bohm & Gavin M. Lee eds., 2018); *State By State Lethal Injection Protocols*, DEATH PENALTY INFO. CTR. (2019), https://deathpenaltyinfo.org/executions/lethal-injection/state-by-state-lethal-injection-protocols.

[3] For detailed assessments of the changes in execution methods historically, see generally Deborah W. Denno, *The Lethal Injection Quandary: How Medicine Has Dismantled the*

The latest method, lethal injection, is now used almost exclusively as states seem to have exhausted alternative methods of execution apart from changing the drugs and procedures of lethal injection itself.[4] With lethal injection proven to be as problematic an execution method as its predecessors, some states have shown a growing interest in reverting back to older methods of execution, seeking to refurbish the older method's image and suggesting that prior difficulties were exaggerated.

The purpose of this chapter is to explore the future of execution methods in light of states' efforts to repeat or borrow from the past. It begins by examining current changes to lethal injection and the move by some states to adopt, reconsider, or modify prior methods. For example, in 2018, Alabama adopted nitrogen hypoxia, a purportedly new execution method that Oklahoma and Mississippi had already approved for circumstances in which lethal injection was rendered unconstitutional or "otherwise unavailable." But, historically, lethal gas techniques have produced some of the most botched and gruesome executions this country has ever experienced. Likewise, in 2015, Utah resurrected the firing squad, which is also allowed in Oklahoma and Mississippi as a constitutional substitute if lethal injection, nitrogen hypoxia, and electrocution are no longer viable. One year earlier, in 2014, Tennessee approved a law that allows the state to use electrocution if lethal injection drugs cannot be obtained. While seven states including Tennessee enable inmates to choose electrocution as an execution method, no other state mandates that inmates be executed by that method, which also has produced horrifying botched executions for over a century. Older lethal injection drugs are also coming back into play. Ohio, for example, has now returned to listing sodium thiopental as a first-drug option in its protocol, even though sodium thiopental is currently inaccessible.[5]

This chapter concludes that, unlike the movie, states cannot go "back to the future"[6] in an effort to re-invent or rebrand problematic execution methods of the past. Ironically, the method that is most humane — the firing squad — faces the biggest rebranding hurdle of all because of society's stereotyped perception of its barbarity.[7] Current execution methods may simply retain a general status quo and eventually follow the same path as hanging: for the first time since this country's birth, no state offers hanging as an alternative method of execution because all three hanging states abolished the death penalty entirely. Such may be the future of all execution methods.[8]

Death Penalty, 76 FORDHAM L. REV. 49–128 (2007) [hereinafter Denno, *Lethal Injection Quandary*]; Deborah W. Denno, *When Legislatures Delegate Death: The Troubling Paradox Behind State Uses of Electrocution and Lethal Injection and What It Says about Us*, 63 OHIO ST. L.J 63–260 (2002) [hereinafter Denno, *When Legislatures Delegate*].

[4] *See infra* Charts 1–4.
[5] *See State By State Lethal Injection Protocols, supra* note 2.
[6] *See* BACK TO THE FUTURE (Amblin Ent. 1985).
[7] *See* Deborah W. Denno, *The Firing Squad as a "Known and Available Method of Execution" Post-Glossip*, 49 MICH. J.L. REFORM 749, 772–93 (2016).
[8] *See infra* Chart 1 at ±.

WHERE WE ARE NOW

Of the twenty-nine existing death penalty states, Chart 1 shows that lethal injection is the sole method of execution in twenty-three states and one of two methods of

CHART 1: *Execution Methods by State 2019**

Single-Method States (23)
Arkansas*** • Arizona* • Colorado† • Georgia • Idaho • Indiana • Kansas • Kentucky* • Louisiana • Mississippi** • Montana • Nebraska • Nevada • North Carolina • Ohio • Oklahoma** • Oregon† • Pennsylvania† • South Dakota • Tennessee* • Texas • Utah* • Wyoming‡
Choice States (10)±
Lethal Injection or Firing Squad (1): Utah* Lethal Injection or Electrocution (6): Alabama • Florida • Kentucky* • South Carolina • Tennessee* • Virginia Lethal Injection or Lethal Gas (3): Arizona* • California† • Missouri Lethal Injection or Nitrogen Hypoxia (1): Alabama
States Without the Death Penalty (21)
Alaska • Connecticut • Delaware • Hawaii • Illinois • Iowa • Maine • Maryland • Massachusetts • Michigan • Minnesota • New Hampshire • New Jersey • New Mexico • New York • North Dakota • Rhode Island • Vermont • Washington • West Virginia • Wisconsin (Also–the District of Columbia)

* The information for this chart is derived from Denno, *supra* note 2, at 436; DEATH PENALTY INFO. CTR., METHODS OF EXECUTIONS 1 (2019), https://deathpenaltyinfo.org/state-and-federal-info/state-by-state. Arizona, Kentucky, Tennessee, and Utah have provisions that are not retroactive and therefore allow choices for some inmates. These three states are listed in both the Single-Method States and Choice States categories. *Id.*

** Mississippi and Oklahoma now allow for the use of nitrogen hypoxia or electrocution only if lethal injection is unavailable or held unconstitutional. These states also allow for the use of the firing squad if nitrogen hypoxia, lethal injection, and electrocution are held unconstitutional or "otherwise unavailable." DEATH PENALTY INFO. CTR., AUTHORIZED METHODS BY STATE 1 (2019), https://deathpenaltyinfo.org/executions/methods-of-execution/authorized-methods-by-state.

*** Arkansas authorizes the use of electrocution only if lethal injection is unavailable or held unconstitutional. DEATH PENALTY INFO. CTR., AUTHORIZED METHODS BY STATE 1 (2019), https://deathpenaltyinfo.org/executions/methods-of-execution/authorized-methods-by-state.

‡ Wyoming authorizes the use of lethal gas if lethal injection is invalidated, held unconstitutional, or is "otherwise unavailable." DEATH PENALTY INFO. CTR., AUTHORIZED METHODS BY STATE 1 (2019), https://deathpenaltyinfo.org/executions/methods-of-execution/authorized-methods-by-state.

† States with Gubernatorial Moratoria. DEATH PENALTY INFO. CTR., STATE BY STATE 1 (2019), https://deathpenaltyinfo.org/state-and-federal-info/state-by-state.

± As of May 2019, the three states that allowed hanging as an execution method (Delaware, New Hampshire, and Washington), have abolished the death penalty. In New Hampshire, the repeal of the death penalty is not retroactive, leaving one person on death row who could potentially still be executed by hanging. *See* DEATH PENALTY INFO. CTR., AUTHORIZED METHODS BY STATE 1 (2019), https://deathpenaltyinfo.org/executions/methods-of-execution/authorized-methods-by-state; *see also* DEATH PENALTY INFO. CTR., STATE AND FEDERAL INFO: NEW HAMPSHIRE 1 (2019), https://deathpenaltyinfo.org/state-and-federal-info/state-by-state/new-hampshire.

execution in ten states (four states fall into both categories).[9] Therefore, every death row inmate must be executed by lethal injection except in those states that allow some inmates a choice between execution methods or that allow another method if lethal injection is rendered unconstitutional or "otherwise unavailable." That said, there is substantial complexity and state-by-state variation in how lethal injection is administered and the contingency plans that states have in place if lethal injection is no longer viable.

Backdrop

Chart 1's surface simplicity masks the extraordinary degree of convolution across states depending on the makeup of their lethal injection protocols — a development that has occurred primarily since 2009 but that springboards from an intricate history. From 1977 to 2009, all states used a similar three-drug protocol: sodium thiopental, a barbiturate anesthetic that causes deep unconsciousness; pancuronium bromide, a muscle relaxant that paralyzes all skeletal muscles, including the diaphragm, which can lead to suffocation; and potassium chloride, a toxin that induces irreversible cardiac arrest. The primary basis for lethal injection challenges was the excruciating pain and suffering caused by the second drug, pancuronium bromide, when the first drug, the anesthetic, was incorrectly administered. Without adequate anesthesia, the inmate would experience conscious suffocation, and would be paralyzed and unable to indicate to the execution team that there was a problem. The inmate's suffering is then exacerbated by the administration of the third drug, potassium chloride, which has been described as having one's veins set on fire.[10]

Courts agreed that if the first drug, sodium thiopental, is ineffective for any of a number of reasons, it would be unconstitutional to inject the second and third drugs into a conscious person. Nonetheless, pancuronium is such a powerful paralytic that, once administered during an execution, inmates cannot exhibit signs of consciousness, pain or suffering to prison officials and executioners.[11] This was the key issue in the litigation that, starting in 2006, successfully prompted death penalty

---

[9] *See infra* Chart 1. Four states, Arizona, Kentucky, Tennessee, and Utah, fall into both the Single-Method State category and the Choice State category because their provisions declaring lethal injection as the sole method are not retroactive and therefore allow choices for inmates sentenced prior to a specific date. Arizona allows inmates sentenced before November 1992 to choose between lethal injection and the gas chamber. Utah allows inmates sentenced before May 3, 2004, to choose between lethal injection and the firing squad. Kentucky allows inmates sentenced before March 31, 1998, to choose between lethal injection and electrocution. Tennessee allows inmates sentenced before January 1, 1999, to choose between lethal injection and electrocution. *See State By State Lethal Injection Protocols, supra* note 2.

[10] *See* Deborah W. Denno, *Lethal Injection Chaos Post-Baze*, 102 GEO. L.J. 1331, 1333–34 (2014).

[11] *Id.*

moratoria and execution stalemates across the country, inevitably leading to the Supreme Court case *Baze v. Rees*,[12] a challenge to Kentucky's protocol.

In 2008, the *Baze* Court upheld the constitutionality of Kentucky's lethal injection protocol under the Eighth Amendment's Cruel and Unusual Punishment Clause,[13] finding that the defendants had failed to show that Kentucky's (then standard) three-drug combination posed a "substantial" or "objectively intolerable" risk of "serious harm"[14] compared to "known and available alternatives."[15] Nevertheless, shortly after *Baze*, an extreme shortage of the first of the three drugs — sodium thiopental—developed in the United States for reasons having nothing to do with the death penalty, but rather issues with the manufacturing of the drugs. Thus, what would otherwise have been an innocuous depletion of an aging drug infrequently used in surgeries would ultimately knock the legs out from under the lethal injection table, as many scholars and courts have documented in detail. States could no longer execute inmates in the way they had done for decades. In addition, the Food and Drug Administration (FDA) and other institutions locally and worldwide curbed the extent to which states could find sodium thiopental for use in an execution.[16]

Ultimately, this drug shortage problem extended beyond the availability of just sodium thiopental, as states attempted to switch to other kinds of lethal injection drugs, which then also became unavailable because of litigation over their humaneness. Along with the reality of diminished or depleted drug supplies and a federal court injunction preventing the importation of sodium thiopental, death penalty states struggled to revise their protocols based on drug availability. While many states continued to search for sources of FDA-approved drugs for lethal injections, some states put lethal injection executions on hold while awaiting a resolution. Still others sought assistance from the U.S. Department of Justice (DOJ). As states' desperation increased, so did their tolerance for risk, as evidenced by a trend toward reliance on "compounding pharmacies" — facilities that create "compounded" drugs under the relatively lax regulation of the states (as compared to the intense oversight of commercial pharmaceutical manufacturers that are regulated by the FDA).[17]

An added risk was that states increasingly used a broad range of drugs — switching from one drug to another — in addition to drugs manufactured by compounding

---

[12] 553 U.S. 35 (2008) (plurality opinion).
[13] The Eighth Amendment provides that "[e]xcessive bail shall not be required, nor excessive fines imposed, nor cruel and unusual punishments inflicted." U.S. Const. amend. VIII.
[14] *Baze*, 553 U.S. at 50.
[15] *Id.* at 61.
[16] *See generally* Denno, *supra* note 10 (discussing the chaos).
[17] *Id.*; *see also* Berry, *supra* note 2, at 1781–95 (providing depictions of states' risk-taking and experimentation).

pharmacies. Executioners were unfamiliar with the potential effects of all these new drugs, bolstering inmates' claims that lethal injection executions were a form of experimentation. One of the most controversial and questionable of these drugs was midazolam, which was involved in several, highly publicized, problematic executions. In 2014, just six years after *Baze*, the Court granted certiorari to determine the constitutionality of Oklahoma's three-drug midazolam protocol. In *Glossip v. Gross*,[18] the Court held that three death row inmates failed to establish that midazolam created "a substantial risk of severe pain" when used as the first of three drugs in Oklahoma's lethal injection procedure.[19] In so concluding, *Glossip* clarified the *Baze* standard and established a two-pronged test in which plaintiffs must prove both that the planned method of execution poses a "substantial risk of severe pain" and "identify a known and available alternative method of execution that entails a lesser risk of pain."[20] In other words, inmates have the burden of establishing another way the state can execute them — one that would substantially reduce the risk of pain and suffering when compared to the planned method.

In 2019, the Court granted *certiorari* in, *Bucklew v. Precythe*,[21] an as-applied challenge to Missouri's one-drug pentobarbital protocol. As opposed to previous cases, which broadly challenged the constitutionality of an execution protocol, *Bucklew* argued narrowly that it would be unconstitutional to carry out his execution using Missouri's protocol because of his unique and rare medical condition. Bucklew suffered from blood-filled tumors in his head, neck, and throat that he argued would rupture and cause him to choke and suffer "excruciating" pain.[22] He also raised questions about the experience, training, and qualifications of the execution team, specifically the extent to which the team was informed about his condition and the extent to which they would make accommodations to reduce the risk of pain and suffering.[23] Although Bucklew identified nitrogen hypoxia as an alternative method of execution, he also argued that prisoners who raise as-applied challenges are not required to proffer an alternative method of execution.[24] Yet, the Court flatly rejected Bucklew's argument that as-applied challenges are subject to a different standard than facial challenges and held that he had not met his burden under the Eighth Amendment.[25] While many commentators found the 5-to-4 decision disturbing, it is difficult to forecast the nature and extent of *Bucklew's* impact given the

[18] 135 S. Ct. 2726 (2015).
[19] *Id.* at 2731. For a thorough and enlightening discussion of *Glossip* and the circumstances that led to it, see generally Eric Berger, *Gross Error*, 91 WASH. L. REV. 929 (2016); Berry & Ryan, *supra* note 2; Jon Yorke, *Comity, Finality, and Oklahoma's Lethal Injection Protocol*, 69 OKLA. L. REV. 545 (2017).
[20] *Glossip*, 135 S. Ct. at 2731.
[21] 139 S. Ct. 1112 (2019).
[22] *Id.* at 1120.
[23] *Id.* at 1131, n.2.
[24] *Id.* at 1121–22.
[25] *Id.* at 1126–29.

opinion's unusual facts and circumstances.[26] Furthermore, neither side in the case sufficiently specified a nitrogen hypoxia protocol, leaving open the question of how the technique would be implemented. The Court's decisions in *Baze, Glossip,* and *Bucklew* have yet to quell litigation challenging lethal injection at a time when there is significant variation in the drug protocols that jurisdictions use to carry out executions.

Multiple Lethal Injection Protocols

The tendency for states to follow what could be considered a typical three-drug lethal injection protocol dissolved when sodium thiopental ceased to be available. The resulting chaos among states in searching for drugs has been well documented,[27] but the protocols continue to vary substantially, and they are ever-changing. Charts 2, 3, and 4[28] serve as a snapshot of the drugs currently used by states in 2019, with a focus on the type of first drug that different states use. Notwithstanding the variability among first drugs, Charts 2 and 4 depict three distinct trends. First, thirteen states still list sodium thiopental in their protocols, despite the fact that thiopental has not been used since 2011, although nearly all of them also list an alternative drug if sodium thiopental is not available.[29] According to the Death Penalty Information Center, nine of those thirteen states seemingly have not changed their lethal injection protocols since their adoption of lethal injection as an execution method, and they have no past protocols listed on the Center's website — the source for most of this Chapter's modern lethal injection information.[30] Of course, states could have changed their protocols and not made that information publicly available. In addition, only four of the thirteen states have executed an inmate after 2010, when there started to be a shortage of sodium thiopental.[31]

The second trend pertains to the kinds of drugs that have replaced sodium thiopental. For example, eight states list midazolam as their first drug, despite the drug's continuing problems, and seven other states list only pentobarbital as their

---

[26] *See* Deborah W. Denno, *Physician Participation in Lethal Injection,* 380 New Eng. J. Med. 1790, 1790–91 (2019).

[27] *See generally* Berry, *supra* note 2; Denno, *supra* note 10; Charts 1–4 infra.

[28] *See supra* Charts 2, 3, and 4.

[29] Those thirteen states are California, Colorado, Indiana, Kentucky, Louisiana, Mississippi, Montana, Ohio, Oregon, Pennsylvania, South Dakota, Utah, and Wyoming. *See supra* Charts 2 and 4.

[30] Those nine states are California, Colorado, Indiana, Kentucky, Montana, Oregon, Pennsylvania, Utah, and Wyoming. *See supra* Charts 2 and 4.

[31] The last executions in those four states were Louisiana (in 2010), Mississippi (in 2012), Ohio (in 2018), and South Dakota (in 2018). *Execution Database,* Death Penalty Info. Ctr., https://deathpenaltyinfo.org/executions/execution-database (last visited Sept. 25, 2019).

CHART 2: *Current Lethal Injection Protocols 2019: Type of First Drug**

1-Drug Protocol Beginning with Only Pentobarbital	Georgia Idaho Louisiana Missouri North Carolina South Dakota Texas
1-Drug Protocol Beginning with Pentobarbital or Sodium Thiopental	Ohio South Dakota
2-Drug Protocol Beginning with Midazolam	Arizona Louisiana
2-Drug Protocol Beginning with Only Sodium Thiopental	Montana
2-Drug Protocol Beginning with Sodium Thiopental or Pentobarbital	South Dakota
3-Drug Protocol Beginning with Etomidate	Florida
3-Drug Protocol Beginning with Only Pentobarbital	South Carolina
3-Drug Protocol Beginning with Pentobarbital or Sodium Thiopental	Colorado Kentucky Pennsylvania South Dakota
3-Drug Protocol Beginning with Midazolam	Alabama Arkansas Ohio Oklahoma Nevada Tennessee Virginia
3-Drug Protocol Beginning with Only Sodium Thiopental	California Indiana** Mississippi*** Montana Oregon Utah Wyoming
4-Drug Protocol Beginning with Diazepam	Nebraska
No Current Protocol in Place	Kansas

* The information in this chart is derived from DEATH PENALTY INFO. CTR., STATE BY STATE LETHAL INJECTION PROTOCOLS 1 (2019), https://deathpenaltyinfo.org/executions/lethal-injection/state-by-state-lethal-injection-protocols.
**Only if Sodium Thiopental is unavailable, then Pentobarbital or Brevital
*** Only if Sodium Thiopental is unavailable, then Pentobarbital or Midazolam
Note: All drug names are derived directly from the states' protocols.

CHART 3: *Current Lethal Injection Drugs Protocols 2019: Types of First, Second, Third and Fourth Drugs**

First (or Only) Drug in Protocol
Brevital (Methohexital Sodium) – 1st Drug (in a 3-Drug Protocol) Diazepam – 1st Drug (in a 3- or 4-Drug Protocol) Etomidate – 1st Drug (in a 3-Drug Protocol) Midazolam – 1st Drug (in a 2- and 3-Drug Protocol) Pentobarbital – 1st Drug (in a 1-, 2- and 3-Drug Protocol) Propofol –1st Drug (in a 1-Drug Protocol) Sodium Thiopental – 1st Drug (in a 3-Drug Protocol)
Second Drug in Protocol
Hydromorphone – 2nd Drug (in a 2-Drug Protocol) Fentanyl Citrate – 2nd Drug (in a 3- or 4-Drug Protocol) Pancuronium Bromide – 2nd Drug (in a 3-Drug Protocol) Rocuronium Bromide – 2nd Drug (in a 3-Drug Protocol) Vecuronium Bromide – 2nd Drug (in a 3-Drug Protocol)
Third (or Fourth) Drug in Protocol
Cisatracurium Besylate – 3rd Drug (in a 3- or 4-Drug Protocol) Potassium Acetate – 3rd Drug (in a 3-Drug Protocol) Potassium Chloride – 3rd Drug or 4th Drug (in a 3- or 4-Drug Protocol)

* The information in this chart is derived from DEATH PENALTY INFO. CTR., STATE BY STATE LETHAL INJECTION PROTOCOLS 1 (2019), https://deathpenaltyinfo.org/executions/lethal-injection/state-by-state-lethal-injection-protocols.
Note: All drug names are derived directly from the states' protocols.

first drug.[32] Two states use drugs that no other state uses: Florida (etomidate) and Nebraska (diazepam). The third trend reflects a change in the number of drugs that states use. Seven states have switched from a three-drug protocol to a one-drug protocol between 2009 and 2019 even though no state had a one-drug protocol before 2009. Nebraska has a four-drug protocol.[33]

For those lethal injection protocols that use more than one drug, the variability does not stop with the first drug. As Chart 3 shows, there are also differences among the second, third, or fourth drugs, depending on how many drugs a particular state has in its protocol. The combined effects of all of these factors — different drugs and different drug combinations — are shown in Chart 4, which provides the current and past lethal injection statutes for all death penalty states that specify the kinds of drugs and their combinations used by departments of corrections in their protocols.

---

[32] The eight states listing midazolam are Alabama, Arizona, Arkansas, Ohio, Oklahoma, Nevada, Tennessee, and Virginia. The seven states listing only pentobarbital are Georgia, Idaho, Missouri, North Carolina, South Carolina, South Dakota, and Texas. *See supra* Chart 2.

[33] Those seven states that switched to a one-drug protocol are Georgia, Idaho, Missouri, North Carolina, Ohio, South Dakota, and Texas. *See supra* Chart 2.

CHART 4: *Current and Past Lethal Injections Protocols by State 2019**

State	Current Protocol	Past Protocol(s)
Alabama	3-Drug Midazolam	3-Drug Pentobarbital 3-Drug Sodium Thiopental
Arizona	2-Drug Midazolam and Hydromorphone	1-Drug Pentobarbital 3-Drug Pentobarbital 3-Drug Sodium Thiopental
Arkansas	3-Drug Midazolam, Vecuronium Bromide, Potassium Chloride	3-Drug Sodium Thiopental
California†	No current protocol in place	3-Drug Sodium Thiopental
Colorado†	3-Drug Sodium Thiopental or Pentobarbital, Pancuronium Bromide, Potassium Chloride	None
Florida	3-Drug Etomidate, Rocuronium Bromide, Potassium Acetate	3-Drug Midazolam 3-Drug Pentobarbital 3-Drug Sodium Thiopental
Georgia	1-Drug Pentobarbital	3-Drug Pentobarbital 3-Drug Sodium Thiopental
Idaho	1-Drug Pentobarbital	3-Drug Pentobarbital 3-Drug Sodium Thiopental
Indiana	3-Drug Sodium Thiopental (or Pentobarbital or Brevital if not available), Pancuronium Bromide or Vecuronium, and Potassium Chloride	None
Kansas	No current protocol in place	None
Kentucky	3-Drug Sodium Thiopental or Pentobarbital	None
Louisiana	2-Drug Midazolam and Hydromorphone 1-Drug Pentobarbital	3-Drug Sodium Thiopental
Mississippi**	3-Drug Sodium Thiopental (or if unavailable, Pentobarbital, if Pentobarbital is unavailable, then Midazolam), Pavulon (Vecuronium Bromide or Rocuronium Bromide), then Potassium Chloride	3-Drug Sodium Thiopental
Missouri	1-Drug Pentobarbital	3-Drug Sodium Thiopental
Montana	2-Drug Sodium Thiopental, Pancuronium Bromide	None
Nebraska	4-Drug Diazepam, Fentanyl Citrate, Cisatracurium Besylate, Potassium Chloride	None
Nevada	3-Drug Midazolam, Fentanyl, Cisatracurium	None
North Carolina	1-Drug Pentobarbital (or other short-acting barbiturate) – this drug is given at two different times	None
Ohio**	1-Drug Pentobarbital or 1-Drug Sodium Thiopental or 3-Drug Midazolam, Vecuronium Bromide (Pancuronium Bromide or Rocuronium Bromide) and Potassium Chloride	2-Drug Midazolam and Hydromorphone 1-Drug Pentobarbital 1-Drug Sodium Thiopental 3-Drug Sodium Thiopental
Oklahoma	3-Drug Midazolam, Pancuronium Bromide, Potassium Acetate	3-Drug Midazolam 3-Drug Pentobarbital 3-Drug Sodium Thiopental

(continued)

CHART 4: (*continued*)

State	Current Protocol	Past Protocol(s)
Oregon†	3-Drug Sodium Thiopental	None
Pennsylvania†	3-Drug Pentobarbital or Sodium Thiopental, Pancuronium Bromide, Potassium Chloride	None
South Carolina	3-Drug Pentobarbital (protocol not publicly available)	3-Drug Sodium Thiopental
South Dakota**	3-Drug Sodium Thiopental or Pentobarbital, Pancuronium Bromide, Potassium Chloride 2-Drug Sodium Thiopental or Pentobarbital, Pancuronium Bromide 1-Drug Sodium Thiopental or Pentobarbital	3-Drug Sodium Thiopental
Tennessee	3-Drug Midazolam, Vecuronium Bromide, Potassium Chloride	3-Drug Sodium Thiopental
Texas	1-Drug Pentobarbital	3-Drug Pentobarbital 3-Drug Sodium Thiopental
Utah	3-Drug Sodium Thiopental, Pancuronium Bromide, Potassium Chloride	None
Virginia	3-Drug Midazolam, Rocuronium Bromide, Potassium Chloride	3-Drug Pentobarbital 3-Drug Sodium Thiopental
Wyoming	3-Drug Sodium Thiopental	None

* The information in this chart is revised and modified from DEATH PENALTY INFO. CTR., STATE BY STATE LETHAL INJECTION PROTOCOLS 1 (2019), https://deathpenaltyinfo.org/executions/lethal-injection/state-by-state-lethal-injection-protocols.
** States that list sodium thiopental in both past and current lethal injection protocols. Ohio is the only state that started with a sodium thiopental-based protocol, then instituted new protocols with different drugs due to the unavailability of sodium thiopental, and then added sodium thiopental back into its most current protocol.
† Moratorium in place, current protocol may not be in place
Note: All drug names are derived directly from the states' protocols.

In addition, Chart 4 shows states' most recent protocols and their previous protocols as enacted by statute, thereby giving a sense of the nature and frequency of state protocol changes.

There is immense variability among the states represented in Chart 4. While some states, such as California, have no execution protocol in place due to a death penalty moratorium, other states, such as Ohio and South Dakota, have several options and allow for a one-drug, two-drug, or three-drug protocol, depending on a drug's availability. Likewise, three states — Mississippi, Ohio, and South Dakota — list sodium thiopental in both their past and current protocols, although the newer statutes seem to have adjusted for its unavailability. Lastly, one state — South Carolina — does not make its most recent drug protocol available to the public, so one can only deduce its current protocol from its most recent lethal injection procedure, which utilized a three-drug protocol beginning with Pentobarbital.

Apart from the trends noted in Charts 2 and 3, however, Chart 4 demonstrates the extent to which states vary from one another and how they have changed over time. Clearly, drug availability is a driving force behind this variability, but the continual changes also signal how risky and experimental the methods really are.

The Federal Government's Protocol

The federal government, meanwhile, rarely uses capital punishment, with no federal execution since 2003.[34] The future of that trajectory, however, was called into question by two developments in 2019. First, the Office of Legal Counsel of the Department of Justice (OLC) released a legal opinion stating that the FDA does not have jurisdiction over the drugs applied in lethal injection executions.[35]

Second, the Bureau of Prisons (BOP) had finalized revisions to its execution protocol and execution dates were set for five federal death row inmates.[36] The revised BOP execution protocol called for use of pentobarbital in a single drug protocol as opposed to the three-drug thiopental protocol used in the three previous federal executions.[37] The federal government claimed that the one-drug pentobarbital procedure was acceptable because a range of states had used pentobarbital either as a single drug or in conjunction with other drugs, and courts had upheld its use as consistent with the Eighth Amendment.[38]

Critics have strenuously objected to these developments, voicing a number of concerns relevant to this chapter's back-to-the-future inquiry. Where will the government acquire pentobarbital given the increasing difficulty states have had in obtaining it? Will the government eventually disclose the source or keep it secret? Will the pentobarbital be created by a compounding pharmacy and thus raise inherent risks of ineffectiveness?[39] The OLC's 2019 memorandum stressed its view that the FDA does not have jurisdiction to regulate drugs used for capital punishment,[40] but critics state that stance contravenes prior policy.

---

[34] *Federal Death Penalty: Overview*, DEATH PENALTY INFO. CTR., https://deathpenaltyinfo.org/state-and-federal-info/federal-death-penalty (last visited Sept. 25, 2019).

[35] *See* Steven A. Engel, *Whether the Food and Drug Administration Has Jurisdiction over Articles Intended for Use in Lawful Executions*, DEP'T OF JUST. (May 3, 2019), https://www.justice.gov/olc/opinion/file/1162686/download.

[36] Press Release, Dep't of Just., Federal Government to Resume Capital Punishment after Nearly Two Decade Lapse, July 25, 2019, www.justice.gov/opa/pr/federal-government-resume-capital-punishment-after-nearly-two-decade-lapse.

[37] *Id.*

[38] *Id.*

[39] *Don't Strengthen the Death Penalty, Abolish It*, FEDERALIST, July 29, 2019, https://thefederalist.com/2019/07/29/dont-strengthen-death-penalty-abolish; *Federal Government Announces New Execution Protocol, Sets Five Execution Dates*, DEATH PENALTY INFO. CTR. (July 25, 2019), https://deathpenaltyinfo.org/news/federal-government-announces-new-execution-protocol-sets-five-execution-dates; *Mixed Response to Federal Execution Announcement: Conservatives, Catholic Bishops Oppose Decision, Arizona Announces Plans to Follow Federal Lethal Injection Protocol*, DEATH PENALTY INFO. CTR. (July 30, 2019), https://deathpenaltyinfo.org/news/mixed-response-to-federal-execution-announcement-conservatives-catholic-bishops-oppose-decision-arizona-announces-plans-to-follow-federal-lethal-injection-protocol. The 2013 D.C. Court of Appeals decision is *Cook v. Food and Drug Administration*, 733 F. 3d 1 (D.C. Cir. 2013).

[40] *See* Engel, *supra* note 35, www.justice.gov/olc/opinion/file/1162686/download.

Together, these two developments indicate a turning point in the nation's history with capital punishment. They have also spurred a flurry of commentary from scholars, politicians, and other pundits questioning what the future of executions will look like.

Are We Heading Backward?

The chaos created by the rapid changes in lethal injection protocols over the past decade belies the extent to which legislatures, courts, and departments of corrections have retained a firm foothold in the past. The discussion below provides an overview of those circumstances, as well as the exceptions.

Lethal Injection Protocols: How the Present Mirrors the Past

Over the three decades following Oklahoma's adoption of lethal injection in May 1977, thirty-nine states would eventually do the same, with many being influenced by one another.[41] However, my research shows substantial variability in how states amended their execution statutes to include lethal injection. For most, there was no clean break from the execution method ostensibly being replaced; in fact, there was often ambivalence about whether there should be a replacement. For example, there were notable differences among states that authorized either retroactive or nonretroactive applications of lethal injection, depending on whether the amending lethal injection statute was enacted after inmates were sentenced or convicted ("pre-enactment prisoners"), or before they were sentenced and convicted ("post-enactment prisoners").[42]

In 1997, twenty years after Oklahoma adopted lethal injection, thirty-two of the thirty-eight death penalty states had adopted lethal injection in some capacity, and the variability in their approaches has relevance today. Twenty-one states offered no alternative method of execution for inmates sentenced or convicted after the date the lethal injection statute was enacted or became effective. Eight states allowed inmates to choose between lethal injection and another execution method (either hanging, the firing squad, electrocution, or lethal gas); in turn, four states provided such a choice only to those inmates sentenced or convicted prior to the statute's enactment. Mississippi was even more unusual in requiring the pre-enactment inmate to use the execution method that was in place when that inmate was sentenced to death, while post-enactment inmates would get lethal injection.[43] While the Court in *Malloy v. South Carolina*[44] held that the Ex Post Facto Clause

---

[41] See Denno, *supra* note 10, at 1341–42.
[42] See Deborah W. Denno, *Getting to Death: Are Executions Constitutional?*, 82 Iowa L. Rev. 319, 378–79 (1997).
[43] *Id.*
[44] 237 U.S. 180 (1915).

was not violated when a new, presumably more humane, method of execution (that is, lethal injection) is retroactive,[45] inmates have unsuccessfully challenged statutes in which the new, presumably more humane, execution method is not retroactive.[46]

With rare exception, all courts — including the Supreme Court — have generally refrained from finding any execution method unconstitutional; rather, legislatures typically circumvent constitutional challenges so as not to acknowledge the problems created by a particular execution method. A primary form of this kind of circumvention involves statutes with what I call "constitutional substitutes." In my 1997 study of the topic, ten states possessed a lethal injection statute that allowed for at least one constitutional substitute if lethal injection were ever rendered unconstitutional or "otherwise unavailable." These substitutes consisted of other execution methods that were considered more problematic than lethal injection (hanging, electrocution, the firing squad, and lethal gas), but that were still constitutional. At the time these constitutional substitute statutes were devised, the motivation was to preclude a potential hiatus in executions in the event there were challenges to lethal injection that would otherwise prohibit executions altogether. That said, three additional states put the responsibility for choosing the execution method with someone other than the inmate (such as the commissioner of corrections) in cases when a method was being challenged or was difficult to enact.[47] In this way, long before there was an actual drug shortage, states were preparing for the possibility that a method might not be available for whatever reason.

The full extent of the constitutional substitute provisions was demonstrated by Oklahoma's lethal injection statute in 1997. If lethal injection were rendered unconstitutional, an inmate would be executed by electrocution. If both lethal injection and electrocution were rendered unconstitutional, an inmate would be executed by firing squad.[48] On the surface, the execution methods are in a hierarchy based on purported humaneness: lethal injection was adopted by states to quell their concerns with electrocution, while electrocution was introduced in 1890 as a method to address perceived problems with hanging and other potential methods, including the firing squad.

It is ironic that states would allow the implementation of a more problematic form of execution if the presumably more humane form could not be carried out. But present-day policies mirror the past in this respect, as a variety of states still have constitutional substitutes.[49] Either bad statutory habits have simply never disappeared, or the states are being reinvigorated in other ways, using other types of methods. The bottom line is that states have never been fully able to let go or render unconstitutional clearly problematic execution methods or statutory strategies.

---

[45] *See id.* at 182–84.
[46] *See* Denno, *supra* note 42, at 378–79.
[47] *See id.* at 379.
[48] *See id.* at 390.
[49] *See supra* Charts 1, 2, and 4.

Rather, states have put them on the back burner only to retrieve them when needed to ensure the continuity of the death penalty. The following examples illustrate how the present mirrors the past.

Sodium Thiopental

As noted in Charts 2–4, thirteen states still list sodium thiopental in their statutes even though that drug has not been available for more than a decade. Even when it was available, sodium thiopental was a controversial and questionable choice from the start, given that it is a "fast-acting barbiturate" and its effects in the execution context were unknown and untested.[50] Still, when faced with drug shortages, many statutes include sodium thiopental in providing several options for the first drug of their lethal injection protocols. For example, a state may allow sodium thiopental, pentobarbital, and midazolam to be used interchangeably. Indeed, Oregon does not even name a specific drug in its statute; it just mentions the use of a barbiturate.

Constitutional Substitutes of Other Execution Methods

In the past, lethal injection protocols provided constitutional substitutes employing other methods of execution that were problematic but still constitutional. The number of such provisions has dwindled in the last twenty years, but Chart 1 shows the states that offer constitutional substitutes. For example, Mississippi and Oklahoma have substitute statutes that enable the application of nitrogen hypoxia. In turn, Tennessee permits the use of the electric chair, and Utah allows the firing squad if the state is unable to access lethal injection drugs thirty days before an execution.

Oklahoma's lethal injection protocol is currently being litigated but, in its present form, the state's statute has added a constitutional substitute since 1997: Nitrogen gas is now listed first in the state's four-substitute hierarchy. Thus, if lethal injection is unconstitutional or unavailable, the Oklahoma statute first authorizes the use of nitrogen gas, followed by electrocution and the firing squad if those methods become unconstitutional or unavailable.[51] Oklahoma's statute aptly illustrates the back to the future phenomenon surrounding lethal injection: nitrogen gas is a new method never before used in any execution in this country. Yet, its method of incorporation into Oklahoma's four-substitute hierarchy reaches back to the statutory framework that Oklahoma originally laid out without apparent regard for humaneness.

---

[50] *See* Denno, *When Legislatures Delegate*, supra note 3, at 98–100.

[51] OKLA. STAT. tit. 22 § 1014. Oklahoma authorizes the use of nitrogen hypoxia if either lethal injection is held unconstitutional or "otherwise unavailable"; then the state authorizes electrocution if nitrogen hypoxia and lethal injection are held unconstitutional or "otherwise unavailable"; finally, the state authorizes the firing squad if nitrogen hypoxia, lethal injection, and electrocution are held unconstitutional or "otherwise unavailable." *Id.*

Constitutional Substitutes of Other Lethal Injection Drugs

Drug substitutions for sodium thiopental started in 2010 with pentobarbital[52] and have continued to include more problematic drugs such as midazolam and, potentially, etomidate.[53] The purpose in allowing such substitutions runs parallel to the goals underlying constitutional substitutes of execution methods. As Chart 4 shows, states commonly keep available a number of "starter drugs" (the sodium thiopental substitutes) while protecting the constitutional viability of even the most troubling ones. If one drug is not available, states often have at least one other contingency drug.

While Charts 3 and 4 appear to present new techniques and procedures for ensuring the continuing application of the death penalty, states' approaches in fact borrow from strategies that were developed when lethal injection was first adopted. Likewise, the seemingly blind pursuit of execution at any cost, even at the risk of experimenting on human beings, is a practice that long has been in place.

Electrocution: An Execution Method That Never Really Goes Away

Electrocution has been widely used in the United States since 1890, peaking in 1949 when a total of twenty-six states made the switch to electrocution due to concerns over the barbarity of hanging. After 1949, however, no additional states adopted electrocution because the method had produced a series of botched and gruesome executions. Nevada switched to lethal gas in 1921, and by 1955, nearly a dozen states had adopted that method because it appeared to be more humane. Still, by 1973, states stopped adopting lethal gas as an execution method because it too led to grotesque accounts of inmates experiencing slow and suffocating deaths.[54]

Lethal injection, first employed in 1977, was quickly adopted by a substantial number of states in its first decade. Even so, a sizeable number of holdout states retained their original execution method; it would take until 2009 for electrocution to cease being the sole method of execution in any state, instead remaining an option in a half-dozen states.[55] Notably, electrocution is the only method of execution rendered unconstitutional by any state. Both Georgia[56] and Nebraska[57] have ruled that electrocution violates their respective state constitutional provisions against cruel and unusual punishment. Since the very start of its use, electrocution has been widely recognized as among the most gruesome methods of execution,

---

[52] *See* Denno, *supra* note 10, at 1358.
[53] *See supra* Charts 1–4.
[54] *See* Denno, *supra* note 42, at 364–68.
[55] *See* Denno, *supra* note 10, at 1341–42.
[56] *See* Dawson v. State, 554 S.E.2d 137 (Ga. 2001).
[57] *See* State v. Mata, 745 N.W.2d 229 (Neb. 2008).

with scores of journalists and witnesses documenting their concerns over flames, burnt flesh, and bursting eyeballs.[58]

Given this trajectory, it is striking that there are inmates who still choose electrocution over lethal injection, thus reverting to a method created before the turn of the twentieth century rather than one introduced eight decades later. Within a ten-year period — from 2009 to 2019 — seven inmates selected electrocution over lethal injection, with an almost even split between Virginia (three inmates) and Tennessee (four inmates).[59] For Stephen West, an inmate to be executed by electrocution (in Tennessee in 2019), the choice was clear: he claimed "that the electric chair is 'also unconstitutional, yet still less painful' compared with the state's preference of a three-drug lethal injection."[60] Two other Tennessee inmates — David Miller and Edmund Zagorski — also chose electrocution over lethal injection in 2018, offering rationales similar to Stephen West's claim. They expressed particular concern over Tennessee's use of midazolam, which they claimed "results in a prolonged and torturous death."[61] West was among a group of four inmates who, in 2018, filed a lawsuit requesting a federal court's permission to be executed by firing squad, given that three states (Mississippi, Oklahoma, and Utah) allow that method under restricted circumstances[62] (see also Chart 1).

"Such madness [with electrocution] should not continue," stressed Justice Sonia Sotomayor's dissent to David Miller's execution.[63] Justice Sotomayor noted that Tennessee's 2018 electrocutions were just a month apart, and electrocution — while preferable to lethal injection — "can be a dreadful way to die."[64] She derided *Glossip v. Gross*'s[65] "perverse requirement" that inmates must provide an alternative

---

[58] For example, in *Dawson*, 554 S.E.2d 137, the Georgia Supreme Court stressed that electrocution's "purposeless physical violence and needless mutilation," *id*. at 143, as well as its "specter of excruciating pain and ... certainty of cooked brains," constitutes cruel and unusual punishment, *id*. at 144. The court also noted that the Georgia legislature had, since 2000, been moving in the direction of a switch, *id*., and that "many states" had changed to lethal injection, "clearly" an "important factor" in determining the constitutionality of "an older method," *id*. at 143.

[59] *See Execution Database*, DEATH PENALTY INFO. CTR., *supra* note 31 (providing data on executions by electrocution from 2009–2019).

[60] *See Tennessee Executes Inmate in Electric Chair for Killing Mother and Daughter in 1986*, CBS NEWS (Aug. 15, 2019), www.cbsnews.com/news/tennessee-electric-chair-stephen-west-execution-today-2019-08-15/. In Tennessee, inmates can choose the electric chair rather than lethal injection if their crimes occurred before 1999. *See supra* note 9 and accompanying text.

[61] Travis Loller, *Tennessee Executes Second Inmate in 2 Months*, AP NEWS (Dec. 6, 2018), www.apnews.com/678772de856c4ba5b453aa49a04a5295.

[62] *See supra* note 60.

[63] Miller v. Parker, 139 S.Ct. 399 (2018). Justice Sotomayor dissented in both cases concerning Tennessee's 2018 electrocution executions. *Id*.; Zagorski v. Parker, 139 S.Ct. 11 (2018).

[64] *Miller*, 139 S.Ct. at 399.

[65] 135 S. Ct. 2726 (2015).

method of execution if the state's standard method violates the Eighth Amendment.[66] In essence, *Glossip* encouraged inmates to return to prior execution methods simply to avoid the perils of lethal injection, notwithstanding that those prior methods were also problematic.

Firing Squad: Is a Method from a "Primitive Era" More Humane Than Our Modern Era's Methods?

Other than hanging, the firing squad is this country's oldest method of execution. (The first documented firing squad execution occurred in 1608.)[67] Justice Sotomayor's dissent in *Glossip v. Gross*[68] supports the proposition that the firing squad may be the most humane of the available execution methods, despite its historically brutal reputation. She sets forth this argument by examining what "a known and available alternative method of execution" could be in light of evidence accessible to death row inmates. In her view, for example, "the firing squad is significantly more reliable than other methods, including lethal injection," and "there is some reason to think that it is relatively quick and painless."[69] Granted, the firing squad "could be seen as a devolution to a more primitive era,"[70] and "the blood and violence that comes with it" as evidence of such a perspective.[71] At the same time, those stereotyped facets of the firing squad do not make the method "unconstitutional"[72] even though the firing squad's "visible brutality" could lead to Eighth Amendment objections.[73] There is strong support for Justice Sotomayor's position that an inmate may consider the "visible yet relatively painless violence" linked with the firing squad "vastly preferable to an excruciatingly painful death hidden behind a veneer of medication."[74] Lethal injection may be even more violent than the firing squad if witnesses could see behind lethal injection's "curtain."[75]

These facts and arguments gain further significance in light of efforts by inmates and states to make the firing squad a viable alternative method of execution. Importantly, Justice Brett Kavanaugh's concurrence in *Bucklew v. Precythe*[76] emphasized that all the Justices agreed that the alternative method "need not be authorized under current state law"; inmates can propose any constitutional method

---

[66] *Miller*, 139 S.Ct. at 399.
[67] Denno, *supra* note 7, at 778.
[68] 135 S. Ct. at 2792–97 (Sotomayor, J., dissenting).
[69] *Id.* at 2796.
[70] *Id.*
[71] *Id.* at 2797.
[72] *Id.*
[73] *Id.*
[74] *Glossip*, 135 S. Ct. at 2797 (Sotomayor, J., dissenting).
[75] *Id.*
[76] 139 S. Ct. 112 (2019) (Kavanaugh, J., concurring).

as an alternative, even one that their own state has not adopted.[77] Justice Kavanaugh added that he did "not prejudge the question whether the firing squad, or any other alternative method of execution, would be a feasible and readily implemented method for every state," but rather only that an acceptable alternative method should be available.[78]

Of course, not all legislatures will be receptive to adopting methods such as the firing squad, even if the courts could conceivably permit them. South Carolina started to consider a bill to allow execution by firing squad, but that bill has seemingly stalled.[79] At the same time, Utah brought back firing squads as a backup method of execution in 2015. While the state's last firing squad execution was in 2010 (that of Ronnie Lee Gardner), inmate Ron Lafferty could have been executed by firing squad at some point in 2020 had he not recently died in prison from natural causes in November 2019.[80]

Hanging: A Method Is Eliminated for the First Time in This Country's History

Hanging is this country's oldest execution method. In 1853, it was the method used by forty-eight states and territories.[81] Nevertheless, when New Hampshire abolished the death penalty in May 2019, it became the last of three states that listed hanging as a potential execution method. The two other states that allowed hanging — Delaware and Washington — also abolished the death penalty in 2016 and 2018, respectively.[82]

Thus, for the first time in this country's history, hanging is no longer an available method of execution. Ironically, the one method that prompted this country to seek more humane alternatives (such as electrocution) has been eliminated, not because of concerns over the method's barbarity and history of botches, but rather because the states that still used it had abolished the death penalty entirely.[83]

---

[77] *Id.* at 1136.

[78] *Id.*

[79] South Carolina Senate Bill No. 176 (123rd sess.) passed the Senate but appears to be stalled in the House Judiciary Committee. *See* S.C. SENATE BILL No. 176, www.scstatehouse.gov/sess123_2019-2020/bills/176.htm. No action was taken on the bill as of the last day of the legislative session ending May 2019.

[80] Associated Press, *Utah Man Featured in "Under the Banner of Heaven" Closer to Death by Firing Squad*, USA TODAY, Aug. 14, 2019, www.usatoday.com/story/news/nation/2019/08/14/utah-death-row-inmate-ron-lafferty-loses-appeal-closer-execution/2006367001/.

[81] Denno, *When Legislatures Delegate*, *supra* note 3 at 82.

[82] *See supra* Chart 1.

[83] Hanging as a method was abolished at the same time that the death penalty itself was abolished in these states except for Delaware, which disassembled the gallows in 2003. Notably, because the repeal in New Hampshire was not retroactive, there is a possibility that the one person left on death row in New Hampshire could be put to death by hanging if lethal injection is not possible. Given New Hampshire's death penalty history, however, it seems unlikely this person will even be put to death and it appears that the state may no longer have an active gallows.

Unlike electrocution and the firing squad, no state has seriously considered hanging as an alternative method today. The most recent hangings occurred in the early to mid-nineties, and in just two states: Washington (in 1993 and 1994) and Delaware (in 1996). It is doubtful hanging will return, and it may be the one execution method that states have clearly relegated to the past.[84]

Nitrogen Hypoxia: When "Past" Becomes "Present"

Three states — Alabama (in 2018), Mississippi (in 2017), and Oklahoma (in 2015) — now provide nitrogen hypoxia as an alternative to lethal injection in an effort to surmount the challenge of acquiring appropriate drugs for lethal injection.[85] However, Alabama is the only state in which an inmate can "affirmatively choose[]" nitrogen hypoxia instead of lethal injection if the inmate gives notice of the choice within a prescribed time period.[86] In contrast, Mississippi[87] and Oklahoma[88] allow for execution by nitrogen hypoxia only as a constitutional substitute if lethal injection is rendered unconstitutional or "otherwise unavailable."

Execution by nitrogen hypoxia has never before been attempted in any state's execution chamber, and no state has dispensed specific information about how the method would be implemented. The idea for the method is attributed to Stuart Creque, a California technology consultant who wrote a two-page article in the *National Review* about a purportedly secure means of inducing unconsciousness painlessly and non-toxically.[89] He based his recommendation on accidents in which individuals died as a result of being exposed to nitrogen, an odorless and invisible gas. If the gas were infused in a contained gas chamber, explained Creque, an inmate would become unconscious almost immediately. Shortly thereafter, the inmate would experience the oxygen deprivation known as hypoxia. The result would be brain injury and then death.[90]

Twenty years later, Oklahoma took Creque's proposal seriously, becoming the first state to allow nitrogen hypoxia as an alternative method if lethal injection or electrocution was rendered unconstitutional or "otherwise unavailable."[91] Although the legislature overwhelmingly passed the bill, the justification for it was based on a skeletal fourteen-page report by three arts and sciences faculty members from East

---

State and Federal Info: New Hampshire, DEATH PENALTY INFO. CTR., https://deathpenaltyinfo .org/state-and-federal-info/state-by-state/new-hampshire (last visited Sept. 25, 2109).

[84] *Methods of Execution*, DEATH PENALTY INFO. CTR., https://deathpenaltyinfo.org/executions/ methods-of-execution (last visited Sept. 25, 2019).

[85] *See supra* Chart 1.

[86] ALA. CODE § 15-18-82.1.

[87] MISS. CODE § 99-19-51.

[88] OKLA. STAT. tit. 22 § 1014.

[89] *See* Stuart A. Creque, *Killing with Kindness*, NAT'L REV., Sept. 11, 1995, at 51.

[90] *Id.* at 52.

[91] *See* OKLA. STAT. tit. 22 § 1014.

Central University. None of these individuals held the medical, scientific, or technical qualifications to assess such a means of putting a person to death, much less the background to advise how such a method would be administered.[92] In light of this lack of detail, it is difficult to accept arguments that nitrogen hypoxia is the most humane and effective way to execute an inmate. In addition, as of 2019, neither Alabama nor Oklahoma has purchased equipment to carry out such executions nor developed a protocol for doing so.

Of course, this country's reliance on lethal gas is nothing new.[93] The American gas chamber was conceived and implemented years before gas chambers were introduced in Nazi Germany.[94] While nitrogen gas is a different type than what the three "lethal gas" states listed in Chart 1 would apply, the concept and conceivably the implementation could be the same. Further, when Russell Bucklew identified nitrogen gas as an alternative method of execution, his argument derived from the Missouri legislature's failure to specify the type of lethal gas that was to be employed in the state's gas protocol. Therefore, nitrogen gas was consistent with the wording of the state's statute.[95]

The Court in *Bucklew v. Precythe*[96] affirmed the decisions of the district court and the Eighth Circuit, rejecting Bucklew's argument that a lethal injection execution would be unconstitutional. Even so, nitrogen hypoxia most resembles a back-to-the-future scenario: it is the only method any state has adopted after lethal injection, despite falling in the footsteps of lethal gas.

CONCLUSION

The future of execution methods is virtually impossible to predict. The secrecy, incompetence, politics, and ignorance that long have enveloped the death penalty in this country maintain a particularly firm grip on how execution methods are created and conducted.[97] The coming years will gauge the extent to which inmates will press for methods beyond the ever changing lethal injection drugs that create risks and constitute experimentation. Of course, it is also possible

---

[92] Scott Christiansen, *How Oklahoma Came to Embrace the Gas Chamber*, New Yorker, June 24, 2015, www.newyorker.com/news/news-desk/how-oklahoma-came-to-embrace-the-gas-chamber.

[93] *See supra* note 57 and accompanying text (discussing the history of lethal gas and the problems associated with it).

[94] Scott Christensen, The Last Gasp: The Rise and Fall of the American Gas Chamber 1 (2010).

[95] *See supra* notes 21–26 (discussing *Bucklew*).

[96] 139 S. Ct. 112 (2019).

[97] For discussions of many of these issues in the context of different protocols, states, and cases over time, see generally Eric Berger, *Lethal Injection Secrecy and Eighth Amendment Due Process*, 55 B.C. L. Rev. 1367 (2014); Berry, *supra* note 2; Berry & Ryan, *supra* note 2; Denno, *supra* note 10; Denno, *When Legislatures Delegate, supra* note 3; Yorke, *supra* note 19.

that drug shortages will become so severe that lethal injections cannot be carried out at all.[98] Given that both Justice Sotomayor and Justice Kavanaugh have mentioned the firing squad as an example of an alternative, that method may start to be more widely applied. The *Bucklew* Court's ruling that inmates can choose methods outside of their own state law frees them from the pronouncements of their state legislatures and opens the door to more possible outcomes. However, the most predictable outcome appears to be a return to the past. The back-to-the-future pattern evident throughout the history of states' execution methods seems destined to play out yet again in the immediate future.

Meanwhile, twenty-one states have now abolished the death penalty, and California's governor has issued a moratorium on executions for the country's largest death row population. President Donald Trump's pro-capital punishment stance is countered by the fact that "[t]he use of the death penalty remained near record lows" in 2019.[99] Indeed, if hanging is any example, abolishment of the death penalty may come faster than states' abilities to change the ways they execute inmates.

---

[98] There have been some commentaries on the topic of the future of execution methods but they do not expand beyond the techniques that this chapter has already discussed. *See, e.g.,* Zaria Gorvett, *The People Rethinking Methods of Execution*, BBC FUTURE (June 6, 2018), www.bbc .com/future/story/20180604-is-there-a-humane-way-to-kill-a-criminal; Carter Sherman & Tess Owen, *Death Penalty States Are Looking for New Ways to Execute People*, VICE NEWS (Jan. 2, 2018), www.vice.com/en_ca/article/gyw5gm/death-penalty-states-are-looking-for-new-ways-to-execute-people.

[99] Matt Ford, *America Is Stuck with the Death Penalty for (at Least) a Generation*, NEW REPUBLIC, July 19, 2018, https://newrepublic.com/article/150036/america-stuck-death-penalty-at-least-generation; Alan Greenblatt, *Why the Death Penalty Has Lost Support from Both Parties*, GOVERNING THE STATES AND LOCALITIES (Apr. 16, 2019), www.governing.com/topics/public-justice-safety/gov-death-penalty-states-new-hampshire.html; *The Death Penalty in 2019: Year End Report*, DEATH PENALTY INFO. CTR., (2019), https://deathpenaltyinfo.org/facts-and-research/dpic-reports/dpic-year-end-reports/the-death-penalty-in-2019-year-end-report.

14

Evolving Standards of Lethal Injection

Eric Berger[*]

INTRODUCTION

Lethal injection has been the dominant method of execution in the United States for several decades, but in recent years, it has changed dramatically. Understanding the evolution of lethal injection shines important light on both the American death penalty's recent history and also its possible future. These changes raise important Eighth Amendment questions, as well as practical issues about the long-term viability of lethal injection and perhaps even the death penalty generally.

A VERY BRIEF HISTORY OF LETHAL INJECTION

Oklahoma became the first state to adopt lethal injection in 1977 when it designed a three-drug protocol consisting of sodium thiopental, an ultra-short-acting barbiturate anesthetic; pancuronium bromide, a paralytic inhibiting muscle movement; and potassium chloride, which induces cardiac arrest.[1] Texas soon copied Oklahoma's protocol, and other states soon mimicked these early adopters.[2] Over the next twenty-five years, thirty-eight states adopted this three-drug protocol.[3]

In 2008, the U.S. Supreme Court upheld the constitutionality of Kentucky's three-drug protocol in *Baze v. Rees*.[4] Kentucky's protocol resembled Oklahoma's

---

[*] Earl Dunlap Distinguished Professor of Law and Associate Dean for Faculty, University of Nebraska College of Law. Special thanks to Will Berry and Meghan Ryan for editing this volume and their excellent suggestions to improve this chapter, and to Ngozi Ndule and Robert Dunham for their maintenance of and guidance with the invaluable databases of the Death Penalty Information Center.

[1] See Deborah W. Denno, *The Lethal Injection Quandary: How Medicine Has Dismantled the Death Penalty*, 76 FORDHAM L. REV. 49, 55 (2007).

[2] *See id.* at 78.

[3] *See* Deborah W. Denno, *Lethal Injection Chaos Post-Baze*, 102 GEO. L.J. 1331, 1342 (2014).

[4] 553 U.S. 35 (2008).

and Texas' protocol. Indeed, at the time of *Baze*, U.S. lethal injection protocols all resembled each other. Thirty-six of the country's thirty-seven death penalty states had lethal injection as their sole or primary method of execution, and lethal injection states carried out executions with this same three-drug protocol.[5] To be sure, there were important differences in how states *administered* the drugs. To this extent, states' *procedures* could differ in important ways. However, the basic *protocols* — that is, the sequence of drugs — were nearly identical across the country.

Just over a decade later, the landscape is very different. Today, lethal injection protocols vary considerably from state to state. Moreover, the three-drug protocol that dominated the landscape a decade ago has fallen out of favor. Some states still retain it (usually in an altered form), but since 2015, there has been a decided trend in favor of a one-drug protocol. This chapter explores that trend and related Eighth Amendment implications.

THE VARIATION OF LETHAL INJECTION PROTOCOLS

In the years since *Baze*, many states have changed their drug protocols. In some cases, they have done so multiple times. Some states also have adopted alternative protocols, stipulating a preferred protocol but permitting state officials to select a different protocol instead, should the drugs for the preferred protocol be unavailable.

Lethal injection protocols today fall into one of three basic categories. States may move between categories over time, and their primary and backup protocols may belong in different categories. Nevertheless, a brief summary of the categories provides a helpful sense of the landscape.

The first category encompasses three-drug protocols, though usually with different drug combinations than in 2008. Like Oklahoma's original procedure, three-drug protocols consist of a drug that ostensibly anesthetizes the inmate, followed by a paralytic, followed by potassium chloride. In the years since *Baze*, states have substituted different anesthetics and paralytics.

Often, these substitutions have been because states have had difficulty procuring one drug or another. Multiple factors explain the drug shortage. In 2010, Hospira, Inc., the sole U.S. manufacturer of thiopental, ceased domestic production of the drug at its domestic plant due to an "unspecified raw material supply problem."[6] Opposition to capital punishment also played a substantial role in the shortage. Starting around 2011 when the Danish pharmaceutical Lundbeck urged an Ohio prison official to discontinue the use of its products in executions, pharmaceutical

---

[5] *See id.* at 53 ("This broad consensus goes not just to the method of execution, but also to the specific three-drug combination used by Kentucky.").

[6] Carol J. Williams, *Maker of Anesthetic Used in Executions Is Discontinuing Drug*, L. A. TIMES, Jan. 22, 2011, http://articles.latimes.com/2011/jan/22/local/la-me-execution-drug-20110122.

companies have tried to prevent states from using their drugs in executions.[7] States have had increasing difficulty procuring death penalty drugs as other pharmaceutical companies, such as Pfizer, have also announced that they would not provide drugs for executions.[8]

As these problems mounted, some states replaced thiopental, the "traditional" three-drug protocol's anesthetic, with a different first drug, such as pentobarbital, midazolam, or etomidate. However, states have often found that such switches are short-lived, because pharmaceutical companies quickly figure out states' new plans and take steps to try to prevent states from obtaining the new execution drug, as well as the old. For example, not long after states started using pentobarbital in executions, pharmaceutical companies, such as Lundbeck, tried to obstruct states from getting that drug.[9]

The second category of lethal injection protocols encompasses one-drug protocols.[10] A one-drug protocol delivers to the inmate an overdose of a single barbiturate anesthetic (or similar drug), such as pentobarbital or thiopental. Whereas the three-drug protocol relies on the third drug to kill the inmate by (painfully) stopping the heart, a one-drug protocol merely puts the inmate into a sleep from which he will never awaken. To this extent, some states moved to a one-drug protocol in an effort to minimize the risk of suffering.[11]

The third and smallest category is a catchall for experimental protocols that do not fall into either of the first two categories. For example, in 2014, both Ohio and Arizona conducted executions using an unusual two-drug protocol. Both of these procedures were botched, resulting in prolonged executions.[12] Neither state has retained these controversial protocols. In 2018, Nebraska used a controversial four-drug protocol including diazepam (valium), fentanyl (an opioid), a paralytic, and

---

[7] *See* Raymond Bonner, *Pharmaceutical Company Bans Sale of Drug for Use in Lethal Injections*, THE ATLANTIC, July 1, 2011, www.theatlantic.com/national/archive/2011/07/pharmaceutical-company-bans-sale-of-drug-for-use-in-lethal-injections/241332/; Adam Gabbatt & David Batty, *Danish Firm Lundbeck to Stop US Jails Using Drug for Lethal Injections*, THE GUARDIAN (July 1, 2011), www.theguardian.com/world/2011/jul/01/lundbeck-us-pentobarbital-death-row (explaining that Lundbeck required anyone buying their product to sign a paper stating that they will not sell the drug to prisons).

[8] Erik Eckholm, *Pfizer Blocks the Use of Its Drugs in Executions*, N.Y. TIMES, May 13, 2016, www.nytimes.com/2016/05/14/us/pfizer-execution-drugs-lethal-injection.html; *Pfizer's Position on Use of Our Products in Lethal Injections for Capital Punishment*, PFIZER (Sept. 2017), www.pfizer.com/files/b2b/Global_Policy_Paper_Lethal_Injection_Sept_2017.pdf.

[9] *See* Gabbatt & Batty, *supra* note 7.

[10] See Eric Berger, *Lethal Injection Secrecy and Eighth Amendment Due Process*, 55 B.C. L. REV. 1367, 1380 (2014).

[11] *See infra* notes 53–63 and accompanying text.

[12] *See* Maya Rhodan, *Arizona Inmate Dies after Nearly 2 Hours in Apparently Botched Execution*, TIME, July 24, 2014, http://time.com/3026551/arizona-execution-botched-lethal-injection/; Lawrence Hummer, *I Witnessed Ohio's Execution of Dennis McGuire. What I Saw Was Inhumane*, THE GUARDIAN (Jan. 22, 2014), www.theguardian.com/commentisfree/2014/jan/22/ohio-mcguire-execution-untested-lethal-injection-inhumane.

potassium chloride. It seems doubtful that the state will use this protocol again.[13] In all events, these two- and four-drug protocols are very much outliers. The vast majority of executions have been with either a three-drug or a one-drug protocol.

THE RISKS OF THE THREE-DRUG PROTOCOL

Many observers and some states have acknowledged the three-drug protocol's risks. Everybody agrees that the third drug, potassium chloride, is extremely painful as it courses through the inmate's veins toward his heart.[14] Some have likened it to being burned alive from the inside.[15] However, the protocol's paralytic can entirely conceal that pain. Moreover, the paralytic also paralyzes the inmate's diaphragm, thereby creating the terrifying sensation of suffocation.

For these reasons, the humaneness of the three-drug protocol hinges on whether the first drug properly anesthetizes the inmate from the suffering caused and concealed by the second and third drugs. There are reasons, however, to doubt whether the first drug will consistently and fully perform its anesthetizing function. For one, because states have had difficulty getting some of the drugs for their protocols, they have substituted for thiopental different first drugs, some of which cannot reliably guard against the excruciating pain that potassium chloride manifestly causes.[16] For example, some states have selected midazolam as their first drug,[17] even though there are serious questions about whether it can realistically protect against severe pain.[18]

Even when the states select a more suitable first drug, such as pentobarbital, the execution team must still successfully administer it. States, however, often fail to properly select, train, and supervise execution team members. As a result, states have made a variety of serious mistakes delivering the drugs, including the anesthetic. For example, some states have failed to set the IV catheter properly, resulting in infiltration — that is, drugs spilling into the tissues surrounding the inmate's veins.[19] Infiltration itself is very painful and can also prevent the inmate from receiving an

[13] *See* Joe Duggan, *Nebraska Says It Can't Replace Key Death Penalty Drug, Which Expires Aug. 31,* OMAHA WORLD HERALD, Aug. 10, 2018, www.omaha.com/news/courts/nebraska-says-it-can-t-replace-key-death-penalty-drug/article_30a6e633-dabf-5b20-a288-6607f1d72cc6.html.

[14] See Eric Berger, *Lethal Injection and the Problem of Constitutional Remedies,* 27 YALE L. & POL'Y REV. 259, 265 (2008).

[15] *See* Glossip v. Gross, 135 S. Ct. 2726, 2795 (2015) (Sotomayor, J., dissenting).

[16] *See* Eric Berger, *Gross Error,* 91 WASH. L. REV. 929, 940 (2016).

[17] Some states have also replaced pancuronium bromide with a different paralytic, such as vecuronium bromide or rocuronium bromide. Unlike the choice of the anesthetic, the selection of one paralytic over another is unlikely to alter the risks of the protocol.

[18] *See In re* Ohio Execution Protocol Litigation, No. 11-106, 2019 WL 244488, at *65 (S.D. Ohio Jan. 14, 2019); Berger, *supra* note 16, at 951–57.

[19] *See* Governor's Comm'n on Admin. of Lethal Injection, Final Report with Findings and Recommendations 8 (2007).

adequate dose of an anesthetic.[20] Other states have also rapidly injected their drugs in quick succession, not realizing that the anesthetic does not take effect instantaneously.[21] At least one state has made mistakes mixing the drugs, unwittingly altering the dosage of the anesthetic.[22] Another state listed certain drugs in its written protocol only to use a different drug by accident in actual executions.[23] In short, for the three-drug protocol to cause painless deaths, states must design and administer it with a degree of competence and professionalism they often lack.

In light of these concerns, experts have repeatedly testified and written that one-drug protocols using a single barbiturate anesthetic (or similar drug), such as pentobarbital, greatly reduce the risk that the inmate will feel excruciating pain.[24] The reason, these experts explain, is obvious: the second and third drugs in the three-drug protocol can each cause great suffering.[25] Moreover, the second drug, the paralytic, can completely conceal that searing pain, removing, as one expert put it, the inmate's ability to "voice the fact that he or she is awake when they are feeling the effects of pancuronium or potassium chloride."[26]

By contrast, in a one-drug protocol, the state administers an overdose of a drug that simply puts the inmate to sleep. This one-drug approach therefore removes from the protocol the drugs that both cause and mask suffering.[27] As one expert anesthesiologist has testified, "[i]f all you're using is an anesthetic-only technique, which is what veterinarians use … the chance of causing an inhumane death is exceedingly remote. Again, you're using a drug that all it does is make you get sleepy and then make you go to sleep and then make you stop breathing and make you die."[28]

The transition in several states from a three-drug protocol to a one-drug protocol, then, has helped reduce the risk that the condemned will suffer an agonizing execution. Of course, it is not always clear whether states have switched protocols out of genuine concern for the condemned or to try to resume executions after drug shortages, botched executions, court orders, or other difficulties. However, even states entirely unconcerned with the inmate's suffering still must consider the three-drug protocol's dangers. Three-drug protocols heighten the risk of botches, which in

---

[20] *See* Berger, *supra* note 14, at 270.
[21] *See* Deposition of Larry Crawford, Taylor v. Crawford, No. 05-4173, 2006 WL 1779035, at 129–31 (W.D. Mo. May 23, 2006).
[22] *See* Taylor v. Crawford, 2006 WL 1779035, at *7 (W.D. Mo. June 26, 2006).
[23] *See, e.g.*, Matt Ford, *An Oklahoma Execution Done Wrong*, THE ATLANTIC, Oct. 8, 2015, www .theatlantic.com/politics/archive/2015/10/an-oklahoma-execution-done-wrong/409762/. Oklahoma's error did not involve the anesthetic, but the incident demonstrates that a state could make such a mistake.
[24] *See, e.g.*, Mark Dershwitz & Thomas K. Henthorn, *The Pharmacokinetics and Pharmacodynamics of Thiopental as Used in Lethal Injection*, 35 FORDHAM URB. L.J. 931, 955–56 (2008).
[25] *See id.*
[26] Deposition of Dr. Mark Dershwitz vol. I, 120–21, Jackson v. Danberg, No. 06-300 (D. Del. Sept. 10, 2007).
[27] *See id.* at 51.
[28] Trial Transcript Excerpt 69, *Biros v. Strickland*, No. 04-1156 (S.D. Ohio Mar. 27, 2009).

turn can cause states to put executions on delay for years. For example, after a badly botched execution and other public difficulties involving lethal injection, Oklahoma halted executions in 2015 and, as of this writing, has still not resumed them.[29] Moreover, because the three-drug protocol heightens the risk of excruciating pain, courts are more likely to hold such protocols unconstitutional.[30] To this extent, the risks of the three-drug protocol likely affect states' decision-making in this area, regardless of the particular state officials' motives.[31]

Botched three-drug executions further help explain the shift to the one-drug protocol, showcasing that that protocol's risks are not merely theoretical. One reporter witnessing Oklahoma's 2014 execution of Clayton Lockett described the inmate's agony.

> Lockett began to breathe heavily. He clenched his teeth. He rolled his head. Then he tried to speak ... Lockett lurched up against the restraints. While the witnesses looked on, he started writhing as if trying to free himself, to get up off the gurney. He struggled violently, twisting his whole body.[32]

While the Lockett execution was particularly horrific, states have also botched other three-drug executions. Angel Diaz's three-drug execution in Florida resulted in large, gruesome chemical burns and blisters on his arms.[33] During Ronald Bert Smith Jr.'s three-drug execution in Alabama, the inmate clenched his fist and heaved and coughed for thirteen minutes.[34] Far from being anomalous, then, Lockett's botched three-drug execution was one of multiple examples.

Indeed, Professor Austin Sarat calculates that seventy-five three-drug lethal injection executions were botched between 1982 and 2010.[35] Professor Sarat's estimation may be on the low side. For one, he concluded his study before some of the most prominent botched three-drug executions, such as those of Lockett and Smith. Additionally, the protocol's paralytic may well have concealed excruciating pain in other seemingly peaceful executions. It is therefore impossible to know precisely

---

[29] *See, e.g.,* Grant Hermes, *Executions Still on Hold in Oklahoma*, NEWS9, April 21, 2017, www .news9.com/story/35215220/executions-still-on-hold-in-oklahoma.

[30] *See, e.g.,* Harbison v. Little, 511 F. Supp. 2d 872, 903 (M.D. Tenn. 2007); Taylor v. Crawford, No. 05-4173, 2006 WL 1779035, at *7–8 (W.D. Mo. June 26, 2006), *rev'd* 487 F.3d 1072 (8th Cir. 2007); Morales v. Hickman, 415 F. Supp. 2d 1037, 1046 (N.D. Cal. 2006).

[31] *See generally* Eric Berger, *The Executioners' Dilemmas*, 49 U. RICH. L. REV. 731 (2015).

[32] Jeffrey E. Stern, *The Cruel and Unusual Execution of Clayton Lockett*, THE ATLANTIC, June 2015, www.theatlantic.com/magazine/archive/2015/06/execution-clayton-lockett/392069/.

[33] *See, e.g.,* Ben Crair, *Photos from a Botched Execution*, NEW REPUBLIC, May 29, 2014, https:// newrepublic.com/article/117898/lethal-injection-photos-angel-diazs-botched-execution-florida.

[34] *See, e.g.,* Kent Faulk, *Alabama Death Row Inmate Ronald Bert Smith Heaved, Coughed for 13 Minutes during Execution*, AL.COM (June 6, 2017), www.al.com/news/birmingham/index .ssf/2016/12/alabama_death_row_inmate_is_se.html.

[35] *See* AUSTIN SARAT, GRUESOME SPECTACLES: BOTCHED EXECUTIONS AND AMERICA'S DEATH PENALTY 177, 197–210 (2014).

how many three-drug executions have resulted in excruciating deaths. The number, however, is likely significant.

By contrast, the one-drug protocol is far less problematic. This is not to say that it is entirely without risks. Some states have procured drugs from the black market or from compounding pharmacies, some of which lack the facilities to manufacture drugs safely.[36] Consequently, there is a risk that even a one-drug protocol can cause pain because of contaminated, impure, sub-potent, super-potent, or otherwise flawed drugs.[37] On balance, though, the one-drug protocol poses far fewer dangers than a three-drug protocol, because it eliminates the paralytic and the potassium chloride.

THE MOVEMENT AWAY FROM THE THREE-DRUG PROTOCOL

This backdrop helps explain why some states have moved from the three-drug to the one-drug protocol (usually with pentobarbital). Execution statistics help demonstrate the one-drug protocol's new prevalence. In 2008, one hundred percent of executions were carried out with the three-drug protocol. Just two years later, in 2010, more than 20 percent of executions in the United States were with a one-drug protocol. Two years after that, in 2012, more than half of all executions used a one-drug protocol.

Over the next few years, reliance on the one-drug protocol became increasingly more common. In both 2013 and 2014, more than sixty percent of executions were with the one-drug protocol. And in 2015 and 2016, that number leaped to eighty-five percent of executions. While the three-drug protocol was used for a modest majority (sixty-one percent) of executions in 2017, the trend against it resumed in 2018 and 2019 when only about thirty percent of executions used a three-drug method.[38]

Recent trends have, thus, steadily favored the one-drug protocol. From the beginning of 2012 to December 1, 2019, only thirty-four percent of U.S. lethal injection executions (eighty of 233) utilized a three-drug protocol. Sixty-three percent have been with a one-drug protocol.[39] This trend has accelerated more recently. From the beginning of 2015 until December 1, 2019, only thirty-four of 116 total executions (twenty-nine percent) utilized a three-drug protocol.

A survey of current protocols further confirms that many states are moving away from the three-drug protocol. Today, only seven states (Alabama, Arkansas, Florida,

[36] *See* Berger, *supra* note 10, at 1384.

[37] *Id.*

[38] *See Execution List 2019*, DEATH PENALTY INFO. CTR., https://deathpenaltyinfo.org/execution-list-2019 (last visited Dec. 1, 2019); *Execution List 2018*, DEATH PENALTY INFO. CTR., https://deathpenaltyinfo.org/execution-list-2018 (last visited Dec. 1, 2019); *Execution List 2017*, DEATH PENALTY INFO. CTR., https://deathpenaltyinfo.org/execution-list-2017 (last visited Dec. 1, 2019). Because Nebraska's four-drug protocol includes both a paralytic and potassium chloride, I am counting it here as a three-drug protocol.

[39] Two executions in 2014 were with a two-drug protocol.

Mississippi, Ohio, Tennessee, and Virginia) currently have in place a three-drug protocol with which they have executed someone since 2011.[40] Thus, just fourteen percent of all states — and only twenty-three percent of death penalty states — currently have a three-drug protocol with which they have executed someone since 2011.[41] Additionally, the federal government, which announced in July 2019 that it would seek to resume executions, has replaced its old three-drug protocol with a new one-drug pentobarbital protocol.[42]

Closer examination reveals that even the short list of three-drug states might be overstating confidence in that protocol. For example, Tennessee, which had not executed anyone since 2009, carried out three executions in 2018 and three more in 2019. The state did use the three-drug protocol for one execution in 2018 and another in 2019. Tennessee law, however, permits inmates to select electrocution as an alternative method of execution. After an expert alleged that Billy Ray Irick felt searing pain during his three-drug execution in August 2018,[43] two other Tennessee capital inmates chose electrocution instead for their 2018 executions.[44] As Justice Sotomayor emphasized in her dissent from a denial of an application for a stay of execution, Edmund Zagorski's decision to be executed by electric chair was "not because he thought that it was a humane way to die, but because he thought that the

---

[40] *See State by State Lethal Injection*, DEATH PENALTY INFO. CTR., https://deathpenaltyinfo.org/state-lethal-injection (last visited Mar. 16, 2019). This count excludes Oklahoma. While Oklahoma used a three-drug protocol as recently as January 2015, it does not currently have a protocol in place due to a court order during pending lethal injection litigation. The state has, in fact, indicated that it plans to turn away from lethal injection and to nitrogen gas for executions. *See* Timothy Williams, *Oklahoma Turns to Gas for Executions Amid Turmoil over Lethal Injection*, N.Y. TIMES, Mar. 14, 2018, www.nytimes.com/2018/03/14/us/oklahoma-nitrogen-executions.html.

[41] Nebraska did carry out its first execution in two decades in August 2018 with a very unusual four-drug protocol that arguably exacerbates the three-drug protocol's risks. *See* Merrit Kennedy, *Nebraska Carries Out 1st Execution Using Fentanyl in U.S.*, NPR (Aug. 14, 2018), www.npr.org/2018/08/14/638250649/nebraska-prepares-to-carry-out-first-execution-using-fentanyl. However, Nebraska has already conceded that two of its four drugs have expired and that it does not anticipate being able to restock those drugs again. *See* Joe Duggan, *Nebraska Prison Officials on the Hunt for More Lethal Injection Drugs*, SCOTTSBLUFF STAR HERALD, Aug. 20, 2018, www.starherald.com/news/regional_statewide/nebraska-prison-officials-on-the-hunt-for-more-lethal-injection/article_caa402f4-4a80-5c3f-934a-054bf0cc5f1.html. It is therefore unclear whether Nebraska will be able to resume executions or what future execution protocols will look like.

[42] *See* Dep't of Justice, Federal Government to Resume Capital Punishment after Nearly Two Decade Lapse, July 25, 2019, www.justice.gov/opa/pr/federal-government-resume-capital-punishment-after-nearly-two-decade-lapse (noting that the federal government's new one-drug execution protocol replaces the three-drug protocol previously used in federal executions).

[43] *See* Adam Tamburin & Dave Boucher, *Tennessee Execution: Billy Ray Irick Tortured to Death, Expert Says in New Filing*, TENNESSEAN, Sept. 7, 2018, www.tennessean.com/story/news/crime/2018/09/07/tennessee-execution-billy-ray-irick-tortured-filing/1210957002/.

[44] *See, e.g.*, Associated Press, *Second Tennessee Prisoner on Death Row Chooses Electric Chair for Execution*, NBC NEWS (Nov. 26, 2018), www.nbcnews.com/storyline/lethal-injection/second-tennessee-prisoner-death-row-chooses-electric-chair-execution-n940341.

three-drug cocktail that Tennessee had planned to use was even worse."[45] While Tennessee did carry out another three-drug lethal injection execution in 2019, it also used electrocution twice more later that year. Indeed, four of Tennessee's six executions in 2018 and 2019 were by electrocution.[46] If anything, then, events in Tennessee confirm misgivings about the three-drug protocol.

Ohio probably belongs on this list even less than Tennessee. While Ohio in 2016 did adopt a three-drug protocol with which it carried out three executions in 2017 and 2018, the state itself had previously expressed a clear preference for the one-drug protocol. In fact, Ohio was the first state to adopt a one-drug protocol. Ohio's prior three-drug protocol came under attack after that state's failed attempt to execute Romell Broom in September 2009. Shortly thereafter, Ohio abandoned its three-drug protocol in favor of a one-drug protocol. At the time it made that switch, the state represented in federal court that it would no longer use pancuronium bromide or potassium chloride for executions.[47] Specifically, Ohio stated then that "[t]here is absolutely no reason to believe that defendants will reinstate the previous 'three-drug protocol' . . . And, more importantly . . . defendants cannot 'go back to their old ways' and execute plaintiffs using the prior procedures."[48] Ohio's subsequent return to the three-drug protocol, thus, was in clear conflict with its stated preference.

Indeed, recent events in Ohio further underscore that state's discomfort with the three-drug protocol. On January 14, 2019, a federal magistrate judge found "as a matter of fact it is certain or very likely" that Ohio's three-drug protocol, which controversially included midazolam as its first drug, would result in "severe pain and needless suffering."[49] The judge, however, did not strike down the Ohio protocol, because the plaintiff did not demonstrate the availability and feasibility of an alternative method, as required by Supreme Court doctrine.[50] Later that same month, though, Ohio Governor Mike DeWine postponed an upcoming execution so that the state could reassess its lethal injection cocktail.[51]

---

[45] Zagorski v. Haslam, 139 S. Ct. 20, 21 (2018) (Sotomayor, J., dissenting from denial of application for stay and denial of certiorari).

[46] *See* DEATH PENALTY INFO. CTR., *Searchable Execution Database*, at https://deathpenaltyinfo .org/executions/execution-database?filters%5Byear%5D=2018&filters%5Byear%5D=2019&filters %5Bstate%5D=Tennessee (last visited Jan. 4, 2020).

[47] *See In Re* Ohio Execution Protocol Litig., 860 F.3d 881, 892 (6th Cir. 2017) (discussing Ohio's representation that it was switching to a one-drug protocol and would not reinstate the three-drug protocol).

[48] *Id.* at 903 (Moore, J., dissenting) (quoting Defendants' Motion for Summary Judgment in Ohio Execution Protocol Litigation).

[49] *In re* Ohio Execution Protocol Litigation, No. 11-106, 2019 WL 244488, at *65 (S.D. Ohio Jan. 14, 2019) (decision and order on motion for stay of execution and preliminary injunction).

[50] *See id.* at *66–70 (concluding that the plaintiff had not satisfied the second prong of the Supreme Court's test in *Glossip v. Gross*, 135 S.Ct. 2726 (2015)).

[51] *See, e.g.*, Jeremy Pelzer, *Gov. Mike DeWine Delays Killer's Execution, Orders Review of Lethal-Injection Drugs*, CLEVELAND.COM, Jan. 25, 2019, www.cleveland.com/politics/2019/01/gov-mike-dewine-delays-killers-execution-orders-review-of-lethal-injection-drugs.html.

As of this writing, it is unclear whether Ohio will ever use its three-drug protocol again.[52] However things end up playing out, the magistrate judge's ruling and the governor's subsequent decision highlight both the three-drug protocol's dangers and Ohio's preference for a more humane method. To this extent, Ohio's inclusion on the list of three-drug protocol states is questionable.

A few other case studies further highlight states' concerns with the three-drug protocol. During the course of litigation challenging its three-drug protocol, the State of Washington switched to a one-drug protocol. As the state explained to the Washington Supreme Court, in light of Ohio's experience with the one-drug protocol and the opinions of experts advising the Washington Department of Corrections, the state adopted a one-drug protocol as its "presumed method."[53] Like the State of Ohio, Washington represented that the "drugs pancuronium bromide and potassium chloride will not be used in the one drug protocol under the amended policy."[54] The state justified its decision by explaining that a one-drug protocol using only thiopental "eliminates the risk of any pain."[55] The Washington Supreme Court has since struck down that state's death penalty entirely.[56] In the meantime, however, the state made clear its preference for a one-drug protocol.

Events in California were similar. A working draft of California's most recent protocol forswore the three-drug protocol. As the state explained, "While CDCR [the California Department of Corrections and Rehabilitation] considered several single and multi-chemical combination methods of execution, it elected to use a single-chemical method because it reduces the risk of pain and possible complications, and addresses constitutional concerns."[57] The state continued by explaining

---

[52] Admittedly, the Sixth Circuit, in affirming the magistrate judge's ruling, said in dictum that the lower court had erred in finding that the plaintiff had met his burden in establishing that Ohio's protocol was constitutionally problematic. *See In re* Ohio Execution Protocol Litigation, 937 F.3d 759, 762-63 (6th Cir. 2019). The Sixth Circuit's decision, however, does not undermine the basic point that Governor DeWine's actions reflected serious concerns about the three-drug protocol. After the Sixth Circuit's decision, Governor DeWine announced that Ohio would not conduct any executions in 2019. *See* Jeremy Pelzer, *Ohio Won't Hold Any Executions in 2019 as Gov. Mike DeWine Issues More Reprieves*, CLEVELAND.COM, Oct. 30, 2019, at https://www.cleveland.com/open/2019/10/ohio-wont-hold-any-executions-in-2019-as-gov-mike-dewine-issues-more-reprieves.html.

[53] *See* Respondents' Motion to Dismiss as Moot 4, *Stenson v. Vail*, No. 83828-3 (Wash. Sup. Ct. Mar. 1, 2010).

[54] *Id.* Washington at this time did retain the three-drug protocol as an option for the inmate but stated that it would not use the three-drug protocol "unless the inmate expressly elects the three drug protocol in writing." *See* Respondents' Motion to Dismiss, *supra* note 53, at 5.

[55] *Id.* at 9.

[56] *See* Mark Berman, *Washington Supreme Court Strikes Down State's Death Penalty, Saying It Is 'Arbitrary and Racially Biased'*, WASH. POST, Oct. 11, 2018, www.washingtonpost.com/news/post-nation/wp/2018/10/11/washington-supreme-court-strikes-down-states-death-penalty-saying-it-is-arbitrary-and-racially-biased/?noredirect=on&utm_term=.086972a64006.

[57] California Dep't of Corrections and Rehabilitation, *Initial Statement of Reasons* 1, Oct. 30, 2015.

that its goal in designing a new protocol was "to develop a humane and dignified execution."[58] California further explained that its proposed one-drug protocol would help eliminate the constitutional concerns raised by a three-drug protocol containing a paralytic and potassium chloride.[59] The state ultimately did adopt a one-drug protocol.[60]

California Governor Gavin Newsom recently issued an executive order withdrawing that protocol as part of a broader moratorium on capital punishment.[61] Consequently, the California protocol, like the Washington one, is no longer active. However, the state's chosen protocol before this development reflects the same strong aversion to the three-drug protocol.

Developments in Arizona reflect similar concerns. The Arizona Department of Corrections (ADC) represented in a settlement agreement with death row inmates that it would never use a paralytic in any future executions and that it would also remove the "three-drug lethal injection protocol from the current and any future version of the ADC's execution procedures."[62] The most recent Arizona protocol, in fact, stipulates that the state use a one-drug protocol.[63]

To be sure, while only fourteen percent of states currently have in place a three-drug protocol with which they have executed someone since 2011, several other states nominally have three-drug protocols. However, it is worth emphasizing that those states have not executed anyone in years. Indeed, many states retaining the three-drug protocol almost never execute anyone. Colorado, Indiana, Nevada, New Mexico, Oregon, Pennsylvania, South Carolina, Utah, and Wyoming all have or have recently had three-drug protocols officially on record, but none of them have executed anyone since 2011. Five of those states (Colorado, Oregon, Pennsylvania, Utah, and Wyoming) have not executed anyone since the 1990s. Two more of those states (Nevada and New Mexico) have not executed anyone since the Supreme Court decided *Baze* in 2008.[64] It should not be surprising that many of the states retaining the three-drug protocol rarely or never conduct executions. After all, states that have capital punishment in name only would have little incentive to revise a protocol they are unlikely to use.

---

[58] *See id.*

[59] *See id.* at 2.

[60] *See* State of California Office of Administrative Law, *In re* Department of Corrections and Rehabilitation, Adopt Sections 3349.1 et al., *12–13 (Mar. 1, 2018).

[61] *See* Tim Arango, *California Death Penalty Suspended; 737 Inmates Get Stay of Execution*, N.Y. Times, Mar. 12, 2019, www.nytimes.com/2019/03/12/us/california-death-penalty.html.

[62] Transcript of Status Conference 7, Wood v. Ryan, No. 14-1447 (D. Ariz. June 12, 2016); *see also* First Amendment Coalition v. Ryan, No. 14-1447, at *3 (D. Ariz. June 22, 2017) (order for dismissal) (prohibiting the state from adopting or employing "any lethal-injection protocol that uses a paralytic").

[63] *See* Arizona Dep't of Corrections, Department Order 710: Execution Procedures, Attachment D at *1–2 (June 13, 2017).

[64] *See* Death Penalty Info. Ctr., *State by State Lethal Injection*, https://deathpenaltyinfo.org/state-lethal-injection (last visited Feb. 4, 2019).

Some of these states arguably do not belong on the list of three-drug protocol states at all. New Mexico voted to abolish the death penalty in 2009. Because the repeal was not retroactive, two men remained on New Mexico's death row, but the state was clearly moving away from capital punishment altogether.[65] Indeed, in 2019 the New Mexico Supreme Court vacated the two remaining death sentences and ordered that both men be re-sentenced to life in prison. Oregon nominally has a three-drug protocol, but it also has had a death penalty moratorium in effect since 2011.[66] Nevada technically does have a three-drug protocol, but it does not include potassium chloride (the drug causing excruciating pain), so it arguably does not belong in this list either.[67]

To be clear, the trend should not be overstated. While the move away from the three-drug protocol has been significant, several states do still use it. Indeed, even today, more states use three-drug protocols than one-drug protocols. That said, the trend away from the three-drug protocol is notable, especially given the ubiquity of that protocol in the 1990s and 2000s. Between 1990 and 2008, thirty-three different states carried out a three-drug execution.[68] As noted above, today just seven (and arguably just six) states have an active three-drug protocol that they have used since 2011.[69] To be sure, the overall decline in the death penalty partially explains the decline. But some of capital punishment's decline is due to problems with the three-drug protocol that have forced states to suspend executions.

Indeed, it is no coincidence that some three-drug states have had to put executions on hold for years.[70] Botches and other problems arising out of three-drug executions are common and therefore prone to interfere with states' abilities to carry out executions. Oklahoma previously carried out executions frequently, but following serious problems with its three-drug protocol, it has put executions on hold for five

---

[65] *See* DEATH PENALTY INFO. CTR., *Death-Row Prisoners by State*, https://deathpenaltyinfo.org/death-row-inmates-state-and-size-death-row-year?scid=9&did=188 (last checked Mar. 16, 2019).

[66] *See* DEATH PENALTY INFO. CTR., *2018 Midterm Elections: Governors in Moratorium States Re-Elected, Controversial California D.A. Ousted*, https://deathpenaltyinfo.org/category/categories/states/oregon (noting the reelection of Oregon Governor Kate Brown, who continued the state's death penalty moratorium).

[67] Nevada's unusual protocol includes midazolam, fentanyl, and cisatracurium. *See* Nevada Dep't of Corrections, *Execution Protocol* 23-25, June 11, 2018, https://deathpenaltyinfo.org/files/pdf/NevadaProtocol_06.11.2018.pdf.

[68] *See* DEATH PENALTY INFO. CTR., *Execution Database*, https://deathpenaltyinfo.org/executions/execution-database?filters%5Byear%5D=1990&filters%5Byear%5D=1991&filters%5Byear%5D=1992&filters%5Byear%5D=1993&filters%5Byear%5D=1994&filters%5Byear%5D=1995&filters%5Byear%5D=1996&filters%5Byear%5D=1997&filters%5Byear%5D=1998&filters%5Byear%5D=1999&filters%5Byear%5D=2000&filters%5Byear%5D=2001&filters%5Byear%5D=2002&filters%5Byear%5D=2003&filters%5Byear%5D=2004&filters%5Byear%5D=2005&filters%5Byear%5D=2006&filters%5Byear%5D=2007&filters%5Byear%5D=2008&filters%5Bmethod%5D=Lethal%20Injection.

[69] *See supra* notes 39–51 and accompanying text.

[70] *See supra* notes 29–32 and accompanying text.

years and counting.[71] Ohio recently put its three-drug protocol on hold after a judge there identified the procedure's dangers.[72] Litigation is also obstructing executions in a number of other three-drug states, including Indiana, Kentucky, Louisiana, and North Carolina.[73] Litigation may eventually obstruct executions in other three-drug states, such as Mississippi.[74] Of course, litigation can also interfere with one-drug executions, but because that protocol substantially decreases the risk of pain, the plaintiff's odds of winning (or even obtaining temporary relief) are lower. The three-drug protocol's own problems, then, have substantially contributed to its decline.

None of this is to say that the current trend will necessarily hold. Perhaps the three-drug protocol will make a comeback; the death penalty is unpredictable. Compared to the landscape at the time of *Baze*, though, the decline of the three-drug protocol is dramatic.

EIGHTH AMENDMENT IMPLICATIONS

These recent lethal injection trends carry Eighth Amendment implications. These trends will not necessarily change judges' approaches to Eighth Amendment lethal injection challenges, but the phenomena discussed here do raise important constitutional issues, which courts will likely flesh out over the coming years. They also both reflect and affect changed attitudes toward the death penalty, which in the long run may matter more than Eighth Amendment doctrine.

It is well known that the Eighth Amendment incorporates "evolving standards of decency."[75] While other areas of constitutional law also change as social norms do,[76] the Eighth Amendment's text uniquely seems to invite some sort of evolution. After all, the Eighth Amendment addresses not only cruelty but also *unusualness*.[77] It therefore views skeptically disfavored punitive practices.[78] To this extent, a

---

[71] *See supra* note 29 and accompanying text.

[72] *See supra* notes 47–52 and accompanying text.

[73] *See* DEATH PENALTY INFO. CTR., *State by State Lethal Injection Protocols*, at https://deathpenaltyinfo.org/executions/lethal-injection/state-by-state-lethal-injection-protocols.

[74] *See* Jordan v. Hall, First Amended Complaint, No. 15-295 (S.D. Miss. Sept. 28, 2015) (challenging constitutionality of Mississippi's three-drug protocol).

[75] *See* Trop v. Dulles, 356 U.S. 86, 101 (1958).

[76] *See generally* BARRY FRIEDMAN, THE WILL OF THE PEOPLE: HOW PUBLIC OPINION HAS INFLUENCED THE SUPREME COURT AND SHAPED THE MEANING OF THE CONSTITUTION (2009); MICHAEL J. KLARMAN, FROM JIM CROW TO CIVIL RIGHTS: THE SUPREME COURT AND THE STRUGGLE FOR RACIAL EQUALITY (2004); Corinna Barrett Lain, *Upside-Down Judicial Review*, 101 GEO. L.J. 113 (2012).

[77] The Court has not fully explicated the meaning of the word "unusual" in the Eighth Amendment. *See, e.g., Trop,* 356 U.S. at 100 & n.32 (noting that the words of the Eighth Amendment "are not precise" and that it "is not clear" whether the word "'unusual' has any qualitative meaning different from 'cruel.'").

[78] *See, e.g.,* William W. Berry III, *Evolved Standards, Evolving Justices? The Case for a Broader Application of the Eighth Amendment*, 96 WASH. U. L. REV. 105, 118–29 (2018) (discussing Eighth Amendment majoritarianism).

punishment that was constitutional in the past might become unconstitutional in the future if society largely abandons it. Changed practices can have constitutional implications.[79]

Recent trends, then, raise new questions about the three-drug protocol's constitutionality. After all, the Court looks to state practices as "the clearest and most reliable objective evidence of contemporary values."[80] The Court in Eighth Amendment cases considers not only the status quo but also "the direction of the change."[81] As we have already seen, the direction of change is clearly against the three-drug protocol.

Admittedly, many states do still retain the three-drug protocol, but most of those are states that never execute anyone. It is possible, of course, that as states continue to have difficulty procuring pentobarbital and other drugs suitable for single-drug protocols, we will see more three-drug executions in future years. On the other hand, the fact that several states and the federal government have moved to a one-drug protocol indicates continued discomfort with the three-drug approach. Moreover, the fact that many three-drug states are having difficulties carrying out executions is further indication that the three-drug protocol is inherently problematic.

Importantly, courts need not consider these evolving practices against the three-drug protocol in isolation. Rather, judges and lawyers should view the move away from the three-drug protocol in conjunction with powerful evidence of that protocol's dangers. In other words, a court need not strike down a remaining three-drug protocol simply because it is the exception. Instead, a court could invalidate a three-drug protocol, because it creates a significant risk of excruciating death *and* because it is becoming unusual.

Given the great — and, often, excessive — deference that courts offer states in lethal injection cases,[82] many courts might reject such an argument, at least today. But today's losing argument can become tomorrow's winning one. Evolving standards of decency, indeed, contemplates this possibility of doctrinal change.[83]

Moreover, even if a court were not willing to invalidate a state's practices solely on these grounds, the trend against the three-drug protocol still has constitutional salience. Faced with Eighth Amendment lethal injection challenges, states often contend that an adverse ruling would effectively kill the death penalty, because they

---

[79] *See id.* at 151 (contending that when jurisdictions abandon particular punishments, courts should examine carefully whether that punishment violates the Eighth Amendment).

[80] Atkins v. Virginia, 536 U.S. 304, 312 (2002) (quoting Penry v. Lynaugh, 492 U.S. 302, 331 (1989)).

[81] *Cf.* Roper v. Simmons, 543 U.S. 551, 566 (2005).

[82] *See* Bucklew v. Precythe, 139 S. Ct. 1112, 1125 (2019) ("[T]he Constitution affords a 'measure of deference to a State's choice of execution procedures' and does not authorize courts to serve as 'boards of inquiry charged with determining best practices for executions.'" (quoting Baze v. Rees, 553 U.S. 35, 51–52 (2008))); Berger, *supra* note 16, at 932–36.

[83] *Cf.* Berry, *supra* note 78, at 151.

would be unable to develop a workable alternative procedure.[84] A ruling against their current protocol, they insist, is an undemocratic blow against capital punishment altogether.

The recent history of lethal injection belies this contention. For one, the variety of lethal injection protocols and the relatively rapid changes in state practices demonstrate that states can and do change their protocols successfully. Many states have had difficulty getting drugs, but the states that have really wanted to continue executions have been able to do so, often changing protocols along the way. Texas, for instance, switched from the three-drug to a one-drug protocol in mid-2012 and, as of this writing, has carried out eighty-four one-drug executions. It is simply not true, then, that the abandonment of one protocol necessarily equates to forgoing executions forever.

Relatedly, the successes of the one-drug protocol highlight that, contrary to some of their claims, three-drug states can find other means to carry out executions. Not only have several three-drug states switched to the one-drug protocol, but also the one-drug protocol has executed many more people in recent years than the three-drug protocol. This fact alone ought to persuade courts not to put too much stock in states' claims that they would be unable to develop a viable new lethal injection protocol were their three-drug protocol invalidated.

Moreover, the availability of the one-drug protocol can help plaintiffs satisfy the Supreme Court's requirement that lethal injection challengers proffer a "feasible, readily implemented" alternative execution procedure.[85] While some states may insist that they could not obtain drugs for a new protocol — and that a proposed alternative is therefore not "feasible" or "readily implemented" — the fact that other states carry out one-drug executions should help demonstrate that it is, in fact, possible to implement a one-drug protocol. In fact, Justice Kavanaugh's concurrence in *Bucklew v. Precythe* emphasized that the plaintiffs' proposed "alternative method of execution need not be authorized under current state law."[86] Quite simply, the recent rise of one-drug executions demonstrates that a plaintiff proffering a one-drug method satisfies the Court's "feasible, readily implemented" requirement.

To the extent that shifts to one-drug protocols reflect concerns about the three-drug protocol, this story also casts doubt on the deference courts often reflexively grant lethal injection protocols and the three-drug protocol in particular. Several states have publicly admitted their concerns about the three-drug protocol's safety. That courts have been willing to bless lethal injection protocols that states themselves subsequently foreswore (due, in part, to safety concerns) raises questions about

---

[84] *See, e.g.*, Transcript of Hearing on Motion to Dismiss, Kelley v. Johnson, No. CV-15-992, 2016 AR S. Ct. Briefs LEXIS 49, at *127 (Ark. Oct. 7, 2015) (stating that "the Department of Correction would have a very difficult time obtaining drugs").

[85] *See Bucklew*, 139 S. Ct. at 1125.

[86] *See id.* at 1136 (Kavanaugh, J., concurring).

whether those judges have crafted and applied a wise Eighth Amendment standard. If judicial deference seemed controversial in 2015 in *Glossip v. Gross*,[87] it seems even less deserved today for those few states that cling to a risky execution method abandoned by peer states.

Of course, courts extend such deference in substantial part because they fear that states forced to adopt a new protocol would be unable to procure new drugs. Judges, on this view, ought not facilitate "guerilla warfare" on the death penalty.[88] But states' concerns about the three-drug protocol, coupled with the successes of the one-drug protocol, should persuade judges that the three-drug protocol is more dangerous and the one-drug protocol more feasible than they had assumed. Admittedly, some states may still have difficulties getting drugs for a one-drug protocol. But because pharmaceutical companies now so uniformly oppose the use of their drugs in executions, these problems now exist for *all* protocols. Indeed, the fact that one-drug executions have substantially outnumbered three-drug ones over the past half dozen years should signal to courts that a ruling against a three-drug protocol is not tantamount to invalidating capital punishment writ large.

The Supreme Court to date has pursued an aggressively deferential attitude toward state choices in this area.[89] Some Justices themselves are likely frustrated that, despite the Court's repeated rulings against lethal injection plaintiffs, many states struggle to carry out executions. While courts tend to overstate states' difficulties getting drugs, these Justices are correct that some states have had trouble finding lethal injection drugs and carrying out lawfully imposed death sentences. To this extent, the Court's decisions in cases such as *Baze*, *Glossip*, and *Bucklew* are understandable, albeit controversial.

Significantly, though, judicial decisions have played only a bit role in the larger saga of lethal injection.[90] Perhaps this fact partially helps explain the Supreme Court's frustration. States' lethal injection difficulties stem far less from unfavorable court decisions than drug companies' refusal to provide execution drugs due to a variety of reasons, such as investor concerns, foreign pressure, and the companies' own moral and institutional norms.[91] Drug companies simply do not want states using their drugs to kill people. Courts' Eighth Amendment rulings have little effect on those companies' values.

---

[87] *See generally* Berger, *supra* note 10.

[88] *See* Transcript of Oral Argument at 58, Glossip v. Gross, 135 S. Ct. 2726 (2015) (No. 14–7955) (question of Alito, J.).

[89] *See* Berger, *supra* note 16, at 944–94.

[90] See Eric Berger, *What about Bucklew? Courts, Culture, and the Future of Lethal Injection* (manuscript on file with author).

[91] *See, e.g.*, James Gibson & Corinna Barrett Lain, *Death Penalty Drugs and the International Moral Marketplace*, 103 GEO. L.J. 1215, 1220–36 (2015); Pfizer, *Pfizer's Position on Use of Our Products in Lethal Injections for Capital Punishment* (April 2016), www.pfizer.com/sites/default/files/b2b/GlobalPolicyPaperLethalInjection.pdf.

While these companies have not fully detailed the nature of their moral objections, they likely are connected, albeit subtly, to shifts in public attitudes toward capital punishment. If Americans overwhelmingly supported the death penalty, companies may be less willing to take a public stand against capital punishment, even if they themselves had misgivings about states using their drugs to kill people. After all, in the 1990s, when public support for capital punishment was much higher than it is today,[92] states did not have trouble obtaining lethal injection drugs. It is likely no accident that drug companies' objections began seriously disrupting American executions around the same time public support for the death penalty began to wane significantly. Right around the time public support for capital punishment hit a four-decade low, investors began pressuring drug companies to stop supplying drugs for executions.[93] To be sure, the execution drug shortage is a complicated phenomenon with many interconnected parts,[94] but changes in public attitudes toward the death penalty likely play a substantial role.

For its part, decline in support for capital punishment is even more complicated, but it likely grows partially out of a greater understanding of the death penalty's numerous problems, such as, among others, wrongful conviction, arbitrary imposition, racial and class bias, and exorbitant cost.[95] Public opinion, state practices, drug company policies, and lethal injection problems, then, are all interconnected, at least somewhat. Increased media and scholarly attention to the death penalty's serious problems surely have played some role in decreasing Americans' support for the practice,[96] which in turn has encouraged investors to pressure drug companies to stop supplying drugs for executions, which has likely played a role in many companies' decisions to take a strong stand against the use of their drugs in lethal injection. Drug companies' practices, in turn, have made it more difficult for states to get drugs, thus resulting in far fewer executions. To this extent, lethal injection problems have been a factor in the sharp decline in executions,[97] a decrease that

[92] *See* Pew Research Ctr., *Public Support for the Death Penalty Ticks Up* (June 11, 2018), www .pewresearch.org/fact-tank/2018/06/11/us-support-for-death-penalty-ticks-up-2018/ (noting that public support for the death penalty in 1996 was at seventy-nine percent in contrast to forty-nine percent in 2016 and fifty-four percent in 2018).

[93] *See* Eckholm, *supra* note 8; Letter from Patrick Doherty, Director of Corporate Governance, Office of the State Comptroller of New York, to Joseph Haggerty, Executive Vice President, Mylan, Inc. (Nov. 7, 2014), *in* LETHAL INJECTION INFO. CTR. https://lethalinjectioninfo.org/wp-content/uploads/2018/02/2014_12_30_priv-NYCRFs-Mylan-shareholder-resolution-2.pdf; Pew Research Ctr., *supra* note 92.

[94] *See, e.g.*, Berger, *supra* note 90; Gibson & Lain, *supra* note 91, at 1236–39 (documenting the role foreign governments and international norms played in the lethal injection drug shortage).

[95] *See generally* BRANDON L. GARRETT, END OF ITS ROPE: HOW KILLING THE DEATH PENALTY CAN REVIVE CRIMINAL JUSTICE (2017); CAROL S. STEIKER & JORDAN M. STEIKER, COURTING DEATH (2016).

[96] It is, of course, impossible (or, at best, extremely difficult) to prove the precise role of any given factor, and other factors, such as the decline in crime, have played a role, too. *See* GARRETT, *supra* note 95, at 89–92.

[97] *See id.* at 195–204.

may contribute to the growing public sentiment that the death penalty is broken and not worth its high price.

These interrelated phenomena are significant, but they also should not be overstated. For one, lethal injection problems are only one small part of a much bigger canvas of death penalty problems. Furthermore, the death penalty is not dead — at least not yet. As drug companies, investors, foreign governments, and other actors continue to make it difficult for states to procure the drugs they need, states face choices.[98] In states where support for capital punishment is lukewarm, drug shortages might push the state toward abolition or a stalemate with a legally valid but practically defunct death penalty. In states where support for capital punishment is stronger, drug supply issues might push the states toward other lethal injection protocols or entirely different methods of execution.[99]

Whatever changes states adopt in the short term could have long-term consequences for both the death penalty and Eighth Amendment law. Any new execution method could open the door to yet more litigation. It might also invite further changes in public opinion, especially if states adopt more transparently violent execution methods, such as the firing squad. Similarly, courts may become increasingly receptive to various Eighth Amendment arguments against capital punishment if the number of executions, death sentences, and death penalty states all continue to decline.

Alternatively, courts might follow the Supreme Court's more reactionary path, erecting numerous hurdles for the lethal injection plaintiff to combat the perceived unfairness of the abolition movement's "guerilla warfare." The Court, for instance, has already heightened the Eighth Amendment's risk standard in method-of-execution cases, requiring that plaintiffs prove that the challenged protocol is "sure or very likely to cause serious illness or needless suffering."[100] Under such a standard, protocols that caused agonizing suffering half the time would seem to pass constitutional muster, an outcome in tension with earlier Eighth Amendment doctrine.[101] This approach also is in tension with the broader societal pressures against capital punishment. Given the Supreme Court's current composition, however, it is entirely possible that Eighth Amendment doctrine and states' comfort with capital punishment will move in seemingly opposite directions.

It is too early to say how this will play out. Eighth Amendment doctrine, though, will ultimately have to respond to real-world developments in lethal injection and the death penalty, just as state lethal injection and death penalty practices have responded to changed social attitudes and Eighth Amendment rulings. This intersection runs in both — indeed, many — directions.

---

[98] *See* Gibson & Lain, *supra* note 91, at 1236–39.

[99] *See* Associated Press, *supra* note 44; Williams, *supra* note 40.

[100] Glossip v. Gross, 135 S. Ct. 2726, 2736 (2015).

[101] *See* Louisiana *ex rel.* Francis v. Resweber, 329 U.S. 459, 463 (1947); *In re* Kemmler, 136 U.S. 436, 447 (1890); Berger, *supra* note 16, at 980–82.

CONCLUSION

Faced with drug supply problems and serious questions about the three-drug protocol's safety, death penalty states have moved from the three-drug protocol toward a one-drug protocol. This evolution raises Eighth Amendment questions about the remaining three-drug protocols. Given that several states have moved away from the three-drug protocol because that protocol creates intolerable risks of excruciating pain, courts should not reflexively defer to remaining three-drug protocols.

Even if these trends do not immediately alter Eighth Amendment doctrine, the forces conspiring to bring about these changes will likely continue to reshape the American death penalty. Many states continue to find it difficult to obtain lethal injection drugs, regardless of their protocol. The switch from one protocol to another may sometimes provide a temporary solution, but as drug companies get wise to states' new plans, they typically take steps that make it difficult for states to get the new drugs as well. While the occasional state, most notably Texas, seems to have found a steady drug supply, many death penalty states frequently seem to be in a panic mode, scrambling to find a new drug supplier or to adopt a new protocol altogether.

Method of Execution Used in U.S. Executions 2008–2019

	3-Drug executions	2-Drug executions	1-Drug executions	Non-LI executions	Total	% Of lethal injection executions using 3-drug protocol	% Of lethal injection executions using 1-drug protocol
2008	36	0	0	1	37	100	0
2009	50	0	1	1	52	98.04	1.96
2010	35	0	9	2	46	79.55	20.45
2011	38	0	5	0	43	88.37	11.63
2012	21	0	22	0	43	48.84	51.16
2013	14	0	24	1	39	36.84	63.16
2014	11	2	22	0	35	31.42	62.86
2015	4	0	24	0	28	14.29	85.71
2016	3	0	17	0	20	15	85
2017	14	0	9	0	23	60.87	39.13
2018	7*	0	16	2	25	30.43	69.56
2019	6	0	14	2	22	30	70
Total	239	2	163	9	413	59.15	40.34

* Nebraska's 2018 4-drug execution is counted here as a 3-drug execution, because it contains a paralytic and potassium chloride.
All statistics gathered at Death Penalty Information Center, Searchable Execution Database and Execution List by Year Database (last visited Jan. 6, 2020).

These phenomena over the long term might push states toward alternative methods of execution or away from the death penalty altogether. Of course, numerous other factors also shape this landscape. As Carol Steiker and Jordan Steiker observe, the death penalty has taken many unexpected turns so far, so perhaps the only thing one can say with certainty about its long-term future is that it is unpredictable.[102] In the shorter term, the trend against the three-drug protocol is a laudable development, because it minimizes the risk of excruciating executions. Courts reviewing the remaining three-drug protocols should keep that trend in mind.

---

[102] STEIKER & STEIKER, *supra* note 95, at 5.

15

The Future of Juvenile Life-Without-Parole Sentences

Cara H. Drinan[*]

INTRODUCTION

Despite inventing the juvenile court model in the late nineteenth century, the United States has become an international outlier in the severity of its juvenile sentencing practices.[1] In 2020 in this country, adolescents are routinely transferred out of juvenile court and into adult criminal court often without any judicial oversight.[2] Once in adult court, children can be sentenced without regard for their youth.[3] Juveniles are housed in adult correctional facilities;[4] they may be held in solitary confinement;[5] and they experience high rates of sexual and physical assault.[6] Until 2005, children convicted in America's courts were subject to the death penalty, and in many states, they still may be sentenced to die in prison.[7] In fact, the United

---

[*] Professor of Law, Columbus School of Law, The Catholic University of America.

[1] *See generally* Cara H. Drinan, The War on Kids: How American Juvenile Justice Lost Its Way (2017). The central thesis of *The War on Kids: How American Juvenile Justice Lost Its Way* is that the United States abandoned the premise of the juvenile court model in the late twentieth century, enacting punitive practices that made it possible for youth accused of a crime to be treated as adults. *Id.*

[2] Anne Teigen, *Juvenile Age of Jurisdiction and Transfer to Adult Court Laws*, Nat'l Conf. State Leg. (Jan. 11, 2019), www.ncsl.org/research/civil-and-criminal-justice/juvenile-age-of-jurisdiction-and-transfer-to-adult-court-laws.aspx (providing an overview of transfer mechanisms by state).

[3] Drinan, *supra* note 1, at 61–65 (describing the impact of mandatory sentences as applied to youth in adult court).

[4] Wendy Sawyer, Prison Policy Initiative, Youth Confinement: The Whole Pie (Feb. 27, 2018), www.prisonpolicy.org/reports/youth2018.html (demonstrating that, among the nearly 53,000 incarcerated youth, more than 4,600 are in adult jails and prisons).

[5] *See generally* Hum. Rts. Watch & ACLU, Growing Up Locked Down: Youth in Solitary Confinement in Jails and Prisons Across the United States (Oct. 2012), www.aclu.org/sites/default/files/field_document/us1012webwcover.pdf.

[6] Drinan, *supra* note 1, at 66–81 (discussing conditions of confinement for youth in juvenile and adult prisons).

[7] *See infra* notes 10–33 and accompanying text.

States is the only country in the world that permits children to be sentenced to life without parole (LWOP).[8]

In recent years, in a series of cases referred to as the *Miller* trilogy, the U.S. Supreme Court has banned juvenile execution and has significantly limited the extent to which states can impose juvenile life-without-parole (JLWOP) sentences. This chapter argues that, despite the moral leadership displayed by the Court in its *Miller* trilogy, JLWOP sentences are here to stay absent comprehensive state legislation that embraces age-appropriate sentencing for youth.

This chapter begins with a brief overview of the *Miller* trilogy. As I explain in the first part, these cases not only limited the extent to which states can impose the most severe sanctions on youth, but also arguably created new substantive and procedural rights for youth serving extreme sentences. The next section of the chapter documents the significant ways in which the *Miller* trilogy has curbed the practice of JLWOP in America. Finally, the chapter concludes by examining the future of JLWOP in America, focusing on the scope of the phenomenon, executive efforts to undermine the *Miller* trilogy, and the current Court's aversion to extending juvenile sentencing limits. This examination leads to the sobering conclusion that, despite the *Miller* trilogy, the uniquely American practice of JLWOP will persist absent state legislation reflecting the fact that "children are constitutionally different from adults for purposes of sentencing."[9]

THE *MILLER* TRILOGY

In a series of cases known as the *Miller* trilogy,[10] the Supreme Court has reined in the states' ability to subject children to the harshest of criminal sentences.[11] In 2005, the Supreme Court held in *Roper v. Simmons* that the Constitution forbids the execution of juveniles.[12] The *Roper* Court examined youth as a group and analyzed whether execution of minors was proportionate given their diminished culpability and greater capacity for rehabilitation.[13] At the same time, the Court looked at legislative trends regarding juvenile execution and exercised its own judgment to rule that the practice violated evolving standards of decency.[14]

---

[8] Josh Rovner, *Juvenile Life Without Parole: An Overview*, THE SENTENCING PROJECT, July 23, 2019, www.sentencingproject.org/publications/juvenile-life-without-parole/.

[9] Miller v. Alabama, 567 U.S. 460, 471 (2012).

[10] This term refers to *Roper v. Simmons*, 543 U.S. 551 (2005); *Graham v. Florida*, 560 U.S. 48 (2010); and *Miller v. Alabama*, 567 U.S. 460 (2012).

[11] I have discussed these decisions in greater detail in prior works. *See* DRINAN, *supra* note 1, at 84–96; Cara H. Drinan, *The Miller Revolution*, 101 IOWA L. REV. 1787 (2016) [hereinafter Miller Revolution]; Cara H. Drinan, *Misconstruing Graham & Miller*, 91 WASH U. L. REV. 785 (2014); Cara H. Drinan, *Graham on the Ground*, 87 WASH. L. REV. 51 (2012).

[12] 543 U.S. 551 (2005).

[13] *Id.* at 569–74.

[14] *Id.* at 574–75.

One aspect of *Roper* is especially noteworthy in the context of the *Miller* trilogy and its downstream effects. Examining juvenile execution for the first time since 1989, the *Roper* Court drew on science to find that children are categorically different from adults.[15] In particular, this science proved that juveniles are lacking in maturity and impulse control; that they are more susceptible to negative peer influences than adults; and that their moral character is still fluid.[16] And because of these developmental differences, the *Roper* Court held that juveniles are less culpable than adults and that the goals of retribution and deterrence cannot justify the death penalty for minors.[17] This component of the *Roper* decision laid important foundation for the *Graham* and *Miller* decisions, both of which were anchored in the scientific fact that children are different from adults.[18]

Five years later, in *Graham v. Florida*,[19] the Court addressed the question whether life without parole is a permissible sentence for a juvenile who commits a non-homicide crime. Writing for the majority, Justice Kennedy explained in *Graham* that the Eighth Amendment bars both "barbaric" punishments and punishments that are disproportionate to the crime committed.[20] Further, within the latter category of proportionality cases, the Court traditionally examined term-of-year sentences on a case-by-case basis, while in the death penalty context it considered categorical restrictions.[21] In a significant methodological departure,[22] Justice Kennedy held that, because *Graham*'s case challenged "a particular type of sentence" as applied "to an entire class of offenders who have committed a range of crimes," the Court should rely upon its (previously capital) categorical approach.[23] Using this approach, and again relying upon the scientific differences between adolescents and adults, the *Graham* Court held that the Constitution precludes a JLWOP sentence for a non-homicide crime.[24]

In 2012, in *Miller v. Alabama*,[25] the Supreme Court held that the Eighth Amendment bars JLWOP sentences even in most homicide cases. Specifically, JLWOP is not permissible unless the sentencing body takes into account "how children are different, and how those differences counsel against irrevocably

---

[15] *Id.* at 569–74.

[16] *Id.* at 569–770.

[17] *Id.* at 571–72.

[18] *See, e.g.,* Miller v. Alabama, 567 U.S. 460, 471–72 (2012)(reviewing the *Roper* and *Graham* discussions of why children are scientifically and constitutionally different); Graham. v. Florida, 560 U.S. 48, 68 (2010)("[D]evelopments in psychology and brain science continue to show fundamental differences between juvenile and adult minds.").

[19] 560 U.S. 48 (2010).

[20] *Id.* at 59.

[21] *Id.* at 59–61.

[22] See, e.g., Alison Siegler & Barry Sullivan, "'Death Is Different' No Longer": Graham v. Florida *and the Future of Eighth Amendment Challenges to Noncapital Sentences*, 2010 SUP. CT. REV. 327 (2010).

[23] *Graham*, 560 U.S. at 61–62.

[24] *Id.* at 74.

[25] 567 U.S. 460 (2012).

sentencing them to a lifetime in prison."[26] Sentencing bodies must analyze the minor's developmental environment,[27] and only if it is determined that the minor is "the rare juvenile offender whose crime reflects 'irreparable corruption,'"[28] is JLWOP constitutional. Finally, in *Montgomery v. Louisiana*, the Court held that its *Miller* decision is retroactively applicable,[29] making thousands of prisoners nationwide eligible for a resentencing or parole hearing.[30]

As an immediate matter, the *Miller* trilogy outlawed juvenile execution, banned JLWOP in non-homicides cases, and significantly narrowed the instances in which states can impose JLWOP even in homicide cases. At the same time, this line of cases arguably created new substantive and procedural rights for justice-involved youth. Specifically, advocates have leveraged the "kids are different" rationale of these cases[31] to argue for reform of the transfer laws that put kids in adult court in the first instance,[32] as well as for conditions of confinement that reflect young people's vulnerability and unique capacity for rehabilitation.[33] Moreover, because the Court held that minors must have a "meaningful opportunity to obtain release,"[34] scholars have argued that they also must have access to education and other rehabilitative services.[35] Relatedly, lawyers and academics have argued that, in order to satisfy the "meaningful opportunity to obtain release" mandate, state parole procedures must be tailored to youthful offenders. For example, parole review boards should employ risk assessment tools specific to the juvenile offender population,[36] and those seeking parole per *Miller* should enjoy procedural rights, such as the assistance of counsel, that do not apply to typical parole proceedings.[37] Finally, in the wake of

---

[26] *Id.* at 480.

[27] *Id.* at 477–80.

[28] *Id.* at 479–80 (citation omitted).

[29] 136 S. Ct. 718 (2016).

[30] The Sentencing Project estimates that 2,100 individuals were sentenced to mandatory JLWOP and became eligible for relief under *Montgomery*. Rovner, *supra* note 8.

[31] Perry L. Moriearty, Miller v. Alabama *and the Retroactivity of Proportionality Rules*, 17 U. PA. J. CONST. L. 929, 949 (2015) (stating that, with the *Roper* decision, "[t]he Court's modern 'kids are different' jurisprudence was born").

[32] *See* Miller Revolution, *supra* note 11, at 1825–26 (discussing *Miller's* erosion of mandatory transfer provisions and related scholarship).

[33] *See, e.g.*, Elizabeth S. Scott, *Children Are Different: Constitutional Values and Justice Policy*, 11 OHIO ST. J. CRIM. L. 71, 101–03 (2013) (discussing appropriate juvenile correctional environments in light of the *Miller* trilogy).

[34] *See generally* Sarah French Russell & Tracy L. Denholtz, *Proportionate Sentences: The Next Wave of Eighth Amendment Noncapital Litigation*, 48 CONN. L. REV. 1121 (2016) (discussing the emergence of the "meaningful opportunity" requirement and state responses).

[35] *See, e.g.*, Beth Caldwell, *Creating Meaningful Opportunities for Release: Graham, Miller and California's Youth Offender Parole Hearings*, 40 N.Y.U. REV. L. & SOC. CHANGE 245, 286–91 (2016) (documenting that youth serving extreme sentences are often barred from rehabilitative programs and arguing for requiring such services to create opportunity for release).

[36] *Id.* at 299–302.

[37] Sarah French Russell, *Review for Release: Juvenile Offenders, State Parole Practice and the Eighth Amendment*, 89 IND. L. J. 373, 421–28 (2014).

Miller, the juvenile defense bar has recognized that a JLWOP sentence is tantamount to a death sentence for a minor, and it has created specific standards of legal
representation for JLWOP cases.[38] In short, the *Miller* trilogy not only abolished
juvenile execution and limited JLWOP but also laid the foundation for a host of
new substantive and procedural rights for youth in the criminal justice system.

JLWOP CURBED BY THE *MILLER* TRILOGY

The central claim of this chapter is that, despite the *Miller* trilogy, JLWOP is likely
here to stay unless legislatures embrace comprehensive juvenile sentencing reform.
I will turn to explaining that claim below, but here let me be clear: the *Miller* trilogy
has significantly curbed the practice of JLWOP in America. First, as discussed
above, the Court's decision in *Montgomery v. Louisiana* determined that the *Miller*
decision was retroactively applicable to cases on collateral review. Because of the
Montgomery ruling, more than 2,000 individuals who had been told as children that
they would die in prison became eligible for a resentencing or parole hearing.[39] This
ruling alone created optimism for thousands of individuals and family members who
had thought all hope was lost.[40] Moreover, as of December 2018, nearly four
hundred people have reentered society and have come home to their families
because of the *Miller/Montgomery* rulings.[41]

At the same time, the language and logic of the *Miller* trilogy highlighted
juveniles' unique capacity for rehabilitation and the related inappropriateness of
JLWOP. State lawmakers, in turn, have paid attention. In 2011, the year before
Miller, only five states banned JLWOP. Today, twenty-three states and the District of
Columbia ban the sentence.[42] An additional five states have no one serving the
sentence.[43] Thus, in a very short period of time, the Court's leadership in the *Miller*
trilogy set in motion a legislative trend away from JLWOP.

In addition to implementing the core holdings of *Graham* and *Miller*, some lower
courts have embraced a more capacious reading of the *Miller* trilogy to ban or

---

[38] *See* CAMP. FOR FAIR SENT'G OF YOUTH, TRIAL DEFENSE GUIDELINES: REPRESENTING A CHILD
CLIENT FACING A POSSIBLE LIFE SENTENCE (Mar. 2015), www.fairsentencingofyouth.org/wp-
content/uploads/Trial-Defense-Guidelines-Representing-a-Child-Client-Facing-a-Possible-Life-
Sentence.pdf.

[39] *See supra* note 30 and accompanying text.

[40] *Cf.* Montgomery v. Louisiana, 136 S. Ct. 718, 736–37 (2016) ("In light of what this Court has
said in *Roper, Graham,* and *Miller* about how children are constitutionally different from adults
in their level of culpability ... prisoners like Montgomery must be given the opportunity to
show their crime did not reflect irreparable corruption; and, if it did not, their hope for some
years of life outside prison walls must be restored.").

[41] CAMP. FOR FAIR SENT'G OF YOUTH, TIPPING POINT: A MAJORITY OF STATES ABANDON LIFE-
WITHOUT-PAROLE SENTENCES FOR CHILDREN 6 (Dec. 3, 2018), www.fairsentencingofyouth
.org/wp-content/uploads/Tipping-Point.pdf.

[42] Rovner, *supra* note 8.

[43] CAMP. FOR FAIR SENT'G OF YOUTH, *supra* note 41, at 5.

curtail sentences outside the narrow holdings of those cases. For example, while the *Graham* Court barred JLWOP for non-homicide crimes, it did not answer the question whether a minor who commits such a crime may be sentenced to a term-of-years sentence that exceeds the minor's life expectancy. Nor did the Court in *Graham* or *Miller* address whether its rulings apply to instances where the minor receives a sentence that exceeds his life expectancy, but the sentence results from *aggregated* term-of-year sentences.

Some lower courts, though, have answered these questions in defendants' favor and have thus further limited the use of JLWOP and other extreme sentences for youth. For example, courts have struck down 45-year,[44] 50-year,[45] 52.5 year,[46] and 110-year[47] sentences under *Graham* and *Miller* even though those sentences were not "technically … life without parole sentence[s]."[48] Moreover, some courts have treated *aggregate* sentences that result in de facto life sentences as also triggering the protections of the *Miller* trilogy.[49]

In these ways, the *Miller* trilogy prompted not only the release of individuals once sentenced to die in prison, but also state legislation tending toward abolition of JLWOP and judge-made law that recognizes that children deserve a "meaningful opportunity to obtain release based on demonstrated maturity and rehabilitation."[50]

WHY JLWOP PERSISTS

Despite these promising developments, JLWOP will likely persist in America absent comprehensive juvenile sentencing reform at the state level. This is true for a number of reasons.

The Scope of the Problem

First, the sheer scale of the JLWOP phenomenon is significant. The Supreme Court did not categorically ban JLWOP in its *Miller* decision, and despite the state legislative trend away from JLWOP, approximately half the states still have the sentence on the books.[51] In these jurisdictions, youth are exposed to this death-in-custody sentence. In addition, there are more than 2,000 individuals nationwide whose cases were squarely within the purview of *Miller*,[52] and relief even for those

---

[44] Bear Cloud v. State, 334 P.3d 132 (Wyo. 2014).
[45] Casiano v. Comm'r of Corr., 115 A. 3d 1031, 1043–44 (Conn. 2015).
[46] State v. Null, 836 N.W. 2d 41 (Iowa 2013).
[47] People v. Caballero, 282 P.3d 291 (Cal. 2012).
[48] *Null*, 836 N.W. 2d at 71.
[49] *See, e.g., id.* at 70–73; *see also* Brown v. State 10 N.E.3d 1 (Ind. 2014) (reviewing aggregate sentences in light of the *Miller* trilogy).
[50] Graham v. Florida, 560 U.S. 48, 75 (2010).
[51] Camp. for Fair Sent'g of Youth, *supra* note 41, at 5.
[52] *See supra* note 30 and accompanying text.

individuals has been unpredictable because of resistant state actors, as I discuss in greater detail below. Moreover, there are thousands of *additional* individuals who were convicted as minors and who are serving de facto life sentences, life sentences with parole in jurisdictions where parole is a meaningless ritual, and life sentences that are a function of aggregate term-of-year sentences.[53] Courts have been split on whether *Miller* provides relief to these individuals,[54] and, unless the Supreme Court clarifies these questions in favor of minors serving extreme sentences, in some jurisdictions individuals will continue to serve disproportionately lengthy sentences for crimes they committed as minors. In sum, those seeking the abolition of JLWOP and its functional equivalent have a steep hill to climb given the continued widespread use of extreme juvenile sentencing.

Resistant State Executive Actors

Second, even among those individuals directly affected by *Miller*, relief has been inconsistent and largely dependent upon geography. While the *Miller* Court did not categorically ban JLWOP, it made clear that "given all [the Court had] said in *Roper*, *Graham*, and [*Miller*] about children's diminished culpability and heightened capacity for change ... appropriate occasions for sentencing juveniles to this harshest possible penalty will be uncommon."[55] Yet, in some parts of the country prosecutors have sought to re-impose JLWOP or similarly extreme sentences on prisoners during re-sentencing hearings. For example, in Michigan, as of 2016, 363 people were serving mandatory JLWOP sentences. State prosecutors have argued that nearly two-thirds of those individuals should be resentenced to LWOP.[56] Prosecutors in Louisiana are seeking LWOP sentences for about one-third of the people eligible for relief per *Miller* and *Montgomery*.[57] That number, however,

[53] *See* Ashley Nellis, *Still Life: America's Increasing Use of Life and Long-Term Sentences*, THE SENT'G PROJECT, 16–18 (May 3, 2017), www.sentencingproject.org/publications/still-life-amer icas-increasing-use-life-long-term-sentences/ (discussing the breadth of extreme juvenile sentencing in America and estimating that nearly 12,000 people are serving a life or virtual life sentence for crimes committed as minors).

[54] Despite the juvenile-friendly decisions discussed above, a number of courts have declined to read *Miller* as providing relief in these cases. *See, e.g.*, Bowling v. Dir., Virginia Dep't. Corr., 920 F. 3d 192, 197 (4th Cir. 2019) (declining to apply *Miller* to sentences of life *with* parole and declining to apply the logic of *Miller* to the parole context); *Null*, 836 N.W. 2d at 73 (addressing cases holding that *Miller* does not apply where the lengthy sentence is the result of aggregate sentences).

[55] Miller v. Alabama, 567 U.S. 460, 479 (2012).

[56] Samantha Michaels, *The Supreme Court Said No More Life without Parole for Kids. Why Is Antonio Spree One of the Few to Get Out of Prison?*, MOTHER JONES, Dec. 26, 2018, www .motherjones.com/crime-justice/2018/12/tony-espree-cyntoia-brown-mandatory-life-without-parole-juvenile-lifers-justice-kennedy-miller-alabama/.

[57] Jessica Pishko, *"We're Basically Guessing on These Cases:" Louisiana's Disastrous Resentencing Hearings*, THE NATION, Dec. 22, 2017, www.thenation.com/article/were-basically-guessing-on-these-cases-louisianas-disastrous-resentencing-hearings/.

masks the fact that, in some counties within Louisiana, prosecutors are seeking to re-impose JLWOP in nearly *all* cases.[58] Similarly, the District of Columbia enacted a law in 2016 providing resentencing opportunities to those individuals who had been convicted before the age of eighteen and who had served at least twenty years in prison.[59] Despite the promise of this legislation, at this writing, the District of Columbia's federal prosecutors have sought to prevent resentencing for *every indi-vidual* who has sought relief under the new law.[60] This is true even in cases where the individual has demonstrated decades of maturity and rehabilitation, precisely the kind of evidence the Supreme Court was focused on in *Graham* and *Miller*. Thus, JLWOP and similarly extreme sentences are persisting in part because of prosecutor-ial resistance to Supreme Court mandates in some pockets of the country.

At the same time, parole has been an equally unreliable path to relief for individuals sentenced to JLWOP. The *Montgomery* Court explained:

> A State may remedy a *Miller* violation by permitting juvenile homicide offenders to be considered for parole, rather than by resentencing them. Allowing those offend-ers to be considered for parole ensures that juveniles whose crimes reflected only transient immaturity — and who have since matured — will not be forced to serve a disproportionate sentence in violation of the Eighth Amendment.[61]

Many states followed the Court's suggestion on this count and have relied upon parole as their path to *Miller* compliance. Some states have permitted individuals sentenced to JLWOP to access standard parole procedures, while a number of states, including Connecticut, Louisiana, Nebraska, California, and West Virginia, have created parole procedures specific to juvenile offenders serving extreme sentences.[62]

In both cases, however, the question of whether such procedures satisfy the requirements of the *Miller* trilogy has generated litigation in state and federal courts. For example, prisoners seeking relief post-*Miller* and post-*Montgomery* have chal-lenged state parole procedures for failing to provide procedural safeguards; for failure to distinguish between adult and juvenile offenders; for decision-makers' primary emphasis upon the gravity of the original offense rather than demonstrated rehabilitation; and for paltry release rates that render parole a hollow remedy.[63] Perhaps the starkest example of this phenomenon is the case of Henry Montgomery himself. Despite his victory before the Supreme Court in *Montgomery v. Louisiana*, Montgomery was denied parole for the second time even though, at seventy-two, he

---

[58] *Id.*

[59] Kira Lerner, *D.C. Shows Mercy for People Who Committed Crimes as Children, but Prosecutors Are Fighting Back*, THE APPEAL (May 23, 2019), https://theappeal.org/d-c-offers-hope-to-people-who-committed-crimes-as-children-but-prosecutors-are-fighting-back/.

[60] *Id.*

[61] Montgomery v. Louisiana, 136 S. Ct. 718, 736 (2016) (internal citation omitted).

[62] *See* Russell & Denholtz, *supra* note 34 at 1131–37.

[63] *Id.* at 1139–50 (canvassing this litigation around second-look procedures).

has served fifty-five years and has an impeccable correctional record.[64] If individuals like Montgomery, who have served decades in prison for crimes they committed as minors and who have demonstrated growth and rehabilitation, cannot obtain parole, then the process itself cannot be the meaningful opportunity to obtain release that the Supreme Court envisioned. While the *Montgomery* Court may have anticipated that parole would be an efficient remedy, in reality many state executive actors are reluctant to grant parole in juvenile homicide cases.

Current Supreme Court Appetite for Limiting Extreme Juvenile Sentences

Finally, it would be imprudent to expect the current Supreme Court to maintain the reform momentum to date, let alone to further extend the limits on juvenile punishment set forth in the *Miller* trilogy. Since its decision in *Montgomery v. Louisiana* in 2016, for the most part, the Court has been reluctant to expand the scope of the *Miller* trilogy and deferential in matters of *Miller*'s implementation. For example, as discussed above, courts are split on whether the *Miller* trilogy applies to de facto life sentences or life sentences that result from aggregate term-of-year sentences, and the Court has declined to squarely address those issues.[65] At the same time, the science on which the *Miller* trilogy relied suggests that adolescent brain development continues into the mid-twenties, and juvenile justice advocates have pushed for policies to reflect that reality.[66] Again, though, the Court does not seem inclined to consider expanding the logic of the *Miller* trilogy to cases in which the defendant is over eighteen.[67] Moreover, in *Virginia v. LeBlanc*,[68] the Court signaled that it would grant states wide latitude in implementing the mandates of the *Miller* trilogy. LeBlanc was sentenced to LWOP for a non-homicide crime at sixteen.[69] He sought relief under *Graham*, but Virginia argued that he did, in fact, have a "meaningful opportunity to obtain release" as required by *Graham* because the state had a *geriatric* release program under which he could seek release at the age of sixty.[70] The Supreme Court held that Virginia's

---

[64] Samantha Michaels, *A 72-Year-Old Lifer Won a Landmark Supreme Court Ruling, But Louisiana Won't Let Him Out of Prison*, MOTHER JONES, April 12, 2019, www.motherjones .com/crime-justice/2019/04/henry-montgomery-juvenile-lifer-louisiana-denied-parole/.

[65] *See, e.g.*, Bostic v. Dunbar, *cert. denied*, 138 S. Ct. 1593 (U.S. April 23, 2018) (No. 17-912).

[66] *See* David Jordan, *Vermont Rolls Out a New Idea to Rehabilitate Young Offenders*, CHRISTIAN SCI. MONITOR, July 6, 2018, www.csmonitor.com/USA/Justice/2018/0706/Vermont-rolls-out-a-new-idea-to-rehabilitate-young-offenders (discussing state reforms that incorporate this brain science).

[67] *Cf.* Tucker v. Louisiana, 181 So.3d 590 (La. 2015), *cert. denied*, 136 S. Ct. 1801 (U.S. May 31, 2016) (No. 15-946) (Breyer, J., dissenting from the denial of certiorari) (noting that the defendant was eighteen years, five months, and six days old at the time of the crime).

[68] 137 S. Ct. 1726 (2017).

[69] *Id.* at 1727.

[70] *Id.* at 1727–28.

decision was not an unreasonable application of *Graham*.[71] Thus, the Court appears to have little appetite either for vigorously enforcing the *Miller* trilogy or for expanding its core holdings.

There is no reason to expect the Court to better protect the rights of juvenile lifers any time soon, and, in fact, there is some reason to fear backsliding given the new composition of the Court. Justice Kennedy was a driving force behind the Court's examination of extreme juvenile sentences[72] and a vocal opponent of broader American criminal justice practices.[73] Among the *Roper, Graham, Miller,* and *Montgomery* decisions, Kennedy authored the majority opinion in all but one case. His retirement has been a devastating blow to juvenile justice advocates before the Court. In addition, since the *Montgomery* decision, Justices Gorsuch and Kavanaugh have been confirmed, establishing a solid conservative majority on the Supreme Court. In light of the Court's transformation after *Miller*, juvenile justice advocates must prepare for diminishing Eighth Amendment protections from the Court.

At the moment, those advocates are focused on the case of Lee Boyd Malvo, in which the Supreme Court recently granted certiorari.[74] At seventeen, Malvo and a much older co-defendant committed ten murders, known as the "DC Sniper" killings.[75] Malvo's co-defendant was executed for the murders in 2009, and Malvo is currently serving a life sentence in Virginia.[76] Malvo's attorneys have argued that, under *Miller* and *Montgomery*, he is entitled to a resentencing hearing at which his youth and other mitigating circumstances may be considered.[77] In other words, he is asking a lower court to determine per *Miller* whether he is, in fact, the rare case of a juvenile whose crimes reflect "irreparable corruption" rather than "transient immaturity."[78] If he is not, then his JLWOP sentence cannot stand.

Virginia, however, claims that the Commonwealth does not impose *mandatory* life-without-parole sentences, and thus Malvo is not entitled to retroactive relief.[79]

---

[71] *Id.* at 1728–29.

[72] Reginald Dwayne Betts, *What Break Do Children Deserve? Juveniles, Crime, and Justice Kennedy's Influence on the Supreme Court's Eighth Amendment Jurisprudence*, 128 YALE L.J. FORUM 743, 744–51 (2019).

[73] *See, e.g.,* Justice Anthony M. Kennedy, Speech at the American Bar Ass'n Annual Mtg., Aug. 9, 2003 (addressing the scale, discrimination and unfairness of American corrections), www .supremecourt.gov/publicinfo/speeches/sp_08-09-03.html.

[74] Mathena v. Malvo, 893 F.3d 265 (4th Cir. 2018), *cert. granted*, 139 S. Ct. 1317 (U.S. Mar. 18, 2019) (No. 18-217).

[75] Domenico Montanaro, *Supreme Court to Take Up DC Sniper Case, Raising Issue of Sentencing Minors*, NPR (Mar. 18, 2019), www.npr.org/2019/03/18/704420800/supreme-court-to-take-up-d-c-sniper-case-raising-issue-of-sentencing-minors.

[76] *Id.*

[77] *Malvo*, 893 F.3d at 270–71 (describing the history and nature of Malvo's habeas claims under *Miller*).

[78] *Id.* at 272 (internal citation omitted).

[79] Pet. for Writ of Cert., Mathena v. Malvo, (Aug. 16, 2018) (No. 18-217), 2018 WL 3993386 at *5.

As Malvo's attorneys pointed out in their brief opposing certiorari, there is no widespread confusion regarding *Miller's* application; a majority of courts have already concluded that *Miller* applies both to mandatory and discretionary JLWOP sentences.[80] Further, as Malvo argued, *Montgomery* and *Miller* made clear that juvenile life without parole is only constitutional when imposed upon "the rare juvenile offender whose crime reflects irreparable corruption,"[81] and no court has made that determination in Malvo's case. The Supreme Court heard the case on October 16, 2019,[82] and it is unclear exactly how the Court will treat the case. Malvo's counsel maintains that Virginia merely seeks to "relitigate *Montgomery*" through the pretext of a retroactivity question.[83] If this is true, and if the Court were to accept the Commonwealth's invitation to do so, then the central holdings of *Miller* and *Montgomery* could be in jeopardy.

In sum, given the new composition of the Court, juvenile justice advocates need to prepare for a much less hospitable audience in Supreme Court cases challenging extreme juvenile sentences. As a champion of the Court's institutional integrity, Chief Justice Roberts can likely hold together the remaining five Justices from the *Montgomery* majority and protect the core of the *Miller* trilogy. But it remains to be seen how Justices Gorsuch and Kavanaugh will shape the Court's juvenile sentencing decisions in the future.

CONCLUSION

In this chapter, I have argued that, absent state legislation embracing age-appropriate sentencing for youth, JLWOP and comparably extreme sentences are here to stay. As sobering as this reality may be, there is good reason to be optimistic that states may, in fact, take up this kind of legislation. First, as discussed above, the number of states that ban JLWOP has more than quadrupled since 2011. To the extent that there is reform momentum in 2020, that momentum resides largely in state legislatures, not the Supreme Court. Second, some state courts and state legislatures have relied upon the science of the *Miller* trilogy to go well beyond the mandates of *Miller* since 2012. For example, two states have banned mandatory minimum sentences as applied to youth across the board,[84] and several states are

---

[80] Respondent's Brief in Opposition to Certiorari, Mathena v. Malvo (Oct. 19, 2018) (No. 18-217), 2018 WL 5263264 at *11–17.

[81] *Id.* at *1 (citation omitted).

[82] Amy Howe, *Court Releases October Calendar*, SCOTUSblog (Jul. 1, 2019, 2:58 PM), www.scotusblog.com/2019/07/court-releases-october-calendar-2/.

[83] Respondent's Brief in Opposition to Certiorari, Mathena v. Malvo, (Oct. 19, 2018) (No. 18-217), 2018 WL 5263264 at *23–27.

[84] State v. Houston-Sconiers, 391 P.3d 409, 420 (Wash. 2017) ("[W]e hold that sentencing courts must have complete discretion to consider mitigating circumstances associated with the youth of any juvenile defendant, even in the adult criminal justice system."); State v. Lyle, 854 N.W.2d 378 (Iowa 2014) (abolishing mandatory minimums as applied to juveniles).

expanding eligibility for juvenile court jurisdiction.[85] Similarly, California recently banned the transfer of youth under sixteen to adult court for any crime.[86] These are remarkable reversals of decades-long harsh treatment of youth, and these reversals are happening in state courts and legislative bodies. Finally, the public seems to have embraced the science that says kids are different, as polling data show strong support for juvenile rehabilitation efforts.[87] In sum, even if the Supreme Court may not be inclined to further extend the *Miller* trilogy, there are signs that state actors may be up for the task and that the electorate may be supportive of continued juvenile sentencing reforms.

In those states where there is public support and legislative interest, ideal legislation would ban the practice of JLWOP altogether and make clear that such a ban applies to any sentence that is likely to result in a juvenile defendant's death in custody. Specifically, this ban would include de facto life sentences, life sentences that result from aggregate sentencing, and life sentences with parole in jurisdictions where the chance of parole is so remote that it is comparable to that of executive clemency. Moreover, such legislation should make clear that, even when youth commit serious crimes, they should be sentenced in an age-appropriate way, and that their sentences should be reviewed early and often. Finally, this model legislation should require states to invest in juvenile rehabilitation and education even when youth are sentenced to lengthy term-of-year sentences. Only with such measures can we hope to finally see an end to JLWOP in America.

---

[85] *See* John Kelly, *Several States Ponder Expansion of Juvenile Justice beyond 18*, Chron. Social Change, Mar. 11, 2019, https://chronicleofsocialchange.org/news-2/several-states-ponder-expansion-of-juvenile-justice-beyond-18/34152.

[86] Sara Tiano, *California Passes Bill Banning Transfer of Juveniles under 16*, Chron. of Social Change, Aug. 30, 2018, https://chronicleofsocialchange.org/justice/juvenilex-justice-2/california-passes-bill-banning-transfer-of-juveniles-under-16/32081.

[87] *See, e.g.*, GBAO Strategies, New Poll Results on Youth Justice Reform (Mar. 18, 2019), https://backend.nokidsinprison.org/wp-content/uploads/2019/03/Youth-First-National-Poll-Memo-March-2019-Final-Version-V2.pdf.

16

Metrics of Mayhem

Quantifying Capriciousness in Capital Cases

Sherod Thaxton[*]

INTRODUCTION

Social science has figured prominently in debates over the constitutional administration of capital punishment for more than a half-century, especially with respect to capricious and biased decision-making.[1] The Court's ruling in *Furman v. Georgia*,[2] responsible for ushering in the modern era of capital punishment by invalidating then-existing capital statutes as violative of the Eighth Amendment's prohibition against cruel and unusual punishment, was replete with references to social scientific evidence documenting inconsistent, irrational, and discriminatory capital charging and sentencing practices.[3] *Furman* contained the most extensive discussion of social science research in any decision up to that point,[4] and all five Justices comprising the per curiam opinion in *Furman* agreed that evidence identifying the

---

[*] Professor of Law, UCLA School of Law.

[1] *See, e.g.,* U.S. General Accountability Office, *Death Penalty Sentencing: Research Indicates Patterns of Racial Disparities,* GGD-90-57 (1990) (reporting that 82% (twenty-three of twenty-eight) of all methodologically sophisticated studies examining capital punishment processes since the *Furman v. Georgia* ruling uncovered evidence of arbitrariness and bias) [hereinafter "GAO"]; David C. Baldus & George Woodworth, *Race Discrimination in the Administration of the Death Penalty: An Overview of the Empirical Evidence with Special Emphasis on the Post-1990 Research,* 39 Crim. L. Bull. 194 (2003) (reporting that nearly all studies of the capital punishment process reveal arbitrary and discriminatory decision-making).

[2] 408 U.S. 238 (1972) (per curiam).

[3] *Id.* at 363 (Marshall, J., concurring) (identifying social scientific evidence to support the claims that (1) most murderers are not sentenced to death, (2) most condemned inmates are not ultimately executed, (3) death is administered in a racially and economically biased fashion, (4) innocent persons have been executed, and (5) many murderers become model prisoners and are law-abiding citizens upon release from prison).

[4] Craig Haney, Death by Design: Capital Punishment as a Social Psychological System 10 (2005) (noting that *Furman* contained more than sixty footnotes citing published social science research on the realities of the death penalty process and that Justices writing for both the majority and the dissent grappled with social science evidence).

capricious imposition of the death penalty provided sufficient justification to impose an immediate moratorium on executions in the United States and then require the commutation of all death sentences for condemned inmates. Yet the weight given to this empirical evidence (or lack thereof) in judicial decision-making has, itself, been irrational and inconsistent.

Twelve years after *Furman*, in its landmark decision in *Pulley v. Harris*,[5] the Court rejected a capitally condemned inmate's claim that California's capital punishment statute violated the Eighth Amendment because it failed to mandate comparative (i.e., inter-case) proportionality review.[6] Many legal analysts perceived the Court as backpedaling on the very procedural protections it had endorsed eight years earlier in *Gregg v. Georgia*,[7] when it seemingly identified comparative proportionality review — required under Georgia's capital statute — as a necessary component of constitutionally valid death penalty schemes.[8] *Gregg* emphasized that the Eighth Amendment, *inter alia*, forbade disproportionate punishment and required procedures that limit the risk of capriciousness.[9] And appellate review of legal actors' discretionary choices appeared to be part and parcel of any statutory framework capable of identifying and correcting constitutional errors. *Pulley* acknowledged that comparative proportionality review was a laudable feature of Georgia's statute and that such review might be necessary if a capital statute was "so lacking in other checks on arbitrariness."[10] The Court reasoned, however, that comparative proportionality was not an indispensable feature.[11] The Court explained that Georgia's capital statute adequately limited and directed the jury's discretion without inter-case review via other procedural protections — namely, bifurcated proceedings (i.e., separate trials for determining guilt and punishment), a limited list of crimes and special circumstances required for death eligibility, and mandatory consideration of mitigation evidence at the sentencing phase.[12] The Court's identification of what it believed to be procedurally sufficient protections was perplexing because the

---

[5] 465 U.S. 37 (1984).
[6] Comparative proportionality review entails a comparison of a death-sentenced inmate's case with sentences imposed in similar cases in order to determine whether the inmate's punishment is proportionate with respect to both the circumstances of the crime and the background of the defendant. Timothy V. Kaufman-Osborn, *Proportionality Review and the Death Penalty*, 29 JUST. SYS. J. 257, 258–63 (2008).
[7] 428 U.S.153, 189 (1976) (plurality opinion).
[8] Georgia's capital statute was closely modeled after the American Law Institute's Model Penal Code. *Compare* 1973 GA. LAWS 74 *and* GA. CODE ANN. § 27-2534 (1973), *with* MODEL PEN. CODE §210.6.
[9] *Gregg*, 428 U.S. at 189 ("*Furman* mandates that ... discretion must be suitably directed and limited so as to minimize the risk of wholly arbitrary and capricious action.").
[10] *Pulley*, 465 U.S. at 50.
[11] *Compare id.* at 45, *with* Walker v. Georgia, 555 U.S. 979 (2008) (Stevens, J.) (noting that the Georgia Supreme Court "carried out an utterly perfunctory review" and a "breakdown in the statutory process" of Georgia's comparative proportionality review).
[12] *Pulley*, 465 U.S. at 45.

initial capital statutes it approved as passing constitutional muster had not been subject to empirical scrutiny by the Court.[13] Instead, the Court based its decisions solely on the assumption that the procedural protections contained therein would eliminate or significantly reduce the rampant capriciousness and bias that had been identified by social scientists and provided the basis for the Court's per curiam opinion in *Furman*.[14] The majority in *Gregg* was careful to note that its approval of any particular capital statute did not constitute a blanket endorsement of any similarly constructed statute and that "each distinct death penalty system must be examined on an individual basis."[15] However, the Court failed to clearly articulate any metric it would use to evaluate whether a system was, in fact, operating as the government promised.[16]

Gregg foreshadowed the Court's capital punishment jurisprudence for the next four decades.[17] *Furman's* strong concerns about actual outcomes of death penalty cases were deemphasized; *Gregg's* assumption that the guided-discretion statutes would result in valid and reliable death sentences was left unexamined; and social science evidence that identified and documented the persistence of the pre-*Furman* era problems was either ignored or significantly minimized.[18] The Court's misplaced confidence in the rational, consistent, and nondiscriminatory administration of the death penalty was highlighted in Justice Brennan's forceful dissent in *Pulley*. According to the Justice, the Court was ignoring available evidence and "simply deluding itself, and also the American public, when it insists that those [capital defendants] have been selected on a basis that is neither arbitrary nor capricious, under any meaningful definition of those terms."[19] Justice Brennan also (1) noted

---

[13] Initial statues were approved in Georgia, Florida, and Texas. Jurek v. Texas, 428 U.S. 262 (1976); Proffit v. Florida, 428 U.S. 242 (1976); *Gregg*, 428 U.S. at 153.

[14] STUART BANNER, THE DEATH PENALTY: AN AMERICAN HISTORY 273 (2002) (noting that the petitioners from Florida, Georgia, and Texas who initially brought challenges against the post-*Furman* capital statutes in *Gregg* emphasized that the states neglected to provide any empirical evidence that these statutes could accomplish what the *Furman* majority unequivocally stated that the Eighth Amendment demanded).

[15] *Gregg*, 428 U.S. at 195.

[16] The Court's view is akin to Justice Potter Stewart's (in)famous statement concerning the definition of obscenity: "I know it when I see it." Jacobellis v. Ohio, 378 U.S. 184, 197 (1964).

[17] Sherod Thaxton, *Un-Gregg-ulated: Capital Charging and the Missing Mandate of Gregg v. Georgia*, 11 DUKE J. CONST. L. & PUB. POL'Y 145, 158 (2016) (describing the Court's repeated marginalization of social scientific evidence of the unconstitutional administration of the death penalty in the aftermath of *Gregg*).

[18] *Id.*; *see also* McCleskey v. Kemp, 481 U.S. 279 (1987) (holding that statistical evidence of racially disproportionate death penalty charging and sentencing, even if believed, was insufficient to deem Georgia's capital statute unconstitutional as applied); Craig Haney & Deana D. Logan, *Broken Promise: The Supreme Court's Response to Social Science Research on Capital Punishment*, 50 J. SOC. ISSUES 75 (1994) (arguing that the Court has frequently ignored psychological data in its death penalty jurisprudence).

[19] Pulley v. Harris, 465 U.S. 37, 62 (1984). *See also* Charles J. Ogletree Jr., *Black Man's Burden: Race and the Death Penalty in America*, 81 OR. L. REV. 15, 34 (2002) (explaining that not only have the Court's incremental procedural fixes to the capital punishment system provided the

that the results of scholarly research necessary to support claims of capriciousness and bias "are being complied into a rapidly expanding body of literature," (2) identified no less than thirteen empirical studies demonstrating the unconstitutional (or constitutionally suspect) administration of capital punishment, and (3) emphasized that disproportionate treatment of capital defendants could be eliminated only after these disparities are identified by a procedural device such as inter-case proportionality review.[20]

Thirty years after *Pulley*, Justice Brennan's sentiments were echoed by Justice Breyer in his landmark dissenting opinion in *Glossip v. Gross*.[21] Justice Breyer remarked that the "arbitrary imposition of punishment is the antithesis of the rule of law" and then urged the Court to re-engage social and empirical facts concerning capital charging and sentencing practices.[22] Describing nearly four decades of social science evidence documenting the capricious and bias operation of capital punishment systems, Justice Breyer believed that the time was ripe for the Court to reopen the question of the constitutionality of the administration of the death penalty and invite full briefing that would allow the Court to scrutinize this relevant empirical scholarship with greater care than it had done it the past.[23]

Three years after *Glossip*, Justice Breyer issued a statement with respect to the denial of *certiorari* in a capital case — *Hidalgo v. Arizona*[24] — that appeared to build upon his prior dissenting opinion.[25] Justice Breyer gave an indication of the types of evidence to which the Court may be receptive in future cases challenging the constitutionality of capital punishment. Of particular relevance was that Justices Kagan and Sotomayor, along with Justice Ginsburg, joined Justice Breyer's statement in *Hidalgo*, whereas only Justice Ginsburg joined Justice Breyer's dissent in *Glossip*.[26] Given the four-vote requirement to grant *certiorari*, Justices Kagan and Sotomayor's endorsement of Justice Breyer's view of the growing relevance of social science to the Court's constitutional calculus makes it significantly more likely that a constitutional challenge to the death penalty, if supported by the requisite evidence, will be heard by the Court (and possibly garner at least four votes). In *Hidalgo*, the petitioner, Abel Daniel Hidalgo, challenged Arizona's capital statute because of, *inter alia*, its inability to meaningfully narrow the class of death-eligible defendants

---

appearance of legality and impartiality, but they also have done little to correct the rampant problems of caprice and bias).

[20] *Pulley*, 465 U.S. at 70.

[21] 135 S. Ct. 2726 (2015). Justice Ginsburg joined Justice Breyer's dissenting opinion.

[22] *Id.* at 2760–62 (Breyer, J., dissenting).

[23] *Id.* at 2759; *cf. Pulley*, 465 U.S. at 67 (Brennan J., dissenting) ("If the Court is going to fulfill its constitutional responsibilities, then it cannot sanction continued executions on the unexamined assumption that the death penalty is being administered in a rational, nonarbitrary, and non-capricious manner.").

[24] 138 S. Ct. 1054 (2018).

[25] *Compare id., with Glossip*, 135 S. Ct. at 2726.

[26] Justice Sotomayor wrote a separate dissenting opinion, joined by Justices Breyer, Ginsburg, and Kagan.

to comport with the requirements of the Eighth Amendment as set forth in *Furman* and its progeny. Petitioner Hidalgo offered empirical evidence indicating that nearly 98% of first-degree murder defendants were death-eligible under Arizona's capital statute.[27] Justice Breyer noted that Hidalgo's "evidence is unrebutted[,] points to a possible constitutional problem[,] [and] warrants careful attention and evaluation."[28] Justice Breyer nonetheless agreed with the denial of *certiorari* because the petitioner's "opportunity to develop the record through an evidentiary hearing was denied [and] the issue presented in this petition will be better suited for *certiorari* with such a record."[29]

Justice Breyer focused on legislative narrowing and was dismissive of the claim that "prosecutors may perform the narrowing requirement by choosing to ask for the death penalty in only those cases in which a particularly egregious first-degree murder is at issue."[30] But Justice Breyer's position appears in tension with *Furman*'s emphasis on ensuring the rational and consistent imposition of the death penalty. Indeed, the majority in *Furman* distinguished its Eighth Amendment ruling in *Furman* from its Fourteenth Amendment due process ruling a year prior in *McGautha v. California*[31] based on the reasoning that a constitutionally permissible process could generate a constitutionally impermissible result;[32] that is, the Eighth Amendment's focus was on actual punishments (distributive justice) and not merely the process by which the punishment was decided (procedural justice).[33] Assessments of the rationality and consistency (or lack thereof) of outcomes that a system produces requires a careful inquiry into decision-making beyond statutory narrowing. This is particularly true because the practical consequence of constraining the discretion of the sentencing authority through guided-discretion statutes was to increase the discretion of front-end and back-end actors in the process.[34]

---

[27] *See also* Steven F. Shatz & Nina Rivkind, *The California Death Penalty: Requiem for* Furman?, 72 N.Y.U. L. REV. 1283 (1997) (noting that California's capital statute fails to meaningfully narrow the class of death-eligible murders, and 92% of non-death judgment first-degree murder cases were factually eligible for the death penalty).

[28] *Hidalgo*, 138 S. Ct. 1054.

[29] *Id.*

[30] *Id.* ("[T]hat reasoning cannot be squared with this Court's precedent — precedent that insists that States perform the 'constitutionally necessary' narrowing function 'at the stage of *legislative* definition.'" (citing Zant v. Stephens, 462 U.S. 862, 878 (1983))(emphasis added)).

[31] 402 U.S. 183 (1971).

[32] *But see* Furman v. Georgia, 408 U.S. 238, 376 (1972) (Burger, C.J., dissenting) (arguing that the issue in *Furman* had already been decided in *McGautha* and that the Court should not revisit the issue so quickly after that ruling).

[33] HANEY, *supra* note 4, at 3–23 (explaining that the style of reasoning in *Furman* suggested that the real facts and actual operation of the death penalty would be at the forefront of any future litigation and judicial decisions that pertained to its constitutionality); Sherod Thaxton, *Disciplining Death: Assessing and Ameliorating Arbitrariness in Capital Charging*, 49 ARIZ. ST. L.J. 137, 147 (2017).

[34] BANNER, *supra* note 14, at 273.

Opponents of the post-*Furman* capital statutes expressly argued that the legislatures were required to craft capital statutes that imposed greater justificatory and evidentiary burdens on prosecutors (charging and plea bargaining) and on governors and pardon and parole boards (clemency). Although the Court dismissed these concerns, claiming that charging and clemency discretion were inevitable components of capital schemes and outside of the effective control of legislatures,[35] in the four decades since the Court's ruling, social scientific evidence has underscored that the Court's confidence in the rational, consistent, and nondiscriminatory administration of the death penalty *at any stage of the process* is unwarranted.[36]

The "full briefing" of the empirical evidence on the operation of the death penalty that Justice Breyer invited in his dissent in *Glossip* must also include relevant evidence on capital charging dynamics. Even assuming, as Justice Breyer does, that "prosecutorial narrowing" cannot salvage a capital statute that fails to genuinely narrow the class of death-eligible murders, *Furman* suggests that irrational and inconsistent capital charging could render a capital statute constitutionally infirm — depending on its magnitude — apart from meaningful legislative narrowing. Justice Brennan emphasized in his dissent in *Pulley* that "we must worry whether, first, we have designed procedures which are appropriate to the decision between life and death and, second, whether we have followed those procedures."[37]

When evidence of, *inter alia*, capricious capital charging decisions was presented to the Court three years after *Pulley*, in *McCleskey v. Kemp*,[38] the five-Justice majority rejected the petitioner's arbitrariness claim. Justice Powell, who authored the majority opinion in *McCleskey*, based his decision, in part, on (1) the perceived benefits that prosecutorial discretion offers criminal defendants in the form of individualized justice and (2) the unprecedented procedural safeguards designed

---

[35] Gregg v. Georgia, 428 U.S. 153, 199 (1976) (plurality opinion).
[36] *See generally* DAVID C. BALDUS ET AL., EQUAL JUSTICE AND THE DEATH PENALTY: A LEGAL AND EMPIRICAL ANALYSIS 316, 328 (1990); John J. Donohue, *An Empirical Evaluation of the Connecticut Death Penalty System Since 1973: Are There Unlawful Racial, Gender, and Geographic Disparities?*, 11 J. EMPIRICAL LEGAL STUD. 637 (2014); Stephanie Hindson et al., *Race, Gender, Region and Death Sentencing in Colorado, 1980–1999*, 77 U. COLO. L. REV. 549 (2006); Barbara O'Brien et al., *Untangling the Role of Race in Capital Charging and Sentencing in North Carolina, 1990–2009*, 94 N.C. L. REV. 1997 (2016); William Alex Pridemore, *An Empirical Examination of Commutations and Executions in Post-Furman Capital Cases*, 17 JUST. Q. 159 (2000); Michael J. Songer & Issac Unah, *The Effect of Race, Gender, and Location on Prosecutorial Decisions to Seek the Death Penalty in South Carolina*, 58 S.C. L. REV. 161 (2006); Jon R. Sorensen & Donald H. Wallace, *Prosecutorial Discretion in Seeking Death: An Analysis of Racial Disparity in the Pretrial Stages of Case Processing in a Midwestern County*, 16 JUST. Q. 559 (1999); Robert E. Weiss et al., *Assessing the Capriciousness of Death Penalty Charging*, 30 LAW & SOC'Y REV. 607 (1996); Marvin E. Wolfgang et al., *Comparison of the Executed and the Commuted among Admissions to Death Row*, 53 J. CRIM. L. CRIMINOLOGY & POLICE SCI. 301 (1962).
[37] Pulley v. Harris, 465 U.S. 37, 39 (1984) (quoting John Kaplan, *The Problem of Capital Punishment*, 1983 U. ILL. L. REV. 555 (1983)).
[38] 481 U.S. 279 (1987).

to eliminate arbitrariness and bias.[39] Justice Powell also deemed the statistical evidence of race-based arbitrariness as insufficiently strong to rise to the level of a constitutional violation,[40] although he would subsequently remark that he had an extremely limited understanding of statistical analysis and regretted his decision in that case after he retired from the Court.[41] Yet as Justice Breyer emphasized in *Glossip*, it is equally true that individualized *injustice* is antithetical to the rule of law.[42] The Court has long held that discretionary choices cannot be left to a legal actor's inclinations, but to their judgment that must be guided by sound legal principles.[43] Claims of capriciousness and bias are predicated on the demonstration that legal actors' judgment is unconstrained (or inadequately constrained) by sound legal principles.

A key obstacle for litigants and scholars raising empirically anchored claims of capriciousness has been the absence of a workable definition from both capital statutes and the courts' analysis of them. How is this phenomenon to be measured and what threshold showing must be made before these claims of constitutional error become cognizable to the Court? The American Law Institute's explicit recognition that *Furman* and its progeny have been ineffective at guaranteeing a constitutionally permissible capital punishment system largely stems from the fact that neither the courts nor legislatures have described, intelligibly, how these systems may satisfy or fail the prevailing constitutional standards.[44] But the Court or legislatures need not be the sole source of guidance on this issue. The science of statistics, at its core, is concerned with drawing inferences from data in the face of various types of uncertainty and therefore provides a useful framework for identifying and quantifying the types of errors relevant to the assessment of the constitutionality of the operation of death penalty systems. In other words, statistical social science facilitates the measurement of the extent of mayhem in capital charging and sentencing that the Court has, in theory, labored to minimize for the past five decades. The purpose of this essay is to describe several statistical techniques that are capable of providing doctrinally relevant and empirically informed assessments of

---

[39] *Id.* at 311. *But see Pulley*, 465 U.S. at 67 (Brennan J., dissenting) ("Simply to assume that the procedural protections mandated by this Court's prior decisions eliminate the irrationality underlying application of the death penalty is to ignore the holding of *Furman* and whatever constitutional difficulties may be inherent in each State's death penalty system.").

[40] Petitioner Warren McCleskey's race-based Eighth Amendment arbitrariness claim was distinct from his Fourteenth Amendment (equal protection) race-based discrimination claim; nonetheless, the majority in *McCleskey* rejected both claims.

[41] JOHN C. JEFFRIES JR., JUSTICE LEWIS F. POWELL, JR.: A BIOGRAPHY 451 (1994).

[42] Glossip v. Gross, 135 S. Ct. 2726 (2015).

[43] United States v. Burr, 25 F. Cas. 30, 35 (Cir. Ct. Va. 1807) ("[A] motion to [the court's] discretion is a motion, not to its inclination, but to its judgment; and its judgment is to be guided by sound legal principles.").

[44] AMERICAN LAW INSTITUTE, REP. OF THE COUNCIL TO THE MEMBERSHIP OF THE AMERICAN LAW INSTITUTE ON THE MATTER OF THE DEATH PENALTY (2009) (withdrawing its endorsement of the Model Penal Code's capital punishment provisions).

the degree of capriciousness in capital charging and sentencing systems that can be "scrutinized [by the Court] with more care" than it had done in the past.[45]

The ensuing discussion is organized into two parts. The first part maps the Court's Eighth Amendment jurisprudence on a conceptual and operational framework that is amenable to social scientific inquiry. It then describes and applies a suite of statistical techniques well suited to quantify the level of capriciousness in capital charging and sentencing decisions. In the interest of space, the application of these approaches focuses, specifically, on capital charging decisions, but the techniques are relevant for assessing *both* capital and non-capital charging and sentencing decisions.

COMPLEMENTARY CONCEPTIONS OF CAPRICIOUSNESS

Capriciousness as Unreliability

From a statistical point of view, capriciousness may refer to the "degree of unpredictability or randomness in the output of any social system, *even if the same inputs are consistently applied.*"[46] In the context of capital charging, "inputs" are the legally relevant defendant, victim, and crime characteristics, and the outputs are prosecutors' decisions to seek the death penalty in a case. Under this definition, capriciousness can take two general forms: similarly situated defendants are treated dissimilarly *or* dissimilarly situated defendants are treated similarly. A common term for this type of capriciousness is *unreliability* or *inconsistency.* Even though prosecutors are permitted to exercise their reasoned discretion in seeking the death penalty, *Furman* emphasized that a highly inconsistent death penalty system cannot be "fair and evenhanded" and is therefore unconstitutional.[47] The guided discretion statutes approved by the Court in *Gregg* were designed to rationalize the capital punishment process via constraining frontline legal actors — namely prosecutors, judges, and jurors.

It must be noted that the unreliability of a capital charging system may have causes that do not call into question the constitutionality of the death penalty. Even under a guided discretion regime, the application of rules to facts will always be subject to interpretation, so decision-makers may reasonably differ as to what constitutes similarly situated cases. So, for example, most capital statutes encompass murders that are "heinous, atrocious, and cruel" or "wantonly vile, horrible, and inhuman," but often there is no obvious line of demarcation, and the Court's prior attempts to provide greater clarity to these terms appear to have only muddied the waters even more.[48] As a consequence, seemingly identical cases may be

---

[45] *Glossip*, 135 S. Ct. at 2759.
[46] Weiss et al., *supra* note 36, at 609 (emphasis added).
[47] Furman v. Georgia, 408 U.S. 238, 309 (1972) (Stewart, J., concurring).
[48] *Compare* Godfrey v. Georgia, 446 U.S. 420 (1980), *with* Arave v. Creech, 507 U.S. 463 (1993).

treated differently not simply because prosecutors are exercising their discretion in an inappropriate manner, but because of the problems inherent in the application of legal rules/categories to facts. Cases may also appear factually similar on all key crime and defendant characteristics but differ with respect to unique (and often formally irrelevant facts) that determine the outcome. This, too, undermines consistency, but the permissibility of such factors will likely turn on the degree of overall inconsistency and, of course, whether these unique factors do not run afoul of the law. To be clear, a system that is highly consistent is not necessarily a system that is fair and rational. The Court emphasized this point when it invalidated the mandatory death penalty statutes enacted by Louisiana and North Carolina.[49] These capital statutes violated *Furman* because, *inter alia*, they prohibited juries from considering mitigation evidence, which, in the Court's view, made those sentences irrational.

Capriciousness as Irrationality

Capriciousness can also refer to a system's truthfulness or accuracy — i.e., its level of rationality/validity.[50] A rational system produces what it is purported and designed to produce. A system typically generates irrational results when it is incorrectly calibrated or actors implementing the system use different procedures and considerations.[51] A rational system, on the other hand, produces outcomes that are supported by theory and evidence.[52] In *Furman*, the majority stressed that constitutionally permissible capital punishment systems must be fair and evenhanded, and the rationality of any assessment is closely related to its fairness.[53] This point was underscored by Justice Brennen in *Pulley* when he argued for the necessity of comparative case review.[54]

Prosecutors' assessments of defendants' culpability should be consonant with the standards set forth in the applicable capital statutes because the statutes provide the prosecutor the criteria upon which culpability assessments are to be made in order to comport with *Furman* and its progeny. Specifically, when the factors enumerated in a capital statute fail to account for prosecutorial charging decisions (within an

---

[49] Roberts v. Louisiana, 428 U.S. 325 (1976); Woodson v. North Carolina, 428 U.S. 280 (1976) (plurality opinion).

[50] BRIAN FORST, ERRORS OF JUSTICE: NATURE, SOURCES, AND REMEDIES 33 (2004).

[51] *Id.* at 55.

[52] Burlington Truck Lines, Inc. v. United States, 371 U.S. 156, 168 (1962) (defining arbitrary government action as the lack of a rational connection between the facts that should govern a decision and the choice being made).

[53] In the educational testing literature, assessments are deemed fair when they assess what is "taught." W. Steve Lang & Judy R. Wilkerson, Accuracy vs. Validity, Consistency vs. Reliability, and Fairness vs. Absence of Bias: A Call for Quality 13 (Feb. 2008) (unpublished manuscript) ("[V]alidity means that assessors are making justifiable interpretations about their data and good decisions.").

[54] Pulley v. Harris, 465 U.S. 37, 60 (1984).

acceptable range), then one can conclude that the system is operating irrationally. Improper crime and defendant characteristics that influence the functioning of a system also undermine its rationality because prosecutors, judges, and jurors are prohibited from considering those factors. In other words, when legally legitimate factors fail to sufficiently explain outcomes *or* legally illegitimate factors do explain outcomes (after accounting for the legally legitimate factors), there is evidence of an irrational decision-making process.

Under an Eighth Amendment analysis, conscious discrimination on the part of decision-makers need not be demonstrated in order to substantiate a claim of an unconstitutionally capricious system.[55] Also, as already mentioned, an irrational system does not necessarily imply an inconsistent system. Indeed, the imposition of the death penalty for non-homicidal rape was extremely consistent throughout American history: African American men accused of raping Caucasian women were almost invariably charged with the death penalty and sentenced to death.[56] On the other hand, an unreliable system will almost invariably imply an irrational system because inconsistency undermines accuracy.

QUANTIFYING UNRELIABILITY AND IRRATIONALITY

Metrics of Inconsistency

A metric of inconsistency captures the degree of instability of legal decision-makers across prosecutors. Numerous measures are available, but three are particularly useful in the capital charging context: *intra-class correlation coefficient, mean absolute deviation,* and *median odds ratio.*[57] Given the decentralized and county-centric nature of death penalty charging authority, these metrics are particularly useful for investigating hierarchically structured data (e.g., individual cases grouped by county), and the Court has emphasized the importance of explicitly examining both

---

[55] McCleskey v. Kemp, 481 U.S. 279, 279 (1987).

[56] M. Watt Espy & John Ortiz Smykla, *Executions in the United States, 1608–2002: The Espy File* (2004) (revealing that, from 1608 to 1964, African American men constituted 90% of the 947 executions for non-homicidal rape); *see also* William C. Bailey, *Rape and the Death Penalty: A Neglected Area of Deterrence Research, in* CAPITAL PUNISHMENT IN THE UNITED STATES 226 (Hugo Adam Bedau & Charles M. Pierce eds., 1976) (explaining that, from 1930 to 1971, 50% of arrests for rape were among non-whites, but 90% of executions for rape (407 of 455) were of non-whites); Office of Planning and Analysis, Georgia Dep't of Corrections, *A History of the Death Penalty in Georgia, Executions by Year 1924–2014,* 5–13 (2015) (noting that, from 1924 to 1961, 97% of executions for rape were African American men); *accord* Marvin E. Wolfgang & Marc Riedel, *Rape, Race, and the Death Penalty in Georgia,* 45 AM. J. ORTHOPSYCHIATRY 658 (1975) (explaining that African American males were much more likely to receive the death penalty than similarly situated Caucasian males even after taking into account fourteen legally relevant case characteristics).

[57] Thaxton, *supra* note 33, at 173.

intra- and inter-jurisdictional processes when assessing the constitutionally of criminal punishments.[58]

The intra-class correlation coefficient (ICC) measures the degree of stability of death charging decisions within a specific jurisdiction (i.e., county or similar administrative unit). When key case factors are taken into account, the ICC measures the total *residual* variability — that is, variability left unexplained by those factors included in the model as determinative of capital charging decisions. The ICC ranges from zero to one, and when the ICC is large, death noticing decisions are more consistent within jurisdictions. Conversely, when the ICC is small, charging decisions within a jurisdiction are inconsistent. There are no bright-line rules for interpreting the magnitude of the ICC statistic, but a general rule of thumb is that an ICC value above 0.7 is indicative of a highly consistent system; alternatively, a value below 0.4 suggests that the system is inconsistent.[59]

My examination of capital charging decisions in Georgia from 1993 to 2000, which included nearly 1,300 death-eligible homicides and considered more than forty case-level variables pertaining to the crime, defendant(s), and victim(s),[60] revealed an ICC of 0.19 (or 19%) — well below the 0.4 cutoff indicating an inconsistent system. That is, 81% of the residual variability in death noticing for factually similar cases is attributable to within-jurisdiction dynamics and only 19% results from cases being tried in different jurisdictions.

The mean absolute deviation (MAD) provides the estimate of the variability in the probability that a similarly situated case is noticed for the death penalty across

---

[58] Solem v. Helm, 463 U.S. 277, 290–92 (1983); Enmund v. Florida, 458 U.S. 782, 794–96 (1982).

[59] Domenic V. Cicchetti, *Guidelines, Criteria, and Rules of Thumb for Evaluating Normed and Standardized Assessment Instruments in Psychology*, 6 PSYCHOL. ASSESSMENT 284 (1994).

[60] The *crime related factors* include circumstances of murder (i.e., commission of felony, domestic altercation, other altercation, gang-related, drug-related, sex-crime related, etc.), murder weapon, statutorily defined aggravating factors, motive for killing, confession evidence, weapon evidence, video evidence, and whether the defendant was ultimately convicted of murder. *Defendant related factors* are the number of defendants, defendant's race/ethnicity, sex, age, level of education, employment status, marital status, number of children, military service, history of drug use, psychiatric status, IQ, Wide Range Achievement Test (WRAT), troubled family history, prior violent felony record, prior felony record, prior murder conviction, and whether the defendant was the trigger person. The total number of victims, victim's race/ethnicity, sex, age, and relationship with defendant (i.e., stranger, intimate partner, family, friend) are *victim related factors* included in the model. Thaxton, *supra* note 33, at 176.

    Prior studies have noted the inclusion of 200+ variables. BALDUS ET AL., *supra* note 36, at 42–46 (1990); Raymond Paternoster et al., *Justice by Geography and Race: The Administration of the Death Penalty in Maryland, 1978–1999*, 4 MD. L.J. RACE, RELIGION, GENDER & CLASS 1, 57 (2004). It must be emphasized that I use a conservative counting method for the total number of variables. In terms of inculpatory/aggravation evidence, I have information on the presence or absence of the eleven statutorily defined special circumstances enumerated in Georgia's capital statute, but rather than count them separately, I count them as a single variable that indexes the total number of statutory aggravating circumstances present in the case.

jurisdictions (e.g., across counties).[61] The intuition behind this measure is that the overall inconsistency of a capital charging system can be obtained by determining the average magnitude of the difference in charging behavior across counties within a state for a typical case. Similar to the ICC, the MAD captures how (dis)similar prosecutors treat similarly situated defendants, but it does so in a slightly different manner. The MAD is especially useful when comparing an unadjusted model that does not include factors determinative of prosecutors' charging decisions (i.e., a "baseline") and an adjusted model that includes the relevant inputs. An adjusted model should yield a lower MAD than the baseline under the assumption that charging decisions in counties across the state will converge toward the statewide average for similarly situated defendants.

Based on my analysis of the Georgia data, the MAD for the baseline model was 0.11 (11%), and the adjusted model was 0.08 (8%). In other words, the jurisdictions in Georgia differed in their charging behaviors for factual similar cases, on average, by eight percentage points, and the inclusion of relevant case-level factors decreased the average statewide deviation by three percentage points. This finding is consistent with the results from the ICC analysis: most of the variability in charging behavior is attributable to within-jurisdiction charging inconsistency. Slightly more informative than the MAD is the actual range of jurisdiction effects. The expected likelihood of a similarly situated case receiving a death notice ranged from 0.11 to 0.59 across jurisdictions in Georgia. In other words, the *probability* of receiving the death notice can be 5.36 times higher depending on the jurisdiction and, equivalently, the *odds* can be 11.5 times greater. This, of course, represents the extreme situation: going from the least punitive to the most punitive jurisdiction. The next measure I describe, the median odds ratio, provides an assessment for the typical situation.[62]

The final inconsistency measure, the median odds ratio (MOR), quantifies the variability between counties by comparing two charging decisions from two factually similar cases that are randomly chosen from two different counties.[63] Some analysts believe the MOR is more interpretable than the ICC or the MAD. The MOR is the typical (median) ratio between the cases with a higher and lower probability of receiving a death notice from different jurisdictions. Intuitively, the MOR captures the increased risk of death penalty notice that would occur if a case moved from one county to another. As with the MAD, comparing the baseline and adjusted measures of the MOR assists the analyst in determining the improvement in consistency when relevant case-level factors are considered. The MOR will always be greater than or equal to one. If the MOR is one, then there is no variation between jurisdictions

---

[61] Thaxton, *supra* note 33, at 176.

[62] A very similar measure, the median absolute deviation, which is more resistant to extreme values from counties, may also be used. According to this metric, the unadjusted and adjusted models are, respectively, 0.09 and 0.07.

[63] Germán Rodriguez & Irma Elo, *Intra-Class Correlation in Random Effects Models for Binary Data*, 3 STATA J. 32, 43 (2003).

because the likelihood of receiving a death notice based on a specific set of case characteristics is, on average, equal across counties. The MOR for the baseline and adjusted models for the Georgia data are, respectively, 2.03 and 2.32. So, on average, a case moving from a lower probability death charging jurisdiction to a higher probability death charging jurisdiction more than doubles the odds of receiving a death notice. Of greater significance, however, is that factually similar cases are treated more dissimilarly across jurisdictions, as indicated by the higher, albeit only slightly, MOR for the adjusted model.

Metrics of Irrationality

A useful and widely accepted statistic for assessing rationality is the *coefficient of determination* (R^2). This metric describes the improvement in the predictive ability of an adjusted model compared to a baseline model and can be interpreted as a proxy for the "rational connection between the facts found and the choice made."[64] Discretionary choices may not lend themselves to highly accurate statistical modeling, irrespective of the comprehensiveness of the model, because of idiosyncrasies associated with charging decisions.[65] Rather than indicating that a statistical model is improperly specified (e.g., the model excludes important determinants of capital charging decisions), a low R^2 may simply underscore the fact that a process is inherently capricious.[66] As noted above, capital charging decisions are jurisdiction-specific, so similar to metrics of consistency, appropriate metrics of rationality must account for the hierarchical nature of the data. This can be accomplished by disaggregating the variability in capital charging decisions into within- and between-jurisdiction components and assessing the level of rationality of each component.[67] Whereas the within-jurisdiction R^2 measures the proportion of variance accounted for in the case-level outcome by the case-level explanatory variables, the between-jurisdiction R^2 assesses the proportion of variance accounted for by the jurisdiction-level averages of those explanatory variables. So, for instance, in a rationally operating capital charging system, jurisdictions that tend to have cases that are more highly aggravated (i.e., greater defendant culpability) should be more likely, on average, to seek the death penalty. R^2 can also be calculated for subgroups and used to assess whether the rationality of the charging decisions differs across

---

[64] *See* Motor Vehicle Mfrs. Ass'n v. State Farm Mut. Auto. Ins., 463 U.S. 29, 43 (1983) (quoting Burlington Truck Lines v. United States, 371 U.S. 156, 168 (1962) and defining arbitrary and capricious action in the context of administrative law).

[65] Sherod Thaxton, *Disentangling Disparity: Exploring Racially Disparate Effect and Treatment in Capital Charging*, 45 Am. J. Crim. L. 95, 147 (2018).

[66] *Id.*

[67] Stephen W. Raudenbush & Anthony S. Bryk, Hierarchical Linear Models: Applications and Data Analysis Methods 109–10 (2d ed. 2002) ("The estimates of the proportion of variance explained from a hierarchical analysis may be quite different from those generated in conventional level-1 or level-2 analyses and may lead to different conclusions.").

these classifications.[68] Death noticing behavior might be said to be irrational, unfair, and uneven when associated with legally illegitimate considerations, such as race/ethnicity and gender.

The R^2 statistics for case- and jurisdiction-level dynamics in Georgia data, adjusting for relevant case characteristics, are 0.44 and 0.21, respectively. That is, the explanatory variables in the model explain approximately 44% of the variability within jurisdictions and 21% of the variability across jurisdictions. The ICC measure discussed earlier, revealed that location accounts for 19% of the variability in death charging, so approximately 4% ($0.21 \times 0.19 = 0.039$) of the total variability in death noticing can be explained by between-jurisdiction differences in case-level factors. Several of the case-level characteristics included in the analysis may be deemed legally suspect, particularly for defendant-related factors. One could argue, for example, that it is improper for a prosecutor to consider defendants' race/ethnicity, gender, level of education, marital status, and employment status (to name a few) when deciding to seek the death penalty. The same may also be said for a victim's gender and race/ethnicity.

In an attempt to determine how much Georgia's capital statute was constraining the behavior of prosecutors, a trimmed model was examined that only included (a) the number statutorily defined aggravating circumstances, (b) defendant's criminal history, (c) the number of victims and defendants, and (d) relationship between the defendant and the victim. The premise of this analysis is that, in a rationally functioning system, the "legal core" of the case should, theoretically, drive capital charging.[69] The trimmed model explains 31% of the variance within jurisdictions and 12% of the variance between jurisdictions.

Finally, given the persistence of race-of-victim effects in capital charging and sentencing behavior — and, to a lesser extent, race-of-defendant effects[70] — the R^2 was calculated for four groupings of cases: Caucasian defendants, non-Caucasian defendants, Caucasian victims, and non-Caucasian victims.[71] The R^2 for the combined sample (i.e., all defendants) was 43%, whereas the R^2 was 59% for Caucasian defendant cases, 42% for non-Caucasian defendant cases, 51% for Caucasian victim cases, and 37% for non-Caucasian victim cases.[72] These results suggest that the

[68] Don Hedeker & Robert D. Gibbons, Longitudinal Data Analysis 158, 195–96 (2006).

[69] *See* Donald J. Black, Sociological Justice 20 (1989) (describing the legal core of a case as "the rules in the face of the evidence ... that can be meaningfully analyzed in the jurisprudential tradition").

[70] Thaxton, *supra* note 65, at 120 (summarizing the empirical literature on race-of-defendant and race-of-victim effects in capital charging and sentencing).

[71] The R^2 statistic needed to be rescaled before comparisons across subgroups in order for the comparison to be valid. *See* Joop J. Hox, Multilevel Analysis: Techniques and Applications 133–34 (2d ed. 2010).

[72] Given that the vast majority of death-eligible cases are intra-racial, the higher R^2 statistics for the Caucasian defendant cases and Caucasian victim cases are likely a function of both of those factors.

identical case-level factors explain approximately 40% *more* of the overall variability in capital charging when the defendant or the victim is Caucasian as opposed to non-Caucasian.[73] In the Georgia data, approximately 98% of the death-eligible cases had either an African American or Caucasian defendant, and nearly 95% of the death-eligible cases had either an African American or Caucasian victim, so the "non-Caucasian" defendant and victim cases are, essentially, African American defendant and victim cases.

Some Qualifications about Quantification

Any assessment of capriciousness will depend on both the quality of the data and analytical model. The process of quantifying unreliability and irrationality will be impacted by (1) improperly measured inputs; (2) incorrectly specified relationships between the inputs; or (3) important omitted inputs. With respect to the first condition, there is a legitimate concern that the overall culpability of a defendant may be mis-measured because, as noted earlier, prosecutors may reasonably disagree over whether a factor is present in a case. One would expect this concern to be more relevant when assessing charging decisions inter-jurisdictionally rather than intra-jurisdictionally due to greater uniformity in the assessment of cases within a particular office, largely due to collaboration between attorneys when evaluating cases or office policies governing the assessment of cases. It is worth (re)emphasizing that 81% of the overall variability in capital charging in Georgia was attributable to within-jurisdiction dynamics, after accounting for important crime and defendant characteristics. This suggests that the impact of mis-measured inputs is not driving the results.

The second condition pertains to the way the analyst posits the inputs impact the outcome (i.e., functional form). Is the relationship uniform through the range of a particular input (linear versus nonlinear)? Does the relationship between the input and the outcome depend on the value of another input (additive versus nonadditive)? Concerns over functional form can be addressed, to a large extent, by specifically examining how assumptions about (non)linearity and (non)additivity impact the measurement. Mild departures from the "true" functional form do not negatively influence the assessment but more dramatic departures may. Most of the inputs in the statistical model are binary (yes/no), so concerns over nonlinearity are not especially relevant. As for the non-binary inputs (e.g., the number of co-defendants, victims, statutory aggravating circumstances, etc.), the Georgia data were reanalyzed using models that relaxed the linearity assumption for these variables, and the results were similar. The impact of the non-additivity assumption was also examined for certain pairing of variables and, again, the results remained unchanged. It must be acknowledged, however, that investigating non-additivity

---

[73] Race of defendant: $[(59 - 42) \div 42] \times 100 = 40.5\%$; race of victim: $[(51 - 37) \div 37] \times 100 = 37.8\%$.

can quickly become exceedingly complex when considering the interaction between more than three variables, and these high-dimensional relationships were not explored, so this issue merits further investigation.

The third condition may pose a significant problem for evaluating capital charging decisions if the model fails to include all relevant variables that legitimately influence a prosecutor's decision. This concern is more pronounced for sentencing decisions than charging decisions because the important predictors of death penalty charging have been well-established,[74] and it has been demonstrated that the likelihood of finding novel and meaningful predictors is very low.[75] It is also worth noting that empirical investigations of capital charging across numerous states and time periods, employing various methodological approaches, and considering different inputs, have produced remarkably similar results.[76] Nevertheless, all of these caveats should be kept in mind not only when adopting the aforementioned metrics but also when engaging in any empirically anchored assessment of capriciousness in capital charging and sentencing.[77]

CONCLUSION

Justice Breyer's recent invitations, in *Glossip* and *Hidalgo*, to potential litigants to develop and present social scientific evidence for the Court to assess when deciding on the constitutionality of the death penalty stand in stark contrast to Justice Scalia's (in)famous memorandum to his colleagues on the Court expressing his intention to vote against a constitutional challenge to Georgia's death penalty more than thirty years ago in *McCleskey*.[78] *McCleskey* provided a vehicle for the Court to consider the most sophisticated and comprehensive statistical study ever conducted on the influence of race on capital punishment, and the evidence overwhelmingly indicated rampant capriciousness and bias at every stage of the process. Justice Scalia informed his colleagues that, in his opinion, no statistical showing of capriciousness and bias — irrespective of its magnitude — would justify ruling Georgia's capital statute unconstitutional. He explained: "[I]rrational sympathies, including racial, on jury deliberations and prosecutorial decisions is real, acknowledged in the decisions of this court, and ineradicable, I cannot honestly say that all I need is more proof."[79]

---

[74] GAO, *supra* note 1.

[75] Weiss et al., *supra* note 36, at 617; *see supra* notes 65–66 and accompanying text (explaining that the low predictive power of a statistical model may not be indicative of a problem with the model but instead reveals a process that is inherently capricious).

[76] Thaxton, *supra* note 65, at 122–23 (summarizing results from over a dozen studies of capital charging behavior and noting strikingly similar results).

[77] *See* McCleskey v. Zant, 580 F. Supp. 338, 361–62 (N.D. Ga. 1984) (describing potential deficiencies with statistical models of capital charging and sentencing decisions due to, *inter alia*, mismeasured and omitted variables).

[78] Memorandum to the Conference from Justice Antonin Scalia in No. 84-6811, *McCleskey v. Kemp* (Jan. 6, 1987), *Thurgood Marshall Papers*, The Library of Congress, Washington, D.C.

[79] *Id.*

Even if some members of the current Court share Justice Scalia's belief that capriciousness and bias are inevitable and ineradicable features of capital punishment systems, it is also abundantly clear that at least three other members of the Court are in alignment with Justice Breyer with respect to the relevance of social scientific evidence for the Court's assessment of the constitutionality of the death penalty. Moreover, the U.S. Supreme Court is not the only plausible site of contestation — state supreme courts appear more willing to dismantle the death penalty based on statistical evidence of capriciousness and bias.[80] Consequently, how much capriciousness exists, whether the amount is intolerable, and what efforts should be taken to reduce it, remain questions of monumental importance.[81]

---

[80] *Compare* State v. Gregory, 427 P.3d 621, 636 (Wash. 2018) (ruling Washington State's death penalty unconstitutional in light of statistical evidence demonstrating that it was administered in an "arbitrary and racially biased manner"), *with* State v. Loftin, 724 A.2d 129 (N.J. 1999) (reasoning that statistical evidence demonstrating significant bias would provide adequate grounds for ruling New Jersey's death penalty unconstitutional); *see also* Note, *Washington State Supreme Court Declares Death Penalty Unconstitutional in Washington*, 132 Harv. L. Rev. 1764 (2019) (noting that the Washington Supreme Court "became the first American court to declare the death penalty unconstitutional based primarily on statistical evidence of racial bias in sentencing").

[81] Weiss et al., *supra* note 36, at 625.

17

Race Discrimination in Punishment

Jeffrey L. Kirchmeier[*]

INTRODUCTION

Unlike some other constitutional amendments, the Eighth Amendment was not drafted expressly to address concerns about race. So, early cases interpreting the Amendment did not consider concerns about racial disparities. The Amendment bars "excessive fines" and bans "cruel and unusual punishments," so unlike the Equal Protection Clause of the Fourteenth Amendment, its plain language seemingly does not allow for concerns about whether the punishment is distributed equally.

But over time, as the U.S. Supreme Court has applied the Eighth Amendment and its meaning has evolved, the Court has interpreted the Amendment in a way that expresses concern about more than just whether or not a punishment is cruel or barbaric. Yet, throughout much of the Court's history, it has been reluctant to grapple with racial disparities in the context of the Eighth Amendment even as attorneys have brought the issue to the Justices since the 1960s.

Race, of course, has been intertwined with punishment in North America even before the United States was formed. In the 1700s and 1800s, many states established more severe punishments for African Americans than for whites for some crimes.[1] After the Civil War, as part of Black Codes aimed at newly freed slaves, southern states enacted "draconian fines for violating broad proscriptions on 'vagrancy' and other dubious offenses."[2] Further, states often provided different procedures in

---

[*] Professor of Law, City University of New York School of Law. J.D., Case Western Reserve University School of Law; B.A., Case Western Reserve University.

[1] See, e.g., JEFFREY L. KIRCHMEIER, IMPRISONED BY THE PAST: WARREN MCCLESKEY, RACE, AND THE AMERICAN DEATH PENALTY, 131–32 (2015).

[2] Timbs v. Indiana, 139 S. Ct. 682, 688–89 (2019) (Thomas, J., concurring) (reasoning that the excessive fines clause is incorporated through the Fourteenth Amendment) (citing MISSISSIPPI VAGRANT LAW, LAWS OF MISS. Sec. 2 (1865), *in* 1 WALTER FLEMING, DOCUMENTARY HISTORY OF RECONSTRUCTION 283–85 (1950)).

prosecuting criminal cases depending on the race of the defendant.[3] And outside the courtroom, many communities took the law into their own hands through lynching, more commonly against people of color.[4]

Today, many problems persist through our system of mass incarceration. With more than two million Americans held in prisons and jails in the United States, African Americans are incarcerated at a disproportionately higher rate than white people.[5] Disparities occur throughout the criminal justice process, fueled by racial profiling, "tough on crime" legislation, sentencing guidelines, and biases in the system through prosecutor and juror decisions.[6] Scholars have argued that mass incarceration in the United States has created a subordinate caste of human beings as a result of racial discrimination.[7]

Ultimately, the Supreme Court did consider whether the Eighth Amendment prohibits racial discrimination when it decided *McCleskey v. Kemp* in 1987.[8] Although the Court took a limited approach to addressing race with the Eighth Amendment, it did leave open the possibility that racial disparities in the distribution of punishment may constitute "cruel and unusual punishments." Thus, the Court has allowed for claims based on racial discrimination to be rooted in the Eighth Amendment, even as it has thus far ruled against the claimants in these cases.

RACE AND EARLY EIGHTH AMENDMENT CHALLENGES

In the early years of the United States, courts did not tie racial discrimination challenges to the Eighth Amendment for several reasons. Interpreters had little guidance because the drafters of the Amendment gave minimal discussion to the meaning of the ban on "cruel and unusual punishments."[9] And, when the Amendment was added to the Constitution, the country still had slavery. Yet, some commentators have argued that the Amendment's ban on "unusual" punishments

3   *See, e.g.,* JOHN F. GALLIHER ET AL., AMERICA WITHOUT THE DEATH PENALTY: STATES LEADING THE WAY 85–86, 101 (2002).
4   *See, e.g.,* JAMES W. MARQUART ET AL., THE ROPE, THE CHAIR & THE NEEDLE, 5–7 (1994); FRANKLIN ZIMRING, THE CONTRADICTIONS OF AMERICAN CAPITAL PUNISHMENT 90–92 (2003).
5   Drew Kann, *5 Facts behind America's High Incarceration Rate*, CNN (Apr. 21, 2019), www.cnn .com/2018/06/28/us/mass-incarceration-five-key-facts/index.html.
6   See, e.g., Nicole Smith Futrell, *Vulnerable, Not Voiceless: Outsider Narrative in Advocacy Against Discriminatory Policing*, 93 N.C. L. REV. 1597, 1599–1602 (2015); K. Babe Howell, *Broken Lives from Broken Windows: The Hidden Costs of Aggressive Order-Maintenance Policing*, 33 N.Y.U. REV. L. & SOC. CHANGE 271, 291–307 (2009); Jason Reed, *Dual Failures: the Role of Race in Eighth Amendment Violations in Prisons*, 31 L. & INEQ. 233, 233–38 (2012).
7   *See, e.g.,* MICHELLE ALEXANDER, THE NEW JIM CROW: MASS INCARCERATION IN THE AGE OF COLORBLINDNESS 175 (2010); Jeffrey Fagan, *Symposium on Pursuing Racial Fairness in Criminal Justice: Twenty Years after McCleskey v. Kemp*, 39 COLUM. HUMAN RTS. L. REV. 5 (2008).
8   McCleskey v. Kemp, 481 U.S. 279 (1987).
9   *See, e.g.,* Furman v. Georgia, 408 U.S. 238, 244 (1972) (Douglas, J., concurring).

"emerged from the drafter's desire to protect against discrimination in the use of severe punishments."[10]

The central litigation surrounding the interpretation of the Eighth Amendment in the context of race originated in the early 1950s. At that time, lawyers at the National Association for the Advancement of Colored People's Legal Defense and Education Fund (LDF) expanded their civil rights work to include challenges to the use of the death penalty. Initially, these challenges were based on the Equal Protection Clause of the Fourteenth Amendment and arguments that in southern states blacks were more likely than whites to be sentenced to death for rape.[11] Eventually, though, the lawyers expanded their attacks on capital punishment to include Eighth Amendment challenges to the use of the death penalty for any crimes.

Part of the basis for these Eighth Amendment challenges was the U.S. Supreme Court's decision in 1958 in *Trop v. Dulles.*[12] Prior to *Trop*, the Supreme Court had done little with the Eighth Amendment's ban on "cruel and unusual punishments," partly because the Eighth Amendment rights did not apply to state court cases prior to the incorporation of these rights through the post-Civil War Fourteenth Amendment. In *Trop*, a non-capital case, Chief Justice Earl Warren wrote for the plurality that the Eighth Amendment "must draw its meaning from the evolving standards of decency that mark the progress of a maturing society."[13] This "evolving standards of decency" language allowed attorneys to argue that, even if the death penalty were constitutional at one time, the meaning of the Eighth Amendment may change over time as society changes.[14]

In 1963, Justice Arthur Goldberg, in a dissenting opinion from a denial of a petition for certiorari in two cases, encouraged attorneys to challenge the death penalty for the crime of rape based both upon the Eighth Amendment's ban on cruel and unusual punishments and upon the Fourteenth Amendment's Due Process Clause.[15] In the short opinion, Goldberg raised three questions about the death penalty, including asking whether the death penalty for rape was still constitutional in light of the evolving standards of decency.[16]

---

[10] See Laurence Claus, *The Antidiscrimination Eighth Amendment*, 28 Harv. J.L. & Pub. Pol'y 119 (2004); Aliza Cover, *Cruel and Invisible Punishment: Redeeming the Counter-Majoritarian Eighth Amendment*, 79 Brook. L. Rev. 1141, 1150–53 (2014).

[11] William J. Bowers et al., Legal Homicide: Death as Punishment in America, 1864–1982 17 (1984).

[12] Trop v. Dulles, 356 U.S. 86 (1958) (plurality opinion).

[13] *Id.* at 101.

[14] *Cf.* Meghan J. Ryan, *Does Stare Decisis Apply in the Eighth Amendment Death Penalty Context?*, 85 N.C. L. Rev. 847 (2007) (explaining that stare decisis does not apply in the traditional manner in Eighth Amendment evolving standards of decency cases).

[15] Rudolph v. Alabama, 375 U.S. 889 (1963) (Goldberg, J., dissenting from denial of petition for writ of certiorari); Snider v. Cunningham, 375 U.S. 889 (1963) (Goldberg, J., dissenting from denial of petition for writ of certiorari).

[16] *Rudolph*, 375 U.S. at 889–90.

Goldberg's final published opinion did not mention the way the death penalty was being applied in a racially discriminatory manner. Prior to publication, he had circulated a memo with his ideas, including a reference to the "well-recognized disparity" in the way the death penalty was applied to African Americans in sexual assault cases.[17] But Chief Justice Earl Warren convinced Justice Goldberg to omit the reference to race in the published opinion. Chief Justice Warren feared that the country would find the claims about racial discrimination and sexual assault too controversial.[18]

Still, attorneys responded to Justice Goldberg's call. Through a number of studies, attorneys recognized the presence of racial disparities in the use of capital punishment. In 1964, LDF attorneys presented courts with information about race from interviews with Arkansas court clerks in the case of an African-American defendant sentenced to death for rape.[19] Later, University of Pennsylvania criminologist Marvin Wolfgang performed a more in-depth study, examining rape convictions from eleven states covering two decades from 1945 to 1965.[20] Among other findings, Wolfgang concluded that black men were much more likely to be sentenced to death than white men.[21] Legal claims based upon this evidence, however, were rooted in the Fourteenth Amendment, not the Eighth Amendment.

In 1970, in two consolidated cases in *McGautha v. California*,[22] the U.S. Supreme Court rejected a Fourteenth Amendment Due Process challenge to death penalty statutes that gave jurors wide discretion in sentencing. The majority did not address racial disparities or the Eighth Amendment.[23] But one commentator later noted that the *McGautha* decision "manifested a willingness to look the other way from any signs of racism creeping into death sentencing."[24]

As attorneys launched more Eighth and Fourteenth Amendment challenges to the death penalty, some of the Justices began to take notice of the evidence of racial disparities in the use of capital punishment. When the Supreme Court eventually addressed the merits of an Eighth Amendment challenge to the death penalty in general, some of the Justices raised questions about the punishment's discriminatory use.

---

[17] Arthur J. Goldberg, *Memorandum to the Conference re: Capital Punishment*, 27 S. TEX. L. REV. 493, 505 (1985).

[18] EVAN J. MANDERY, A WILD JUSTICE: THE DEATH AND RESURRECTION OF CAPITAL PUNISHMENT IN AMERICA 25–28 (2013).

[19] KIRCHMEIER, *supra* note 1, at 140.

[20] *See* Maxwell v. Bishop, 398 F.2d 138, 141–42 (8th Cir. 1968), *vacated and remanded on other grounds*, 398 U.S. 262 (1970).

[21] *Id.* at 143.

[22] McGautha v. California, 402 U.S. 183 (1971). The California case was consolidated with one from Ohio: *Crampton v. Ohio*, 402 U.S. 183 (1971).

[23] *See McGautha*, 402 U.S. at 226 (Black, J., concurring) (asserting that any Eighth Amendment challenge would fail because capital punishment was a common penalty at the time the Amendment was adopted).

[24] BARRETT J. FOERSTER, RACE, RAPE, AND INJUSTICE 107 (2012).

Thus, in *Furman v. Georgia*,[25] the Supreme Court held that the existing death penalty statutes violated the Eighth Amendment. At the heart of the problem was that the statutes gave complete discretion to juries in sentencing. The Court, however, was unable to come up with a unified reason for the result, with each of the nine Justices writing separate opinions in the 5-4 decision.

In the decision, some of the Justices in the majority raised the issue of racial disparities in the administration of the death penalty in their separate opinions. For example, Justice Potter Stewart, while reasoning that the Eighth Amendment did not allow for a death penalty applied in a wanton and freakish manner, asserted that "racial discrimination has not been proved" so he was putting that issue aside for the time being.[26] But Justice Thurgood Marshall noted there was a higher rate of blacks being executed and asserted that "there [was] evidence of racial discrimination."[27]

Justice William Douglas spent more of his Eighth Amendment analysis on the issue of race, concluding that the death penalty statutes were "pregnant with discrimination" in a way that was incompatible "with the idea of equal protection of the laws that is implicit in the ban on 'cruel and unusual punishments.'"[28] He explained that the use of the death penalty is "unusual" if it is used in a way that discriminates based on race or other improper reasons.

Even some of the dissenting Justices acknowledged concerns about racial discrimination. Chief Justice Warren Burger noted that statistics suggested that, historically, African Americans were sentenced to death more often than whites in many states, especially for sexual assault crimes. Also in dissent, Justice Lewis Powell referenced statistics showing a racial disparity in the way the death penalty had been used for rape in some states.[29]

Despite the lack of a majority opinion discussing the country's long history of racial prejudice, many knew that such history supported *Furman*'s outcome. Many years later, Justice Harry Blackmun asserted, "*Furman* aspired to eliminate the vestiges of racism and the effects of poverty in capital sentencing."[30]

Then, in 1976, four years after *Furman*, the Supreme Court upheld against Eighth and Fourteenth Amendment challenges new death penalty statutes that provided some guidance to jurors in the form of factors or questions. The plurality reasoned that the new statutes addressed the Eighth Amendment arbitrariness

---

[25] Furman v. Georgia, 408 U.S. 238 (1972) (per curiam).

[26] *Id.* at 309–10 (Stewart, J., concurring).

[27] *Id.* at 364 (Marshall, J., concurring).

[28] *Id.* at 242, 256, 257 (Douglas, J., concurring).

[29] *See id.* at 289 (Burger, C.J., dissenting); *id.* at 449 (Powell, J., dissenting). Powell indicated that claims based on race could be brought under the Equal Protection Clause while referencing a claim of discrimination made in Maxwell v. Bishop, 398 F.2d 138 (8th Cir. 1968), *vacated and remanded on other grounds*, 398 U.S. 262 (1970). *See Furman*, 408 U.S. at 449.

[30] Callins v. Collins, 510 U.S. 1141, 1148 (1994) (Blackmun, J., dissenting from denial of petition for a writ of certiorari).

concerns discussed in *Furman*.[31] But in *Gregg v. Georgia* and the other 1976 cases on capital punishment, those Justices failed to examine racial disparities in their Eighth Amendment analyses.[32]

The Supreme Court would have needed to look no further than the state at the center of both *Furman* and *Gregg* to recognize how a history of racist lynching illustrated bias that continued with the use of legal executions. The simple statistics were alarming on their own, with Georgia executing 337 black people compared to seventy-five white people between 1924 and 1972, the year *Furman* was decided.[33] But the Court saw the new death penalty statutes as the start of a new era in capital punishment, with guidance to jurors that would eliminate, or at least curtail, arbitrariness, bias, and racism.

For a long time after the death penalty's return, the Supreme Court avoided addressing the issue of the role of race in the context of Eighth Amendment challenges. For example, in 1979, the Court held in *Coker v. Georgia* that the death penalty for the crime of raping an adult woman violated the Eighth Amendment.[34] In that case, attorneys argued that the Constitution was violated because of the wide disparity between the number of black men executed for rape and the number of white men executed for the same crime. For example, as Justice Marshall had pointed out earlier in *Furman*, of the 455 people executed for the crime of rape since 1930 when the Justice Department started keeping track, 405 — or eighty-nine percent — were black.[35] But when the Justices issued their majority opinion in *Coker*, they did not mention the stark racial disparity.[36]

The Court did consider claims about racial discrimination in criminal cases under other constitutional amendments. For example, the Court addressed racial bias during the jury selection process in the 1986 case of *Batson v. Kentucky*[37] and in subsequent cases.[38] The challenges in *Batson*, however, were based upon the Sixth

---

[31] Gregg v. Georgia, 428 U.S. 153 (1976) (plurality opinion) (upholding Georgia's death penalty laws that provided jurors with aggravating and mitigating factors during a bifurcated sentencing hearing).

[32] *See, e.g.*, Jurek v. Texas, 428 US. 262 (1976) (upholding Texas's death penalty statute that provided sentencing jurors with questions); Proffitt v. Florida, 428 U.S. 242 (1976) (upholding Florida's death penalty statute); *Gregg*, 428 U.S. 153; *see also* Roberts v. Louisiana, 428 U.S. 325 (1976) (striking down Louisiana's death penalty statute); Woodson v. North Carolina, 428 U.S. 280 (1976) (striking down North Carolina's mandatory death penalty statute).

[33] Stephen B. Bright, *Discrimination, Death and Denial: The Tolerance of Racial Discrimination in Infliction of the Death Penalty*, 35 Santa Clara L. Rev. 433, 441 (1995) (citing Prentice Palmer & Jim Galloway, *Georgia Electric Chair Spans 5 Decades*, The Atlanta J., Dec. 15, 1983, at 15A).

[34] Coker v. Georgia, 433 U.S. 584, 587 (1977) (plurality opinion).

[35] Furman v. Georgia, 408 U.S. 238, 364 (1972) (Marshall, J., dissenting).

[36] Scott W. Howe, *Race, Death and Disproportionality*, 37 N. Ky. L. Rev. 213, 225 (2010).

[37] Batson v. Kentucky, 476 U.S. 79 (1986).

[38] *See, e.g.*, Miller-El v. Dretke, 545 U.S. 231 (2005) (granting habeas corpus relief on a challenge under *Batson*); *see also* Barbara D. Underwood, *Ending Race Discrimination in Jury Selection: Whose Right Is It, Anyway?*, 92 Colum. L. Rev. 725, 727–28 (1992).

and Fourteenth Amendment rights to a fair jury trial and the Fourteenth Amendment right to equal protection.

Yet, Eighth Amendment claims based on racial discrimination did not go away. Capital defense attorneys continued to raise such arguments. And experts continued to analyze and study the impact of race in capital cases.

In 1977, LDF lawyers obtained a stay of execution for a white defendant named John Spenkelink based on a study showing that defendants who killed white victims were more likely to get the death penalty than defendants who killed black victims.[39] But ultimately, courts rejected such claims of arbitrariness and capriciousness that were grounded in both the Eighth and the Fourteenth Amendments.[40]

Courts were critical of many of these early studies on race and the death penalty. Critics attacked studies such as the one used in Spenkelink's case for not accounting for every possible variable. Similar arguments were made about a 1980 study of death sentences in Florida, Georgia, Texas, and Ohio that found disparities based on the race of the victim.[41] Attorneys soon realized that it would take a much more sophisticated study for the Supreme Court to evaluate the Eighth Amendment implications of racial bias in sentences.

THE SUPREME COURT ADDRESSES RACIAL DISCRIMINATION IN THE EIGHTH AMENDMENT CONTEXT IN *MCCLESKEY V. KEMP*

Experts completed a more detailed study about race and punishment in 1982 and then later expanded it. Known collectively as "the Baldus study," the project was the work of law professor David L. Baldus, professor of statistics and actuarial science George G. Woodworth, and law professor Charles A. Pulaski. The three men analyzed more than 2,400 Georgia homicide cases covering 1973 through 1980, breaking them down into more than four hundred variables.[42]

Using multiple regression analysis, they found the race of the defendant had some effect on the outcome of cases, but the race of the victim had an even more significant impact on who received the death penalty in the state. The study concluded that someone accused of a capital crime had his odds of getting the death penalty multiplied by 4.3 if the victim were white instead of another race. Although the Supreme Court and commentators later illustrated some confusion about the actual numbers, missing the difference between odds and probabilities,

---

[39] *See* KIRCHMEIER, *supra* note 1, at 109, 141.

[40] Spenkelink v. Wainwright, 578 F.2d 582, 612–14 (5th Cir. 1978).

[41] Smith v. Balkcom, 671 F.2d 858 (5th Cir. 1982) (noting that "[t]he leap from that [statistical] data to the conclusion of discriminatory intent or purpose leaves untouched countless racially neutral variables"); *see also* William J. Bowers & Glenn L. Pierce, *Arbitrariness and Discrimination under Post-Furman Capital Statutes*, 26 CRIME & DELINQ. 563 (1980).

[42] See, e.g., William J. Bowers, *A Tribute to David Baldus, a Determined and Relentless Champion of Doing Justice*, 97 IOWA L. REV. 1890 (2012).

the study's conclusion was clear.[43] Baldus and his colleagues found that the race of the victim was more of a factor in determining whether someone received a death sentence than several legitimate aggravating factors.

The Baldus study found racial disparities throughout the capital decision-making process, not just at the jury stage. For example, the report revealed "that prosecutors sought the death penalty in 70% of the cases involving black defendants and white victims; 32% of the cases involving white defendants and white victims; 15% of the cases involving black defendants and black victims; and 19% of the cases involving white defendants and black victims."[44]

Across cases, capital defense attorneys began making Eighth and Fourteenth Amendment arguments based upon the sophisticated Baldus study. Ultimately, the case that would take the issue to the U.S. Supreme Court involved a Georgia capital defendant named Warren McCleskey.

In 1978, McCleskey had been convicted of a furniture store robbery and the murder of a police officer. While four men were robbing the store, a white police officer had entered the store to investigate. He was then shot and killed. Although there was some debate about which of the four robbers had done the killing, McCleskey was sentenced to death after one of his codefendants testified against him.

McCleskey's lawyers used the Baldus study during McCleskey's habeas corpus proceedings, and the federal district judge held extensive hearings on the study. While the district court judge ultimately rejected the findings of the study, the U.S. Court of Appeals for the Eleventh Circuit assumed the statistics were correct.[45] But the appeals court ruled against McCleskey, concluding that the numbers were not enough to constitute a Fourteenth or Eighth Amendment violation.[46]

The U.S. Supreme Court decided to review the case, and, on April 22, 1987, the Court issued its opinion in *McCleskey v. Kemp*. The majority opinion was written by Justice Lewis F. Powell Jr. and joined by Justices Byron White, Sandra Day O'Connor, Antonin Scalia, and Chief Justice William Rehnquist.

In evaluating McCleskey's claims, the Court first had to address the Baldus study and its findings. The majority stated that it was assuming for the sake of its constitutional analysis that the Baldus study findings were accurate. One reason that the Court may have made this assumption was that, during deliberations among the Justices, Justice Scalia had written a memo to his colleagues where he disagreed with any strategy of dismissing the findings of the study. He reasoned that the Court

---

[43] *See* KIRCHMEIER, *supra* note 1, at 142–46. *See also* McCleskey v. Kemp, 481 U.S. 279, 287 (1987) (incorrectly summarizing the finding as probability instead of odds).

[44] *McCleskey*, 481 U.S. at 286–87.

[45] *See* McCleskey v. Kemp, 753 F.2d 877 (11th Cir. 1985); McCleskey v. Zant, 580 F. Supp. 338 (N.D. Ga. 1984).

[46] *McCleskey*, 753 F.2d at 891 (reasoning that the Baldus study was "insufficient to show irrationality, arbitrariness and capriciousness under any kind of Eighth Amendment analysis").

could not ignore "that that the unconscious operation of irrational sympathies and antipathies, including racial" operated upon jury and prosecutor decisions.[47]

The Court then rejected McCleskey's equal protection challenge under the Fourteenth Amendment. The Court explained that a person who argues that there was an equal protection violation must bear the burden of proving purposeful discrimination that had a discriminatory effect on the person.[48] Here, McCleskey relied upon the Baldus study as opposed to evidence of specific intentional instances of racism during his trial. The Court found that the Baldus study did not prove that any of the decision-makers in McCleskey's case had acted with discriminatory purpose, and McCleskey failed to show that the Georgia legislature acted with such purpose.[49]

In its Eighth Amendment analysis, the Court recounted the history of its major Eighth Amendment decisions, including *Trop*'s command that the Court consider the "evolving standards of decency that mark the progress of a maturing society."[50] The Court reiterated that cases like *Furman v. Georgia*, *Gregg v. Georgia*, and *Proffitt v. Florida* require states imposing the death penalty to "narrow the class of murderers subject to capital punishment"[51] through "specific and detailed guidance to the sentencer."[52]

Additionally, the Court stressed another Eighth Amendment principle. A court or legislature cannot prevent a sentencer from weighing mitigating factors regarding "any aspect of a defendant's character or record and any of the circumstances of the offense that the defendant proffers as a basis for a sentence less than death."[53]

Finally, in outlining the constitutional requirements for imposing the death penalty, the Court noted that a state may not impose the punishment if there is a national consensus that the punishment is disproportionate for a certain offense.[54] These principles laid the foundation for the Court's analysis of McCleskey's Eighth Amendment arguments.

Using these principles, the Court addressed McCleskey's two Eighth Amendment arguments. First, McCleskey argued that his punishment was disproportionate to sentences in other murder cases. But the Court reasoned that, in comparing his case

[47] Memorandum to the Conference from Justice Antonin Scalia of 6 Jan. 1987, at 1, McCleskey v. Kemp Case File, No. 811-6811, Basic File, Justice Lewis F. Powell Jr. Archives, Washington and Lee University, Lexington, VA, http://law2.wlu.edu/deptimages/powell%20archives/McCleskeyKempbasic.pdf (last visited June 26, 2019).
[48] *Id.* at 292.
[49] *Id.* at 297–98.
[50] McCleskey v. Kemp, 481 U.S. 279, 300 (1987) (quoting Trop v. Dulles, 356 U.S. 86, 101 (1958) (plurality opinion)).
[51] *Id.* at 303 (quoting Woodson v. North Carolina, 428 U.S. 280, 304 (1976) (plurality opinion)).
[52] *Id.* at 303–04 (quoting Proffitt v. Florida, 428 U.S. 242, 253 (1976) (joint opinion of Stewart, Powell, and Stevens, J.J.)).
[53] *Id.* at 304 (quoting Lockett v. Ohio, 438 U.S. 586, 604 (1978) (plurality opinion)).
[54] *Id.* at 305–06.

to other cases that did receive the death penalty, it could not find that his sentence was disproportionate. The Court stressed that, because it had previously upheld the procedures for imposing the death penalty in Georgia, it would assume his death sentence was not disproportionate under the Eighth Amendment.[55]

Second, McCleskey argued that, because racial factors may influence death penalty cases in Georgia, the state's death penalty system "is arbitrary and capricious *in application*, and therefore his sentence [was] excessive."[56] The Court conceded that "[a]pparent disparities in sentencing are an inevitable part of our criminal justice system."[57]

The Court then stressed that the capital punishment process featured the protections of the current Eighth Amendment requirements discussed above, as well as other constitutional procedural requirements designed to eliminate arbitrariness. For example, according to the Court, a capital jury plays an important role in protecting against racial discrimination. Thus, the Court stressed the importance of discretion, not only among jurors, but also among prosecutors.

While discretion may be misused, the Court explained that its "consistent rule has been that constitutional guarantees are met when 'the mode [for determining guilt or punishment] itself has been surrounded with safeguards to make it as fair as possible.'"[58] Thus, because of (1) procedural safeguards to minimize racial bias, (2) the value of jury trials, and (3) the benefits that defendants receive from discretion, the Court found no Eighth Amendment violation. It concluded, "the Baldus study does not demonstrate a constitutionally significant risk of racial bias affecting the Georgia capital sentencing process."[59]

Finally, the majority opinion raised two other "concerns" that affected its Eighth Amendment analysis. First, the Court feared that a ruling in favor of McCleskey would lead to a large number of similar Eighth Amendment claims for other punishments and for other discrepancies besides race. Second, the Court asserted that the racial evidence in the Baldus study would be better addressed by legislatures instead of by the Court applying the Eighth Amendment.[60]

Considering wide problems with mass incarceration and its disparate impact on people of color, one might understand the Court's fear that allowing a successful Eighth Amendment claim based upon race or other factors might bring down the entire criminal justice system. The majority feared the potential endless litigation that may have resulted from studies showing all of the disparities in capital

---

[55] *Id.* at 306–08.
[56] McCleskey v. Kemp, 481 U.S. 279, 308 (1987) (emphasis in original).
[57] *Id.* at 312.
[58] *Id.* at 313 (quoting Singer v. United States, 380 U.S. 24, 35 (1965)).
[59] *Id.* at 314.
[60] *Id.* at 315–19; *cf. id.* at 348–49 (Brennan, J., dissenting) (responding to the point about legislatures by arguing that it is the role of the Constitution to protect unpopular individuals when popular majorities do not).

Joseph, Bailey, National Geographic, Courtesy of the Supreme Court of the United States

sentencing, perhaps preventing anyone from ever being executed or any case from becoming final. Yet, the Court could have limited litigation and drawn lines due to the uniqueness both of the death penalty and the problem of racial prejudice in the country.[61]

Although a majority of the Court rejected McCleskey's Eighth Amendment arguments, four of the nine Justices dissented. Justice William Brennan addressed the Eighth Amendment analysis in a dissenting opinion that was joined by Justices Thurgood Marshall, Harry Blackmun, and John Paul Stevens.[62] The dissenters stressed that the Baldus study "reveals that the risk that race influenced McCleskey's sentence is intolerable by any imaginable standard."[63]

In his analysis, Justice Brennan recounted some of the findings of the Baldus study and the Court's past Eighth Amendment cases that did not require a defendant

[61] *See id.* at 339–40 (Brennan, J., dissenting) (asserting that the Court was ignoring "both the qualitatively different character of the death penalty and the particular repugnance of racial discrimination, considerations which may properly be taken into account in determining whether various punishments are 'cruel and unusual'").

[62] *McCleskey*, 481 U.S. at 325 (Brennan, J. dissenting); *see also id.* at 345 (Blackmun, J., dissenting) (addressing the equal protection claim in a separate dissenting opinion in the case).

[63] *Id.* at 325 (Brennan, J., dissenting). Justices Blackmun and Stevens joined Justice Brennan's opinion except for a short section where Justice Brennan stated his belief that the death penalty violated the Eighth and Fourteenth Amendments in all cases. *See id.* at 320–21.

to show arbitrariness in an individual case. "We have required instead that they establish that the system under which they were sentenced posed a significant risk of such an occurrence,"[64] he stated. The dissenters saw such a showing here from the Baldus study.

For additional support, Justice Brennan evaluated the study's findings in light of Georgia's history. For example, he discussed Georgia's history of differentiating crimes and punishments based upon race. Weighing all the evidence, he reasoned that "sentencing data, history, and experience all counsel that Georgia has provided insufficient assurance of the heightened rationality we have required in order to take a human life."[65]

Thus, in *McCleskey v. Kemp*, the Supreme Court did not outright reject that the Eighth Amendment may be violated when a punishment is applied in a racially discriminatory way. But the majority concluded that the Baldus study failed to support such a conclusion under the existing capital punishment system. The Court gave great weight to the belief that the criminal justice system was set up in a way to minimize arbitrariness and discrimination. As such, it found that the detailed statistical analysis did not demonstrate a constitutionally significant risk of racial bias in the system. Importantly, and disturbingly for many Court observers, the Court accepted not only that discretion is part of the system, but also that such discretion inevitably leads to apparent disparities.[66]

RACIAL BIAS AND THE BAN ON CRUEL AND UNUSUAL PUNISHMENTS AFTER *MCCLESKEY V. KEMP*

The U.S. Supreme Court has not directly addressed any Eighth Amendment challenges based upon race after its decision in *McCleskey v. Kemp*. Many years later, though, Justice Powell, who wrote the majority opinion in that case, was asked by his biographer if he had regretted any of his decisions. The retired Justice Powell stated that he regretted his decision in *McCleskey* and had come to believe that the death penalty should be abolished.[67] Had he come to that view earlier, the Court might have found that the racial discrimination demonstrated in *McCleskey* violated the Eighth Amendment.

Many commentators have been critical of the Court's decision in *McCleskey*. Anthony Amsterdam, a prominent capital defense attorney in several landmark decisions, called the *McCleskey* decision "the *Dred Scott* decision of our time."[68]

---

[64] *Id.* at 324.

[65] *Id.* at 329, 335.

[66] *See, e.g.,* ELIZABETH HINTON, FROM THE WAR ON POVERTY TO THE WAR ON CRIME: THE MAKING OF MASS INCARCERATION IN AMERICA 326 (2016) (stating that the *McCleskey* ruling resulted in allowing racial bias and profiling in various areas of the criminal justice system).

[67] *See* JOHN C. JEFFRIES JR., JUSTICE LEWIS F. POWELL, JR.: A BIOGRAPHY 451 (1994).

[68] Adam Liptak, *New Look at Death Sentences and Race,* N.Y. TIMES, Apr. 29, 2008.

Professor Sheri Lynn Johnson called the decision "shocking."[69] Another attorney has stated that the Court "ignored racism hidden in plain sight."[70]

Because the Supreme Court made it difficult for petitioners to successfully raise Eighth Amendment challenges based upon racial bias, and because lower courts must follow the Supreme Court's interpretation of the Eighth Amendment, some legislatures have attempted to address racial bias in sentencing in other ways. For example, the U.S. Congress considered but failed to pass a Racial Justice Act that would have barred the use of the death penalty where the punishment was applied in a racially disproportionate pattern, which could be shown by statistical proof.[71]

In contrast to the federal government, Kentucky and North Carolina did pass their own versions of the Racial Justice Act. Yet, so far, states' attempts to address the issues raised in *McCleskey* have met mixed success. Kentucky's 1998 law allowing the use of statistical evidence to show that a prosecutor engaged in purposeful discrimination still places a high burden on defendants.[72] By contrast, North Carolina's 2009 Racial Justice Act allowing courts to consider statistical evidence of racial disparities in death penalty cases did result in some reversals of death sentences. But, perhaps because the law was effective, state legislators subsequently watered it down and then in 2013 repealed it.[73]

Following the Baldus study, various studies in other states have found similar evidence of racial bias.[74] But despite the growing evidence of racial bias in criminal sentencing, the Court has not shown a desire to revisit its Eighth Amendment analysis. And lower courts continue to reject racial bias claims because of *McCleskey*.[75]

One may wonder how the Supreme Court may address future Eighth Amendment challenges based upon the continuing development of new studies showing arbitrariness and racial bias in the sentencing system. Although the Court may continue to make it extremely difficult to bring Eighth Amendment challenges

---

[69] Sheri Lynn Johnson, *Unconscious Racism and the Criminal Law*, 73 CORNELL L. REV. 1016, 1016 (1998) (saying the decision was "shocking, but not surprising").

[70] Michael Mello, *Ivon Stanley and James Adams' America: Vectors of Racism in Capital Punishment*, 43 CRIM. L. BULL. 1 (Fall 2007).

[71] H.R. Rep. No. 103–458 (1994).

[72] KEN. STAT. ANN. Sec. 532.300 (1998).

[73] Matt Smith, *"Racial Justice Act" Repealed in North Carolina*, CNN (June 21, 2013), www.cnn .com/2013/06/20/justice/north-carolina-death-penalty/index.html.

[74] *See, e.g.*, KIRCHMEIER, supra note 1, at 310–15; John H. Blume & Lindsey S. Vann, *Forty Years of Death: The Past, Present, and Future of the Death Penalty in South Carolina (Still Arbitrary after All These Years)*, 11 DUKE J. CONST. L. & PUB. POL'Y 183, 196 (2016); Raymond Paternoster et al., *Justice by Geography and Race: The Administration of the Death Penalty in Maryland, 1978–1999*, 4 MD. L.J. RACE, RELIGION, GENDER & CLASS 1 (2004).

[75] *See, e.g.*, Taylor v. Simpson, No. CIV.A. 5:06-181-DCR, 2014 WL 4928925, at *112–13 (E.D. Ky. Sept. 20, 2014).

based upon such evidence, another alternative exists in the form of state constitutions, as shown by a recent decision of the Washington Supreme Court in *Washington v. Gregory.*[76]

In *Gregory*, defense lawyers presented the Washington Supreme Court with a detailed study of capital punishment in the state. Among the study's findings, according to the court, was that "black defendants were four and a half times more likely to be sentenced to death than similarly situated white defendants."[77] Attorneys argued that the study's findings revealed that the Washington death penalty was applied in an unconstitutional manner.

The Washington Supreme Court's decision finding the death penalty unconstitutional rested upon the Washington state constitution, not the U.S. Constitution. The relevant section of the Washington Constitution states, "Excessive bail shall not be required, excessive fines imposed, nor cruel punishments inflicted."[78] State constitutions may be interpreted more broadly than the U.S. Constitution, and the Washington Supreme Court did just that.[79]

So, the Washington Supreme Court, not bound by *McCleskey*, evaluated statistical evidence to conclude that the state's death penalty was administered in an arbitrary and racially biased manner. And because the death penalty was applied in that way, the death penalty also failed to serve penological goals of retribution and deterrence. Thus, the court found the death penalty as administered was a "cruel punishment" in violation of the state constitution. The court explained that it was not holding that the death penalty was per se unconstitutional, meaning that if the state were able to eliminate the racial bias and arbitrariness with a new law, that new law would not be unconstitutional.[80]

Unlike the U.S. Supreme Court, the Washington Supreme Court not only accepted a statistical study revealing racial bias in the administration of the death penalty, but it also took "judicial notice of implicit and overt racial bias against black defendants" in Washington.[81] Where the Supreme Court in *McCleskey* championed its prior decisions on race as reasons for believing that there were adequate procedural protections in place to thwart significant racial bias and thus an Eighth Amendment claim, the Washington Supreme Court came to the opposite conclusion. Citing decisions addressing racial bias in jury selection and prosecutor misconduct cases, the Washington court reasoned that those

---

[76] Washington v. Gregory, 427 P.3d 621 (Wash. 2018); *see* Katherine Beckett & Heather Evans, *The Role of Race in Washington State Capital Sentencing, 1981–2014* (Oct. 13, 2014), https://perma.cc/3THJ-989W.

[77] *Gregory*, 427 P.3d at 630.

[78] WASH. CONST. Art. I, §14 (West 2019).

[79] *Gregory*, 427 P.3d at 631–32.

[80] *Id.* at 633–37.

[81] *Id.* at 635.

decisions provided added support to the study's findings about the existence of racial discrimination.[82]

While the Washington Supreme Court decision was based upon a state constitution provision similar to the Eighth Amendment of the U.S. Constitution, the state court also interpreted the state provision in light of the "evolving standards of decency that mark the progress of a maturing society," just as the U.S. Supreme Court interprets the Eighth Amendment.[83] Thus, as society develops greater understanding about racial bias in the criminal justice system, the Supreme Court may be similarly open to reconsidering its Eighth Amendment analysis in *McCleskey* in light of evolving standards.

There has been a growth in understanding of the role that race plays in American life and in the criminal justice system in particular — especially how racism has contributed to problems of mass incarceration. Not only might the Court revisit its Eighth Amendment analysis in light of the racial impact of capital sentencing, but also it could use the Eighth Amendment to evaluate discriminatory sentencing that results in disproportionate prison populations.[84] Currently, though, courts generally find that claims related to non-capital sentencing and racial bias are better addressed under other constitutional amendments.[85]

CONCLUSION

Although for much of its history the Supreme Court has failed to address racial discrimination in the context of the Eighth Amendment, it clarified in *McCleskey* that racial discrimination in sentencing could possibly amount to a constitutional violation of the prohibition on "cruel and unusual punishments." But in that narrow decision, the Court also made it difficult for such claims to be successful.

Yet, because there is an opening for such claims, it is important to remember that the Eighth Amendment is interpreted in light of evolving standards of decency as society itself evolves. Thus, the Court can eventually evaluate the growing body of evidence of racial bias in the criminal justice system and reconsider its narrow holding on the Eighth Amendment.

Several former Supreme Court Justices and a number of states have reconsidered the arbitrariness of the modern death penalty. Often, part of the reason judges and legislators have reevaluated the death penalty is the recognition of the role that race

---

[82] *Id.* at 635 (citing, e.g., City of Seattle v. Erikson, 398 P.3d 1124 (2017)) (peremptory challenge); State v. Walker, 341 P.3d 976 (2015) (Gordon McCloud, J., concurring) (prosecutor's use of racially charged images).

[83] *Gregory*, 427 P.3d. at 635 (quoting State v. Fain, 617 P.2d 720, 725 (Wash. 1980) (quoting Trop v. Dulles, 356 U.S. 86, 101 (1958) (plurality opinion)).

[84] *See* Reed, *supra* note 6, at 240, 254, 257–61.

[85] *See, e.g.*, Hernandez v. Cate, 918 F. Supp. 2d 987, 1015 (C.D. Calif. 2013) (holding that a prisoner's claims of discrimination based on his ethnicity and Spanish surname should be raised under the Equal Protection Clause, not under the Eighth Amendment).

plays in society and in criminal justice.[86] For example, in addition to Justice Powell — the author of the majority opinion in *McCleskey* who ultimately changed his mind — two other Justices eventually changed their minds too. In 1994, Justice Blackmun announced that he believed the death penalty was unconstitutional in all cases. And in 2008, Justice Stevens also came to conclude that the death penalty is "patently excessive and cruel and unusual punishment violative of the Eighth Amendment."[87] In their opinions announcing their change in views, both Justices Blackmun and Stevens — who along with Powell had voted to uphold the death penalty in *Gregg v. Georgia* — referenced the Court's failed Eighth Amendment analysis of race.[88] Therefore, as the Court's Eighth Amendment analysis evolves, more Justices may fully come to recognize and address the ongoing damage caused by racial bias throughout our criminal justice system.

[86] *See, e.g.*, Kirchmeier, *supra* note 1, at 315–61 (discussing judges and legislators that have changed their positions on capital punishment); Kevin M. Barry, *The Law of Abolition*, 107 J. Crim. L. & Criminology 521, 553–54 (2017) (noting some judges who have raised concerns about the role of race in the use of the death penalty); William W. Berry III, *Repudiating Death*, 101 J. Crim. L. & Criminology 439 (2011) (exploring the shifts in views about the death penalty of Powell, Blackmun, and Stevens).

[87] *See* Baze v. Rees, 553 U.S. 35, 86 (2008) (Stevens, J., concurring); Callins v. Collins, 510 U.S. 1141, 1145, 1153 (1994) (Blackmun, J., dissenting from denial of petition of writ for certiorari).

[88] *Baze*, 553 U.S. at 83–86 (Stevens, J., concurring); *Callins*, 510 U.S. at 1153.

18

Science and the Eighth Amendment

Meghan J. Ryan[*]

As time hurtles forward, new science constantly emerges, and many scientific fields can shed light on whether a punishment is unconstitutionally cruel and unusual, or even on whether bail or fines are unconstitutionally excessive under the Eighth Amendment. In fact, in recent years, science has played an increasingly important role in the Court's Eighth Amendment jurisprudence. From the development of an offender's brain, to the composition of lethal injection drugs, even to measurements of pain, knowledge of various scientific fields is becoming central to understanding whether a punishment is unconstitutionally cruel and unusual. There are a number of limits to how the Court can weave science into its decisions, though. For example, relevant data are difficult to come by, as ethical limitations prevent a wide swath of focused research that could be useful in this arena. Further, the Justices' understandings of the complicated science that can help inform their Eighth Amendment decisions are limited. This chapter examines the relevance and limitations of science — both physical and social — in Eighth Amendment analyses.

EIGHTH AMENDMENT DOCTRINE

The Eighth Amendment's meaning and applications continually evolve. As the plurality in *Trop v. Dulles*[1] explained, "the words of the Amendment are not precise, and ... their scope is not static."[2] Instead, "[t]he Amendment must draw its meaning from the evolving standards of decency that mark the progress of a maturing society."[3] To measure the existing standards of decency at any particular point in time, courts have traditionally examined both objective and subjective indicia.

---

[*] Associate Dean for Research, Altshuler Distinguished Teaching Professor, and Professor of Law, SMU Dedman School of Law.

[1] 356 U.S. 86 (1958) (plurality opinion).

[2] *Id.* at 100–01.

[3] *Id.* at 101.

The primary objective indicium of decency is jurisdictions' legislation. In other words, how many jurisdictions have adopted the practice at issue, and how many have rejected it? Also relevant is how often juries and judges have actually imposed the punishment in practice. Occasionally, the Court has suggested that examining opinion polls, the opinions of professional organizations, and foreign law could also play into an objective assessment of a punishment under the Eighth Amendment.[4]

As for a subjective assessment of the current standards of decency, the Court has taken it upon itself to bring its own independent judgment to bear. In examining this question, the Court has primarily looked at whether the punishment serves retributive and deterrent purposes. For example, where offenders suffering from intellectual disabilities are facing capital punishment, the Court has found that they are less culpable and less deterrable than other individuals without intellectual disabilities, rendering them ineligible for the ultimate punishment.[5] In more recent cases, though, the Court has examined other considerations, such as whether the punishment serves the goal of rehabilitation. In *Graham v. Florida*,[6] for example, the Court found that it is unconstitutional to impose the punishment of life without the possibility of parole (LWOP) on juvenile offenders who committed non-homicide offenses in large part because "the penalty forswears altogether the rehabilitative ideal."[7]

Over time, the Court's interpretation of the Eighth Amendment has changed, just as the plurality dictated in *Trop*. Jurisdictions' laws change with citizens' and lawmakers' views of punishment.[8] Perhaps the citizenry — whether influenced by religion, the media, politicians, or something else — have determined that a punishment is just too cruel to be imposed any longer. Or perhaps a jurisdiction has moved away from a particular punishment simply because it has proved to be too expensive — just as New Jersey abolished capital punishment in large part because of the exorbitant costs associated with it.[9] At the same time, the frequency with which sentencers impose a particular punishment can vary over time. Maybe the nature of offenses has shifted. Perhaps the values and identities of judges and juries have changed. Regardless, as the laws and sentences change, this shapes the meaning of the Eighth Amendment prohibition on cruel and unusual punishments.

---

[4]   *See* Atkins v. Virginia, 536 U.S. 304, 316 n.21 (2002).
[5]   *See generally id.*
[6]   560 U.S. 48 (2010).
[7]   *Id.* at 74.
[8]   In fact, many citizens' views on crime and punishment are cyclical in nature — at least with respect to certain types of offenses — rather than necessarily evolving toward more lenient treatment of the criminal behavior. *See* Meghan J. Ryan, *Taking Another Look at Second-Look Sentencing*, 81 BROOK. L. REV. 149, 163–65 (2015).
[9]   *See* N.J. DEATH PENALTY STUDY COMM'N, N.J. DEATH PENALTY STUDY COMM'N REP. (Jan. 2007), www.njleg.state.nj.us/committees/dpsc_final.pdf; Richard Williams, *The Expense of the Death Penalty Has Lawmakers Reconsidering an Old Debate*, NAT'L CONF. OF STATE LEGS. (July/Aug. 2011), www.ncsl.org/research/civil-and-criminal-justice/the-cost-of-punishment.aspx.

In addition to laws and sentences changing, the ways in which the Court applies its independent judgment changes as new Justices fill Supreme Court seats and even as long-term Justices' ideals change with greater experience. These fluctuations, too, shape the meaning of the Eighth Amendment.

Another important change agent is science. As more data about how jurisdictions implement punishments and how punishments affect offenders (and perhaps even other individuals)[10] become available, citizens', juries', and judges' opinions about punishment may change. If, for example, new neuroscientific evidence were to make clear that a criminal action were the result of a physical abnormality in one's brain rather than the product of an offender's free will, many individuals might find it unjust — even cruel and unusual—to punish that individual with as harsh of a sentence as would ordinarily apply, or perhaps even to punish that individual at all. Or, if it becomes clear based on new science that, for example, current methods of execution create a significant amount of excruciating pain that is avoidable by employing an alternative method, then current Eighth Amendment doctrine would suggest that the punishment is unconstitutional.[11]

SCIENCE, THE OFFENDER, AND PUNISHMENT

New science is likely to have an effect on punishments under the Eighth Amendment in at least two categories. First, this new information could provide insight on what types of offenders are eligible for particular punishments. Second, the information could spur innovations in punishment and also provide greater understanding about how punishments affect those being punished, which could bear on the acceptability of the punishments.

Offender Characteristics

The Supreme Court has long worried about how the state of one's mind relates to punishment. In *Ford v. Wainwright*,[12] the Court chronicled the history of the prohibition on executing "insane" persons, finding that "[t]he bar against executing a prisoner who has lost his sanity bears impressive historical credentials" and explaining that "the practice consistently has been branded 'savage and inhuman.'"[13] Perhaps not surprisingly, then, the *Ford* Court found that the Eighth Amendment

---

[10] *See generally* Meghan J. Ryan, *Proximate Retribution*, 48 HOUS. L. REV. 1049 (2012) (arguing that harms proximately caused by criminal wrongdoing should be considered in retribution-based sentencing).

[11] *See* Glossip v. Gross, 135 S. Ct. 2726, 2738 (2015) ("Our first ground for affirmance is based on petitioners' failure to satisfy their burden of establishing that any risk of harm was substantial when compared to a known and available alternative method of execution.").

[12] 477 U.S. 399 (1986).

[13] *Id.* at 406.

prohibits the practice. Although the historical reasons for the ban are not entirely clear, the Eighth Amendment prohibition is grounded in the idea that an offender should understand what is happening to him and why.[14] And "insanity" could very well prevent an offender from understanding the details of his execution and also why he is being put to death.

Over the years, the Court has expanded the classes of persons who are not eligible for certain punishments. For example, in *Atkins v. Virginia*[15] and *Roper v. Simmons*,[16] the Court held that intellectually disabled persons and juvenile offenders cannot constitutionally be executed. And in *Graham*, the Court held that sentencers cannot constitutionally impose LWOP on juvenile non-homicide offenders.[17]

In supporting these conclusions, the Court has relied on society's views of punishment through the measuring stick of the objective indicia of the standards of decency. It is not entirely clear why societal views of these punishments as related to these particular offenders changed, and, in fact, the Court has been accused of engaging in some creative accounting in concluding that a societal consensus had formed against these punishments. For example, in *Atkins*, Justice Scalia criticized the Court for "miraculously extract[ing] a 'national consensus' forbidding execution of the mentally retarded, from the fact that 18 States — less than *half* (47%) of the 38 States that permit capital punishment (for whom the issue exists) — have very recently enacted legislation barring execution of the mentally retarded."[18] He characterized this as "embarrassingly feeble evidence of 'consensus.'"[19] Despite any shortcomings in the Court's assessment of the objective indicia of decency in these cases, a majority of the Court found the relevant changes in legislation, sentencing, and the like sufficiently persuasive. The majority thus moved on to the subjective assessment of decency, which the dissenters suggested was actually driving the Court's conclusions in these cases anyway.

Indeed, the Court's views on the punishments in cases like *Atkins*, *Roper*, and *Graham* also had evolved such that the Court, in its own independent judgment, found the punishments unconstitutional. Some of this may be the result of shifting membership on the Court, but the Court (perhaps not surprisingly neglecting to

---

[14] *See* Panetti v. Quarterman, 551 U.S. 930, 957 (2007) (explaining that *Ford* prohibits executing offenders who do not understand the punishment imposed on them and why it was imposed); *Ford*, 477 U.S. at 417 ("It is no less abhorrent today than it has been for centuries to exact in penance the life of one whose mental illness prevents him from comprehending the reasons for the penalty or its implications.").

[15] 536 U.S. 304 (2002) (prohibiting the execution of intellectually disabled persons).

[16] 543 U.S. 551 (2005) (prohibiting the execution of juveniles).

[17] *See* Graham v. Florida, 560 U.S. 48 (2010).

[18] *Atkins*, 536 U.S. at 342 (Scalia, J., dissenting) (internal citations omitted); *see also, e.g., Roper*, 543 U.S. at 608 (Scalia, J., dissenting) (arguing that the Court "finds, on the flimsiest of grounds, that a national consensus . . . solidly exists" and stating that "[w]ords have no meaning if the views of less than 50% of death penalty States can constitute a national consensus").

[19] *See Atkins*, 536 U.S. at 344 (Scalia, J., dissenting).

acknowledge that Supreme Court decisions often follow popular opinion)[20] has explained the changes by outlining how the various punishments no longer serve the relevant punishment goals. For example, in *Roper* and *Atkins*, the Court described how executing juveniles and intellectually disabled persons does not serve the punishment goals supporting the death penalty. It does not serve deterrence goals because these persons are generally less deterrable than the average person, and it does not serve retributive goals because these persons are generally less culpable than the average offender. In *Graham*, the Court explained that imposing the punishment of LWOP on juvenile non-homicide offenders similarly does not serve retribution or deterrence goals. Further, it is incompatible with incapacitation, and, probably most importantly, undercuts rehabilitation because "[t]he penalty forswears altogether the rehabilitative ideal."[21] Certainly, new science did not establish that the purposes of punishment fail to support these particular punishments for these particular groups of offenders, but, by the time these cases were decided, there was evidence that these goals were weaker under these conditions. For example, deterrence theory depends on rational decision-making by would-be offenders, but, if these individuals' decision-making is impaired — as the science suggests is often true for juveniles and intellectually disabled persons — then the deterrence rationale for punishment would be diminished in these circumstances. Accordingly, changing understandings about punishments' effectiveness and offenders' competency, culpability, and deterrability can very well shift the Court's independent judgment about the constitutionality of a punishment.

New science can contribute to our understandings about when offenders are unable to perceive what is happening to them and why, the extent to which particular offenders are less culpable than others, how deterrable certain offenders are, and the effectiveness of rehabilitation efforts. In some of its most recent cases, the Court has turned to the realms of psychology and neuroscience to further support the notion that some persons should not be not be subjected to particular punishments.[22] For example, the Court's decision in *Roper* points to the "scientific and social studies" that illustrate juveniles' "lack of maturity" and "underdeveloped sense of responsibility."[23] It further refers to juveniles' particular "vulnerab[ility] or

---

[20] *See generally* BARRY FRIEDMAN, THE WILL OF THE PEOPLE: HOW PUBLIC OPINION HAS INFLUENCED THE SUPREME COURT AND SHAPED THE MEANING OF THE CONSTITUTION (2009); Meghan J. Ryan, *Justice Scalia's Bottom-Up Approach to Shaping the Law*, 25 WM. & MARY BILL RTS. J. 297, 317 (2016) ("There is evidence that the Court, at least to some extent, follows public opinion.").

[21] *Graham*, 560 U.S. at 74.

[22] *Cf.* Laurence Steinberg, *The Influence of Neuroscience on US Supreme Court Decisions About Adolescents' Criminal Culpability*, 14 NATURE NEUROSCI. 513, 513 (2013) ("References to neuroscience in the Supreme Court's thinking about adolescent culpability have become more frequent, just as neuroscience has become more influential in legal policy and practice more generally.").

[23] *Roper*, 543 U.S. at 569.

susceptib[ility] to negative influences and outside pressures,"[24] as well as the transitory, or unfixed, nature of their characters or personalities. These special juvenile characteristics established children as a unique class requiring greater scrutiny and rendered juveniles ineligible for capital punishment. In *Graham* and *Miller v. Alabama*,[25] the Court doubled down on its previous examination of juvenile brain development. In *Graham*, the Court explained that "developments in psychology and brain science continue to show fundamental differences between juvenile and adult minds," such as the continued maturation of parts of "the brain involved in behavior control."[26] And in *Miller*, the Court recited the facts underlying *Roper* and *Graham*, explaining that these "decisions rested not only on common sense — on what 'any parent knows' — but on science and social science as well."[27] Moreover, the *Miller* Court noted that "[t]he evidence ... indicate[d] that the science and social science supporting *Roper*'s and *Graham*'s conclusions ha[d] become even stronger."[28] This led the Court to conclude that, even though mandatory sentences other than the death penalty are generally constitutional, mandatorily imposed LWOP sentences are impermissible for juveniles.

Neuroscience, psychology, and other disciplines contributing to our understandings of competency, culpability, and deterrability often provide us with the possibility of individualized assessments, which can pose a challenge for existing Eighth Amendment doctrine. Although the Court has held that, at least to some extent, the Eighth Amendment requires individualized sentencing,[29] the Court has been hesitant to strike down mandatory sentencing outside the capital context and has generally found Eighth Amendment relief for petitioners in only a categorical manner. For example, the Court has exempted a number of classes of individuals from capital punishment, and it has exempted juveniles from LWOP sentences, but the Court has generally not found long sentences or the death penalty to violate the Eighth Amendment as applied to a particular individual who was not part of a special class.[30] Instead, as in *Atkins*, *Roper*, *Graham*, and *Miller*, the Court has exempted groups of offenders from punishments because of their class characteristics. This categorical approach to the Eighth Amendment could very well clash with the Court's embrace of individualized scientific evidence about competency, culpability, and deterrability. The tension between the categorical approach and the use of individualized scientific evidence is apparent in *Roper*, where, although the

---

[24] *Id.* at 569.
[25] 567 U.S. 460 (2012).
[26] *Graham*, 560 U.S. at 68.
[27] *Miller*, 567 U.S. at 471.
[28] *Id.* at 472 n.5.
[29] *See generally* Woodson v. North Carolina, 428 U.S. 280 (1976) (plurality opinion); Ch. 4.
[30] The Court has, however, exempted certain offenses from death penalty eligibility. *See, e.g.,* Kennedy v. Louisiana, 554 U.S. 407 (2008) (striking down capital punishment for the crime of child rape); Coker v. Georgia, 433 U.S. 584 (1977) (plurality opinion) (striking down capital punishment for the crime of adult rape).

Court exempted juveniles from capital punishment as a categorical matter, it acknowledged that this approach was subject to objections: "The qualities that distinguish juveniles from adults do not disappear when an individual turns 18. By the same token, some under 18 have already attained a level of maturity some adults will never reach."[31] Nevertheless, the Court explained, "a line must be drawn."[32] If the Court continues ushering neuroscience, psychology, and other disciplines capable of individualized assessments of competency, culpability, and deterrability into its decision-making and opinions, it will need to more squarely confront the tension between the possibilities of improved accuracy by way of individualized determinations and the Court's hesitancy to look at these issues on a case-by-case basis.

As a discipline, modern neuroscience is still in its infancy, and researchers have much to learn about brain development, abnormalities, and injuries. As we learn more about the human brain — how decisions are made and how brain capabilities and functions differ — this information could well be relevant to the competency, culpability, and deterrability concerns that the Court has expressed in its Eighth Amendment opinions. Some commentators are troubled by the possibility that, as we continue to learn more about our brains, we could very well discover that criminal actions generally correspond with physical changes or differences in the brain. Indeed, some of the science suggests that it is the physical brain, rather than free will or the mind, that causes our actions and thus criminal behavior. For example, in 1983, Benjamin Libet et al. reported on their study showing that subjects' brain activity associated with movement occurred several hundred milliseconds before they reported intending those movements.[33] This finding was interpreted to prove that there is no free will — that the brain, rather than the mind, caused the movement.[34] The study and its conclusions have since been roundly criticized, but this question about the existence and extent of free will remains. More recently, neuroscientists have been studying prisoners' brains using functional magnetic resonance imaging (fMRI) and have found aberrant brain activity in "criminal psychopaths," suggesting that perhaps it was the offenders' brains, not

---

[31] Roper v. Simmons, 543 U.S. 551, 574 (2005).

[32] *Id.*

[33] *See* Benjamin Libet et al., *Time of Conscious Intention to Act in Relation to Onset of Cerebral Activity (Readiness-Potential): The Unconscious Initiation of a Freely Voluntary Act*, 106 BRAIN 623 (1983); *see also* Stephen J. Morse, *New Neuroscience, Old Problems, in* NEUROSCIENCE AND THE LAW: BRAIN, MIND, AND THE SCALES OF JUSTICE 169 (Brent Garland ed., 2004) (stating that "Libet's exceptionally creative and careful studies demonstrate that measurable electrical brain activity associated with intentional actions occurs about 550 milliseconds before the subject actually acts, and for about 350–400 milliseconds *before* the subject is consciously aware of the intention to act").

[34] *See* Libet et al., *supra* note 33, at 640–41 (suggesting that the evidence "would appear to introduce certain constraints on the potential of the individual for exerting conscious initiation and control over his voluntary acts").

their minds, that caused them to commit criminal acts.[35] Some commentators are concerned that this and similar findings could completely undermine the fundamental moral basis of criminal law that each of us has free will and should be held responsible for our actions.[36] Other commentators are less concerned, concluding that the causation issue to which neuroscience is relevant — whether the physical brain or rather free will caused the criminal behavior — is distinct from the responsibility issue on which the law is based.[37] These are different views stemming from science's suggestion that the culpability basis of criminal law may be eroding. But the science is not so clear. Often, neuroscientists' findings leave even a simpler causation question unanswered. We do not know whether the offenders' brains caused them to commit their crimes or, rather, whether the offenders' criminal activity or their time in prison caused the physical abnormalities in their brains. Without knowing the answer to this, and other related questions, the provocative science cannot shed too bright of a light on the legal questions, let alone answer them. In fact, science alone cannot answer these legal questions. Science is amoral. It can only provide us with additional factual information that one can use in deciding these very difficult legal questions.

The Characteristics of Punishment

Beyond assessing which groups of offenders are ineligible for particular punishments, the Court has also been concerned about the constitutionality of certain types and methods of punishment. For example, the *Trop* Court struck down the punishment of denationalization because, "more primitive than torture, ... [the punishment] destroys for the individual the political existence that was centuries in the development" — it strips the "expatriate [of his] right to have rights."[38] However, despite the fact that the punishment of death is generally thought to be more severe than denationalization — a reality acknowledged by the *Trop* majority[39] — the Court

---

[35] See Kent A. Kiehl, *A Cognitive Neuroscience Perspective on Psychopathy: Evidence for Paralimbic System Dysfunction*, 142 PSYCHIATRY RES. 107 (2006); *see also* John Seabrook, *Suffering Souls: The Search for the Roots of Psychopathy*, NEW YORKER, Nov. 1, 2008.

[36] See, e.g., Joshua Greene & Jonathan Cohen, *For the Law, Neuroscience Changes Nothing and Everything*, 359 PHIL. TRANS. R. SOC. LOND. B 1775 (2004) ("Cognitive neuroscience, by identifying the specific mechanisms responsible for behaviour, will vividly illustrate what until now could only be appreciated through esoteric theorizing: that there is something fishy about our ordinary conceptions of human action and responsibility, and that, as a result, the legal principles we have devised to reflect these conceptions may be flawed.").

[37] See, e.g., Morse, *supra* note 33, at 181 ("[U]nless neuroscience demonstrates that no one is capable of minimal rationality — a wildly implausible scenario — fundamental criteria for [legal] responsibility will be intact.").

[38] Trop v. Dulles, 356 U.S. 86, 101–02 (1958) (plurality opinion).

[39] See id. at 99 ("Since wartime desertion is punishable by death, there can be no argument that the penalty of denationalization is *excessive* in relation to the gravity of the crime." (emphasis added)).

has repeatedly refused to strike down capital punishment as unconstitutional.[40] This is a result of the punishment's entrenchment in both American history and the U.S. Constitution itself.[41]

The Court has commented on particular methods of execution, however. It has explained that methods of execution have generally evolved over time as states have applied new science and technology to create more humane punishments. At the time of the country's founding, hanging was the ordinary mode of carrying out executions. This method was thought to be "more humane than some of the punishments of the Old World," although "it was no guarantee of a quick and painless death."[42] Firing squads were also used during this time.[43] "Through much of the 19th century, States experimented with technological innovations aimed at making [executions — particularly hangings —] less painful."[44] Toward the end of the century, in seeking out "the most humane and practical method known to modern science," the State of New York settled on electrocution.[45] Several other states followed, also adopting electrocution. About half a century later, also perhaps in pursuit of "the most humane manner known to modern science," Nevada adopted a new method of execution: lethal gas.[46] Again, other states followed suit. Well into the twentieth century, states carried out their executions using a variety of these techniques, including hanging, firing squad, electrocution, and lethal gas. By the 1970s, though, there were concerns about the barbarity of various execution methods like electrocution and gas. Further, maintaining electric chairs and gas chambers had become expensive. Spurred by these considerations, an Oklahoma

---

[40] *See, e.g.,* Bucklew v. Precythe, 139 S. Ct. 1112, 1122 (2019) ("The Constitution allows capital punishment."); Glossip v. Gross, 135 S. Ct. 2726, 2732–33 (2015) ("[B]ecause it is settled that capital punishment is constitutional, it necessarily follows that there must be a constitutional means of carrying it out." [internal quotations and alterations omitted]); Baze v. Rees, 553 U.S. 35, 47 (2008) (plurality opinion) ("We begin with the principle, settled by *Gregg*, that capital punishment is constitutional."); Gregg v. Georgia, 428 U.S. 153, 169 (1976) (plurality opinion) ("We now hold that the punishment of death does not invariably violate the Constitution.").

[41] *See* U.S. CONST. amend. V (referencing "capital ... crime[s]"); *see also Glossip*, 135 S. Ct. at 2731 ("The death penalty was an accepted punishment at the time of the adoption of the Constitution and the Bill of Rights."); *Gregg*, 428 U.S. at 168–87.

[42] *Bucklew*, 139 S. Ct. at 1124.

[43] *See* Deborah W. Denno, *The Firing Squad As "A Known and Available Alternative Method of Execution" Post-Glossip*, 49 U. MICH. J.L. REFORM 749, 778 (2016) ("Along with hanging, the firing squad is this country's oldest method of execution.").

[44] *Bucklew*, 139 S. Ct. at 1124.

[45] *In re* Kemmler, 136 U.S. 436, 444 (1890). As Professor Deborah Denno has pointed out, though, "[c]ompelling evidence suggests that the [decision] was influenced heavily by a financial competition between Thomas Edison and George Westinghouse concerning whose current would dominate the electrical industry: Edison's DC current or Westinghouse's AC current." Deborah W. Denno, *When Legislatures Delegate Death: The Troubling Paradox Behind State Uses of Electrocution and Lethal Injection and What It Says about Us.*, 63 OHIO ST. L.J. 63, 72 (2002).

[46] State v. Jon, 211 P. 676, 682 (Nev. 1923).

state senator asked Dr. Jay Chapman, the state medical examiner, and Dr. Stanley Deutsch, the University of Oklahoma College of Medicine's Anesthesiology Department chairman, to investigate an intravenous method of execution.[47] Dr. Chapman and Dr. Deutsch then advised on the particular drugs to use, with Dr. Deutsch concluding that "[w]ithout question this is . . . extremely humane in comparison to either electrocution or execution by the inhalation of poisonous gases."[48] Based on this proposal, Oklahoma, and then other states, soon adopted lethal injection as their primary method of execution, and this remains the primary mode of execution in the United States today.

Thus far, the Court has not found any method of execution to violate the Eighth Amendment. The Court has stated that it has specifically upheld death by firing squad and electrocution, although close readings of the relevant cases create questions about the precedential value of these holdings.[49]

In recent years, the Court has focused on the cruelty involved in lethal injection.[50] Over the past decade or so, the Court has decided three cases on the topic. In *Baze v. Rees*,[51] the Court upheld the then-popular three-drug protocol — consisting of injecting the offender with sodium thiopental, then pancuronium bromide, and finally potassium chloride — for carrying out executions. In *Glossip v. Gross*,[52] the Court denied a preliminary injunction request to stop an execution using midazolam, rather than sodium thiopental, as the first drug in the three-drug protocol. And in *Bucklew v. Precythe*,[53] the Court upheld a single-drug lethal injection protocol using only the sedative pentobarbital.[54] In each of these cases, the Court has made clear that, at least today, the death penalty is generally a constitutional punishment. But there could be instances where the punishment is carried out in such a way that renders it

[47] *See* Denno, *supra* note 45, at 95; Josh Sanburn, *Creator of Lethal Injection Method: "I Don't See Anything That Is More Humane,"* TIME, May 15, 2014, https://time.com/101143/lethal-injection-creator-jay-chapman-botched-executions/.
[48] Denno, *supra* note 45, at 95 n.207 (quoting the February 29, 1977, letter from Senator Bill Dawson to Dr. Deutsch); Sanburn, *supra* note 47.
[49] *See Bucklew*, 139 S. Ct. at 1123–24 (referencing the In re *Kemmler* and *Wilkerson v. Utah* decisions); Denno, *supra* note 43, at 761–62 (suggesting that the Court did not uphold the methods of electrocution and firing squad under the Eighth Amendment in In re *Kemmler* and *Wilkerson v. Utah*).
[50] The Court and commentators often refer to the various "methods" of carrying out lethal injection. Because lethal injection is a "method" of execution, though, the various ways of carrying it out are perhaps better referred to as "techniques." *See* William W. Berry III & Meghan J. Ryan, *Cruel Techniques, Unusual Secrets*, 78 OHIO ST. L.J. 403, 411 (2017).
[51] 553 U.S. 35 (2008) (plurality opinion).
[52] 135 S. Ct. 2726 (2015).
[53] 139 S. Ct. 1112 (2019).
[54] *Bucklew* was actually an as-applied challenge to the execution protocol in question. *See generally id.* (explaining that Bucklew "accept[ed] . . . that the State's lethal injection protocol [was] constitutional in most applications" but argued that, "because of his unusual medical condition, . . . the protocol [was] unconstitutional as applied to him").

unconstitutional. In particular, the Court has been focused on the pain, or the risk of pain, involved in these executions.

The *Baze* plurality explained that, for a method of lethal injection to violate the Eighth Amendment, "there must be a substantial risk of serious harm" that is "objectively intolerable."[55] A petitioner could potentially establish this by suggesting an alternative method of execution — one that is "feasible, readily implemented, and ... significantly reduce[s] [the] substantial risk of severe pain."[56] Piggybacking on *Baze*, the *Glossip* Court explained that a petitioner may prevail on his claim that a method of execution is unconstitutional only if he can "establish[] that the State's lethal injection protocol creates a demonstrated risk of severe pain" and "that the risk is substantial when compared to the known and available alternatives."[57] The *Bucklew* Court pushed this even further, emphasizing that it is the petitioner's burden in every method-of-execution case to propose an alternative method of execution and clarifying that the petitioner also bears the burden of establishing that the alternative can be readily implemented.[58] Despite the state having already statutorily adopted the petitioner's proposed alternative of execution by lethal gas in *Bucklew*,[59] the Court concluded that the petitioner had failed this test because he had not provided details about the necessary concentration of the gas, its administration, and the like.[60] (Never mind that the state would have better access to this information, especially considering that Bucklew was in prison.[61])

As with the characteristics of an offender, like his competency or culpability, science can potentially tell us something about the pain associated with particular punishments. With respect to the death penalty, for example, science can potentially provide us with information about how the deadly drugs are administered, how they interact in a person's body, and even the meaning of a defendant's

---

[55] *Baze*, 553 U.S. at 50 (internal quotations omitted).

[56] *Id.* at 52 (opinion of Roberts, J.).

[57] *Glossip*, 135 S. Ct. at 2737 (quoting *Baze*, 553 U.S. at 51–52).

[58] See *Bucklew*, 139 S. Ct. at 1129.

[59] See MO. REV. STAT. § 546.720 (2007) ("The manner of inflicting the punishment of death shall be by the administration of lethal gas or by means of the administration of lethal injection."); *see also Bucklew*, 139 S. Ct. at 1142 (Breyer, J., dissenting) ("Bucklew identified as an alternative method of execution the use of nitrogen hypoxia, which is a form of execution by lethal gas. Missouri law permits the use of this method of execution. Three other States — Alabama, Mississippi, and Oklahoma — have specifically authorized nitrogen hypoxia as a method of execution." (internal citations omitted)).

[60] See *Glossip*, 135 S. Ct. at 2737; *see also* Garrett Epps, *Unusual Cruelty at the Supreme Court*, ATLANTIC, Apr. 4, 2019, www.theatlantic.com/ideas/archive/2019/04/bucklew-v-precythe-supreme-court-turns-cruelty/586471/ (criticizing the *Bucklew* Court for placing this burden on the petitioner).

[61] See Epps, *supra* note 60 ("This seems like a questionable assignment of the burden — an indigent inmate, locked 24 hours a day in a solitary cell, has fewer means of acquiring information than the state does."); *cf.* Berry & Ryan, *supra* note 50, at 427 (making this same point regarding the burden of establishing a substantial risk of serious harm).

outward reactions to the drugs. In *Glossip*, the Court took something of an uncharacteristically deep dive into the state's use of midazolam as the first drug in its three-drug lethal injection protocol. It ultimately found that midazolam "can render a person insensate to pain" and was thus sufficient to meet Eighth Amendment requirements.[62] In reaching this conclusion, the majority emphasized that it owed deference to the district court and that the petitioner bore the burden to present evidence that midazolam (in the relevant dose) could not sufficiently render someone insensate to pain — at least so much so that the Eighth Amendment was violated. Even the *Glossip* Court recognized, though, that it lacked the expertise to properly assess the science in this arena. In fact, there is a pressing need for further scientific research and study about the interactions and effects of these drugs in humans.

Concentrating the Eighth Amendment analysis on pain poses several additional difficulties. First, we currently do not have a good way to measure pain. And, even if we did, at what point would a particular amount of pain — or the risk of that pain — become so severe that Eighth Amendment protection is warranted? And is it an individual's subjective experience of pain or an objective measure of pain that matters in the Eighth Amendment calculus? Indeed, one individual may suffer significant pain as a result of the same treatment that causes very little pain to someone else. Although we know little about pain, we do know — from experience — that pain is subjective.

Neuroscience could have a role to play here. Although we are still waiting on even more robust useful information in this area, the field could have much to say about how much pain an individual is experiencing. Through measuring blood-oxygen levels in different parts of the brain, which experts correlate with neural activity,[63] fMRI could reveal how different punishments activate different parts of the brain and the level of intensity involved. Research into the "pain center" of the brain, which at least one expert has pinpointed as the dorsal posterior insula,[64] could help experts assess and scale this pain. Of course, difficulties with this project abound. For example, does increased activity in this part of the brain indicate increased pain or, rather, could a lower level of activity suggest that the subject has become conditioned to pain and thus the pain does not register as well in the dorsal posterior insula or other areas of the brain? Again, questions also arise about whether a particular offender's pain matters or whether the average pain of an individual subjected to a punishment should be what counts.

---

[62] *Glossip*, 135 S. Ct. at 2741.

[63] *See* Owen D. Jones et. al., *Brain Imaging for Legal Thinkers: A Guide for the Perplexed*, 2009 STAN. TECH. L. REV. 5, 17 (2009).

[64] *See* Andrew R. Segerdahl et al., *The Dorsal Posterior Insula Subserves a Fundamental Role in Human Pain*, 18 NATURE NEUROSCI. 499–500 (2015). *But see* Karen D. Davis et al., *Evidence against Pain Specificity in the Dorsal Posterior Insula*, F1000RESEARCH (2016), https://www.ncbi .nlm.nih.gov/pmc/articles/PMC4566284/.

Another problem with the Court's focus on pain in its method-of-execution cases is related to the multiple layers of secrecy shrouding today's executions.[65] First, in contrast to the historical public spectacle of executions, modern executions are generally kept hidden from the public. Only a small number of invited observers may be present. Second, states often refuse to disclose the identities of their executioners, the drugs used to carry out lethal injections, and the manufacturers of those drugs. Third, where states still use a paralytic in their execution protocols, this drug hides the effects of the lethal cocktail on the person being executed by preventing the individual from screaming or writhing like might otherwise occur. These many layers of secrecy work to inhibit further understanding about the painful effects of the lethal injection protocol, as well as the associated risks of causing pain, that could result from an executioner's lack of skill or experience, sloppy manufacturing practices and loose governing regulations, or the potency of the drugs themselves.

Certainly, more information related to the particulars of execution methods and techniques is important to providing content to the Court's standards set forth in *Baze*, *Glossip*, and *Bucklew*, but obtaining reliable data is difficult in this area. There is not enough research on the bodily effects of the drugs and dosages used in lethal injections today. In part, there is not a significant market for deadly drugs used in humans that would drive research in this area. More importantly, though, there are significant ethical constraints on conducting this type of research. In most circumstances, one cannot ethically enroll human subjects to participate in a study about the extent to which injecting them with deadly drugs at lethal dosages causes pain. As additional executions are carried out using a particular technique, at least some data on the pain associated with these executions could multiply, but state secrecy related to executions will hamper this effect.

As with other areas of the law, injecting science into Eighth Amendment analyses can perhaps lead to more informed judgment about whether punishments — or even bail or fines — are unconstitutional. However, science can provide only the data and not conclusions about legal questions. As the Court attempts to buttress new Eighth Amendment decisions with science, it will have to confront additional difficult legal questions, particularly questions dealing with the objectivity versus subjectivity of brain structure and function, pharmacological effects in the body, and experiences of pain.

DATA AND STATISTICS

Beyond science related to the offenders and punishments themselves, perhaps the richest source for more informed Eighth Amendment decision-making lies in broader troves of data and statistical analyses of that data. In recent years, there has been an explosion in the government's and others' formal use of data to inform

---

[65] *See* Berry & Ryan, *supra* note 50, at 422–25 (outlining these layers of secrecy).

important decisions. For example, online platforms like Facebook and Google employ user data to target advertisements to individuals most likely to be interested in the product. The medical industry uses data to improve treatment outcomes. And judges in the criminal justice system often use data-powered algorithms to make more consistent decisions about bail, sentencing, and parole. Greater access to data and more prolific use of it could be used to help decide Eighth Amendment questions as well. For example, one could employ statistical analyses to conduct more robust studies about the deterrent value of various punishments. One could dig into data related to the effectiveness of rehabilitative efforts inside and outside of prisons. And better information about the role that prejudices — on race, sex, religion, ethnicity, or other factors — play in sentencing outcomes could help answer questions about whether punishments are imposed in an unconstitutionally arbitrary and capricious fashion.

Historically, though, the Court has not relied too heavily on data and statistics. In the Fourth Amendment context, for example, the Court generally does not look to data or statistics on popular conceptions of privacy when assessing the reasonableness of searches or seizures and, relatedly, "reasonable expectations of privacy."[66] In the Eighth Amendment context, the Court similarly has been hesitant to rely on data and statistics in its decision-making. To be sure, the Court often examines how many jurisdictions have accepted or rejected a practice in determining the constitutionality of a punishment, but several Justices and commentators have characterized the Court's state-counting in this regard as anything but scientific.[67] When invited to decide Eighth Amendment cases based on other types of data, the Court has been less hospitable to such an approach.[68]

In *McCleskey v. Kemp*,[69] the Court explained the shortcomings of statistics in establishing that the death penalty was applied in a discriminatory way such that it violated the Eighth or Fourteenth Amendments. When the petitioner alleged that his death sentence was imposed in a discriminatory fashion — because a statistical study showed, for example, "that black defendants, such as McCleskey, who kill white victims have the greatest likelihood of receiving the death penalty"[70] — the

---

[66] *See* Meghan J. Ryan, *Juries and the Criminal Constitution*, 65 ALA. L. REV. 849, 851, 867 (2014).

[67] *See, e.g.,* Roper v. Simmons, 543 U.S. 551, 608 (2005) (Scalia, J., dissenting) (referring to the Court's evidence regarding state counting as "flims[y]"); Meghan J. Ryan, *Does the Eighth Amendment Punishments Clause Prohibit Only Punishments That Are Both Cruel and Unusual?*, 87 WASH. U.L. REV. 567, 588 n.115 (2010) (noting "the Court's inconsistency in its counting practices"); Tom Stacy, *Cleaning Up the Eighth Amendment Mess*, 14 WM. & MARY BILL RTS. J. 475, 552 (2005) (referencing the Court's "creative jurisdiction counts"); *see also* *supra* text accompanying notes 18–19.

[68] *But see* CRAIG HANEY, DEATH BY DESIGN: CAPITAL PUNISHMENT AS A SOCIAL PSYCHOLOGICAL SYSTEM 10 (2005) (pointing out the prominent role of social science in the various Justices' opinions in *Furman v. Georgia*, 408 U.S. 238 (1972) [per curiam]).

[69] 481 U.S. 279 (1987).

[70] *Id.* at 311.

Court rejected the persuasive value of the statistical evidence.[71] It explained that the statistics failed to prove intent to discriminate, as they did not provide evidence of intent to discriminate in McCleskey's specific case. Although in some contexts the Court has allowed statistical evidence showing a pattern of discrimination to establish such intent, the *McCleskey* Court indicated that the capital context is different, because a uniquely composed jury, considering a variety of factors, makes each capital decision on an individualized basis. Accordingly, the Court concluded that "the application of an inference drawn from the general statistics to a specific decision in a trial and sentencing simply is not" dispositive in these cases.[72]

While these arguments might be relevant to the equal protection issue, one might have expected the statistical study in *McCleskey* to have greater impact on the Eighth Amendment decision, considering that, in *Furman v. Georgia*, the Court had struck down capital punishment as applied throughout the United States because it was imposed in an arbitrary and capricious manner.[73] Yet, when facing the Eighth Amendment question, the *McCleskey* Court again found the statistics unpersuasive. The Court explained that the cases resurrecting capital punishment after *Furman* allowed for, indeed even required, guided discretion for juries making capital sentencing decisions. Not only is some measure of discretion necessary in these cases, the Court continued, but also it is often advantageous for defendants. The Court pointed out that the statistical study did not "*prove* that race enters into any capital sentencing decisions or that race was a factor in McCleskey's particular case."[74] "At most," the Court said, "the ... study indicate[d] a discrepancy that appears to correlate with race."[75] The Court conceded that the statistics suggested "some risk of racial prejudice influencing a jury's decision in a criminal case."[76] However, the Court explained that such risks, as well as "[a]pparent disparities in sentencing," are inevitable where jury discretion is involved.[77] "The question," the Court said, "is at what point that risk becomes constitutionally unacceptable."[78] The Court found that this was not the case here, and it emphasized that the data did not demonstrate the type of "major systemic defects" that led to the Eighth Amendment

---

[71] For the purpose of its analysis, though, the *McCleskey* Court assumed that the statistical study at issue was methodologically sound. *See id.* at 291 n.7.

[72] *Id.* at 294.

[73] *See* DAVID L. FAIGMAN, LABORATORY OF JUSTICE: THE SUPREME COURT'S 200-YEAR STRUGGLE TO INTEGRATE SCIENCE AND THE LAW 259–60 (2004); *see also* Furman v. Georgia, 408 U.S. 238 (1972) (per curiam).

[74] *McCleskey*, 481 U.S. at 308.

[75] *Id.* at 312.

[76] *Id.* at 308.

[77] *Id.* at 312.

[78] *Id.* at 308–09. Moreover, in a later case, the Court reminded us that, even if statistics can provide insight to the risk of harm, the petitioner must also establish that the risk of harm is one that society will not tolerate — it is "so grave that it violates contemporary standards of decency." Helling v. McKinney, 509 U.S. 25, 36 (1993).

violation in *Furman*.[79] Moreover, accepting the petitioner's argument condemning the discretion that contributed to any disparities in sentencing would be "antithetical to the fundamental role of discretion in our criminal justice system," the Court said.[80] Adopting such a position could completely undermine the entire system.

Even though there has been a recent explosion of available criminal justice data — some that could perhaps inform Eighth Amendment decision-making — the Court has not rushed to embrace what statistical studies might suggest about various punishments and their constitutionality under the Eighth Amendment. Although this information could contribute to assessments about, for example, the true deterrence value of a punishment or the effect of a defendant's race on sentencing, it has had little direct impact thus far. Paying attention to these studies could potentially build the foundation for a more evidence-based Eighth Amendment jurisprudence, but of course understanding the many nuances and full implications of these studies poses a challenge. The Court will likely have to wrestle with such information and the challenges that come along with it sometime soon.

THE COURT'S COMPETENCY WITH SCIENCE

A significant hurdle to the Court's reliable and accurate use of science and data in its Eighth Amendment cases is the Justices' general lack of fluency with these materials. The Justices have historically had difficulty understanding some of the science-based issues that have been relevant in a handful of the cases before them. For example, in the 2010 case of *City of Ontario, California v. Quon*,[81] a couple of the Justices demonstrated their lack of understanding of pager and text technologies. In oral arguments addressing a civil rights complaint against the city wherein a police officer asserted that his department's review of his text messages violated the Fourth Amendment prohibition on unreasonable searches and seizures, the Justices asked several questions to better understand the technology.[82] Chief Justice Roberts asked: "Maybe — maybe everybody else knows this, but what is the difference between a pager and e-mail?"[83] Justice Kennedy asked what would happen if someone were to send a text message to an individual while he was texting with someone else: Does the individual have "a voice mail saying that your call is very important to us; we'll get back to you?"[84] These somewhat humorous questions take on a very serious tenor if a lack of understanding about science or technology can affect life-and-death decisions as is often the case in the Eighth Amendment context. For example,

---

[79] *Id.* at 313.

[80] *McCleskey*, 481 U.S. at 311.

[81] 560 U.S. 746 (2010).

[82] *See* Ryan, *supra* note 66, at 884 (relating some of the Justices' questions from oral argument).

[83] Transcript of Oral Argument at 29, Ontario v. Quon, 560 U.S. 746 (2010) (No. 08-1332), www .supremecourt.gov/oral_arguments/argument_transcripts/2009/08-1332.pdf.

[84] *Id.* at 44.

Justice Powell — the author of the *McCleskey* opinion — admitted to his biographer that he did not understand statistics very well.[85] And one commentator has said that "it [is] clear from [Justice Powell's] opinions that he had no interest in obtaining any [such understanding]."[86] Is it possible that, had Justice Powell and his colleagues better understood the statistical study introduced in that case, McCleskey's life would have been spared?[87] A lack of scientific competency by the Court leaves a disquieting fog about whether a better understanding of the science could have caused the Court to reach a different conclusion.

Even when the Court has given greater credence to the science, though — as in *Roper, Graham,* and *Miller,* where the Court relied on psychology and neuroscience — there are still questions about the appropriateness of the Court's actions. For example, in *Roper,* Justice Scalia pointed out that the majority relied on "scientific and sociological studies, picking and choosing those that support[ed] its position," but "[i]t never explain[ed] why those particular studies are methodologically sound," and "none [of them] was ever entered into evidence or tested in an adversarial proceeding."[88] And in *Graham,* Justice Thomas, while not entirely convinced that the Court's reliance on "developments in psychology and brain science" was appropriate, accused the Court of "misstat[ing] the data on which it relie[d]."[89] Further, he explained that scientific evidence does not support the *moral* conclusion that forms the Court's independent judgment. Whether a lack of competency with science could cause the Justices to overlook relevant information or whether it might steer the Court in the wrong direction, a lack of scientific understanding could lead to questionable or even erroneous Eighth Amendment outcomes.

Perhaps the biggest effect of the Justices' lack of competency and resulting lack of confidence with science is its regular deference to state legislatures and lower courts on these scientific matters. With regard to insanity and intellectual disability, for example, the Court has historically left it to the various jurisdictions to define these terms, leaving the Court's determinations that insane and intellectually disabled persons cannot constitutionally be executed as hollower promises than they could be. The Court has somewhat rectified this possible misstep in recent cases, though, outlining some minimal requirements at least for jurisdictions' definitions of intellectual disability.[90] Another example of the Court providing significant deference to lower courts can be seen in the *Glossip* decision's reliance on the district court's assessment of whether the use of midazolam in its three-drug lethal injection

---

[85] *See* FAIGMAN, *supra* note 73, at 258.

[86] *Id.*

[87] Later in his life, Justice Powell explained that, if he could change his decision in just one opinion, it would be in the *McCleskey* decision because he "ha[d] come to think that capital punishment should be abolished." JOHN C. JEFFRIES, JR., JUSTICE LEWIS F. POWELL, JR. 451–52 (1994).

[88] Roper v. Simmons, 543 U.S. 551, 616–17 (2005) (Scalia, J., dissenting).

[89] Graham v. Florida, 560 U.S. 48, 117 (2010) (Thomas, J., dissenting).

[90] *See, e.g.,* Moore v. Texas, 137 S. Ct. 1039 (2017); Hall v. Florida, 572 U.S. 701 (2014).

cocktail created a substantial risk of severe pain. The Court justified this deference not only by the standard of review generally accorded to lower court factual determinations but also by explaining that "federal courts should not embroil themselves in ongoing scientific controversies beyond their expertise."[91] Unfortunately for the petitioner, this also led the Court to require the *petitioner* to bear the burden of establishing a substantial risk of severe pain.[92] Overall, this deference to legislatures on the science underlying the Court's Eighth Amendment decisions creates concerns about a lack of uniformity in some Eighth Amendment baseline for punishments and also the risk of the Court creating powerful precedential case law based upon erroneous fact-finding.

A CHANGING LANDSCAPE

The Eighth Amendment landscape is ripe for change. As the Court has made clear, the meaning of the Amendment shifts as society evolves. And society is regularly undergoing significant transformation, especially today when advances in science and technology are accelerating at an astonishing pace. Science and the information it produces can create change by facilitating greater understanding of offenders and punishments and also by affecting the mechanics of punishment practices. Further, science can help measure societal change. Fully understanding the changes that science precipitates, or even measures, is a challenge. Generally untrained in the various scientific disciplines, the Supreme Court Justices, and judges in general, are confronted with the difficult task of attempting to understand this new information and its implications for important questions like the constitutionality of bail, fines, and punishments under the Eighth Amendment. Although the Court has not, in recent years, squarely faced a head-on challenge with data like it did in *McCleskey*, our dynamic societal landscape and changing punishment practices may require the Court to more directly wrestle with these knotty issues sometime in the near future.

---

[91] Glossip v. Gross, 135 S. Ct. 2726, 2740 (2015); *see also* Baze v. Rees, 553 U.S. 35, 51 (2008) (plurality opinion) (referring to the problem of "embroil[ing] the courts in ongoing scientific controversies beyond their expertise").

[92] *See Glossip*, 135 S. Ct. at 2740.

Index

THE GOLDSMITH'S DAUGHTER

*Another intriuging historical mystery
featuring Roger the Chapman*

Richard, Duke of Gloucester, is determined
to save one brother, George, from being put
to death by the other, Edward IV, King of
England. Roger Chapman must act quickly
and, in a complex case like this one, and
with the pressure of Richard of Gloucester
upon him, he can't simply rely on his intuition.

THE GOLDSMITH'S
DAUGHTER

THE GOLDSMITH'S DAUGHTER

Kate Sedley

Severn House Large Print
London & New York

This first large print edition published in Great Britain 2002 by
SEVERN HOUSE LARGE PRINT BOOKS LTD of
9-15, High Street, Sutton, Surrey, SM1 1DF.
First world regular print edition published 2001 by
Severn House Publishers, London and New York.
This first large print edition published in the USA 2002 by
SEVERN HOUSE PUBLISHERS INC., of
595 Madison Avenue, New York, NY 10022

British Library Cataloguing in Publication Data

Sedley, Kate
    The goldsmith's daughter. - Large print ed.
    1. Roger the Chapman (Fictitious character) - Fiction
    2. Peddlers and peddling - England - Fiction.
    3. Monks - Fiction
    4. England - Social life and customs - 1066-1485 - Fiction
    5. Detective and mystery stories
    6. Large type books
    I. Title
    823.9'14 [F]

    ISBN 0-7278-7131-5

Printed and bound in Great Britain by
MPG Books Ltd, Bodmin, Cornwall.

One

In a long life, it has seemed to me that there are two things which excite the popular imagination above all others. The first is a royal wedding, the second, a royal scandal; and just before Christmas of the year of Our Lord, 1477, information reached us in Bristol that the country was shortly to be edified by both.

With my wife, Adela, and our two small children, Elizabeth and Nicholas, I was paying a Sabbath visit to the Redcliffe home of my erstwhile mother-in-law, Margaret Walker, when I first heard the news. We were all returning to her cottage from the nearby church of Saint Thomas, where we had stood, crowded cheek by jowl, with the rest of the weaving community for morning Mass, when we were overtaken by Jack Nym.

By trade, Jack was a carter and had, until six months earlier, worked mainly for the late Alderman Weaver, bringing bales of raw wool from the Cotswold pastures to the Redcliffe weaving sheds, or carting the finished cloth to its various destinations. But now that the alderman was dead, his looms and house sold, his wealth passed into the hands of his younger brother who lived in London, Jack Nym took work wherever he could find it, and had, he was pleased to inform us, but recently returned from delivering a cartload of merchandise to the capital.

'Yes,' he said, puffing out his skinny chest with pride, 'it was a very important order. Thirty ells of our special red Bristol cloth to be shared amongst the aldermen and guildsmen of London, so that they can replace the shabbiest of their gowns before the royal wedding.'

'What royal wedding?' Adela and Margaret demanded almost in one breath. 'Come inside, Jack, and take a cup of ale before you go home,' Margaret went on eagerly, unlocking her cottage door and holding it wide. 'And while you're refreshing yourself, you can tell us all about it.'

'Yes, please do,' urged Adela. Glancing round, she caught my mocking glance and had the grace to blush before tilting her chin and adding defiantly, 'We shall be most interested to hear your news.'

As she shepherded the children before her, I reflected that these first six months of my second marriage had been the happiest of my life. And I reflected, too, on how lucky we were that my three-year-old daughter and Adela's three-year-old son (Nicholas was the elder by just one month) were so fond of one another; were such good playmates in spite of their frequent disagreements. And fortune had also favoured us insofar as my wife was cousin to Margaret Walker, who had planned and worked for the match from the moment she knew that Adela had been widowed. Margaret, therefore, had experienced no difficulty in accepting Nicholas as her grandson, for neither woman had any other kinsfolk worthy of the name, and for that reason alone the blood-tie, though tenuous, was strong.

Once inside the cottage, Jack Nym sniffed the air, his nose twitching appreciatively at the rich smells of rabbit and herbs and newly baked bread. His goodwife, I seem to remember, was something of an invalid and not favourably disposed towards the cooking pot, so Jack was always hungry and accepted sustenance whenever and wherever it was offered. And once safely perched on the stool nearest the fire, he was happy to sample a plate of Margaret's honey cakes as an accompaniment to his mazer of ale.

'Now,' said the former, seating herself at one end of the long bench and taking Elizabeth on her lap, 'let's hear this news of yours, Jack. A royal wedding, eh? But who in God's name is to be married? I thought all members of the royal family were safely leg-shackled years ago.'

'It's the Duke of York. He's to be wed to the Lady Anne Mowbray, the late Duke of Norfolk's daughter,' Jack informed us thickly, through a mouthful of cake.

Margaret let out a screech that made Elizabeth jump like a startled hare. 'Little Prince Richard? But he's only a child,' she protested. 'He can't be more than four years old now, surely? Five, at the most. I remember distinctly that he was born the same year as the Duke of Gloucester's son, Prince Edward. I recollect saying to Goody Watkins at the time that the two brothers must be very close for each to name his son after the other.'

Jack Nym cleared his mouth with an effort. 'Ay, you're right,' he agreed. 'I overheard someone say that the Duke was only four years of age. And she – Lady Anne, that is – is six. Of course,' he continued knowledgeably, as befitted a man who visited the capital at regular intervals, and who was on more than a mere nodding acquaintance with London ways, 'they won't be living together for a long while yet. Not for years and years and years.'

'Then what's the point of marrying the poor little souls?' Margaret demanded indignantly. 'It could blight their lives if they should happen to grow up and fall in love with two other people.'

Jack Nym shrugged. 'It's the nobility's manner of doing things,' he answered vaguely. 'It's not for us to question why.'

'The late Duke of Norfolk was a very rich man,' I cut in, 'and I believe this girl is sole heiress to his fortune. The King would naturally be anxious to harness all that wealth to the Crown. Hence this marriage.'

'Well, I still think it's a wicked thing to do,' Margaret said severely, glancing down at Elizabeth, who was for once sitting quietly, docilely sucking her thumb. 'Imagine forcing this baby into marrying anyone!'

'When is the wedding to take place?' Adela asked from her seat on the opposite side of the table. 'Or don't you know, Jack?'

I looked round at her with narrowed eyes. There was a purposefulness in her tone that roused my suspicions.

'The fifteenth day of next month,' the carter answered promptly, anxious to dismiss any suggestion of ignorance on his part. He added for good measure, 'In Saint Stephen's Chapel at Westminster. Two days after the feast of Saint Hilary and the day before the Duke of Clarence is brought to trial in Westminster Hall.'

'Brought to trial!' I exclaimed, almost dropping my mazer of ale in astonishment.

11

'Duke George is being brought to trial?'

Jack nodded, pleased by my reaction to his news. To have captured my interest was, he plainly felt, a feather in his cap. 'That's right,' he said.

I leaned forward, compelling his attention. 'You're sure of this?' I urged.

'Of c-course I'm sure!' he spluttered. 'There's not much else being talked about in the London alehouses and taverns, I can tell you. Even the Duke of York's wedding, and the tournament that's to be held the following week, have taken second place – and a poor second place at that – to news of the trial. It seems that until recently no one thought that it would happen. Ever since last June, when the Duke was arrested and sent to the Tower, most people have been expecting to hear of his release.'

I nodded. 'I have, myself. The King has forgiven his brother so often in the past that there seems no reason why he shouldn't do so this time. I thought that imprisoning him in the Tower was just meant to frighten him.'

'Perhaps,' Adela suggested, 'the Duke will be acquitted. Or, if not, maybe King Edward will pardon him afterwards. This is to be a lesson not lightly forgotten.'

Jack Nym shrugged and finished his ale, wiping his mouth on the back of his hand.

'That's not the current opinion of the

12

Londoners. The feeling now is that the rift between the brothers is more serious than was realised; that the Woodvilles are baying for Clarence's blood, and refuse to be appeased this time.'

Margaret slid Elizabeth off her knees and rose to her feet. Taking her big ladle, she stirred the contents of the iron pot that hung above the fire, and the cottage was once more filled with the savoury smell of rabbit stew.

'Why would the King want to bring his brother to trial the day after his son's wedding?' she asked curiously. 'It's bound to throw a damper over the jollifications.'

'Probably,' I suggested, 'because most of the nobles will be in London for the wedding. It's the sensible thing to do, if you think about it carefully. It will save them all another journey later on.'

Margaret sat down again, looking around for Elizabeth, but my daughter had seized the opportunity to slither away to play with Nicholas. 'A strange business,' she remarked thoughtfully after a moment's silence. 'But the King wouldn't dare put his own brother to death, surely? Imagine the scandal! And what would be his mother's feelings, poor lady? You met her once, Roger. What is she like?'

I tried to conjure up a picture of that redoubtable dame, the Dowager Duchess of

York, as I had seen her six years ago in a room at Baynard's Castle, but the essence of her eluded me.

'I'd say that she's a very strong-minded woman,' I answered slowly, 'who has known a great deal of tragedy in her life. My guess would be that whatever happens, now or in the future, she will cope with her grief.'

Jack Nym was regarding me with sudden respect. 'I didn't know you'd ever met the Duchess Cicely, Chapman.'

'Oh yes! And the Duke of Clarence,' Margaret told him proudly, before I could prevent her. 'While the Duke of Gloucester is very nearly a bosom friend.'

'Mother,' I interrupted swiftly, 'you know that's not true. I've had the honour to do a service or two for Duke Richard in my time, but I assure you, Master Nym, there's nothing more to it than that.'

Adela, noting my discomfort, came to my rescue as she so often did. 'How I wish I could see this wedding,' she sighed. 'I've never been to London, and everyone who's been there says it's a wonderful place. I should love to go.'

Jack Nym turned to me. 'Why don't you take her, Chapman? I'm going that way again on the sixth day of January. I'm carting a load of soap to the Leadenhall for Master Avenel, and I'll gladly take you both along.'

14

Adela looked at me, her eyes alight with excitement, and I answered hastily, 'That would be impossible, I'm afraid. We have two young children to care for.'

'If that's all that's bothering you,' Margaret said at once, 'shut up your cottage and leave Elizabeth and Nicholas here with me. I shall be thankful for their company. It gets very lonely in the dead of winter, even though I do see you and Adela almost every day. And by your own admission, Roger, you've had a profitable season so far. Spend a little of your hard-earned money, my lad. Don't be miserly. You're only young once.'

'Mother,' I protested irritably, 'you've just said yourself that it's the dead of winter, with all the bad weather still to come. Do you think I'm so irresponsible that I'll allow my wife to go junketing about the country-side in...' I caught Adela's eye and pulled myself up short. 'In January?' I finished lamely.

For once in her life, Margaret Walker allowed her own needs to overrule her better judgement. So fond was she of the two children, and so desirous of some human company during the long dark evenings ahead, that she made light of a journey that she would normally have condemned as foolhardy, if not downright insane.

'Adela's a strong woman. Make sure you're both wrapped up warmly and you'll

15

come to no harm. After all,' she added with a conclusive gesture, 'you both walked from Hereford to Bristol at this same time last year, and carrying Nicholas as well.'

And that had also been her doing, I reflected. Margaret was quite ruthless when it came to getting her own way, as had been Lillis, her daughter, my first wife and Elizabeth's mother. And as was Adela, Margaret's cousin.

My wife smiled triumphantly at me as she began to make plans with Margaret and Jack Nym. I said nothing then, for I had given my promise to keep our secret until Adela should give me leave to speak; but that evening, in the privacy of our own cottage in Lewin's Mead, and as soon as the two children were in bed and fast asleep, I remonstrated with her.

'Adela, this idea of going to London is utterly foolish, and you know it. You're three months pregnant.'

She laughed and, rising briefly from her chair, kissed me lightly on the forehead.

'Who should know that better than I? But my early morning sickness has passed, and I feel as well as I have ever done in my life. Margaret's right, I'm strong in body. I always have been.'

'But the journey will be tiring,' I protested, 'even if we go all the way in Jack Nym's cart.'

16

She rested one elbow on the table between us, cupping her chin in her hand and regarding me with that faintly mocking stare that never failed to unnerve me.

'My dearest,' she said, 'while you are out peddling your wares each day, I clean the cottage, make the bed, cook the food, chop the kindling, fetch water from the well, go to the market. Above all, I deal with the tempers and tantrums, bickering and squabbling of two small children who constantly vie with one another for my attention. Have you never considered that all that might be much more tiring than a journey to London?'

I had to admit that such a thought had never occurred to me. Baking, sweeping, looking after home and children was the normal business of women; what God intended them for in His earthly scheme of things. I must have looked puzzled, for she laughed again – that deep, full-throated laugh that was so peculiarly hers – and came round the table to sit on my lap, entwining her arms about my neck.

'Master Nym has assured me that we shall travel at a steady pace, taking frequent rests. He knows all the religious houses along the route and says that we can take our pick of where to rest up. Roger, with *three* small children to look after in the future, this may well be my last chance to see London for many years to come.'

'But what about the return journey?' I asked, still determined to make difficulties if I could. 'And where shall we stay?'

'At a decent inn,' she answered with some asperity. 'I'm sure there are many such in London. Indeed, you've told me yourself that there are. What Margaret said is true. You've worked hard since you came back from Devon in the autumn. You've been out on the road every day from dawn to dusk, rain or shine, at a time of year when most pedlars use any excuse to remain under cover. We have a little savings in the hiding place under the floor, so we can afford to put up at an inn. And Jack Nym will bring us home again, he said so. I can see the wedding – and you can see the Duke of Clarence's trial.'

The witch had found my weak spot. She had known, of course, from the moment that the trial was mentioned, that I must be longing to attend. I knew both Clarence and the Duke of Gloucester, had spoken to them face to face, had served each of them to the best of my ability, the latter on more than one occasion. I had even been offered a position in his household.

My devotion to Richard of Gloucester, a young man with whom, according to my mother – God rest her soul! – I shared my birth day, the second day of October, 1452, was as great as that of any of those who served him personally. But I had never wanted to give up my freedom and independence of will, and so I had declined his proposal. Nevertheless, knowing his fierce loyalty to both his surviving brothers – *Loyauté me lie* was, appropriately, his motto – and his equally fierce hatred of the Woodvilles, I could only guess at what his feelings must be now that the long struggle for power between the King's family and the Queen's was nearing its climax. I suspected that, at what must be the bitterest moment of his life so far, he would need the prayers of all those friends who wished him well. (Was it presumptuous of me to consider myself his friend? I did not think so; nor did I believe that he would, either.)

'Well?' Adela asked, kissing me again. 'Are we to go or not? If you don't wish to stay at an inn, there are those friends you've mentioned so often, Philip and Jeanne Lamprey. Perhaps we could lodge with them.'

This time I was able to speak with decision. 'No, for unless fortune has favoured them since we last met, their cottage is too small to accommodate even one extra person, let alone two. We shall certainly call upon them, for they would never forgive me if I didn't take you to see them, but there is no question of being their guests.'

Adela pulled away from me a little, her

dark eyes glowing with excitement.

'Does this mean that we are to go to London? That you have agreed?'

I realised that I was now as eager to make the journey as she was, but I made one last, desperate stand on the side of common sense.

'Suppose the weather turns bad? We might be snowed in for weeks on the road.'

'Master Nym assures me that that isn't likely to happen,' my wife said, getting up and going to pour me some ale. 'I was questioning him while you were drawing water for Margaret, and he's adamant that it's as mild a winter as he can remember, and thinks it almost certain that it will remain that way. All the signs point to it, he says.' She put the overflowing beaker down on the table beside me and went to fetch a cloth to mop up the overspill. This done, she knelt down by my stool. 'Roger, my love, just this once let's take the risk. The children will be well cared for by Margaret. You know as well I do that we need have no fears for them. And when we're old and grey, I'd like to have something to look back on. When you're deaf and doddering around with a stick, when I'm bent double, when the children are grown up and beginning to treat us as though we're not safe to be out alone on the streets, we'll be able to laugh and say to each other, "Do you remember when we were young enough and mad enough to travel to London in the depths of winter with Jack Nym and his cartload of soap? Do you remember the wedding of the little Duke of York and the Lady Anne Mowbray? Do you remember the trial of the Duke of Clarence?"'

I knew I had lost the argument. I knew that, stupid and hare-brained as the adventure appeared, I was suddenly as committed to it as was Adela. I sighed and pulled her back on my lap.

'And when does Jack Nym think of returning?' I asked.

'He's hoping to stay long enough to see the wedding tournament on January the twenty-second. In the meantime, he intends to tout around for someone who needs a load transported back to Bristol.'

This, I calculated, meant at least a week in the capital, and I could not help wondering if our meagre savings were sufficient to support us for such a length of time. Then I reflected that if I took my pack with me, I could earn money by selling my goods. I had done it before in London on more than one occasion. I could do it again.

I smiled at Adela, putting up a hand to smooth her cheek. 'Don't look so worried. We'll go.'

The twelve days of Christmas were over,

and still the weather held, crisp and dry and bright.

Adela and I shut and locked our cottage in Lewin's Mead, warned our neighbours and the Brothers at Saint James's Priory that it would be standing empty for some weeks, took what few valuables we possessed, such as pots and pans and bedlinen, to Margaret Walker's for safety, saw the children happily ensconced in her tiny house and, on the sixth of January, not without some lingering misgivings on my part, set out for London, sitting up beside Jack Nym on the front board of his cart. Behind us, locked in by the tailboard, the crates of grey Bristol soap rattled and clattered and bumped.

I suppose I ought to have guessed what lay ahead, but for once I was lulled into a sense of false security. I presumed that God, if not sleeping, had forgotten me. He had, after all, a lot at present to keep Him busy elsewhere. It never occurred to me that He might have another job for me to do.

Two

Sometime around midday on the fourteenth of January, Jack Nym brought his cart to rest before the strange, wedge-shaped building of the Leadenhall, announcing with relief, 'Here we are at last.' Inside were innumerable market stalls, a granary, a wool store, a chapel in which Mass was celebrated every morning for the stallholders, and the great King's Beam, where goods were weighed and sealed by the customs men.

I knew from past experience that every sort of commodity was on offer within, from iron to cloth, lead to soap, food to second-hand clothing. And it was this last reflection, as well as a sense of obligation, that made me offer to assist Jack Nym to haul his crates of soap indoors.

Our nine-day journey had been uneventful, confounding all my prophecies of doom. The weather had stayed mainly fair with only two or three scattered showers of rain; and after Adela had taken Jack into her confidence regarding her condition, he had behaved with the greatest concern, making sure that at all the places where we found shelter along the route, she was treated with the highest degree of care and attention. Now, however, having reached our destination, we were to part – Jack, once he had made his delivery, retreating to a kinsman's alehouse in that insalubrious, riverside quarter of the city known as Petty Wales, whilst Adela and I had to seek out a cheap, but clean and comfortable inn.

This was partly the reason why I accompanied Jack into the Leadenhall, in the hope that it might be one of Philip Lamprey's days for serving behind his old-clothes stall in the market; for he, if anyone, could advise me where best to look. Adela had borne up remarkably well under the rigours of the journey, but I noticed that since passing through the Lud Gate, some half an hour earlier, she had begun to look pale and strained. No doubt she had thought herself fully accustomed to the noises, smells and heaving masses of a large city. But London had three or four times the number of people crowded within its walls than did Bristol. Furthermore, unless you knew what to expect, the continuous clamour of the bells, the constant, full-throated cries of the street traders and the deafening clatter of iron-rimmed wheels over cobbles could come as an unpleasant shock to the first-time visitor.

Added to all that, the stench of the gutters seemed to assault the nostrils far more pungently than it did at home. We were fortunate that, by the time of our arrival, the rakers had already done their early morning rounds, carting away the previous day's refuse either to the pits outside the various city gates or to the river, where boats were moored, waiting to ferry it out to sea. But the filth was already piling up again, and by nightfall the mounds of stinking rubbish would be just as high as they had ever been. Keeping the London streets clean, then as now, was a never ending struggle.

Inside the Leadenhall it was a little quieter than without, but not much. I seated Adela on an empty, upturned wooden box while I helped Jack to locate his buyers, two soap merchants who sold not only tablets of Bristol grey, but also both the expensive white Castilian sort and the cheap black liquid kind. Then, with Jack's instructions ringing in my ears – 'We meet again here, the day after the tournament, the twenty-third of January, around midday' – I went in search of Philip Lamprey.

I was lucky enough to find him almost immediately, haggling loudly with an elderly woman over a pair of tattered, particoloured hose which I should not have considered worth even the carrying home; or which, if I had, Adela would most certainly have consigned to the dust heap.

'Philip, you old rogue,' I said, putting an arm about his shoulders, 'surely you're not going to charge this poor soul for that disgusting old garment?'

He whipped round, a martial light in his eyes, but this faded as soon as he saw who it was that had addressed him.

'Roger, you great lump!' He threw his arms around me. 'What are you doing in London? But whatever the cause, I'm delighted to see you. And Jeanne will be as pleased as I am.' He turned to his customer. 'All right, mother, you can have 'em for nothing. Go on, put 'em away before I change my mind.'

He looked the same as ever, small and wiry with the thinning grey hair that made him appear older than his forty-four years. His voice still retained that rasping quality, which reminded me of iron filings being rubbed one against the other, and his weather-beaten skin was as heavily pock-marked as I remembered it. And when he moved, he still walked with the military gait he had acquired as a young man while soldiering in the Low Countries.

As soon as I had made him free of the reason for my being in the capital, and as soon as he understood that I had married again, nothing could stem the tide of his enthusiasm. He immediately shut up his stall, ignoring the line of waiting customers, and piled his unsold clothes into a basket to take back to his shop.

'Where is this wife of yours, then?' he demanded. 'Come along! Lead me to her and then you're both going home with me.' As I started to jib about his loss of trade, he slapped me on the back. 'Don't talk such blethering nonsense, man! Jeanne would never forgive me if I didn't bring you to see her right away.'

Jeanne Lamprey was indeed as pleased to see us as Philip had promised, and even more excited than her husband, if that were possible, at the news of my marriage. In the one room daub-and-wattle cottage behind their shop in the western approaches to Cornhill, she embraced us both fervently and plied us with meat, bread and ale, despite our assurances that we had eaten a good dinner at ten o'clock.

I could see that Adela, in spite of being forewarned by me what to expect, was at first somewhat taken aback by our hostess's youth and vitality. This little, bustling body, with the bright brown eyes and mop of unruly black curls, was, at that time, not yet twenty-one years of age and a most unlikely wife for someone like Philip. But she loved him deeply, ruled him with a rod of iron, had curbed his excessive drinking habits and pulled him up from penury and the gutter to be a respectable trader with a shop and a stall of his own.

Her unreserved pleasure at meeting me again I found touching, considering that the last time we had met, a year ago, I had placed Philip in danger of his life. But Jeanne Lamprey was not one to bear a grudge, and one of her many qualities was her loyalty to friends. She was also extremely observant, and within quarter of an hour of being introduced to Adela, had wormed her secret out of her.

'Well, I think you're very brave to journey all this way in your condition in winter,' she said, kissing my wife's cheek. 'But,' she added accusingly, turning on me, 'I can't understand Roger allowing you to do it.'

'You mustn't blame him. He was given no choice,' Adela answered quietly. 'I was determined to come. I'd never been to London and I badly wanted to see it. And I also wanted to see the little Duke of York's wedding.'

Philip expressed surprise that this news had reached us in Bristol as long ago as Christmas. 'But in that case,' he continued, 'you must also have heard that Clarence is about to be brought to trial. With one event following immediately after the other, it's difficult not to speak of both in the same breath.'

I acknowledged that we had heard, and for the next ten minutes or so he and I were engrossed in the inevitable speculation as to why King Edward had at last decided to take action against his troublesome brother – when he had forgiven him on so many former occasions.

'It's all very well people saying that he's just lost patience with the Duke,' Philip remarked, thoughtfully rubbing his chin, 'but it's my opinion that there's something more to it than that, although I doubt we'll ever get to the bottom of what that something is. However, I did hear one titbit of gossip that might have some bearing on the mystery. Yesterday, when I was over by the Moor Gate ... Which reminds me, Jeanne! Don't, as you value your purse, go anywhere in that direction. They're rebuilding and repairing stretches of the wall on either side of the gate, and the locals are out rattling their money boxes, waylaying anyone and everyone for contributions. But as the Common Council's already decided that each household has to pay fivepence a week towards the cost, I told 'em straight that I'd be damned if they got anything extra out of me, or out of any of my friends.'

He seemed inclined to brood darkly on this enormity until his attention was gently recalled by his wife.

'You were telling us what you heard yesterday, Philip, about the Duke of Clarence.'

'Oh ... Yes! Although it wasn't exactly to do with him.' Philip cleared his throat impressively. 'I was told that the Bishop of Bath and Wells had been arrested and imprisoned round about the same time as the Duke, but was released after paying a heavy fine. This man – the man I was talking to – seems to think that the two events might have some connection, although I honestly can't see why they should. But I was wondering if you'd heard anything in your part of the world, Roger?'

I shook my head. 'Not a whisper. It must have been a very brief imprisonment. But then, I reckon Robert Stillington's a man who'd buy his way out of trouble as quickly as possible. All the same,' I added slowly, 'your informant could have grounds for thinking there was a link between the two arrests.' And I told Philip of the meeting I had witnessed some eighteen months earlier between the Bishop and George of Clarence at Farleigh Castle.

We were all sitting around the Lampreys' table, and out of the corner of my right eye I saw Jeanne shift uneasily on her stool. Philip must have noticed it, too, because he laughed and said, 'You've always known too much for your own good, Roger, ever since

30

we first met, which is almost seven years ago now. You're a dangerous person to be around, as I've found out to my cost. So, if you're up to anything on this visit to London, we'd rather not be told.'

'He isn't, I promise you both,' Adela quickly reassured them. 'Our sole purpose is for me to see London, especially the Duke of York's wedding procession. And Roger would like to attend the Duke of Clarence's trial.'

'We'll all go to see the wedding,' Jeanne announced, clapping her hands together like a child suddenly proffered a treat. 'We'll shut up shop tomorrow and make it a holiday. But in the meantime, we must find somewhere for you to stay.' She glanced around at the cramped conditions of the tiny cottage before turning an apologetic face towards Adela and me. 'I only wish we could offer you a lodging here, but you can see how very little room we have.'

'We wouldn't dream of imposing on you,' my wife answered firmly. 'But we should be very grateful if you could suggest a decent inn that won't cost too much.'

'The Voyager!' Philip exclaimed suddenly, snapping his fingers. 'Its proper name is Saint Brendan the Voyager, and you'll find it not far from here, in a street called Bucklersbury. The landlord's name is Reynold Makepeace, and he has the reputation for fair dealing and for not overcharging his guests. Go to the Great Conduit, where The Poultry runs into West Cheap, and Bucklersbury is on your left, running down to the Walbrook. The Voyager's about halfway along, crammed in between all the grocers' and apothecaries' shops. Its sign is the saint in his coracle, perched on top of a huge sea snake.'

We thanked him and prepared to take our leave, not without protests from both our hosts. But I felt that the sooner we were settled, the happier I should be, so without more ado I picked up the big linen satchel in which we had brought a change of clothing and slung it over one shoulder. (I had not, after all, brought my pack, having been dared to do so on pain of my wife's deepest displeasure. And an unexpected gift of money from Margaret Walker had made it easier for me to comply with Adela's wishes.)

We left matters that if the Lampreys heard no more from us before nightfall, they could safely assume that we had been successful in finding lodgings at the Voyager, and that they would call for us there the following morning. Adela and I would spend the remainder of the short January day exploring the delights of West Cheap.

January the fifteenth dawned cold and grey,

with a dank mist rising slowly from the river. But the weather in no way dampened the spirits of the crowds gathered in the vicinity of the Chapel of Saint Stephen at Westminster.

My wife and I had been successful in finding lodgings at the Voyager in Bucklersbury, and had taken an immediate liking to the landlord. Reynold Makepeace was a short, stocky man of some fifty summers, with a large paunch, sparse brown hair, bright hazel eyes and surprisingly good teeth, who exuded warmth and friendliness; and he had offered us a small but cheap and clean room, opening off an outside gallery that ringed three sides of the inn's inner courtyard. The bed, which took up most of the space, had a goosefeather mattress and big, down-filled pillows, with the result that we had slept like logs and risen that morning refreshed both in body and spirit.

Mind you, we had been very tired, having spent the rest of yesterday's daylight hours as we had intended, exploring the delights of West Cheap. Adela had drunk at the Great Conduit, rebuilt and enlarged during King Edward's reign, its crystal-clear water piped in from the spring whose source is to be found in the fields around Paddington. Then we had given thanks for our safe arrival at the Church of Saint Mary-le-Bow, so called because of its underpinning of stone arches. And, finally, as we approached Saint Paul's, visible at the top of Lud Gate hill, its steeple crowned with a copper-gilt weathercock, we had feasted our eyes on the magnificent display of wares in the windows of the goldsmiths' shops.

I've heard it said that there are more goldsmiths' shops crowded together in West Cheap, and spilling over into neighbouring Gudrun and Foster Lanes, than there are in the whole of Milan, Rome and Venice put together. Whether this claim is justified or not I have no means of knowing, never having visited any of those three cities; but I do know that even on a dull January afternoon, our eyes were positively dazzled by the gleam of gold and silver, of precious and semi-precious gems. Rings, necklaces and brooches, ewers, mazers and plates, ornately decorated salt-cellars, chalices and candlesticks all glittered in the fading light.

Outside each shop had stood the apprentices, touting their masters' wares, but secretly, I suspected, longing for curfew and the chance to remove themselves and the merchandise indoors. One undersized lad with a shock of wavy brown hair, who seemed to have no companion, had given up even the pretence of attracting custom, and was leaning against the door jamb, idly watching the passers-by and yawning behind his hand. Adela, smiling sympathetically, had drawn my attention to him, and even as I followed her pointing finger, an elderly man, spectacles perched on the bridge of his nose, had leaned from an overhanging upstairs window and severely reprimanded the boy.

After that, we had had just time enough to walk along Paternoster Row, where the rosary makers have their shops, and where there are also one or two fine private houses, before the bells had rung for Vespers, and we had made part of the mass of people crowding into Saint Paul's. Even the lawyers, who daily conduct their business in the cloisters, had stopped advising or haranguing their clients in order to join in the service; although as soon as it was over, they returned eagerly to the business in hand. (Time, I have often heard it said, is money where the legal fraternity is concerned.)

Now, with a good night's rest behind us, and a breakfast of bacon collops and oatmeal cakes to warm our stomachs, we were outside Saint Stephen's Chapel awaiting the arrival of the bride and groom. True to their word, Philip and Jeanne Lamprey had called for us at the Voyager, and during our walk to Westminster, Adela had had her first good look at the Strand with its splendid dwellings, their gardens running down to the water's edge, and at the beautiful, if crumbling, Chère Reine Cross, that monument to the power of true love.

We had, fortunately, arrived early enough to position ourselves close to the main entrance to the chapel, and so had a clear view of the interior, ablaze with candles, the walls glowing with the rich reds and greens, purples and blues of tapestries. Jeanne, with womanly forethought, had brought a cushion, so that Adela, whenever she grew tired of standing, was able to sit down on the steps.

Jeanne could also enlighten us as to the identity of some of the guests and members of the royal family. The little Prince of Wales, she said, was not present, being, presumably, hard at work at his lessons in distant Ludlow Castle; but the magnificent gentleman just entering the chapel door was his guardian and uncle, Earl Rivers, the Queen's eldest brother. And behind him were the Queen's two sons by her first marriage, the Marquess of Dorset and *his* younger brother, Lord Richard Grey. And here were the four princesses, sisters of the groom. The eldest, Elizabeth, some eleven or twelve years old, was clutching the hand of the baby, Anne, and turning every now and then to frown at the other two – 'Mary and Cicely,' Jeanne hissed in Adela's ear – who showed a deplorable tendency to shuffle their feet and cough and admire one another's dresses in high-pitched, penetrating whispers, much to the amusement of the crowd.

There were many more guests, some of whom I remember clearly, and some of whom I cannot recollect at all. Amongst those I do recall are the little bride's mother, the Dowager Duchess of Norfolk, resplendent in violet cloth-of-gold, and the King's sister, Elizabeth, talking animatedly to her husband, the Duke of Suffolk. His heavy, surly features unexpectedly creased into a grin before they disappeared inside the chapel, the Earl of Lincoln, their eldest son, hard on their heels. The Duke of Buckingham was eye-catchingly attired in silver and green, and arrived in the company of Lord John Howard, a cousin of the Mowbrays (or so someone behind conveniently informed us). They were followed by a plump, but very pretty woman, in a gown and veil of pale blue sarcenet that defied the January cold, and which seemed to sparkle as she moved. At her appearance, a low murmur of disapproval rippled through the crowd.

'Who's that?' asked Adela.

'The King's chief mistress, Jane Shore,' was the prompt reply. 'The people don't care for her because she isn't noble. She was plain Jane Lambert, daughter of a London mercer, before she married a goldsmith by the name of William Shore. They say she first caught the King's eye on his return from France, two and a half years ago. And I've heard it rumoured,' Jeanne continued, warming to her theme, 'that the Marquess of Dorset and Lord Hastings – that was Lord Hastings who went in earlier, in the scarlet and black – are both extremely enamoured of her and are hoping that the King gets tired of her very soon.'

My wife's smiling face told me that she was enjoying her visit to London even more than she had expected to do. These intriguing glimpses into the lives of the royal family and the court made her feel part of a wider, less parochial world than the one she normally inhabited.

Next came a procession of guildsmen in all their fur-trimmed finery, followed by the Lord Mayor and his aldermen in their glory of scarlet hoods and gowns. And then a great fanfare of trumpets heralded the approach of the bride.

She walked, a small, upright figure between the Duke and Duchess of Gloucester, glancing coldly to right and left, seemingly finding it difficult to move, so weighed down was she by her gown of cloth-of-gold and a multitude of jewels. All I can remember of her expression was the look of blighting indifference she cast at the crowds. Not so the Duke and Duchess, who smiled and nodded and occasionally offered a hand to be kissed. But their greetings were mechanical, and I thought how haggard they both looked. Prince Richard's face, in particular, was pinched and lined with worry, its pallor accentuated by the rich crimson and purple of his wedding robes. Today, he must appear happy and joyful; but tomorrow, his brother would be brought to trial on a charge of high treason.

As the royal party drew nearer, I withdrew suddenly into the shadow of the chapel doorway, wishing that we had not placed ourselves to such advantage. I had no wish to be noticed by the Duke, previous encounters between us having invariably resulted in my undertaking some commission for him – commissions that had led me into personal danger. I therefore breathed a sigh of relief as he, together with the Duchess and the bride, passed into Saint Stephen's Chapel without seeing me.

And now here at last was the little bridegroom, flanked by the King and Queen, and looking every bit as indifferent as his future wife. Boredom was written large on a face that had not yet lost the dimpled curves of infancy, and as we all watched, he gave a tremendous yawn, not bothering to conceal it behind his hand. His mother said something to him sharply, and his face puckered as if he were about to cry. Only the sudden weight of the King's hand on his shoulder seemed to deter him, and he fought back the tears. I recollected Margaret's strictures on the marriage of two such young children, and my heart went out to them.

Mine, it appeared, was not the only one; for while we waited outside in the cold for the Nuptial Mass to be celebrated, the general buzz of conversation was of the iniquity of such a wedding. But then, as Jack Nym had argued, it was the nobility's way, and who were we to say it was wrong, so long as it had the sanction of the Church?

Suddenly the chapel doors were flung open, once more revealing the great cavern of warmth and light and colour, spilling out its radiance into the grey January morning. The bride and groom emerged, followed by the King and Queen and the Duke and Duchess of Gloucester. Two attendants advanced, carrying bowls of coins into which King and Duke dipped their hands, tossing a shower of gold to the waiting people.

Everyone was trying to catch as many coins as possible, and I, momentarily throwing caution to the wind, reached up with the rest. Because of my height, I towered over my neighbours and might have caught more than I did but for the fact that, glancing round, I found myself looking straight into the eyes of the Duke of Gloucester.

Three

I don't know what I expected from this exchange of glances; that Timothy Plummer would suddenly materialise at my elbow, perhaps, with orders that his master wished to see me without delay? Of course, no such thing happened: my lord of Gloucester's Spymaster General was nowhere to be seen.

Nevertheless, I could not shake off a feeling of uneasiness. The Duke's smile had been accompanied by a long, hard stare, and, in consequence, I was unable to enter into Adela and Jeanne's excitement at this sign of royal recognition. It was a source of congratulation, and of some self-importance, to the two women for quite a while after the newly-wed couple and their guests had vanished into Westminster Hall for the wedding feast. But I could see that Philip was unimpressed and shared my worry.

'You want to make yourself scarce, my lad,' he growled in my ear, as we made our way towards the cook shops, all of us hungry from the cold and ready for our dinner. 'The Duke of Gloucester's nothing

41

but a source of trouble where you're concerned.'

I nodded. 'The same idea has already occurred to me. But, on reflection, I believe we're both being over-cautious. He has too much on his mind at this present to think up any commissions for me to do. Tomorrow's trial of the Duke of Clarence must be weighing heavily on his mind. There can be no room in his thoughts for anything else.'

'You won't go to the trial, though, as you originally planned? You wouldn't be so foolish as to tempt fate in that way, now would you?' Philip urged.

'Oh ... I'll make sure I'm not noticed,' I answered evasively, loath to forgo my purpose.

Philip sighed heavily. 'In that case, I wash my hands of you,' he said.

We exchanged no further words on the subject, but my old friend's disapproval was plain.

We caught up with our wives at one of the many stalls selling hot meat pies and steaming ribs of beef, and Adela, now that we had a little extra money on account of the two gold coins I had managed to catch, wanted to try a dish of baked porpoise tongues, a delicacy that had not before come in her way. I dissuaded her, however.

'They may not agree with the child,' I suggested, patting her stomach.

42

Reluctantly, she agreed, and settled for a meat pie instead. But then, against my advice – or, maybe, because of it – she insisted on drinking a cup of hot, spiced ale to warm her. I thought it a mistake, but was wise enough to make no further protest. Adela was too independent a woman to be driven in any direction she did not wish to go, and must be allowed to learn her lessons in her own way. I did venture to mention that the Westminster alemongers put a liberal sprinkling of pepper in their beer, but my comment was ignored.

It was no great surprise to me, therefore, as the day wore on, and as we pushed and fought our way from stall to stall through the jostling holiday crowds, to note that Adela's face was contorted every now and then in spasms of discomfort. Eventually, it became obvious that she had lost all interest in the hats and ribbons, laces, shoes and petticoats, and in the hundred and one other goods being offered for sale, wanting nothing so much as to lie down and be quiet.

'I'm sorry,' she confessed at last, 'but I've the most terrible burning pain in my breast. It's the child, of course. You were right, Roger. I should have listened to you and not touched that ale.'

Jeanne Lamprey was immediately all concern, and she and Philip insisted on accompanying us nearly all the way to the Voyager in spite of our urging them to stay where they were.

'There's no good reason why we should spoil your holiday,' Adela protested.

But they would have none of it, persuading us, with, I believe, some truth, that they were tired and would be glad to return home.

'There are too many thieves and pickpockets about on these occasions,' Philip grumbled. 'A man's hard-earned money isn't safe.'

They went with us as far as the Great Conduit, where we parted company with mutual promises of seeing one another again within the next few days.

'And take my advice,' Philip whispered to me at parting. 'Don't go to Westminster Hall tomorrow.'

I went to bed worried about Adela, and with the idea of following his advice. But when, the next day, my wife declared herself so much better, and only wishful of a morning in bed in order to recover fully from yesterday's exertions, I found myself with time on my hands. The consequence was well-nigh inevitable.

Westminster Hall was crammed to suffocation, and there was not a seat to be had anywhere. Outside, the bitter January wind was whipping through the streets, making the assembled crowds blow on their red, chapped hands and stamp their feet in an effort to combat the cold. But, by arriving early, I had just managed to squeeze through the doors, and now stood at the back of the hall in company with two dozen or so equally determined curiosity seekers. I could already feel the prickle of sweat under my arms and down my spine.

Others were also suffering from the heat generated by this press of bodies. The Duke of Buckingham, appointed Lord High Steward for the occasion, was wiping his neck with a silken handkerchief, while the Duke of Suffolk's fleshy face was suffused with blood, looking like nothing so much as a piece of raw meat. But it was not simply the warmth that was making us sweat. There was another emotion abroad, ugly and dark; the expectation, the anticipation of death.

On some countenances, like that of the Duke of Gloucester, it took the semblance of fear; fear for the death of a loved one. On others, it reflected the shame that two brothers, one of them the King, should be about to rend each other in public. And on still others, as on the face of John Morton, Master of the Rolls, it had twisted itself into a look of greed for the skill and thrill of the chase and the final destruction of the quarry.

The sound of muted cheering heralded the arrival of King Edward; and as soon as he had taken his place on the central dais, the Duke of Clarence, who had earlier been brought by water to Westminster from the Tower, was led to the bar. I was shocked to see how thin and pale he had grown, but at the sight of his old arrogant, contemptuous smile, I guessed that however much his appearance might have altered, no real inward change had taken place.

The King gestured for the proceedings to begin, and the Chancellor, Thomas Rotherham, Archbishop of York, rose ponderously to his feet to deliver a sermon on – if my memory serves me aright – the subject of fidelity towards one's sovereign. When he had finished, he sat down again, drawing his episcopal robes about him, rather like a bird folding its wings after flight, and King Edward indicated that the Bill of Attainder should be read.

The Duke of Buckingham, whose task this was, was noticeably nervous, his breath catching in his throat on more than one occasion, and twice faltering almost to a stop. Finally, he had done, and a profound silence settled over the hall, broken only by the occasional cough or a shuffling of feet. The King waited, his steely gaze resting on first one face and then another, but nobody moved: everyone sat as though carved out of stone. At last, when it became apparent that no one was willing to continue the proceedings, he stood up himself, with a suddenness that made his neighbours jump.

Brother faced brother across the hall.

It began quietly, the King reproaching the Duke for his constant treachery and reminding him of his own constant forgiveness. The Duke answered, in a tone equally subdued, that a divided family had naturally resulted in divided loyalties; and as he spoke, he glanced towards the serried ranks of Woodvilles. There, said his look, was the real cause of the division between himself and his elder brother.

The King hesitated, then shifted his ground. Had he not always loved George and treated him well? Had he not given him more money and lands than any King of England had ever before bestowed upon a brother? Had he not made him one of the two richest men in the kingdom after himself? And how had the ungrateful George repaid him?

'By depriving me of my crown and driving me out of the country! Me! Your own flesh and blood!'

Clarence laughed at that, and I saw the Duke of Gloucester flinch from the sound. I could guess what he was thinking; that the Duke's last hope of throwing himself on the King's mercy had gone. And so it proved.

The polite, civilised masks were torn off and cast away. It was no longer brother and brother, no longer subject and overlord. It wasn't even man and man, but two animals, fanged and clawed.

'You are malicious, unnatural and loathsome!' shouted the King.

'And you are a bastard!' yelled the Duke. 'Hasn't our own mother more than once offered to prove you so?'

'Leave our mother's name out of this! Did you not unlawfully order the execution of the Widow Ankaret Twynyho?'

'And did you not retaliate by hanging Thomas Burdet, an innocent man?'

'He was not innocent! On your orders, he maligned the Queen and members of her family!'

Clarence's features were suddenly contorted into a barely recognisable mask of hatred. 'No one could malign that Devil's brood,' he all but screamed. 'Everyone knows that they indulge in the most extreme forms of all the black arts!'

The people in the hall were now avoiding one another's eyes, but glancing furtively every now and then at the Duke of Gloucester, where he sat staring at the ground and biting his underlip. Only the foreign envoys and ambassadors looked on with interest at the unedifying spectacle before them, storing up all the details for their royal masters in their next dispatches.

There was a momentary lull in this exchange of insults, while the two protagonists paused to draw breath. Then, in a torrent of foam-flecked words, the King began reciting all Clarence's many sins: his desertion to Warwick; his marriage to Warwick's elder daughter, Isabel Neville, without his brother's consent; his invocation of the statute of 1470 in order to lay claim to the throne; his attempt to marry Mary of Burgundy (a lady now safely the wife of Maximilian of Austria) until finally...

'I could have forgiven you all this,' the King roared, 'but for your last, malicious, more dastardly treason!'

An air of expectancy hung over Westminster Hall. This, surely, must be the moment we had all been waiting for; the moment when we should at last learn the truth; the real reason for the Duke of Clarence's indictment and trial. The charges which had been adduced so far were old tales: they did not account for the King's sudden decision to rid himself of his brother. A few of those present might believe that Edward had genuinely reached the end of his tether, but not very many. Most of us felt that some new and so far undisclosed treachery, something that struck at the very heart of his right to the throne, would now be revealed.

But then, suddenly, it was all over: I never

quite fathomed how. A flurry of half-sentences on the part of the King; a bewildered Duke of Buckingham pronouncing a verdict of 'Guilty'; warders closing in on their prisoner, leading him away from the bar, and it was finished.

Abruptly, the Duke of Gloucester was on his feet, shouting his brother's name. For a brief moment Clarence turned, looked steadily at him across the intervening space, raised one hand in farewell and then was lost to view amongst his guards. Prince Richard, his naturally pale face now the colour of parchment and seamed with sweat, sank back into his chair, sightlessly scanning the crowds at the back of the hall. But then his eyes suddenly focused themselves, and he half rose again from his seat. It was with a sinking heart that I realised he was looking directly at me.

'So,' exclaimed Philip Lamprey, 'Brother George was found guilty, but is not yet sentenced. There's time enough still for a reprieve.'

I shook my head. 'Somehow I don't think so. Not on this occasion. Unless you were there, you can't begin to comprehend the animosity – no, more than that, the sheer, unadulterated hatred – that flowed between those two. I can only liken it to a festering sore that one day bursts, letting out all the poison and pus that has been accumulating inside.'

'As bad as that, eh?' said Philip ruminatively, scratching his head. He had come that afternoon to seek me out at the Voyager to enquire on Jeanne's behalf after Adela's state of health, and to satisfy his own curiosity as to the outcome of the trial. 'For I knew that against all my good advice you'd be bound to go and see for yourself,' he had chided me. He added now, 'I trust you kept yourself well hidden and did nothing to attract my Lord of Gloucester's attention?'

'Nothing at all,' I answered truthfully, but being less than candid. 'And both the wedding and the trial now being safely over, Adela and I can spend our remaining days in London in a more leisurely fashion, and go where the fancy takes us. She has a desire to visit Leadenhall market again this afternoon, not having seen much of it the day before yesterday.'

'Then you must promise to have supper with us afterwards,' Philip insisted. When I demurred, knowing that hospitality did not come cheap, he said impatiently, 'Jeanne will be only too delighted to see you, and any information you can give her about the trial will be ample reward for such victuals as we can offer you.'

It was impossible to withstand such an invitation; and so, after browsing amongst

51

the stalls and shops of the Leadenhall, and after the purchase of a whip and top for Nicholas and a doll for Elizabeth, Adela and I walked up Bishop's Gate Street, eventually turning in amongst the narrow alleyways of Cornhill to the cottage behind the Lampreys' shop. There, we were afforded such a warm welcome that it was late into the evening, some hours after curfew and the closing of the city gates, before we returned to Bucklersbury.

We were met on the threshold of the Voyager by a perturbed Reynold Makepeace, who at once took my arm, drawing me to one side.

'There's a man here who says he must speak to you urgently,' he said in a low voice, trying to prevent his words from reaching Adela's straining ears. 'The man,' he added impressively, 'wears the Duke of Gloucester's livery.' Reynold's bright hazel eyes were round with curiosity and also with fear.

'Timothy Plummer!' I exclaimed disgustedly. 'What in Heaven does he want?'

'Did I hear my name mentioned?' asked a well-remembered voice, and, a second later, Timothy emerged from the landlord's private parlour, just to the right of the inn's front door.

'So it is you,' I sighed. 'For one blessed moment, I was praying I might be wrong.'

'That's not a very friendly greeting,' he reproached me. 'And you've been particularly hard to find. I was asking for a lone chapman. I didn't expect you to be in company with your wife.' His smile faded. 'And the cursed annoying thing is that you've been almost on the Duke's doorstep all along.'

'What do you mean by that?' I demanded irritably. 'We're a long way from Baynard's Castle.'

'We're not at Baynard's Castle,' Timothy snapped back, reverting, as he so often did when pomposity got the better of him, to lumping himself together with the Duke. 'We're staying at Crosby Place, in Bishop's Gate Street.'

As he spoke, I recalled the splendid house and garden Adela and I had passed earlier in the evening, on our way to the Lampreys' cottage. I had mentioned it, in the course of our conversation, to Philip, who had told me that it belonged to Sir John Crosby, an extremely rich wool merchant, who rented out the place to visiting dignitaries. Foreign ambassadors often resided there for a season. Both the French and Danish envoys had certainly done so. And now it appeared that the Duke of Gloucester had hired Crosby Place for the duration of his present unhappy stay in London. I had no idea whether or not Duchess Cicely was in the city; but if she were, I guessed that Duke Richard might feel he had enough sorrow to bear, without having to cope daily with his mother's grief as well.

'Am I to assume that His Grace the Duke of Gloucester wishes to see me?' I asked sarcastically, and incurred Timothy's immediate ill-will.

'I'm not out scouring London on a bitterly cold, windy, sleety January night for my own pleasure,' he rasped. 'Of course His Grace wants to see you.'

'What for? Did he say?'

'No, of course he didn't say! Nor did I ask him. It's not my place. You just come along with me and you'll find out soon enough.'

I put my arm around Adela. 'And what about my wife?'

Timothy raised his eyes to heaven. 'She'll have to stay here until you return. She's surely capable of doing so! She looks like a sensible woman. Which reminds me.' His eyes lit with a malicious pleasure. 'I rather fancied, when I saw you in Keyford last year, that you were after a different quarry.'

'A mistake on my part,' I answered serenely, thanking my lucky stars that I had told Adela all about Rowena Honeyman, and that I therefore had nothing to hide. 'But how did you know? I'm ready to swear I didn't say a word about the lady.'

'It's my job to know everything about

everyone,' Timothy replied curtly, disappointed that his barb had missed its mark.

This uncharacteristic spitefulness indicated to me something of his perturbed state of mind, and probably denoted the general anxiety and misery of the Duke's entire household. If the master were deeply unhappy, his servants would be, too.

I kissed Adela. 'I must go, sweetheart,' I said. 'I have no choice. Go to bed and get some rest. Are you all right, now? No more heartburn?'

She shook her head and kissed me back. 'Don't worry about me, Roger. I'm perfectly well, only a little tired.' She smiled up at me, but I could see the worry in her eyes. Lowering her voice, she added, 'Don't undertake anything dangerous. Promise me.'

I didn't feel that I could make any promises that I might be called upon to break, so I just kissed her again without making answer. Then, handing her over to the care of Reynold Makepeace and his wife, and roundly cursing my foolhardiness in going to Westminster Hall that morning, in defiance of Philip's advice and my own common sense, I wrapped my cloak more securely about me and instructed Timothy Plummer to lead the way.

There could not have been a more marked

contrast between the cold, dark street without, roofs and window panes drummed by the onset of a thin, lashing rain, and the great hall of Crosby Place.

The leaping flames of a huge fire burning on the hearth sent shadows flickering across the richly carved ceiling and the delicate tracery of the musicians' gallery. High walls and spacious, lofty windows spoke louder than words of the modern approach to building, and of the fortunes to be made in the wool trade. Sir John Crosby was a man of substance and intended that the world should know it.

The hall was empty except for two young people who were playing spillikins in front of the fire. The elder was a very pretty, dark-eyed girl some twelve or thirteen years of age, the younger a sturdy boy of about ten. It was nearly seven years since I had seen them last, but they were both instantly recognisable; the girl because she was so like her father, the boy on account of the strong resemblance he bore to his physically more powerful uncles, the King and the Duke of Clarence. These were Richard of Gloucester's two bastard children, the Lady Katherine and the Lord John Plantagenet.

They glanced up as Timothy Plummer and I entered, brushing the rain from our cloaks, smiled and then continued with their game. But within seconds, a large, comfortable-looking woman, who was plainly their nurse, bustled in and began to shepherd them away.

'Time for bed,' she said as they protested. 'You can play again tomorrow.' And she swept up the spillikins, dropping them into a capacious pocket. 'Make your courtesies to Master Plummer and the gentleman.'

But this they had already done without any prompting, and allowed themselves to be hustled through a door and out of our sight. I stored up the incident to relate later to Adela; a moment to treasure and remember in old age, when two scions of a royal Duke made obeisance to a common chapman.

When Adam delved and Eve span,
Who was then the gentleman?

Timothy indicated that I should take a seat near the fire while he went to find the Duke, but I preferred to stand. When he had disappeared through the same door as the children, I noticed how quiet it was. In a great household there was usually constant noise and movement, but today it was as if someone had died and everyone was already in mourning.

The door opened once again and Richard of Gloucester came in.

Four

He was wearing a long, green brocade robe, trimmed with sable, over hose and a shirt bleached so white that it made his skin appear the colour of old parchment. I thought that I had never seen him look so fragile. He had always been small of stature and of slight physique, two facts that belied the depth of his determination never to give in to the ill-health that had dogged him since he was a child; but that evening, he seemed sick in mind as well as body. The almost black hair and dark eyes were lacklustre, and his nervous habit of twisting the rings on his fingers more pronounced. We were the same age, twenty-six, but I felt myself to be many years younger than Richard of Gloucester.

He gave me his hand to kiss and sat down; then, bidding me be seated in a chair opposite his own, he smiled, and, as always, that smile revealed a different man, infusing his rather austere features with warmth and kindliness.

'Thank you for coming, Roger,' he said, although he must surely have expected me to obey his summons. An attendant entered, carrying a silver flagon and two crystal goblets which he placed on a small table at the Duke's elbow, before making a stately exit. 'Will you take some wine? This is an excellent malmsey, although a little too sweet for my taste, I must confess. My bro ... Some people, I know, prefer it for that reason.'

'I'll take your word for it, my lord. I know nothing of wines.' I accepted the brimming goblet with its silver-gilt rim engraved with a scene of Bacchanalian revels, and waited for him to fill his own.

When he had done so, 'To the absent,' he said quietly, raising it in salute.

'To the absent,' I repeated, avoiding his eyes.

'You must be wondering why I've sent for you,' he went on, after a moment's hesitation. 'I understand from Timothy Plummer that your wife is with you here, in London. I'm sorry to intrude upon your visit like this, but I have need of your special powers.'

Richard of Gloucester was a man liked, in many instances loved, by everyone who took the trouble to know him properly. All the same, in spite of his gentleness and thoughtfulness towards friends and servants, there was a ruthless streak in his nature. When he decided that he wanted something done, no consideration for the convenience or feelings of others would deter him from getting his way.

After a few seconds, while he contemplated the crackling flames on the hearth, he raised his eyes to mine.

'You attended the Duke of York's wedding yesterday. I saw you, outside Saint Stephen's Chapel.' He did not wait for my affirmation before continuing, 'You therefore cannot have failed to notice Mistress Jane Shore.'

'I saw a woman I was told was Mistress Shore. She was dressed in a pale blue gown that seemed to sparkle as she moved.'

'I couldn't say,' was the terse reply. 'I took no notice of what she was wearing.'

The Duke plainly disapproved of the King's chief leman, as he no doubt disapproved of all Edward's other mistresses, and of the sybaritic life that had turned his adored eldest brother from the magnificent, clean-limbed hero of his youth into the man he was today; still immensely tall, still golden-haired, but running to fat, the blue eyes dimmed by boredom and excessive drinking, the once handsome features blurred by too much good living, the sharp mind blunted by constant flattery from sycophantic courtiers. I reflected, as I had done once or twice before, that there was a deep-rooted streak of puritanism in Richard of Gloucester's nature that no doubt made him many enemies. His ability to see things only as good or evil, right or wrong, could one day cause him great suffering, if, that is, it had not done so already.

He interrupted my train of thought to ask, 'What else do you know of Mistress Shore?' While I cudgelled my brain to remember what Jeanne Lamprey had told me of the lady, the Duke went on, obviously not expecting an answer, 'She is the daughter of a mercer called Lambert, and she married a goldsmith by the name of William Shore.' He refilled both our goblets. 'She was not, however, the only female of the Lambert family to marry into that particular trade. It seems that a cousin of her father's also married a goldsmith, one Miles Babcary, who still owns a shop in West Cheap. This couple – so my information runs – had an only child, a daughter who, in due course, married a man, whose name I can't remember.' The Duke was growing impatient, wanting to be done with the tale. 'The long and the short of it is, Chapman, that some months ago this girl – or woman, as I think she now is – was suspected of murdering her husband. She was never arrested, never charged with the crime – partly, I am told, for lack of evidence; and partly, I suspect, because of influence brought to bear by Mistress Shore upon the King. But the taint of suspicion still surrounds her, poisoning her life.'

There was another silence as the Duke's attention again began to stray, the expression on his tired face becoming ever more haunted.

I cleared my throat. 'And Your Highness wants me to discover the truth of this matter, if I can?'

'What? Oh ... Yes! That's why I sent for you, Roger. Mistress Shore is very unhappy that her cousin is still being whispered about by her neighbours.'

My thoughts were racing. Why was the Duke of Gloucester interesting himself in this affair? He disliked the King's mistress, so why was he hoping that I might be able to clear the name of one of her kinswomen? What did any of it matter to him, especially at a time when he had far greater worries to occupy his mind?

But of course! Fear for the Duke of Clarence was the reason. He was convicted but not yet sentenced. There was still time for clemency on the part of the King. And what my lord of Gloucester needed above all else was as many voices as possible raised on Clarence's behalf; as many people as he could muster to plead for the Duke with King Edward in order to counteract the influence of the Queen and her family. And who would be listened to with more sympathy than a favourite leman? But first he had to find an inducement, a lure, in order to persuade Jane Shore to embrace his brother George's cause. So if, at his instigation, I could clear her kinswoman of the suspicion of having murdered her husband, then he would have the necessary bait.

Duke Richard laughed suddenly. 'Your face, Roger, is as easy to read as an open book. You've guessed, I think, why I'm asking for your help in this matter.'

I gulped down the rest of my wine, half rose and replaced the empty goblet on the table beside him, then subsided again into my chair.

'But what if this cousin of Mistress Shore *is* guilty of murdering her husband, my lord? What then? What good will that be to you?'

He sighed, pushing the curtain of hair out of his eyes. 'Then at least we shall know the satisfaction of having brought a criminal to justice,' he said heavily. And when I did not answer, he asked, 'Well? Will you do this for me?'

'Do I have a choice, my lord?'

'You always have a choice, Roger. You know that.'

But I was not so certain that I did. People of the Duke's standing never realise how used they are to being obeyed until someone challenges their authority. Not that I was about to do so. For one thing, my loyalty to Richard of Gloucester was as strong as ever, my affection for him undiminished; for another, however hard I tried, I could never quite suppress the feeling of excitement that invariably overwhelmed me when presented with a challenge to what the Duke had flatteringly called 'my special powers'. Wherever there was a mystery, I could not rest until I had solved it.

I thought guiltily of Adela. I had come to London to show her the city, and now here I was proposing to desert her for part of that time; maybe a great deal of that time. I thought even more guiltily of the Lampreys, and wondered if Jeanne would be kind enough to take my abandoned wife under her wing. I could imagine all too well what Margaret Walker would say when we returned to Bristol and the truth was revealed.

This reflection prompted me to say, 'My lord, my wife and I are due to leave London a week today with the carter who brought us here. If it should happen that I've not solved this problem by then...?'

'You will stay until you have done so, and I shall make all necessary arrangements for you and your wife to be conveyed home to Bristol once the matter is successfully concluded. Before you leave Crosby Place tonight, Timothy Plummer will take you to see my treasurer, who will ensure that you have sufficient money for any extra expense you may incur. Now, is there anything else you wish to ask me?'

I glanced at him to see if he were serious; then protested indignantly, 'My lord, you have told me practically nothing! Merely that there is a goldsmith living in West Cheap whose daughter is suspected of murdering her husband. What is this woman's name? What were the circumstances of the husband's death? Who else might possibly have had a reason for killing him? How many people are there in the household? And how am I to make their acquaintance?'

The Duke laughed again, but there was neither mirth nor warmth in the sound.

'You must forgive me, Roger. My wits are gone wool-gathering.' He thought for a moment before enquiring, 'Where are you staying in London?'

'At the sign of Saint Brendan the Voyager, in Bucklersbury, not far from West Cheap.'

'Ah! Then someone will call upon you there sometime tomorrow morning, to conduct you to Mistress Shore's house in the Strand. She is the best person to tell you anything you need to know.' A faint spasm of distaste contorted his features. 'I will make all the necessary arrangements tonight.' He rose to his feet and I rose with him. He held out a hand once again, but when I would have kissed it, he stopped me and gripped one of mine instead, as if I were a friend. 'Do your best for me, Roger. As

65

you've guessed, I need Mistress Shore's help in ... in a certain matter.'

Mistress Shore lived in one of the magnificent houses that border both sides of the Strand, hers being one of those whose gardens run down to the river. The young man, dressed in the Duke of Gloucester's blue and murrey livery, who had presented himself at the Voyager soon after dinner that morning, was obviously expected, and had no difficulty in gaining entry for the pair of us.

When I had returned to the inn the previous evening and told Adela all that had passed between the Duke and myself at Crosby Place, she had made no difficulties and uttered far fewer recriminations than I felt I merited. For this, two reasons were, I think, responsible. Firstly, in her condition, she was finding London noisier, busier and more tiring than she had expected; secondly, she had become close friends with Jeanne Lamprey, who was proving a restful and sympathetic companion, solicitous, as only another woman can be, for Adela's welfare. A very early morning visit by myself to their old clothes shop in Cornhill had put both Jeanne and Philip in full possession of the facts, and provoked the latter into lecturing me on the folly of not heeding good advice when it was offered.

'I warned you, Roger, not to attend the Duke of Clarence's trial! You'd already been spotted once by my lord of Gloucester at the wedding. To risk bringing yourself to his notice for a second time was the purest folly. You've got no more than you deserve.'

Jeanne told him to hold his tongue and promised to take care of Adela during those hours that I should necessarily be forced to spend in West Cheap. And I had a suspicion that both she and my wife continued to relish this glimpse into the lives of those normally so far above them, and were not altogether displeased by the turn of events.

The Duke of Gloucester's envoy and I were shown into a lofty hall where, surprisingly, a homely spinning wheel stood close to the hearth on which a bright fire burned, welcome on such a cold and cheerless winter's morning. An embroidery frame and coloured silks lay scattered over the central table of carved and polished oak, while an ancient, moth-eaten dog was ensconced in one of the hall's three armchairs, dribbling contentedly into a red satin cushion. My companion, to my amusement, eyed it askance. Like me, he had no doubt expected the King's favourite mistress to own an elegant little greyhound, bedecked in a jewelled collar and velvet coat.

My heart began to warm towards Mistress

Shore, even before she put in an appearance. But when she finally arrived, hot, somewhat flustered and full of apologies for her tardiness in receiving me, I knew that whatever the Duke of Gloucester felt about this woman, I liked her, and was willing to serve her for her own sake, as well as his.

The young man who had brought me to the house made me known to Mistress Shore and then, with a bow and a flourish, took his leave. When he had departed, she gave me a conspiratorial smile.

'Now we can be comfortable.' She looked me up and down. 'You're very good looking,' she said, but without any hint of invitation or coquettishness in her tone. 'You remind me of the King when he was younger.'

I could feel the hot blood rising in my cheeks. 'Y-you're very kind,' I stammered.

She only smiled and shook her head. 'Shall we have some ale? I prefer ale to wine. His Highness says that that's because I have low tastes, and of course, he's perfectly right.' She giggled.

I thought her enchanting, and could see why most men – with one very notable exception – would find her so. Jane Shore had a happy disposition.

After she had called a servant and given orders for the ale to be brought, she grew serious, settling herself in one of the two unoccupied armchairs and inviting me to sit in the other. She patted the ancient dog's head as she passed, and he briefly opened a bleary eye and twitched his ragged stump of a tail before going back to sleep again.

'His Grace of Gloucester tells me that you are a solver of mysteries,' she said. 'He has told you a little, has he not, about my kinswoman, Isolda Bonifant?'

'A very, very little,' I replied earnestly. 'That is why I am here this morning, to learn, I hope, a great deal more from you.'

The ale arrived and she poured it into two pewter beakers, wishing me good health before she drank. 'It was fate,' she said, 'that brought you here; fate that the King should have discussed my cousin's plight with his brother. I hope that you will be able to help Isolda, Master Chapman, for it's no pleasant thing for her to have neighbours, and even friends, whispering about her behind her back. Which she knows they must do by the way they grow embarrassed in her company, or avoid her altogether if they can.'

'That I can well imagine. Now then, if you please, will you tell me the background to the story?'

It was a straightforward enough tale. As Duke Richard had said, a cousin of Mistress Shore's father, one Susannah Lambert, had

69

married a goldsmith, Miles Babcary of West Cheap. The couple had had only one child, Isolda, born in June, 1448, the year after their marriage. This girl, according to my companion's account, had never been pretty, even as a child, and had grown plainer as she grew older, a fact which had made it difficult to find her a husband. She was also, it appeared, fiercely independent, the mother having died when her daughter was only thirteen, and Isolda having assumed the role of woman of the house from that day forward.

Two weeks after her twenty-fourth birthday, she had finally married. Her husband, Gideon Bonifant, was ten years older than his bride and of inferior status, having been no more than assistant to an apothecary in Bucklersbury before the wedding. But Miles Babcary had been so relieved to see his only child settled and happy at last that he had, as well as welcoming Gideon into his home, also taken him on as a partner, patiently teaching his new son-in-law the business of goldsmithing from the lowliest task to the most complex. Master Bonifant had proved himself to be an apt pupil and the business throve, the one sadness being that after five years of marriage there was no sign of a grandchild for Miles; no immediate heir after Isolda to inherit his shop and his money.

The Babcary household, as well as an apprentice and maid-of-all-work, also consisted of Miles's niece and nephew, his younger brother Edward's orphaned children. Edward Babcary had died at the battle of Tewkesbury fighting for King Edward in the spring of 1471, and his wife had died of plague two months later. At that time, Christopher Babcary had been thirteen years of age, his sister only eleven, and with typical generosity, Miles had offered them the shelter of his roof. His nephew he had taken on as a pupil in the shop, while Eleanor Babcary had proved a useful assistant to Isolda in the running of the house. Even after Isolda's marriage the following year, no serious changes were deemed to be necessary, and the domestic and business arrangements of the Babcary household had carried on in much the same way as before, except that with both his son-in-law and his nephew learning the trade, Miles had needed only one apprentice.

And so matters had continued for the next five years, until the autumn of 1477.

'I have to admit,' Mistress Shore said, her colour slightly heightened, 'that although I used to be a frequent guest of my father's cousin and his daughter, I have lost touch with them of late, for the past three years in fact, since ... since I came to live here, in this house,' she finished.

I nodded understandingly: she had had less to do with the Babcarys since becoming the King's mistress. But she was not a woman who would ever consider herself of so elevated a status that she would ignore her kinsfolk completely. Some contact had been maintained with the family, and when Isolda Bonifant had been suspected of murdering her husband, Mistress Shore had brought all her considerable influence to bear upon the King in order to ensure that no charge was brought against her cousin.

'For I didn't, and still don't, believe Isolda guilty of such a crime,' she said belligerently, jutting her chin and daring me to question her judgement. 'There has to be another explanation, and if people weren't so bigoted, they'd see that for themselves. Friends and neighbours who've known her all her life must know that she isn't capable of killing anyone. It isn't in her nature.'

Such blind faith made me uneasy. 'How did Master Bonifant die?' I asked.

'He was poisoned.' Mistress Shore sounded defiant, as well she might. 'Oh, I know what you're thinking! That poison is a woman's weapon.'

'It's easier for them to use than either the dagger or the cudgel,' I pointed out. 'On the other hand, I've known women who have resorted to both those methods, and men who have administered poison. They say it's

72

a favourite means of despatching enemies in Italy. Do you know what poison was used?'

Mistress Shore hesitated. 'I think it was aconite, monkshood, or so Miles Babcary informed me. I'm not sure how he knew. I suppose the physician or the apothecary who was called recognised certain symptoms.'

'Undoubtedly. I believe it causes burning pains in throat and stomach, and the victim has great difficulty in swallowing. The muscles of the neck stiffen, and after ten minutes or so, breathing becomes impossible.'

Jane Shore gave a little shiver. 'How horrible! But there were other people in the house as well as Isolda. It might have been one of them. I believe that Christopher Babcary didn't get on well with Master Bonifant. They had had many disagreements.'

'Do you know why?'

My hostess did not reply at once, looking down at her hands, clasped in her lap. Finally, after a few moment's silence, during which the only sounds to be heard were the old dog's wheezy snores and the crackling of the fire on the hearth, she raised her head and looked me in the eyes.

'Master Chapman, I must be honest with you. The King doesn't wish me to be too closely concerned in this business. Until my kinswoman's name is cleared, he prefers that I have nothing to do with the Babcary household.' She sighed. 'I can understand that. He feels that he has done enough by bringing his influence to bear and preventing charges being brought against Isolda. Therefore, if I give you my cousin's direction in West Cheap, you would earn my deepest gratitude if ... if—'

'If I were to confine all my enquiries to the family, and not bother you until I have reached a conclusion,' I finished for her.

She smiled mistily at me. 'Indeed, I feel ashamed of making this condition, but I cannot bring myself, at this difficult time, to go against His Highness's wishes.'

'And how will the Babcarys like me poking and prying about? Do they even know of my existence?'

'Yes. Yes, they do, and all of them are anxious for your assistance. They want to know the truth as much as I do.'

It occurred to me that there must be one person who already knew the truth and whose welcome would be a sham: the murderer. But I said nothing. Instead, I rose, kissed the little hand that was offered me and promised Mistress Shore that I would do everything in my power to discover who had really killed Gideon Bonifant.

Five

I recognised the place at once. It was the house where Adela and I had seen the lazy apprentice being scolded from an upper window by his bespectacled master.

Following Mistress Shore's directions, I had walked almost to the end of West Cheap, where, at the Church of Saint Michael at Corn, it joins Paternoster Row to the south and the Shambles to the north.

'Look for a shop and dwelling close to the Church of Saint Vedast,' she had instructed me. 'A representation of two angels is painted on the plasterwork between the third-storey window and the roof. I sent to my cousin this morning to warn him of your arrival. You will be expected.'

So there I was, a pallid winter sun struggling to break through the leaden clouds, my cloak and boots splashed with mud and filth from carts driving too near the central gutter, my ears deafened by the babel of street cries – 'Hot sheep's feet!' 'Ribs of beef!' 'Clean rushes!' 'Pots and pans!' 'Pies and pasties!' and dozens more. Every few yards of my journey from the Strand, hands had clutched at my sleeves and whining voices had assailed my ears, pleading for alms. Some beggars were hale and hearty, others hideously disfigured, either by nature or by the cruelties of civil punishment and war, and all excited pity. I gave what I could, but there were too many suppliants, and eventually I had been forced to ignore their importunities. I reached my journey's end with some relief and entered the shop.

A long counter faced me as I stepped inside, and beyond this was the workroom. A youth, the same boy I had seen three evenings since, was working the bellows at a furnace built into a wall, while the same elderly man was admonishing him in an exasperated tone.

'No, no, no, Toby! A light pressure, if you please! You want to fan the coals gently into flame, not blow great clouds of smoke out through the vent to choke the passers-by! Good God, lad, don't you ever attend to any of the instructions that you're given?'

Another man, not so very much older than the apprentice, was hammering out a piece of gold on an anvil, which stood on a bench in the middle of the room. As I watched, he laid down the hammer and picked up a pair of tweezers, beginning to pull and tease the hot metal into shape. Near at hand lay a chisel and a rabbit's foot, while further along the bench were what looked like a pair of dividers, a saw, a file and a number of small earthenware dishes. An array of other tools was ranged along a shelf to my right.

It was the older man, whom I rightly guessed to be Miles Babcary, who saw me first, bustling forward in the hope of a sale, his face falling ludicrously as soon as he noted my homespun apparel.

'Master Babcary?' I asked, holding out my hand. 'I'm Roger Chapman. Mistress Shore told you, I think, that I should be coming?'

I judged him to be about sixty (he later told me that he had not long celebrated his fifty-eighth birthday), a ruddy-cheeked, somewhat corpulent man with thinning grey hair in which gleams of chestnut brown could still be seen. His pale blue eyes, magnified by the spectacles perched on the bridge of his nose, blinked at me, owl-like, but at my words, his kindly features brightened.

'So she did! So she did! Walk around the counter, Master Chapman. You are more than welcome. We shall be very glad, believe me, to have this hateful business cleared up once and for all. You can have no idea what it's like for my daughter to be whispered about behind her back.'

'Master Babcary,' I warned, 'I may not be able to arrive at any firm conclusion. Or...' I hesitated. The elder of the two younger men had now drawn near and was listening intently to our conversation. I continued, 'Or I might reach the wrong conclusion as far as you're concerned.' I saw from Miles Babcary's slightly puzzled expression that he did not fully understand my meaning, and I began to flounder. 'What I mean is ... What I am trying to say...'

The young man came to my rescue. 'Are you suggesting, Chapman, the possibility that my cousin Isolda might really have poisoned her husband?'

Both his age and a fleeting likeness to Miles told me that he must be the nephew, named by Mistress Shore, if my memory served me aright, as Christopher Babcary. I nodded, and there was an immediate explosion of protest from his uncle.

'No, no! I won't have it! My dearest girl could never have done anything so terrible! Master Chapman, you are here to prove her innocence.'

'I will if I can, sir,' I assured him. 'But you must have realised by now that if Mistress Bonifant isn't guilty, then someone else is.'

Again, I encountered that bewildered stare, and again it was Christopher Babcary who interpreted my meaning.

'What the chapman is saying, Uncle, is that if Isolda didn't murder Gideon, then someone else in the house must be the killer; one or the other of us who was present here that day, at Mistress Perle's birthday celebration.'

This idea, although I could see that it was not a new one to the nephew, plainly had not occurred before to Master Babcary. So absorbed had he been in trying to prove that his daughter was not a murderess that the implication of her innocence had quite escaped him. For a moment he looked as if he might burst into tears, but then pulled himself together, his face taking on a mulish expression.

'I – I want Isolda exonerated,' he stuttered at last. 'She didn't do it. I know she didn't. She loved Gideon, whatever he might have said to the contrary. I'm sorry, Christopher, my boy, if it means that you and others fall under suspicion. But if it's of consolation to you, I don't believe that anyone who was present here that day is guilty, either. In fact, I'm very sure no one is.'

Christopher Babcary glanced at me, then back at Miles. 'But it stands to reason, Uncle, that one of us must have poisoned Gideon. Besides himself, there were nine of us in the house that evening, and apart from those nine, no one else could have put the monkshood in his drink. The shop was locked and shuttered as soon as the guests had arrived.'

Miles Babcary put a hand to his forehead, growing more confused by the minute. One half of his mind could not help but acknowledge his nephew's logic, but the other half refused to accept it. If Miles could have his way, Gideon Bonifant's murder would prove to have been an accident or suicide; or, better still, the handiwork of a passing stranger who had mysteriously managed to gain access to the house.

I said gently, 'Master Babcary, we cannot continue to stand here in the shop where every passing fool can gape at us through the open doorway. Can we be private? In spite of talking to Mistress Shore, I am still ignorant of many details concerning this murder.'

'Yes, yes! Of course! But you must wait a few moments, if you please. Toby, is the gold melted yet? If so, bring it over here immediately.'

The boy lifted a pot out of the furnace with a pair of tongs and carefully transported it to the work bench, his tongue protruding from one corner of his mouth, his young body taut with concentration as he tried not to spill any of the precious liquid. Meantime, Miles Babcary had drawn towards him a thin sheet of copper on which innumerable circles were shallowly engraved; and within each circle a bird or a flower, the figure of a saint, a face or the wheel of fortune was also scored into the metal. It was plainly a mould of some sort, but what

80

purpose was served by the final product – delicate, paper-thin, filigree golden medallions – I could not imagine.

Christopher Babcary, noting my puzzled frown, enlightened me.

'They are sewn on women's gowns. They make the material shimmer as my lady walks.'

'So that's what it was,' I said. 'I'm remembering how Mistress Shore's robe glittered at the Duke of York's wedding.'

'As did every other lady's gown, I should imagine,' Christopher amended. 'We and the rest of the goldsmiths hereabouts sold out of our entire stock of medallions during the preceding weeks.'

His uncle, meanwhile, had been filling the circular moulds with the molten gold, the surplus being caught in a narrow runnel fixed to the edge of the bench. The boy addressed as Toby began to scrape at the lumps and flakes as they hardened, gathering them up and carefully depositing them in some of the earthenware bowls.

'Where does the gold come from?' I asked.

'Mostly from Hungary and Bohemia,' Miles Babcary answered, removing his leather apron and hanging it up on a nail. 'These days, it's brought into the country in the shape of coins, which are thought preferable to the old-fashioned ingots ... Well now, Master Chapman, perhaps you'd like to accompany me upstairs where we can be comfortable, and I'll tell you all you need to know about this unfortunate affair.'

He paused long enough to issue instructions to his nephew and the boy, Toby, on what needed to be done during his absence, then led the way through an inner door to a passageway beyond. Here, to our right, a staircase spiralled upwards, while, straight ahead, lay what I supposed to be the kitchen quarters. As if to prove my assumption correct, a young girl appeared, entering from the yard at the back and carrying across her shoulders a yoke from which two buckets were suspended, some of their contents spilling on to the flags in great splashes of clear, sweet water.

'Ah! Meg!' Miles Babcary beckoned her forward. 'This is Roger Chapman who will be in and out of the house and shop for a while. He may want to ask you some questions, but there's no cause to be afraid of him. Just tell him what you know. He won't get angry or hurt you.'

The girl unhitched the yoke from her shoulders, lowering it and the buckets to the ground before approaching us with such caution that she literally inched her way along the wall, arms outstretched, fingers splayed against the stone.

'She's very wary of strangers,' Miles informed me, but not loud enough for the girl herself to hear. 'She's a foundling, and was, I'm afraid, mistreated at the hospital on account of her appearance. She's also slow of speech and understanding.' He tapped his forehead significantly. 'You have to be patient with her.' He added as an afterthought, 'Meg Spendlove's her name.'

I held out my hand and said gently, 'I'm pleased to make your acquaintance, Mistress Spendlove.'

Her only answer was a goggle-eyed stare. She was so small and thin that it was impossible to be certain of her age, and I doubted very much if even she knew how old she was. (Although Master Babcary told me afterwards that they thought her to be in her sixteenth year as, according to the nuns of the hospital, she had been abandoned, at only a few days old, in the same month that Queen Margaret had invaded in the north.) She was unprepossessing to look at, someone at sometime having broken both her nose and jaw, and the bones having knit together very badly. Because of this, her mouth hung almost permanently open, and when it was shut, she breathed in a painfully wheezing fashion. Contrary to expectation, however, there was a hint not only of intelligence but also of shrewdness in the dark brown eyes, if you took the trouble to look for it.

'You're a good girl,' Miles said, patting her

shoulder. 'Try to remember what I've just told you concerning Master Chapman. Now, off you go and finish your work or you'll have Mistress Bonifant on your tail, and you don't want another scolding, do you?'

The girl shook her head and went back to pick up her pails, disappearing with them through a second door which, as I later discovered, led into the kitchen.

My host and I proceeded up the twisting stairs as far as the first-floor landing, where two doors were set in the wall, side by side. Miles pushed open the right-hand one, ushering me into what was plainly the family living-room. It was as spacious as the narrow confines of the building would allow, and was, I guessed, the largest chamber in the house. A solid oaken table stood in the middle of the rush-strewn floor, a leather-topped bench, piled with brightly coloured cushions, occupied the window embrasure, and a corner cupboard displayed not the usual collection of silver and pewter ware, but, as was only to be expected, items of gold taken from Master Babcary's stock. A fire burned brightly on the hearth, a good supply of logs stacked close by, ready to replenish it when necessary. Two armchairs, several stools and a carved wooden chest, which stood against one wall, completed the furnishings.

'Sit down. Sit down, Master Chapman,' my host invited, with that repetition of speech which I was soon to learn was characteristic of him. I had hardly done so, drawing up a stool to the fire, glad to warm my cold hands at the comforting blaze, when the door opened and someone else came into the room; and before I could turn my head, Master Babcary continued, 'Ah! Here's my daughter.'

Isolda Bonifant was not as I had imagined her. Mistress Shore had described her as being plain; plain enough, in fact, to find difficulty in attracting a husband. And indeed, no one could have described her as a pretty woman. Her best feature was a pair of deep blue eyes that returned my gaze with a candid stare, but no trace of resentment at my obvious curiosity. Otherwise, it was a strong, almost mannish face with thick, dark eyebrows, a high-bridged nose and a stern, unsmiling mouth. And yet I was immediately attracted to her. She reminded me in some way of Adela, a woman who, once she had committed herself, would give you her full loyalty and support. I could understand why her father thought her innocent of this terrible crime.

I pulled myself up short with a silent admonition. I knew, none better, that first – and sometimes even second and third –

impressions could be deceptive. Master Babcary was making me known to his daughter, and I rose from my stool to return her greeting.

'Mistress Bonifant,' I said, bowing. 'God's peace be with you.'

'I hope it may be,' she answered frankly, advancing into the room. She looked me up and down. 'You're a very strange chapman. I've never met one before who is intimate with princes and the King's chief whore.'

'Isolda!' Her father's reprimand was harsh. 'You won't talk like that, if you please, while you're under my roof. Mistress Shore is your kinswoman by blood and mine by marriage. She has done, and is doing, her best to help us. I wish you will remember that without her assistance you could well have been accused of Gideon's murder.'

Mistress Bonifant shrugged. 'Perhaps it would have been better if I had been. At least, by now, I would either have been proved innocent or be dead.' She moved further into the room, coming to stand beside me, and I saw the dark shadows beneath her eyes. 'But that still doesn't explain how the chapman here is acquainted with our cousin.'

And so, not for the first time, and certainly not for the last, I gave brief details of my history and the circumstances that surrounded my friendship with the Duke of Gloucester. As always, my listeners expressed surprise that I had not chosen to better myself by taking advantage of the Duke's ever increasing cause for gratitude; and, as always, I reiterated my reasons for not doing so.

'I like my independence too much, the freedom of being my own master. I want no one set in authority over me.'

Master Babcary admitted that he could see the force of such an argument, and Isolda also conceded that, were she a man, she might feel the same way. Having said this, she begged me to be seated again and brought forward another stool for herself, placing it alongside mine.

'Well, and what conclusions have you come to regarding the murder of my husband, Master Chapman?'

'Good Heavens, girl!' her father protested. 'He hasn't been in the house but half an hour, and as yet knows very little of what happened last December. I brought him up here for some peace and quiet and in order to make him acquainted with the facts.'

'Then I shall stay to help you.' And Isolda sat down with a rattle of the household keys fastened to her belt.

Miles Babcary must have seen the expression on my face, for he said nervously, 'Do you think that a good idea, my dear? You are, after all, the one most nearly concerned and ... and...' His eyes rolled in my direction, seeking guidance.

Mistress Bonifant laughed suddenly, sounding genuinely amused. 'And you think it would be better if I didn't remain to plead my own cause?'

Miles Babcary and I assented with almost one voice.

'Very well then,' she agreed, rising to her feet, but just at that moment the door opened for the second time and a young girl came in.

I judged her to be some sixteen or seventeen years old, about the same age as I had learned Meg Spendlove to be, but there all similarity ended. There could not have been a greater contrast than between those two. One was plain – some might even call her ugly – unloved and had probably never known an act or word of simple human kindness until she had come to this house to work. The other was a beautiful, blue-eyed, creamy-skinned peach of a girl, obviously cherished by all who knew her. Miles Babcary's face lit up at the mere sight of her face, and Isolda went forward to kiss her cheek.

'Nell, my love, you must be chilled to the marrow. Was it very cold outside? Come to the fire and warm yourself.'

At the same time, Miles Babcary turned to

me and said, 'This is my niece, Eleanor. You have already met her brother, Christopher, downstairs. Nell, my sweetheart, this is Roger Chapman who has been sent to us by Mistress Shore. He has agreed to try to solve the mystery of poor Gideon's death.'

Eleanor Babcary gave me a smiling, incurious glance, putting back the hood of her cloak to reveal an abundance of chest-nut-brown hair. An effort had been made to tame it into two long plaits that hung down over her shoulders, but a profusion of little curls were everywhere escaping their con-finement, tendrils that she vainly, if absent-mindedly, tried every now and again to smooth into place.

'I wasn't at all cold,' she said in answer to Isolda. 'This lovely fur-lined cloak that you and Uncle Miles gave me for Christmas has kept me warm.' She reached out to take one of Master Babcary's hands in hers, pressing it gratefully to her cheek.

My host's smirk of pleasure reminded me of nothing so much as a callow schoolboy who has been praised by a favourite tutor, and my suspicions were confirmed that Eleanor Babcary was the darling of the household. What I was not so sure of was whether she was aware of this fact, or if she used the knowledge for her own advantage. Only time would tell. What was plain, how-ever, was that Isolda, like her father, doted on her cousin, and somehow I did not think her a lady who would be easily fooled by a pretty face and a charming manner.

'Was Mistress Perle at home?' Miles Babcary demanded. 'Did you speak with her? Did she agree to take supper here this evening?'

'I saw her, yes, and spoke with her.' Eleanor tenderly squeezed her uncle's hand which she was still holding in one of her own. The blue eyes filled with facile tears that spilled over and ran down the velvety cheeks. 'But she still refuses to eat with us, Uncle. She repeated that she thinks it better that she sees us as little as possible until this business of Gideon's death is satisfactorily resolved. Those were her very words: I took particular note of them. "Until this business of Gideon's death is satisfactorily resolved."'

Disappointment and bewilderment were visible in every line of Miles Babcary's face. 'Why does she persist in this answer?' he asked angrily of no one in particular. 'It's over a month and a half now since the murder, and still she refuses to set foot across my threshold. Why?'

Neither of the women seemed inclined to answer this question, Eleanor looking sympathetic, but vacant, Isolda closing her lips tightly as if there was much she could have said, but chose not to do so. It was left to me to offer a solution.

'Master Babcary, your nephew said in my hearing that your son-in-law died during Mistress Perle's birthday feast, so I presume that the celebration took place in this house?'

My host nodded. 'That is correct. It was the fourth of December, the feast of Saint Barbara, after whom Mistress Perle is named, and I had invited her to sup with us that evening.'

A slightly foolish smile curled his lips and he sighed sentimentally. I began to understand his attachment to this Mistress Perle. My guess was that he had been courting her, hoping to make her his wife, and that the lady had not been unwilling. Her present rejection of him was therefore all the harder to bear.

I said gently, 'Don't you think that her reluctance to see you might be the result of your fierce protestations concerning your daughter's innocence? As Master Christopher was saying to you a short time ago: if Mistress Bonifant didn't commit the murder, then someone else who was in the house that evening did. It follows, therefore, that Mistress Perle may feel herself to be the object of your suspicion.'

Master Babcary's florid countenance turned pale. 'She couldn't possibly think such a thing! She couldn't!' But a moment's consideration showed him the truth of my words. He grabbed my arm and shook it. 'Master Chapman, you must find out what really happened! Come! Draw closer to the fire and I'll tell you about the events of that evening.'

Six

The two women left us, Eleanor allowing herself to be led away by Isolda without once questioning the older woman's decision. Yet again, I wondered if she were always this docile; and if so, did she resent the fact that uncle and cousin seemed to treat her as though she were still a child?

'Now,' said Miles Babcary as the door closed behind them, 'you've met all the members of my household, Master Chapman – all those who remain, that is. But I don't need to remind you that until the evening of the Feast of Saint Barbara, last December, there was another, my son-in-law, Gideon Bonifant. He—'

'Did you like him?' I asked, interrupting my companion's flow of words and thus flustering him. I have often found this a useful tactic for getting at the truth.

'What?' Miles stared at me, mentally thrown off balance. 'I ... He was ... Why should I not like Gideon?' was the belligerent response. He fidgeted uncomfortably for a moment or two before adding, 'To be honest, he was not someone you could like or dislike with any great fervour. He was not a man anyone could get to know very well. His emotions were always kept strictly in check, and what sort of a husband he made I have no idea. But he seemed to make Isolda happy, and that was all that mattered to me.'

'Mistress Shore hinted that perhaps Gideon was not a good enough match for your daughter. An apothecary's assistant, so she said, from Bucklersbury.'

'Well, well, and what if he was?' Miles let his irritation show at this second interruption. 'You've seen Isolda. As you can guess, she didn't attract men easily, even when young. You know that she's ... that she's not a handsome woman. To be truthful, she's plain. She's very plain. Added to which, she has an independent turn of mind, which is not surprising when you consider that she has been sole mistress of this house since the age of sixteen. That was when my last housekeeper left me because, she said, she and Isolda could no longer share the same roof without falling out every day.'

I asked curiously, 'And yet – forgive me if

I am being too bold – you are thinking of marrying again?'

This time, Miles's annoyance was palpable. 'Master Chapman, it is only just over two weeks since I celebrated my fifty-eighth birthday. I am not yet in my dotage. I am still a virile and active man. A comfortable and well-run home is not the only consideration for someone of my age and appetites. I must admit that until Mistress Perle was widowed two and a half years ago, the thought of remarriage had not entered my head. But I have known and been fond of Barbara for a very long time; and once her period of mourning was over and she was able to take up the threads of her life again, I realised that my liking for her had turned into something stronger. And from one or two very broad hints that she dropped, I had every reason, until recently, to believe that she was entertaining similar thoughts about me. I talked the matter over with my daughter and Gideon, and told them that if Mistress Perle should do me the honour of agreeing to become my wife, I would buy her house in Paternoster Row and give it to them to live in. They seemed agreeable enough. I think Isolda, particularly, was beginning to feel it time that she had an establishment of her own.'

'Mistress Perle and her husband had no children?' I enquired, although I had already guessed the answer.

'No, none.' Miles's irritation increased still further. 'But why am I telling you all this? What has it to do with Gideon's death?'

'In a case of murder,' I assured him apologetically, 'there is no saying what might eventually prove to be of importance in solving the crime. Please forgive me if I have probed too deeply into matters that you feel do not concern me.'

He appeared somewhat mollified by this explanation, although a little resentment still lingered.

'Very well! Very well! Let us now return to the evening of Gideon's death. As I have already told you, it was Mistress Perle's birthday, December the fourth, the Feast of Saint Barbara, and I had invited her to celebrate the occasion here, with my family; the family that I hoped would also soon be hers. She was only too happy to agree, provided that she could bring with her her two great friends and neighbours, Gregory and Ginèvre Napier.'

'Ginèvre Napier!' I exclaimed. 'And she lives in Paternoster Row? Then I know the lady. Or perhaps I should rather say that I met her once, some years ago, when I was enquiring into the disappearance of two children from their home in Devon. I came to London to speak to Mistress Napier, who had been a friend of the children's mother.'

'Well, well! Goodness me! Upon my soul! Upon my soul! Here's a coincidence!' Master Babcary exclaimed. 'If it is indeed the same person.'

'A lady,' I replied, selecting my words carefully so as not to give offence, 'past the first flush of youth, but determined to hold the ravages of time at bay.'

'That's her! That's her!' my host declared. He added, not bothering to pick and choose *his* words, 'A painted hussy I've always thought her, no better than she should be. And so I've often told Mistress Perle, for it troubles me that Barbara should make a companion of such a woman, although I believe the Napiers were very kind to her during Edgar Perle's last illness. But Barbara is unpersuadable in the matter, and continues to be close friends with the couple. It's the only subject on which we don't see eye to eye, so I suppose I can't complain. Man and wife will never agree on everything – if, that is, we ever become man and wife,' he finished gloomily.

'Tell me about the evening of the murder,' I invited.

'That's just what I've been trying to do for the last ten minutes,' he retorted indignantly, 'only you keep on interrupting me, Chapman.'

I said I was sorry, hoping that he would not detect the insincerity in my tone. 'Pray continue, sir.'

'Very well! Very well! Mistress Perle, Ginèvre and Gregory Napier were to share our supper with us, and the shop was shuttered and locked before they arrived. Being December, it was almost dark by four o'clock, and I felt that I should lose very little custom by closing an hour or so earlier than usual. It was, in any case, very nearly time for the curfew bell.' He took a breath and then continued, 'The meal had been laid here, in this room, with the best napery and cutlery and the set of silver plates that I made for my poor wife when first we were married. The very *finest* silver, you understand, from the mines at Kuttenberg, which lie somewhere between Prague and the borders of Muscovy, or so I'm told. And, as on all festive occasions, each member of the family had his or her especial goblet.'

'Especial goblet?' I queried.

For answer, my companion got to his feet, went to the door and opened it. 'Isolda!' he shouted. 'Come here, if you please. I want you!'

There was a short delay, then I heard the patter of feet descending the second flight of stairs from the floor above. Isolda's voice asked, 'What's the matter, Father?'

'The key, girl! The key to the corner cupboard, let me have it.'

There was the chink of metal against

metal as Isolda slipped the key from the ring attached to her girdle; then, having come back into the room and again shut the door, Miles proceeded to unlock the fretted panels of the corner cupboard, behind which could be seen the gleam of gold and silver. He stooped to one of the lower shelves and, when he stood upright once more, he was holding a crystal goblet with a silver foot and stem and a carved golden rim, very like the one from which I had drunk at Crosby Place. He carried it over to the fire and handed it to me.

'This is mine,' he said, resuming his seat. 'If you look carefully, you will see amongst the chasing around the lip my initials, M.B.'

Turning it slowly and reverently between my hands, watching as the flames from the fire struck myriad rainbow-hued sparks from the crystal bowl, while a hundred reflected lights burned deep in the heart of the golden rim, I saw amidst the carved bunches of grapes, gambolling nymphs and trailing swags of vine leaves the intertwined initials M and B, just as my host had claimed.

'I see them,' I said. 'Master Babcary, this is as beautiful a piece of craftsmanship as I have ever beheld.'

A faint flush of pleasure mantled his cheeks, although he must have been used to such praise, and from far greater connoisseurs of the goldsmith's art than I was.

'It's one of six,' he told me. 'And I hope that one day it will be one of seven.' He went on, by way of explanation, 'When I was first married, I embellished two goblets as a wedding gift for my wife; one with her initials carved into the rim, the other with mine. Then, when Isolda was born, I decorated another such goblet for her as a christening present. When my nephew and niece were orphaned and came to live with me, I did two more, and, finally, the following year, one for my son-in-law. Susannah's I have put away at the back of the cupboard and no one uses it now, but I am hoping to replace it soon with one bearing the initials B.B. For Barbara Babcary,' he added, in case I was in any doubt as to his meaning.

'And each member of the household uses his or her own goblet,' I murmured.

'Not every day! They are not for everyday use,' he reproved me. 'They are taken out only on special occasions.'

'And Mistress Perle's birthday was just such an occasion,' I suggested.

'Of course! The five goblets were set out on the table along with others that I keep for guests.'

'I understand. Pray continue,' I urged.

'After the shop was closed for the night, and all the merchandise removed from windows and locked away, we retired to our bedchambers to change into our Sunday clothes before the guests arrived; all, that is, except my daughter, who was still downstairs in the kitchen, helping Meg prepare the food. It ... it was very unfortunate that this should have been so, but you've seen Meg Spendlove, Master Chapman, and can probably guess that she is not the most reliable of servants. But Isolda won't hear of turning her out, and says it's not important that Meg is simple because she – Isolda – prefers to keep an eye on everything herself.' He sighed. 'And that is true. My daughter is a most efficient housekeeper.'

'You say you all retired to your bedchambers. Where are these rooms situated, sir?'

My host bent down and threw another log on the fire. Some resin caught alight and flared up in a bright blue flame.

'My chamber is on this floor, next to the room we are now sitting in. Isolda's room – and Gideon's room as it also was then, of course – is on the next floor at the front of the house, immediately overhead, while my niece, Eleanor, sleeps in the bedchamber behind it, above mine. Finally, the two rooms on the third floor, beneath the eaves, are occupied by my nephew at the front and Tobias Maybury, my apprentice, in the little attic at the back. Meg has her own bed in a cupboard in the kitchen.'

'And do you know at what time Mistress Bonifant eventually came upstairs to change her gown?' I asked.

My companion's mouth suddenly shut like a trap and he began drumming with his fingers against the arms of his chair. He looked distressed and uncomfortable, and, to my mind, was silently debating whether or not to lie.

I leant forward. 'Master Babcary,' I pleaded, 'you must tell me the truth if you want my help in finding an answer to this mystery. Concealing what really happened won't benefit either you or your daughter, and falsehoods may result in my pointing the finger of suspicion at an innocent person. I feel sure you wouldn't want that.'

For a moment or two he made no answer, merely passing his tongue between his lips as if they needed moistening. At last, however, he said reluctantly, 'I heard Isolda come upstairs just as our guests knocked at the outer door. She must have come in here to check that all was well, because as I quit my room she left this one. We passed each other, she going towards the upper flight of stairs as I was going towards the lower.'

'Did she say anything?' I asked.

Again there was that hesitation while he once more considered the advisability of a good round lie. But he decided, sensibly, against it.

'Isolda told me that everything was ready, that the table was set and that she had poured wine into the goblets so that we could drink Mistress Perle's health as soon as we were all assembled. She said that there was only the food to bring up from the kitchen, and she would help Meg with that whenever we decided to sit down to eat, but she thought I might want to give Barbara her birthday present first.'

'Did you make any answer?'

Master Babcary lifted suspicious eyes to mine, patently uneasy that I had made no comment on the information I had just been given.

'I think I agreed with her, then went downstairs to the shop to let in our guests.'

'Did you meet anyone coming up?'

Master Babcary shook his head. 'No, I told you that with the exception of Isolda, everyone had already retired to his or her room to change into Sunday clothes.'

'Not everyone,' I pointed out. 'Meg Spendlove was still below.'

'Oh, Meg! Meg doesn't count, surely! What reason would she have to murder Gideon? Besides, as I said, her bed is in the kitchen. She'd have no reason to go upstairs until the food was called for.'

'In a case of murder,' I retorted, 'I've

found it wise to discount no one. Meg might have had some cause to dislike your son-in-law, hate him even, that the rest of you know nothing about.'

My companion shrugged and got up to light the candles in a branched candlestick of latten tin that stood in the middle of the table. The January day was growing dark outside, with rain now drumming steadily against the window panes. 'Oh, as to that,' he replied, resuming his seat and drawing it a little closer to the fire, 'I can tell you that there was no love lost between them. Gideon was a man who put great store by good order and hard work. Now, Meg is hard-working enough, and more than willing to do her fair share of domestic chores if supervised and treated kindly, but she tends to be untidy and careless if left to her own devices. Her slatternly ways irritated my son-in-law, sometimes beyond endurance, and he could never understand Isolda's tolerance in the matter. There were disagreements between them on the subject. I won't call them quarrels, because Gideon was a difficult man to quarrel with, simply folding his lips and walking away when any one of us did something that angered him.'

'And had there been any unpleasantness between him and Meg in the days before the murder?' I asked.

My host frowned. 'I don't think so;

nothing, at least, that I can recollect. But then, I have so many calls upon my time,' he added self-importantly, 'that I probably wouldn't remember. You must quiz the women about that sort of thing. Those events loom larger in their lives than they do in men's.'

'But was there any chance,' I persisted, 'that while you were welcoming your guests and letting them into the shop Meg could have crept upstairs and put poison in your son-in-law's wine? For I am assuming that that was what happened, that the monkshood was put into Gideon's cup as it stood, unattended, on this table.'

Master Babcary shivered and then nodded, his pomposity draining away as he contemplated the terrible climax of that December evening.

'I can't honestly say that I saw Meg during the time before Mistress Perle and I, together with Master and Mistress Napier, came up here to the parlour. But that doesn't mean,' he added musingly, 'that she couldn't have slipped upstairs and down again without anyone noticing, for we stood a few minutes in the shop exchanging greetings while they all took off their cloaks, and the two women removed their pattens.' He looked a little ashamed of this sudden about face, but I could well understand that he would rather the blame for the murder was laid at Meg Spendlove's door than at his daughter's.

'What happened next?' I asked. 'Who was here and who was absent when you and your guests entered this room?'

Miles screwed up his face in an effort of concentration. 'Gideon was here and Toby – Tobias Maybury, my apprentice – and...' he paused, willing himself to remember. 'And Nell and Christopher. Isolda made her entrance a few moments later. As I've told you, she had been the last one to go to her room to change.'

'So what happened next?' I prompted, as Miles seemed disinclined to proceed with his story.

He shivered and held his hands again to the flames. 'Next, I gave Mistress Perle her birthday gift. A jewelled girdle,' he went on unnecessarily, as though anxious to postpone reaching the awful moment of the murder as long as possible, 'of pale blue leather, studded alternately with Persian sapphires and Egyptian turquoises. She was delighted with it' – as well she might be, I thought – 'and I could see that Mistress Napier was very envious of her friend.' (A fact, I decided, that must have given the gift added value in the eyes of Barbara Perle.)

'And then,' I said, 'presumably you all drank Mistress Perle's health?' My companion nodded mutely. 'And that was when your son-in-law died?'

'Yes.' Miles's voice was so low that I had to strain my ears to catch the word.

'Can you remember exactly what happened?'

'I shall never forget it as long as I live.' He raised his eyes from contemplation of the fire, where a woodlouse was just escaping as fast as its legs could carry it from the terror of the flames, and looked directly into mine. 'I went to my accustomed place at the head of the board and raised my goblet. "To Mistress Perle," I said. "May she have long life and happiness."'

'I'm sorry, but I must interrupt you yet again,' I apologised. 'Do you always sit in the same order around the table?'

'We are creatures of habit,' he said, 'as, in my experience, are most families. Every household has its own little rituals, its simple jokes and allusions that mean nothing to outsiders.' Master Babcary was more astute than he looked. 'When we are on our own, I always sit at the head of the board, with Isolda at the foot. My nephew sits to my right, beside Tobias, and opposite him, to my left, his sister. When ... when Gideon was alive, he sat on the same side of the board as Nell, between her and his wife. But that evening, with company present, Isolda had arranged the table so that she was on my right hand, and, alongside her,

106

Gideon and then Nell. Mistress Perle was seated to my left, Gregory and Ginèvre Napier, in that order, to *her* left. Christopher was at the foot of the table. Toby, as on all occasions when we entertained, would take his meal with Meg, downstairs in the kitchen.'

'So it was Isolda who directed you where to sit?' I asked, and Miles Babcary reluctantly agreed. 'You said she also set the table, so would she have made sure that each of the family goblets was correctly placed?'

Once again, a muttered and reluctant assent was wrung from my host, and I felt that it was hardly surprising Mistress Bonifant had been suspected of her husband's murder. Indeed, the surprise was that, even with the power of the King being brought to bear on her behalf, she had never been charged with the crime. On the other hand, there was one vital question that I had not yet posed, and the answer to it might make a world of difference. I was not, however, ready to ask it for the moment.

'You all went to the table and took your places, after which you raised your goblets, already filled with wine by your daughter, and proposed the birthday toast to Mistress Perle. What then, sir?'

'What then? Why, we drank, of course.'

'Did Master Bonifant collapse at once?'

'Not immediately. We all sat down – we

107

had been standing to drink Barbara's health, you understand – except Isolda, who left the room to go down to the kitchen. The rest of us began to talk: Master Napier and I about the new tariffs that the Poitevins have imposed on the exports of silver from Melle; and the women about such items of gossip as were current last December, whatever they may have been. Gideon was exchanging a few remarks with Christopher, which surprised me because they had been somewhat at loggerheads for the past few months, when suddenly he struggled to his feet, trying desperately to get his breath. Neither could he swallow; his throat and lips were stiff as boards and his face was turning blue. He tried to speak, but all that came out was a terrible croaking sound. I'll never forget it. It will haunt me until the day I die.' And Miles Babcary covered his eyes with his hands.

'What did you do?'

'What could any of us do? Mistress Perle was almost fainting in horror, and I had to give her the better part of my attention. It was Mistress Napier, I think, who told her husband to go for the apothecary who lives in Gudrun Lane. She has a cool head on her shoulders, I'll grant you that. Before he could leave the room, however, Isolda and Meg came in carrying the trays of food. It took them a moment or two to understand what was happening but, as soon as they did, Meg screamed and dropped her tray with an almighty crash, exactly as one would expect her to behave.'

'And Isolda,' I asked, 'what did she do?'

There was a silence of several seconds, then Miles said slowly, 'She just stood there, as though turned to stone, while Gideon raised his hand and pointed a finger at her, his eyes filled with horror and absolute terror. Then he pitched headlong across the table. By the time the apothecary was fetched, he was dead.'

Seven

A log crackled, the flames leapt up the chimney and shadows were sent scurrying and curtseying across the tapestried walls. After a moment's silence, I cleared my throat and asked the question that had been gnawing away at the back of my mind for the past half an hour or more.

'Master Babcary, was there – *is* there – any good reason why your daughter should be suspected of murdering her husband? So far, you have painted the picture of a couple happily, or at least contentedly, married, even if that marriage was not a love match.'

'Who says it was not a love match?' My companion's bottom lip jutted dangerously.

'Are you claiming that it was?' I demanded, meeting his attack with counter-attack, a strategy that I have frequently used to good effect.

The lip was withdrawn, indicating defeat. 'Perhaps not,' he conceded. 'But they both liked each other well enough. It's true that Gideon drove a hard bargain; an equal partnership in the shop, although he knew nothing of goldsmithing, and senior status to Christopher, who had been learning the trade for a full year before Gideon's arrival in the house.' Resentment coloured Miles's tone and, as if suddenly aware of it, he made an effort to laugh off his son-in-law's pre-sumption. 'Of course, there was nothing in that, when all's said and done! He was Isolda's husband, and would one day inherit the shop and everything in it in her name. It was only natural that he would have to learn what was what, and that he should expect to be more important to me than my nephew.'

Nevertheless, you did not like him the better for it, I thought to myself. Aloud, I asked, 'Was your daughter happy that matters should be thus arranged?'

'She wasn't consulted,' Miles replied simply. 'Her assured inheritance of all that is mine was a part of her dowry, along with the sum of money I settled on her and Gideon at the time of their wedding. These are men's concerns, not women's. She was sufficiently content to be married at last, after years of being a maid.' He tried to compose his features into an expression of acceptance for a situation that had plainly irked him. Miles had not cared for his son-in-law, I decided, however much he might have tried to persuade himself and the world otherwise.

'You haven't yet answered my question, sir,' I reminded him, as a further squall of rain spattered against the windows.

'Question? What question?' Brooding upon Gideon's shortcomings, he had forgotten what it was that I had asked him.

'Was there any good reason why Mistress Bonifant should have been suspected of murdering her husband?'

Once again, the short-sighted, pale blue eyes looked into mine while their owner debated whether or not to tell me the truth.

'There was none on her part,' Miles answered at last. 'Isolda's affection for Gideon in the weeks and months leading up to the murder appeared to be what it had ever been, I'll swear to that. And so will everyone else in the house.' Or incur his undying displeasure was implicit in his tone, although the words remained unspoken.

'In that case, what can you tell me about

Master Bonifant? Did you have any reason to believe that his affection for your daughter had altered in any way? Did he ever give you any hint that all might not be well between them?'

Rain pattered down the chimney and hissed among the burning logs like a plague of snakes. The silence stretched, thin as a tautly drawn wire, but at last Master Babcary shrugged resignedly.

'Gideon had told me some weeks, maybe a month or so, before the evening of his death that he suspected Isolda of cuckolding him with another man.'

I was betrayed into a gasp, hastily suppressed. 'And did he happen to mention this other man's name?' I asked.

'No, not directly, but he did tell me on a separate occasion that he had overheard Christopher boasting to his sister of being in love with an older woman, and that he – Christopher, that is – was almost certain that his love was requited.'

I thought about this. 'You were not the only person in whom Master Bonifant confided his doubts about your daughter and nephew, obviously.'

'Why do you say that?' Miles's tone was accusatory. 'Have you been talking to other people before you came here?'

I shook my head. 'Only to Mistress Shore, but you know about that. No, I'm judging

112

by the fact that if you had been the sole recipient of Gideon's confidence, his accusation would not have become generally known. You would have said nothing that would in any way have incriminated your daughter, and certainly not once your son-in-law had been murdered.'

'Why should I? I had no idea if the slander were true or false,' was the indignant rejoinder. 'Would you expect me to repeat something detrimental about my own child for which I only had Gideon's word?'

'I'm not blaming you,' I said hurriedly. 'I have a daughter of my own, and whatever might be right in the eyes of God or the law, I know that I could never do anything that might harm her.'

'Not even if you thought she had committed some great sin?' Miles Babcary asked in a voice so low that I almost failed to hear him.

'No, not even then,' I admitted, 'for that's the nature of the tie between my child and me.' He nodded to show that he understood, and I continued, 'So who else did your son-in-law confide in?'

'In Gregory Napier, the last person in the world I should ever have wished to be privy to my family's affairs.' Miles spoke bitterly, and I could see that his hands had begun to tremble. 'There were also one or two others who came forward to say that Gideon had

113

made them free of his suspicions. One was his former master, Ford, the apothecary, whose shop is in Bucklersbury.'

'And what was Mistress Bonifant's response to these accusations?'

'She just laughed at them. She said they were absurd and that we must be making them up. At first, she didn't seem to grasp how serious they were, especially after Gideon had been poisoned.'

'And when she did?'

'She was completely bewildered, poor girl. She couldn't begin to imagine why Gideon would have wanted to spread such lies about her, and demanded to know the identity of the man with whom she was supposed to have been unfaithful.'

'And when it emerged that it was her cousin, what did your nephew have to say?'

Master Babcary rubbed the side of his nose with his finger. 'Kit denied it furiously. He also denied that he had ever told his sister that he was in love with an older woman, and that the woman might be in love with him. Nell, of course, upheld his story.'

'Of course! But did you believe her?'

Master Babcary pursed his lips. 'Ye-es,' he said, but with a lack of conviction that made me raise my eyebrows. Reluctantly he confessed, 'Nell has led a very sheltered life, first with her father, then with me. She is inclined to get flustered when she is hostilely questioned, or feels herself under threat in any way.' He stared long and hard into the burning heart of the fire. 'Sometimes, she sounds as though she's lying when she isn't. There are people like that, you know,' he added eagerly. 'She's very shy.'

I agreed that there were indeed people in whom the mildest interrogation aroused the strongest sensation of guilt, even when they were entirely innocent of any wrongdoing. Eleanor Babcary could well be one of them, but it was also possible that, on this particular occasion, she might *not* have been telling the truth in order to protect her brother. I suspected from his general demeanour that her uncle had thought her denial less than ingenuous. But when I suggested this possibility to him, Miles sprang hotly to her defence.

'I'll swear that she wasn't lying. You don't know that girl as I do, Master Chapman. She is as open and as honest as the day. She abhors untruths, I tell you. She simply gets confused, as I have already explained, when faced with a barrage of questions.'

'And who questioned her?'

'One of the Sheriff's officers, naturally, for of course we were obliged to send for the Law as soon as we realised that my son-in-law had been poisoned. The officer wasn't as gentle with Nell as he might have been, and consequently her attitude persuaded him that she was lying.'

'But she stuck to her story?'

'Oh, yes! That, more than anything, convinced me that she must be telling the truth.'

I refrained from pointing out that if Eleanor Babcary abhorred untruths, as her uncle had just maintained, he would have needed no convincing: he would have known for a fact that his niece was not lying. Moreover, I believe that the person has not been born who is totally incapable of telling a falsehood. Surely, if for no other reason, we all instinctively make the effort to protect those whom we love.

The door opened and Mistress Bonifant's voice sounded calmly through the gloom, unperturbed by the fact that she knew we must have been talking about her.

'It's nearly four o'clock, Father. Will Master Chapman be staying to supper?'

'I – er – I have no idea, my dear.' He turned to me. 'Master Chapman, would you care to share our evening meal with us? You would be very welcome.'

'I was unaware that the day was so far advanced,' I said, getting to my feet. 'Thank you for your offer, Mistress Bonifant, but I must go back to the Voyager and take supper with my wife. This visit to London was to

116

have been a holiday for both of us, and I cannot neglect her any further this evening. Tomorrow being Sunday, I shan't disturb your Sabbath peace, but, with your permission, Master Babcary, I'll return on Monday and question the other members of your household.'

'If you think you can solve the riddle of my son-in-law's death, we shall be glad to see you,' he answered heavily. He glanced somewhat shamefacedly at his daughter, where she still stood framed in the open doorway. 'I'm sorry, my dear, but I've had to tell Master Chapman everything.'

'If by that you mean that Gideon seems to have gone around accusing me of adultery,' Isolda replied evenly, 'it's only what I should have expected you to do, Father. There's no need to apologise. Thanks to the testimony of Gregory Napier and Master Ford, the apothecary, everyone in Cheapside has heard about it.'

I half expected her to plunge into a hot denial of her late husband's allegation, but she did no such thing, and I began to realise that heat and Isolda Bonifant were strangers to one another. She was a woman of even greater self-control and self-containment than my Adela but, then, according to Master Babcary, Gideon had been of a similar temperament, and they seemed to have been eminently well suited to one another. It was possible, however, that one of them had been acting a part.

I took my leave of Mistress Bonifant and was conducted downstairs again by my host. As we turned towards the inner shop door, Meg Spendlove emerged, and at the sight of me, she shied like a startled horse. The tin tray she was carrying by her side clattered against the wall, and her thin, white face puckered as though she were about to burst into tears.

'There, there, my good child,' Miles Babcary said soothingly, 'that will do. There's no need to be frightened. No one's going to hurt you. Have you taken Master Kit and young Toby their ale? That's all right, then. Off you go to the kitchen before something boils over and puts out the fire.' He added, so that only I could hear, 'Not an infrequent occurrence, I do assure you, Master Chapman.'

Christopher Babcary and Tobias Maybury were still at their work, the interior of the shop lit now by lamps and candles, the flames reflected a hundred times over in the depths of the various gold and silver objects and precious gems. Many more of the sparkling golden medallions had been made, ready to be bought and sewn on the silk and velvet gowns of London's wealthiest ladies, so that they could ripple with light whenever they moved. No doubt, I thought bitterly, there was some sumptuary law that restricted the medallions' use to noble-women only, but then I had to smile as I considered that probably no such law was necessary. For what good would these fragile, wafer-thin golden discs be to women who wore homespun and coarse, thickly woven linen?

Master Babcary was looking around in obvious satisfaction, his troubles momentarily forgotten. He was a man who plainly loved his trade, and who was never happier than when he was in his workshop. He would have had little time, then, for a man like Gideon Bonifant, who seemed to have regarded the art of goldsmithing merely as a means of making money. And as if to confirm that impression, Miles had taken my arm and was drawing me towards a small table where a coronet of entwined gold and silver ivy leaves was taking shape.

'For my kinswoman, Mistress Shore,' he said, picking it up and holding it lovingly between both hands, 'to be worn next week at the Westminster Tournament, in honour of the new little bride and bridegroom. It is to be set with these Scottish pearls and Egyptian emeralds.' He sighed wistfully. 'I would have designed a grander circlet if only she would have permitted it. But Jane gave strict instructions that I should make nothing for her that would in any way outshine the jewels to be worn by the Queen or any of Her Highness's sisters.'

He replaced the coronet on the table and linked one of his arms through mine, giving it a little squeeze, well away by now on what was obviously his favourite hobby horse. 'One of the finest examples of the goldsmith's art that I have ever had the privilege of seeing was the wedding coronet of our own Princess Margaret, when she married the Duke of Burgundy ten years ago this summer. Alas, I had no hand in the fashioning of it – I only wish that I had – but it was put on display with other items of her dowry, including all her jewellery, in the Goldsmiths' Hall in the weeks before her wedding. It was small and was meant to perch on the top of her head to show off that beautiful long, fair hair of hers. It was made of gold and decorated with enamelled white roses, rubies, emeralds and sapphires. In the front was a diamond cross and a huge pearl set in another white rose; and all along the lower edge, "C"s and "M"s were wrought in gold and linked by lovers' knots. Oh, it was a splendid piece of work, Master Chapman, I can tell you! It made me proud of my calling and of my fellow goldsmiths who had made it.'

I encountered Christopher Babcary's amused glance, and he winked at me.

'I think the chapman wants to be off,

Uncle. It's wet and dark outside. He's wanting the comforts of the Voyager, I reckon.'

'Of course! Of course! My boy, you should have said. But beauty delights me.'

He led me towards the street door and the display booth, where the glitter of precious metal still enlivened the darkness. Soon everything would be taken inside and safely locked away for the night but, for the moment, the windows of the goldsmiths' shops in West Cheap continued to sparkle like so many heavenly constellations.

As I was about to escape into the murk of the January evening, Master Babcary grabbed my arm and detained me yet again.

'My father, you know,' he said, his eyes glowing with excitement, 'saw the crown brought to this country by King Richard's first queen, Anne of Bohemia, at the end of the last century. He told me that it was the most exquisite thing he had ever laid eyes on in the whole of his life. He said it was six inches tall at its highest point, straight-sided and set with the most glorious array of jewels: scores of diamonds, rubies and sapphires and more than a hundred pearls.' Master Babcary's transports suddenly died away in a heavy sigh. The light left his eyes and his shoulders sagged. 'It's gone from these shores now, alas! It was given away by the usurper, Henry of Bolingbroke, as a part of his daughter's dowry when he married her to Ludwig of Bavaria.'

'Uncle!' Christopher Babcary had come to stand beside us and slipped an affectionate arm around the older man's shoulders. 'Master Chapman needs to be off, and we have to start packing up for the night. Besides, it's suppertime and I'm ravenous. My stomach is positively rumbling with all those delicious cooking smells wafting in from the kitchen.'

My host was contrite. 'You must forgive me, lad. My family have heard all my tales so often that they derive no pleasure from hearing them any more, so a stranger is a godsend to me. Well, well! We shall see you again on Monday then.' He shook my hand vigorously and swung round on his heel, immediately berating the unfortunate apprentice for some sin of omission or commission, I wasn't sure which.

Christopher Babcary grinned as he opened the outer door. 'You musn't mind Uncle Miles,' he apologised quietly. 'His enthusiasm for his work can become a little wearisome after a while, and you have to ask him – politely, of course, but firmly – not to repeat all the anecdotes that you've heard a hundred times before. But don't you worry! I'll make sure he doesn't bore you too much while you're here.'

I thanked him, but assured him that I really didn't mind. 'How did his son-in-law take Master Babcary's stories?'

Christopher's face lost its animation. 'Gideon was never one to wrap things up in clean linen. He would tell my uncle bluntly to hold his noise; that he had no interest in what he was saying. Indeed, Gideon made no secret of the fact that he found goldsmithing itself extremely irksome. He once told Uncle Miles to his face that he would sell the shop as soon as he was master here.'

I nodded. I should have liked to continue the conversation, but instinct told me that it was not the right time. Christopher wanted to be away to his supper, and I needed to go back to the inn to find out how Adela was faring. I therefore bade him goodnight and stepped out into the wind and the rain.

Both had increased in intensity during the last few minutes, and there was also a hint of sleet in the air. The cobbles gleamed wetly between the piles of refuse that had mounted up everywhere during the day, and their surface was treacherous and slippery. I trod warily, using my cudgel as a walking stick rather than holding it at the ready as a weapon. A sudden, particularly fierce gust of wind almost tore my cloak from my back, and I clutched at it with my free hand, holding the edges together at the neck as best I could, but unable to pull up my hood, which now lay, a soggy weight, across my shoulders. I silently cursed Master Babcary for delaying me, but reflected yet again on how much he and Gideon Bonifant must secretly have disliked one another. To be compelled to live and work together, day in, day out, under the same roof, and, at the same time, be forced to present a complaisant face to the world for Isolda's sake, must have been purgatory for both of them. Had it eventually been enough of a spur to drive Miles Babcary to murder?

I was too tired and too preoccupied with the elements to give the idea further consideration just then, and I pushed on along West Cheap in the direction of the Poultry. The rising storm had driven most people to seek either permanent or temporary shelter indoors, and there were only two or three other intrepid walkers like myself still battling against the squalls of wind and rain. Many of the wall cressets had been doused or blown out, but shafts of light from shops and houses slabbed the darkness.

I was approaching the entrance to Gudrun Lane, a gaping mouth of blackness on my left, illuminated solely by a lamp hanging high over the doorway of a stable. As I pressed forward, my head bent against the ever increasing force of the wind, I was suddenly convinced that, out of the corner of my left eye, I had seen a movement – someone or something had retreated into the alleyway. Common sense told me that there was little significance to be attached to this fact: a man, a child, a dog, a cat was taking cover from the storm. But I discovered that for no apparent reason I was nervous. Fear slithered across the surface of my skin.

I had suddenly recollected that halfway along its length, Gudrun Lane was connected, by a little street running at right angles to it, to Foster Lane. And Foster Lane, at its southern end, joined West Cheap by the church of Saint Vedast and Master Babcary's shop. I also remembered something else that I had lost sight of during the last two or three hours, whilst making the acquaintance of Miles Babcary's family and servants: a member of that household could well be a murderer who would be terrified that I might discover the truth about him or her. Had someone left the house as soon as I had taken my own departure, hurrying by that circuitous route to waylay me at the entrance to Gudrun Lane?

I spun round, my cudgel gripped firmly in my right hand and raised to do whatever combat was necessary. My heart began beating faster as I entered that black void of the lane, lit by its solitary beam of light from overhead.

Eight

Keeping close to a row of three-storeyed houses that made up the left-hand wall of Gudrun Lane, I crept forward, my cudgel at the ready, my feet squelching through puddles and piles of garbage. Once, a thin cat, disturbed from its scavenging by my approach, shot across my path with a screech of fury, making me start back and almost knocking me off balance, my heart pounding so hard that I was scarcely able to breathe. Another time, a dog, as wet and bedraggled as I must have looked myself, came sniffing and snapping around my ankles, until I kicked it away with a curse. But apart from these two incidents, nothing broke the silence except for the drumming of the rain and the gusting of the wind.

I was beginning to doubt the existence of this alley that connected Gudrun and Foster Lane – how did I know about it, anyway? I must, at sometime or another, have been this way with Philip Lamprey during one of our forays into the city – when suddenly, there it was, to my left, as narrow and as noisome as memory had painted it. I hesitated for a long moment before turning the corner, every muscle tensed in readiness for a sudden assault upon my person. But nothing happened. No one was lying in wait for me, and the wet cobbles stretched away into the darkness, lit by the pallid gleam of a torch fixed to the wall of one of the cottages and set in a sheltered nook, out of reach of the wind. The piles of rubbish were even higher here than in West Cheap, and I had to step with extreme caution so as not to lose my footing.

Beyond the range of the torchlight, I paused again, convinced that I had heard a noise some little way ahead of me: a cough, perhaps, or a sharp intake of breath.

'Who's there?' I called, but there was no reply. Seconds later, a huge rat scuttled close to one of my boots and disappeared into another mound of offal and rotting vegetables a few yards behind me.

Three or four more paces brought me into Foster Lane. I turned left towards the looming bulk of Saint Vedast, and within moments was back in West Cheap, standing outside Master Babcary's shop. I could hear voices from within raised in cheerful conversation, and the sudden peal of a woman's laughter, but the shutters were up and there was nothing, no movement of any kind, to suggest that anyone was lurking in the surrounding shadows. Either whoever had come after me, with the intention of warning me off, had then thought better of it, or I had been a victim of my own overheated imagination. I was reluctant, however, to admit that it might be the latter.

The storm had abated somewhat, and I was gripped by a burning desire for the warmth and safety of the Voyager – its ale, its excellent food and the company of my wife. Moving as far into the centre of the thoroughfare as I dared without danger of stumbling into the open drain, I strode out as fast as I could, looking straight ahead of me and ignoring as much as possible all the black, gaping mouths of the streets and alleyways on either side of the road. Ten minutes later, I reached the Great Conduit and the entrance to Bucklersbury.

'You've had a long day,' Adela observed.

She was curled up on the bed, watching me devour a huge, steaming hot meat pie, together with a bowl of dried peas and onions. Both dishes had been served, on the orders of Reynold Makepeace himself, in the warmth and comfort of our room. My wife, who had eaten her supper before my arrival, assured me that she was feeling a great deal better, and insisted that we talk about the rigours of *my* day – although I fancied that there was an unusual touch of

128

acerbity in her tone.

'As a matter of fact, I have had a very tiring few hours,' I answered defensively. 'First, if you remember, I had to visit Mistress Shore at her house in the Strand—'

Adela, who had indeed forgotten this fact, immediately interrupted. 'Tell me all about it!' she commanded.

And I was allowed to go no further with the account of my doings until I had described my meeting with the King's mistress in the the minutest detail. Adela was particularly taken with my description of the old dog on his red satin cushion, and at once pronounced Mistress Shore to be a woman very much after her own heart.

'Jeanne Lamprey tells me that she's popular both with the common people and at court.' Adela tilted her head to one side. 'So why doesn't the Duke of Gloucester care for her, do you suppose?'

I stared consideringly at my plate. It was a question that had been nagging away at the back of my own mind ever since my meeting with the King's mistress and the realisation that she was, in truth, as kind and as merry and as unassuming as her reputation made her out to be. Why then did the man I admired – worshipped, almost – above all others obviously have so little liking for her?

'I think,' I said at last, raising my eyes to my wife's, 'that Duke Richard regards

Mistress Shore in the same light as he regards members of the Queen's family, the Queen herself, Lord Hastings and so many others who surround the King. He sees them all as responsible in their various ways for his brother's physical and moral decline. Oh, Edward's handsome enough even now, I grant you, but seven years ago, around the time of the battle at Tewkesbury, he was magnificent; lean as a greyhound, strong as an ox and with a mind sharp enough to outwit all those powerful barons who had robbed him of his throne and driven him into exile.

'But now, while he'll never be fat on account of his great height, he's growing corpulent, he has a double chin, he's a pensioner of King Louis of France – a fact of which the Duke of Gloucester bitterly disapproves – and, if the gossips are to be believed, he devotes more time to pleasure than the Council Chamber. And to top everything else, he seems, finally, to have turned against his brother, George of Clarence.'

'Your Duke sounds to me a rather puritanical young man,' Adela observed dryly, wriggling into a more upright position on the bed, her back supported by the banked up pillows. 'Almost a prig, but not above overlooking Mistress Shore's faults – real or imagined – when he needs to make use of her and of her influence with the King.'

I resented any criticism, however oblique, of the Duke of Gloucester.

'He's trying to save his other brother's life,' I protested vigorously. 'Surely a compromise with his conscience is justified under such circumstances.'

'It depends what the Duke of Clarence has done to turn the King so irrevocably against him at last.' Adela gave her sudden, disarming smile. 'But don't let's quarrel when I haven't seen you all day, and when I'm unlikely to see much of you for as long as it takes you to resolve this mystery. What happened at the goldsmith's? Do you have any idea as yet whether or not the daughter really committed the crime?' She patted her stomach. 'Tell your son and me all about it.'

'It might be another daughter,' I said, somewhat rattled by her insistence that the child she was carrying was a boy. 'What I want is a girl who looks like you.'

'It's a boy,' was the confident answer. 'And Margaret agrees with me.'

'I don't see how you can possibly be so sure,' I retorted, and was rewarded with what I called her 'knowing' expression – a slight smile of contempt for my male ignorance, accompanied by a look of pity. A shake of her head implied that it would be fruitless to continue a discussion in which I was so plainly at a disadvantage.

As I had come to realise over the years that all pregnant women, however rational in other ways, adopt this omniscient attitude towards the mysteries of childbirth, especially when addressing a man, I let the subject drop and launched into a recital of everything that had happened at Master Babcary's shop.

'So you see,' I said when I had finished, 'there are still many enquiries to make before I can offer an opinion as to Mistress Bonifant's guilt or innocence. To begin with, apart from the family and servants, there were three other people present in the house on the night of Gideon's death – three neighbours to whom I have not even spoken as yet.'

Adela reached over and took the bowl containing the remains of the dried peas and onions from the tray on my knees, and began scooping the vegetables into her mouth with the wooden spoon provided.

'I can't help it,' she laughed, noting my raised eyebrows, 'I'm hungry all the time. The trouble is that, although I know peas and onions will probably give me a violent colic later, I can't resist eating them. But go on. What do you make of the story that Gideon Bonifant was spreading just before his death? The story that Isolda was unfaithful to him with her cousin, this – this—'

132

'Christopher Babcary,' I supplied. I propped my chin on my hands and stared into the heart of the small sea-coal fire where the flames burnt blue and yellow, and for whose warmth and light and comfort we had agreed to pay the landlord a small extra daily charge. 'Why would a man spread such a story if it weren't true, particularly as he and his wife seem to have spent five reasonably contented years together?'

Adela put the now empty bowl back on the tray and shifted her position in order to make herself more comfortable.

'On the other hand,' she said after a moment or two, 'even if we accept that the story is true – and, as you say, a man doesn't claim to have been made a cuckold without good reason – infidelity doesn't necessarily turn a woman into a murderess.' She chewed her bottom lip thoughtfully. 'You say that both Isolda and her cousin deny the charge that Gideon levelled against them?'

'Yes, but they have to, don't they, unless they wish to brand themselves poisoners in the eyes of the world? They'd be fools to admit it.'

'But if Mistress Bonifant *did* kill her husband, how did she hope to get away with it if he had already told people about her infatuation with Christopher Babcary?'

'Because she had no idea that he'd done so. Her father confirms that he never

133

mentioned Gideon's accusations to Isolda. And the other people in whom her husband confided – his old master, the apothecary, and Master Napier – were hardly likely to have confronted her with the story.'

Adela rubbed her stomach and grimaced. 'That's true,' she agreed. 'But what about this cousin? Was he never suspected of being the murderer?'

'He might have been, I suppose, in due course. But Mistress Shore seems to have implored the King for his intervention too rapidly for the Sheriff's officers to have levelled accusations at anyone, or for any kind of investigation to have got under way. King Edward, not wishing, I imagine, for his chief leman to be implicated, even by association, in anything so sordid as murder, halted all enquiries immediately. But it's not so easy, of course, to stop the whispering of neighbours and erstwhile friends, as it is to give orders to officials. And so here I am, once more embroiled in what, in a very roundabout way, has become the Duke of Gloucester's concern.'

Or God's, I added silently. For it wasn't Duke Richard who had brought me to London at this particular time. It was the Almighty yet again, manipulating my thoughts and desires; or, at least, if not mine, then Adela's. But I was learning at last not to feel resentful – well, not too resentful

134

– for I had come to appreciate that I might find my day-to-day existence very humdrum without these adventures of mine.

I emerged from my brief reverie to realise that Adela was speaking, echoing something of my own uneasiness.

'...but you mustn't lose sight of the fact, Roger, that *somebody* committed that murder, whether it was Isolda Bonifant or no. And whoever it is, is probably very frightened by your investigation and the possibility that you might discover the truth.'

'Only "might"?' I protested, quizzing her and laughing at her discomfiture. 'No, no! You're quite right, my love! It would never do for a wife to be too confident of her husband's abilities, or she would cease to have the whip hand.' Then, seeing that my teasing was genuinely distressing her, I plunged, without thinking, into an account of what had occurred on my way back to the inn.

But this, of course, only served to worry her even further, as I ought to have known it would.

'Do you really believe that you were being followed?' she demanded anxiously.

I shook my head. 'I honestly don't know. I could find no evidence of it, and yet—'

'And yet?' she queried, her voice trembling a little.

'And yet, at the time, I was certain that I

135

had heard or seen something suspicious. And when I remembered that connecting alleyway between Foster and Gudrun Lane, I was conscious that anyone from the Babcary household could have caught up with me without following me directly from the shop. But I might have been mistaken. There are sufficient cats and rats foraging among the rubbish to account for any number of apparently mysterious movements and noises. I mustn't let my imagination run away with me.'

But my wife remained unconvinced. Once it had dawned on her that a murderer was still at large, and that I might pose a danger to him or her, she was unable to be easy in her mind. I could see her wrestling with the urge to demand that I disoblige the Duke of Gloucester and give up my enquiry into the killing of Gideon Bonifant. But Adela was also wise enough to know that even if she prevailed this once, she was unlikely to do so the next time – or the next.

So she contented herself with giving me a wintry smile and saying, 'Take care! You already have three, and will soon have four, people dependent on you for their daily bread. None of us can afford to lose you.'

I rose to my feet, stretching and yawning. 'It's nice to know that I'm appreciated as a breadwinner, if nothing else,' I grinned.

I was rewarded with a look of deep

hostility. 'You know perfectly well what I mean.'

'Of course I do.' I sat down on the edge of the bed and put my arms around her.

'What will you do tomorrow?' she asked, slewing round to kiss my cheek. 'You said you've promised the Babcarys that you won't disturb their Sabbath peace.'

'Neither shall I.' I returned her kiss. 'But I've a fancy to see this Master Ford, the apothecary who was Gideon Bonifant's former master. Undoubtedly, he will go to church. But which one does he favour, I wonder.'

There were at least four churches of importance in the area, any one of which Master Ford might attend, although none in Bucklersbury itself.

In adjoining Needlers Lane stood the churches of Saint Pancras and of Saint Benet Sherehog. Walbrook, at the eastern end of Bucklersbury, boasted Saint Stephen Walbrook, while Saint Mary Woolchurch served the inhabitants of the Stock's Market and the Poultry.

'Where does Master Ford, the apothecary, worship of a Sunday?' I asked Reynold Makepeace after breakfast the following morning.

He scratched his nose while giving the matter his full consideration.

137

'Now there you have me, Master Chapman, for I don't know, I'm sure. Wait here a moment and I'll enquire in the taproom. Someone there might be able to help you.'

He returned a few minutes later, however, shaking his grizzled head.

'I'm afraid no one seems to know for certain, although Peter Paulet, who lives in Soper Lane, thinks he remembers that the late Mistress Ford used sometimes to worship at Saint Mary Woolchurch.'

I thanked him for his trouble and enquired about the exact location of Master Ford's shop.

'Now that I can tell you,' my host said with satisfaction, wiping his hands on his best Sunday linen apron. 'You'll find it on this side of the street, at the Walbrook end, almost directly opposite a large stone-built house on the southern side, called the Old Barge. A strange name for a house, you might think, but ships used to tie up there before that part of the Walbrook was paved over. But Master Ford's shop won't be open today, if, that is, you're needing any remedies from him.' The kindly face clouded with anxiety. 'It's not Mistress Chapman, is it? If there's anything wrong, you must let me send for the local midwife. She'll be by far the best person to advise you.'

'No, no! My wife is in excellent health,' I assured him, which was true except for a somewhat disturbed night, the result of Adela's craving for dried peas and onions. 'I just wanted a word with Master Ford about – about something,' I finished lamely.

Fortunately, Reynold Makepeace was not a curious man, and made no attempt to discover why I had this sudden urge to speak to one of the Bucklersbury apothecaries, or, indeed, how I even came to be aware of his existence. He simply nodded and hurried away to attend to his customers in the taproom, one or two of whom were vociferously demanding his services.

Quarter of an hour later, my wife and I left the inn, walking eastwards towards Walbrook. The storm of the previous evening had, thankfully, blown itself out, giving way to a cold, but not frosty, morning, and a thin sun struggled to break through the leaden clouds. Adela, wrapped in her thick woollen cloak with its fur-lined hood, a garment purchased especially for this visit to London, assured me that she was as warm as it was possible to be in January, while her pattens kept her feet out of the mud and rubbish. (For being Sunday and a day of rest, there were no street cleaners to remove yesterday's accumulated filth. Cleanliness and godliness, alas, do not always go hand in hand.)

The clamour from the bells was deafening, for London, or so I'm told, has well over a hundred churches within its walls, not to mention those proliferating outside its pale. Adela had to raise her voice to make herself heard.

'Why do you wish to speak with this Master Ford?'

'If Gideon Bonifant was once his assistant, he must know something about the man. Anything he can tell me might prove useful. Wait!' I paused, gripping her arm and pointing to the opposite side of the street where Bucklersbury ran into Walbrook. 'That big house must be the one that Landlord Makepeace mentioned. And Master Ford's shop, he said, is almost directly opposite.'

This information, however, was not as valuable as it at first seemed, for the frontage of the Old Barge was the width of at least four or five shops on the northern side of the street, three of them belonging to apothecaries. But even as we watched, people began leaving home for church in answer to the bells' summons. A family of six – father, mother and four children – emerged from one of the apothcaries' shops, setting off westwards, in the direction of Needlers Lane, while from another, a middle-aged couple headed for Saint Stephen Walbrook. Minutes later, a tall, thin man appeared in the remaining apothecary's doorway, turned smartly to his left and had vanished round the corner into

Walbrook before I had time to gather my wits together.

'That must be him,' Adela hissed, nudging me painfully in the ribs. 'Reynold Makepeace told us, if you remember, that Master Ford is a widower, and both of the other two men had wives.'

'I think you're probably right,' I nodded. 'And that's the way to the Stock's Market and Saint Mary Woolchurch, where, again according to Master Makepeace, the late Mistress Ford sometimes worshipped.'

'Then what are we waiting for?' my wife demanded, slipping her hand once more within my arm. 'In that case, that's where *we* shall worship.'

'And we'll probably have the added pleasure of seeing Jeanne and Philip as well,' I said.

For I had recollected that Saint Mary Woolchurch was also adjacent to the old clothes market, and consequently was the church most often attended by the Lampreys. (Although they did occasionally honour Saint Benet Fink, on the corner of Fink's Lane, with their presence.)

Adela's step quickened at the prospect of a possible meeting with our friends, even though she expressed doubt about finding them very easily amongst the attendant congregation. But in this she was wrong, for almost the first people we encountered in the crowded nave, standing at the back near one of the pillars, were Jeanne and Philip Lamprey, both of whom greeted us as if they had not seen us for a month, instead of only the previous day.

Once the Mass had started, and I could whisper in Philip's ear without being overheard by all around us, I asked him if he knew Master Ford, the apothecary. Philip nodded.

'Is he here?'

My friend craned his neck and stretched up on his toes in an effort to see over the heads of all those in front of him. Finally, he gave a grunt of triumph.

'I can just see the top of his hat. It's the one he wears every Sunday. I recognise the feather coiled around the brim. Why do you want to know?'

I countered with another question of my own.

'Are you well enough acquainted with Master Ford to introduce me to him when the service is over?'

Philip rolled suspicious eyes towards me. 'Not really, but that needn't stop me. However, that's all I'm doing. I've already told you once, Roger, you're not involving me in any of your schemes. They're usually far too dangerous.'

Nine

Master Ford seemed a little disconcerted to be claimed as an acquaintance by Philip Lamprey for, as Philip bluntly informed him, he had not been in Master Ford's shop above twice in his life, those being the only two occasions on which he had previously spoken to the apothecary.

'But I've often seen you among the congregation here, and Mistress Ford, also, when she was alive.' My friend's tone was hearty as he pumped the other man's hand up and down. Philip was doing his best for me, even if he did not wish to get involved.

Jeanne went one better. Put in the picture by my wife, she bewildered Master Ford still further by inviting him to take his dinner with us at the Voyager, where, in a whispered conversation during the service, I had invited the Lampreys to eat with Adela and myself. Quick to follow this lead, I added my entreaties to hers, but decided to be honest with the apothecary and give him a chance to decline should he wish to do so.

'Hmmph,' he grunted when I had finished

143

a somewhat halting explanation. 'I wondered how long Mistress Shore and her kinsfolk would be content to let the matter of poor Gideon's murder rest, before trying to find out the truth.' We began to move slowly towards the church porch, impelled forward by the crowd of people surrounding us. 'It's all very well the King bringing pressure to bear on the Sheriff's officers to proceed no further with their enquiries but, in the end, it's always unsatisfactory not knowing what really happened.' The nostrils of his long, thin nose, set in the middle of his long, thin face, flared in disapproval.

We emerged into the Stock's Market to discover that the day had grown brighter, the sun forcing its way through a break in the leaden clouds and diffusing sufficient warmth to dry the slimy cobbles.

I turned once again to my new acquaintance. 'What's your answer, then, Master Ford? Will you give us the pleasure of your company at dinner?'

He hesitated, but only for a second: Reynold Makepeace had a well-deserved reputation for serving some of the best food for streets around.

'Thank you,' he said in his courteous, rather stately fashion. 'I should be pleased to accept your kind invitation.'

His tone was still a little wary, but who could be surprised at that? To be accosted

144

by two complete strangers and two known to him only by sight, and, in addition, be pressed into dining with them, must have been a bewildering experience. But I suspected that dinner at the Voyager, even with four unknowns, was preferable to his own lonely table. Besides, it turned out that he was well acquainted with Reynold Makepeace, and the pair of them greeted each other with the easy familiarity of old friends.

By the time we had walked the length of Bucklersbury, it was past ten o'clock, and the long trestles and benches of the Voyager's dining parlour were already filling up. In deference, however, to the fact that Adela and I were guests at the inn, and that I was known to have some connection with His Grace of Gloucester, the landlord ushered the five of us into a private room overlooking the main courtyard, and saw to it that we received the best and promptest of attention. (The look he gave Philip was a puzzled one, unable, probably, to reconcile this pock-marked, unsavoury-looking individual with my more noble connections.)

We ate boiled beef with buttered vegetables, a curd tart accompanied by a dish of raisins steeped in brandy, and a sweet cheese flan, all washed down with the Voyager's best home-brewed ale. It was a dinner to remember, as, indeed, I have remembered it down through the years with pleasure and nostalgia. (Food today isn't what it was. There's no flavour to anything any more, although my children – quite wrongly, it goes without saying – attribute this fact more to my age and loss of taste than to the inferior quality of the viands.)

During the course of the meal, I was able to talk to Master Ford, who was seated next to me, about Gideon Bonifant and the murder.

'Gideon was my assistant for only a year before he married Isolda Babcary and went to work for his father-in-law,' the apothecary said, between mouthfuls of boiled beef and buttered vegetables. 'The marriage was a great stroke of good fortune for him, and raised his prospects beyond anything he could otherwise have hoped for. Indeed, until Mistress Babcary took a fancy to him, Gideon had no prospects that I could see, and seemed destined to remain my assistant for the rest of his life. After all, it seemed highly unlikely that anyone in the local community of Isolda's standing and expectations would ever glance in his direction.'

'On the other hand,' I interrupted, 'is it not true that Isolda Babcary had met with no success in finding a husband before she met Gideon Bonifant? I've met the lady, and while I should be reluctant to describe her as ugly, she is certainly no beauty. Moreover, as her father was at pains to inform me, she is of a very independent disposition. And the combination of lack of good looks and strong-mindedness seems to have deterred the other men of her acquaintance from proposing matrimony, even though, or so I imagine, she was possessed of a substantial dowry.'

Master Ford, with great dignity, wiped a dribble of gravy from his chin and ladled another helping of boiled beef and vegetables on to his plate. He then turned his head slowly in my direction, staring reproachfully down that long, patrician nose of his.

'Are you suggesting that Gideon was prepared to overlook these defects in Isolda Babcary in order to avail himself of her fortune?' he demanded.

'Well, he wouldn't be the first man to have done so,' Philip cut in, waving his knife and spoon excitedly in the air and saving me the trouble of replying. 'There's many a poor man who's improved his lot by marrying for money. And no shame to him for doing so, either! It isn't something I'd be happy to contemplate, but the poor must look out for themselves in any way they can. That's my motto!'

'I daresay!' The apothecary's expression grew even more disapproving. 'But Gideon Bonifant was a very pious, very God-fearing man who told his rosary several times a day and always said his prayers before going to sleep at nights. He was not the sort of person to put financial considerations above all others.'

Philip grimaced. 'Sounds like a bit of a dullard to me,' he sniggered.

He was seated opposite me, next to his wife, and I kicked out with my foot in an effort to restrain him. Unfortunately, from the spasm of pain that contorted Jeanne's features, I realised that I had missed my target. Turning back to Master Ford, I hastily changed the subject.

'You say that Master Bonifant had worked as your assistant for only a year before he married Isolda Babcary, yet I recall Mistress Shore telling me that he was ten years older than her kinswoman at the time of the wedding. And Isolda herself was twenty...?'

'Twenty-four.' Master Ford nodded. 'Yes, you are quite correct. Gideon had turned thirty-four when they married. So you see,' he added, directing a censorious glance at Philip, 'he was not a youth to have his head turned by the prospect of wealth and social betterment. He did not marry Isolda Babcary for her money.'

Philip snorted and opened his mouth, doubtless to say what I felt inclined to say myself, that advancing years might have made Gideon more, rather than less, desperate to improve his lot. But I refrained and looked at my friend, silently imploring him to do the same. To my great relief, he got my message and addressed himself once more to his plate.

'The point I am trying to make,' I said, turning yet again to our guest, 'is that Master Bonifant was not a *young* man when he first went to work for you. He must have been at least thirty-two or maybe thirty-three years of age. Do you know anything about his life before that date?'

The apothecary laid his spoon and knife together on his empty plate and, for a moment or two, allowed his attention to wander to the curd tart and sweet cheese flan that one of the inn servants had just placed on the table, together with the brandy-soaked raisins and a jug of fresh ale. Once having satisfied himself of their excellence, he politely gave me all his attention.

'Gideon was not a native of this city,' he said. 'He had lived, until such time as he came to work for me, in Southampton. But the unexpected death of his young wife, some months earlier, had given him a distaste for the place. So he left, and set out for London, in an effort, I imagine, to put the tragedy behind him.'

I stared in surprise at my informant. 'Master Bonifant had been married before? Neither Mistress Shore nor Master Babcary told me that he was a widower.'

The apothecary looked somewhat non-plussed by this remark, then shrugged.

'Perhaps,' he suggested, 'they saw no need to mention it. After all, it's hardly relevant to his death. Nevertheless, I feel sure they must have known. I can't believe that Gideon would have kept the fact a secret.'

'No, indeed,' I answered thoughtfully.

Adela glanced up from her plate and laughed. 'My husband likes to know every little detail, Master Ford, whether it has any bearing on his enquiries or no.'

'He's just plain nosy,' Philip said, 'and it can land him in a lot of trouble.' He added feelingly, 'It can land other people in a lot of trouble, as well.'

'Each fact, however irrelevant it appears, may be of importance,' I retorted sententiously. 'But pray continue, Master Ford. How did Master Bonifant come to be in your employ? Had he been an apothecary's assistant in Southampton?'

'So he told me, and I saw no need to doubt his word. He seemed to know the business, and quickly proved to my satisfaction that he could mix lotions and make up unguents as well as I could myself. He knew the properties of all the different herbs, and was good at discussing the ailments, as well as the necessary remedies, with my customers, particularly the older ones. He had, in fact, become invaluable to me during that short twelvemonth, and I was extremely sorry to part with him when the time came for him to marry.'

'How did you meet him, and what happened to your previous assistant?' I asked.

Master Ford managed a thin-lipped smile. 'I see what your friend means about your nosiness. Are such facts really important in attempting to solve the mystery – if indeed there *is* a mystery – of Gideon's murder?'

'Probably not,' I admitted. 'But as I have already pointed out, I cannot tell what might be of value and what might not. And it's true, I'm curious by nature.'

'"Nosy" was what we said,' Philip grinned.

With an effort of will, I ignored him, but I was beginning to tire of his pleasantries. Leaving my curd tart untouched on my plate, I twisted my head even further in Master Ford's direction, in spite of the fact that such a posture was giving me a severe pain in my neck. 'I'd be grateful for an answer to my question.'

The apothecary sampled the sweet cheese tart and it seemed to have a mellowing effect upon him.

'My previous assistant was my wife,' he explained. 'She had inherited her considerable knowledge of ailments and their treatments from her father, who was also an apothecary, and so I had never had need of any other help in the shop. She had been

151

dead only three or four months when Gideon came asking me if I was in want of an assistant.' Master Ford heaved a sigh. 'The similarity of our situations, both of us so recently bereaved, may, originally, have inclined me to employ him, but I never had any cause to regret my decision.'

'Of all the apothecaries in London,' I asked, 'how did he come to pick on you? There must be a dozen in Bucklersbury alone.'

Master Ford shook his head sadly, as though he were dealing with an idiot child. 'I was not the first shop at which he had offered his services. Gideon told me later that he had, in fact, been trudging around the city for several days. It was, oddly enough, the apothecary in West Cheap, in Gudrun Lane, who advised him that I might be glad of his assistance.'

'Why do you say "oddly enough"? What was strange about the apothecary in Gudrun Lane?'

'Jeremiah Page was summoned to the goldsmith's house the night that Gideon died.'

'Ah, yes!' I refilled my beaker with ale and finally managed to consume a mouthful or two of curd tart. 'I remember Master Babcary mentioning that fact.' I frowned. 'Why was an apothecary sent for and not a physician?'

Master Ford shrugged. 'That I cannot tell you. I wasn't there. You must ask members of the household for an answer. Maybe there's no physician who lives close enough at hand. Maybe those present weren't sure that Gideon was really dead, and hoped that an apothecary might have an antidote to revive him. Maybe ... But I repeat, I wasn't there. I don't know what anybody said or thought. I only heard the rumours and the stories that circulated afterwards.'

'You were shocked by the news of Gideon Bonifant's murder?'

'Of course I was shocked.' Master Ford hesitated a moment or two before continuing, 'Shocked, but not altogether surprised.'

'And why was that?' I queried, although I could guess the answer.

The other three had by now finished their meal and, with nothing else to distract them, were listening intently to the conversation.

Master Ford, who had also eaten his fill, eased his thin buttocks into a more comfortable position on the bench and pressed a thumb and forefinger to the bridge of his nose as though considering his reply. At last he said, 'A few weeks before his death, Gideon confided in me his suspicion that his wife was being unfaithful to him with her cousin, Christopher Babcary.'

'And you believed him?'

Once again, the apothecary hesitated over his answer. 'At the time, I thought him completely sincere in his belief, but mistaken.'

'Why did you think him mistaken?' Jeanne Lamprey wanted to know.

Master Ford spread his long, thin hands, with their elegant, tapering fingers.

'I don't know Christopher Babcary all that well, you understand. I've only spoken once to him at any length, and that was at Gideon's wedding to Isolda. He was some fourteen years of age then, all spots and pimples as such callow youths generally are. But I've caught sight of him many times since, when I've been in West Cheap, and over the past five and a half years, he's grown into a good-looking young fellow.

'Now, it seemed to me, when Gideon first told me of his suspicions concerning him and Isolda, highly improbable that such a man, who cannot lack for female companionship, would fall in love with a woman older than himself by some ten years, and one, moreover, who is so plain that she found it difficult to get herself a husband in the first place.' Master Ford bit his lip. 'But I should have had more faith in Gideon's knowledge of the pair. I repeat, he was a God-fearing man and would never have made such an accusation lightly.'

'You think then that Mistress Bonifant is guilty of her husband's death?'

'Either she alone or she and her cousin together.' Master Ford turned to stare defiantly at me. 'Don't think me ignorant of the details of the murder. I made it my business to find them out. I was fond of Gideon – or as fond as I could be after only a year's close acquaintance. He was not a man anyone could get to know easily, for he was reluctant to talk freely about himself. His grief at the death of his first wife went too deep for idle prattle, and I honoured him for that. I understood his reticence. I'm just sorry that chance put Isolda Babcary in his way.'

'How did that happen?' I asked.

The apothecary shook his head. 'I don't know. All I do know is that one day she came into the shop asking for Gideon. I called him from the back room where he was mixing up some lotions for me, and I could see at once that they were no strangers to one another. The only thing that surprised me, as it appeared to surprise Gideon, was that she had come seeking him out. I thought it unmaidenly and forward.'

'Did you think then that romance might be in the air?'

'It was the last thought to cross my mind. She was twenty-four years old and plain. She had nothing to recommend her to a man like Gideon.'

'Except her money and the fact that her

father was a goldsmith in West Cheap,' Philip said, unable to resist the temptation to say his piece yet again.

'Philip! Hold your tongue!' Jeanne was before me with her admonition. 'Nevertheless,' she went on, smiling apologetically at Master Ford, 'you must admit that there is some truth in what my husband says.'

'Well...' Won over by her charm, the apothecary wavered. 'Maybe Gideon was a little flattered at being singled out by a woman of standing and fortune. But I'd be willing to swear to his sincerity when he told me that he was extremely fond of her. He said she had a sweet and pious nature, and that in his estimation that was of far greater importance than her lack of physical beauty.'

I could see that Philip was about to make some jibe or other, but Jeanne forestalled him.

'Indeed, I must confess to feeling precisely the same way when I married my husband,' she said, causing Philip's jaw to drop open in astonishment at such an unexpected broadside. But her remark, cruel as it may have been, had the desired effect of ensuring his silence.

I carefully avoided looking at Adela, who was shaking with suppressed laughter, and kept my eyes fixed firmly upon the apothecary, who had obviously seen nothing amusing in Jeanne Lamprey's remark.

'Did you remain friendly with Master Bonifant after his marriage?' I asked.

'We were always on speaking terms,' the apothcary answered slowly. 'If we met one another in the street, we exchanged more than the time of day. Gideon would enquire after my health, and I after his and that of Mistress Bonifant. And in the first year or so succeeding the wedding, he would occasionally visit my shop, rather than the one in Gudrun Lane, if he or his wife needed any medicaments. But, understandably, as the years went by, those visits grew less and less until they ceased altogether. Latterly, I saw nothing of him unless, by chance, we met out of doors.'

'Why do you say "understandably"?' I wanted to know.

Master Ford shrugged and once again regarded me as though I were slightly simple.

'Because,' he explained slowly and clearly, 'Gideon became a part of the Babcary household. He was learning the goldsmith's craft from his father-in-law and had no more interest in the apothecary's trade. I didn't blame him. He didn't wish to be constantly reminded of his lowlier past.'

'Did it surprise you that he and Isolda had no children?'

'No, it didn't!' Master Ford exploded

angrily. 'I never thought upon the subject. It's God's will that many couples remain childless. It was His will that my dear wife and I should have no progeny. Really, Master Chapman, your curiosity gets the better of you and I think, if you and your friends will excuse me, that I shall be going.' He rose from the bench and made courteous bows to both Adela and to Jeanne. 'Thank you for a very fine dinner, but now I must be on my way.'

He was gone before I could do anything to stop him. I heard his voice upraised in the passageway as he took his leave of Reynold Makepeace.

'Well,' remarked Philip with great satisfaction, 'you can't pretend that it was *my* fault Master Ford went away. That was entirely your doing, Roger! You asked one question too many as you always do. That long nose of yours is still getting you into trouble.'

I nodded in vexation. 'I should have guessed that he and Mistress Ford were childless when there was no mention of a son or daughter.'

'You weren't to know,' Adela soothed, patting my arm. 'So! Did your questions yield anything apart from the fact that Master Bonifant had been married before?'

I considered her question. 'Oh, I think so. I know now that Gideon was a pious,

God-fearing man—'

'Or passed as one,' Philip sneered, his experience of life before he met and married Jeanne not having made him think very highly of his fellow creatures in general.

'Or passed as one, as you say,' I agreed. 'And he certainly showed very little gratitude to the man who had given him both shelter and employment when he was destitute in London. Master Ford should surely have been treated as a friend after the marriage put Gideon on an equal footing with him.' I sighed. 'But apart from his accusation against his wife and her cousin, I know as yet of no other reason why anyone should wish to murder Gideon Bonifant.'

Ten

We spent the rest of the day in the company of the Lampreys, sitting for a while longer, after Master Ford's departure, over our ale at the Voyager, and then, when the weather improved still further and the afternoon became dry and bright, we went for a walk at Adela's request.

'For I shall be nothing but a bladder of

wind if I sit here any longer,' she protested, 'like one of those footballs that boys kick around in the streets.' She eyed me with mock severity as she rose to her feet. 'Here I am, barely three months pregnant, and already this child is causing me more discomfort than Nicholas did in nine. He's going to take after his father, a restless soul.'

'As long as he isn't as nosy,' Philip said, and I forced myself to laugh, although I could feel my hackles rising. My old friend was becoming a regular source of irritation to me.

We walked the length of Walbrook and down Dowgate Hill to the Baltic Wharf, where the great foreign ships from that northerly region of Europe drop anchor near the Steelyard to unload their cargoes of timber and furs and dried fish. There were plenty of people about, some still dressed in their church-going clothes, ready to be pleased by the unexpected and fragile burst of good weather.

A couple standing near to us on the dockside, and talking loudly enough for the woman's part in the conversation to be easily overheard, had apparently made the journey to Saint Stephen's church at Westminster that morning in order to see the little Duke and Duchess of York at Mass. It seemed, however, that the newly-wed children had been the two persons of least

160

interest to the lady, whose discourse was all of fashion and of what had been worn by which dame of consequence, with disparaging remarks falling as thick as leaves in autumn – much to the fascination of my wife and Jeanne Lamprey who had edged closer to the couple in order not to miss a word.

The speaker, although she was at present swathed in the concealing folds of a dark woollen cloak, plainly considered herself enough a woman of the *beau monde* to pass such strictures, and oozed self-satisfaction. Her companion, whose back was towards me, also seemed happy with her company if his over-zealous attentions were anything to judge by. From where I was standing, I could just make out his companion's features beneath her hood: a handsome, world-weary face, the thin cheeks too pale even for the January cold, and undoubtedly daubed with the white lead used by the more sophisticated women of our society to conceal the effects of sun and wind on their complexions.

Eventually, Philip and I, weary of contemplating the ships, gestured to our still eavesdropping wives that we should move on and, as they reluctantly obeyed our summons, the couple also decided that they had remained stationary long enough. The man swung round, offering the woman his arm, and I came face to face with Christopher Babcary.

'Master Chapman!' He greeted me without enthusiasm, but, at the same time, was obviously gratified to be seen with such a companion. He made no effort to introduce the lady, however, and was beginning to walk away when he paused and turned back. 'We shall meet again tomorrow then, in West Cheap, unless, that is, you've changed your mind.' Abruptly, he released himself from the woman's clasp and stepped closer to me, lowering his voice so that only I could hear his words. 'And wouldn't it be wiser if you did so? All these questions can do no good: they only stir up trouble for Isolda. She's had enough to bear since Gideon's death, with all the hints and whispers and rumours circulating amongst our neighbours.' He suddenly turned aggressive and added violently, 'Leave us alone, Chapman, or you may live to regret your interference.'

He spun on his heel and rejoined his companion who had been waiting for him with ill-concealed impatience. She said something to him that I could not catch, but from his hangdog expression, it was plainly a reprimand.

'Bad-tempered harpy!' Philip grunted sourly, staring after their retreating backs. 'But there! If the lad fancies that sort of woman, what can he expect? Who is he? One of the Babcary family I should guess.'

'You would guess correctly,' I answered, also watching the couple's progress towards Dowgate Hill, the lady still visibly incensed and refusing, with much head tossing, to take her escort's hand. 'That's Christopher Babcary, the goldsmith's nephew.'

Adela came to stand beside me, slipping her hand into the crook of my arm.

'So that's the man accused by Gideon Bonifant of cuckolding him, is it?' she enquired, having overheard my answer. 'Well, if that's the kind of woman young Master Babcary prefers, I can't imagine, at least not from your description of Isolda, that he would entertain anything but a cousinly affection for her.' My wife went on thoughtfully, 'Of course, that doesn't mean to say that Gideon was wrong in his assumption that his wife was betraying him with another man. He might simply have picked on the wrong person. You'll have to bear that in mind when pursuing your investigations, Roger.'

I bit my tongue and maintained my composure with an effort. First, I had been forced to endure Philip's jibes about my 'nosiness', and now here was Adela telling me how to conduct my business, instructing me in what I should do well to remember. It only needed Jeanne Lamprey to add her mite for my cup of humiliation to run over.

Jeanne was busy keeping an eye on the weather, which was changing yet again, black clouds piling up the Thames from the east, bringing with them a freshening wind and a smell of sleet and rain in the air.

'We'd better make for shelter,' she decided, pulling up the hood of her cloak and holding it firmly together under her chin. 'Adela shouldn't be out in a storm, Roger, not in her delicate condition.'

I made no answer, except to put an arm around my wife. It seemed that I was not to escape advice on how to be either a solver of mysteries or a good husband, and I found myself looking forward to the morrow when I could once more be my own man.

We parted from the Lampreys on the corner of Bucklersbury, Philip having promised to fetch Adela early next morning and to escort her to their shop. There, in return for all their kindness, she would spend the time before dinner helping Jeanne to sort and mend the old clothes collected by Philip over the past few days and now ready for reselling.

'And after we've eaten,' Jeanne said, reaching up to kiss Adela's cheek, 'provided that Philip can manage on his own for a while, and if you feel fit enough, I'll take you to see the wild animals in the Tower.'

Adela thanked her, returning the kiss, and

a few moments later, we were hurrying along Bucklersbury, making for the inn as fast as we could, the icy spears of rain already beginning to sting our faces. Once within the comfort of our room, we lit the candles and closed the outer shutters against the cold, shaking the dampness from our cloaks and hanging them from the wall pegs to dry.

'And now,' said Adela, seating herself on the edge of the bed and eyeing me accusingly, 'what was Christopher Babcary whispering to you on the quayside, there? And you needn't think to lie to me, either, Roger. I couldn't hear what he was saying, but I could see by the expression on his face that he was giving you some kind of warning.'

'Not a warning exactly,' I muttered. 'But I admit he was trying to persuade me to change my mind. He thinks that my questioning could do Mistress Bonifant more harm than good. And he's right, of course, if she should prove to be guilty of her husband's murder.'

'Was that all he said?' My wife regarded me with her clear, unwavering gaze.

I sighed. I had discovered very early on in my married life that it was almost impossible to lie to Adela. 'No, he advised me to leave the family alone or I might live to regret my interference.'

'But you won't take his advice, of course.'

165

It was a statement, not a question.

'My dearest, I can't,' I protested, sitting beside her on the bed and putting my arms around her. 'I can't possibly disoblige the Duke.'

'Can't or won't?' she asked, but immediately turned to plant a kiss on my lips. 'Forgive me, I shouldn't have said that. I don't know what's got into me lately. It must be my condition, I'm allowing myself to become a prey to odd humours and fancies and doing what I said I'd never do. I'm interfering.'

I held her closer, murmuring endearments. I knew that I was at fault, that I should have refused the Duke's commission. I ought not to be abandoning her in a strange city, dependent for amusement on two comparative strangers. But I was as selfish then as I am today (or, at least, so my children tell me). Once presented with a mystery, I could no more leave it unresolved than I could grow wings and fly.

The next morning, after breakfast, I saw Adela off to Cornhill in the company of Philip Lamprey, and then, with an uncontrollable lightening of the heart and a spring in my step, set out myself for West Cheap. The sky was leaden grey, there was a sprinkling of snow on the ground and the wind was bitter, but nothing could diminish

166

my spirits at the sheer pleasure of being on my own again, of being my own master, of being able to order my own actions exactly as I chose. The world about me was already humming with activity: church bells were tolling, street cleaners shovelled yesterday's steaming refuse into their carts, traders took down shutters and opened up their shops, pedlars and piemen shouted their wares, lawyers, in their striped gowns, hurried past on their way to Saint Paul's. As I was caught up and borne along on this tide of humanity, I was prodded into the realisation of just how good it was to be alive, and I thought with sudden poignancy of those prisoners, like the Duke of Clarence, languishing in prison, many under sentence of death. But it also reminded me of how wrong it is to rob another human being of the life that God has given to him or her; the life that is our pathway to heaven.

I experienced a stab of guilt. Since my brief conversation on Saturday with Christopher Babcary about the murdered man, and now after talking to Master Ford, I had begun to feel a certain antipathy towards Gideon Bonifant, resulting almost in indifference as to the identity of his murderer. But even supposing those feelings concerning him were justified, murder was never warranted, however unpleasant the victim might have been. And all I could reasonably say of Gideon just at present was that he seemed to me an ungrateful, rough-tongued man, with an eye to his own advancement by any means at his disposal. But of how many hundreds of others could that also be said? It did not mean that any one of them could be killed with impunity and nobody care.

The furnace had already been lit in Master Babcary's workshop by the time that I arrived, and young Tobias Maybury was assiduously working the bellows, forcing the flames to leap higher and higher up the chimney. Christopher Babcary was seated at the bench in the middle of the room, burnishing a golden belt buckle with his rabbit's foot, and brushing the tiny particles of loosened metal into his leather apron. Master Babcary himself was standing at the long bench, which also served as a counter on which to display the finished goods, thoughtfully rubbing his chin as he alternately scrutinised Saturday's batch of golden medallions and a lump of amber that either he or one of the other two had begun to chisel.

At my entrance, they all looked up from their work, the apprentice, after a cursory glance, returning to his bellows. Christopher Babcary gave me an enigmatic stare before resuming his polishing, and only Master Babcary evinced any pleasure at seeing me again. He left his bench and came towards me, hand outstretched.

'Master Chapman! You've kept your word and come back to us, then.'

'Did you doubt that I would?'

'No, no! At least, I didn't. However, Kit, there, thought that you might have had second thoughts, didn't you, lad? I don't know why.'

His nephew grunted something unintelligible without pausing again in what he was doing, but it seemed to satisfy his uncle. The older man turned back to me.

'Well, I don't suppose you need to talk to me for a second time, Master Chapman. You heard all I had to say the day before yesterday. But of the rest of my household, who would you like to speak to first?'

I hesitated about making demands, and had rather hoped that Miles would have made his own suggestion. Having been invited to state a preference, however, I said reluctantly, 'With your permission, sir, Mistress Bonifant would seem the obvious choice.'

My host nodded vigorously. 'Precisely my own conclusion. So I've told Isolda to hold herself in readiness in the upstairs room. She's there now, I believe, so you can go up straight away.' His face assumed an anxious expression. 'I'm sure she'll be able to convince you of her innocence.'

169

I made no answer to this last remark, but with my hand on the latch of the inner door, I paused and turned round.

'Master Babcary, who do *you* think murdered your son-in-law?' I asked.

The question took him by surprise, as I had intended that it should.

'Wh-what do you mean?' he stammered.

'You don't deny that Master Bonifant was poisoned?'

'N-no! Of course I don't.' He began to fidget uncomfortably. 'What's this all about? I don't understand. What are you getting at?'

'I'm asking for your opinion – if, that is, you truly believe your daughter to be innocent – as to who you think the real murderer might be. Surely you must have some suspicions of your own.'

'No,' he snapped, the good-humoured smile vanishing from his face. 'I suspect no one.'

'To suspect no one is to suspect everyone,' I pointed out gently, 'including Mistress Bonifant.'

Miles Babcary was no fool: I could see by the expression in his eyes that he was perfectly capable of following my logic, but he was not prepared to admit it.

'I don't know what you mean,' he shrugged. 'You're talking in riddles.'

To continue to press him would have been

foolish and only antagonise him further, and as master of the house I needed his goodwill. Besides, I should be no more successful in getting him to admit to his suspicions, if he had any, than I had been on Saturday. I felt sure that he was as uncertain of his daughter's innocence as he was of anyone else's guilt, but he was never going to say as much to me. For the time being, I must leave well alone.

'Forgive me, sir,' I apologised, 'I didn't mean to upset you. I'll go up now and talk to Mistress Bonifant.' But once again I paused and called across to Christopher Babcary, 'I hope you and your lady got home safely yesterday without either of you getting too wet.'

He replied briefly that they had, while his uncle raised his eyes to heaven.

'And which lady is this, pray?' Miles asked. 'No, don't bother telling me, boy, for I'm sure I shall be none the wiser.' He shrugged and turned back to me. 'I've never known such a lad for fancying himself in and out of love every few weeks or so. First it's one woman, then it's another. I suppose that one of these days he'll decide it's time to settle down and make up his mind who it is he really wants to marry, but not just at present.' He took a pace towards me, lowering his voice. 'Which is why that story my son-in-law was putting about in the months

171

before his death was so much moonshine.'

But was it? I wondered, as I climbed the stairs to the first-floor landing. Might not Christopher Babcary, at one time, have fancied himself in love with his cousin? He appeared to like older women, if the lady I had seen him with the previous day was anything to judge by. On the other hand, not only were Isolda Bonifant's looks against her, but the familiarity of living under the same roof with someone, each day and all day, year in and year out, seemed to me to make this an unlikely possibility.

Yet I knew from past experience that I could rule nothing out, that the improbable happened in life far more often than one imagined. Perhaps young Master Babcary's fancy had once strayed towards Isolda, and perhaps she had been flattered by his unexpected attentions. On the other hand, she must have known of his reputation for fickleness. How could she not have, living in the same house and watching him grow up? Would she, therefore, have allowed herself to succumb to his charms? But maybe she had genuinely fallen in love with him, and could not help herself.

But as yet there was no answer to any of these questions, and I knew that neither Isolda nor her cousin could be expected to admit to betraying Gideon, even supposing there was any truth in the accusation. Yet why should Gideon Bonifant lie? No man worth his salt wants to appear as the cuck-olded husband, and is therefore hardly likely to make up such a story. But he could have been mistaken in the identity of Isolda's lover, a person in whom I was beginning to believe. Her plain features may well have proved a barrier to the finding of a husband when she was a maid, but five and a half years of marriage could have given her a confidence and an air of invita-tion lacking in a single woman.

I stood still for a moment at the top of the first flight of stairs, looking at the two doors facing me. The left-hand one, if I remem-bered rightly, led into Master Babcary's bedchamber at the back of the house; the other, beside it, opened into the family living-room, where they spent their evenings and the long winter hours of darkness together. Above me, on the second and third floors, the rest of the household slept; close quarters for five people, six when Gideon had been alive, and that was without including the little maid, Meg Spendlove, whose domain, waking and sleeping, was the kitchen.

I walked the few paces along the landing to the second door, then raised my hand and knocked before lifting the latch and going inside.

Isolda Bonifant was seated to the left of

the fireplace, in one of the two armchairs, and her cousin, Eleanor Babcary was seated in the other. I was somewhat taken aback not to find my quarry alone, but the younger woman immediately rose to her feet and began to edge towards the door.

'I'm just going,' she said nervously.

'Oh, sit down again, Nell,' Isolda scolded, half amused, half irritated. 'Master Chapman won't eat you, you goose! Besides, he'll want to talk to you as well as to me. He can talk to us both together.'

I didn't know what to say. The last thing I wanted was to have the older woman prompting her cousin, putting words into her mouth, which would almost certainly be the case if Eleanor Babcary stayed. I glanced from one to the other, thinking, not for the first time, what cruel tricks nature could play. The Babcary blood, which they both shared, gave them a certain similarity of feature, enough at any rate to suggest that they were related. Yet Eleanor, with her creamy skin, blue eyes and profusion of curly auburn hair, was extraordinarily pretty – some might even think her beautiful – while Isolda could never be described as anything but plain. And the Lambert blood, which bound the latter to Mistress Shore, had also worked in her disfavour. Yet her candid blue gaze, her strength of character, her direct mode of speech, gave her, to my mind at least, an attraction that the gentle, timid charm of her cousin did not. But I suspected that not many men would agree with me.

Eleanor, obviously used to obeying her cousin, but sensing that I wished her to go, hesitated, unsure what to do. Her long, slender fingers played nervously with the pendant that she wore, twisting it round and round on its thin gold chain.

'Nell, sit down!' Isolda commanded. 'And stop fiddling with that thing around your neck. It's so delicate that you'll break it, if you're not careful. Draw up a stool, Master Chapman, and ask us what you want to know.'

I did so reluctantly, as Eleanor Babcary, with equal reluctance, resumed her seat by the fire, but perched on the very edge, as though ready for instant flight. I could see the pendant clearly now, a fragile circle of gold holding a true lover's knot set with tiny sapphires.

'That's very beautiful,' I said.

'It was a present from all of us on her seventeenth birthday, last October,' Isolda told me. 'My father made it, but we all had a hand in it somewhere. Even I was allowed to help in a very small way, although my big hands are so clumsy that Gideon was doubtful about letting me anywhere near it. He—' She broke off, staring in dismay at her young cousin's trembling underlip. 'Nell! Dearest! What's the matter? What have I said to upset you?'

She had half risen from her chair and would have gone to Eleanor, but the younger woman was already on her feet.

'It's nothing! Nothing!' she protested, in a voice choked with sobs. Then she fled from the room, and we heard the patter of her feet as she ran upstairs, followed by the slam of her bedchamber door.

Isolda slowly sank back into her seat. 'Now what on earth's got into Nell?' she wondered.

Eleven

There was a moment's reflective silence while Isolda Bonifant and I were busy, each with our own thoughts. I had no clue to my companion's, for her face gave nothing away but, for my part, I was wondering what had been said to provoke such a violent reaction on the part of the younger woman. Had it been the mention of Gideon? Had Eleanor Babcary been fonder of her cousin's husband than she had a right to be? Or was it simply that the manner of his death had distressed an impressionable young girl to such a degree that any allusion to him upset her? But the answer, of course, was not apparent and would have to wait until I knew more about her.

I decided to make no mention of the incident. There was no point in wasting my time listening to Isolda's lies and prevarications.

'Mistress Bonifant,' I said, leaning across and reclaiming her attention with a gentle tap on the arm, 'your father has made me free of his recollections concerning the evening of your husband's death. Will you now give me yours?'

She had jumped at my touch, startled out of her reverie, blinking at me for a second or two as though uncertain where she was.

'Master Chapman! I'm sorry, I was daydreaming. Firelight sometimes has that effect on me.' She drew a deep breath and smiled bravely. 'Please forgive me. What is it that you want to know?'

'Will you tell me what you remember about the evening Master Bonifant died?'

'Very well,' she agreed after a slight hesitation. 'What exactly has my father told you?'

'I'd rather hear your version of events first, if you please, independently of his.'

She sighed and looked down at her hands, which were clasped loosely together in her lap. Absent-mindedly, she began to twist her wedding band round and round on her finger.

'It was Mistress Perle's birthday,' she began at last, 'which is also her saint's day – December the fourth, the feast of Saint Barbara. My father had asked her to celebrate the occasion here, with all of us, and I think she would have agreed at once but for the fact that she wanted her friends and neighbours, Gregory and Ginèvre Napier, to be of the party.' The heavy lids were suddenly raised and the cool blue eyes looked directly into mine. 'Perhaps you may have realised for yourself, since your talk with my father, that he is hoping to make Mistress Perle his wife.'

'Master Babcary admitted as much. He also told me that, if such an event took place, he intended to buy the Widow Perle's present home in Paternoster Row for you and your husband to live in. He believed you both to be happy with such an arrangement. Indeed, he implied that you, in particular, were more than happy, that it was your wish to have an establishment of your own.'

Isolda cradled her chin in one hand, supporting her elbow with the other.

'I shouldn't have objected,' she agreed after a moment's contemplation of the fire. 'That is to say,' she added honestly, 'I couldn't possibly have remained here if

178

Father had married again.' Once more she raised her eyes to mine. 'I've been mistress of this house too long – ever since the age of sixteen or thereabouts – and I couldn't share the management of it with another woman.'

My curiosity got the better of me. 'What would you do if Master Babcary and Mistress Perle were to be married sometime in the future?'

Isolda smiled serenely. 'I should hold my father to his promise and remove to Paternoster Row, taking poor little Meggie with me. She'd never suit Mistress Perle's notion of a kitchen maid, and, in any case, Barbara would undoubtedly bring her own highly competent servants with her. And I should ask Nell to live with me – that is, until she gets married. Which she undoubtedly will, because she's so beautiful.'

'Does she not care for Mistress Perle, either?'

My companion threw back her head and gave a hearty, full-throated chuckle.

'Nell likes everyone,' she said, dropping her hands back into her lap. 'But you're quite right with your "either", Master Chapman. I'm not enamoured of my father's choice of bride. Did I make it that apparent?'

I shifted uncomfortably on my stool. 'Well—' I was beginning awkwardly, but

179

Isolda cut me short.

'You mustn't worry about it,' she assured me. 'People are always telling me that I'm not good at concealing my feelings. But please don't mistake me. I know nothing against Barbara Perle. The truth is that I'm piqued because I never thought my father would consider marrying for a second time. Now, what else did you wish to ask me?'

'Well, I know from Master Babcary that Mistress Perle finally agreed to his suggestion that she celebrate her birthday here, on condition that she could bring her friends, Gregory and Ginèvre Napier with her ... Your father doesn't care for the Napiers, particularly the lady, does he?'

'No, indeed! If, that is, one can call her a lady!' Isolda gave me a sidelong, somewhat shamefaced grin. 'Now I'm being catty, Master Chapman. But you must make up your own mind when you see her. As you say, Barbara won the argument, and consented to my father's proposal.'

'The three guests arrived, or so I understand from Master Babcary, sometime around four o'clock, after the shop was barred and shuttered for the night. Prior to that, the merchandise had been removed from the windows and locked away, and then everyone but you retired to change into their Sunday clothes. Where were you, Mistress Bonifant?' I enquired with an assumed ignorance.

'I was still in the kitchen,' was the somewhat tart reply, 'cooking the food. My father had insisted that we have all Barbara's favourite dishes and, as there are quite a goodly number of them, I had spent most of the day there. Meg was helping me, but her assistance is often more of a hindrance than otherwise.'

'And, earlier, you had come upstairs to this room to lay the table. You had unlocked that cupboard over there and put out the special family goblets, each with its identifying set of initials worked into the gold around the rim. And you had filled them with wine.'

She did not respond immediately, and I began to wonder if she were going to answer at all. For a while, the only sounds to be heard were the crackling of logs on the fire and the rustle of the wall tapestries as they billowed in a sudden draught. From below, Master Babcary's voice was raised, calling for Meg Spendlove, but after that all was quiet again until Isolda suddenly swivelled in her chair to face me.

'Damning, isn't it? Enough, probably, to have brought me to the stake but for my cousin's intervention on my behalf with the King. Yet the fact is that I often filled our cups with wine – or ale, or water, or whatever else we were drinking – before we ate, because it meant that I could then top up the pitcher, so saving us from the annoyance of having to send down to the kitchen for more drink during a meal. And, in addition, on that particular evening, I wanted us all to pledge Mistress Perle's health as soon as we were assembled.'

'And afterwards, when you had finished laying the table, you returned to the kitchen?' She nodded. 'But when you eventually came upstairs again to change your gown, did you go straight to your bedchamber?'

'No, I came in here for a last look round, just to make sure that I'd forgotten nothing. I knew how much the occasion meant to my father.'

'And did you encounter anyone else while you were doing this?'

'Yes, my father himself. He was coming out of his room just as I was leaving this one. His bedchamber, as you probably know, is next door, so we passed one another on the landing. I told him that everything was ready and he grunted. He was in a hurry to get downstairs. I think he said that the guests had just arrived.'

So far, her story tallied in most essentials with that of Master Babcary. Either they were both speaking the truth, or they were in collusion, and adept at telling lies.

I asked abruptly, 'What did your husband think of your father's intention to remarry?'

She seemed somewhat put out by this change of direction, but gave the impression of answering as openly and as honestly as she could.

'Gideon was a little – what can I say? – a little worried by the idea at first. But when my father explained to him that I should in no way be the loser by the marriage – that although he would have to make provision for his wife, the shop and all its contents would still be left to me – my husband grew more reconciled to the match.' She added hastily, 'You must understand that Gideon was only concerned with protecting my interests.'

I assured her that I did. And she might well have been right: I was in no position, just then, to judge the truth of her assertion, even though I might doubt it.

'How did Master Bonifant get on with the rest of the household?' I asked, startling her once again and making her uneasy.

'He – he got on well enough, why do you ask?' And when I refrained from answering, she added defensively, 'Gideon was a very reserved man, who only made friends with difficulty. Even after five and a half years of marriage, I can't pretend that I ever really knew what he was thinking. Nevertheless, he was a kind husband: considerate, f-faithful.' She stumbled slightly over the final word.

I pretended not to notice. 'What about your cousins?' I queried. 'Was Master Bonifant fond of them? Were they fond of him?'

There was another infinitesimal pause before Isolda could bring herself to reply.

'The three of them rubbed along together, but I don't know that there was any deep affection on either side.' She scratched one cheek consideringly. 'You have to remember that when Gideon came to live here, after our marriage, Kit wasn't quite fourteen years of age, while Nell was only eleven. They were children in the eyes of a man of thirty-four, and so they have remained ever since.'

I thought that while this might well be true on Gideon's side, Eleanor Babcary, whose flower-like innocence made her appear a lot younger than her years, was now a young woman of seventeen and, after her outburst just now, I couldn't help wondering yet again what her feelings had been towards her cousin's husband.

'What about the young apprentice?' I asked. 'Tobias, isn't that his name? And your maid, Meg Spendlove, how did Master Bonifant get along with them?'

'Oh, come now!' Isolda was incredulous. 'You can't possibly imagine that either of those two had anything to do with Gideon's death!'

'I rule no one out who was in the house that evening. Someone killed your husband, Mistress Bonifant and, if, as you claim, it wasn't you—' I broke off, shrugging.

She looked unhappy and began to fidget with the leather girdle that encircled her waist. It was fully a minute before she answered, and I had time to wonder what her response would be. Eventually, she gave herself a little shake and sat up straighter in her chair.

'So be it,' she sighed. 'I didn't murder my husband, Master Chapman, however black things might look against me, so I'll tell you what you want to know.'

'To be honest with you,' I said, 'your father has already informed me that Master Bonifant found Meg's slatternly ways difficult to tolerate, and that you and he had had differences of opinion on the subject.'

My companion seemed vexed, but admitted reluctantly, 'Father's right. Gideon was extremely neat and orderly in all his ways. A girl like Meg was bound to irritate him, and he couldn't understand why I didn't dismiss her and employ someone more efficient.'

'Why didn't you?' I queried.

Isolda was indignant. 'Meg has been with us since we took her from the Foundling Hospital when she was ten years old. And if

185

you had seen her then, you'd know how happy and well fed she is now, in spite of her appearance. I could no more turn Meggie into the street to fend for herself than I could Eleanor.' She looked away from me, staring once again into the heart of the fire, and added in a low voice, 'I know what it is to be plain and unattractive.'

I was at a disadvantage. If I refuted her statement, my protests would ring hollow, and the more I tried to convince her of their sincerity, the less I would be believed. It was better, I decided, to say nothing on the subject.

Instead, I asked hurriedly, 'Do you know if Master Bonifant had had cause to take Meg to task shortly before he died?'

Her head turned sharply in my direction, and I could see the answer in her face.

'Who told you?' she demanded accusingly. 'Was it Father?'

'No, nobody told me. I merely drew a bow at a venture.' And the arrow, I added to myself, has found its mark.

Isolda tapped one of her feet angrily, annoyed with herself for falling into the trap.

'Yes,' she conceded at last. 'There had been an unpleasant scene between my husband and Meg some few weeks before the murder.'

'What was it about?' I prompted when she

186

seemed disinclined to continue.

My companion slumped back in her chair as though suddenly very tired.

'It was the occasion of Nell's last birthday feast,' she said wearily, 'on the thirty-first of October, All Hallows' Eve. I wasn't very well that day, and had left the setting of the supper table to Meg while I lay down upon my bed. Woman's trouble,' she added, looking me straight in the eyes before I could embarrass her by asking a tactless question. 'I had given her the key of the corner cupboard and told her to be especially careful when putting out the gold and crystal goblets. (I have discovered over the years that if you trust Meg to do something, she will give of her best. What she resents most is being treated as though she's a fool.)

'I had gone over with her again and again where everybody sat, so that each person would get his or her own goblet. But, unfortunately, Meg still managed to make a mistake, although, as I insisted at the time, she could be forgiven for it. She had mixed up Gideon's and Christopher's goblets, but the initials G.B. and C.B. are very alike, especially with all that carved foliage surrounding them.'

'But Master Bonifant was angry with her?'

Isolda frowned. 'He was excessively angry for a man who normally showed his displeasure merely by folding his lips together

187

and walking out of the room. He ranted and raved, saying the most appalling things to poor little Meg, just as though all the frustration of years had suddenly burst into the open. I can remember Father and Nell and Kit, and even Toby Maybury, staring open-mouthed, as though they couldn't believe their ears; as though Gideon had suddenly taken leave of his senses. Of course, after a few minutes, when he saw how everyone was looking at him, he took himself in hand, calmed down and apologised to Meggie.'

'And how did she react to this burst of temper?'

'Very much as you might expect. There were floods of tears and instant denials. But then, that's Meg's way of dealing with every unpleasant situation in which she finds herself. Nothing is ever her fault, but always that of some other unidentifiable person.'

'Did she accept Master Bonifant's apologies?'

Isolda smiled sadly. 'Of course not! He had always made his disapproval of her plain, although in his customary austere fashion, and, as a consequence, *she* had never liked *him*. She was, I think, even a little afraid of him. But,' my companion added hastily, seeing the trap into which she was falling, 'her dislike was not enough to make her poison him, if that's what you're thinking.'

I said nothing in response to that. A simple soul like Meg Spendlove was just the sort to harbour a grievance and brood upon injustice. For most of her short life she had been the butt of other people's unkindness, and it would not be surprising if, one day, a particular act of hostility had proved too much for her. Had she, after weeks of turning the incident over in her mind, found herself, on the occasion of Mistress Perle's birthday, with the opportunity to get rid of her tormentor once and for all, and taken it? But that posed another problem. Where had she obtained the poison?

That question, however, would have to wait. 'What were your feelings,' I asked Isolda Bonifant, 'about your husband's uncharacteristic outburst?'

She answered, this time without any hesitation whatsoever. 'I thought it all part of a general deterioration in Gideon's health that had been worrying me over the preceding two or three months.'

'He was ill?' Master Babcary had mentioned nothing of this. 'What was the matter with Master Bonifant? Had anyone else noticed that he was ailing?'

'No, I don't think so.' Isolda answered my last query first. 'It wouldn't have been so obvious to other people. But Gideon hadn't been eating as well as usual. He had always been a hearty trencherman, even though he

189

put on no flesh to show for it, yet for many weeks before his death, he had started to leave food on his plate at every meal. It's true that Kit remarked on the fact to me one day, asking what was wrong with Gideon's appetite, but I don't think he assumed it to be a sign of poor health, only that my husband was preoccupied about something or other.'

'You thought differently, however?'

'I might not have done so had it not also been for his broken nights. Gideon had always been a sound sleeper, but quite suddenly, about the same time that he started losing interest in his food, he began to be very restless. I would wake in the small hours to find him gone from my side, and when I went to look for him, he was prowling about the house, unable, he said, to sleep.' She had a drawn, unhappy look that I had noticed once or twice before during the course of this conversation. 'But when, on the first occasion that this happened, I begged him to come back to bed and to tell me if there was anything troubling his mind, he answered with such savagery, at the same time raising his hand as though ready to strike me, that I never interfered again. When I woke and he wasn't there, I just waited until he returned. And I learned to pretend to be asleep when he did so.'

'Did these nightly wanderings occur very often?'

'With increasing regularity. To begin with, I suppose I would find him gone perhaps once in a couple of weeks. But later, it was almost every night.'

'And he never hinted at what was worrying him?'

Isolda shook her head, avoiding my eyes. 'But I know now, don't I? Father has told you what Gideon was saying about me.'

'About you and your cousin Christopher, yes!' There was another long pause, this time while I plucked up courage to ask the necessary question. 'Mistress Bonifant,' I said at last, '*was* there any truth in your husband's accusation?'

'Of course not!' Her tone almost scorched me with its furious denial. She went on, more calmly, 'Oh, Kit likes women, but not my sort of woman. I agree that he prefers them to be older than himself but, apart from the fact that he has always looked upon me as another sister, he is only attracted by worldly and sophisticated women. They flatter him and persuade him that he, too, is worldly and sophisticated – but I suspect that they make use of him. And behind his back, they're probably laughing at him.'

I thought she could well be correct. But there was another question, more difficult than the first, that I must now put to her.

'Were – were there any grounds for your husband's suspicion that ... that he was being betrayed?'

Isolda turned once more to look at me, and her eyes widened, but whether in anger or astonishment I was unsure.

'By me? With another man, you mean?' And when I nodded, she burst into mocking laughter. 'Master Chapman, are you blind? I'm a plain, some would say an ugly, woman, who had enough difficulty in finding *one* man who wanted to bed me. Where would I have found another?'

Such candour was endearing – if it were genuine.

'You do yourself a great injustice,' I said, repairing my earlier omission, 'and I will repay your frankness with some of my own. You are not beautiful, not even pretty, but there are many men who would find you easy to love. So I ask you again, did Master Bonifant have any reason for his suspicions?'

Isolda drew a deep breath. Then, 'No,' she answered a trifle unsteadily, 'he did not. I swear to you that whatever grounds he thought he had for suspecting me of infidelity, they were entirely false. Where they could have come from, I have not the least idea – unless some secret enemy of mine, or of his, put them into his head for his or her own wicked purpose.'

192

Twelve

'Do you know of such an enemy?' I asked after a few moments, when Isolda's last words had had time to sink in.

She shook her head. 'No, although it's not for want of thinking about it. But no particular person springs to mind. Of course, it would be foolish to presume that Gideon and I were loved, or even liked, by all our acquaintances, or even by all those who professed themselves to be our friends. Yet I'm unable to think of a single soul who would wish either of us so ill that he or she would be prepared to tell a lie that could result in so much distress and misery.'

'Nevertheless, somebody did just that.'

She sat forward in her chair, stretching her back as though it were aching. 'I know,' she answered quietly. 'That's what I find so frightening.'

'And your husband never mentioned this accusation to you? Did you indeed know nothing of it until after Master Bonifant's death?'

'Gideon never said a word to me. Had he

done so, I should have been able to refute the accusation. And I hope that I should have been able to set his mind at rest.' She shivered and held out her hands to the blaze. 'That's what disturbs me most, Master Chapman, that he seems to have had such belief in this tale, accepted it so readily, that he never even asked me to prove my innocence.'

I nodded sympathetically. If she were telling the truth, this omission of Gideon's did appear odd, to say the least of it. But was she telling the truth? I had only her word for what had passed between herself and her husband. I should never now hear his side of the story.

'What did you do that evening,' I asked, 'when you had changed your gown?'

'I came downstairs, naturally, to this room, to join in the celebration.'

'And who was here when you entered?'

'Everyone – except Meg, of course. She was still down in the kitchen.' Isolda ticked off the assembled company on her fingers, screwing up her eyes a little as she once more conjured up the scene in her mind. 'My father, Mistress Perle, Gregory and Ginèvre Napier, both my cousins and, of course, Gideon. Oh yes, and our apprentice, Tobias Maybury,' she added on a faint note of surprise. 'I recall wondering at the time why he was present.'

'Shouldn't he have been?'

'If it had been a normal mealtime, with just the family, yes. He always eats with us. But not when we entertain. Then he has his food downstairs in the kitchen, with Meg. And I remember now...'

'Go on,' I urged as her voice tailed away into silence. 'What do you remember?'

'Oh, it probably means nothing,' she protested, 'but it occurred to me that he looked ... well, flushed, as if he were feeling guilty about something or other. It was probably my imagination, for he didn't remain long in the room after my arrival, and he seemed perfectly himself when I saw him some fifteen minutes later, down in the kitchen. He and Meg were whispering and giggling together. At least,' she amended, 'Toby was giggling. Meg, come to think of it, looked rather flushed and indignant.'

'I see. Now, according to Master Babcary, you instructed everyone where to sit.'

Isolda smiled thinly. 'So I did, because I had laid the table and knew where I had placed each person. Yes,' she continued, bitterly, 'I can quite see why suspicion points so heavily in my direction.'

I was unable to reassure her. 'Pray continue,' I entreated. 'What happened next?'

'We all took our places around the table to drink Mistress Perle's good health. Oh, but I'm forgetting. Before we did so, Father presented Barbara with her birthday gift, a leather girdle studded with sapphires and turquoises. It's very beautiful and very costly and would, I think, have apprised us of Father's intentions towards her, had we not known them already. Neither Gideon nor Kit, as I recall, looked as though he much approved.'

'After which you all drank the lady's health in the wine already poured out by you?'

'Yes.'

'And then?'

'And then I went down to the kitchen to help Meggie bring up the trays of food.' Isolda took a deep breath to steady her voice. 'As I re-entered this room, Master Napier was just coming out. He looked grey and sweating, and I thought he'd been taken ill, but I know now, of course, that he was going for the apothecary in Gudrun Lane. I didn't realise at first what was happening, until I saw Gideon. He was standing beside his chair, struggling desperately for breath. His face was turning blue. He couldn't speak, and his lips and throat seemed so stiff that he could neither swallow nor talk. All he could do was to make a terrible croaking sound.' Isolda covered her face with her hands and remained like that for several seconds. When she raised her face again, however, it had been wiped clean of all emotion. 'Meggie screamed and dropped her tray, while Gideon ... Gideon raised his hand and pointed at me.' She shuddered. 'Dear Mother in Heaven! I'll never forget his eyes. They were so full of hatred.'

By eleven o'clock, dinner had been eaten and cleared away, the men coming upstairs from the shop one at a time: first Master Babcary, followed by his nephew and, lastly, by the apprentice, Toby Maybury.

I had found it strange eating with the family and not being relegated, as I usually was, to the lowlier company of the kitchen. But as someone known to be in the employ of Mistress Shore and, even more importantly, in that of the Duke of Gloucester, I was treated as a guest rather than as a nosy, interfering pedlar – although I suspected that the Babcarys were beginning to regard me in that light.

Eleanor had reappeared at dinnertime, looking pale and wan, but with an unimpaired appetite. She ate daintily, but heartily, making short work of a plate of mutton stew and dumplings, three honey and saffron tarts and a mazer of ale. All the same, she managed to convey the impression that she had just risen from her sickbed and was treated accordingly, with much tenderness and loving affection, by her cousin, brother and uncle. In these circumstances, I felt I must delay questioning her until such time as she was showing a more robust face to the world, and consequently requested that I might be allowed to talk to Meg Spendlove.

'Then speak to her in the kitchen,' Isolda advised me. 'Meg won't be happy anywhere else. Not that I think you'll get very much out of her, even there. She's very wary of strangers, particularly of men.'

We were once more alone, the men having returned to the workshop and Eleanor Babcary having withdrawn again to her bedchamber, complaining of a headache.

'I'll do my best to overcome her prejudice,' I said. 'But before I go downstairs in search of her, there is one thing, Mistress Bonifant, that I have so far failed to ask both you and your father. How do you think the monkshood was obtained? Would you or any other member of the household know?'

Isolda hesitated, then answered reluctantly, 'My father, who's not so young as he was' – I couldn't help reflecting how indignantly Master Babcary would have taken issue with this statement – 'uses an oil, made chiefly from the root of the monkshood plant, to ease his aching joints. Long hours bent over his workbench has given him rheumatic pains in his arms and back. This liniment, provided for him by Master Page of Gudrun Lane, gives him great relief when rubbed well into his shoulders and the surrounding flesh.'

'And who performs this service for him?' The colour crept up under her skin and then receded, leaving her very pale.

'I do sometimes,' was the reply. 'At other times, it's Kit.'

'But everyone in the house is aware that Master Babcary uses this embrocation?'

'I suppose so.'

'And also that it is extremely poisonous?' She nodded. 'Master Page made it plain both to Father and to me that it could prove fatal if swallowed, and we naturally made sure that the other members of the household were also told. And because of that warning, Father always keeps the bottle containing the liniment locked in a cupboard in his room.'

'And where does he keep the key to this cupboard?'

Isolda bit her lip. 'In a little wooden box in the chest at the foot of his bed. Unfortunately,' she added, 'everyone knows that it's there and which cupboard it unlocks.'

'So anyone could have taken the bottle and poured some of the contents into Master Bonifant's wine?'

'Yes, I'm afraid that's true.'

I thought about this. 'My mother used to use a liniment made from the root of the monkshood plant,' I said after a short silence, 'for her rheumatics, and my recollection of it is that it had a pungent smell. Why, I wonder, did Master Bonifant not notice it as he drank?'

Isolda began to collect the dirty dishes together and stack them in a pile. After a long moment, she replied, without raising her eyes from what she was doing, 'The oil was very potent, and Apothecary Page warned us that even a drop could prove fatal. Kit and I were to wash our hands thoroughly every time we so much as touched it, and we were never to use it if we had a cut or scratch or any kind of abrasion on our skin. So I suppose it needed only a very small amount to kill Gideon. And the wine itself had a strong bouquet.' She gave an uncertain little laugh and finally met my gaze. 'You see, I'm being perfectly candid with you, Master Chapman.'

Was she also being very clever? I asked myself, but was unable to make up my mind.

'I appreciate your frankness, Mistress Bonifant,' I replied. 'After the – after your husband's death, did you or Master Babcary check the bottle containing the monkshood oil to see if any of it was missing?'

'We did, but it was impossible to tell. The bottle is of thick, smoked glass with a very tiny neck. And, as I told you, only the smallest drop would have been necessary to kill Gideon. Why do you ask?'

'Because it occurs to me that it may not have been your father's liniment that was used. If, for instance, the murderer was from outside this house, then the poison must have been obtained elsewhere.'

Isolda gave me a quick, sidelong glance. 'You're thinking of Barbara Perle and the Napiers. But what motive could one of those three possibly have had for wishing my husband dead?'

'That I don't know at present, but there may have been a reason. And now, if you'll allow me to carry that tray downstairs for you, I'll speak to Meg Spendlove.'

Isolda shook her head. 'You'd do better to let me come with you and introduce you properly as a friend. Besides,' she added, picking up the heavy wooden tray, loaded with its stacks of dirty dishes, as though it were a featherweight, 'I don't trust you with your hands full on that twisting stair. You're more than liable to drop the lot. In domestic matters, men are clumsy creatures – or, at least, so they pretend.'

On which slightly sour note, she led the way down to the kitchen where Meg Spendlove was already scouring out the cooking pots ready for the preparation of the evening meal.

The maid's eyes had widened with fright as soon as she saw me, and she retreated to the opposite side of the stone bench on which she was working when Isolda explained that I wished to talk to her about the murder.

'I don't know anything, Missus,' she muttered. 'I wasn't there.'

Isolda lowered her burden on to one end of the bench and put water to heat over the fire in order to wash the dirty plates.

'No one's accusing you of anything, Meggie,' she said soothingly, adding, with a significant glance in my direction. 'Master Chapman knows that you had nothing to do with Master Bonifant's death. He just wants to ask you a question or two. Now, sit down quietly on that stool and listen to what he has to say. Don't be afraid. I shall be right here, beside you.'

I would far rather have spoken to Meg alone, but I had enough sense to realise that without Isolda's comforting presence I should probably get nothing out of her at all. It was therefore the lesser of two evils, and I resigned myself to putting up with a certain amount of interference from my hostess.

'Meg,' I said gently, not quite sure where I should begin, 'what ... what were your feelings about Master Bonifant?' She stared at me blankly. 'Did you like him?' I asked.

I had expected prevarication, and was unprepared for her blunt, 'No! I didn't. I hated him.'

'Now, Meggie dear!' Isolda interrupted hurriedly. 'You know that's not true. You didn't always get on well with him, I agree, but you didn't hate him.'

'Yes, I did,' was the uncompromising retort. The little face was suddenly filled with loathing. 'I'm glad he's dead. I thank God every night for it when I say my prayers.'

There was no arguing with such conviction, and Isolda stood, irresolute, not knowing what to say for the best, nor how to put Meg on her guard for what she probably guessed would be my next question.

'Did you know that the liniment used by Master Babcary to ease his aches and pains is poisonous?'

Meg nodded vigorously, a belligerent gleam in the brown eyes.

'Yes, 'cause Missus Isolda told us all when the 'pothecary first brought it to the house. And I know where it's kept, and where the key to the cupboard is.' Having made this admission, however, all her bravado seemed to desert her and she burst into noisy sobs. 'But I didn't kill Master Gideon. I didn't! I didn't!'

Isolda flew to her side, putting a protective arm around her shoulders.

'Of course you didn't, Meggie! Nobody would ever accuse you of such a thing, would he, Master Chapman?' And she stared at me defiantly, daring me to contradict her.

This assurance seemed to have the opposite effect on Meg to the one intended, and the sobs grew louder. I had to wait several minutes for the noise to abate, but the delay afforded me an opportunity to ignore Isolda's question without her realising it.

'Meg,' I said, even more gently, when the fit of crying had eventually subsided, 'I know that you and Mistress Bonifant spent most of the day in the kitchen, preparing the food for Mistress Perle's birthday feast but did you, for any reason, go up to the parlour after the table had been laid?'

'I've already told you that she didn't,' Isolda put in quickly.

I tried to recollect whether she had done so or not, but I need not have worried. Meg Spendlove was too simple to take a hint.

'I didn't go up *after* the table was laid,' she answered, frowning slightly. 'But I did go up with the Missus aforehand. She said if I was good, she'd let me put the special cups on the table. Missus told me where to put them, so I shouldn't get 'em mixed up again.'

Isolda sighed resignedly. 'She loves those goblets. She likes to look at the carving around the rims, the clusters of grapes and vine leaves, the nymphs and shepherds dancing.' She glanced at the girl and shook her head. 'Why did you have to go and blurt that out, Meggie? No one need have known you were there.'

Meg seemed puzzled. 'Toby knew,' she said. 'He peeped round the door while you were telling me where to put the things on the table.'

It was Isolda's turn to frown. 'I didn't know that. I didn't see him.'

'You wouldn't. You had your back to him,' Meg answered. 'But I saw him and he saw me. He winked at me, then went away again.'

'Was he there for long?' I asked. 'Long enough, say, to overhear what Mistress Bonifant was saying and to watch where you placed the goblets?'

'I dunno. I suppose so.' Meg had stopped being frightened and was beginning to grow surly at all this questioning.

But I hadn't quite finished with her yet.

'Later on,' I said, 'after Mistress Perle and her friends had arrived, Toby came down to the kitchen to have his supper with you, as he always did when there were guests. Mistress Bonifant has told me that when she entered the kitchen, you and he were whispering together. Toby was laughing. What were you talking about?'

The rich colour surged into her face.

205

'Nothing!' she exclaimed fiercely. 'Anyway, I can't remember.'

'Then how do you know that it was nothing? Something must have amused Toby,' I urged. 'What was it?'

Meg's face, from which the tide of red had now receded, became expressionless. 'Can't remember,' she repeated.

'Try,' I pleaded.

Meg simply shrugged her thin shoulders and looked away.

Isolda smiled mockingly. 'Master Chapman, you might as well save your breath. You'll get no more out of her now that she's made up her mind not to tell you. She can be as obstinate as a mule.'

I had no doubt that she was right. I have invariably found that simple people, like Meg Spendlove, possess a tremendous strength of will and determination.

'Did you poison Master Bonifant, Meg?' I asked abruptly, hoping to catch her off her guard.

She thrust out her underlip and her eyes sparked with anger. 'No! But I wish I had,' she answered.

There seemed nothing more to be said. Meg was in a thoroughly recalcitrant mood and I should get no more from her. I could have persisted, but it would have done no good. I glanced at Isolda, who gave an almost imperceptible, discouraging shake of her head.

'We'll leave you alone then, Meggie,' she murmured. 'I'll come back later and give you a hand with the dirty dishes.'

'No need to,' Meg replied, her tone surly. 'I can do them on my own.'

'Well, at least she isn't frightened of you any longer,' Isolda smiled as we left the kitchen. There was a crash from somewhere behind us as an iron cooking pot was carelessly dropped on the stone-flagged floor and we both laughed. 'Now, what do you want to do next? Do you wish to speak to Toby Maybury? If you'll return upstairs, to the parlour, I'll see if Father can spare him from the workshop.'

'I do want to speak to him,' I agreed, 'but I also need to speak to both your cousins.'

Isolda pursed her lips. 'I suppose Nell *might* be feeling well enough to answer a few questions by now,' she said doubtfully. 'I'll ask her if you like. But don't be surprised if she declines. She's not very strong, you know. She has always suffered from delicate health.'

It was on the tip of my tongue to protest that a girl who had such a hearty appetite was probably as strong as a packhorse, but I restrained myself. I should gain nothing by antagonising these people, and it was obvious that Eleanor Babcary was a privileged person in the household.

'I should be very grateful for your help in this matter, Mistress Bonifant,' I said. 'I should like to have a word with Mistress Eleanor, if I may. Master Toby can wait a while.'

Isolda accompanied me up the first flight of stairs, leaving me outside the parlour to continue on up to the second storey, where her cousin's bedchamber was situated next to her own. I pushed open the door, closing it carefully behind me, and once again approached the fire, thankful for its warmth after the dank chill of the kitchen.

I sat down in the armchair, recently vacated by my hostess, and stared into the heart of the flames. So far, I had no idea who had killed Gideon Bonifant, but was very much inclined to think that Isolda was innocent of the crime. Yet I was well aware that this was to ignore the most telling evidence, and was simply because I liked her. Moreover, I knew that my judgement was often at fault, and on several occasions before this, I had been drawn to women who had turned out to be far more evil than any man. Her apparent frankness might mean that she was just a clever dissembler, and it was therefore vital that I remain on my guard where Isolda was concerned.

I had guessed that Eleanor Babcary would take some persuading to leave her bed, but it now seemed a very long time since my hostess had left me at the parlour door. I got up from my chair, stretching my arms and legs, which were beginning to ache from inactivity, unused to this cloistered, sedentary life. I turned my back to the fire, letting its heat seep into my bones, and it was while I was standing thus that I suddenly realised how quiet, all at once, the house was. It was true that the door of the room was closed, but surely I had previously been able to hear some sounds through it. But now there was nothing; not so much as the echo of a distant voice, not even the creak of a floorboard. I could hear no footfall from the rooms overhead, no faint crash from the kitchen regions.

The hairs began to rise on the nape of my neck, and I again felt as I had done the night before last, on my way back to the Voyager. It was as though some evil presence was very close at hand, and I reflected with dismay that I had left my cudgel downstairs, in the shop. So I clenched my hands into two sizeable fists and rocked forward on the balls of my feet, ready to launch myself at whatever was threatening me.

The silence seemed as impenetrable as ever. Then the latch of the door was slowly lifted.

Thirteen

Yet again, my worst fears were not realised. It was Eleanor Babcary who entered the room, closely followed by Isolda. I breathed a sigh of relief, but, at the same time, wondered why my imagination was playing me such tricks.

It was plain that Eleanor had accompanied her cousin against her will. There was a pout to the soft lips, a sullen expression in the blue eyes that clearly indicated her reluctance, and I wondered what arguments Isolda had used to cajole her into talking to me. Perhaps she had pointed out that it would be wiser to submit to my questioning now and get it over with, than to wait in uneasy anticipation of the ordeal still to come.

'I hope you're feeling better, Mistress,' I said with as much concern as I could muster, convinced in my own mind that there was nothing really wrong with the girl except for an irritation of nerves which I could not, at present, explain. 'Won't you sit down?' And I pointed to the armchair nearest the fire.

She glanced over her shoulder at Isolda, who nodded encouragement.

'Do as Master Chapman says, Nell. I'll sit here, opposite you, and then you'll have no need to be afraid.'

'I hope Mistress Babcary knows better than to be afraid of me,' I responded with some asperity. 'I've done nothing that I'm aware of to inspire fear in any member of this household.'

'You're looking for the truth concerning a murder,' Isolda answered drily. 'That's enough, surely, to frighten us all.' She moved to the other armchair and sat down.

Her cousin followed suit, but held herself erect, fidgeting nervously, as she had done earlier, with the pendant around her neck. I drew forward a stool and seated myself midway between the two women.

'Mistress Babcary,' I invited, 'tell me all you can – anything that you remember – about the evening that Master Bonifant died.'

Eleanor's story, told haltingly, agreed with both her cousin's and her uncle's version of events, and was recounted with almost no prompting from the former, and with very few glances in her direction.

Eleanor had, she said, gone up to her bed-chamber to change from her workaday into her best clothes at the same time as the other members of the family – excepting, of course, Isolda – and had returned here, to the parlour, to see Mistress Perle presented with her birthday gift and to drink her health.

'Mistress Bonifant was late putting in an appearance because she had been delayed in the kitchen,' I pointed out. 'What did you all talk about while you were waiting for her arrival?'

The younger woman furrowed her brow. 'I can't remember. Mistress Napier spoke to me, but I have no recollection of what she said, because I wasn't listening to her very closely. Toby was winking and mouthing something at me from behind her back, but I couldn't make out what it was he was saying.'

I leant forward a little, my interest quickening. 'Winking and mouthing, was he? And did you ever find out what it was that he'd been trying to tell you?'

Eleanor shook her head. 'I never asked him.' Her face grew bleak. 'With everything that ... that happened afterwards, I'd forgotten all about it until now.' She had at last stopped tugging at her pendant and was gripping the arms of her chair so hard that the knuckles of her hands gleamed white.

'He wasn't supposed to be here, was he? When your uncle entertains guests, Toby takes his meals in the kitchen.'

'Yes, with Meggie.' Eleanor raised her lovely eyes to mine. 'I don't know why he was in the parlour. He shouldn't have been.'

I did not press the matter. I could winkle the truth out of young Toby later. Meantime, I had a more important question for Eleanor Babcary, but one which I was loath to put to her in Isolda's presence. Fortunately, just at that moment, there was the sound of feet pounding up the stairs and, a second or two later, Toby himself put his head around the door. The sound of distant wailing reached our ears.

'You'd best come, Mistress,' he said to Isolda. 'Meg's dropped half a dozen eggs on the kitchen floor and is crying her eyes out. She won't be comforted by anyone but you.'

My hostess stifled what could have been an unladylike curse as, with a better grace than I think I could have mustered in the circumstances, had I been in her shoes, she rose and accompanied the apprentice downstairs. She did falter as she reached the parlour door, but, to her credit, her hesitation was only momentary. A second later, I heard the click of the latch.

I turned back to Eleanor to find her eyeing me askance. It was almost as if she knew what I was going to ask her.

'Mistress Babcary,' I said, 'what were your feelings for Gideon Bonifant?'

'My feelings for him?' Her eyes were

warier still.

'Yes. Did you like him? Were you ... Were you fond of him?'

I noticed with interest that at my reference to the murdered man, one of Eleanor's slender white hands had risen, almost unconsciously, to finger yet again the pendant on its thin gold chain. Her voice, when she answered, was somewhat constricted.

'He was Isolda's husband. Of course I liked him, for her sake.'

'Was that the only reason? Did you not like him for his own sake?'

'I don't know what you mean.' She sounded slightly breathless. 'I – I didn't think much about him. He was years older than I was. He was ten years older than Isolda. Gideon always seemed to me to be more of Uncle Miles's generation, although I suppose he wasn't really.' She blinked unhappily. 'Kit and I had only been here a year when he and Isolda were married and he came to live here, too. So ... Well, I was used to him, you see. He was just another member of the household.'

I reflected for the second time that while this had probably once been true of Eleanor's attitude towards her cousin's husband, it was possible that her feelings for him might have undergone a change. I don't know what put this idea into my head, except that she refused to meet my eyes when speaking of Gideon, and continued, in the same restless, nervous way, to fiddle with her pendant. There was also the memory of her earlier tears.

I said, 'According to Mistress Bonifant, that jewel of yours was a birthday gift from all of them – herself, your uncle, your brother and Master Bonifant. Everyone had a hand in making it, is that not so?'

Eleanor looked bewildered by this change of subject, and for a second or two could do nothing more than nod her head. Finally, however, she answered, 'Yes. Uncle Miles was responsible for most of the work because he insisted that it must be done properly, that it had to be perfect for me. But they all had a hand somewhere in the fashioning of it.'

'And what was Master Bonifant's contribution, do you know?'

I heard the breath catch in her throat and her eyes suddenly widened with an emotion whose nature still eluded me.

'I – I was told he set the sapphires in the lover's knot.'

'And who told you that?' I queried gently.

'What?' She had been temporarily lost in some dream world of her own and I had to repeat my question. 'Oh,' she replied, once she understood, 'I can't remember. Uncle Miles, I expect. Or Kit perhaps. Or maybe even Isolda.'

'But not Master Bonifant himself?'

The door opened and Isolda returned to seat herself again in the chair opposite her cousin's.

'What a mess!' she exclaimed, torn between annoyance and laughter. 'Six eggs running everywhere among the rushes, and a bowl broken into the bargain. That's Meggie's second accident today. She cracked an earthenware cooking pot earlier on. Those are the sort of accidents that so infuriated Gideon.' Isolda grimaced and shrugged resignedly. 'Well, Master Chapman, and have you finished questioning Eleanor yet?' She cast one shrewd look at her cousin's face and continued, 'Nell, dearest, you look tired. I think you should lie down until suppertime. Come along!' She got up, holding out an imperious hand. 'I'll help you up to bed.'

Eleanor rose obediently and, I fancied, with relief. Isolda addressed me over her shoulder.

'I've told Toby to come up here to see you. He shouldn't be long; only a minute or two, or until he's finished whatever task it is that Father has set him.'

'And Master Christopher?' I murmured. 'I still haven't spoken to him.'

She heaved another sigh. 'Don't worry! I'll make certain that you do. You might as well finish your enquiries here all in one day.'

She didn't add, 'And then you won't have to come back,' but I could hear the unspoken comment in her voice.

When the two women had gone upstairs, I waited several minutes before deciding to go in search of young Toby for myself. I wished to speak to Miles again, as well as to Christopher Babcary and the apprentice, and guessed that I should find them all together in the shop, which indeed I did.

The three men were busy and looked none too pleased at my uninvited appearance amongst them.

'Toby was just coming up to the parlour,' Miles said testily. He was bent over his workbench, putting the finishing touches to the coronet of gold and silver ivy leaves for Mistress Shore.

I ignored this remark and asked him why he had failed to mention the scene between his son-in-law and Meg Spendlove only some five weeks before the murder.

He answered sourly, 'Because I'd forgotten about it, that's why. I told you, I have too many calls upon my time to take much notice of such domestic squabbles. But yes, I do recall the occasion now that you jog my memory. Gideon indulged himself in a display of bad temper that was quite unnecessary in my opinion.'

'In everyone's opinion,' his nephew put in, looking up from the other end of the bench, where he was sorting and grading a bag of pearls.

'And you don't think that maybe Meg bore Master Bonifant a grudge for this unwarranted dressing-down?'

It was Toby's turn to abandon the tray of wax, in which he was drawing a pattern of leaves and flowers, and come forward to stand in front of me, his lower lip jutting aggressively.

'Meg wouldn't harm a fly,' he said. 'You let her alone.'

'That will do,' his master reproved him. 'Get back to your work.'

'No, no!' I said, putting a detaining hand on the apprentice's shoulder. 'I want to know, Toby, why you were in the parlour on the evening of the murder. I understand that when there are guests, you eat in the kitchen. So what were you doing upstairs? Both Mistress Bonifant and Master Babcary, here, have testified to your presence, as I'm sure Master Christopher could also do, if asked.'

'That's true enough,' Christopher confirmed. He glanced curiously at the apprentice. 'I hadn't really thought about it until now, but what *were* you doing skulking about in the parlour, when you should have been down in the kitchen with Meg?'

Toby glared defiantly at the three of us. 'I just went in to have a look at the table,' he said. 'At the goblets, really. They're so beautiful. I like to touch them. I like to feel the carving round the rims.'

Miles Babcary mellowed visibly in the face of this unlooked-for tribute. 'The boy has a natural eye for craftsmanship. I'll make a goldsmith of him yet.'

Toby simpered virtuously.

'And was that the only reason you went into the parlour?' I asked.

His eyes met mine for a fleeting moment before his glance slid sideways. 'Yes,' was the truculent reply.

'And did anyone else enter the room while you were there?'

This was an easier question to answer.

'Master came in with Mistress Perle and the other lady and gentleman, a few minutes after Master Bonifant and Kit and Nell. Mistress arrived last of all, and then I went downstairs.'

I noted that while Christopher and Eleanor were referred to with familiarity, Gideon had evidently remained on more distant terms with a lowly apprentice.

Toby, feeling that he had satisfied my curiosity, would, at this point, have squirmed free of my hand and returned to his task, had I not tightened my grip on his shoulder.

'Just a minute! According to Mistress Babcary, something else happened before you left the parlour. What was it that you were

219

trying to tell her behind Mistress Napier's back? She says you were mouthing words at her and making signs.'

There was a tell-tale pause before Toby retorted defiantly, 'I was not!'

'She says you were, and I don't see why she should tell me a lie.'

'No, indeed,' Christopher cut in. 'My sister's a very truthful person.'

Toby went a guilty red. 'I'm not saying she lied,' he protested. 'I'm just saying she must have been mistaken.'

'How could she possibly be mistaken about such a thing?' I asked severely.

He then changed tack, claiming that his memory was at fault, and that he could remember nothing of the matter. But that, he conceded generously, didn't mean to say it wasn't true. And in spite of all my perserverance and the derision of uncle and nephew, we could not persuade him to alter his story. It was obvious, to me at least, that he was lying but there was nothing I could do against his obstinate persistence that he was unable to recollect the incident, and that, therefore, whatever it was that he had been trying to convey to Eleanor had been of no importance. Eventually, I gave up and released him, whereupon he retired again to his workbench with a heartfelt sigh of relief.

I turned my attention to Christopher.

'Master Babcary,' I said, 'perhaps you

would tell me what you remember of that evening.'

He shrugged his broad shoulders and continued deftly sorting the pearls, assembling them into three different groups by size.

'I expect I'm only telling you what you have already heard,' he said, without looking up. 'We shut the shop early that evening and then went upstairs to change into our Sunday clothes, it being Mistress Perle's birthday feast.'

'Did you all leave the shop together?' I asked.

Christopher glanced at the older man, frowning. 'You went first, I think, Uncle Miles. If I remember rightly, you wanted to be sure that you were ready before Mistress Perle and her friends arrived.'

'That's true,' Master Babcary confirmed. 'And as well that I did. I went straight to my room but, even so, I was barely dressed before I heard Barbara's knock.'

'And then?' I prompted. 'Who was the next to leave?'

Once again, Christopher shrugged and grimaced, implying that he was unable to remember. 'Is it of any importance?' he sneered.

'It might be,' I replied, trying to keep my temper. 'In any case, I should be interested to know the answer. Was it you or Master Bonifant or young Toby, here?'

'It was Master Bonifant,' Toby said, giving me a winning smile in order to make up for his former intransigence.

'Are you sure of that?' I asked.

'Of course I'm sure. He'd been applying some gilding to that silver chalice Master had made for Saint Pancras's church, and I remember him saying, "I've had enough of this! I'm off upstairs. I'll finish it in the morning." Only of course he never did. Master finished it himself a week or so later.'

There was an uneasy silence while Christopher, Miles Babcary and Toby avoided one another's eyes and I looked thoughtfully at the three of them. Finally, I enquired of Christopher, 'Is that your recollection, too? Was Master Bonifant the next to go upstairs?'

He nodded. 'Yes. Now I think back, I can recall Gideon using precisely those words. He'd been in a bad mood all day, more than usually grumpy and taciturn, although his temper seemed to have improved a bit by the time we were all assembled in the parlour.'

'And did you or Toby go upstairs next?'

Christopher glowered at me, irritated by my persistence. Once more, it was the apprentice who answered for him.

'I did. I knew Master would want me to look tidy, even if I wasn't eating with the family.'

222

'And how long after Master Bonifant's departure was that?'

Toby pulled a face and raised his eyebrows at Christopher. 'Ten minutes, would you say?' And when the other man did not answer, he went on, 'Yes, about ten minutes. Maybe a little longer.'

'Your bedchamber's on the top floor, so I've been told.'

Toby nodded. 'Next to Kit's.'

'You went straight up there from the shop?' Again he nodded. 'And did you see anyone else on the stairs?'

'No. Well,' he amended, 'I saw Master Bonifant when I reached the second landing. He was just going into his room. He said he'd been to the kitchen to have a word with Mistress Bonifant, which was why he'd been delayed.'

'And did you believe him?'

Toby blinked in surprise. 'Why shouldn't I believe him when he said so? Where else could he have been?'

For some reason that I was unable to explain to my own satisfaction, the delicate, flower-like features of Eleanor Babcary swam before my mind's eye. Had there been a brief, secret lovers' tryst between her and Gideon? Or was I, as ever, letting my imagination run ahead of common sense? I had no evidence – at least, not so far – to suppose that either was in love with the other. All the same, I would check with both Meg and Isolda to discover if this statement of Gideon's was true.

I turned back to the apprentice. 'And it was after you had made yourself fit to be seen in company that you sneaked down to the parlour?'

'Yes. I told you, I went to look at the goblets. I always do, when they're taken out for feast days and holidays.'

My host looked even more gratified than before.

'Master Babcary,' I asked abruptly, 'did you know that your son-in-law had been married previously? That your daughter was his second wife?'

He raised his eyes from Mistress Shore's coronet and looked both astonished and indignant that I could suppose him ignorant in this matter.

'Of course I knew. It's not the sort of circumstance a man would conceal.'

I bowed my head in agreement. 'So I should suppose. But I was curious as neither you nor Mistress Bonifant had mentioned the fact.'

He threw up his hands in exasperation. 'Why should we? It can have no bearing on his murder. The lady herself died many years ago, and can hardly have had anything to do with his death. Who told you about her?'

'Master Ford, the apothecary, Master Bonifant's old master.' I shifted my gaze to the nephew. 'Master Babcary, did you know, before Gideon's death, of the stories he was spreading concerning you and Mistress Bonifant?'

Christopher's fingers were suddenly stilled amongst the pearls that he had been so busily sorting. A tide of blood suffused his face. Miles Babcary nervously adjusted his spectacles.

'Of course I didn't,' the younger man answered with a menacing quietness. 'Had I done so, I should have made it my business to refute such an evil slander.'

I plucked up courage to ask, 'There was, then, not the slightest vestige of truth in the rumour?'

'None whatsoever!' His tone was venomous, and his eyes, now fixed on my face, dared me to pursue the subject.

I braved his wrath and said, as apologetically as I could, 'Master Bonifant also claimed to have overheard you boasting to your sister of being in love with an older woman, and of being almost certain that your love was requited. Was this true?'

Never, in my estimation, was guilt written more plainly on a man's face than it was at that moment on Christopher Babcary's but, having denied the charge in the past, and, presumably, having persuaded his sister to lie for him, he could do no other than refute it now, even though it was doubtful that he would wish to.

'Whatever Gideon thought he heard, he was mistaken.'

'I see. And do you know of any other man whose' – my tongue fumbled for a word – 'whose friendship with your cousin might have misled Master Bonifant into imagining that you were his betrayer? Or convinced him that he was indeed being betrayed?'

'I know of no one!' came the furious response.

'No one! No one!' echoed Miles Babcary, equally angry.

'But Master Bonifant must have got this idea from somewhere!' I cried despairingly. 'Something must have made him suspect that his wife was being unfaithful to him.'

Two mouths shut like traps; the looks from two pairs of eyes would have struck me down if they could. But I was there at the instigation of the King's mistress and of the Duke of Gloucester, and neither man dared to send me packing from the house, as I had not the smallest doubt he wished to do.

I swung round and faced the apprentice, who had given up all pretence of working and was staring at me, goggle-eyed.

'Do you know of anyone, Toby?'

Toby pulled himself together and gave my question his gravest consideration. But after some long, hard thought, he slowly shook his head.

'No,' he said, 'there's no one I can think of. Mistress was always a loyal wife as far as I could see. Besides,' he added with all the candour of youth, 'men just don't fancy her, do they? Not like Mistress Nell. But,' he added, his eyes suddenly sly, 'I did think, at one time, as how Master Kit was partial to Mistress Napier. I used to see the way he mooned at her whenever she visited the shop. And once, I caught him trying to kiss her.'

Fourteen

'And what happened then?' my wife enquired, her face alight with interest and curiosity. 'Did Christopher Babcary admit to the truth of Toby's accusation?'

I had returned to the Voyager just as dusk was falling, and was now cosily ensconced in our little room in front of a glowing fire, which Reynold Makepeace had insisted be lit for Adela's comfort, after what had proved to be a somewhat tiring day in the company of Jeanne Lamprey.

True to her promise, Jeanne, leaving Philip

227

in charge of their shop, had taken my wife to see the wild animals in the Tower. But the walk from Cornhill, the cold, the noise, the crowds of people and the densely packed traffic of the streets, particularly around the Tower itself, had left Adela feeling, as she herself phrased it, 'like a wrung-out dish-cloth.' She had arrived back at the inn sometime in the mid-afternoon, her exhausted appearance immediately exciting our host's ready sympathy. He had sent one of the pot-boys scurrying to set a lighted taper to the wood and coals freshly laid on our hearth, while the cook despatched two kitchen maids to our bedchamber with hot broth and rosewater jelly.

I was now drinking a bowlful of the same broth, together with a large slice of good wheaten bread and a couple of collops of bacon, all washed down with Reynold's best ale, glad to be free of the Babcarys' house and what I felt to be the family's growing hostility towards me. But Adela was anxious to know everything that had happened during the day, and so, between mouthfuls of food, I had regaled her with the facts. But when I reached the point of Toby's revelation concerning Christopher Babcary and Ginèvre Napier, I had been forced to go through to the taproom in search of more ale. I had, however, barely seated myself once again in my chair before my wife, stretched out on the bed, her aching back propped against the pillows, compelled me to continue my story by answering her question.

I laid down my spoon. 'Christopher denied it hotly at first, as you might imagine. But Toby was so persistent in declaring that what he had told us was correct, and Miles Babcary and I made it so obvious that we believed him – both of us having experience of the kind of woman preferred by Christopher – that, in the end, he grudgingly conceded it to be the truth. And finally, rather than allow me to question his sister again, he confessed that he had indeed boasted to Eleanor that he was in love with an older woman – although without naming her – and that he was certain that his love was returned. He had no idea at the time that his remark had been overheard by Gideon but when he learned how the other man had misinterpreted it, his one thought was to deny ever having said such a thing, and to persuade his sister to deny it, also.'

'So much,' Adela said, nodding sagely, 'for Miles Babcary's conviction that his niece was incapable of lying.'

I picked up my spoon again. 'I have no doubt at all,' I agreed, 'that she is as capable of telling untruths as anyone else, when it suits her to do so. I'm quite certain that she is concealing something concerning herself and Gideon Bonifant, but what that something is, I've as yet no real inkling. I can only guess that she was in love with him and won't own to it for her cousin's sake.'

'But do you think that Gideon was in love with her? Were they, in fact, lovers?'

I finished my broth and wiped my mouth on the back of my hand.

'I should think it well nigh impossible in a house with so many people in it,' I answered. 'Besides, as far as I can gather, he showed no interest in her except as his wife's cousin. The impression I've gleaned of Master Bonifant – although I admit it could be wrong – is of a cold, calculating man who probably married Isolda for no other reason than her dowry and the place in society that she could bring him. Had she not been so plain, she would most likely never have considered him as a husband, but he took advantage of her lack of suitors and her desire to be married to carve out for himself a comfortable niche in life. And I doubt that he would have jeopardised his position as Miles Babcary's son-in-law by betraying Isolda with Eleanor.'

I could see that Adela was not wholly convinced. She said something about people like Gideon having hidden fire in their souls, a remark I instantly derided as far too fanciful and romantic to have been uttered by anyone as sensible as herself, and put it down to her condition (which, as all men know, makes women a little unbalanced).

Adela gave me one of her quizzical looks, accompanied by a small, secret smile that somehow made me feel like a foolish schoolboy. But all she said was, 'What will you do next?'

'Next, I must talk to Mistress Perle and the Napiers,' I answered, adding guiltily, 'Will you go to the Lampreys' again tomorrow?'

My wife shook her head. 'They've very kindly asked me to do so, but I've refused. A day spent here, in the inn, will do me more good. Besides, I'm sure Jeanne and Philip need a rest from *my* company. I'll join them again the following day, if necessary.'

'I'm afraid it will be necessary,' I replied gloomily. 'As yet, I've no idea what really happened that December afternoon, only the conviction that nothing was as straightforward or as simple as it seemed.'

'You don't believe, then, that Mistress Bonifant murdered her husband?'

'Without proof that she really did have a lover, she appears to have had no motive for doing so.'

'And you've decided that, if she did, Christopher Babcary wasn't the man?'

I shrugged. 'He denies it, Isolda denies it, although that, of course, is only what I should expect them to do. But you saw for

231

yourself the woman he was with yesterday, on the quayside – a woman as unlike Mistress Bonifant as it is possible to imagine. Miles Babcary also tells me that his nephew fancies himself in love with a different lady every few weeks. Why, then, would Gideon regard any flirtation between his wife and her cousin, supposing there was one, as seriously meant? No, I find it far easier to believe that Christopher was talking about Mistress Napier to his sister.'

Adela was silent for a few moments. 'That's probably true,' she said at last. 'But why, when Master Bonifant overheard that remark, did he instantly assume that Christopher Babcary was referring to his cousin?'

I pushed my chair back from the fire, which was now proving too hot for me.

'Because,' I answered slowly, reasoning things out as I spoke, 'he already believed Isolda to be unfaithful to him, and Christopher's confession to his sister simply confirmed his suspicions. Gideon jumped to the over-hasty conclusion that Christopher Babcary was the man.'

'But that still doesn't explain,' Adela argued, 'why Master Bonifant believed Isolda to be cuckolding him in the first place.'

'No,' I agreed, rubbing my forehead. 'I have already come to the conclusion that I

232

shall have to go back and question Eleanor Babcary again, for if Isolda confided in anyone, I'm sure it would have been in her beloved Nell. But as it's already been proved that the young lady will lie to protect those she loves, I doubt I have much hope of finding out the truth.' I sighed. 'And where does young Toby Maybury fit into the events of that afternoon? What was he doing in the parlour? If it was just to look at the chasing on the goblets, as he claims, what was he trying to convey to Eleanor behind Ginèvre Napier's back?'

Adela turned on to her side. 'And the maid, Meg Spendlove, she had a grudge against Master Bonifant, you say?'

I finished my ale. 'She did. And I haven't really established whether or not she had an opportunity to return to the parlour on her own after helping Isolda to lay the table. Yes, I'm afraid I've no choice but to go back to Master Babcary's after I've visited Mistress Perle and the Napiers.'

'And when will that be?' asked Adela, sliding off the bed and coming to sit on my knees.

'First thing tomorrow morning,' I said, kissing her cheek.

But I had barely scraped the overnight stubble from my chin, and had only just returned from holding my head under the courtyard pump, when Reynold Makepeace came knocking urgently at our bedchamber door.

'A messenger's here from His Grace of Gloucester,' he announced breathlessly when my wife had opened it in answer to his summons. 'He says he must speak with Master Chapman.'

'Then he must wait on me in here,' I called out testily. 'I've not yet finished dressing.'

A few moments later, the same young man who had shown me the way to Mistress Shore's house three days earlier was ushered in by a deferential Reynold Makepeace, whose only reward was a dismissive flick of the fingers.

'The Duke wishes to speak to you,' the young man announced, addressing me and ignoring Adela. 'You must accompany me immediately to Crosby Place.'

'His Grace will have to possess his soul in patience until I've had my breakfast,' I snapped, annoyed by this cavalier treatment of my wife.

'No,' the young man answered levelly. 'Now! My lord is in no mood to be kept waiting. You can eat in our kitchens afterwards, if you're so hungry.'

There was something in his tone, even though he had not raised his voice, that made me think twice about my gesture of defiance, and Adela also begged me to go.

'You must do as His Grace commands,' she urged.

I finished dressing as slowly as I dared with the young man's impatient eyes fixed upon me, then I kissed my wife, assuring her that I should be back within a very short space of time.

'I'll return here before I visit Paternoster Row,' I told her.

Two horses were tethered outside the inn, such, apparently, being the Duke's impatience to see me that he could not wait for us to make the journey to Bishop's Gate Street on foot. My guide swung himself into the saddle of one of the beasts and signed to me to mount the other.

'You can ride, I suppose?' he asked as an afterthought.

I assured him that I could, although it was not usually my lot to be mounted on such a spirited, thoroughbred animal.

We arrived at Crosby Place very speedily, a path through the teeming streets miraculously opening up for us at the sight of my companion's azure and murrey livery and his badges of the White Boar and the Red Bull. The mansion looked even more impressive by daylight than it had done at night: a large, strongly constructed house of stone and timber, built around a courtyard and surrounded by what would, in spring and summer, undoubtedly be a beautiful garden. I was again shown into the great hall with its oriel window, marble floor and arched roof decorated in red and gold.

'Wait here,' I was instructed. 'Someone will be with you very shortly.' And the young man disappeared through a door beneath the minstrels' gallery.

A number of servants and attendants passed through the hall, eyeing me with either curiosity or indifference, before the Duke's secretary came to escort me to his master. We found the Duke seated at a table, writing, in one of the smaller chambers, but he threw down his pen and swivelled round to greet me as soon as John Kendall had announced me and withdrawn.

'Roger! Thank you for coming so quickly.'

I felt ashamed of my former ill-humour and, at the same time, was shocked at Duke Richard's appearance. If he had seemed unwell four days earlier, I thought him positively haggard now. The dark circles under his eyes were almost black, the eyes themselves sunk deep into their sockets. His face was all bone and no flesh, while his furred gown hung so loosely about him that it was plain to see that he had lost more weight. The hand that he gave me to kiss was skeletal.

He motioned me to the window seat and sat down beside me; or, rather, he perched on the edge, getting up to walk restlessly around the room every few minutes or so.

'How are your investigations proceeding?' he asked, coming straight to the point. 'Have you been able to prove the innocence of Mistress Shore's cousin?'

'Not yet, my lord,' I answered, adding defensively, 'these matters take time. In any case, after a lapse of so many weeks, it may not be possible to uncover any proof that will solve the mystery one way or the other.'

He began to pace the floor, beating his clenched right fist into the open palm of his left hand.

'I must have something soon that will enable me to persuade Mistress Shore to use her influence with the King in favour of saving my brother's life.'

'If you'll forgive me for saying so, my lord,' I ventured, 'having met Mistress Shore since we last talked on this subject, I don't believe you need a bargaining counter in order to enlist her help. She strikes me as a tender-hearted lady who wishes no one any harm.'

The Duke rounded on me almost as though I had spoken blasphemy.

'Do you expect me to beg a *favour* of that woman?' He returned to sit beside me on the window seat, and I could see that he was trembling with anger. After a moment or two, however, he controlled his emotions and raised a faint smile. 'Forgive me, Roger!

But for my own peace of mind I must have a bargaining counter, as you call it. Give me the truth about this murder, and I shall be able to enlist Mistress Shore's support without loss of face.'

'But what if Mistress Bonifant – Mistress Shore's kinswoman – is indeed guilty?' I queried.

My companion was once more on his feet, restlessly roaming from window to table, from table to door and back again. The agitation of his mind would not let him be still.

'In that case,' he answered, swinging round to face me, 'I shall use that fact as a threat to force her to do my will. I shall threaten to have her cousin arrested unless she does as I request.' The Duke gave a laugh that cracked in the middle. 'Oh, you needn't look so outraged and reproachful, Roger. Wouldn't you use any means in your power to try to save the life of someone you love?' He again sat down, seizing and gripping one of my wrists so hard that the marks of his fingers remained for hours afterwards. 'Don't put me on a pedestal, my friend. I can be as ruthless as any other man when it comes to something that is important to me.'

'Would His Highness really have his own brother put to death?' The words were jerked out of me before I had time to think.

I had hardly expected an answer to so impertinent a question, but Duke Richard was once more on his feet, banging with his fist against the wall until the knuckles were skinned and bleeding.

'Not left to himself, no! I feel sure of it! But with the Queen and all her family determined on George's death and constantly whispering in Edward's ear—' He broke off, suddenly aware of the impropriety of talking to me so openly, and stood, gnawing his underlip and nursing his injured hand. Then he went on harshly, 'My brother of Clarence was born in Dublin, did you know that? The Irish are wild men, untameable, and it's as though some of that wildness rubbed off on George. But they're charming, too, with the gift of the gab, and he also has both those attributes in abundance.' The Duke continued, talking now more to himself than to me. 'George has always been like a child, grabbing what he wanted with both hands and then relying on his silver tongue to get him out of trouble. But he looked after me when I was young, protected me, comforted me, during those terrible years of our childhood when we never knew what fresh disaster the next day would bring. I owe him more than I can ever repay.'

I said softly, fearing that I was intruding on private grief, but not knowing what else to say, 'It's small wonder that Your Grace is

239

fond of him.'

Duke Richard turned to stare at me, blinking a little, as though he had been unconscious of my presence for the past few minutes, before sitting down again on the window seat.

'I'm fond of both my brothers, that's the difficulty, and to see them at odds like this—' He broke off, giving a shaky laugh. 'At odds, did I say? Now there's an understatement! They're both hell bent on one another's destruction.'

It was on the tip of my tongue to ask how George of Clarence could destroy the King, but I thought better of it. My companion had already confided in me more than he should have done, and I could tell by his suddenly wary expression that he thought so, too, and was probably beginning to regret his frankness.

I stood up. 'Your Highness may trust me. I hope you know that.'

He nodded, giving me his hand to kiss in farewell.

'Let me know as soon as you have resolved this mystery, Roger.' He added, half to himself, 'Even then, it may be too late.'

I wanted to say, 'Go to Mistress Shore, today, and ask her to intercede for the Duke of Clarence's life. She won't despise you for begging this favour.' But I knew that he would never do so. He was too proud. For reasons of his own, he disliked the King's leman too much to enlist her help without being able to offer her an inducement in return. So I merely bowed and promised to bring him word as soon as I had reached a conclusion regarding the death of Gideon Bonifant.

'I'm depending on you, Roger,' were his parting words.

Which was all very well, I reflected peevishly, as I made my way back to Bucklersbury and the Voyager, but if there was no proof to be had, all the dependence in the world couldn't produce any.

It was a bitterly cold day, with low-scudding clouds and a sleety rain that stung the face and hands, and I flung what alms I could spare to the blue-faced beggars, shivering in their scanty rags. I found Adela huddled over the fire in our bedchamber, her long, thin hands spread to the blaze, but otherwise contented and cheerful. She had been dozing, for pregnancy made her extremely sleepy, and was quite happy to doze again when I had gone. But first she wanted to hear all that had passed between the Duke and me.

When I had finished telling her, she grimaced. 'He's asking too much of you, Roger.'

Her assumption that I might fail Duke Richard irritated me and blew away my own pessimistic mood.

'Well, I shan't learn anything new by wasting my time here,' I answered briskly, and bent to kiss her. She laughed, but refused to tell me what it was that she found so amusing. Instead, she patted my cheek and instructed me to run along, just as though I had been Elizabeth or Nicholas. (I sometimes had the impression that she regarded me as another of her children.)

Having once again obtained her assurance that she could manage very well on her own for the next few hours, I promised that I should be back before nightfall.

'Send to Paternoster Row if you need me, to the house of either Mistress Barbara Perle or to that of Gregory and Ginèvre Napier,' I told her.

Paternoster Row, which, as I have already said, is where rosaries are chiefly made, is on the north side of Saint Paul's church-yard. But interspersed with the shops are several private dwellings, one of which I instantly recognised, four storeys high, the carved timbers of its gable picked out in scarlet, blue and gold. The upper windows were made of glass, three of them decorated with leaded trefoils and three with circles within triangles, both signs of the Blessed Trinity. This was the Napiers' house, and I had last been inside it three years earlier, when I was investigating the disappearance of a brother and sister from their home in

Devon. Circumstances, as I had told Master Babcary, had brought me to London to question Ginèvre Napier, who had been a friend of the children's mother.

Before renewing my acquaintance with Mistress Napier, however, I first wished to speak to her next door neighbour, Barbara Perle, but realised that I had no idea if her house were to the left or to the right of the Napiers'. I was still trying to decide which dwelling to approach first, standing well back in order to view them better, and unconsciously edging further out amongst the traffic, when the rattle of wheels and the sound of people shouting assailed my ears. The next moment, I was caught unceremoniously around the waist and dragged out of the path of a runaway horse and cart.

'That was a close run thing,' panted my rescuer, a stocky youth with a broken nose. 'You want to watch what you're doing, Master. You could've been killed.'

I acknowledged the fact and grasped his hand in gratitude; but it was not until after more passers-by had come to congratulate me on a narrow escape from death that a feeling of unease began to possess me. Despite my well-wishers' assurance that such accidents were commonplace in London owing to the general carelessness of the drivers, I was unable to rid myself of the suspicion that someone might deliberately have tried to kill me. No one seemed to have taken particular note of the carter's appearance, or be able to describe him, but considering the speed at which he had been travelling, this was hardly surprising.

I told myself that I was being foolish. Running me down would be a risky method of trying to dispose of me, and as far as I knew, the Babcarys owned neither horse nor cart. And yet, surely by now the murderer of Gideon Bonifant should have made some move to stop me enquiring further...

'Have you come to interrogate Mistress Perle?' a voice asked in my ear, and swinging round, I found Christopher Babcary standing at my elbow.

'Where have you sprung from?' I asked.

He looked at me, obviously surprised by my belligerent tone, and indicated the basket he was carrying.

'I've been delivering her coronet to Mistress Shore, in the Strand,' he answered, preparing to move on. 'If you want Barbara Perle's house, it's that one, there.' And he pointed to the one to the right of the Napiers'.

I thanked him mechanically, and stood staring after him as he turned away and continued walking along the street.

Fifteen

The skinny young maid who answered my knock informed me that the mistress had stepped out for a moment or two to visit a sick neighbour, but that she would return before long if I cared to come inside and wait. I accepted the offer, following the girl up a flight of stairs to a parlour on the first floor, a room similar in size and content to that of Master Babcary's house. On the face of it, there would seem to be little difference between his and Mistress Perle's respective fortunes.

The maid bade me be seated, but then, instead of leaving to continue with her household chores, she lingered, looking at me with suppressed excitement, plainly desirous of talking to someone.

'Do you know what today is, sir?' she asked shyly.

'The Feast of Saint Sebastian?' I hazarded.

'It's also the Eve of the Feast of Saint Agnes,' she said, her eyes sparkling with anticipation. 'They do say that on this night, if you do what you're told, you'll dream of your future husband.' She giggled nervously. 'I hope he's as handsome as you.'

'And what is it that you have to do?' I enquired, laughing.

'It's not a joke, sir,' she reproved me. 'Young girls like me do see things in dreams, you know. First of all, I have to fast throughout the day – though that'll not be easy – and I mustn't let anyone kiss me, not even a little child. Then tonight, before I go to bed, I have to take a hard-boiled egg, scoop out its yolk and fill the hollow with salt, then eat it, shell and all. After that, I've to put on a clean nightgown and walk backwards towards the bed – I can't turn round and look at it, or the spell will be broken – and I must say this verse.' She screwed up her face and, with a great effort of memory, recited.

'Fair Saint Agnes play thy part,
And send to me mine own sweetheart,
Not in his best or worst array,
But in the clothes of every day.'

The sound of the street door opening and closing recalled her to her duties.

'That'll be the mistress now,' she said hurriedly. 'You won't mention anything about what I've been telling you, will you sir? She'd say it's all nonsense and the waste of a good egg, but I say you never know! I'd like to see the man I'm going to marry, whoever he is.'

I promised faithfully that her secret was safe with me, and was still smiling and shaking my head, like some old greybeard, over the naivety of young girls, when the parlour door opened and Mistress Perle came in.

She was a good-looking, well-built woman with a broad, handsome face marred only by the fleshiness of her nose. It needed a second, possibly a third, glance to notice the network of fine wrinkles around the blue eyes, and to realise that she was not quite as young as she at first appeared. She was, I finally decided, in her middle fifties, just the right age for Master Babcary.

'You must be Master Chapman,' she said taking a seat at the table and motioning me to sit opposite her. 'Miles sent to warn me you might be arriving sometime or another, and here you are! What is it you want to know?' She evidently intended to waste no time on the usual courtesies.

I explained as briefly as I could the circumstances and reasons for my visit while she listened attentively, not revealing by so much as the flicker of an eyelid whether or not she was already in possession of these facts. Indeed, there was something unnatural about her general stillness, although

I was conscious of the uneasy clasping and unclasping of her hands, as they rested on the table-top in front of her. But when she spoke, her voice was full and steady.

'I repeat, what is it you want to know?'

'Can you tell me what you remember about the afternoon of Master Bonifant's death?'

She was silent for a while, staring into space, but at last she shrugged and nodded her acquiesence.

Her account of the events leading up to the moment when Gideon died was in substance the same as that told by everyone else.

'When they had drunk my health,' she said, 'they all sat down. Oh, except Isolda, of course, who left the parlour in order to go down to the kitchen. That Meg of theirs can never be trusted to do anything properly by herself.' The small, full mouth was pursed in disapproval. 'Why Miles doesn't get rid of her I cannot understand. I've spoken to him often enough on the subject.'

'What happened next?' I interrupted, afraid that she was about to wander from the point.

'Oh, the men began talking – about the new tariffs on silver imported from Poitou, I think. They wouldn't be happy unless they'd something to grumble about. Ginèvre started ed telling Nell Babcary some rigmarole concerning a length of velvet she'd bought just that morning and which, when she got it home, she'd found to be flawed.'

Mistress Perle paused in order to clear her throat, so I took the opportunity to say, 'And Gideon Bonifant was talking to Christopher, or so Master Babcary informed me. Is that correct?'

My companion considered this. 'I don't recall that Gideon was actually *speaking* to Kit. It was more ... more that he was staring fixedly at him. I remember thinking later that perhaps Master Bonifant had already begun to feel ill.'

'Was Christopher Babcary speaking to *him*?'

'He might have been,' she answered slowly. 'I do recollect that Kit was looking puzzled. Almost—'

'Almost?' I prompted.

'Almost as if something hadn't happened that he was expecting to happen.' She shrugged. 'But maybe I'm talking non-sense.'

I made no answer, but privately consider-ed that if Mistress Perle were right, then it was possible that Christopher Babcary had put the monkshood in Gideon's cup, or known that Isolda had done so, and had been anxiously watching his victim for the first signs of the poison taking effect.

'Pray continue,' I begged.

Mistress Perle shivered. 'You must know what happened next. Miles and Kit have surely told you. You don't need a description from me.'

'I should like to have one, all the same.' I added with a flattering smile, 'Women notice so much more than men.'

'Oh – very well. Gideon suddenly staggered to his feet, clutching his throat. He was plainly choking and, at first, I thought that some of his wine had gone down the wrong way. Then I saw that his face was turning blue. I could also see that he was trying to swallow, but couldn't. His throat appeared to be as stiff as a board. His lips, too, because when he tried to speak, he was unable to form the words.' She hesitated, frowning a little. 'And yet I thought at the time that I did hear something that sounded like "aconite".'

'So you think he realised immediately that he'd been poisoned?'

'Perhaps,' she conceded. 'He was desperately afraid, I could see that. But also—'

'But also?'

Mistress Perle put a hand to her forehead. 'Oh ... I don't know! It's difficult to explain. There was an expression on his face that I can only describe as ... as *outrage*. It was as if he couldn't really believe what was happening to him.'

'I should imagine death, particularly

violent death, would make us all feel like that,' I replied gently. 'But please continue.'

'What? Oh ... very well! Ginèvre told Gregory to run for the nearest apothecary. That would be Jeremiah Page in Gudrun Lane. In the doorway he almost collided with Isolda and the girl. They'd just come up from the kitchen with the food.'

'And what did they do?'

She snorted. 'Meg behaved exactly as you would expect her to – she screamed and dropped her tray, the stupid creature! Isolda simply stood and stared. Then Gideon – I swear I'll never forget it as long as I live – he raised his hand and pointed at her.' Mistress Perle gave an exaggerated shudder. 'It was obvious what he meant. He was accusing her of his murder.'

There was silence. My companion, lost in her own thoughts, continued to clasp and unclasp her hands, while I recollected Miles Babcary's words. 'Mistress Perle was almost fainting in horror, and I had to give her the better part of my attention.' It occurred to me that for someone in such a distraught condition, Barbara Perle's memory of events was remarkably detailed, and I wondered if her distress had been assumed for her lover's benefit, or if Master Babcary had been mistaken in the nature of her agitation. Stealing another look at her while she was still lost in her reverie, it struck me anew that she was ill at ease, and had been ever since the beginning of our conversation. I noticed that there was a film of sweat across her forehead, and the constant restlessness of her hands implied an unquiet mind. Did she have something to conceal?

I asked suddenly and loudly, 'Who do you think murdered Gideon Bonifant, Mistress?'

She jumped and glared at me for a moment as though I was some unknown intruder. Then she answered with an unnatural vehemence, 'Isolda of course! There's no doubt about it! Probably aided and abetted by that cousin of hers.'

'Do you mean Christopher Babcary?'

'Of course I mean Christopher Babcary! Who else? I'm not likely to be talking of Nell! Although come to think of it, she's the sort who could be persuaded into anything. She hasn't the brains of a goose. Hasn't Miles told you what Gideon said to him about Kit and Isolda a short time before he was murdered? Yes, he has: I can see the answer in your face. Only Miles has probably persuaded you that it's all a lot of nonsense. He won't listen to anything against his precious daughter. But of course she did it! Who else had such opportunity, both to obtain the monkshood and put it in the wine, as she did?'

There was a false, slightly hysterical note

to Mistress Perle's anger, as though she were trying to convince herself, more than me, of Isolda's guilt. But I nodded as if in agreement and thanked her for her time.

'I have to call on your neighbours now,' I said, rising. 'Fortunately, Mistress Napier and I have met before, so we are not total strangers.'

My hostess gave me a look of startled enquiry, and I was forced, for politeness's sake, to repeat the story of my previous encounter with Ginèvre. It did nothing to reassure Mistress Perle, however, who appeared even more agitated than before, demanding to know if it were really necessary that I visit the Napiers. And it was not until I had made it perfectly plain that I was not to be dissuaded, that she reluctantly summoned her servant to conduct me to the door.

I followed the girl downstairs.

'Don't forget all you have to do tonight,' I whispered, and left her giggling on the door-step.

Mistress Napier was, by great good fortune, at home, and, claiming to be an old acquaintance, I was shown by the same young woman into the same downstairs parlour that I remembered from three years earlier. The red and gold painted ceiling beams were slightly more smoke-blackened than they had been then, the tapestries covering the walls were a little dustier; but the three richly carved armchairs, the fine oaken table and the corner cupboard, with its display of bowls and cups and plates all crafted in gold or silver-gilt, were exactly as memory had preserved them. The filigree pendants of the candelabra, suspended over the table, still tinkled in every draught.

Ginèvre Napier, too, was true to my recollection of her, except that time had not dealt kindly with her. The lines around the grey-green eyes were more obvious, the brown spots on the backs of her hands more numerous. The plucked eyebrows and shaven forehead only emphasised her age, just as the many gold chains encircling her neck showed up the scrawniness of her throat.

She was seated near the window, busy with a piece of embroidery, but the heavy, almond-shaped eyelids were opened to their fullest extent as I entered the room, so that she could scrutinise me better.

'I know you,' she said in her husky voice. 'We've met before.'

'Some time ago,' I answered. 'You were so gracious as to answer some questions for me about Lady Skelton and her second husband, Eudo Colet. Her two children had been murdered.'

'Of course! Now I remember! And did you

ever get at the truth of the matter? Sit down and tell me all about it.'

So, at her bidding, I pulled up one of the other armchairs and regaled her with a brief account of the events in Devon three years previously. Happily, she was not a woman given to exclamations of dismay or demands for repetition, merely remarking, when I had finished my tale, 'Rosamund always was a fool.' She added, looking me up and down, 'You've put on weight since last we met. You have the appearance of a contented man. You had a wife and little girl, as I recall.'

'I was in fact a widower at the time, but I've married again since then. I now have a stepson and another child of my own on the way.'

Ginèvre laid aside her embroidery and leant back in her chair. She regarded me from beneath the heavy, half-closed lids.

'I do hate people who are happily married,' she mocked. 'They're so horribly smug. But then, a big, virile fellow like you could keep any woman happy between the sheets, I'll be bound.' I felt myself beginning to blush and she laughed. 'All right, Master Chapman, I'll spare you further embarrassment. I know why you're here, although until you walked in, I'd no idea that you were the same chapman whom I'd met before. Barbara Perle heard from Miles

Babcary that you were asking questions about the death of Gideon Bonifant, and warned me in her turn.' She frowned. 'These enquiries are on behalf of the Duke of Gloucester, as I understand it. Now why on earth should His Grace be interesting himself in the matter?'

I explained and Mistress Napier sniffed derisively.

'If you want my opinion,' she said, 'the man's deluding himself if he thinks that Mistress Shore or anyone else can influence his elder brother on this score. Clarence has been making a nuisance of himself for years, and I think King Edward will now grasp any opportunity to rid himself of Duke George once and for all. However, let us return to our sheep, as our French cousins so quaintly put it. What do you want to know about Gideon Bonifant's murder?'

'Anything that you can tell me,' I answered. 'Everything that you can recall.'

Savoury smells were beginning to emanate from the Napiers' kitchen, reminding me not only that it was nearly dinnertime, but also that I had had no breakfast that morning. My empty stomach was starting to rumble.

'Are you hungry?' Ginèvre asked abruptly, and when I nodded, went on, 'Then you can eat with me.' She picked up a small silver handbell and rang it. 'Lay another place in the dining parlour,' she ordered when her maid answered the summons, and rose to her feet. 'Come along,' she said briskly. 'Gregory's at the shop and won't be home until this evening. I dislike eating alone.'

I followed her to a room at the back of the house and within easy reach of the kitchen, so that the food came hot to table, an arrangement many other households would do well to emulate.

'We can eat while we talk,' my hostess remarked, sitting down and indicating that I should do likewise. 'So! You want to know anything and everything about the afternoon that Gideon Bonifant died.'

A rich pottage of beef and vegetables was set before us and Ginèvre picked up her spoon. She did not, however, immediately fall to, but sat absent-mindedly stirring the contents round and round in the bowl, obviously immersed in her own thoughts. I waited in silence. Indeed, I was so busy cramming my mouth with lumps of bread soaked in this delicious broth that I doubt if I could have spoken even if I'd tried.

Arriving at a decision, Ginèvre suddenly raised her head and looked at me across the table. I was surprised to see an ugly, vindictive twist to the thin, heavily painted lips.

'Who have you talked to?' she asked, and when I named them, nodded. 'In that case, I don't suppose there's anything I could add about the events of that afternoon that you haven't been told already. But something I can tell you is that, even supposing Isolda did have a lover, as Gideon claimed, she wasn't the only one present at Barbara's birthday feast who had a reason for wanting to dispose of Master Bonifant.'

I paused in the act of conveying yet another hunk of bread to my gaping mouth, and stared at her. 'If you mean Christopher Babcary or Meg Spendlove,' I began thickly, but was allowed to get no further, being interrupted by a scornful laugh.

'Kit Babcary! And who's Meg Spendlove, pray?' My hostess didn't wait for a reply, but continued, 'No, I'm referring to my husband and the woman I foolishly, trustingly, thought was my bosom friend, Barbara Perle.'

My mind turned somersaults. 'Are you saying that ... that Master Napier and ... and Mistress Perle were ... were—?'

'Oh, for heaven's sake don't be so mealymouthed,' Ginèvre snapped, slamming one hand down on the table so hard that her spoon jumped out of her bowl. 'Gregory and Barbara have been lovers this past year or more.' She yelled for her maid and, when the girl appeared, ordered her to remove the broth. 'Bring us something we can get our teeth into,' she said.

'Why are you telling me this?' I asked

slowly. 'What does it have to do with the death of Master Bonifant?'

Ginèvre laughed. 'He found out about them. I don't know how, and I haven't bothered to enquire. But he had a long nose and a mean mind. He threatened to tell both Miles Babcary and me about their liaison. Liaison,' she repeated, smiling mirthlessly. 'What a splendid word that is. What respectability it bestows on something that is merely the adulterous humping around in a seamy, sweaty bed. However, let us once again return to our sheep. Gregory immediately told Gideon that he would confess to me himself.' Her lip curled. 'He knew he had little to fear. There had been too many other women in the past. They meant nothing to him, as Barbara Perle meant nothing. He'll never leave me, nor do I wish him to. He's a good provider. I bawled him out and called him all the names I could lay my tongue to, and that, as far as I was concerned, was the end of the matter.'

'But it was different for Mistress Perle?'

Venison steaks, stewed in red wine and peppercorns, were set before us, and then the maid slipped quietly from the room.

'Of course it was different for Barbara. Gideon Bonifant was threatening to tell Miles, and that would have meant the end of all her hopes to become the second

259

Mistress Babcary.'

'What did Gideon want? Money?' I asked, before filling my mouth with the deliciously tender meat.

'No. He wanted Barbara's promise to refuse Miles's offer of marriage, should he make one.'

I could see that such a demand made sense to a man wishing to protect his wife's inheritance and his own place in the Babcary household. His father-in-law's proposal to buy the house in Paternoster Row and give it to him and Isolda, generous as it was, had no appeal for Gideon. He wanted no outsider, in the shape of Barbara Perle, influencing any of Miles's future decisions. For who could tell what he might or might not be persuaded to do if neither his daughter nor his son-in-law was present to restrain him?

'So what course of action did Mistress Perle decide on?' I wanted to know, as soon as I had emptied my mouth.

Ginèvre lifted her thin shoulders in a disdainful shrug. 'She didn't. All she could think of doing was to come bleating like a frightened sheep to Gregory. Oh yes, he told me. Once the affair was out in the open, he saw no need to keep anything a secret from me.'

'And what was Master Napier's solution?'

'Oh, he could think of nothing but to offer

Gideon money – a very large sum of money – to keep him quiet.' My hostess looked as if she were about to spit. 'I soon put a stop to that, I can assure you. I didn't mince my words. I told Gregory that if he parted with so much as a single groat to Gideon Bonifant, I should make Miles free of the whole sordid affair.'

I thoughtfully chewed another slice of venison. 'And that's how matters stood last December, on Mistress Perle's birthday?'

I understood now Mistress Perle's vehement assertion that Isolda had murdered her husband and her apparent unease throughout our talk together. My new-found knowledge also explained her attempt to dissuade me from speaking to Ginèvre. She had rightly been afraid that her friend, in a moment of pique and spite, would reveal to me the truth about herself and Gregory Napier.

'So you see' – my hostess was speaking again – 'Barbara had quite as good a reason as either Kit Babcary or Isolda to wish for Gideon's death.'

'And so had you,' I thought, but did not say so aloud.

Nevertheless, there was a possibility that Ginèvre might have come to the conclusion that Gideon was better dead than alive. Perhaps Gregory had, after all, decided to defy her and made up his mind that he would try to buy the blackmailer's silence. She was astute enough to realise that if Gideon agreed, it could result in far more than a single payment, and I guessed that she was too proud a woman to put an end to such a situation by blabbing all to Miles Babcary. Furthermore, it was extremely likely that her husband had already confided to her Gideon's accusation against his wife and Christopher; an accusation that would immediately point the finger of suspicion at Isolda, leaving everyone else as seemingly innocent bystanders.

But if Gregory or Ginèvre Napier or Barbara Perle was the murderer, where had they obtained the monkshood? But of course the answer to that was simple. From the same source as Miles Babcary: a liniment for aches and pains procured from Jeremiah Page of Gudrun Lane.

Sixteen

I glanced up to see my hostess eyeing me narrowly. Before she could say anything, however, I asked quickly, 'Do any of your friends and acquaintances in these parts own a horse and cart, Mistress?'

She was obviously startled by this un-looked-for change of subject, and stammered a little over her reply.

'No ... Yes ... What I mean is that Hugo Perle used to keep both horse and cart in the stables just around the corner, in Old Dean's Lane. But I believe Barbara sold them after his death. Why do want to know?'

'Do you have any idea who bought them?' I went on, ignoring her question and posing another of my own.

'No. No, I don't. I'm not absolutely certain that Barbara did decide to sell.' Ginèvre had recovered her poise and was growing irritable. 'Although ... Wait a moment! Now I think about it, I seem to recollect her mentioning that Miles Babcary was the purchaser. Or am I mistaken?' she added to herself.

'Have the two families, the Perles and the Babcarys, always been friends?'

Ginèvre swallowed a mouthful of venison, frowning at this continuing diversion.

'Of course. Barbara is a Lambert by birth and a cousin of the late Mistress Babcary.'

It was my turn to frown. This fact had not previously been revealed by either Isolda or her father. To be fair, it had probably seemed irrelevant to them, but it could account for some of Gideon's hostility towards the marriage between his father-in-law and Mistress Perle. His late wife's kinswoman might well exert a stronger influence over Miles than a perfect stranger, who knew nothing of the family's affairs, would do.

'Why did you wish to know about the horse and cart?' my hostess asked, pushing her plate aside with a slice of venison still uneaten. I averted my greedy gaze and explained that I had almost been run over outside her house, but she made little of this. 'If you were standing in the middle of the thoroughfare, as you say you were, then I'm hardly surprised. People drive recklessly in London, with scant regard for life and limb. I doubt very much if it was a deliber-ate attempt on your life, if that's what you're thinking.'

I had to admit that she was right. I told her of the other two occasions on which I had felt, if not exactly in danger, then threatened by some unseen presence.

'Yet it seems you were wrong both times,' she said. 'On your own admission, there is no evidence of harmful intent towards you on anyone's part.'

'No, but there ought to be,' I blurted out.

Ginèvre smiled shrewdly at me, raising her plucked eyebrows, her thin lips lifting slightly at the corners. 'You mean that Master Bonifant's murderer should be trying to prevent you asking any more questions?' I nodded and she gave her low, throaty chuckle. 'I take your point. There might, of course, be an explanation, but I must admit that I can't see...' Her voice tailed away and she stared at me unblinkingly for a moment before shaking her head decisively. 'No! Impossible!'

'What's impossible?'

But she refused to say another word on the subject, resisting all my pleas for her to tell me what was in her mind on the score that she had to be wrong, and that what she was thinking made no sense. And with that I had to be content.

I finished my dinner and took my leave of her, no nearer a solution to the murder of Gideon Bonifant than I had been yesterday or the day before that. I walked as far as the stables in Old Dean's Lane and questioned a couple of the ostlers there. They both confirmed that Master Babcary had indeed bought the horse and cart belonging to Hugo Perle after the latter's death, but also assured me that neither had left the premises so far that day. And they pointed to a placid cob, looking over the door of a stall in one corner of the yard, and to a cart lined up with three others against the northern wall. When I told them the reason for my curiosity, both men were unanimous in agreeing that the horse and cart that had so nearly run me down probably belonged to a brewer living in Knightrider Street, who had driven abroad that morning and whose recklessness was a byword in the area.

Once again, my fears had proved groundless. Gideon's murderer, whether Isolda or another, seemed to feel sufficiently secure to allow me to pursue my investigations unhindered. All the same, I wondered, as I walked slowly back along Paternoster Row, if I were not being lulled into a false sense of security. And what was that impossible something that had occurred to Ginèvre Napier that had not yet occurred to me?

This thought reminded me that I had not so far spoken to Gregory Napier, but I doubted if he were at his goldsmith's shop in West Cheap or he would surely have returned home for dinner. And if I were truthful with myself, I had to admit that I was in no mood, just at that moment, to listen to a further account of the events leading up to Gideon Bonifant's death. I needed somewhere to sit and think quietly about what I already knew, and to try to make sense of it all.

I directed my steps towards Bucklersbury. I did, however, make one more call before returning to the Voyager. As I had to pass the entrance to Gudrun Lane in my journey along West Cheap, I decided that I might as well pay a visit to Jeremiah Page and enquire if either of the Napiers or Mistress Perle had bought any monkshood liniment from him lately. A question and a groat to a legless beggar, squatting on his little trolley at the corner of the lane, quickly ascertained the exact whereabouts of the apothecary's shop, and a few minutes later, I was standing in its dim interior.

Master Page was a small man with a luxuriant auburn beard and a pair of sharp, beady eyes that regarded me suspiciously the second I mentioned the names of Perle and Napier.

'If it's to do with the murder of Master Babcary's son-in-law,' he snapped, 'I've said all that I have to say on that subject. I told the Sheriff's officer what I knew – which wasn't much – at the time. I'm not being dragged into it any further.'

'I'm making enquiries on behalf of His

267

Grace, the Duke of Gloucester,' I said importantly.

'And I'm the great Cham of Tartary,' was the scathing response.

It took me a few minutes to convince Master Page that I was serious, but in the end I managed it. His manner became a little more unbending, although not by much, and in reply to my original question, he said that nearly everyone in the area who was over a certain age bought his monkshood liniment.

'And when you're as old as they are, my young master, you'll know the reason why. Joints get stiff and painful with the passing years, and my embrocation is the best.'

'I'm sure it is,' I answered soothingly. 'Does that mean Master and Mistress Napier and Mistress Perle also buy it?'

'They might,' he admitted cautiously. 'I'm not saying they don't. But why do you want to know? None of them were implicated in Master Bonifant's killing. It was that wife of his, or her cousin, or both. I'd lay any money on that, especially after what Gideon confided to me about the pair of them.'

'Ah! So he told *you* that story as well, did he?' I asked.

The beard jutted angrily. 'No story, was it, in view of what happened subsequently? Lucky for Mistress Bonifant that she has a kinswoman who's leman to the King. At least, that's *my* opinion for what it's worth.'

I ignored this remark. 'When you reached Master Babcary's shop that afternoon, was Gideon Bonifant dead?'

This time the beard waggled up and down in affirmation. 'But only just. The body was still warm. However, there was nothing I could do to revive him, so I sent for the physician, who, in turn, called in the Sheriff's officer. It was too late to make Master Bonifant sick – although that remedy can often do more harm than good because, of course, the throat's so stiff, it's well-nigh impossible to make the victim swallow an emetic.'

'What were the Babcarys and their guests doing when you entered the parlour?'

Jeremiah Page hunched his shoulders. 'That girl of theirs – Meg I think they call her – was having hysterics, and Miles Babcary was flapping about like a demented hen. The rest were looking as though someone had taken a poleaxe to them.'

'Even Mistress Bonifant?'

'Even her,' the apothecary admitted grudgingly. He stroked his beard thoughtfully. 'Oddly enough...'

'Go on,' I urged. 'Oddly enough...?'

'Well ... It's just that you've made me think; made me picture the scene again in my mind. Most of them, as I said, were staring at Master Bonifant, who was

269

slumped face downwards across the table, as if they couldn't believe their eyes. But then the younger woman, Master Babcary's niece, suddenly smiled. I don't think anyone saw her but me; they were all, as I've said, looking elsewhere.'

'What sort of a smile?' I asked, intrigued.

The beard twitched from side to side as its owner considered the question.

'It was very fleeting, you understand. It had vanished in less time than it takes to tell. But I'd say it was a smile of ... of relief. Yes, that's it! It was definitely a smile of relief.'

'You mean ... as though she were glad that Master Bonifant was dead?'

'I'd say so, yes.'

'You might have been mistaken, of course.'

'I might have been. But somehow I don't think I was.'

He remained adamant, and I walked the rest of the way back to the Voyager lost in thought. Why would Eleanor Babcary be relieved that Gideon was dead? If she had been in love with him, she should have been deeply upset. But was the apothecary's interpretation of what he had seen correct? According to him, the girl's expression had been fleeting, barely long enough for it to have registered as a smile.

My head was beginning to ache by the time I reached the inn. The bitter cold and intermittent showers of sleet were partly responsible, but I was also concerned by my lack of progress. I had accepted the Duke of Gloucester's request to investigate the death of Gideon Bonifant four days ago, and every passing hour brought the sentencing of George of Clarence that much closer. If only Duke Richard would beg Mistress Shore to intercede for his brother without feeling that he had to offer her an inducement, all might yet be well. But he wouldn't: that was one thing of which I could be certain.

To add to my worries, there were now only two more days, the second being the day of the tournament at Westminster, before Adela and I were due to meet Jack Nym at Leadenhall market to begin our journey home to Bristol. As things stood, Adela would have to go alone, and while I trusted Jack to take every care of her, the prospect was not one I relished. Moreover, I could well imagine the tongue-lashing I would receive from my quondam mother-in-law when I finally arrived home – particularly if I had not managed to solve the mystery and it had all been for nothing.

The Voyager was quiet when I entered, most of its customers being gripped by a post-prandial lethargy. I made my way to our chamber and found that my wife, too, was lying supine upon the bed and gently snoring. Without more ado, I kicked off my boots and stretched out beside her. Less than two minutes later, I was sound asleep.

It was dark when, with a snort and a violent twitch, I awoke to find Adela sitting beside the fire, watching me in some concern. A tray with the remains of her supper and all of mine, now gone cold, reposed on the floor at her feet.

'God's teeth!' I exclaimed, swinging my legs off the bed. 'What time is it?'

'The church bells are ringing for Vespers,' she said. 'You must have been asleep for hours.'

I cursed softly. 'I meant to return to the Babcarys' shop this afternoon. There are still some questions I want to put to the family.'

'You're going nowhere,' Adela retorted in a very wifely spirit, pushing me back on to the bed. 'You're worn out and, Duke of Gloucester or no Duke of Gloucester, you're remaining here for the rest of the evening.'

I knew that there was no arguing with her in this mood. Not that I was prepared to put up much of a resistance anyway: I did indeed feel worn out. Furthermore, I needed to think or, preferably, to talk things over, so I settled myself once more against the pillows and, when I had filled myself up with bread and cheese and other cold viands from the tray and drunk the ale, patted the empty space beside me invitingly. Adela was only too happy to cuddle up, and understanding enough to accept that I was, at present, in no mood for lovemaking.

'Tell me what's troubling you,' she commanded.

My first and most pressing worry, that she would, in all likelihood, be forced to travel back to Bristol without me, she dismissed as a mere nothing.

'I shall be perfectly safe with Jack Nym. And even if it weren't for the children and taking them off Margaret's hands – for I'm sure she must have had a surfeit of their company by now – I still wouldn't accept the Duke's offer for me to remain in London until this matter is satisfactorily concluded. I think you'll feel far less trammelled on your own.'

I couldn't argue with her, at least, not convincingly, so I simply gave her a hug. In reply, she sent me one of those half-mocking glances that never fail to remind me of my late mother.

'Will you listen while I talk?' I asked.

'Of course,' she answered readily. 'Tell me everything.'

So I recounted all I knew about the Babcary, Perle and Napier households, what I had gleaned from Masters Ford and Page, and all the details, insofar as I knew them, of the afternoon that Gideon Bonifant died. When I'd finished, we sat in silence for a while, watching the flames of the fire flicker and curtsey on the hearth, spurting now blue, now red and yellow.

'That means,' Adela murmured at last, 'that apart from Isolda, there were at least two other people present that afternoon who would have been happy to see Gideon Bonifant dead: Mistress Perle and Gregory Napier.'

'There may have been more than just those two,' I pointed out. 'If Isolda had been cuckolding her husband with her cousin, as Gideon claimed, then Christopher Babcary must be a suspect, also. Then there's Meg Spendlove, who had been so upset after Gideon had verbally chastised her for mixing up the family goblets at Eleanor's birthday feast. She may well have borne him a grudge that grew in her mind until it was out of all proportion to his offence. And what about Miles Babcary? I don't say that there's a strong case to be made against him, but it's obvious to me that he didn't much care for his son-in-law, and if he had entertained any inkling that Gideon disapproved of his proposed marriage to Barbara Perle and was trying to prevent it, I don't think we could rule him out.'

Adela nodded in agreement. 'And, from

what you've told me of her, perhaps it might also be unsafe to discount Mistress Napier. She sounds a formidable woman. And if she were afraid that her husband was about to defy her and offer Gideon a large sum of money to hold his tongue, she might have decided to take matters into her own two hands and end the blackmailer's life. And if I understood you correctly, Apothecary Page intimated that his monkshood liniment has been bought by both the Napiers and Mistress Perle, so the means would have been there, handy.'

I frowned. 'But not easy to administer. After their arrival, the three guests were conducted upstairs by Miles Babcary to the parlour, where the table was already laid. But at that point only Isolda knew where each person was sitting. It was she who later directed them to their various places.'

'Couldn't the guilty person have worked out which was Gideon's seat by the initials on his cup?'

I shook my head emphatically. 'Impossible! The carving around the rims is so ornate that only a close inspection can reveal to whom each one belongs. From even a short distance, they all look the same. Moreover, there were already four people in the room when Miles Babcary and his guests entered the parlour: Christopher and Eleanor, Gideon and the apprentice, Toby

Maybury. Isolda arrived a few moments later. Neither Gregory nor Ginèvre Napier nor Barbara Perle could have found the opportunity to drop poison into any of the cups.' I sighed despondently. 'It looks as though it *has* to be one of the Babcarys, and Isolda seems the most likely suspect.'

'What about the other cousin, the girl, Eleanor?' Adela asked.

'I can't find any reason why she should have wanted to murder Gideon Bonifant. If I'm right, she was in love with, or at least very fond, of him.'

'But if the apothecary's right, then she was relieved that he was dead.'

'Mmmm ... But did Master Page see what he thought he saw?' I muttered doubtfully.

Adela nestled her head against my shoulder. 'We haven't mentioned the apprentice yet. What was it, do you think, that he was trying to tell Eleanor behind Ginèvre Napier's back?'

I grimaced. 'I don't know. And Toby isn't going to tell me. So unless I can work it out for myself...' I shrugged and let the sentence go.

There was silence while my wife and I each pursued our own thoughts. Then Adela asked suddenly, 'You don't think that Toby could have been in league with either Mistress Perle or one of the Napiers? That *he* put the poison in Gideon's cup, then got

276

frightened and was trying to warn Eleanor of what he'd done?'

'No, I don't.' I bent my head and kissed her. 'My darling, I think you're grasping at straws. I don't want the murderer to be a member of the Babcary household, because I like them all, but I must remember that my emotions have misled me before. The fact that the Napiers and Mistress Perle had very strong reasons for wanting Gideon dead mustn't blind me to the fact that they had no opportunity for poisoning his wine.'

'Could Gregory Napier have managed to do it while Mistress Perle was being presented with her birthday gift?' my wife suggested after a pause. 'All eyes would surely have been on her and this jewelled girdle that Master Babcary had ornamented for her.'

I considered the idea, but it would have involved an extraordinary sleight of hand, and I reluctantly shook my head.

'No, I don't think so. The sad fact is that it was Isolda who laid the table, deciding where everyone should sit. It was Isolda who poured the wine into the goblets. It was Isolda who had the time and opportunity to enter her father's bedchamber, next door, and who knew where the bottle of liniment was kept. The only thing I can't be sure about is that she had a good reason for killing her husband. Was Gideon telling the truth when he accused her and Christopher of cuckolding him?'

'Why would he lie?' Adela wanted to know, echoing my own thoughts and the thoughts of so many others. 'He may have been a far more despicable character than you realised at first, but no man is deliberately wishful of making himself look a fool without good reason.' She added after a pause, 'Apart from the three immediately involved, does anyone but you know of the liaison between Mistress Perle and Gregory Napier?'

'I shouldn't think so. If as much as a hint of it had reached Miles Babcary's ears, I doubt he would still be so anxious to marry Dame Barbara.'

'Why do you suppose that Ginèvre Napier confided in you?'

'I've been asking myself that question, and I can only think that she suddenly felt the need to tell someone. She's bottled up the secret for all these months and today, at last, she could bear to do so no longer.'

'I wonder she wasn't afraid that you'd inform the Babcarys or the Duke or the Sheriff's men, and so implicate her and Gregory in Gideon's murder.'

'I don't believe that, at that particular moment, she cared. She just wanted to share the knowledge of her friend's and her husband's perfidy with another person, and to do them a mischief. But I feel sure that when she's had time to think things over, I shall hear from her again, begging for my discretion.'

'She hasn't yet sworn you to secrecy,' my wife pointed out, 'nor even extracted a promise that you'll keep her confession to yourself. Don't you think, therefore, that you should inform the Sheriff's officers of what you know?'

I again shook my head. 'Not until I'm absolutely sure that one of them is the murderer. At the moment, I cannot see how any of them could have administered the poison, and until enlightenment dawns – if it ever does – it would be wrong of me to entangle three possibly innocent people in the coils of the law. If Isolda stood in imminent peril of being arrested and tried for her husband's murder, that would be a different matter.' I leant back against the pillows. 'I wish I could rid myself of this feeling that the quarrel between Gideon Bonifant and Meg Spendlove has a significance that I have somehow overlooked.'

Adela made no answer and her head was growing heavy on my shoulder. When I glanced down, I saw that her eyelids were beginning to droop and that her lower jaw was slack. I roused her gently.

'Time to get undressed and ready for bed.' She made a feeble attempt to resume our conversation, but it was very half-hearted and by the time I had carried our supper tray back to the kitchen – explaining to the cook why my bowlful of broth was untouched – and returned to our bedchamber, my wife was between the sheets and sound asleep. I stripped off my boots and outer clothing and thankfully rolled in beside her.

Seventeen

I was dreaming.

As always, I knew that I was dreaming, but, at the same time, everything that happened seemed very vivid and very real.

I was in the Babcary house, walking upstairs from the shop, Toby Maybury hard on my heels.

'He was just going into his room,' Toby kept saying. 'He was just going into his room.'

As we reached the top of the first flight of stairs and emerged on to the landing, Isolda came out of the parlour, and although she looked straight at us, she appeared to see neither myself nor the apprentice. She simply turned to her right and mounted the second flight of stairs to her bedchamber. I glanced over my shoulder to speak to Toby, but he had disappeared and when I pushed open the parlour door and went inside, he was already there, standing beside the table.

'We mustn't let Meg be blamed,' he said – then was abruptly transformed into Mistress Perle's maid.

The girl had on a clean nightgown and was holding a hard-boiled egg, one half in each hand. The yolk had been scooped out and replaced with salt and, as she began to walk backwards, away from me, I noticed that she was wearing Eleanor Babcary's pendant around her neck.

I moved towards the table, which was ready laid for a meal, stretching out my hand for one of the gold-rimmed goblets that stood beside each place.

'Don't!' a voice exclaimed behind me. 'I've just poisoned the wine in that cup.'

I spun round with a great cry – only to find myself sitting up in bed, sweating profusely, and Adela shaking my arm.

'Roger! What is it? Have you been having one of your dreams?' She smoothed back the damp hair from my forehead.

I nodded mutely, then became aware that someone was tapping gently on our bed-chamber door.

'Master Chapman, is everything all right?' whispered Reynold Makepeace. 'Is Mistress Chapman well?'

I got out of bed and opened the door a crack. 'I was riding the nightmare, that's all, I'm sorry if I disturbed you.'

Reassured, the landlord crept away and I went back to Adela, slithering down beside her and, by now, shivering with cold. She held me in her arms and soothed me, but I had no sooner fallen asleep again than I was back in the Babcarys' house, and this time Isolda was standing beside me, outside the closed parlour door.

'Have you seen Gideon?' she asked me, adding with a frown, 'He wanders about the house at nights, you know. He says he's unable to sleep.'

She vanished, and now I was inside the room, gripped by fear, convinced that someone who wished me dead was waiting outside on the landing; someone who would kill me, given half a chance. In a sudden access of bravado, I wrenched the door open, only to find myself face to face with Ginèvre Napier, who was convulsed with merriment.

'There's no one here except me,' she laughed. 'No one wants to harm you.'

'But someone *ought* to want to harm me,' I argued. 'Someone should be trying to prevent me asking any more questions.'

She looked both knowing and amused and to the sound of her throaty chuckling, I woke to find the first grey shreds of daylight rimming the shutters of our room.

Adela was asleep beside me, her face, framed by the pillow, calm and peaceful in its repose. I sat up in bed and looked down at her, thanking God, as I did each morning, for sending her to me, and for bringing me to my senses before I let her slip through my fingers and marry another man. After a while, as though suddenly becoming conscious of my gaze, she opened her eyes and smiled.

'You had a restless night,' she said, wriggling into a sitting position and kissing my unshaven cheek. 'Did your dreams bring you any enlightenment?'

'Not yet,' I admitted, returning her kiss. 'But give them time and they might become clearer. What will you do today?'

'I've promised to visit the Lampreys. It will be my last chance, because tomorrow, we are going to watch the tournament at Westminster, and the day after that, I, at least, must start for home.' She tilted her head to one side and looked sidelong at me. 'What are your plans?'

I sighed. 'I must go back to West Cheap and talk to the Babcarys yet again. To Eleanor especially. There's something that I haven't yet discovered concerning her relationship with Gideon, but which I feel in my bones holds a vital key to this mystery. And tomorrow,' I added defiantly, 'I shall accompany you to the tourney ground. The

King is hardly likely to decide Clarence's fate on such a day, and I refuse to be parted from you during your final hours in London.' I was suddenly racked with guilt, and took her in my arms. 'Sweetheart, I'm afraid this visit, which you looked forward to so keenly, has been spoilt by this business of Gideon Bonifant's death.'

'It's not your fault,' she murmured consolingly. 'As you said, if your Duke could only bring himself, like a sensible man, to appeal directly to Mistress Shore for her intervention on behalf of his brother, you need never have been involved in this murder. You mustn't blame yourself.'

But that was just what I was determined to do. 'I should have refused,' I said.

'No, no!' On that point, Adela was adamant. 'It never does to offend those in authority, particularly anyone so highly placed as the Duke of Gloucester. We're poor people, Roger, of no account except unto God. And one day in the future, who knows but that we may be glad of Duke Richard's protection? It was certainly fortunate for Isolda Bonifant that her kinswoman is leman to the King.'

But still my sense of guilt would not be assuaged.

'I haven't even bought you a keepsake to remind you of your visit to London,' I moaned.

Adela clapped a hand to her mouth, the childish gesture making her look, all at once, absurdly young.

'What is it?' I asked, bewildered.

For answer, she freed herself from my embrace, got out of bed, shivering with the sudden cold, and padded over to our travelling chest, where it stood in a corner of the room. She opened the lid and took something from inside.

'I forgot to tell you. I bought this from a stall in the Leadenhall market, on Monday. Jeanne Lamprey and I went there before she took me to see the animals in the Tower.'

Adela climbed back into bed and snuggled up to me, warming her now icy feet on mine and ignoring my yelp of protest. She was holding a small leather bag which, having released its drawstring, she upended on to the white linen quilt. Some sort of necklace fell out which, when my wife held it up, resolved itself into a chain and pendant.

'The man I bought them from swore they were silver,' Adela laughed, 'but I don't think they can be. They were much too cheap.'

I took them from her and was about to examine the metal from which they were made more closely, when I paused, my attention arrested by the design of the pendant: a true lover's knot enclosed within a circle.

'What's the matter?' asked my wife, studying my face. 'Are you angry with me for buying them? As I said, they didn't cost a lot.'

'No, of course not,' I answered. 'It's just that this is a replica of Eleanor Babcary's pendant, only hers is fashioned in gold and studded with tiny sapphires.'

Adela was intrigued. 'The man who sold it to me said that it's a very old design, and one that's imbued with magical powers. If a woman wears it in bed, she'll see the man she's going to marry.'

'I thought that was only on Saint Agnes's Eve,' I protested. 'And something to do with a hard-boiled egg—' I broke off, demanding indignantly, 'Why would you want such information? You're already married!'

Adela burst out laughing. 'Do you think I've forgotten that fact? I just think it's pretty. The pendant, I mean. And anyway, I'm far too old and sensible to believe in such nonsense.' She sighed wistfully, 'I was old at sixteen. I grew up early.'

'But that doesn't happen to all women,' I said reflectively. 'Some women are protected and cosseted and retain their innocence to a much greater age.'

'Are you speaking of Eleanor Babcary?'

'Yes.' I handed the pendant and chain back to Adela. 'Wear it today and to the tournament tomorrow.' I kissed her again.

286

'And don't dream of any man but me.'

'I haven't since the moment I met you.' She must have seen the self-satisfied smirk on my face, for she gave one of her sudden laughs. 'Don't let that admission go to your head, my love. There's plenty of time for me to change my mind and plenty more fish in the sea.' But the kiss she planted on my cheek, before getting out of bed, drew the sting from her words.

Half an hour later, just as we were finishing breakfast in the taproom, I asked, 'Are either Philip or Jeanne Lamprey coming to fetch you this morning?'

My wife shook her had. 'No, I forbade it. It's not far, and by now, I'm sufficiently familiar with the streets around here to be able to find my own way to their shop.'

'Good,' I said. And in answer to her enquiring lift of the eyebrows, went on, 'Will you come with me first to the Leadenhall and point out the stallholder who sold you the pendant?'

She looked mystified, but asked no questions and willingly agreed. Consequently, fortified by Reynold Makepeace's hot, spiced wine and wrapped warmly in our cloaks, the hoods pulled well up around our ears, we set out as the church bells were beginning to ring for Tierce. The street cleaners were already hard at work, shovelling yesterday's evil-smelling refuse into their carts, their hands blue with cold beneath the grime. But, in general, they were a cheerful bunch of men, calling and waving a greeting as we passed.

The Leadenhall was a hive of activity, as always on those days when 'foreigners' from outside the city limits were allowed in to set up their stalls. That day, too, a load of wool had arrived from the Cotswolds to be weighed on the King's Beam and sealed by the customs men before being carted down to the wharves. To add to the crowds and general confusion, a fine but icy rain had begun to fall as we were turning out of Bucklersbury into the Stock's Market, and many people had pushed their way into the Leadenhall for shelter. By the time we entered, the place was packed to the doors, and Adela doubted that she would be able to locate the man we were seeking.

In the event, however, she found him with surprising speed, a tall, lanky fellow selling cheap jewellery made from base metals, which, with barefaced effrontery, he declared to be silver and gold. I pushed my way to the front of the little crowd gathered around his stall, and indicated the lover's knot pendants, hanging by their chains from one of the horizontal poles that held up the canopy.

'Are those of your own making, friend?'

'They are.' He smiled, displaying a gap

between his two front teeth. 'But the design is magical, and was shown to me by an ancient who had brought it back, at great risk to his own life, from the lands of Prester John.'

I forbore, with difficulty, from remarking that it looked like a perfectly ordinary English love knot to me, and asked what magical property the pendants possessed.

'If a maid wears one in bed, she'll see the face and form of the man she's going to marry,' was the prompt response.

'And do you tell this tale to every woman who buys a pendant from you?' I sneered.

'Ay, and also to those who just come here to waste my time. Like you, I fancy,' the man added, his expression turning sour.

'My wife has already bought one,' I said, urging Adela forward. She obligingly opened her cloak to show the stallholder the pendant clasped around her neck.

The man was mollified but, when asked, denied all knowledge of anyone by the name of Babcary or Bonifant.

'I'm from Paddington village, a fair way west of here. I know no one personally hereabouts.'

'But you set up your stall in the Leadenhall every week?'

'I do, and have done for the past year or more.'

I thanked him and, taking Adela's arm,

moved away. My wife regarded me curiously.

'So, what have you learned?' she asked, as we stood in the shelter of the porch, looking out at the lancing spears of rain.

I put my arm around her. 'I've learned that any member of the Babcary household could have heard our friend's story about the magical properties of his pendants any time during the past twelve months. So which of them suggested a pendant of the same design when it came to deciding on Eleanor's birthday gift?'

'Is it important?'

'I'm not sure,' I answered slowly, 'but I think it might well be, especially if that person was aware that Eleanor herself had visited the jeweller's stall in Leadenhall market and believed what she had been told by the owner.' I nodded to myself. 'Which she probably would, being the innocent that she is.'

Adela hugged me. 'Then you'd better be off to West Cheap immediately to find out what you can. Don't worry about me. The Lampreys' shop isn't very far.'

The goldsmith's shop was empty except for Toby Maybury, busy about the necessary but monotonous task of stoking up the furnace with the bellows. He glanced over his shoulder as I entered and scowled when he saw who it was.

'Oh, you're back again, are you? What do you want this time? Why don't you leave us alone?'

I remained determinedly friendly, ignoring his hostile manner.

'Toby, my boy, I need your help. You've proved yourself to have a good memory; to be a bright, observant lad. So tell me, who suggested the design of the pendant that was made for Mistress Eleanor's birthday?'

Won over by my flattery, the apprentice put down the bellows and strolled across to talk to me, his young face puckered in a thoughtful frown.

'I believe it was Gideon,' he said after a moment or two's reflection. 'Yes, the more I think about it, the surer I am that it was Master Bonifant. Wait!' There was a pause, then he went on triumphantly, 'I definitely remember now! It was one afternoon towards the middle of last October. The master called the other two over to the main counter here, and asked what they thought he should make Mistress Nell for her seventeenth birthday. Master Kit didn't have any suggestions to offer. Well, he wouldn't, would he? He's like all brothers. Not much interested in the likes and dislikes of a sister. But Master Bonifant, he knew at once. "She bought a cheap pendant off some stall in Leadenhall market," he says, "that seems to

291

have taken her fancy. Let's refashion it for her in gold." And then he went on about it being a simple design of a lover's knot in a circle, easy to do. In fact, the master thought it was too simple and decided that the centre of the pendant – the knot itself – should be studded with sapphires.'

'Master Bonifant didn't mention anything about such a design possessing magical powers?' I enquired.

Toby regarded me pityingly. 'Of course not! Why should he? Lovers' knots are as common a design in jewellery as they are in embroidery.'

I apologised profusely, admitted that I had been scatterbrained since childhood, and deferred to his superior knowledge.

'Pray continue,' I begged.

Toby shrugged my foolishness aside. 'That's nearly all there is to tell. Mistress Bonifant, urged on by her husband, went to look for the original pendant in Mistress Nell's room, when she was absent from the house one day, but couldn't find it. But Master Bonifant's description was good enough for the master. The gold replica was easily made.'

'And was Mistress Babcary pleased with her gift?'

Toby thrust out his bottom lip. 'Funny you should ask that,' he said after a few seconds' musing. 'Now that I come to think of it, she wasn't as pleased as I should have expected her to be. But at the time, I put it down to the fact that we were all upset by Master Bonifant's outburst against Meg for getting the goblets mixed up. No one was in very good spirits after that.'

'But did Mistress Babcary wear the pendant very often?' I persisted.

Toby considered the question. 'She's worn it a lot lately,' he said.

'Since Master Bonifant's death?'

'Well ... Yes, I suppose so. But she might have worn it just as much before. I don't recollect.'

Miles Babcary, followed by his nephew, came into the shop. The former beamed for a moment until he realised that it was not a customer who was claiming the attention of his apprentice, but the same nosy chapman whose constant poking and prying and questioning was becoming so unwelcome. Afraid to vent his ill-humour on me – the emissary of the Duke of Gloucester and the King's favourite leman – he shouted at Toby instead.

'If you've let the fire go out, you stupid boy, I'll have the skin off your back! Get back to that furnace and those bellows immediately.' He turned to me. 'And what do you want this time, Master Chapman?'

'That's exactly what I asked him,' Toby proclaimed, not noticeably cowed by his master's displeasure. But all the same, he scuttled off to the furnace and worked the bellows with renewed vigour.

'I just want another word or two with Mistress Eleanor,' I answered humbly, 'if I may.'

I think that Miles Babcary, prodded in the back by Christopher, would have refused his permission had not Isolda, just at that moment, entered the shop from the back of the house. She was hot and flushed, wearing a big linen apron and holding a ladle in one hand. She was obviously in the middle of preparing dinner, the wholesome smell of cooking hanging about her, and lovelier by far to my nostrils than any exotic perfumes of the East.

'What's going on here?' she demanded, and I repeated my request before either her father or her cousin could reply. 'Oh, very well,' she agreed. 'You'll find Nell upstairs in the parlour, busy at her embroidery.' Her menfolk started to protest, but she cut them short. 'The sooner Master Chapman finds out what he wants to know, the sooner he'll leave us in peace,' she said, and vanished again in the direction of the kitchen.

Her common sense prevailed and I was given grudging permission by Miles to proceed upstairs to speak to his niece.

Eleanor was seated in front of her embroidery frame, which had been set up close to the fire, two large working candles, in silver candlesticks, on the table beside her. She looked round as I opened the parlour door and remained, needle poised above the canvas, staring at me.

'Master Chapman,' she murmured warily, 'why are you here?'

'I've come to speak to you,' I answered, drawing up a stool and sitting down beside her.

'I've told you all I know about Gideon's death.' Her voice had acquired a shrill note and I noticed that her hands were trembling.

'Not quite all,' I demurred. 'Sometime or another, you bought a pendant in Leadenhall market, and the man who sold it to you told you that it had magical properties. If you wore it to bed, you would see the face and form of the man you would one day marry. Isn't that true?' She nodded, looking at me with round, frightened eyes. 'And you confided this secret to Gideon Bonifant?'

'Yes,' she whispered.

'So let me guess,' I went on. 'It was after you began wearing the pendant to bed that you started seeing him in your room each time you woke up. Am I right?'

Eleanor gave a shudder. 'I'd be asleep, and then something, a touch on my cheek or forehead, would rouse me just in time to see his likeness gliding out of my room. Of

course, I realised that this was a hallucination of the Devil. How could Gideon
possibly be my future husband when he was
already married to Isolda? I didn't know
what to do.'

'And you couldn't confide in her, as you
would have done about anything else that
was troubling you, because she was the
person most nearly concerned. Did you
think of saying anything to Gideon himself?'

The colour flooded her cheeks. 'No, I
couldn't. That would have been worse than
telling Isolda. It might have looked as
though ... as though...' Her voice tailed away
into silence.

'As though you might have been making it
up as a way of offering yourself to him,' I
suggested.

Eleanor covered her face with her hands
and nodded.

'So you said nothing to anyone?'

She raised her head again. 'No, but I
didn't wear the pendant in bed any more.
And when that didn't stop the visitations, I
threw it away.'

I wondered how Gideon had found out
about this, but I was convinced that
somehow he had done so.

'And then your uncle and cousins gave
you a pendant made to the selfsame pattern
for your birthday. But this was made of
gold, studded with sapphires. You couldn't

possibly throw this one away.'

'No.' She was trembling so much that I put an arm about her shoulders for comfort. 'And then, of course, I started seeing Gideon's likeness in my room again each night.'

I asked as gently as I could, 'And did it never occur to you that it could be Gideon himself whom you were seeing? That it was a flesh and blood man and not some hallucination, as you call it, of the Devil?'

Eleanor turned her head slowly to stare at me. 'You mean...? You mean that Gideon was coming to my room every night *in person*? That it was a trick to frighten me? But why on earth would he want to do that? No, no! He would never have been so un- kind.'

'I don't think it was meant as unkindness,' I answered. 'Quite the opposite. I believe he was hoping to make you fall in love with him by planting the idea in your mind that you and he would one day be married.'

Eighteen

'But how could we ever have been married?' Eleanor asked. She pushed aside her embroidery frame with shaking hands. She repeated, 'He was married to Isolda.'

I shrugged. 'But who knew what the future held? Fatal illness, accidents, both these things are everyday occurrences, which, by his reckoning, could have happened to your cousin at any time. He wished to accustom you to the idea that, one day, you and he could possibly be man and wife. But Gideon was like all of us: while he could quite easily envisage the death of somebody else, he regarded himself as immortal.'

Eleanor considered this idea for a second or two, then emphatically shook her head. 'No! You're wrong! Isolda and Gideon were happily married.'

It was my turn to demur. 'Maybe Mistress Bonifant was happy, but I wouldn't be certain about her husband. My guess is that he'd fallen in love with you. You were only a child when they were first married but, over the years, you'd grown into a beautiful woman. I suspect that he suddenly – perhaps to his own surprise – found himself attracted to you. Maybe, to begin with, it was against his will. Let us give him the benefit of the doubt and say that he struggled to suppress his feelings for a while, but that, eventually, they proved too strong for him. That was when he started to spread rumours about Isolda and your brother.'

Eleanor lifted her lovely eyes to mine. 'You mean that he was lying?'

'Have you never considered the possibility that he might have been?'

My companion drew a deep breath. 'I thought Gideon was mistaken about the man being Kit, who has never been enamoured of ... of ... well, ugly women.' Eleanor pressed her hands to her cheeks and hung her head. 'That's a horrible thing for me to say about Isolda, but ... but...'

'Why be ashamed of stating the truth?' I soothed her. 'I know very little of your brother, but judging by the woman who was hanging on his arm last Sunday, I would be prepared to wager good money on Master Christopher feeling nothing for Mistress Bonifant beyond normal, cousinly affection. But please go on. You were implying that while you thought Gideon to be wrong about the identity of Isolda's lover, you nevertheless believed that there might, in fact, have been one.'

Eleanor raised one hand to her forehead. 'Did I imply that? Yes, I suppose, to be truthful, I did.'

'You thought Isolda was in love with someone other than her husband? What made you think so?'

My companion, however, seemed to have no clear idea why she had entertained such an idea and, as far as I could make out, it rested on nothing more than the belief, already expressed to me by my wife, that no man would claim to be a cuckold without good reason.

'But who could your cousin's lover possibly have been? Were there any men that you knew of with whom she was particularly friendly?'

It seemed there was no one to whom Eleanor could immediately put a name, and she was too anxious to return to the subject of Gideon and his nocturnal prowlings to give the idea any positive thought.

'Are you serious in your suggestion, Master Chapman, that what I imagined was a ... a spirit haunting my room, was really Gideon himself, in the flesh?'

'I'm convinced of it,' I answered gently. 'Mistress Bonifant herself told me that, over the past months, Gideon had risen from his bed on many occasions and gone wandering about the house at night. This sleeplessness was one of the reasons why she had begun to fear for his health. In reality, of course, he was not ill, merely lovesick. And he had seen a way to turn your confidence about the magical properties of the original pendant – the one you bought in Leadenhall market – to his advantage. He would enter your chamber which, I believe, is next to his and Mistress Bonifant's, touch you lightly on your cheek or forehead in order to rouse you and, then, before you were properly awake, remain just long enough for you to recognise him before slipping from the room and hurrying back next door.'

'But – but the visitations stopped after I threw the pendant away.'

'Not for long, I should guess. Only until you received the new one for your birthday. Am I not right?' And when she nodded, I continued, 'According to Toby Maybury, it was Gideon who not only proposed a pendant as the family gift, but who also suggested the design for it. Did you know that?' This time she shook her head, an expression of increasing horror on her face. I asked softly, 'Were you fond of Gideon Bonifant?'

'No!' Eleanor shivered, wrapping her arms around her body for comfort. 'No, I wasn't. I didn't dislike him, not for years, and he was always kind to me, although he could be sharp-tongued with other people. But I was never fond of him. There was always something about him that, deep down, I didn't really care for. That's why I was so distressed when ... when these nightly visitations started. I wouldn't have wanted him for my husband even if he'd been free, but I thought that fate had ... had decreed that I should marry him one day.' She gave a little laugh that faltered in the middle. 'I was worried for Isolda's life, not his. I was afraid, as you said just now, that she was the one who was going to die. Every time she left the house or complained of a headache I was worried. And then, after all, it was Gideon who died, who was poisoned.'

'Tell me honestly,' I said, 'do you believe your cousin discovered that Gideon was in love with you and murdered him as a consequence?'

'Yes, tell Master Chapman honestly, Nell, my dear, what you really think.' Isolda Bonifant's voice sounded behind us, although there was no rancour in her tone.

Neither of us had heard her enter the parlour and we both started with surprise. Eleanor gave a muffled cry, jumped up, pushing past her cousin, and fled from the room. Isolda made no attempt to detain her.

'How long have you been there, Mistress?' I asked, when I had recovered my breath.

'I've been listening outside the door, which you failed to close properly, for quite some time,' she admitted unashamedly. 'Long enough to understand what Gideon was up to.' She moved towards the fire, sitting down in her cousin's vacated chair and idly playing with the needle that Eleanor had left jabbed into the canvas of the embroidery frame.

'And did you ever suspect that your husband was in love with Mistress Babcary?' I asked bluntly.

She made no answer for a moment or two, then suddenly shrugged and looked me full in the face.

'I had my suspicions, but I didn't want to believe it was true. He was twenty-two years older than she was, and I'd managed to convince myself that what he felt for her was no more than the affection of, say, an uncle for his niece.' She laughed and looked away again. 'What a self-deluding fool I was! But as for his attempt to persuade her into thinking of herself as his future wife in the manner you've just explained to Nell, of that I had no idea.'

'Had you known, what would you have done?' I asked.

She regarded me straitly. 'I should have done my utmost to put a stop to such nonsense – but not by murdering Gideon.'

And suddenly, I found myself believing her without any of my former reservations. There was something about Isolda Bonifant that commanded my respect. She might be considered ugly by many men's standards of beauty – although not by mine – but her mind was like her face, strong and honest. And there had been too many others, that night of Barbara Perle's birthday feast, either around the table in the parlour or downstairs in the kitchen, who benefited from Gideon Bonifant's death. For Miles Babcary it removed a son-in-law uninterested in the goldsmith's trade, and who would quite possibly have sold the shop the moment it became the property of his wife. It rid Meg Spendlove of one whom she saw as a tyrannical master, and prised a thorn from Toby Maybury's side. Eleanor Babcary was freed from a continuing nightmare, while her brother was no longer the target of Gideon's false accusations. The Napiers ceased to suffer from the threat of exposure, he as a philandering husband, she as a cuckolded wife (surely something not to be borne by a woman as proud and as vain as Ginèvre). Most important of all, however, Barbara Perle's future as the second Mistress Babcary still lay before her whenever she chose to accept Miles's proposal of marriage. She would neither be forced to give up her pretensions to being his wife nor revealed as an adulteress. Of all of those around that supper table, she, perhaps, had more to gain than anyone else.

I suddenly realised that if I went to the Duke of Gloucester with as much knowledge as I now possessed, he could lay enough evidence before Mistress Shore to convince her that her kinswoman was far from being the only possible murderer of Gideon Bonifant, and demand his favour in return. On the other hand, if these facts became common property, they would not only throw suspicion on the innocent as well as the guilty, they would also destroy at least two lives, Miles Babcary's and Barbara Perle's. It was therefore my duty, if I could, to unmask the real murderer, even if it meant giving up a chance to return home with Adela the day after tomorrow.

'You're looking pensive, Master Chapman.' Isolda's voice broke through my thoughts, making me jump. 'Have you come to the conclusion that I'm speaking the truth?'

'I might have,' I answered cautiously. I longed to tell her the whole story, but there were secrets that had to be preserved, at least until the truth was exposed. And perhaps – who could tell? – even after that revelation. I leaned forward, resting my elbows on my knees. 'Mistress Bonifant,' I asked abruptly, 'why do you think no one has tried to kill me?'

'Why has no one tried to kill you?' she repeated blankly.

'Yes. Oh, several times I've thought my life was in danger, but on each occasion so far, it seems to have been a false alarm, arising out of a natural expectation on my part that the murderer of Master Bonifant would try to prevent me discovering his – or her – identity. After all, a person who has killed already has less reason to fear killing again. However many your victims, you can only be hanged once.'

'Master Chapman!' Isolda rose to her feet. Her face was white and strained, like someone who was holding her emotions on a very short rein. 'This has been a trying morning. I have found out things about my husband I would far rather never have known – or at least not known for certain – so I have no wish to be further burdened by talk of hanging. It's almost ten o'clock and dinner will soon be ready. Will you stay and eat with us?'

I declined her invitation, wanting to get back to the Voyager to spend as much time with Adela as I could before her departure the day after next.

'But there is one more question I should like to ask you,' I murmured apologetically. Taking Isolda's resigned expression as permission to proceed, I said, 'On the evening of the murder, did Master Bonifant visit you in the kitchen before going upstairs to change into his Sunday clothes?'

She frowned. 'I don't recollect his doing so, but I may have forgotten the incident if it was of no significance. Who claims that he did?'

'Toby Maybury. He says that he saw your husband going into your bedchamber some while after he had left the shop. According to Toby, Master Bonifant explained away his tardiness by saying that he had been to the kitchen to have a word with you.'

Isolda gave a crack of laughter. 'If I were you, Master Chapman,' she advised, 'I wouldn't believe a word that Tobias Maybury says.' She spun on her heel and made for the parlour door, where she paused, her hand on the latch. 'That boy is a menace and always has been. Well, I doubt if we shall run into one another tomorrow at the tournament. The crowds will be far too dense. But in case we do, promise me that, just for once, we won't talk about my husband's murder.' She passed a hand wearily across her forehead. 'And now I must go to Nell and reassure her that what I overheard this morning will not affect my fondness for her. None of it was her fault. And I have been used to hearing myself described as ugly throughout my life.'

Isolda's prediction that the tourney ground at Westminster would be crowded proved to be correct.

It was a bright, clear day, warmer than of late, but still with a sharp wind blowing off the river; a day necessitating woollen cloaks, stout boots and pattens for the women, but one also that encouraged people to be out of doors rather than languishing at home.

The Duke and Duchess of Gloucester were notable only by their absence, and the Duke of Clarence mouldered in the Tower, still uncertain of his fate. But the lack of the King's family was amply compensated for by Mistress Shore, wearing her ivy-leaf coronet, and by the multitude of Woodvilles, their courtiers and sycophants, who surrounded him and the infant Duke and Duchess of York, not only in the loges, but also in the arena. Leading the Party Without were the Queen's brother, Anthony, Earl Rivers, and her elder son from her first marriage, Thomas Grey, Marquess of Dorset, while the ranks of the Party Within were swollen by others of her numerous relatives, including Sir Richard Haute, who was to win one of the principal prizes.

In accordance with the rules laid down by the first Edward, two centuries earlier, no contestant could be accompanied by more than three armed knights or squires, and the carrying of knives, clubs and daggers was strictly forbidden. Heralds and spectators had to be weaponless, and a fallen participant was allowed time to rise. Even so, some ugly injuries were sustained, and the sight of these, together with the noise, dust and incessant clash of arms, were enough to test the strongest nerves. I was not surprised, therefore, when Adela apologised to the Lampreys, who had accompanied us, and insisted that she and I leave the tourney ground and go in search of quieter pleasures. In her condition, peace and rest were becoming daily more essential.

As usual at these affairs, the vendors of drinks and hot pies were doing a roaring trade but, although I bought two meat pasties, one for each of us, Adela said that all she wanted was to quench her thirst, so I was obliged, with very little persuasion, to eat them both. We discovered a man selling cups not only of ale but also of primrose wine, and having purchased one of the former for myself and one of wine for Adela, we retired to some tables and benches that had been placed near Westminster Gate under a makeshift awning. At that distance, the sounds of the jousting were muted.

'Ah, that's better,' Adela sighed, some of the colour coming back into her cheeks. She took another sip of her wine, then leant across the table, proffering me her cup. 'Try this, Roger. It's very good. You'd like it.'

I gave a decided shake of my head. 'No, I shouldn't. I hate primrose wine. You know I do.'

'But this is different. I don't know what's in it, but it has a more pungent smell to it and a stronger flavour than any other primrose wine I've ever drunk. I'm sure you'd agree with me if only you'd taste it.'

Once again, I shook my head vehemently, setting down my beaker of ale on the table between us, while I finished off the second of the two pasties.

'Primrose wine is primrose wine,' I observed thickly, through a mouthful of pastry.

Adela never argued with me when I was in one of my unreasonable moods. She had other methods of dealing with my obstinacy.

My attention was momentarily distracted by a brawl between a couple of drunkards which was taking place some twenty paces distant, the distraught wives hanging on to their husbands' jackets and vainly trying to separate them. Not that there was likely to be much physical damage done: it was mostly hot words and posturing. Grinning to myself, and keeping my eyes on the contestants, I put out my hand, picked up my cup and raised it slowly to my lips ... The flavour burst, like a golden bubble, inside my mouth. There was a delicate hint of sage, of rosemary, of wild arum, like nothing I had ever previously tasted. It was like drinking the essence of spring.

'Delicious, isn't it?' demanded my wife.

'I ... What? That isn't my ale.' I stared indignantly from the table to Adela, who was smiling at me and looking ineffably smug.

'I switched the cups while you were watching those two men. Be honest, Roger! Admit it! That primrose wine is like no other you've had before.'

'It's better than Margaret's or Goody Watkins's, I'll give you that,' I answered grudgingly, unwilling to concede her the victory. Our eyes met and she held my gaze. After a moment or two, I burst out laughing. 'All right! You win! It does indeed have the most wonderful flavour, and just to prove to you that I'm sincere, I'll buy myself a cup.'

I swung my legs over the bench and went in search of the wine-seller. I found him eventually, his tray slung around his neck by its leather strap, but its contents diminishing fast. In response to my request for the recipe for the primrose wine, he shook his head lugubriously.

'I don't know what's in it, friend. I'm not allowed to know. My goody makes it, and the secret's been in her family for generations, handed down from mother to daughter. But it sells well, which is the most important thing as far as I'm concerned.'

I was elbowed aside by other customers returning for second cupfuls, and I made my way back to Adela, who had now been joined by the Lampreys.

'We've come to say goodbye,' Jeanne said, stooping to kiss my wife's cheek. 'We must get back to the shop and I've had enough of men playing at being warlords. Adela, my dear, we shan't see you again as you're off home tomorrow. I hope you have a safe journey with only this Jack Nym, or whatever his name is, for company.' She raised her head and stared at me accusingly. 'I suppose we might see you, Roger, as you're remaining in London on the Duke of Gloucester's business.'

It was only later that I pieced together what she had been saying because, at the time, I was like a man in a dream. For no apparent reason, I had just recalled a remark made earlier by Adela, and this had inspired a train of thought concerning Gideon Bonifant's murder that had absorbed my whole attention. All at once, it was as though a candle had been lit in a darkened room: suddenly, I could begin to see my way forward.

Philip, ever sensitive to an atmosphere of female disapproval, pressed my hand in sympathy as we took our farewells, but it was a gesture whose significance was lost on me at that particular moment.

'You're very quiet,' Adela remarked, as we made our way back to the Voyager. 'Do you regret not going home with me tomorrow?'

Most ungallantly, I shook my head. 'No, I trust Jack Nym.' I was scarcely conscious of what I was saying. 'My love,' I went on, putting an arm about her shoulders as we pushed against a strengthening wind, 'I must leave you at the inn and go on to Crosby Place. I need to borrow a horse from His Grace's stables.'

'A horse?' Adela stopped in the middle of the Strand, forcing me to do likewise. She knew that I was a poor rider and was puzzled. 'Why do you want to borrow a horse?'

'I have to go to Southampton,' I answered, urging her forward. 'If I walk, it will take me over a week to get there and the same amount of time to return. On horseback, each journey can be accomplished in two or three days.'

'But why do you have to go to South-ampton at all?' my wife demanded, none too pleased by this unexpected development in my plans.

I couldn't explain until I was more certain of my ground.

'It's where Gideon came from,' I said feebly. 'He lived there before he moved to London, after his first wife died.'

Adela glanced doubtfully at me, but she was wise enough not to ask any more questions. I guessed that her anxiety stemmed from her concern that something might happen to me during my travels, and I hastened to reassure her.

'Don't worry, sweetheart. I'm in no danger. I know that now.'

She made no further comment, but her sleep that night was broken, and I suspected that my words had been of little comfort to her. With the coming of daylight, she was no less preoccupied, and said almost nothing as we made for the Leadenhall, our box loaded on to a handcart pushed by one of Reynold Makepeace's cellarmen. (I had extracted my few belongings from the box earlier and stuffed them into a canvas sack lent to me by our ever-accommodating host.)

Jack Nym was before us, and, at first, viewed my intention to remain behind with even greater disapproval than that shown by Jeanne Lamprey. But once he understood my reasons, and that no less a person than the King's brother was involved in my decision, he changed his tune, assuring me that he would take every care of Adela, and that not the smallest risk would be taken that might endanger her health.

'Trust me, Roger!' he exclaimed, clapping me on the shoulder. 'Trust me!'

I told him that I did, embraced Adela passionately, helped her mount to sit beside Jack, and watched the cart until it was out of sight, lost among the noonday crowds as it crawled towards the New Gate, the village of Holborn and the open countryside beyond. Then I went back to the Voyager, where I paid our shot, saddled the horse lent to me from the Crosby Place stables the previous day, settled the canvas sack containing my belongings on my back, where it felt instantly at home, and set out, crossing to Southwark by London Bridge before turning the roan's head in a south-westerly direction.

Nineteen

My late start on Friday, coupled with the fact that I rested myself and the horse for the whole of Sunday at a wayside inn somewhere between Farnham and Winchester, meant that I did not reach Southampton until Monday afternoon.

I entered through the squalid suburbs of Orchard Lane, and, inside the walls, the perilous state of the streets had not altered since I was last in the town three years previously. My mount stumbled frequently over the broken paving stones and potholes in the road. There was the usual number of foreign sailors wandering aimlessly about (the babel of different tongues making me suddenly homesick for the Bristol Backs), while the shopkeepers and stallholders vied for their custom.

From East Street, I turned south, carefully

studying the gabled ends of the houses that faced on to High Street, the small court-yards to the side and rear of each dwelling forming narrow alleyways between them. When I saw the public latrine, I knew I was nearing my journey's end, although my nose had warned me of the fact sometime earlier. The scents of newly baked pies and pasties, boiled ham, braised beef and roast fowl had been assailing my nostrils for several min-utes past. I directed my tired horse along the little passageway that separated the latrine from the neighbouring building, to where, some twenty paces in, and set at right angles to the other houses, stood John Gentle's butcher's shop.

Master Gentle himself, in spite of the coldness of the day, had set out his wares on a large trestle table in front of his booth, and was directing the purchase of a leg of mut-ton by a respectable dame who, I guessed, was housekeeper to one of the local gentry. Time somersaulted backwards and it was once again the summer of the English in-vasion of France, that invasion which ended in the humiliation of our troops and a fat annual French pension in King Edward's pocket.

I had no idea if Master Gentle would remember me but, as soon as he glanced up, the round, weather-beaten face split into a welcoming grin and the hazel eyes twinkled.

'Well, well! Roger Chapman, as I live and breathe.' He eyed my horse and grimaced. 'You've come up in the world since last I saw you. It used to be Shank's mare for you.' He turned his head, yelling for his wife. 'Alice! Come and see who's here!'

Mistress Gentle, as small as her husband was large, appeared round the side of the booth from the cottage at the rear, her mild brown eyes blinking in puzzlement.

'What is it, John? What's the matter?' Then her glance alighted on me and her delicate features were instantly creased with pleasure. 'Master Chapman, come in! Come in!'

I had to excuse myself for a time while I located the nearest livery stable and made sure that the Duke's horse would be looked after for the night, or for as long as it was necessary for me to remain in Southampton. Then I returned to the Gentles' shop. The customer had gone and no other had as yet arrived to demand the butcher's attention, so he and his wife were both waiting for me in the cottage kitchen, where a bright fire burned and a pan of stew was warming amongst the flames.

We spent the next hour catching up on one another's news, Master Gentle having routed out a neighbour's son, who, for a consideration, was willing to watch over the stall and booth and shout for John whenever he was needed. So it was they learned that I had married again, had a stepson as well as a daughter, with a third child on the way. They also learned that I was at present on an errand for the Duke of Gloucester, which intrigued them, but without eliciting a torrent of prying questions. They were a discreet couple, content with such snippets of information as came their way.

In return, I heard that their only child, Amice, with whom I had once fancied myself just a little in love, was still a seam-stress in the household of the King's mother, the Dowager Duchess of York, and that she was happy with the young groom of the stables whom she had eventually married. After which, I was invited to share their meal and the three of us sat down to an early supper of beef stew and herb dump-lings, a good strong cheese and slices of wheaten bread. The Gentles lived well, if simply.

'And now,' asked the butcher when we were all replete and the empty dishes pushed to one side, 'what do you *really* want with us?' He added with a self-mocking grin, 'Apart, that is, from the pleasure of our company?'

I grinned back at him. 'It's a very great pleasure to renew our acquaintance, Master Gentle,' I said. 'But, of course, you're right. There is another purpose to my visit. Do you by any chance remember – or do you know of anyone who might possibly remember – a man, an apothecary's assistant, by the name of Gideon Bonifant, who once lived in this town? He left here some seven years ago, after the death of his wife.'

John Gentle furrowed his brow in thought, but his wife knew immediately of whom I was speaking. Women are invaluable in matters of gossip, even after such a lapse of time.

'I know who you mean!' she exclaimed, clapping her hands together in triumph. 'You recollect him, John, surely! He worked for Apothecary Bridges, who has a shop in All Saints' Ward.' She turned back to me. 'The shop's on this side of High Street, but above All Saints' Church, towards the Bar Gate.'

Her husband shook his head. 'I know Apothecary Bridges, of course. Who doesn't in S'ampton? But he's had so many assistants, and seven years is a long time to remember them all. I don't recall this Gideon Bonifant.'

Alice Gentle grew impatient.

'Yes you do, John,' she insisted. 'Long-faced, pious fellow with very cold, staring, grey eyes. I never much liked being served by him whenever I had need to go into the shop, which was more frequently than I cared for. I preferred Apothecary Godspeed in French Street, except that he was too often drunk to serve me. He was always saying that he'd give up the ale, but—'

'Do you remember Gideon Bonifant's wife?' I interrupted, afraid that my hostess was about to digress and treat me to a dissertation on the failings of the unknown Master Godspeed.

'Oh yes,' was the ready response. 'She was from All Saints' Ward as well, but from the poorer part, outside the walls. A buxom enough girl, all the same, when Gideon Bonifant married her, but after a year or so she became ill and just wasted away. A sad sight, she was, by the time she died.'

'And Master Bonifant, so I understand, couldn't bear to remain in Southampton any longer, once she was in her grave.'

Alice Gentle raised her eyebrows. 'And who told you that, pray?'

'Apothecary Ford of Bucklersbury, in London. He employed Gideon as his assistant when Master Bonifant arrived in the city looking for work.'

My informant frowned. 'That's not quite how I remember it,' she protested. 'My recollection is there was more to it than that. I rather fancy Master Bonifant left Southampton because there was a good deal of whispering and gossip about him – but I can't recall exactly what at this distance of time.'

'Glory be!' exclaimed John Gentle, laughing. 'Wonders will never cease! I've never known your memory to fail before, girl, in such matters.'

His wife joined in the laughter. 'No, that's true enough. There must have been something else occupying my mind at the time of his departure. Seven years ago, you said, Master Chapman, since he left here?'

I nodded. 'The year of the battle at Tewkesbury and the subsequent death of King Henry.'

'That would be it then. That was the summer that Amice fell sick of a fever and nearly died.' She sighed. 'I'm sorry, Master Chapman, but if you want more information, you'll have to find someone else.'

'Can you advise me as to who might know the whole story?'

It was the butcher who answered.

'Apothecary Bridges' dame is the person you need. She's an even bigger gossip than my Alice, here.' He squeezed his wife's arm affectionately, robbing the words of any sting of criticism. 'She'd certainly have known what was going on in the life of her husband's assistant. I'm willing to bet my own on it.'

Once again, Mistress Gentle nodded. 'And that's no lie! You'd best go to see her now, lad. They'll be shutting up shop soon. The evenings are drawing out a little, but not by much. By the way, where are you staying tonight? You're welcome to sleep here, in Amice's old bed, if you wish. We've only the one bedchamber, but neither John nor myself snores, so far as I know.'

I accepted her generous offer with the proviso that it was only for a single night. If I had to stay longer in the town, I would find myself accommodation elsewhere. But somehow, I did not think that much of a possibility: I felt I was already in possession of the facts and all that was needed now was confirmation of my suspicions. I would set out for Apothecary Bridges' shop immediately.

I set off up High Street, past All Saints' Church, towards the Bar Gate, and, following Alice Gentle's carefully detailed instructions, found Apothecary Bridges' shop without much difficulty. One mention of Mistress Gentle's name and I was welcomed effusively by the good lady of the house, who was minding the counter while her husband, so she instantly informed me, was in the back room making a brew of wild basil and calamint for a customer with a bad chest infection – a certain Master Simmons of Blue Anchor Lane.

Such a willingness to impart information augured well. And, indeed, as soon as I made known to her the reason for my visit she was only too eager to reveal all she knew concerning Gideon Bonifant.

'It's a long time ago now, as you say, since Gideon was assistant to my dear husband, but I remember him very clearly – and that poor wife of his.'

'What did she die of?' I interrupted. Mistress Bridges pursed her lips. 'You may well ask. But you'll be fortunate if you can find anyone to give you an answer. Marion Sybyle was a fine-looking girl when Gideon married her, and they were happily wed for five years or more, although they weren't blessed with any children, more's the pity.'

Here she was forced to break off in order to serve a customer, complaining of an upset stomach, with a packet of powdered limestone and chalk.

'Mix it with a little goat's milk, my dear,' she instructed the woman, 'and swallow it straight down. It'll do the trick all right.' She turned back to me. 'Where was I?'

I jogged her memory, adding, 'Why did you say "more's the pity" when referring to Gideon Bonifant's and his first wife's lack of children?'

'Because it might have prevented him having an eye for other women,' was the censorious reply. 'Oh, things were fine between them, as I said, for five years or so, before Marion began to get a bit scrawny and lose her looks. She'd been a very pretty young woman – she had three or four lads after her at one time, as I remember – but as she got older, her features started to coarsen. It might not have mattered so much if Geraldine Proudfoot hadn't come on the scene.'

Another customer arrived for some feverfew tablets and to gossip about a neighbour, leaving me once again to contain my impatience as best I could. Eventually, however, she departed and I was able to resume my conversation with Mistress Bridges.

'Who was Geraldine Proudfoot?'

'She moved here with her parents from over Winchester way. Beautiful she was, too good for an apothecary's assistant, even supposing Gideon had been free to marry her, and so I told him. "Her father's a lawyer. She's not for the likes of you," I said. Of course he denied having any interest in her, but I knew better, and so did anyone else who had an eye in her head. And I understood Master Gideon well enough by that time to know that Geraldine's superior status was more than half her attraction for him. That man always thought himself worthy of a better fate than the one that God had planned for him.'

A third customer, a man this time, bought some water parsnip seeds, but, thankfully, proved disinclined to talk and left the shop within a very few minutes.

'Water parsnip seeds, taken in a little wine,

are an excellent relief for hernia,' Mistress Bridges whispered confidentially, leaning towards me across the counter. 'If you happen to have one, let me recommend—'

'No, I don't,' I assured her hurriedly. 'Pray continue telling me about Master Bonifant.'

'Well, I suppose there really isn't much more to tell. I couldn't honestly say – nor could any of my friends – that I ever saw Gideon and Geraldine Proudfoot together, except in the way of business. The elder Mistress Proudfoot was a sickly creature and Geraldine used to come into the shop to buy medicines for her mother. I don't think she was aware of Gideon but as the person who most often served her, my husband, you understand, being kept busy in the back, making up the potions and pills. But she and Gideon did chat together, and I saw the way he eyed her up and down when he thought she wasn't looking. As I told you just now, I did my best to warn him off, but he'd simply stare right through me as though I hadn't spoken.' Mistress Bridges chuckled. 'Oh, he'd have liked to tell me to mind my own business, interfering old gossip that I am, but he didn't dare for fear of losing his job.'

There was a further diversion while she sold a young girl a poultice of rue and borage for a swelling on the knee, but finally, having enquired after the health of

every single member of the girl's innumerable family, she was free to give me her
attention once more.

'Mistress Gentle told me that Gideon's
first wife just seemed to waste away,' I said.

'That's true.' Mistress Bridges nodded her
head emphatically. 'She was a fine, buxom
wench when he married her, but as I
remarked a while back, Marion did lose a
bit of weight as she got older. Nothing in
that: her mother was like a rasher of wind.
But then it got worse – much, much worse.
Before she died, Marion was a walking
skeleton, and in constant pain. Of course,
there was gossip. I told one or two of my
greatest friends what I'd observed concerning Gideon and Geraldine Proudfoot,
but naturally I swore them to secrecy. My
husband had dared me to repeat my suspicions. And I have to admit that the way
Gideon nursed his wife silenced a lot of the
whispering.'

'But you still suspect that he might have
poisoned her?'

Yet again, Mistress Bridges nodded, but
this time she glanced uneasily over her
shoulder towards the room behind the shop,
and put a finger to her lips.

'Well, it wouldn't surprise me to learn that
he had,' she answered, lowering her voice.
'Most people thought him no more than a
rather humourless and taciturn young man,

but I knew him better than that. There was a ruthless streak in Gideon Bonifant. There was a stray dog that used to hang around the shop. I encouraged him, I have to confess, by putting out scraps. But then he started to make a nuisance of himself, coming into the shop and barking if he didn't get his food on time, until, one day, in a fit of bad temper, my husband said he wished that someone would get rid of the animal. That dinnertime, Gideon offered to prepare the dog's meal in order, he said, to save me the trouble. He'd never suggested doing so before, and I should have been suspicious, but I was very busy that morning. By mid-afternoon, the dog was dead, stretched out stiff and cold beside his half-empty plate. When I accused Gideon of deliberately poisoning the poor creature, he just laughed.'

'What happened after the death of his wife?' I asked. 'I know he went to London, but I was told that it was because he was so grief-stricken, he was unable to remain in Southampton any longer.'

Mistress Bridges laughed shortly. 'If he was grief-stricken, it was on account of Geraldine Proudfoot's marriage to young Oliver Braine, a highly suitable young man of her parents' choosing. Not that she was averse to their choice, and a very happy, blushing bride she made. It was after her wedding that Gideon announced he was off to London to try his fortune there.' She eyed me shrewdly. 'What's this all about? Has he been accused of poisoning someone else?'

'No-o,' I answered slowly, and stood for a moment, lost in thought. Then I added, 'Didn't I say? It was Gideon himself who was poisoned.'

'Gracious Mother of God!' gasped Mistress Bridges. 'There's divine justice for you!'

I smiled. 'You really are convinced that he murdered his first wife, aren't you?'

'I am.'

She would have said more, but the sudden appearance of her husband effectually put an end to our conversation. Apothecary Bridges peered at me short-sightedly over the top of his spectacles and asked if I were being attended to.

'Not that you look to be ailing from anything much,' he added drily. 'I've rarely seen a healthier specimen of young manhood.'

'I – I've got what I came for, thank you,' I answered hastily, opening my cloak and patting the pouch at my waist as though there were something in it. 'Goodbye, then, Mistress, and my gratitude for all your help.'

I quit the shop swiftly and in a very cowardly fashion, leaving Mistress Bridges to think up the answer to her husband's inevitable question of what was wrong with me. But I was indeed genuinely grateful to her. As I walked back to John Gentle's butcher's shop, pushing my way through crowds making last-minute purchases, or heading for an evening's convivial drinking in the local taverns, I reflected that I could start for London first thing the following morning. I had learned more about Gideon Bonifant than I had dared to hope for when I had set out from the capital the preceding Friday.

I was sure now that I had the answer to who had murdered him. I might never be able to prove it to the total satisfaction of a lawyer or a Sheriff's officer, but my reasoning must surely be sufficient to raise doubts as to Isolda Bonifant's guilt in the most prejudiced of legal minds. And as soon as I had imparted my knowledge first to the Babcarys and secondly to the Duke, I should be free to set out for Bristol. I would be home by the middle of February.

I began to whistle tunelessly to myself.

It was again late afternoon when, on Thursday, I crossed London Bridge and made my way once more to Bucklersbury, to beg a room from Reynold Makepeace.

Having heard my request, he took a deep considering breath. 'We're very full, Roger, and I've had to let the chamber you shared with Mistress Chapman to someone else. Will it be for long?'

'Two nights only. Tomorrow should see my business in London completed. I'll be on the road at daybreak on Saturday.'

'In that case, you can share my bed-chamber for two nights, if you've no objections to sleeping in the same bed as me.'

I assured him that I hadn't. 'And I've another favour to ask you,' I added. 'Can you spare one of your pot-boys to take a message to Master Babcary in West Cheap? I'm too tired, or I'd go myself.'

Reynold, somewhat reluctantly, agreed and, when the lad at last appeared, he also muttered under his breath about the inconvenience of being dragged from his work. But when he understood that my request entailed a journey for which I was prepared to recompense him, he cheered up considerably.

'Tell Master Babcary,' I said, 'that I shall be with him first thing tomorrow morning, and ask him to ensure that he and all his household are present. Tell him that I believe I have the answer. He'll understand.'

The boy sped away, reporting back to me an hour or so later with Miles Babcary's reply.

'He says he'll do as you ask, Master, and he'll keep the shop closed until after your visit. But he hopes as how it'll be worth it, because he doesn't like losing money.'

I spent a restless night, trying not to disturb my host too much with my tossing and turning. Fortunately, Reynold was so tired from his day's exertions that he slept like a child, barely moving on his side of the goosefeather mattress. Was I correct in the assumptions I was making? Much would depend on the testimony of Toby Maybury. If he confirmed my suspicions, all would be well. And on this thought I finally fell into an uneasy doze.

I rose with Reynold at the crack of dawn and breakfasted on dried herrings and oatmeal, standing up at one of the tables in the Voyager's kitchen, too anxious even to sit down, as the harassed kitchen maids begged me to do, forced as they were to work around me. But eventually, I was off, making my way through the already crowded streets to West Cheap.

I need not have worried that I might be too early. Master Babcary and every member of his household were awaiting my arrival. They all laid claim to a disturbed night on account of my message, and Isolda, especially, looked pale and strained.

'Come up to the parlour,' Miles said without preamble, seizing me by the arm the moment I entered the shop and forcing me towards the stairs.

He had no time for the niceties of formal greetings, and the others closed in at my back to make sure that I did as I was told. In the parlour, a fire was already burning on the hearth, for it was a cold morning and there was a touch of frost in the air. I was very glad to stoop and warm my hands.

'Now then, Chapman,' Master Babcary said, closing the door behind him and coming forward, 'no beating about the bush, if you please. Tell us straight out which one of us you suspect of murdering my son-in-law.'

A definite atmosphere of menace pervaded the room, and I wondered fleetingly what might have been my fate had my answer been any other than it was. But I had no need to worry. I straightened my back and turned to face them all.

'Gideon Bonifant poisoned himself,' I said.

Twenty

For several seconds there was total silence, then Miles gave an incredulous laugh, echoed nervously by Isolda. But it was Christopher who first found his voice.

'Are you trying to tell us that Gideon committed suicide?' he asked in a tone of cautious relief; cautious because he could not yet permit himself to believe that I was serious.

'Oh, no,' I answered. 'It was an accident. The person he intended to kill was you.'

Christopher looked dazed. 'Me? Why me?' he demanded. 'Are you sure this isn't just a farrago of nonsense, Chapman?'

'I can't prove anything,' I said, 'I can only guess at what happened from the facts at my disposal. But I think what I'm about to tell you would raise considerable doubt concerning Mistress Bonifant's guilt in the minds of any lawyer or Sheriff's officer. Indeed, I hope that it would convince them of her innocence. And when I leave here, I shall go straight to the Duke of Gloucester and lay my conclusions before him, which he can then pass on to Mistress Shore, thus setting him free to ask his favour of her.'

'Oh, never mind the Duke or Cousin Shore,' Miles Babcary interrupted impatiently. 'For goodness sake, sit down, Roger, lad – everyone sit down! – and explain matters to us.'

I noted that within a very brief space of time I had progressed from 'Master Chapman' to 'Roger, lad', and suppressed a smile. I was no longer a potential enemy, but their possible saviour.

Obeying Miles's instructions, we all, with the exception of Meg Spendlove, seated ourselves around the table, Meg preferring to crouch over the fire to make the most of this unaccustomed source of warmth. I glanced at the circle of eager, and now friendly, faces, reflecting that I had been right not to ask for the presence of Mistress Perle or the Napiers at this gathering. Neither Miles nor any member of his household had the least suspicion that any one, let alone all, of those three had a motive for murdering Gideon, and it was kinder to let sleeping dogs lie. It was not my place to reveal the affair between Gregory Napier and Barbara Perle, and if the latter did ever become the second Mistress Babcary, the subsequent domestic upheaval was for Miles and his daughter to sort out between them.

'Well, Roger? Well?'

Miles was growing red in the face and looked as though he might swell up and burst if he were starved of the facts for a moment longer. I cleared my throat and began.

'Since last Friday, I've been in Southampton – returning late yesterday afternoon – and first I must tell you what I discovered.' I repeated all that Mistress Bridges had told me about Gideon, his first wife and the girl called Geraldine Proudfoot. 'So you see,' I concluded, 'although there is no definite proof that Gideon poisoned Marion Sybyle, I believe it to be the truth in view of what happened here last November.'

Isolda shook her head. 'No, no! You're wrong, Master Chapman. You must be. I lived with Gideon for over five years. He wasn't, I freely admit, the most loving of husbands, but, then, he didn't marry me because he loved me, I'm quite aware of that. But I can't and won't think that he would ever commit murder. Besides, you said his intended victim was Kit. It doesn't make sense.'

'It does if *you* were accused of the murder,' I answered. 'It was, I believe, a very subtle plan. But we're going too fast. We must return to when Gideon first arrived in London.

'He came here a disappointed man. The woman he had hoped to wed, with a view to raising himself in the world, had married someone else: he had killed his wife for nothing. But then, a year later, he met you, who – who fell in love with him.'

Isolda put her elbows on the table and cupped her chin in her hands, sending me a fierce, almost contemptuous glance.

'We might as well be honest about it, Roger. There was no love on either side. I'm a plain woman whom men have never fancied and I was desperate to be married. Gideon knew that, just as I knew that he wanted me for the position I could bestow and the inheritance that I should one day bring him as my husband. It was a marriage of convenience for us both, but that doesn't mean to say that we were unhappy.'

There was a pause before I continued, my voice rough with pity, 'Your husband, I suspect, was content only until he fell in love with Mistress Eleanor. When you married, she was only a mere child of twelve, but then she grew up into ... into—'

'A beautiful young woman,' Isolda supplied drily, ignoring her cousin's murmur of distress.

'Exactly,' I hurried on. 'But there was a difficulty. Gideon also wanted Master Babcary's money, and the only way he could achieve that was to ensure that Mistress

Eleanor became her uncle's sole heir. So not only you, but also Master Christopher had to be removed. What better way was there than to have you arrested, tried and executed for *his* murder?'

'But would anyone believe that I wanted to do away with Kit?' Isolda demanded to a general murmur of agreement.

'Of course not. Gideon meant to make it seem that you had intended to poison *him*, but had accidentally killed your cousin instead. Before that happened, however, he had to persuade Mistress Eleanor that fate had decreed that they were eventually to be man and wife. As you and she already know, he saw a way to do that after she bought a pendant in Leadenhall market and confided to him her belief in its magical powers.' And for the sake of Miles Babcary, his nephew and apprentice who, by the blank expression on their faces, were totally bewildered, I repeated the story of the two pendants.

'Gideon did *what*?' thundered Miles, springing to his feet. 'He dared to enter my niece's bedchamber, while she was sleeping! Isolda, did you know about this?'

'No, certainly not, Father. I knew Gideon was restless and had taken to wandering around the house at night, but I thought he was ill. I had no idea that he was playing such a trick on Nell, and I'm hurt and angry that you could think otherwise.'

Miles had the grace to apologise, and resumed his seat looking shamefaced. 'Pray continue,' he muttered, glancing at me.

I inclined my head. 'Gideon's next step was to put about the story that Isolda was cuckolding him with her cousin. He told you, Master Babcary, he told his former master, Apothecary Ford, and he told Gregory Napier. There may have been others, also, to whom he talked in confidence, tavern acquaintances and the like. And as people have pointed out to me, a man doesn't willingly admit to being a cuckold unless he is both sure of his ground and deeply shocked and hurt by his wife's conduct. Gideon counted on this fact to command his listeners' belief in the tale. Everyone knew that Mistress Bonifant was not really the sort of woman preferred by Master Kit' – Christopher shifted uncomfortably on his stool – 'but, with the exception of you, sir,' I nodded at Miles, 'they all accepted the truth of the story.'

I paused to clear my throat again, and a chorus of impatient voices urged me to continue. I was only too willing to oblige.

'Having prepared the ground,' I went on, 'fate then played into Gideon's hands when, at Mistress Eleanor's birthday feast, last October, Meg mixed up the two goblets belonging to him and Master Christopher.

As Mistress Bonifant once pointed out to me, the initials G.B. and C.B. look very much alike amid all that elaborate carving around the rims.'

Meg Spendlove rose like an avenging fury from where she was crouching in front of the fire.

'I did not mix them up!' she screamed, seizing my arm and shaking it violently.

'Meg, behave yourself!' Isolda exclaimed wrathfully. 'Release Master Chapman this minute! As he has so kindly reminded us, it's very easy to confuse those two sets of initials.'

'But I didn't!'

'Wait,' I said, removing Meg's hand from my sleeve and holding it soothingly between both of mine. 'She could be telling the truth, you know. Why shouldn't Gideon have switched the goblets himself? Yes, yes! The more I think of it, the more I wonder that I didn't consider the possibility earlier. It established in your minds a precedent for such a mistake being made.' I heard the girl's sharp intake of breath as she prepared to make further protest, and squeezed her hand reassuringly. 'No, Meg, no one's blaming you. Master Gideon switched the cups himself, I feel almost certain of it. Go and sit down by the fire again.' When, somewhat sullenly, she had complied, I leant forward excitedly. 'You all said that Gideon's explosion of anger was unusual, that, normally, he didn't indulge himself with such displays of rage. But on the occasion of Mistress Eleanor's birthday feast, it was necessary for him to do so in order to impress upon you all what had happened, and to ensure that you wouldn't be surprised if the same error was repeated.'

Miles Babcary nodded, a grim expression on his face. 'I'm beginning to understand what you're getting at, Roger, lad.' He sucked in his breath. 'To think that all those years we were harbouring a cold-blooded killer in our midst and didn't know it – a killer with such an evil, devious mind.'

'Well, I don't understand,' Isolda protested defiantly. 'You'll have to explain matters more clearly for me, Master Chapman.'

I answered as gently as I could, 'It's as I said just now, Mistress. Your husband planned to poison your cousin and lay the blame on you, admitting to the Sheriff's officer – with the greatest reluctance, I'm sure – that you must really have intended to murder him. I can only guess, but I feel as certain as it's possible to do in the circumstances, that he would have claimed *you* put the poison in his cup, but that Meg had somehow muddled it up with Master Kit's when she was helping to set the table.'

'When, in fact,' Christopher interrupted, also beginning to see the light, 'it was Gideon himself who put the poison in his own goblet and then switched it with mine. That's what he was doing after he left the shop and why he took so long to reach his bedchamber.'

'Exactly,' I said. 'Something delayed him.'

'Wait a minute!' Miles exclaimed peremptorily, holding up a hand. 'Aren't you forgetting that it was *Gideon* who was poisoned? If he'd switched his own goblet with Kit's, someone must have switched them back again.'

I nodded and looked across the table at the apprentice, whose cheeks had suddenly flamed with colour.

'I think it's time you owned up, Toby. Don't be frightened. There's nothing to be ashamed of in what you did. You simply thought that you were helping a friend, isn't that so?'

All eyes swivelled in his direction. He had now grown very pale, and I repeated my assurance that he had done nothing wrong. Eventually he seemed to accept my word.

'I came up to take a look at the table, like I told you. I know I'm not supposed to be in here when there's company coming, but those goblets are so beautiful, real craftsman's work, and I don't get the chance to see them very often.' I could guess that

Miles was ready to forgive the boy anything after that paeon of praise, even if Toby admitted to murdering Gideon himself – which, in a way, he had. The apprentice went on, 'While I was admiring everything, I remembered the awful fuss Master Bonifant had made at Mistress Nell's birthday feast, just because Meg had mixed up the cups.'

'And what did you do, Toby?' I asked hurriedly, before Meg could proclaim her innocence afresh.

'I examined the rims of all the goblets carefully, and, sure enough, I discovered that Meg had made the same mistake again. She'd given Christopher Master Bonifant's cup and Master Bonifant Christopher's. So I changed the two over. It was difficult to do without spilling the wine, but I managed it – and only just in time. Next moment, Master Bonifant appeared. Then the master came in with Mistress Perle and Master and Mistress Napier, followed by Christopher and Mistress Nell.'

I glanced anxiously at Meg to see how she had taken Toby's assumption that it was her carelessness that had caused the mix-up, but she was staring at him open-mouthed, an expression of adoration on her small, pointed face. For a moment, I was at a loss to interpret it, but then I understood. Toby had cared enough for her welfare to risk getting into trouble himself, for if he had spilled the wine and ruined all Isolda's careful table arrangements, he would probably have received a thrashing. But he had been willing to take that chance for her sake. From now on, he would be a hero in her eyes.

I turned my attention back to Toby, now basking in the approval of both Miles Babcary and Meg Spendlove, and said, more as a statement of fact than a question, 'And that is what you were trying to tell Mistress Eleanor while she was talking to Ginèvre Napier, that you had averted another unpleasant scene between Meg and Master Bonifant.'

'Yes.' Toby's tone was unusually subdued for one in such high favour. 'I killed Master Bonifant, didn't I?' he asked unhappily.

'He killed himself,' Christopher answered warmly. 'You saved my life, Toby, and I shan't forget it. Next time I'm tempted to berate you for some stupidity or other, I must try to curb my tongue.'

Eleanor rose from her place and went round the table to kiss the apprentice's cheek.

'You have my undying gratitude, too, Toby. What would I do if I lost Kit?'

Isolda caught my eye and sighed. 'Holy Mother preserve us,' she muttered. 'At this rate, the boy will soon be too big for his breeches. Roger, tell us what made you first suspect that Gideon might have accidentally poisoned himself.'

I scratched my head. 'The idea grew on me very slowly, and it's not easy to pinpoint one particular thing. Odd as it may seem, I found it strangely worrying that no one was trying to kill me or do me harm. I did suffer two or three false alarms, but that was all they turned out to be. It was logical to assume that if one of you was Gideon's murderer, that person would be eager to prevent me discovering the truth. Even if you, Mistress, were the culprit, you wouldn't want people's suspicions confirmed. Yet nothing happened.

'Then there was something that Mistress Perle told me. She said that after everyone had drunk her health, and while you were waiting for Mistress Bonifant to return from the kitchen with the food, Gideon was staring fixedly at Master Christopher, as though he were expecting something to happen – which, of course, he was.'

'That's right!' Christopher Babcary exclaimed. 'I remember now. His look puzzled me. Later on, however, it slipped my mind.'

I nodded and went on, 'Mistress Perle also commented on the expression on Gideon's face after the poison had begun to work. She said he looked outraged, as if he

344

couldn't really believe what was happening to him. She also thought, probably correctly as matters have turned out, that she heard him mutter the word "aconite", but of course his lips were so stiff by that time that she couldn't be sure. Furthermore, Mistress Perle was not the only person to mention Master Bonifant's expression of horror – understandable, you may think, in the circumstances – but it suggested to me that he knew at once what had happened. He knew that somehow or other he had drunk from his own cup and that he would be dead within a very few moments. No one mentioned an expression of surprise or bewilderment. A small thing, perhaps, and of no significance on its own, but it added to the sum of knowledge that was slowly coming my way.

'There was also Mistress Bonifant's alleged infidelity with her cousin. The source of this rumour was Gideon, and only Gideon. I could find no evidence for his claim, and nothing, either, to support the idea that he might simply have hit upon the wrong man. No one could suggest anyone with whom she might have been cuckolding her husband.'

I saw Isolda wince, although I doubt if the others noticed. They were too busy pondering on all that I had just told them.

'What made you think that the goblets

might have been switched over?' Miles Babcary asked me.

'It was something that happened while
my wife and I were at the Westminster
tournament,' I explained. 'She changed my
cup for hers while we were eating our
dinner, for reasons that are too uninterest-
ing to burden you with. Suffice it to say that
the incident suddenly opened my eyes to
what might really have happened on the
evening of Master Bonifant's murder. From
what Mistress Eleanor had confided in me
about the pendants, and Master Bonifant's
behaviour, I guessed that he had fallen in
love with her and determined to make her
his wife. That, in its turn, made me wonder
if something similar could have happened
before, with his first wife, and was the
reason I decided to visit Southampton. I
was well rewarded.

'And now,' I added, rising to my feet, 'I
must take my leave of you and go to beg an
audience of Duke Richard at Crosby Place.'

They were loath to let me go and profuse
in their thanks for solving the mystery, for
the Babcarys, like myself, were convinced
that they now held the answer.

The Duke, having listened intently to my
story, was of the same opinion.

'Well done, Roger,' he said quietly, offering me his hand to kiss. 'I shall make sure
that Mistress Shore is in possesion of the

facts before nightfall, after which—'

He broke off, declining to say more, unwilling, possibly, to raise his hopes too high. I don't think he entertained any doubt that Jane Shore would intercede with the King on behalf of his brother George, especially in view of the favour he, Richard, would just have done her, but I do think he was beginning to have misgivings concerning Edward's eventual clemency. There was a bitterness in his tone when he spoke of the King that I had never heard before, and deep worry lines had carved themselves into his face from nose to chin. The Richard Plantagenet I had known until then always had a lurking twinkle in his eyes, as though he could see the ridiculous side of life even while coping with its grim, and often dangerous, reality.

But the man who prowled around the great hall of Crosby Place, listening to my story, was a different creature; an animal at bay, surrounded by enemies all snapping and snarling at his heels, not knowing what the next moment would bring. I reasoned that if the King pardoned the Duke of Clarence yet again, Duke Richard would return to his normal self; the gay and gallant young man who had survived an uncertain childhood, plagued by ill health, to become the chief stay and prop of his elder brother's throne. But if the Queen and her family persuaded the King to sign Clarence's death warrant, then I feared for Duke Richard's future, not so much at the Woodvilles' hands, but as a victim of his own embittered nature.

Then, suddenly, he was smiling his usual sweet smile, and I dismissed my bleak thoughts as fancies.

'You must forgive me, Roger, for spoiling your wife's visit to London. How will you return to Bristol?' he added. 'Do you wish to retain the horse?'

I shook my head vigorously. 'My lord, I'm happier on my own two feet. Horses and I have never seen eye to eye, and I find them uncertain beasts at the best of times. With good weather, good luck and some friendly carters, I should be home by the middle of next month.'

He laughed and again held out his hand. But this time, when I would have knelt to kiss it, he stopped me, saying, 'Shake the hand of your friend, Roger, for you are one of the few people I count on for un- questioning loyalty. Tell me I'm not wrong.'

'You're not wrong, my lord,' I promised. 'Whatever happens, now or in the future, you may rely on my friendship.'

The weather, luck and the whole fraternity of carters were with me on that journey back to Bristol. I was home by the second week in February.

I was greeted with joy by my children, with warm and loving affection by my wife and was soundly scolded by my quondam mother-in-law. But Margaret's original indignation and anger at my allowing Adela to return home without me had long since cooled, and her remonstrations were only half-hearted. Secretly, she was proud of my involvement with those in high places, and I had to describe over and over again my visit to Mistress Shore's house. Adela was far more interested in the outcome of the mystery, and, once she was in possession of the facts, agreed that my conclusion was probably the correct one.

'I've no doubt at all that you're right, my love. You're a very clever man. Now! We need fresh kindling chopped, water fetched from the well and then it's time you were out on the road once more. We are short of money.'

So life had settled back into its normal pattern by the end of the month, when the knowledge of what had happened in London first burst upon us. As so often, information reached the castle before the town, and it was Adela's former admirer, the Sheriff's officer, Richard Manifold, who brought us the news.

'Well,' he said, seating himself at our table and accepting a mazer of ale, 'it's done then.

The Duke of Clarence is dead; executed, presumably, but no one as yet knows how. Rumour talks of drowning in a butt of malmsey wine, but I don't know that one can put much store by such a tale.'

I sat down slowly on the stool opposite him. 'King Edward signed his brother's death warrant?' I asked incredulously.

'Must have done.' Richard Manifold wiped his mouth on the back of his hand. 'As far as I can gather from the messenger who brought the news, the sequence of events was as follows. On the seventh day of this month, the Duke of Buckingham, as Lord High Steward, passed sentence of death upon Clarence. But even at that late stage, the King hesitated for so long about signing the warrant that, on the eighteenth, the Speaker of the Commons requested that whatever was to be done, be done quickly. And on the very same day, the Duke was executed in the Tower, having first offered up his Mass penny and been shriven. After that, all's secrecy and mystery. They say that even his mother, the old Duchess of York, doesn't know for certain how he died. But he is dead, that's for certain. But as for details, we'll have to contain our souls in patience for a while longer.'

So it was done, I thought to myself. The Woodvilles had triumphed. Those three brothers who had been through so much together were now only two, and I wondered what Duke Richard was feeling. Did he fear that the Queen's rapacious family would one day turn on him?

I grieved silently for him. He faced a lonely and very dangerous future.